☆☆☆☆☆☆☆☆☆☆☆☆☆☆☆☆☆☆☆☆☆☆☆☆☆

From Hayes to McKinley

National Party Politics, 1877–1896

☆☆☆☆☆☆☆☆☆☆☆☆☆☆☆☆☆☆☆☆☆☆☆☆☆

MORGAN, H. Wayne. From Hayes to McKinley; National Party Politics, 1877–1896. Syracuse, 1969. 618p il bibl 69-17074. 12.95

CHOICE   SEPT. '69

History, Geography &
Travel

   North America

Morgan, author of *William McKinley and His America* (1963) and editor of *The Gilded Age: A Reappraisal* (1963), focuses in this study upon the reorganization of politics from the inauguration of Hayes to the election of William McKinley. National consolidation characterized several areas of American life in the period: economics, technology, and diplomacy are matched in this study by the emergence of an effective national party system which integrated the congeries of local baronies each party represented in 1877. The Republicans, using the tariff, Federal regulation, and the currency as unifying issues, forged a successful national organization. Democrats, still committed to a decentralist, agrarian rhetoric, floundered in a morass of localisms. Based upon extensive research in manuscripts and newspapers, as well as upon the plethora of secondary accounts of the period, Morgan's study is a major corrective to older views of the era as one of issueless, "dead-center" politics. Morgan's lively style and incisive portraits of leading figures enhance the work. Extensive endnotes, an excellent bibliographical note, and index.

☆☆☆☆☆☆ ☆☆☆☆☆☆☆☆ ☆☆☆☆☆☆☆☆☆☆☆

Other Books by
H. Wayne Morgan

☆☆☆☆☆☆ ☆☆☆☆☆☆☆☆ ☆☆☆☆☆☆☆☆☆☆☆

The Gilded Age
A Reappraisal (1963) (Ed.)

William McKinley and His America (1963)

American Writers in Rebellion
From Mark Twain to Dreiser (1965)

America's Road to Empire
The War With Spain and Overseas Expansion (1965)

☆☆☆☆☆☆☆☆☆☆☆☆☆☆☆☆☆☆☆☆☆☆☆☆☆☆

From Hayes to McKinley

National Party Politics, 1877–1896

☆☆☆☆☆☆☆☆☆☆☆☆☆☆☆☆☆☆☆☆☆☆☆☆☆

H. Wayne Morgan

SYRACUSE UNIVERSITY PRESS

Copyright © 1969
by Syracuse University Press, Syracuse, New York

All Rights Reserved

FIRST EDITION

Library of Congress
catalog card number: 69–17074

Manufactured in the United States of America

Preface

The last generation of the nineteenth century fills a peculiar place in American thinking. It seems remote and grandfatherly, but its problems and ideals are still real. It radiated optimism in a time of great change, but seldom trusted what the twentieth century calls "idealism." Frankly materialistic, it was aware of human limitations, and assumed that well-being both reflected and created progress. These ideals spread through all levels of society, not just among those who ruled. Millions who hoped to rise, and often did, clung fervently to ethics symbolized by successful men.

All this confuses scholars, who usually dismiss the period as an interlude between the Civil War and Progressivism. Historians have recently re-examined the era's diplomacy, economy, and culture, but few have studied party politics. General accounts and textbooks too often repeat facile conclusions that make every businessman a robber baron and all politicians humbugs. This usually reflects poor information. Detailed studies are scarce, and fragmentary sources make research into politics difficult. A generation of men more interested in power than fame kept poor records. Bitter struggles within and between parties to retain and consolidate support put a premium on the quiet compromise and unwritten understanding among leaders, which hampers historical investigation. A predominantly Republican era has also found few partisans among historians who tend to be "liberal" Democrats.

These politicians seem genteel and bland, but the issues they met were deeply significant, attesting to America's emergence as a great industrial state and international power. Tariff protection, free silver, and civil service reform only sound archaic. As reciprocity, inflation, and bureaucracy they are very much alive, and still unsettled. It is fashionable to avoid the era's politics with the comforting view that no basic issues divided the parties, but politics was an ever-present, vivid, and meaningful reality to that whole generation. Men believed fervently that wide differences separated Republicans and Democrats. We ought to do them the justice of examining the proposition, and any close study of the problem reveals fundamental and important party differences. Broadly speaking, the Republicans spoke for the emerging businessman-skilled labor-prosperous farmer coalition that triumphed in 1896. They believed in federal economic subsidy, and a workable amount of regulation for the national interest. Democrats, however, clung doggedly to ancient ideals of local rule—negative government that protected alleged individualism—and never understood the changes that covered America after the Civil War.

This book has two major purposes: (1) to detail and unify the events of national politics between 1877 and 1896, the years that produced a working national party system; and (2) to show how parties differed, and how each met the major issues of the time. This is not a thesis book, though the theme of an emerging national party system helps unify the narrative. Party politics developed a coherent national form and direction in this period. This helped to unify the United States by providing an overriding symbolic loyalty, material rewards, and a stake in government for millions of people. At the conclusion of the Civil War, the country was still a collection of regions, ethnic groups, and clashing local loyalties. At century's end, economic development, diplomacy, and the emergence of a national party system all worked toward national unity. Government activity in the twentieth century could not have grown without that foundation.

The book develops in a cumulative, analytical narrative. I try to avoid distracting authorial interruptions, hoping my viewpoint emerges from the narrative as the events themselves develop. The book is obviously not a history of the period, and concentrates on national politics. I discuss some important laws that reflected deeper currents of thought, and deal with foreign policy and economics only as they impinged directly on politics. The bibliography cites pertinent works covering these problems. Of necessity, I have shortened my treatment of many famous incidents and issues like pension legislation, the Pullman Strike, and Populism, especially where adequate secondary literature is available. The book is essentially a view of politics *at* the top, and *from* the top. This necessitates a good deal of attention to developments within the parties as well as between them. Since the Republican party was most active in meeting the era's issues, and underwent many changes while seeking a national constituency, it necessarily figures more largely than the opposition.

Most students of the period focus on reform movements, which obscures the events, personalities, and issues important to most people at the time. I have therefore centered the discussion on major parties and problems, and, for instance, offer only a summary of Populist development, which I feel sets that question in better perspective than most studies of the period. I also assume the reader has a working knowledge of problems like Reconstruction, the South, and economics. I have also tried to humanize and broaden the subject's appeal by including a considerable amount of relevant information on personalities and the social aspects of public life which greatly interested the era's reading and voting public. At all times, I hope the reader gains a sense of presence and development as they might have appeared at the time. It is always helpful to recall the White Queen's remark: "It's a poor sort of memory that only works backwards."

To avoid cluttering the pages with explanatory symbols, I have altered punctuation and spelling without notice where such changes did not affect the text's meaning. I have also written only a brief bibliographical guide to easily available secondary sources, with a few suggestions for further research and writing. Documentation at specific points in the footnotes may also be useful to the interested reader.

So many people have helped make this study possible that listing their names would make another book and still not repay my debts. I am genuinely grateful to the staffs of every library mentioned in the notes, who gave me special attention for several years, but I must thank some individuals. Mr. Watt P. Marchman, Mrs. Ruth Ballenger, and Mrs. Rose Sberna of the Rutherford B. Hayes Library in Fremont, Ohio, are among the best librarians in the profession. Their quiet efficiency and courtesy make any stay at the Library a rewarding experience. The staff of the Manuscripts Division of the Library of Congress is always helpful and knowledgeable. I am deeply grateful to Mr. Edwin A. Thompson, now at Johns Hopkins University, for both his aid and friendship when he worked at the Division.

Several organizations assisted me financially. The American Philosophical Society awarded a summer grant. The Ohio State University gave me a year's leave with its Elizabeth Clay Howald Fellowship. The University of Texas provided leave from teaching, research assistance, and secretarial help.

Mr. John L. Gaddis and Mr. Calvin W. Hines obeyed regal commands and deciphered strange handwriting to make the manuscript presentable. Karl and Susan Conrad helped in the book's last stages. My good friends and colleagues, Norman D. Brown and Lewis L. Gould, were of much aid. The result, of course, is my responsibility.

H. Wayne Morgan

Austin, Texas
Fall, 1968

Contents

☆☆☆☆☆☆☆☆☆☆☆☆☆☆☆☆☆☆☆☆☆☆☆☆

From Hayes to McKinley

National Party Politics, 1877–1896

☆☆☆☆☆☆☆☆☆☆☆☆☆☆☆☆☆☆☆☆☆☆☆☆

Prologue

On the afternoon of March 1, 1877, the regular Pennsylvania Railroad run to Washington added two special cars at Columbus, Ohio. Fine coachwork and lavish appointments indicated the occupants' importance. A large crowd gathered to witness the train's departure, and hear a former governor's farewell address as he left to become President of the United States. Sporadic cheers announced his arrival, and in due course Rutherford Birchard Hayes and party arrived at trainside. He smiled through a full beard, and doffed his hat enthusiastically. The crowd rustled in anticipation, and from the rear platform Hayes spoke briefly of national unity and his hope that everyone would help end sectional conflicts that had dominated the country for so long. He waved again, bowed slightly, and the train moved down the tracks, leaving behind a flurry of cheering and a backdrop of flags and colorful uniforms.

At other stops in Ohio, Hayes repeated these generalities. In Pittsburgh, where the train switched, he made a more substantial but similar speech to a large crowd. It was all part of the American tradition of bidding a private citizen farewell as he assumed the nation's highest office. The modest, judicial Hayes played the role well, knowing the whole country listened to his words and tone. The circumstances surrounding the trip were unique in American history. The facts did not yet support Hayes' calm assumption that he was President.

The tracks unrolled methodically behind the train, but the events that brought Hayes to this trip were not so neatly arranged. Between November, 1876, and this moment, unwound the most tortuous trail in American political history. For four months men gave differing judgments, warned of conflict, and expressed grave doubts over the results

1

of a disputed presidential election. Partisans of Hayes and the rival claimant, Democrat Samuel J. Tilden, alternately threatened war and offered to compromise. As the traditional date for inauguration approached, none quite knew the outcome. Promises of patronage, an end to federal presence in the South, and bipartisan politics all swirled finally into the magic word "compromise" that assured Hayes' election through extraordinary machinery to count the presidential ballot.

As Hayes crossed Ohio and Pennsylvania, the final proceedings of the Electoral Commission in Washington insured his election. Fortified with tacit promises from political leaders, the Commission now reported to Congress after weeks of labor that Hayes was President by a single electoral vote. While his party rested fitfully aboard their moving train, weary men filed into the House chamber to hear Thomas W. Ferry of Michigan, President *pro tem* of the Senate, announce the results. It was nearly dawn, March 2, and murky light fell on men with worn faces, their clothes rumpled and unkempt from sleeping in unaccustomed postures and places. Not all members stayed; some left to rest, nurse grievances, or sigh with relief that it was all over.[1]

The new President's train rocked gently toward the great prize, and near Harrisburg took on a telegram announcing the final vote. Nervous aides eagerly read the small paper, then shouted with relief. A staff member read the news to Hayes through the door to his compartment. He responded with a kind rebuke: "I hear you; don't wake up everybody in the car. Good night." [2]

At a fashionable address in Gramercy Park, New York City, a different drama ended. Samuel J. Tilden resigned himself and his friends to the results. Better this compromise and possibly advantageous martyrdom than civil strife or deadlock. There would be other elections. He was not a man to struggle against great odds if he could delay for later victory. Now his face and demeanor showed no emotion as he listened to friends, surveyed the elegant library, talked softly of *objets d'art,* and waited. It was over.

Later that morning the President-elect arrived in Washington, showing no signs of strain or doubt. A crowd was at the station, and prominent statesmen paced the platform. Hayes alighted with a springy step and quick smile, and shook hands all around. The formalities over, he took the arm of John Sherman, close confidant and ranking Ohio Republican, and walked to a carriage that would take him to the Senator's home. Mrs. Hayes, laden with flowers and radiating charm, followed with General William T. Sherman. President Grant did not appear, at Hayes' request, and he politely declined to stay at the White House. He would avoid acting like a president before the inauguration. Grant should have noted this early independence, and unwillingness to lean on the departing Administration.

After a brief rest, Hayes visited Grant, then went to the Capitol for an informal reception among old friends. Many men were surprised to see him, having predicted he would be a recluse, fearful of assassination. It was not an idle thought. In the last weeks, leaders of both parties talked too easily of violence. Southern firebrands threatened to march on Washington and install Tilden with force, or inaugurate him separately and fight it out. Some Republicans replied with equal fervor, dreading the prospect of a pro-southern administration. "If we are to have a war in order to settle the question if we are to become Mexicanized or not, then let it come now, that our children may live in peace," wrote one of General Sherman's correspondents.[3] Sensational newspapers virtually invited someone to shoot Hayes.[4] The mail brought threatening letters. One evening in Ohio, the family was startled at dinner when a bullet broke a window. The authorities found no suspects. Hayes calmly assumed it was the work of cranks, but his son Webb carried a pistol thereafter when they walked together for evening exercise.[5] Now, nothing unusual marred his informal visits in Washington. He noted with a quiet smile that General Sherman drew larger crowds than he because more people recognized him. The President-elect was an unknown quantity to most Americans.[6]

On Saturday, March 3, President Grant went to the Capitol for a last day of formal dealing with Congress. Veiled in cigar smoke, he signed bills, shook hands with friends and some foes, and bade farewell to this aspect of political power. He was reserved and taciturn, methodically signing papers while secretaries blotted ink.[7] Back at the White House, he helped Mrs. Grant with final details for the customary state dinner to his successor.

One small problem remained. March 4 was Sunday and Hayes would not take the oath until Monday. Fearful of any interregnum, Grant and Secretary of State Hamilton Fish persuaded him to take an early oath of office. "I did not altogether approve," Hayes recalled, "but acquiesced."[8] When the President-elect's party arrived for dinner that evening, they moved through ornate rooms filled with famous guests. Flowers brightened tables, diplomatic and military uniforms vied with ladies' dresses for color and pomp. Before the company went to dinner, Hayes and Grant stepped quietly into the Red Parlor. Chief Justice Morrison R. Waite read the oath of office. Hayes responded, then they joined the company, not remarking that two presidents sat down to dinner.

Sunday passed quietly, and inaugural Monday dawned cold and

cloudy, but the sky brightened at noon. Grant was sure the settlement was final, but arranged maximum security. Like a good soldier, he muted the precautions. Not many people realized that plain clothes-men mingled with the crowds. At noon, Grant walked with Hayes onto special platforms facing east from the Capitol. Hayes' step was firm, his eyes bright, and voice steady as he intoned his administration's plans. He spoke as a nationalist, asking all men to join in ending sectional strife. He would enforce national laws, and asked only that everyone obey them. If southerners guaranteed civil rights for the Negroes under state governments, he would not interfere. Reiterating earlier campaign pledges to improve government administration, he promised reasonable changes in the civil service. To both politicians and office-seekers he offered suitable rewards that did not conflict with national policy, but he firmly reminded them, "he serves his party best who serves his country best." The rest was routine, but Hayes obviously believed all reasonable people would follow his lead, a tone not every-one caught or understood. He would be "moderate" and "conciliatory," the terms that won this victory. But moderation was not weakness, and he proposed to lead other men, willing or not.

The ceremonies ended, distinguished groups left, and Washington celebrated with a mixture of relief and joy. At the White house, a lavish luncheon awaited, and the Grants departed after this last social duty. The Hayes family was moving in, and statesmen jostled with porters. Everyone relaxed and celebrated as the day's festivities continued. Crowds milled along Pennsylvania Avenue to watch parades march past like bright beads on an endless chain. That night, Hayes reviewed a torchlight parade that wound around the White House, ending in a serenade that lent a rustic touch to the day's pro-ceedings. He spoke briefly, then fireworks burst overhead, covering the new Administration with a dome of many-colored lights.[9]

In a way it was anti-climactic, but a good sign. Better firecrackers than cannonades; better Hayes than further doubt or war. Now that it was all over and the great crisis-winter past, most people accepted the results. They wanted order and release from tension. They liked the harmonious tones of Hayes' remarks, and appreciated his easy self-assurance. Partisan strife was temporarily suspended. There were promises to keep and men to satisfy, measures to pass and errors to correct, but for now, the public would wait and see.

☆☆☆☆☆ ☆☆☆☆☆ ☆☆☆☆☆☆☆☆☆

Part One
1877–1884

☆☆☆☆☆ ☆☆☆☆☆ ☆☆☆☆☆☆☆☆☆

I

☆☆☆☆☆☆☆☆☆☆☆☆☆☆☆☆☆☆☆☆☆☆☆☆☆

Hayes: Harmony and Discord

☆☆☆☆☆☆☆☆☆☆☆☆☆☆☆☆☆☆☆☆☆☆☆☆☆

Washington exemplified the best and worst aspects of the Republic, resting as it did on a partially fulfilled grand design. An elaborate street plan was barely sketched in at the edges, and too hastily built up in the center. The war halted orderly progress, and later developments mushroomed the city too quickly for tasteful planning. Marble and granite palaces of the newly rich stood near dreary shantytowns of an ever-growing Negro population. Government buildings seemed perpetually unfinished because of shoddy work and poor design. The Capitol and White House showed signs of wear, and hosted an endless stream of visitors who thought the national capital was community property. Behind the White House, the stately monument to the nation's father remained unfinished. A simple and embarrassing lack of funds left it an awkward, truncated shaft poised in mid-thrust toward grandeur.

A man could buy a fine meal and taste superb wines here. He might drive blooded horses ahead of a carriage with a coat of arms on the doors. He could wear high fashion to match a powerful public position but stepped in mud walking to his office, and met a horde of rude favor-seekers once there. Dignity and snobbery had their place, but tourists saw Supreme Court justices riding horse-cars, and senators' wives shopping in markets. A visitor could stay in an expensive hotel room, and dodge flying tobacco juice in the lobby. Few Americans were strangers to the spittoon, and carpets would do if no brass bowl was near. "They use plenty of tobacco at these Washington hotels," a correspondent noted. "The floor of an office is often made a general spittoon, where if one dropped a coin, he would want to put on a glove before picking it up." [1]

The city was noted for dinners, balls, and picnics, where men transacted deals and made arrangements with a democratic ease that
shocked foreigners. Success rather than pedigree reigned. With money
and power, anyone entered society. "The skeletons in Washington
closets are legion, and the paint and powder that adorn many a beautiful face cannot cover up the story that lies underneath," Frank Carpenter noted. "But Washington seldom bothers itself about the skeletons
in its inhabitants' closets. Lucifer himself will be welcomed if he will
dress well, keep his hoofs hidden in patent leathers, and his tail out of
sight." [2] These stark contrasts made the city distasteful to diplomats accustomed to European elegance. Lord Bryce called it "a wilderness of
mud and Negroes." [3]

The Founding Fathers designed the city for politics, and it pursued
that industry with obsessive zeal. It was always crowded, half-finished,
and self-conscious; sure that political chaff in the winds of conversation
was the stuff of history. The Hayes family seemed an odd one to dominate such a city, and few in high society expected to adopt their tone.
They were almost boastfully addicted to "country living," simple food,
Sunday hymns, Temperance, and the easy dealings of small town politics.

The departing Grants were hardly cosmopolitan, but the General
had developed a certain social flash. He drove a fancy rig, visited the
race track, summered in elegant watering places, and hobnobbed with
millionaires. A curious lack of focus on either simple or lavish living
keynoted both his private and public life, puzzled observers, and told
much of the sudden elevations of democratic politics. Many of Grant's
friends and actions alienated the country, but Washington took him
in stride. He was a welcome relief from the war years and the dreari-
ness of Andrew Johnson. The capital would miss him, while quietly
cheering the departure of less savory or interesting cronies.

The new First Family remained unknown. The contested election
had been tortuous and unnerving, and both Tilden and Hayes receded
into the background as the struggle took on a separate life. Reporters
and politicians cautiously praised Hayes' apparent firmness and personal courage. They knew at least the bare outlines of his past. He had
a good war record, and was sensible in his few public statements. But
the dominant tone in national politics was flaccid; most observers assumed he would drift with events.

Hayes interested the public, but was hardly a man to draw a crowd.
He cultivated a quiet demeanor that seemed dull, but used it both as

armor against criticism or flattery, and to show other men he meant business. He stood just under six feet, with reddish-brown hair, and bright blue-grey eyes. He smiled readily, and had a fund of stories to ease tension or change the subject. He wore the dark, plain clothes convention decreed, sported no jewelry except a wedding ring, and had no idle hobbies. Careful living kept him well, though he complained when old war wounds ached. He was easily accessible in his office or on the streets, but preferred not to waste time in idle conversation.[4]

Hayes was a self-contained, controlled personality. A posthumous son born in Delaware, Ohio, in 1822, he grew up among protective women, but took masculine example from a favored uncle, Sardis Birchard, a New Englander by birth, moderately wealthy, with a taste for study and an eye on the main chance in real estate investments. As a child, Rutherford played little because of poor health. In school, he gorged on copybook maxims, but later took them with a judicious grain of salt. For a frontier youth, he had an elegant upbringing, studying at Kenyon College and Harvard Law School. In the process, he acquired a Whiggish tone, believing in man's essential rationality, but understanding his weaknesses and the limitations of wishful thinking. To many he never seemed young. He studied law in Columbus, but practiced in Fremont, Ohio, where his home sat in a stately grove of trees; away from the rush of cities, but near the developing Great Lakes and Ohio River Valley.

His personality seemed well integrated and family connections smoothed the path of a rather ordinary life, but appearance was deceptive. As a youth he suffered from insomnia and was sometimes "melancholy," but he had mastered internal doubts. "My tendency to nervousness in my younger days . . . gave some uneasiness," he recalled years later. "I made up my mind to overcome it, to maintain steady nerves if possible under the most trying circumstances." Like all men, he privately imagined fabulous success, complete with martial glory. In later years, he boasted almost pathetically that he cross-examined as a lawyer, fought as a soldier, and had a tooth filled without anesthetic.[5] He matured with a fixed sense of stable values, wanted the "best people" to rule, and had a trace of innocent snobbery. But he believed in change and efficiency, and had a strong sense of social obligation. He would make a mark, perhaps to show people who thought him bland. As a close friend once noted: "Underneath his laughing face and cheerful smile, there is a big engine of human nature at work all the time. He has himself under constant control, however.

Control of his temper and tongue, coupled with an even, balanced brain—not a brilliant one, but sound and strong; and ambition and energy have been the secrets of his power and success." [6]

Hayes had a small career in Ohio politics and was a successful lawyer, but he almost welcomed the Civil War as a release for personal tension and a good cause. His Whiggish demeanor let him condemn slavery without wishing to abolish it forcibly, but he was an early Republican. As a volunteer officer, he fought bravely in western Virginia, and was severely wounded in the leg and arm at South Mountain in 1862. Inevitably, he became a political figure in Ohio. In 1864, his congressional district sent him to the national House, but he refused to take the seat unless the war ended. [7] It did, and he served from December, 1865, until he ran for governor of Ohio in 1867. Two terms gave him a reputation in Ohio Republican circles, and started a rise to national prominence. He declined a third term in 1871, and retired to Spiegel Grove in Fremont. By now, he was familiar at county fairs, ox roasts, and Grand Army reunions; all rungs on the political ladder. In the process he developed a geniality that let him "pat and praise every man's pumpkin at an agricultural fair." [8]

In 1875, with the assistance of a small but shrewd group of friends, he secured a third gubernatorial term that automatically made him a contender for the presidential nomination in 1876. During the campaign, he told his diary laconically: "If victorious, I am likely to be pushed for the Republican nomination for president." [9] As a popular and able governor, he let men like John Sherman and James A. Garfield foster a boom that beat party leaders James G. Blaine, Roscoe Conkling, Oliver H. P. Morton and Benjamin Bristow. He came to the presidency as a moderate on almost all issues, including the southern problem and civil service reform.

Few men knew best how to approach Hayes, and this lack of familiarity caused many personal problems that thwarted good intentions. He "willingly hurt the feelings of no one," but resisted all efforts to bypass or use him. [10] He knew other Republicans were more popular, and that men like Conkling thought him weak. In a quiet way, he would show them otherwise. "If elected, the firmest adherance to principle against all opposition and temptations is my purpose," he said in 1876. "I shall show a *grit* that will astonish those who predict weakness." [11] He said it to his diary, and others had to discover for themselves his attachment to principles.

Hayes dealt poorly with opponents. His silence and formidable manner chilled many for whom a genial remark, the promise of reward, or a moment's chaff might have softened the blow. To a nervous man like Blaine, he seemed incredibly slow; to a contemptuous one like Conkling, he was impossibly dull. Hayes thought both men shallow and pretentious. He angered opponents by his refusal to quarrel, in an era that doted on personal invective.[12] The President seemed to ignore critics, quoting Lincoln's maxim: "It seems to be a comfort to them and doesn't hurt me."[13] Whatever his private thoughts, he avoided public confrontations, but candidly admitted: "Few men are worried less than I am by hostile criticism and abuse, and few men enjoy more than I do kind words."[14]

Hayes' desire to master the facts of every situation made him seem hesitant. "Hayes makes haste slowly but surely," Carl Schurz wrote a critic. "You will soon wake up and see things done. Hayes is a general like old Thomas; wants to have his wagons together when he marches, but loses no battles."[15] It seemed a poor prediction in 1877, but patience won him victories. An interview could be unnerving unless the visitor had his facts straight and made a lucid argument. The President had a fondness for silence when facing a man or problem he disliked. (The stenographer sitting nearby was also unwelcome to loose-tongued politicians.) He had a keen sense of prerogative, but did not hesitate to pressure congressmen or other politicians, which surprised and irritated powerful men who thought him a nonentity.[16] His use of clever subordinates like Sherman and Garfield, as well as the refusal to fight, did not sweeten the dose.

Hayes was a hardworking, well-informed executive. He wanted details on everything, and correspondence from the "folks back home" told of political changes and support for his acts. As time went on, he traveled widely, talking harmony in such an orderly and prosaic way that people liked it. He toured the South, and made several trips through the Midwest and Old Northwest. The President valued the time away from Washington's cloying atmosphere, enjoyed meeting people, and was a shrewd propagandist. In his last year in office he visited the Far West, and spent so much time on trains that friendly critics chided "Rutherford the Rover."[17]

Hayes remained an enigma to his generation. Many people of all persuasions admired his ideals, but his causes did not attract the banners and bugles of a conquering host. The nation wanted peace and harmony, prosperity, and an end to party strife. Hayes was well suited to this task as a national figure, but he never mastered the art of buying people without their knowledge. He could not have done much differently. The Republican party was delicately balanced among its component parts, tired from the strains of war and Reconstruction, facing new challenges without full answers, raising a fresh set of leaders, and not eager for firm leadership. At best, Hayes could accomplish a kind of negative progress through defensive attacks, depending on public opinion to goad politicians to action. He knew there would be no dramatic change in his term, but he could outline for the future. He trusted time, believing that great social changes came in grey disguises. The colorful moment, however luminous, faded. Politics was a process, not a crusade. Men would only do so much at a given moment, and sometimes the wise leader governed by example.

Every Tuesday and Friday afternoon from twelve to two, Hayes presided over regular Cabinet meetings. The seven men who sat with him around a big table were the Administration's heart. He chose each for a purpose: to represent a party interest, speak for a geographical section, handle a technical problem, or advise on general policy. Choosing a Cabinet consumed much of any new president's time; keeping it together was equally burdensome. The men involved were not mere administrators. Each was a politician with friends and foes whose activities might ruin even the best beginning. Hayes usually stepped into the room after the men arrived. They were congenial and chaffed each other until the President goodnaturedly ended "this ten minutes of boys' play before school." [18] It was an interestingly assorted group, for all the conviviality. Old Simon Cameron of Pennsylvania complained of the "damn literary fellers" around Hayes, and some newspapers remarked drily on a Cabinet of "rare and quaint mosaics." [19]

At Hayes' right sat William Maxwell Evarts, Secretary of State, famous as a lawyer and punster. He early opposed slavery, and helped build New York's Republican party. After the war, he served briefly as Andrew Johnson's attorney-general, and was a brilliant chief counsel during the President's impeachment trial. He had fought the Tweed Ring, and was a Republican legal authority during the contested election of 1876. The premier portfolio was a reward for services well rendered. His chief political handicap was antagonism toward New York's powerful Senator Roscoe Conkling.

Evarts' modest popular reputation rested on a famous wit. He was the delight of hostesses and bane of opponents. A famous sally explained that Washington threw a dollar across the Rappahannock because "the dollar went much farther in those days." Confronting a group of office-seekers, the Secretary remarked: "This is the largest collection for foreign missions I ever saw." And he threatened to put a sign above the door: "Come, ye disconsulate." He was smooth and genial, but vain. "He's very witty and a great bore," Mrs. Henry Adams snapped. "He insisted that he was Alpha and Omega," Thomas Donaldson recalled.[20] Evarts was already planning to upgrade the foreign service and expand foreign trade. He was not an imperialist, but believed in commercial expansion. Before he left office, Evarts made important technical improvements in departmental information releases, staff appointments, and contacts in the business world.

The seat across from him held Secretary of the Treasury John Sherman. First a Whig, then a Republican, he entered the national House from Ohio in 1855, and was a senator from 1861 to 1877. As a moderate Republican and masterful legislator, he was an architect of Hayes' victory, and deserved reward. Sherman understood national finance better than any other politician. Hayes knew the Administration must fund the national debt, resume specie payments, and probably beat the demand for free silver. Sherman would be invaluable in all these struggles, and functioned brilliantly as an administration intermediary with Congress and the business community.

To Evart's right sat Iowa's George W. McCrary, Secretary of War. He had a reputation for civil service reform and moderation toward the South, and advised Hayes on western politics. McCrary's counterpart, Navy Secretary Richard W. "Uncle Dick" Thompson, was Indiana's Cabinet spokesman. He was a valuable link to the "Old Whig" element and understood shifting politics. He had never been aboard ship, however. While touring a vessel, to the astonishment of accompanying officers, he thumped the deck with his cane and exclaimed: "Why, the durned thing's hollow!"[21] The press dubbed him "The Ancient Mariner of the Wabash." His political advice was valuable, but Thompson was a weak appointment, and he departed good-naturedly in 1880, when Hayes opposed his efforts to sell Panama Canal Company stock.

The Attorney-General, Charles Devens of Massachusetts, sat next to Thompson, and was his opposite in temper and background. He had connections in the Boston oligarchy, but did not wither into eccentricity or social aloofness. Though a brave volunteer soldier, he declined Hayes' offer of the War Department and took the legal portfolio, and could be counted on for sound legal advice. An inveterate bachelor and favorite diner-outer, Devens dressed with meticulous care. "The Beau of the Cabinet," Hayes called him, "our fixey young man."[22]

Further down to the President's right, Postmaster-General David

M. Key of Tennessee turned a bearded but lively face to the proceedings. He represented the South and the Democrats in this Republican administration, and Hayes expected him to dispense patronage below Mason and Dixon's line. As a moderate Democrat, he supposedly knew who to reward. He testified to Hayes' hope of integrating the South into the nation with federal offices, economic subsidies, and bipartisan politics.

At the foot of the table, peering through thick glasses, sat the Cabinet's most controversial member, Interior Secretary Carl Schurz. His career was a personal success story spanning several countries. Fleeing Germany after the revolutions of 1848, he lived in France, Switzerland, and England before coming to the United States in 1852. He settled in Wisconsin and was active as a Republican organizer among German-Americans. During part of the war he was minister to Spain, but returned to be a general of volunteers, with important political connections. He toured the South for President Johnson, was a journalist in St. Louis, and served one senatorial term after 1869.

Schurz made enemies as he blundered through life. He never grasped the meaning of American partisanship, and drew wrath from powerful men to whom party fidelity was the original virtue. His greatest single crime in their eyes was the Liberal Republican bolt of 1872, which he led out of disgust with Grant. "The Flying Dutchman of American politics," one foe said; "the Dutch viper," and "Mephistopheles with Whiskers," another remarked. To simpler folk who disliked his dangerous party irregularity, Schurz was "that crout-eating Greeleyite." New York's Thomas C. Platt best stated the personal animosity of party regulars, calling him "a lively German peddler of apples of discord, and a retail dealer in vinegar, manufactured from the juice of sour apples." [23] Schurz had a biting tongue and acid pen. He could also be narrow-minded, pompous, and isolated from the main currents of changing times and issues. He was a technical reformer, but a philosophical conservative. As of 1877, he offered Hayes contacts among civil service reformers and influence in the Midwest. Through the Interior post, he wished to help Indians, reform land laws, and generally improve government service.

These were Hayes' principal advisers. The President allowed each man latitude, and wisely involved all in major decisions. They were able men, though only Sherman left a major impression on history. Hayes could not have chosen advisers otherwise, but the group was politically weak. Evarts and Schurz offended party regulars like Conkling and Blaine. Some people distrusted Sherman, and many Repub-

licans opposed the bipartisanship Key symbolized. But the group
represented Hayes' effort to realign party politics; the Cabinet was
decidedly moderate in attitude. Hayes was willing to represent geography and major party blocs in the Administration, but not with
possibly antagonistic men. He would not risk fancied or real domination by choosing an agent of Conkling or Blaine.

Unofficial advisers were equally important. Men like Garfield in the
House, and Stanley Matthews in the Senate, managed congressional
problems and often visited the White House. William Henry Smith,
head of the Western Associated Press and Collector of the Port of
Chicago, was a link between the Midwest and Washington. Murat
Halstead of the *Cincinnati Commercial* was an equally valuable source
of political information. Moderates like Andrew Kellar of the *Memphis
Avalanche* were tactful presidential agents in the South.

Hayes' immediate advisers indicated his approach to politics in a
time of balanced strength, dangerous personal tensions, and uncertain
directions. He would be Republican but moderate, dividing the burden
between known and unknown men. He dominated the group, and they
loyally supported his policies. The choices necessarily slighted some
political sensibilities, and announced that "this man Hayes" would
jealously guard Executive prerogatives. It was not a welcome idea to
powerful senators and the lords of customhouses.

The public cared more about the First Family than Cabinet appointments. Newspapers soon purveyed stories on White House life, and
usually applauded the family's simplicity, noting the absence of flashy
military aides and blooded horses.[24] The President followed a spartan
regimen that appealed to many. He rose early, did a few exercises,
and worked over papers until breakfast at 8:30. After family prayers
and play with the children, he saw callers until about noon. A visitor
might join him in a light lunch. Unless the Cabinet met, he read more
reports, took a brief drive and short nap, had dinner, then worked
until midnight. He attributed his good health to exercise, avoidance
of tobacco and alcohol, and light foods.[25] Hayes worked easily with
the staff, liked young people, and often watched clerks and telegraphers play ball on the lawn during the noon hour. William T. Crump,
his former army orderly, oversaw routine paper work; another personal friend, William K. Rogers, was private secretary. Webb Hayes
substituted when his father dealt with sensitive matters.

Hayes often received callers amid a litter of papers and books as if
he were in a country law office. When Thomas Eakins painted him in

shirtsleeves for the Union League Club, horrified members stored the picture. On numerous tours, he was calm and goodnatured during inevitable embarrassing emergencies. If drapes refused to part, fireworks failed to fire, or horses bolted, he usually joked and lent a helping hand.[26] His self-assurance and sense of humanity were infectious, and eased the daily routine and many politically tense moments.

The family was a welcome change from political dealings. The second son, Webb C. Hayes, recently graduated from Cornell, stayed at the White House much of the time. Two younger children, Fanny and Scott, punctuated important conferences with demands for pocket money, chased down corridors, and kept the gardeners busy. At vacation times, Birchard came down from Harvard Law School, and Rutherford from Cornell. Miss Emily Platt, a niece from Columbus, was a frequent visitor until her lavish White House wedding in 1878. This large and varied family fortified Hayes' public image as a typical American.

Lucy Hayes soon captured public fancy. Time had filled out her figure, but she was a handsome matron, with an attractive face and dark hair. A few snobs thought her "too familiar and not dignified enough for the Mistress of the Mansion. . . ," but she easily won public approval.[27] She preferred good works to politics, and quietly managed the household and her husband's needs. The family was religious without being sanctimonious. Few people criticized the Sunday hymn-fests because they were a normal part of the family personality. It seemed quite natural to see Vice-President Wheeler, Senator Sherman, and Congressman and Mrs. William McKinley grouped around a piano singing psalms. And more popular strains might be heard when that obligation ended.[28]

Public curiosity fed on rumors that Mrs. Hayes would dry up the wine cellar. It seemed inconceivable, especially after the popular image of Grant, but it was true. Temperance was one of the few subjects that roused her stubbornness. "You know there is a warlike side to her sympathetic nature," Hayes warned Schurz.[29] Rumors of heavy drinking in foreign embassies, especially among young people, and a fair knowledge of the people around the last administration fortified her determination to set an example for Temperance. She hid sideboards, stored potted plants in the billiard room, and entertained ladies from the WCTU. They wanted to give her a water fountain, but bought a portrait instead. While she favored Temperance, the decision on liquor at the White House rested with the President.[30]

Hayes hesitated; might it not look foolish? He took an occasional drink of light wine, and was not a total stranger to heavier vintages, but had abstained in recent years. It was not an unmixed blessing. "In avoiding the appearance of evil," he said later, "I am not sure but I have sometimes unnecessarily deprived myself and others of innocent enjoyments." [31] Six weeks after inauguration he had not settled the problem, and served wine for a visiting Russian prince, in the interests of speeding treaty negotiations. After that, wine lists did not accompany menus, and the press referred to "Lemonade Lucy." Critics blamed the WCTU, though Mrs. Hayes was not a member; others said wrongly that Hayes was too cheap to pay a liquor bill. In fact, the experiment was part of his desire to set good examples. He would not force anyone to follow his lead.[32]

The papers depicted a cheerless White House, and urged guests to make private arrangements in hip-pockets. "She went from the farm house to the White House," a newsman later wrote of Mrs. Hayes, "and drank catnip tea all the way." [33] The presidential couple calmly ignored criticism. "They did unpopular things, as their wineless dinner-giving," an Ohio acquaintance recalled, "but it was with such thoroughbred courtesy that no one could resent it." [34] Lack of bottled spirits did not inhibit White House entertainment, and few predecessors gave such lavish dinners. The presidential salary equaled the task, but Hayes had few other resources. Gossip said falsely that he was rich and a penny pincher. He had some Ohio investments, but saved little. "We spent in hospitality, charities, and generous living the whole amount," he recalled.[35] Mrs. Hayes carefully supervised the elaborate state affairs, and added to the Mansion's plate and silver; an old chair covering, worn carpet, or faded drapery always demanded attention.[36]

The Hayes family was not spectacular, but seemed comfortable to the public. In that sense, they set a tone for the nation's middle class. With all the gentle insularity of small-town origins, they refused to let either power or place turn their heads. They assumed their values were best, and would prevail, but easily tolerated different views. The President talked much of teaching by example. Men of flashier tastes smiled in amused cynicism, but that calm respectability was just what the country wanted.

The press joked about "Lemonade Lucy," and printed details of White House life, but politicians thought of larger things. One question dominated everything: Would the new Administration solve the southern problem? Between November and March, intermediaries in all camps worked out an elaborate but tacit compromise, with Hayes' silent blessing, that averted violence and promised to end Reconstruction. Its salient points were well known: A Republican president would remove federal soldiers from Louisiana and South Carolina, the last remaining "unredeemed" states, and recognize local rule; as part of a long-term program, Republicans would extend federal patronage to the South, construct levee and harbor improvements, help complete the Texas and Pacific Railroad, and welcome the South into national life; southern politicians would not obstruct certain Republican programs, would help elect Garfield speaker of the House, obey the Constitution, and guarantee Negroes civil rights. If this arrangement succeeded, the South could expect northern private capital, which in turn could gain liberal financial terms; southerners would get a new standard of living, and quit political bickering to rebuild their states and section. A restored Union in the best sense of the word would follow. "The Southern people are to be made to feel that they are a part of the great American republic, and to this end they are to be aided in the establishment of honest and economical local government," the *New York Tribune* noted as Hayes read his inaugural address.[37]

Hayes made few public statements on this arrangement, but friends and leading Republicans supported it. Those who thought Hayes weak had some grounds for doubt. A man with his war record might not abandon emotions surrounding the noblest moments in his life. He once told William McKinley that a GAR button was "the grandest decoration he ever had." [38] And he still thought the war "the divinest . . . that was ever waged." [39] But he knew war was "a cruel business [with] brutality in it on all sides." [40]

His ardor for Radical Reconstruction had soon cooled, and as federal intervention wore on, he thought there was another way to change the South. As early as 1871, he concluded that material progress would do more for both whites and Negroes than martial law.[41] As the disputed election unfolded after November, 1876, he agreed that peace would in fact pacify the South. The business community would help politicians establish order. Education, internal improvements, full governmental representation, and patronage would ease the transition to responsible local rule. By December, 1876, Hayes told a visitor that "carpetbag governments had not been successful; that the complaints of the southern people were just in this matter." [42]

Almost everyone who advised him insisted that Reconstruction must end. If he took the lead, after suitable arrangements with southerners, the problem would terminate on a just, if not happy note. Powerful groups in the North thought the experiment had failed; public opinion would not support it any longer. The real problem was not to end Reconstruction, but to avoid disrupting the Republican party. By January, 1877, President Grant had assured advisers that, while he would not withdraw the last troops, he favored ending military rule.[43] All this fortified Hayes' own attitudes. Like most men, he believed what he wanted to believe; but he saw hundreds of letters from all kinds of men after November, 1876, promising that southerners with adequate federal support would slip quietly back into the national stream. This alone could bring any kind of justice, harmony, and economic well-being to the Negro.

To Hayes, the dominant theme in this discordant symphony was the simple fact that northern public opinion would not support a federal military presence in the South. The whole problem disrupted national economics and politics. The Negro had made little progress with token federal protection, and a large body of opinion was indifferent or frankly hostile to more sacrifices for full emancipation.[44] Even Republican officials in the South knew the game was over. Daniel Chamberlain, carpetbag governor of South Carolina, admitted as much. "The North is *tired* of the Southern question, and wants a settlement, no matter what." [45] Just how to change the South remained the insoluble problem of the age. Hayes might well have agreed with the observation: [46] "The South says to Hayes what the school-boy thinks at his teacher—

> Talkin' don't do no good,
> Lickin don't last long—
> Kill me you daren't.

Would southern leaders fulfill their promises? Critics called them "Bourbons," dismissing talk of "redeeming" the South as a means of restoring pre-war rule. Like the Frenchmen, they supposedly had neither forgotten nor learned. This stereotype was not quite accurate, however. The group did not include old rebels like Jefferson Davis, Alexander H. Stephens, or Robert Toombs. The Bourbons talked about the Lost Cause, knowing its political value, but saw the line between reality and fantasy. They were largely self-made men, interested in railroads, lumber yards, mines, wharves, and levees, rather than constitutional debates or plantations. They were pompous and conservative, but not enough to harm material self-interest. They wanted to govern and develop a redeemed South; in return they promised order.

Hayes' belief that Whiggery might restore southern stability and material wealth reflected his interest in bipartisanship, and personal optimism. The idea had some hope of success. Though leftover zealots in the North opposed withdrawal, their own program of military occupation failed to change the South, truly free the Negro, or help poor whites. By 1877, all but two states were in local hands. Hayes' idea was fundamentally sound. Only material prosperity and political stability could help anyone in the South. If he could entice enough old Whigs, moderate Democrats, and reasonable Republicans into a new arrangement, if not a new party, the compromise might work.

Nervous politicians feared Hayes would not fulfill his agents' promises. Pressures were great to discard the arrangement, now that he was successfully elected. He might ruin the GOP if he moved quickly; but delay invited Democratic attacks and renewed guerrilla warfare in national politics. Speaker of the House Samuel J. Randall wrote a fellow Democrat, Senator Thomas F. Bayard of Delaware, to put off confirming Hayes' Cabinet until he withdrew troops from New Orleans and Columbia.[47] Hayes' usual silence, and the soft footfalls of arriving and departing advisers, fortified an impression that he might wait too long for comfort's sake.

The President was merely getting his wagons together. He wanted to mollify colleagues, sound opinion, and cushion the shock when carpetbag regimes fell. He started the whole process with a firm attitude of mind, though not a detailed plan: "My policy is trust, peace, and to put aside the bayonet." [48] He saw four alternatives: The Administration might force new elections in the states, accepting the results; this would take time, and perhaps renew debate on both sides with unfortunate consequences. He could recognize local legislatures, ignore carpetbaggers, and let events develop; this might bring violence, and compel intervention. He could "acknowledge Packard and Chamberlain, and leave them to their own state remedies"; that would also provoke violence. Only the last choice was realistic: "Withdraw troops and leave events to take care of themselves." [49]

No one in the Cabinet but Devens favored even token force, and he did not press the issue. Evarts thought the whole arrangement was unconstitutional, since the people of Louisiana and South Carolina had duly elected legislatures. The rest simply wanted to ease out, and the President had little popular support for any other course. "If this leads to the overthrow of the *de jure* government in a state, the *de facto* government must be recognized." [50]

Hayes turned first to South Carolina because the situation there was the least explosive. Rival governments, one with federal support under Daniel H. Chamberlain, the other under the tutelage of Wade Hampton, tensely awaited Washington's recognition. Chamberlain's regime controlled a few buildings and no one's loyalties outside his own circle. "No intelligent man, who is politically sane and has watched the situation in the South, can have any sort of doubt that the Packard and Chamberlain governments would dissolve like the baseless fabric of a vision and vanish into thin air as soon as the federal authority should declare that it would no longer protect them," a New York paper warned.[51]

On March 23, Hayes invited Chamberlain and Hampton to Washington. Chamberlain arrived on March 27; Hampton came two days later, his progress north a latter-day triumph, complete with florid speeches from a railroad car. After a Cabinet meeting on March 31, Hayes announced that when the two men returned to Columbia, federal troops would retire. On April 3, in a formal letter to the Secretary of War, he ordered the soldiers to their barracks. Though he called on northern friends for help, Chamberlain left office quietly. At noon, Tuesday, April 10, he surrendered papers and state effects to Hampton, ending military rule in the Palmetto State.[52]

In Louisiana, a more complex situation awaited the President. The state was important because of New Orleans' role in national trade and as an investment center for the South. Its customhouse and other federal offices made it an enclave of Republican power in a Democratic wilderness. Contending state governments were ensnarled in threats and confusion, and delay or the wrong tone might trigger violence, but after fifteen years of federal control of one kind or another, the carpetbag government ruled an acre of the state. Stephen B. Packard, awaiting succession with federal support, warned that withdrawal would leave Negroes at the mercy of ravenous mobs, and asked northern Republicans to thwart Hayes.

The President's caution served him well, despite carping criticism from Democrats. On March 21, Hayes announced that he would send a special commission to investigate the confused situation. He hoped several prominent southerners like John M. Harlan and L. Q. C. Lamar might serve, but they declined, as did Vice-President Wheeler. Hayes chose a reasonably balanced group of moderates that critics thought was the limit of his reach, and which friends praised for avoiding controversy with powerful leaders. By April 19, the commission favored withdrawal. Last minute conferring convinced Hayes "that the colored people shall have equal rights to labor, to education, and to the privileges of citizenship. I am confident this is a good work. Time will tell." [53] The wish fathered the thought, but on April 24, the soldiers returned to barracks. The effort to reconstruct Louisiana and the South was over.

While these public events fell into place, Hayes read private reports from friends en route to New Orleans that first heartened, then disappointed him. Andrew Kellar said the business element in cities along the Mississippi, and especially in New Orleans, would fulfill political promises. He even held out the hope that businessmen would join a coalition of old Whigs and moderate Democrats. Hayes' friend James M. Comly, editor of the *Ohio State Journal* in Columbus, drifted down the Mississippi in euphoric mien, sure that "Henry Clay Whiggery" would revive when the formalities of withdrawal ended. But less than two weeks later, arriving in New Orleans where local forces were in firm control, reality dawned. He wrote Hayes a fitting epitaph for the grand design: "The 'old Whig' sentiment I spoke of petered out before we reached New Orleans. There is nothing to hang an old whig party on. The truth is there does not seem to be anything except the Custom House to hang *anything* on." [54]

Nervous tension in the South gave way to relief as white elements took command in the name of "local rule." Tremors ran through the Republican party while moderates and radicals alike awaited conciliation's effects. For a nervous moment, Senator James G. Blaine of Maine, easily the GOP's most commanding public figure, attacked Hayes' moderation. Long a deft matador with the bloody shirt, Blaine reacted instinctively to the accomplished fact of troop withdrawal, though during the preceding winter he seemed to favor the settlement. On March 6, he spoke openly against the policy, and Garfield tried to mollify him for days, asking only that he give it "a fair trial." [55] Blaine had gained too many votes on the issue to drop it quietly; but he earnestly suspected southern intentions regarding the Negro. "I can't go the new policy," he wrote Whitelaw Reid. "Every instinct of my nature rebels against it and I feel an intuition amounting to an infatuation that the North is adopting it against the day of wrath. In any event, its success means the triumph of the Democratic party—against which I wage eternal war!" [56] The intensity of the outburst indicated his doubts, though he knew the days were passing rapidly when that purely emotional cry "Vote the way you shot!" would build parties.

The southern problem was a major factor in life; but as an echo, not a battle cry.

Most Americans agreed with a Thomas Nast cartoon: "Stand back and give the President's policies a chance." [57] Hayes hoped to satisfy the inarticulate masses' desire for rest; whatever he did alienated someone. He knew enough of human psychology to understand the remark of a former abolitionist: "My judgment clearly approves the policy of Mr. Hayes, yet my feelings rebel." [58] Hayes did not agonize over the decision. "My judgement was that the time had come to put an end to bayonet rule," he later noted. "I saw things done in the South which could only be accounted for on the theory that the war was not yet ended. . . . My task was to wipe out the color line, to abolish sectionalism, to end the war and bring peace." [59]

Hayes started the process of conciliation with high hopes, and clung tenaciously to the idea of a new southern political group that might vote Republican if the North used carrots instead of sticks. He thought the "pacification policy" would determine affairs in North Carolina, Maryland, Virginia, Tennessee, and Arkansas. In unguarded moments, he expressed hopes about Louisiana, South Carolina, and Florida.[60] Once released from the imprisoning uncertainty of his first month in office, Hayes embarked on a series of personal appearances that refuted the straw-man caricature. On Memorial Day in 1877, he decorated Union and Confederate graves in Tennessee. In June he went to Boston with Evarts, Schurz, Key, and Devens to seek support. In September he visited Ohio, Kentucky, Tennessee, Georgia, and Virginia, spreading the gospel of harmony, urging everyone to forget the past, tacitly promising assistance for the future.[61] His ventures into the South surprised reporters, politicians, and even southerners. People who allegedly thought him a fraud, turned out in droves.[62]

The ceremonial and social aspects of the trips were all very well, but the President knew their political value. He convinced himself that southern cities would soon welcome Republican doctrine. Leaving Richmond, he noted: "There are thousands of intelligent people who are not Democrats, and who would like to unite with the conservative Republicans of the North." [63] A little later, Secretary Sherman summed up the reasonable partisan ideals behind Hayes' policy: "What we wish is to combine, if possible, in harmonious political action the same class of men in the South as are Republicans [elsewhere]; that is, the producing classes, men who are interested in industry and property." [64] It was a fine idea, and could help both the South and the Republican party, but it was utterly unrealistic. The South was no sooner free of federal influence than it lapsed into sectionalism. Part of this was spasmodic, but most of it inhered in the situation. The Republican party was identified with military rule and Negro rights. Those two simple propositions spelled its doom in southern history.

Hayes sweetened the pills with the sugar of patronage. In five months, a third of his southern appointments were Democrats. True, he sometimes violated civil service principles, and appointed to federal posts members of the 1876 returning boards and carpetbaggers, but that was natural in political life. He was more than generous to southerners; Secretary Key sent them considerable Post Office patronage.[65] Hayes did not try to build a Negro faction, and frankly counseled freedmen to stay in the South even though in segregation, as long as whites obeyed the law.[66]

Both the original compromise and its fulfillment required cooperation between Democrats and Republicans. In the fall of 1877, when Congress convened in special session, the spirit of conciliation disappeared with unseemly speed. The Democrats refused to elect Garfield Speaker, as he had predicted. The President already had doubts about the Texas and Pacific Railroad, and wanted to avoid "any more Credit Mobilier operations."[67] But Republicans were not as obstructive as the Democrats who controlled the House. Southern demands for internal improvements frightened economy-minded northern Democrats. Some of the proposals for spending federal money in the South savored of Mark Twain's best sketches. Southerners suggested a tunnel through the Alleghenies to Virginia; a canal across Florida to link the Gulf and the Atlantic; useless roadways, bridges, and levees. Between October and December, they introduced 40 such bills in the Senate, and 267 in the House.[68] Many northern Democrats did not want a revived, and perhaps dominant, southern party. Republicans and some Democrats did not welcome southern opposition to tariff protection, the gold standard, and industrialization. "We must conciliate the solid South, undoubtedly," remarked the *New York Tribune*. "But what will it cost?"[69]

State and local elections in the fall of 1877 returned Democratic slates in the South, forecasting things to come in national contests. More and more of the President's associates turned from his dream of harmony when it failed to pay dividends. Garfield candidly wrote a friend in February, 1878: "The policy of the President has turned out to be a give-away from the beginning."[70] He soon repeated the talk of Capitol corridors and hotel suites: "The impression is deepening that he is not large enough for the place he holds." [71] From the party regular's viewpoint, the real fault in Hayes' program was a failure to make political gains. Garfield said Hayes seemed to act alone in dealing with the South. "It would have been more just and more politic to have associated his party with the proffers of good will." [72] The genteel *Nation* summed it up: "The Democrats have thus far managed to make the President's southern policy appear quite as much a Democratic victory as a voluntary and patriotic scheme of his own." [73]

The proof of prediction came in the congressional elections of 1878. The Democrats won Congress, and voted an almost solid South. Garfield's only consolation was a solid North, whose electoral votes would choose a Republican president. Hayes told the press: "I am reluctantly forced to admit that the experiment was a failure," though in his annual message a month later he urged patience.[74] Thereafter, he spoke more harshly of the South, both publicly and privately, and had less time for visiting dignitaries from that area. The results provided Hayes' opponents with an excuse to attack his policies. Old Abolitionists were most vocal. Wendell Phillips had already said: "Half of what Grant gained for us at Appomattox, Hayes surrendered in Washington on the 5th of March." [75] Early in the new year, William E. Chandler, never reconciled to any "new Republicanism," published correspondence with William Lloyd Garrison. Like a relic stranded on the beaches of Time, Garrison cried: "The bloody shirt! *In hoc signo vinces!*" [76]

Friends of the Negro agonized over his fate. Critics accused Hayes and the Republicans of "abandoning" him,* but the whole process of American history abandoned the Negro. No significant body of opinion now sustained military rule, an understandable, if distressing, attitude. The southern problem had dominated American life for over a generation, and most expedients with any support had their trial. Nothing seemed to work, short of a massive effort at total physical, economic, and social reconstruction which northern opinion would not support even in 1865. A man of fifty in 1877 had spent most of his adult life worrying over the South and the Negro; first in the great compromises of the 1850's, then in four years of war, then in twelve years of "recon-

---

*Most historians make this claim, and then pass on to condemn Republicans for trying to revive the issue with the "bloody shirt." How the party was to use the issue without discussing it is a mystery, and how they could discuss it without reviving wartime issues is a greater mystery. Few historians ever point out that the "bloody shirt" had a more potent appeal in the South than in the North, and that politicians in grey used it far longer than those in blue.

struction." A man of thirty had spent all his adult years listening to the subject. A maturing man of twenty-one remembered little else. Hard times, new issues, and the sheer weight of time made the problem seem increasingly less relevant or soluble. "[Garrison] may go on saying hard things about Mr. Hayes, and there will be multitudes to shout Amen," the *New York Times* commented. "But does he really imagine that outside of small and suspicious circles any real interest attaches to the old form of the southern question?" [77]

More significant for moderate Republicans, powers within the party began to assail the President. Blaine was unhappy, and Conkling had long argued that Hayes hoped to create a personal party, alternately calling the President a weakling and a tyrant.[78] The southern question was subsiding in northern politics, though its fierce rhetoric lingered like a stubborn echo.

Events rapidly confounded predictions that Hayes would spend a quiet term in the White House. The nagging southern issue consumed time and energy, raising grave problems in both major parties. In the summer of 1877, however, public apprehension and attention focused on the first great outbreak of labor violence in American history. The long depression naturally frustrated workers, and some prophets of gloom predicted a war between labor and capital, as industrialization enveloped American society. In mid-July, railroad workers on the principal lines passing through Maryland, Pennsylvania, and West Virginia struck to gain union recognition, better working conditions, and higher pay. Tension easily flashed into violence, and in Pittsburgh strikers and militia fought until state governors requested federal troops.*

Unrest reflected deeper problems in the lengthening depression.[79] The President's responsibility was simple; he must maintain order, whatever his private views. Secretary Sherman blamed the railroad companies for obtuseness and speculation that forced wage cuts,[80] but local officials, nervous politicians, and the propertied middle class favored more repressive measures than either state or federal authorities permitted. The chilly *Nation* thought the whole affair "a national disgrace. . . ," and saw "a widespread rising, not against political oppression or unpopular government, but against society itself." [81] Workers bitterly accused the railroads of oppression, and had similar visions. "A Striker" warned that cries for law and order would not move men whom unjust laws and attitudes restricted. "We are sick of this game,

---

*This story is brilliantly recounted in Robert V. Bruce, *1877, Year of Violence* (Indianapolis: Bobbs, Merrill, & Co., 1959).

are soul-weary of looking around for some sympathy or spirit of justice; and finding none, we turn to each other and form brotherhoods and unions, depots of the army of labor, officered by the skilled mechanic." [82] It was a perceptive remark, warning that labor like business reserved the right to combine and compete in larger units.

Hayes reluctantly supported state authority with token forces of federal troops, realizing they would inevitably help break the strike, but his constitutional obligations were clear; he had to meet appeals of state authorities for federal troops. He took only modest comfort with the usual diary entry. "The strikes have been put down by *force*, but now for the real remedy. Can't something be done by education of the strikers, by judicious control of the capitalists, by wise general policy to end or diminish the evil? The railroad strikers, as a rule, are good men, sober, intelligent and industrious." [83] It was an unrealistic suggestion, emphasizing education and rationality—factors seldom at the disposal of bitter and desperate men.

So the summer passed. The first public acceptance of the President's southern policy mixed with apprehension and struggle. Behind the scenes, a fight opened within the Republican party. Men and ideas clustered around the calm words "civil service reform" in patterns that threatened to disrupt the Republican party.

Hayes probably never heard of Ambrose Bierce, or read the sharp, cynical observations later in *The Devil's Dictionary*, but he would have liked the definition for *lighthouse:* "A tall building on the seashore in which the government maintains a lamp and the friend of a politician." Hayes wanted to reform a civil service that *only* maintained politicians. The party platform in 1876 favored competent appointments, but Hayes opposed officeholders' service in campaigns, assessments on salaries, and political rotation. "I need hardly assure you that if ever I have charge of an administration, this whole assessment business will go up, 'hook, line, and sinker,'" he told Carl Schurz during the campaign.[84] In the inaugural address, he disturbed some listeners by proposing reform "that shall be thorough, radical, and complete; . . ." Yet he never opposed partisan appointments. Like most moderate reformers, he wanted to abolish assessments, appoint qualified persons, and grant tenure.

Most politicians assumed, like the *New York Times*, that "preference will be given to a Republican, all other things being equal." [85] Opponents of change quietly hoped the southern question, needs of party harmony, and other pressures would make Hayes drop the subject, but the President had reformers in the Cabinet, and he discussed the idea even while settling the southern problem. Men like Senator Conkling soon stayed away from the White House rather than seek patronage. The daily mail brought Hayes both encouragement and warnings from reformers.

These proponents of change, soon to wear the derisive name "Mugwump," were a small but vocal group, with influence in the professional and business worlds that spilled over into workaday politics.* Their leading spokesmen, like Edwin Lawrence Godkin, editor of the *Nation,* George William Curtis, editor of *Harper's Weekly,* and Secretary Schurz, were familiar to the reading public. They were not unknown to politicians now demanding the usual grease for the wheels in the political machine. These men were not a party, but they were a movement, staging conventions, writing articles, and speaking for reform. The typical Mugwump was well educated, more involved in professional or financial interests than industry. Efficiency and competition were twin gods, and he distrusted government regulation and subsidization. He favored free trade and the gold dollar. He distrusted combinations of labor as much as those of capital or big government. He disliked immigrants, and wavered in supporting full social participation for the Negro. Looking at bad city government, he suspected democratic control and universal suffrage.[86]

The movement's leaders were older men, but younger people of the same type moved against entrenched organizations. The whole movement also reflected the usual desire of younger men for power as each generation passes. Old issues were fading; those who sharpened new ones could rule, and just as importantly, set the tone of society.[87] These were gentlemen, but they matured in the sharp American system and gave as good as they got. Godkin never turned the other cheek without a good reason, and many a contemptuous politician bore marks of his retaliatory assaults. The *New York Evening Post* under his editorship, and the *Nation,* his chief love, breathed truculence. Joseph H. Choate called the former "a pessimistic, malignant, and malevolent sheet, which no good citizen goes to bed without reading." One elderly lady always felt safe with the *Post* on the doorstep because "it just lay there and growled all night." [88]

Their audience was important. The gospel of efficiency satisfied some businessmen with political influence. Cries for retrenchment rallied a propertied middle class complaining of high taxation and

*Technically speaking, the term "Mugwump" identifies Republicans who left their party in 1884 to support Grover Cleveland. I realize the dangers of using the term too inclusively, but it seems applicable, since the bolt of 1884 concerned a type of man and a body of thought well established in the 1870's.

poor government. A desire to make government more efficient appealed to people tired of political factionalism. A few politicians favored a merit system to lighten the burden of sifting office-seekers, and the dangers of appointing the wrong people. Around the edge of the Mugwump doctrine ran the unifying moral principle that "spoilsmanship" was inherently wrong. It bred paternalism, and marked a spiritual decline from the days of the Fathers.[89]

The reformers lived in cities, where the worst examples of popular rule were in evidence, and transferred this attitude to all government. They were amazed that bossism and corruption flourished with such complacency. How long would the masses tolerate bad city services, immorality, high taxes? Was the voter satisfied to receive only crumbs from Government's table? He often was. The uneducated immigrant at least saw material benefits in a bossism that accepted him on his own terms. He voted for men who held court on shoeshine stands and in lodge halls rather than in board rooms or paneled libraries.

Mugwumps never understood the full meaning of patronage. Men who gave it, and men who won it had power and stature. It symbolized success and acceptance, and denoted a role in the party structure. Organizations which reformers busily condemned as inefficient and corrupt rested on human contacts, and increased the small man's stature. The teeming masses of Philadelphia, small-town businessmen, and prairie farmers often gained a satisfying status in defying their "betters." Mugwumps returned the hostility, talking darkly of coming revolutions and the "lower classes." Men usually admire and respect either individuals or humanity as an abstract whole. Anything in between seems a mob. Reformers hoped that governmental efficiency and economy would balance a tendency to ruthless social mass. Permanent policy-making, and official tenure would control growth and keep power in the hands of those fitted to rule.

The Mugwumps remained ingrown, reading each other's books, talking similar rhetoric, making the same proposals. They could not command a mass following, but relied on propaganda and contacts among moderate men who did rule. "The best elements of society," as they modestly styled themselves, were not likely to set the public afire. Charts, graphs, and figures were less real than a letter of appointment or bag of groceries. Charles Francis Adams, George William Curtis, Charles Eliot Norton, were not lightning rods of public appeal. Irritating self-righteousness did not help. "When I am in a small minority I believe I am right," William Everett of Massachusetts noted smugly. "When I am in a minority of one, I know I am right."[90]

Few lines of communication and none of affection linked them to professional politicians. Neither side had any illusions about the brewing fight as Hayes took office. "The politicians who have long lived by the use of official patronage will not surrender it without a fierce and desperate resistance," Benjamin Bristow warned Schurz.[91] Talk of competitive examinations irritated ward bosses and state barons. George Washington Plunkitt, Tammany Hall's great sidewalk-philosopher, later reviewed the whole thing with horror. A man might not get a job without answering "a list of questions about Egyptian mummies and how many years it will take for a bird to wear out a mass of iron as big as the earth by steppin' on it once in a century."[92] Horace Porter of New York said a Mugwump was a person educated beyond his capacities. Others saw reform as a way of creating an impersonal elite and disappointing the common man:[93]

> We shall see some queer mutations
>   and improvements not a few
> Firemen now must know equations
>   and be up on Euclid too.
> Practical we are, not narrow—
>   here the proof of that appears;
> Men who wheel the nimble barrow
>   must be civil engineers.

Politicians berated the "part-your-hair-in-the-middle-George William Curtis frauds."[94] Powers like Tom Platt of New York ridiculed the whole thing as a disguise for high-toned office-hunters. "Hungry expectants of office stand on street corners and shout the shibboleth [of civil service reform] until they are hoarse and weary. The independent journalist rolls it as a sweet morsel under his tongue, and daily blurts it in the face of a nauseated public."[95]

Politicians rebutted Mugwumps with a philosophy that appealed to many Americans. The people, they held, wanted no impersonal government, however efficient. Officials should be responsible to constituents, and the threat of removal kept them on their toes. Assessments from their salary were legitimate campaign contributions. Above all, as a correspondent warned Hayes: "Every free government is necessarily a partisan government."[96] Permanent tenure would breed arrogance and perhaps inefficiency in office-holders. It would do for the Prussians or English, but not Americans. They preached the gospel of "every man an expert," with a right to government employment if he could get it.[97]

The whole doctrine and controversy stirred dormant factionalism in both parties. Senators, Congressmen, and local officials saw that a

permanent civil service might weaken localism in politics, and emphasize loyalty to party over individual leaders. It could also increase the
president's powers to mold a national party at the expense of other
leaders. He might easily say he had no jobs to offer, thanks to the
civil service rule; or appoint his own man, safe from later removal.
Those suspicions prompted fierce opposition. The waspish *New York
Sun* warned: "What Hayes and Schurz and the rest of the fraudulent
administration mean by civil service reform is to put their own political friends in office and foist them on their successors for life." [98]

Mugwump doctrine was full of contradictions and twisting turns of
logic. It preached efficiency, but in small ways. Seeking order, it channeled growth narrowly. Better government could not live apart from
a free-wheeling democracy that savored politics. Politicians understood the double threat in civil service reform, since it would deprive
them of patronage and campaign funds. But just as importantly, in an
era of close elections and bitter strife, organized civil service reformers
might gain the balance of control. In the hands of secure men commanding an influential audience, reform dominated parts of the business
community, college classrooms, pulpits, lawyer's offices. None of these
groups alone could threaten partisan victory, but if an issue combined
them, power might pass to those "who foraged between the lines."
This was the politician's fear.

Civil service reform did not become an issue accidentally. In a time
of bewildering change it offered some hope of social control and
predictable growth. It promised reason in governmental administration, just as efficient management brought order to business. It would
found a government useful for an unknown future, when no man
could tell what the state might have to do. The Mugwump vision of
America as a whole was distorted and narrow, but the reformers were
right, if often for the wrong reasons. Civil service reform was an ironic
paradox for the men who proposed it. A radical suggestion within the
context of American party development, it would perform a conservative function.* It might also let expert government expand beyond
the Mugwumps' desires.

"Now for civil service reform," Hayes wrote on April 22, 1877. "We
must limit and narrow the area of patronage. We must diminish the

---

*In 1898 the English Fabian Socialist Beatrice Webb toured the United States,
and after noting its chaotic politics, observed: "If such a civil service could arise
in the United States and gain permanence of tenure, it will become the most powerful and untrammeled bureaucracy in the world." (See *Beatrice Webb's American
Diary*, 1898, 38.)

evils of office-seeking. We must stop interference of federal officers with elections. We must be relieved of congressional dictation as to appointments." He ordered Sherman to investigate the customhouses in New York, Boston, San Francisco and Philadelphia, and the Secretary dispatched a group to New York under John Jay. On May 24, it recommended a reduction of staff and removal of the customhouse from politics. Sherman passed the report to Hayes, agreeing with the subsidiary recommendations, but cautiously asking for presidential advice on removing employees. Hayes was firm—officeholders must not be assessed and must be fit for their work. Later in the week, Sherman told Collector Chester A. Arthur to reduce the staff and avoid partisan activity. The directive recommended rather than instructed on most points. The Secretary, and apparently the President, wished to avoid a confrontation with the New York Republican organization. Perhaps Arthur would take the hint and set his customhouse in order.

Reformers sighed; it all sounded like the ritualistic noises General Grant had made about reform. Perhaps Hayes was as weak as his enemies said. Behind the scenes, Sherman tried to convince friends that self-help was better than party warfare. The President was silent for a month, then on June 22, issued an executive order forbidding federal officeholders "to take part in the management of political organizations, caucuses, conventions, or election campaigns." He put teeth in the rhetoric: "No assessment for political purposes on officers or subordinates should be allowed," and applied the ruling to the whole civil service.[99] Reformers applauded, and filled editorials with praise, but Sherman continued politicking, and Hayes waited on events. Everyone expected a battle, and no one was eager for it.

All parties concerned might well hesitate, for Hayes had challenged the lordliest Republican, Senator Roscoe Conkling of New York. The subject of miles of newspaper coverage, he was the chief ornament of a gaudy era's public life. His Republican credentials were as good as any man's, and better than most. Born in 1829, he rose quickly in Utica's legal and political circles. He served in the national House from 1859 to 1867, except for one term in 1863–65. He stood between Thaddeus Stevens and threatening foes, who promptly departed, knowing Conkling's agility in the boxing ring. A staunch war Republican and Radical, he earned a reputation for rigid political allegiance and cutting invective. When William H. Seward remained loyal to Andrew Johnson, Conkling gained control of the major faction in the New York party. After his first election to the Senate in 1867, he increasingly dominated the state organization, and became a friend of Presi-

dent Grant, who offered him the position of Chief Justice of the
United States in 1873. Conkling declined, preferring politics to the
Bench. His personal machine rested on the simple tenets of loyalty,
uncompromising if undefined Republicanism, and the sheer tension of
winning in the chaotic Empire State. He summed up his philosophy
in one line: "I do not know how to belong to a party a little." [100]

The public knew Conkling more as a personality than politician,
and small wonder, in view of the image he cultivated. He was tall,
graceful, and took pride in his hair, one "Hyperion curl" dangling
carefully over a broad forehead. Disdaining sober black, he was a
bird of paradise in a barnyard of duskier fowl. Green trousers and
a scarlet coat, mauve waistcoats with gold lace, striped shirts, and
yellow shoes, were all part of "Lord Roscoe's" legend. Though charming when necessary, he generally fulfilled a reputation for arrogance.
His few empty letters unrolled in purple ink through florid lines on
suitably embossed paper. If he needed a page boy in the Senate, he
clapped his hands like a Roman senator. On more than one day, he
strode scowling to his seat amid adoring sighs from ladies in the gallery, and nodded curt thanks for baskets of roses. Foes sneered at
"the curled darling of Utica," but he dismissed criticism as envy.[101]

Most of Conkling's surface personality was an elaborate front; but
the act was merely larger than life, and reflected his true tastes and
values. He was hostile to the world, and suspected every man's motives. The wonder was that a defense mechanism controlling these
tensions let him develop as a public figure. But within him, like a
clearing in a jungle, was a hidden capacity for warmth and respect.
Like many formidable men, he helped the less fortunate without
publicity. He was a lifelong friend of the Negro, and Blanche K.
Bruce, black senator from Mississippi in Radical days, named a son
after him. Conkling seldom answered opponents, but quietly thanked
those who did. Many people of differing views attested to his generosity, and to his clear, if usually cold, understanding of their problems.[102]

The press covered his activities as it reported an earthquake—
amply but without approval. He returned the favor, esteeming reporters somewhat lower than the angels. He announced with a sneer
that only two of heaven's creatures could rightly employ the term
"We"; newspaper editors and men with tapeworms. He was not the
typical politician, whose public enemies are often private friends. A
foe was a foe, and they did not speak as they passed by. It extended
even to the household. His daughter married a man he disliked, whom

he called "Mrs. Conkling's son-in-law." [103] He was not the beer-hall, song-fest, county-fair politician, shaking hands all around, and sampling every lady's pie. He believed in a good measure of contempt for followers, and noted "the spaniel-like element of human nature" that liked to follow a great man's lead.[104] Conkling enjoyed money, but was not corrupt. "You see these rooms," he told a visitor to his hotel. "They are the best I can afford, and by the utmost economy it is as much as I can do to make the strap and buckle meet at the end of the year." [105] He played the game for power and publicity, to feed a starved nature he could never expose. Fortunately, a group of able men like Arthur explained away his whims and crotchets, mollified tempers, and bandaged emotional bruises.

Conkling's organization seemed impregnable to the idle observer, but the Senator covered its real gaps with a good deal of bluff. New York's electorate shifted constantly, and a man with a power base in the countryside and upstate towns ran hard just to survive. He could not rule New York City, but its minority vote resting on federal patronage would give him a state-wide majority. Conkling was now in trouble. His disinterest in fresh issues and distrust of new men threw him back on old methods of maneuver and talk. Nervousness made him over-react to Hayes' proposed reforms, and it was not in his nature to compromise.

Conkling could not find words to sketch his contempt of reformers, but had not always disliked Hayes. He sought the nomination in 1876, and some friends touted an eastern-midwestern alliance:

> Conkling and Hayes
> Is the ticket that pays.

He did not campaign actively in 1876, because of eye trouble, and resented the nomination of New York's William A. Wheeler for vice-president.[106] After the election, his emissaries spread tales about the two men. Hayes thwarted Conkling's hope of naming a Cabinet member by appointing two of his enemies, Evarts and Schurz. Evarts had pretensions in New York politics and would not regret Conkling's ruin.[107] Within a month of the inauguration, the Senator's friends were openly condemning "the old woman policy of Granny Hayes." Conkling said Hayes would knife everyone who helped him, suggesting darkly that he had "a disturbed mind." [108] Hayes reciprocated,* and

---

*After Conkling's death in 1888, Hayes noted: "An inordinate egotism and self-will were too much for his judgement. If he could not rule, he would not 'play.' He was unfaithful to his party when-ever he could not control it." (Hayes Diary, April 19, 1888, HML.)

matched Conkling's open contempt with stubbornness, remarking later that it was "useless to attempt to conciliate such a person." [109] As their jousting began, harmonizers like Sherman hoped for a quiet settlement. With a solid South in the offing, the party dared not lose New York.

The fight was bitterly personal, but also reflected different views of politics. Hayes knew Republicans must expand their national base. He wanted the party to face new issues, and civil service reform was a necessary beginning. More importantly, he wanted to enhance the presidency in national leadership. The party could not survive at the mercy of men like Conkling, willing to sacrifice wider interests for regional dominance. The Senator was a holdover from pre-war days, when powerful local leaders dictated national policies. Hayes would attack him with patience, the appointment power, and public opinion. In the process, he hoped other Republicans would see the danger of Conkling's style. As Murat Halstead warned: "The Cameron, Morton, Conkling, Grant party cannot be maintained. It must have a broadened base and reinforcements, or it is gone and the Democratic party will come into power for a generation. If you and I live to see it out of power, we will be old men." [110]

Any movement against the New York customhouse automatically involved the Collector, Chester Alan Arthur, a major figure in eastern Republican circles. "Chet" Arthur was a large, elegant man; even-tempered, and an ideal lieutenant for Conkling. He had patience and tact to explain away hurts his chief inflicted. Among his thousand employees, he was "a good natured and popular man," noted for knowledge of the revenue system. He made a great reputation for administrative vigor during the war, when he organized New York State's effort in cooperation with the federal government. Arthur was not a spoilsman so much as a partisan who saw nothing wrong in rewarding Republican fidelity. President Grant persuaded him to take the post of Collector in 1871, and $40,000 a year in fees and moieties made him a ranking government official until Congress fixed a salary of $12,000 a year in 1874, still a princely sum. [111] Arthur managed the most important single post in the federal revenue system. The Port of New York handled most American imports; during his tenure, some $840,000,000 passed through the office. The Port was a national institution, another reason for Hayes' refusal to leave it to local politicians. Arthur had a reputation as a reasonable partisan, but the business community distrusted customs authorities. The staff was often lax, and occasionally corrupt. Many employees were ill-equipped for technical duties. Businessmen would not risk open warfare on the Custom House, but quietly pressured congressmen and officials for reform.[112]

Secretary Sherman, in whose jurisdiction the matter rested, was eager to avoid a party battle, but would change the system. He hoped Arthur could make Conkling cooperate, because he "preferred to try to execute the proposed reforms with him in office rather than [with] a stranger." [113] Arthur's resistance to change stiffened as the summer waned. He would not step aside, and he could not desert Conkling. Like his chief, he hoped political friends would thwart the assault. Sherman's idea of retaining him in office was illusory anyway. Reformers insisted he must go; he represented a system, and should be its martyr. To leave him in charge would give the lie to reform. "Mankind at large will not believe that the Ethiopian can change his skin or the leopard his spots," Charles Eliot Norton warned the President.[114]

Hayes wanted to teach Conkling a lesson, and perhaps start liberalizing the New York party. Disturbing reports also came from William Henry Smith, collector in Chicago. Midwestern businessmen distrusted the New York Custom House. Its staff allegedly changed duties or delayed shipment of competing goods to interior markets. Hayes also knew this step toward change would pacify nagging Mugwumps and gain public support for a more general program.[115] Sherman continued efforts to avoid a clash, but on September 6, the Cabinet agreed to proceed against Arthur and his immediate subordinates. Hayes, leaving on a southern tour, would send in new appointments when Congress convened in special session in mid-October. Arthur's refusal to resign or cooperate crystallized the fight.[116]

Conkling was vacationing in Europe, where he regaled dinner guests with assaults on "snivel service reform," and vowed New York's party would not endorse Hayes' Administration at the forthcoming state convention. On Friday, August 10, he returned to New York. Reporters with sharp pencils chugged out to the ship in fireboats, but got only evasive replies to questions. The Senator alternated between idle talk and waving a small flag at friends on the dock. The trip upstate was a triumphal progress, and Conkling received guests at home in the quaint splendor of a garden party with oriental lights. He knew, of course, that some senatorial friends expected and wanted him to challenge the Administration.[117]

Newspaper speculation divided between fears that he would split the party with some foolish, vindictive move, and hopes that he would not resist reform. George William Curtis would offer the national convention a motion praising Hayes' southern and civil service policies. That was more than Conkling could take. He wrote a speech, showed it to friends, and refused to moderate the tone. As delegates gathered in Rochester on September 26, few people knew exactly what he would do.[118] Visitors saw a crowded hall, decked with bunting and strewn with flowers. A large stuffed eagle spread its wings symbolically, either for flight or attack. Conkling's presiding lieutenant, Thomas C. Platt, quickly set the tone, roasting reformers as traitors, and referred unkindly to the national Administration.

Then the great moment came, and Lord Roscoe rose coolly, scrupulously dressed, calm while the cheering subsided. "Administrations do not make parties, parties make administrations," he said. "Parties go before administrations, and live after them. The people make parties." Delegates were respectful but the galleries hissed, and the sight of Curtis angered Conkling. Warming to the subject, he exhausted the theme with point and counterpoint. The hot lava of his contempt splashed on "the dilettanti and carpet-knights of politics, men whose efforts have been expended in denouncing and ridiculing and accusing honest men, who in storm and sun, in war and peace, have clung to the Republican flag and defended it against those who have tried to trail and trample it in the dust." Amid mingled cheering and booing, he delivered a famous sally:

> Some of these worthies masquerade as reformers. Their vocation and ministry is to lament the sins of other people. Their stock in trade is rancid, canting self-righteousness. They are wolves in sheep's clothing. Their real object is office and plunder. When Dr. Johnson defined patriotism as the last refuge of a scoundrel, he was unconscious of the then undeveloped capabilities and uses of the word "Reform."

Open vowels lingered in the air, but he did not pause. "They forget that parties are not built up by deportment, or by ladies' magazines, or gush." As for Hayes, "The new president has been surrounded and courted by men who have long purred about every administration, some of them for more years than many of you have lived." [119]

Curtis remained in his seat, murmuring to friends: "What an exhibition!" "Bad temper!" "Extraordinary!" After the event, he fell back on olympian paternalism. "It was the saddest sight I ever knew, that man glaring at me in a fury of hate, and storming out his foolish blackguardism. I was all pity. I had not thought him great, but I had not suspected how small he was." [120] Curtis lost the motion to endorse Hayes, but many of Conkling's friends thought he went too far, and reluctantly entertained the opposition's idea: "Mr. Conkling will discover shortly that he has had one personal convention too many." A large proportion of the galleries clearly favored the Administration. The President was philosophical. Conkling later rumbled: "Yes, there are about three hundred persons here who believe themselves to 'occupy the solar walk and milky way,' and even lift up their skirts very carefully for fear even the heavens might stain them." [121]

Hayes fired the next shot and, on October 24, named Theodore Roosevelt, Sr., to replace Arthur as Collector; L. Bradford Prince to replace Alonzo B. Cornell as Naval Officer; and Edwin A. Merritt to be Port Surveyor. All were moderate Republicans, though hardly reformers. Hayes and Sherman thus hoped to strike a balance within the New York party, but Lord Roscoe saw it otherwise. On November 30, his Senate Commerce Committee unanimously rejected the nominees. A group of ranking New York Republican congressmen visited Hayes, hoping for a compromise, but the President silently pointed to the civil service plank in the 1876 platform. On December 12, after issuing threats, cashing political IOU's, and rallying anti-reform senators in the name of senatorial courtesy, Conkling defeated Roosevelt and Prince, but let Merritt pass.[122]

Conkling savored the victory, little noting that he used most of his power to attain it. His arrogance and narrowness began to rankle colleagues. If it came to choosing between his Republican party and Hayes', they might follow the President. But it was largely the reformers' turn to criticize Hayes in the spring of 1878. His subordinates did not prevent "voluntary" contributions to campaign funds; partisanship in the departments and post offices did not cease. Hayes now seemed disinterested, and told Curtis realistically, "we have only a percent on our side—not enough to quarrel, or sulk about things. Let us get together. The harshest blows many crotchety reformers strike are against each other. Many of the blows are in sheer ignorance of facts." [123]

In the intervening months, a number of state conventions endorsed the Administration. Vacationing congressmen at Christmas-time found constituents either disinterested or hostile toward senatorial delay. With issues like free silver, depression, and the South, didn't Congress and Republicans have better things to do than quarrel over customhouses? Hayes was right. "In the end the claim of a single senator to control all nominations in his state will be found so preposterous that it will fall of its own weight." [124] The reformers began praising Hayes again after July 11, when he removed Arthur and Cornell, with interim appointments for Merritt and Silas W. Burt.

In December, he sent the nominations to the Senate's regular session. Conkling delayed, storming in committee rooms and corridors, but he was running scared. Sherman made more promises, pulled wires, and secured enough Republicans and Democrats to pass the appointments on February 3, 1879. The confirmation had a bipartisan tone, but many Democrats like Thomas F. Bayard simply wished to thwart the abusive Conkling.[125] An air of quiet triumph surrounded Hayes. The President's critics said Cabinet members danced on tables and "the buttermilk flowed at the White House like water." [126] Godkin had a moment of sweet revenge: ". . . the destruction of the Arthur-Cornell question must have left a great void in [Conkling's] intellectual life. *That* he had thoroughly mastered. He was familiar with all the literature on it, ancient and modern. If an Arthur-Cornell Chair had been founded at a university, he would have been the only man competent to fill it." [127]

Hayes drafted new rules for the civil service, stressing efficiency and a reasonable partisanship. "Let no man be put out merely because he is Mr. Arthur's friend, and no man put in merely because he is our friend." [128] He later repeated the basic purpose in the fight. "The first step in the reform is to abolish congressional patronage—to restore to the executive the appointing power which has been usurped by Congress, and especially by the Senate." [129] Hayes meant it, but the big words did not fool anyone. Patronage and localism had not magically passed out of national life. Hayes had political aims and did not abolish partisanship. Lowly village postmasters and lordly collectors remained powers. But it was a beginning that normal political processes would extend. The Mugwumps complained of half a loaf, showing how little they comprehended representative politics, expecting Hayes to topple the system in a year, or even a term. They should have rejoiced. Hereafter, presidents and parties would not ignore civil service reform and all it symbolized.

Conkling was hardly finished. His organization remained a crucial factor in national elections, and in January, 1879, the Legislature gave him a third term. Cornell went on to be governor. Aides like Platt and Arthur continued their rounds. But something went out of Conkling. The realization that he could lose, biting publicity, and a small understanding that times were changing made him morose and magnified his worst qualities. Aloofness became isolation; arrogance a dangerous unwillingness to listen to reason. He withdrew further into himself, and seemed irritable and petty.[130] He sulked, and was a trifle discouraged, but the world would hear from him again.

The fight over the customhouse appointees and all it represented was sharp and important, but the general public had other worries in 1877 and 1878. President Grant left the Senate in special session, the usual courtesy to an incoming Administration. It adjourned in March, after confirming appointments, and Congress would not normally meet again until December. Hayes called a special session for mid-October to handle the backlog of business that had accumulated during the contested election, an unwelcome but inevitable move. The Democratic House would probably inflame the southern question, the Senate would support Conkling, and many members would strike for free silver and against resumption.

The currency debate inevitably centered on Secretary Sherman. "Prester John," "the Ohio Icicle," "the greatest financier since Hamilton," were among his informal titles. He was now in the prime of life, rising to national eminence from Ohio, where he was born in 1823. He and his famous elder brother William Tecumseh were rambunctious youths, and did not gain a great deal from books. William Tecumseh always retained a nervous vigor, but an early aging process made John one of the staidest men in politics. A taste for mathematics took him into Ohio's canal country as a young surveyor.

Ambition made him drop roistering ways, and he put on a mask that seldom changed during a long career. Moving to Mansfield, he studied law, worked in Whig politics, and attained national distinction in the Republican wave that bore up so many young men in the 1850's. After serving in the national house from 1855 to 1861, he replaced Senator Salmon P. Chase in 1861, and retained the seat until Hayes called him to the Treasury post.* During the war, he helped create the national banking system. After the war, he stifled a natural desire for conciliation, and accepted most Republican policy on the South. On questions of finance, he remained moderate, favoring specie resumption, but opposing contraction of the greenbacks, easily assuming the two were compatible.

Behind his severe grey beard and cool eyes, lurked no hint of a seething personality. He looked the part he played, the national statesman, careful not to break anyone's eggshells, sure to survive with knowledge and political legerdemain. "No man ever slapped him on the back and said, 'Hello, John!'" an acquaintance recalled.[131] He professed to have no sense of fun but occasionally a facial expression could have been called a smile. Men respected Sherman, but few

*Sherman was Secretary of the Treasury for Hayes, 1877–81; senator from Ohio, 1881–97; secretary of state for McKinley, 1897–98; and died in 1900.

liked him. "People will be knocked down for calling Blaine a thief," a constituent wrote James A. Garfield, "but who ever heard of anyone knocked down for calling Sherman a thief?" [132] It might have been otherwise, but as he once drily remarked, "hypocrisy is foreign to my nature." [133] He probably meant "flattery"; after all, he was a politician.

This personality fitted the needs of his constituency. A man did not enter Ohio politics lightly, or expect to survive without what safer colleagues loosely called "trimming." Republicans from New England and Democrats from the South could afford firm stands on divisive issues, but in Ohio, with its polyglot population and varied economy, only the political compromisers stayed alive. Sherman's greatest personal feat was to combine an innate caution and conservatism with an instinctive understanding of the restless people of Ohio. It contained southerners from across the river, easterners in the Western Reserve, new immigrants, and old families. It had been a major frontier area, but now boasted a settled civilization. Offering urban culture, its strength was in the countryside. Shipping plied its lakes and river traffic was in its veins of commerce. It mined metals and produced oil, manufactured iron and grew wool. All its people drew on an older tradition of rustic independence, and devoured generations of politicians. Few congressional districts were safe, and any senatorial or presidential candidate courting Buckeye favor had to walk softly. The state produced a special type of politician whom critics dismissed too easily. In sharpening the arts of compromise in local affairs, people like Sherman, Garfield, and McKinley illustrated in microcosm the evolution of their party and country. They understood coalition politics and became constructive nationalists.

Sherman had principles, but readily delayed a struggle over the whole in order to gain it piece by piece. He might shade the truth to suit his needs, and made few speeches if he could talk privately to better advantage. The slow and awkward system of legislation and politics was a fact; it would not change in an afternoon. It did not always work for the best, but it could work for the most people. The constructive politician therefore compromised. Sherman often stated why he personally opposed a measure, and then voted for it to satisfy constituents. A man with such attitudes was open to misrepresentation, but through a long and brilliant career he did much patient and unpublicized work while others talked. Sherman was a Senator of the United States, not merely a senator from Ohio.

His verbal caution was legendary. He coined the phrase "mending fences" to explain a trip to his Mansfield farm without making political comment. Mugwumps condemned his foggy utterances, "made up of sense and nonsense in about equal parts, but so commingled that the former should be made effective in legislation and the latter useful on the stump." [134] It was an inadvertently shrewd observation on a technique not without merit. Others were less kind: [135]

> There was an old Prester named John,
> On finance essentially gone.
>   In prestidigitation
>   He beat all creation—
> And failed to be President John.

That was equally astute, for he wanted desperately to be president, and never really had a chance. He was thwarted by his cold personality, inability to unify Ohio delegations, the technicalities of his financial expertise, and more popular opponents.[136]

Publicly, he wore a dry fatalism. Privately, he expressed a realistic material philosophy that explained much of his lack of popular appeal: [137]

> Undoubtedly the tendency of all civilizations is to make the rich richer and the poor poorer, with sudden fluctuations and changes in life beyond the control of prudence and care, but these have always existed and always will exist in any society where property is protected. Labor becomes more abundant and cheaper, property increases and the fortunate few enjoy the greater share of the blessings of life. He would be a wise man who could change this course of civilization, and a very bold one to try to do it.

A man with that opinion would not raise a crowd in America, where everyone supposedly equaled every task, and a bigger dollar lay just around the corner.

Opponents labeled Sherman a front man for nefarious big business, but the charge was wide of the mark. He was a shrewd operator in real estate, and more properly typified the small-town boomer; the man in the corner grocery; the farmer with a new barn, selling produce in town; the lawyer or doctor in offices above the bank. His real estate firm dealt in carefully plotted lots and sure speculations. He corresponded with bankers, dealers in patent medicine, tobacco, crockery, woollens, and iron products. He was a typical American middle-class paradox; a conservative optimist, believing in progress and change, with a keen sense of stable values and social hierarchy. A friend put it in good contrast: "Sherman was popular with the businessman, the banker, and the thinker; Blaine was the idol of the rank and file, of the men in the trenches." [138] This combination of frank but constructive materialism and political skills armed Sherman well for the task at hand, stabilizing the federal currency without disrupting his party.

Congress opened on October 15, organizing for business in a flurry of talk and a sea of complimentary flowers. Visitors in both houses saw all the famous men. Senator Blaine—"the Plumed Knight"—represented Maine, scarcely noting an equally famous antagonist, "Lord Roscoe." Lesser figures talked and read. In the House, old hands like William D. "Pig Iron" Kelley, Pennsylvania's staunch protectionist, shared attention with Samuel J. Randall, soon to be Speaker again. There were new southerners, and promising freshmen Republicans. Among the former, John G. Carlisle of Kentucky showed a Roman profile. Amid the latter, William McKinley of Ohio exercised a famous charm. Thomas B. Reed of Maine filled a chair with a lively bulk. The members were genial, but behind them stood the stresses of hard times. Rising public demands for monetary inflation marked the steady decline of Reconstruction's issues in favor of economics that would reorient political parties.

The problem Sherman faced seemed simple enough. A Republican Act of 1875 directed the Treasury to redeem greenbacks in gold on January 1, 1879. Behind that action lay years of struggle, involving debtor and creditor interests, sectionalism, and various definitions of morality. Wavering Republican control of Congress perpetually jeopardized the law. Redemption day loomed over Hayes and Sherman, with political uncertainty and hard times making it doubtful they could accumulate enough gold to cover $346,000,000 in greenbacks.

The American people always ignored the currency question's fiscal complexities in favor of moralistic slogans. Despite dullness, it had a long life, reflecting the interests of every man's pocketbook. Since the days of Alexander Hamilton, Andrew Jackson's fight on the Bank, and wartime inflation with paper money, farmers and bankers discussed the subject with equal fervor and prejudice.* "There are as many financial sects in America as there are parties in Spain," Henry Watterson of the *Louisville Courier-Journal* noted. "Every man has a theory on finance of his own and is indifferent to any other," Sherman said. The high-toned *Nation* was right for once in noting that financial "knowledge of the public takes the form of an impression rather than a clean-cut idea." Men debated the abstruse subject for decades, and people adopted conflicting firm opinions. Richard Croker of Tammany

---

*I am not concerned here with the fiscal soundness of either silver or gold, but with the bases of their appeals and their effects on political parties after 1877.

Hall may have summed up the average man's view: "What's wrong with silver money? I'm in favor of all kinds of money—the more, the better." [139]

The issue had important moralistic overtones involving basic questions of honesty and contract, but was decidedly personal. Some favored inflation to reduce debt burdens and raise prices of goods they sold. Others opposed it to maintain purchasing power of money they lent, and feared inflation that would harm everyone. Silver's supporters endlessly praised "the dollar of the daddies," noting that the white metal had reigned with the yellow since Hamilton, forgetting he paid debts in gold. The issue commanded larger audiences the further west one traveled from Philadelphia. "We do not want a Wall Street silver dollar, but a people's silver dollar," Murat Halstead's Cincinnati paper exclaimed, "a Mississippi Valley dollar, a dollar with an eagle on it, whose right wing shall fan Washington City while his left wing wafts the dust along the streets of San Francisco, and his tail spreads over Hudson's Bay, while his beak is dredging the mud from the stream between the jetties at South Pass." [140] Silver's proponents generally disliked paper money, and saw the metal as part of resumption. If the government granted it full legal-tender status, and subsidized production with a purchase plan, no one would question its relation to gold. "Silver money and resumption should be the battle cry of the country today . . . ," a prominent paper exclaimed. Others held out a simple compromise: coin silver dollars, and inflationists would not oppose resumption.[141]

The movement "to do something for silver" rose in the Ohio and Mississippi Valleys after 1873. The area expanded rapidly after the war with the help of eastern credit. It felt the depression more than the East because much of its economy led a marginal existence. As a friend warned Hayes: "The West is going to ruin as fast as possible and the people are getting desperate and ready to jump onto any party or hobby horse that promises relief." [142] Politicians heard confusing rumbles. Many creditor interests that favored "sound money" in the East liked "soft money" in the West. An economy built on future growth found insurance in continuous expansion. Western bankers and businessmen opposed contraction, and many favored silver.[143] Political elements in the South long friendly to inflation, now threatened to join western radicals and weaken both major parties.[144] Most significant for Republicans, a Greenback Party sapped marginal strength in the ever-doubtful Midwest. If Republicans did not produce a national compromise for silver, they might lose a disproportionate amount of congressional power.

Debt was a key issue, as the depression increased past obligations by appreciating the dollar's value. "The suggestion that the silver dollar is a dishonest dollar is met with the statement that gold has appreciated, and to make the gold dollar the standard measure is to rob the debtor class for the benefit of the creditor class," William Henry Smith wrote Hayes. "Debts contracted when paper was at 80, 50, 20 and 10 percent discount should not now be paid in gold—the effect with a single standard. This argument reaches the masses, and there is no effective way of answering it." [145] The proposition that the creditor lending money in boom times against doubtful collateral should profit from risk found little support among debtors.

War changes easily to nostalgia, letting men recall only exciting but safe moments, reducing the need to judge in the comfort of mass action. It provides a total experience, marking the high point of many people's lives with a glamor and commitment that seldom come in peacetime. Inflation that caused resentment in wartime now looked good during depression, and was part of the inflationists' answer to critics. "Our workingmen are captured with the proposition that when we had a great volume of depreciated currency in circulation, during and after the war, times were good and everybody had plenty of work," one of Schurz's friends wrote.[146] Wartime shortages, scarcities of men and material, and expanding markets produced that prosperity. But people recalled only the rustle of greenbacks when they lived in a seller's market for labor and a buyer's market for long term debts. Wartime experience, familiar to all Americans, cut both ways. Millions of other people did not want inflation's uncertainties, or to have to check the dollar's value in the morning paper.

During most of Reconstruction, Republicans defeated fiat money, illustrating an important tendency to control the divisive question. The frustration of western and southern inflationists easily spilled into a conspiracy thesis. A powerful press, with editors often highly placed in politics, referred to "the New York Gold Ring," and condemned "the New York financial regency." [147] Midwestern and southern resentment at dependence on the East flared into bitter talk. "We do not want the New York Exchange, the greatest gambling hole in the United States, to rule the whole world," a correspondent told Hayes.[148] Politicians warned against letting an eastern Secretary of the Treasury excite western animosity, and Sherman from Ohio was a good compromise. Men who worked hard envied and condemned those who seemed to make fortunes from shuffling papers and selling stocks.*

The greatest conspiracy in the minds of silver inflationists centered on "The Crime of '73," when a coinage act discontinued the standard silver dollar. The law ostensibly only reflected silver's disuse, and the simple fact that it was slightly above par with gold. But men from the Rocky Mountains and the South saw an international conspiracy that combined English gold and Wall Street compliance. After years of debate and miles of newspaper treatment, partisans proved only that some men in government in 1873 wished to avoid flooding the United States with foreign silver, and wanted to adopt and maintain the world-recognized gold standard. It was a rather open conspiracy, involving congressional hearings and knowledge of the facts among politicians of both parties, including silverites.[149] Gold advocates countered with a conspiracy thesis: Mine owners wanted to sell excessive silver to the government, to stabilize its value. The bonanza kings of Nevada, Idaho, Colorado, and California bought propaganda, and had excessive representation in the Senate, but they did not create public demand for silver inflation. Neither conspiracy thesis explained the issue. Hard times, the attraction of cheap dollars to settle debts and raise producers' prices, and the natural allure of quick commercial expansion based on easy credit underlay the controversy.

Neither businessmen nor farmers supporting silver wanted uncontrolled inflation. They rejected paper and accepted coined dollars with "intrinsic value." Political moderates warned opponents that silver was a reasonable compromise. Failing to get it, the people might demand and obtain paper money. Any demagogue could raise a mob on the issue in time. People were familiar with silver, which would insure its stability. The supply was also limited, and could not pour from printing presses.[150]

---

*"It is with some alarm that we see the persistent efforts of the jobbers, robbers, and wreckers of Wall Street to control the National Treasury Department. These men are non-producers—necessary evils, not to be encouraged. The Treasury should be in the hands of some competent man from the Valley of the Mississippi— that fertile region sending abroad the products which pay our national debt. The center of political power in the future will be the grain producing regions westward of Ohio. From thence will come a race of intellectual and physical giants. Great cities are rather inimical to the perpetuity and safety of the government, and in my judgement the executive of the nation should be watchful and jealous of the plottings and conspiracies of brokers and money-changers of the East. Jesus of Nazareth did not like them overmuch, nor do the people at large." (John Livingston to Stanley Matthews, January 24, 1881, Hayes HML; see also Unger, The Greenback Era, 340.)

Men follow myths and symbols, and gold was mankind's oldest standard of value. Its friends colored arguments with as much outrage and moralism as those who pushed the white metal's claims. Spokesmen of propertied interests and the expanding middle class saw inflation as an attack on long-term investment that bordered on a loosely defined "communism." If irredeemable currency brought steady and uncontrollable inflation, men with money to invest would raise interest rates, stiffen terms, and hoard capital. This would retard growth and defeat the silverites' purposes.[151] Advocates of gold appeared deceptively united because of their powerful press and social positions, but they talked a great deal to cover weaknesses.

In general, men in credit-hungry businesses favored moderate inflation. Very few businessmen wanted contraction; they sought slow inflation on a gold standard. Their strength centered in northeastern cities—New York, Philadelphia, Boston, and their tributaries.[152] Men dealing in international trade usually favored a settled standard. Fluctuations in the price of gold could cheapen inventories or raise the cost of foreign exchange. Many were equally sure a double standard would drive gold out of circulation, as Gresham's law operated, and make foreign trade even harder.[153]

That was an impressive point, while America needed and got foreign investment and sold bonds abroad. In the 1870's most European powers went on the gold standard, and dumped silver in the world market. Without gold redemption, could the United States trade effectively abroad or maintain price parity at home? Gold symbolized prosperity and stability: ". . . the farmer's grain, the planter's cotton, the Chinaman's tea are all interchangeable on a common basis of value, and, as every venture is thus relieved of the element of uncertainty, enterprise becomes less hazardous and therefore freer," a business journal proclaimed.[154] As industrialization steadily triumphed in the United States, with confusing directions and imbalanced emphasis, gold naturally acquired both practical and ideological significance as the world's safe standard of exchange.

The Northeast set the nation's intellectual and moral tone. As a center of education, religious teaching, and publishing, its pronouncements radiated across the country. Most of these worked toward stability and fixed morality in public affairs, heavily favoring the gold standard. The clergy, editors, famous writers and teachers, furnished gold adherents a potent body of doctrine and rationalization. Talk of the solemnity of contract, rewards of labor, individual competition, the possibilities and responsibilities of wealth all echoed from pulpits and rostrums. President Hayes and men of his background saw that part of the question simply: "To attempt to pay the public debt in depreciated silver coin is a violation of the public credit and public faith." [155]

The controversy crossed party lines, finding no simple solution. Neither major party commanded full support for its professed stand, and all groups simplified logic for public consumption. Silverites were partially correct in urging credit expansion, but the answer was a new banking system and changed attitudes toward credit, rather than manipulation of the money supply. Like the tariff question, currency reform agitated the whole generation, requiring the talents of able men merely to avoid politically dangerous action. To politicians, it required harmonization of conflicting interest groups. This produced legislative enactments that slowed discussion but satisfied no one. Moderates now worked toward both "doing something for silver" and gold redemption.

Congress settled to the task with both determination and weariness. "The old soft money folly seems to have gained in strength since the last Congress," Garfield noted. "Our final defense will probably be a veto." [156] Renewed debate on free silver was bad enough, but Republicans might not control even their own party. Hayes' battles for civil service reform and his southern policy were already costly. "The truth of the matter is that the administration has no party in the Senate," a Washington paper reported.[157] The President's own views were obscure. As an "Ohio man," he never took an ironclad oath for either metal, but he favored resumption on the date scheduled, and opposed paper money.

Missouri's Richard Parks "Silver Dick" Bland managed a House free coinage bill. He had secured passage of a measure in 1876, though the Senate killed it, and was determined to win full victory. Eastern critics called him a "silver fanatic," but his section needed credit and debt relief, and he spoke for a large body of public opinion. He also wanted an assay office, mint, and vault storage facilities in St. Louis. The West liked and trusted him. A Montana paper proclaimed proudly: "Silver, so long prostrate, rises to its feet in Congress at last, with a smile that is childlike and Bland." [158] On November 5, the House passed a free coinage bill with the ratio of 16 to 1, by a vote of 167–53. Only 6 members from the West and South opposed it; only 9 from New England and the mid-Atlantic states favored it. But 92 members did not vote. This and congressional efforts to repeal the Resumption Act unnerved the Administration, and Sherman made daily trips to Capital Hill. The President was noncommittal until the annual message of December 3. Arguing that laws could not maintain parity of money, and that agitation threatened resumption, Hayes wished Congress would let the bill die. If it passed, he insisted that it require payment of the existing debt in gold.

House silverites were confident, but should have known how devious the Senate could be. The bill went to Iowa's William B. Allison, champion of the soft-shoe in politics. With his meticulous clothes, and noble head, Allison looked like "a Roman Senator with American business shrewdness added to his dignity." [159] Colleagues said he could cross the Senate floor wearing wooden shoes and make no more noise than a fly on the ceiling. Iowa, like Ohio, was not a safe place for doctrinaires. "I always like to vote, if I can," he said, "so as not to be called upon to explain too much at home." [160]

Sherman urged Allison to produce a quick compromise. The Secretary was painfully accumulating a gold reserve, and nervousness in the banking community and abroad might raise costs at best, and wreck his plans at worst.[161] Allison soon cooled the House's ardor; he had enough Republicans and hard-money Democrats to beat free coinage. They had best compromise. He worked through December and January, and Bland's followers quickly capitulated.[162] The final bill required Treasury purchase of not less than $2,000,000 and not more than $4,000,000 of silver monthly, coined into standard dollars of 412½ grains. These were convertible to silver certificates, and both were legal tender unless contracts specified otherwise. The law directed the President to seek an international conference to work for bimetallism. In mid-February, it went to the White House.

Would Hayes veto, consent, or let it become law unsigned? Some friends like Stanley Matthews openly favored silver, and supported congressional attacks on resumption. Sherman allegedly said Hayes would "permit it to become law." Others urged him to accept it as the best workable plan. Tom Ewing of Ohio thought Hayes would be canny. If Congress would obviously override, he would veto the bill for the public record; otherwise he would let it pass. The measure avoided free coinage, did not assault resumption, and would pacify both sides. That was about the gist of the Cabinet's advice. Sherman feared a veto's effects on the money market; other members felt Congress would get the blame for anything bad that happened.[163]

Hayes had privately decided to veto any bill that did not insure gold payment of the public debt. On February 28, he returned the measure to Congress on those grounds, and because he thought it economically dangerous and morally unsound. The House was angry. Few members thought he would dare reject such a popular measure. The waspish S. S. Cox of New York said the message was "the charge of a fraud by a fraud," but the speaker struck the remarks. The House overrode, 196–73. A special messenger took it to the Senate, which followed suit, 46–19. The bill was law two hours after leaving Hayes' office.

Later that night, Hayes joked about congressional speed and made some remarks at his own expense. The shouting died rather quickly, as the press wearily asked for relief from debate. The silverites accepted the facts of coalition politics, and seemed content. Whatever its economic aspects, the Bland-Allison Act was good politics. In effect, the GOP got credit for helping silver, favoring moderate inflation, and yet guaranteeing resumption. It was an especially effective move in the Midwest, which had critical votes for 1880, and blunted the edge of Greenbackism, though that party won 14 House seats in the November congressional elections. The controversy rounded out Hayes' first year in office. "The year, if I think of the scenes through which I have passed, seems an age," he noted laconically.[164]

Throughout the debates, Sherman worked with bankers to build a gold reserve, and develop confidence. Hayes justly gave him high marks for political shrewdness, sharp bargaining, and effective propaganda.[165] In April, he negotiated a $50,000,000 sale of gold bonds with New York bankers. In July, he told friends nothing could stop resumption but repeal of the law, "and this I do not anticipate."[166] The economy rose from the trough of depression. Summer exports of wheat, flour, meat and cotton brought gold from Europe, where crops moldered in bad weather.

January 1, 1879, was a Sunday. Sherman had about $133,000,000 in gold to cover over three times as much in greenbacks, and there was some apprehension on Monday, when payment began. Wall Street wore bunting, and its statuary trailed bright ribbons as a sign of confidence. The Custom House and other federal buildings displayed colors, while crowds looked at piles of shiny gold coins in tellers' cages. At the Subtreasury building, a lone customer changed $210 in greenbacks for gold. At day's end, some $132,000 in paper had come in; but about $400,000 in gold changed for paper. It was anticlimactic to hear Robert Ingersoll say: "I am thankful to have lived to see the day when the greenback can raise its right hand and declare 'I know that my Redeemer liveth.'"[167]

Sherman basked in unusual popularity, receiving callers with a smile. Even opposing congressmen, hearing the sounds of returning prosperity, admitted his reputation would rise. In a year the presidential booms would begin, and he was in the running. Sherman knew public acclaim easily turned to catcalls, but he had widened his base of political support. He would remain silent and wait upon events, turning wheels behind the scenes.[168]

Hayes reported in December that resumption and restored confidence had turned the price indexes upward. The country was tasting prosperity again. The silver cloud no bigger than a man's hand that grew to threaten whole political parties had moved, but it remained a cloud. Hayes left the subject with an introspective warning. Banks were always unpopular, and silver might create a new party. Probably not now, "but if all the discontented could be embodied in one party, with cheap money and plenty of it as its watchwords, the power of such a party would be ample for mischief, and it might for a time, rule the country." [169]

The impatient American people seldom respected Congress, even when demanding a great deal of it. The quarreling between Capitol and White House that marred Reconstruction, and the tension of Hayes' first months, compounded public aversion to debate. Hayes usually looked better than Congress, because he kept his temper and did his apparent duty. The legislators had a bad press. "You can't use tact with a Congressman!" a Cabinet member told Henry Adams during Grant's term. "A Congressman is a hog! You must take a stick and hit him on the snout!" Members of the upper house were little better. "If a Congressman is a hog, what is a senator?" [170]

The very nature of representative politics clouded the atmosphere around legislative proceedings. Lobbyists were powerful, members blocked pet peeves and pushed favorite whims, and talk enveloped the process until the public agreed with cartoonists that Congress was a vast snail. Legislators' personal conduct did not help matters. "The Hole in the wall," or members' refreshment bar between the House and Senate, served more than lemonade. Senators generally had elegant pretensions, but House members lounged with feet on desks, reading hometown newspapers while one of their number passionately supported a lost cause. Ladies in the gallery fanned aside a stale haze of cigar smoke, and often left hurriedly to avoid showing open contempt for the proceedings.[171]

Amid struggles over specie resumption and civil service reform, lesser fights with larger symbolism drew coverage from the press.

Western representatives had long advocated ending Chinese immigration, despite the Burlingame Treaty of 1868. Hayes knew that most unions and workingmen favored restriction of cheap labor that undercut wages, but when Congress passed a bill virtually abrogating the treaty and restricting immigration, he vetoed it with a dual admonition. Law was not the remedy when it violated a treaty; and the Executive alone conducted foreign affairs. Despite an outcry from the Pacific Slope, he stood firm and had the satisfaction of negotiating new treaty terms that gave the United States regulatory rights.

The irritations and frustrations of the disputed election would not down, and Democrats reopened the controversy for the coming presidential election. They focused on an unlikely target, the Army. It had long since dwindled from blue legions to some 25,000 professionals, policing nearly 13,000 miles of border, and protecting federal property. In their most useful role, soldiers chased Indians across deserts and through rocky mountains. In more colorful roles, they stood ceremonial guard at White House functions, enlivened parades, and staged funerals for war heroes. Democrats rumbled about reducing the Army, and left it unpaid for months at a time. In the spring and summer of 1879, they skirmished against the federal authority which soldiers upheld and symbolized. Amendments to appropriations bills forbade the use of soldiers and federal marshals at the polls, another clear sign that the southern question was not dead. Hayes' friend, Guy Bryan in Texas, said the riders' only purpose was to assure that no successor would revive Grantism.[172]

Hayes and congressional managers saw it differently. Garfield condemned the "effort of Congress to coerce the President," a theme Hayes knew by heart.[173] Sharp debates in the spring of 1879 brought strange champions to the President's side. Blaine attacked the measures. With appropriate sarcasm, he calculated that in the South, only 1,155 soldiers pitched tents or paced quarters, bored from lack of anything to do. The only active soldiers policed the Mexican border at the request of state authorities, and endured hardships without notable complaint and little pay. New York City had more policemen than the South had soldiers. New England, he said heavily, had 120 federal soldiers per million population, and was far more oppressed than the southern brethren. The whole debate was a "prodigious and absolute farce," aimed to catch votes and bully the Negro.[174]

The usually patient Garfield rather testily attacked the Democrats' "perfidious treatment of the president, their still worse treatment of the Negroes, their persistent efforts to praise the 'lost cause' . . . and you mistake our resistance to them for an attempt on our part to re-awaken dead issues." [175] Hayes defended his prerogatives and national authority with spirit. "Of course I don't believe in test oaths, and do not care to use the military," he told William Henry Smith. "But the states rights heresy that the nation cannot enact safeguards for its national elections, and the still more dangerous doctrine that a bare majority in the two houses can absorb all the powers of all the departments of the government, cannot be under any conceivable circumstances approved where embodied in legislation." [176] He quickly decided to veto any bills that infringed on his rights as commander-in-chief or president. Evarts took a legalistic view, presuming Congress could pass such laws. "He doesn't seem to see," Hayes snapped, "that it is merely a new form of the old conflict between ultra-states rights and the national doctrines." [177] As bills ground through the legislative mill, he read a veto message to Garfield and the Cabinet. In April, 1879, he began a series of vetoes that roused ire in Congress, but steadily gained public favor.[178]

The opposition talked loosely of insurrection. Garfield hesitantly suggested the Democrats were "in a hole," and could not back down without losing face. Should the Republicans compromise, and avoid stalling Congress and leaving the Army unpaid indefinitely? In late May, with more vetoes pending, McKinley, Garfield, and Smith talked it over with Hayes, who said acidly: "A square backing down is their best way out, and for my part I will await that result with complacency." [179] The Democrats blustered, but finally voted pay for the Army, blandly pronounced against force at the polls, and refused to vote salaries for federal marshals.

The Democrats thus created no new issues, and made a disorderly and obstructive spectacle. "Was there ever anything more ridiculous?" Secretary Evarts told reporters. "They began by saying to the President, 'Sign our political measures or we will withhold $46,000,000 of the appropriations for running the government.' 'That does not frighten me,' replied the President: 'I shall go ahead and do my duty just the same.' 'Very well,' said the Democrats, 'if that's your intention, we will keep back $20,000,000.' Finding the President still unmoved, they cried out 'If you don't back down, we will refuse you $10,000,000.' As this threat had no effect, they finally held back $600,000 [for marshals' salaries] and ran away. It was a remarkably well-developed case of the small end of the horn." [180]

Even allowing for partisanship, the press was right in calling Hayes "the only real gainer" from the whole affair. His calm defense of presi-

dential authority and nationalism looked both safe and vigorous beside
the quarrelsome Congress. "There is a growing impression among the
Republicans that Mr. Hayes is a remarkably cool hand," the *New York
Herald's* special Washington correspondent wrote. "[He is] patient,
wary, not capable of getting scared, a shrewd and long-headed politician, and a far wiser and safer party leader than the irate Senators
who have vainly battled against him so often." [181] Such talk was good
news for Hayes and the party.

Early in the summer of 1877, Samuel J. Tilden went to Europe for a
change of scenery. In October, he returned to face well-wishers. From
the steps of his Gramercy Park mansion, he spoke in a high-pitched
voice of "fraud," and vowed to resume the fight for Democratic success. He smiled wanly, shook a few hands, and disappeared inside to
await the presidential sweepstakes of 1880. Neither party had allowed
the compromise of 1877 to work, and neither forgave or forgot what
preceded it. In the South, local courts violated the tacit agreement and
prosecuted former Republican officeholders connected with the last
days of Radical government. In the North, partisans like William E.
Chandler of New Hampshire, and important people in Congress and
the press would not let the problem subside. It was too much to expect
otherwise of human nature, or of men who had matured on all that
the southern question symbolized.

After 1878 the Democrats wanted to assault Hayes' title, and create
an issue for 1880. In May, they secured a select House committee
under Clarkson N. Potter of New York to examine the settlement that
made Hayes president. The move ironically reflected desires both to
increase and lessen Tilden's stature in the Democratic party. Tammany
Hall wanted to avoid the "fraud issue" and Tilden; a thorough airing
might make him "unavailable." His friends cultivated the martyr's role;
an investigation would put the Republicans on the defensive. Hayes
deprecated the whole business; and it made him a little nervous. He
rationalized it away as bad for sectional harmony, and unsettling to
business. Much of the press on both sides agreed. He held simply
that he *was* the President; the issue closed on March 5, 1877. Congress
could try to impeach him, but they must risk a public trial.

The investigation proceeded with a packed committee, rehashing
old information. In October, the *New York Tribune* burst the balloon
with a series of "Cipher Dispatches." Decoded telegrams taken from
Western Union in 1876 showed that Tilden's nephew, William T.
Pelton, had offered to buy electoral votes. Tilden's response that it was

news to him caused some smiles. Pelton lived in his uncle's house
during the election contest, and it seemed unlikely that "Whispering
Sammy" did not know what was going on.

Republicans were jubilant, wishing to extend the committee's work
to other dark corners. The investigation took a sharp turn in December, 1878, when Congress assembled for the regular session. Through
January, the committee heard a wider variety of witnesses than Democrats desired. Pelton and Smith M. Weed, a Tilden lieutenant and
son of Thurlow Weed, admitted indiscretions. At his own request,
Tilden appeared and denied all charges, but recalled some dealings
over South Carolina's electoral votes. He had ordered Pelton to stop
the bargaining.

Public reaction did not favor Tilden, though no one came out of the
investigation the better for wear. With the air full of boomerangs,
Democrats let the committee end its work inconclusively. Luck, cryp-
tography, and careful selection of texts had blackened Democratic
eyes, and made Hayes the martyr instead of Tilden. By summer, with
the Army vetoes sustained and the Potter Committee looking elsewhere for work, Hayes could safely note: "I am now experiencing
one of the 'ups' of political life. . . . Of course it will not last. But I
think I have the confidence of the country." [182]

Friends and advisers had counseled against confronting Congress,
but Hayes' political sense was right. He sustained Executive rights,
enlarged political nationalism with impressive firmness, and created
little public rancor. Most irritation settled on Congress, which looked
parochial and obstructive. It seemed intent on fulfilling Mark Twain's
dictum that had Congress been present when the Deity said "Let there
be light," mankind would never have had any. Republicans regularly
warned the public not to trust the Democrats, saying they were disorganized, negative, and unable to rule. On the eve of a critical presidential contest, they proved the charge.

As 1879 closed, Hayes knew attention would turn to fresh contenders for his office. Out of the running by choice, he clearly favored
Sherman, but was publicly silent. He added up his achievements with
a genial smugness. He had started a southern policy that might yet
succeed; at any rate, it was the best available. The public credit was
sound, with some of the debt refunded at lower interest rates. In the
silent labyrinths of departmental policies, subordinates had begun
more liberal policies on land, Indians, and the foreign service.[183]

Hayes had tested Republican opponents, and won part of the struggle to broaden the party's base. The civil service reforms were not spectacular but marked a path for successors. He successfully defended his office against Congress. Above all, he typified the most popular and constructive aspects of his party's nationalism with skillful publicity. In only a narrow sense could critics grant him "negative greatness." He prevented some unfortunate events, and advertised good causes in preparation for the day when people would accept them. The tactics were necessarily unglamorous; he could not afford boldness in a tired nation. The party's hold was tenuous, and its internal stresses grave. Hayes did not move suddenly, but he moved, and the public credited that accomplishment to the GOP. The party and the country were better for his holding office. Hayes revealed a shrewd understanding of politics and public temper: "We are in a period when old questions are settled, and the new ones are not yet brought forward. Extreme party action, if continued in such a time, would ruin the [Republican] party. Moderation is its only chance. The party out of power gains by all the partisan conduct of those in power." [184]

By being respectable, patient, and active, Hayes helped restore presidential authority and boosted the process of nationalizing party politics. He increased respect for government after years of ineptitude and scandals, and enlarged public faith in Republican power to rule through rational compromise. It was not an easy task. Hayes had to quietly but firmly avoid Grantism, demilitarize the South, and face divisive issues like civil service reform and silver without disrupting the party. He did a remarkable job, and enhanced Republican chances for 1880.

As spring came on, he listened to political talk; a relaxed tone entered his conversation. He would regret leaving the White House, but welcomed the shady grove at Fremont. Being an ex-president had compensations; he could enjoy a certain respected stature without nagging responsibility. He and Mrs. Hayes entertained guests with the usual courtesy. Old friends like Mr. and Mrs. William Dean Howells came for dinner and a folksy visit. "Well," Mrs. Howells remarked, "you will soon be out of it." The President paused a moment, and smiled: "Yes, out of a scrape, out of a scrape." [185]

II

Presidential Sweepstakes: 1880–Style

When he stepped from a carriage, crossed a hotel lobby, or dined out, a crowd gathered. His mere presence made men lift their hats in silent respect, and his name stirred both memory and controversy in millions of people. Not many foreigners, unfamiliar with American mythology, would expect him to produce those reactions. He was short, stout, and unexciting. Neither place nor power persuaded him to change a fundamental indifference to clothing. Greeting guests, welcoming dignitaries, within his family, he remained impassive. But admirers knew that apparent indifference was a mask for shyness, and nothing he did changed their regard and affection. His name was Ulysses Simpson Grant, and for nearly a generation he was a presence in the minds of men, reminding them of a personal past they had escaped and promising a success they might attain. As conquering general, Savior of the Union, President of the United States, he was first citizen to most Americans.

Grant was that rare human phenomenon, a symbol who remained flesh and blood. Every schoolboy knew by heart the details of his career, a legend that fulfilled the American dream of rags to riches, obscurity to fame, helplessness to power, without losing a rustic quality that appealed to those who hoped to follow the path. Becoming modesty, and few and carefully chosen words in an era of profuse comment, made silence seem wisdom and calmness strength. Grant was a strange but not unusual amalgam of humanity and detachment, commitment and withdrawal, force and vacuum. They all reflected contradictions in a personality that poverty, ridicule, and family misunderstanding warped early in life. To protect a sensitive nature he adopted the rituals of diffidence. Outwardly, the sudden fame of war leadership did not change him, but behind the steady gaze and calm appearance was a pathetic desire for approval and hunger for recognition—forces too strong to admit, and so alloyed with contradictions of behavior.

As a general he favored mass and steady assault. There was little dash and no glamor in his view of war, and perhaps of life. Inured to the demands of battle, he did not lose sight of individual feelings, and could not abide the sights and sounds of pain. "I couldn't stand the amputations and had to go out into the rain and sit for most of the night against a tree," he said after visiting a hospital tent.[1] He understood men and was one of them.

At war's end, he took charge of the dwindling army, combining military and civil duties in a way that made him seem an ideal non-politician to the masses. Wearing the country's highest honors, he seemed to serve no single group. He stayed human, oblivious to the glitter of a blatant homage, "the undismayed hero of a thousand receptions." [2] Not even the presidency after 1869 changed the personality. He greeted equally famous people diffidently. The silence was part of an inner sense of unworthiness, fortified with a wonder at how he got there, and a certain distrust of the world. "It seemed to him immodest to uncloak himself to the world, or even entirely to his most intimate friend," a faithful aide remembered.[3] But he was not immune to expressions of respect. James G. Blaine was right: "He liked popular applause more than any man I ever knew." [4]

The secret of his early success as president was not hard to define. He represented order, non-partisanship, stability, and the dream of everyman for fame. People sick of war and weary of reconstruction turned gladly to one whose philosophy seemed to rest in a compelling sentence: "Let us have peace." The ideal faded quickly. The military hero had no place in everyday political life, and Grant betrayed a weakness for sycophants and bad advisers in this unfamiliar realm. Great scandals cast a dark pall over the man and his party: The Whiskey Ring, Indian frauds, Salary Grab, and the Credit Mobilier all thwarted the good he might have done. Grant had a weakness that hurt his Administration more than personal corruption—the inability to disavow dishonest or incompetent men. It was easy work for every hypocrite to say that opponents attacked him through his friends. A personality insecure and thwarted for so many years could not abandon those who held him up to fame. The public remained sure that "If only Grant knew!" these things would pass away, but others in politics were less kind. "Early in 1869 the cry was for 'no politician,'" Governor William Claflin of Massachusetts wrote privately, "but the country did not mean 'no brains'!"[5]

Even the Liberal Republican bolt of 1872 did not stir Grant's desire to master political or administrative arts. He merely thanked Providence for a close escape. Friends could only call him "a man of the best intentions, profoundly desirous to govern wisely and justly, and profoundly ignorant of the means by which good government is secured."[6] The creeping blight of personal abuse robbed a second term of glamor. Confused advice, ceaseless problems, lack of momentum, emptied the presidency of its earlier charm. In 1876, he somewhat bitterly accepted the consensus against a third term and remained silent during most of the disputed election. A note of almost pathetic apology crept into his last annual message of December 5, 1876. He cited his political inexperience and how politicians he trusted had misled him, and shifted blame to subordinates. He claimed "only that I have acted in every instance from a conscientious desire to do what was right, constitutional within the law, and for the very best interests of the whole people. Failures have been errors of judgement, not of intent."

On leaving office, he told Thomas Nast: "I am tired of abuse, and of being a servant of the people. I am going to feel once more how it seems to be a sovereign, as every American citizen is."[7] But no man can be a private sovereign, and the public never relinquishes a hero. People soon forgot his bad judgment and political ignorance, and recalled only the silent figure—deceptively strong—representing power, Union, patriotism. He was a living flag, a collective memory for that generation. "The people feel that in honoring Grant they are honoring all that is best in themselves."[8]

"The General," as he was popularly known after 1877, was restless. He and his family departed for Europe, planning a two-year world trip. He toured England with the status of a former sovereign, ranking only below the Royal Family. Doors opened magically, and once more he sat stolidly through dinners, lawn parties, public receptions, not as a former president, but as the hero of the Union. He crossed Europe, from Denmark to Greece, but wearied of echoing museums. He found more of interest in railways and dams than in Madonnas and bibelots. In Berlin, he added a cubit to his stature by quietly refusing the Emperor's suggested parade: "A military review is a thing which I hope never to see again."[9] He betrayed a small gift for humor that some mistook for ignorance, remarking that Venice would be attractive if the streets were drained. It was an eminently practical, if undiplomatic suggestion.

All this increased Grant's stature at home, where politicians, disgusted with Hayes and moderation, bade him rally the faithful "Stalwarts" in the GOP. Travel would broaden his appeal. He might leave as a national hero wearing a little tarnish, but would return an international figure, more knowledgeable, appealing, stable. The caravan slowly unwound across the Holy Land, to India, China, and Japan. His few speeches made some sense, for he talked of trade and good will, of the future not the past. Every day's paper detailed his progress to Americans. John Russell Young of the *New York Herald* was in the party, writing dispatches that became a best-selling book. In ornate hotel suites, Grant opened letters that told of popular appeal and party needs, but put them aside with apparent indifference. Now and then he answered them in the same tone: [10]

> I note what you say about the prospects for '80, and hear the same thing from other sources, letters, and papers. But with the revival of business all this will be forgotten, and I am very sure it will be gratifying to me. I have had all the honors, and would like to avoid the vexations of political life for the future. Although not sensitive to the abuse of opponents—who slander without regard to facts—I do not care to be a constant antagonist. I have children—and children's children, in a small way—who may be affected by these things, and I want to spare them.

He seemed frank in remarking of politicians: "They have designs for me which I do not contemplate for myself." [11] Distance lent enchantment on both sides, and as he crossed the Pacific many men talked of a third term. No amount of denial removed him from the sweepstakes. His disavowal of political intentions to reporters in Hong Kong only raised the alarm in some circles at home. "[It] may possibly do for the Chinese, but for Americans it is too thin," a midwestern paper noted.[12]

Grant's antipathy to Hayes and "moderation" was no secret. The new President's appointment of "Greeley soreheads" irritated him. Civil service reform left him cold. Senator Conkling, and Pennsylvania's powerful Senator James Donald Cameron were advisers. Across the country, scattered newspaper voices rose steadily in a chorus of comment on his intentions. In October, 1877, partly to revive flagging circulation, the *St. Louis Globe-Democrat* began to criticize Hayes and moderate Republicans. On May 28, 1878, it launched a third term boom for Grant in 1880.[13]

Response was ragged. High-toned Mugwumps raised hands in horror; Grant's coterie would wreck the country, kill the Republican party, and set back the modest beginnings of change. He would restore local bosses, revive the southern question, make rascals supreme. Practical politicians waited upon events. Others slowly stirred to life, hoping to stop Grant with a moderate Republican. But who? In the wake of hard times, labor troubles, and drifting politics, more and more people favored a firm hand. "We need a strong government in Washington," a Chicago clergyman snapped, "and General Grant is an army of one." [14] His supporters began a chorus: Now he was ready to be president—a curious backhanded compliment with considerable public appeal. Professionals gravitated to his camp, but did not manufacture the boom. "The backbone of the movement, without which it could have only a forced, sickly, sensational existence," an eastern paper admitted, "lies in Grant's popularity with the masses of the Republican party. They have already forgotten his many errors of judgment." [15]

Late in September, 1879, the General's party landed in San Francisco. The Slope's aristocracy, not far removed from the mining camps that made it rich, provided a lavish welcome.[16] Political talk weaved around the edges of ballrooms filled with corseted and feathered ladies and elegantly attired swains, sometimes drowning out the waltz music, other times filling private rooms. President Hayes' friend James M. Comly talked to Grant until 2 A.M., and Grant said he did not know what awaited him. He spoke cordially of Sherman, Hayes, Blaine— nearly everyone. "I do not want to run again. I would rather somebody else would be nominated. I do not think I am *needed* for a candidate. I would rather they would take somebody else." He smoked, sipped wine, talked in a monotone, gestured eloquently. "I would not turn my hand over either way." [17]

The more Grant protested, the less effect it had. He said he did not seek the nomination, not that he did not want it. It looked as if he would not have to turn over a hand or do anything but stay alive to gain the nod. The trip east was a continuous ovation. Mere rumor of his arrival filled railroad stations. In formerly hostile cities like Louisville, he drove down avenues jammed with cheering humanity. Ladies hung from windows to wave handkerchiefs, men shouted themselves hoarse, stars and stripes hung from buildings and lampposts. In Chicago, veterans gathered for an Army of the Tennessee reunion, and the city showered him with plaudits and honors. The one stable factor in it all was his stolid figure and brief, eventless speeches. To emo-

tional men like Mark Twain, he brought back all the glorious memories. "My sluggish soul needs a fierce upstirring, and if it would not
get it when Grant enters the meeting-place, I must doubtless 'lay' for
the final resurrection." [18]

But a hero could enter a limited number of cities in triumph, greet
just so many GAR veterans, and give only a few innocuous thanks
before attention waned. He came home too soon; there were nine
months before the convention. "The ovation business palled upon the
public taste," the genteel *Atlantic Monthly* noted gratefully.[19] He said
nothing of political plans, and as far as friends knew, proposed only to
rest in the South, tend weakened finances, and return to his home in
Galena, Illinois. "I am not a candidate for any office," he wrote privately en route, "nor would I hold one that required any manoevering
or sacrifice to obtain." [20] He warned relatives against ostentatious wel-
comes. "But don't be having dinner parties and other entertainments
to take up all the time. I want to get out to the farm and see the horses
and colts." [21]

There was no denying the enthusiasm for Grant. Crude polls in the
Midwest showed him ahead of all other contenders. If an organization
focused this diffuse urge, he could win the nomination.[22] Support rose
in unlikely places. The South devoted much newspaper coverage and
platform oratory to extolling his virtues. Uneasy about even "moderate" Republicanism in Washington, many former carpetbaggers and
some other elements favored Grant. Ironically, a war hero schooled in
the ways of peace might give the South more harmony than compromising politicians. Early in the year he toured the section, to par-
take of sun and sound opinion. He talked his brand of harmony,
assuring audiences the war was over and local rule must prevail. He
seemed to offer Hayes' moderation plus glamor to a people hungry
for both. Reporters wired north that "The people of the south are getting crazy about Grant. It's Grant! Grant! Grant! everywhere!" [23]

Roscoe Conkling commanded those who would make Grant president and capture the Republican party. It was hardly accidental. His
personal admiration of Grant never wavered. In 1872, he had helped
beat off Liberal Republicanism, and exercised a famous invective in
defending the President. "A war of mud and missiles has been waged
for months, . . ." he told crowds. "Every thief and cormorant and
drone who has been put out—every baffled mouser for place and
plunder—every man with a grievance or a grudge—all who have
something to make by a change, seem to wag an unbridled tongue or
to drive a foul pen." [24] The fight with Hayes, and growing fear of

Blaine and the "Half-Breed" Republicans who wished to work for the future rather than live in the past, impelled Conkling to organize Grant's boom.

In spite of the attacks on his organization, Conkling seemed secure in 1880. This was true, in the sense that decline was now inevitable. His strength was largely the evidence of things merely visible. There was always about him an air of the baroque and grandiloquent, but it had once reflected real political power. As he stood now to challenge the fresh attitudes that men like Hayes represented he seemed antique, outdated. But he controlled New York, and her convention votes were a long step toward victory. His strategy was simple. Take rotten boroughs in the South; that would ruin Sherman and gain delegates. Invade the West with a power base from Illinois, Grant's home; that would weaken Blaine. Build in the East on New York and Pennsylvania. Other candidates would awake in mid-spring to a *fait accompli*.

The Keystone State boasted a brilliant, if not always lovable, organization man in the form of J. Donald Cameron. Now forty-seven years old, the elegant "Don" controlled the state with an impressive firmness inherited from his father. President Lincoln had made old Simon Cameron Secretary of War, then later sent him as far away as he could, as Minister to Russia. But whatever criticism the old fox raised among the circumspect, he was a charming man. "He had the graces of age without its infirmities, . . ." Blaine recalled.[25]

It must have run in the family. The son had the same demeanor, with added elegance and style that made him a familiar figure at fashionable spas or counting rooms. He could afford European travel and a leisurely existence that gave entree to intellectual and artistic circles. He was a friend of Henry Adams and John Hay, who overlooked his service as Grant's Secretary of War in 1876–77, and could talk about pictures and books, but preferred party management. As a senator from Pennsylvania between 1877 and 1897, he was a stubborn partisan, but tended to constituents' needs while making himself powerful. In January, 1880, Cameron was elected chairman of the national committee. Opponents, still dozing in their camps, suddenly talked of harmony. Sherman praised him as "by all odds the best man for the place, . . ." and started mending fences.[26] The Pennsylvania state convention endorsed Grant in February after "the familiar Cameronian methods." Cameron then looked to the delegations in the Border states.[27]

In Utica, on February 25, the New York state convention heard Conkling praise Grant and move to commit the delegation for a third term. As a clerk read the resolution, an onlooker in the galleries cried "Blaine!" and Conkling answered: "The shallows murmur, but the deeps are dumb." The roll obeyed his summons, 216–183. It was not a safe margin; the delegation was never fully under his control. He was steadily using up ammunition early in the game. Opposing Democrats said the convention hastened "like a well-trained dog obeys a circus clown, to roll itself in the mud at his command."

Others noted Lord Roscoe's heavy touch. "Mr. Conkling has a good hand for the machine, but no finger for the pulsations of the popular heart." [28] The Senator revealed a dangerous arrogance that marked him for destruction. In the little time he had for socializing, Conkling tried to fill the old *beau ideal* role, but charm wore a little thin. It did not take much to set him off against opponents. "I really believe if their plans go astray," a lady noted after an exhibition of his temper, "the New York senator will go up in spontaneous combustion, from sheer fury." [29] In another month, "The Boom" was well underway, with lines of communication threading the Midwest and South. Blaine was among the first to score the big talk rising there. ". . . wherever Republican success is most hopeless, there Grant enthusiasm runs highest." [30]

While state conventions met and wrangled, the candidate appeared unconcerned. Others made speeches and discussed his apparent views. He evinced an elaborate disinterest in things public. In private, he guarded the boom, corresponded with managers, and coveted the nomination. If things went wrong, he was irritable. On good days he smiled while pacing the room, press dispatches in one hand and a cigar in the other. By May, it seemed the nomination would be his without an open struggle. John Logan, after leaving Elihu B. Washburne, told reporters the faithful would stand fast, no matter how many ballots it took to choose Grant.[31]

Of course, there was irritating criticism. The prospect of a third term unnerved many, and not only Democrats. Republicans wondered if the party could survive four more years of Grant's friends, no matter how much he might have changed. More virulent opponents saw in him an informal monarch, awaiting the crown, never to take it off. More than that, honest men disliked the "scaly set" Grant would bring to public office.[32] The fiction that he was solely the people's choice evaporated under the heat of rigged conventions and boss dictation. From a hero, he changed to a front man for the political element Hayes was battling with growing public approval. He was no longer above criticism, and many newspapers let fly.

Discontent within the party finally focused, with quiet help from the Administration and Grant's opponents. In St. Louis on May 6, a convention of independents, including many personal admirers of Grant, condemned the third term idea. Senator John B. Henderson of Missouri, an independent Republican, chaired the proceedings. Much of the press ridiculed the gathering as a collection of powerless malcontents. The *New York Times* said it consisted of "four assorted Germans, a carefully selected Pole, General Henderson, and a number of persons heretofore more or less closely connected with the Republican party." [33] Perhaps. But the opposition was organizing, advertising, undermining Grant's image, sowing doubts among the electorate.

In a more practical way, Conkling was reaching the end of his string. He read headlines: "Anything to Beat Grant." In private conferences, especially among westerners, he met a baffling evasiveness, a disturbing unwillingness to cut the cards. He was reduced to peddling embassies and judgeships under a future Grant administration. The balloon was at its maximum. It was impressive as balloons went, but could burst more easily than expand. As convention time approached, he descended to dealing.[34] The experience was new to Lord Roscoe. He had never worked quite this way before. In fact, it was an admission of defeat. Had Grant gone his limit? Or could skillful and even brutal last-minute dealings take him over the top? Conkling heard, of course, that none of the big contenders would win. Already, men were writing letters to Congressman Garfield, busy managing John Sherman's boom, telling him to expect lightning. ". . . all anti-machine Republicans . . . see that the only safety for the Republican party is in making some man such as yourself our candidate," [35] Pennsylvania businessman Wharton Barker wrote him. Conkling's arrogance was a cover for fear. What if he lost? At his back, like time's wingéd chariot, he heard the sounds of James G. Blaine.

In January, 1876, Senator James G. Blaine of Maine, offered an amendment to a pending measure restoring certain civil rights to rebel southerners. He was already famous, and easily the front runner for his party's presidential nomination. Blaine spoke rapidly in a fine clear voice, moving to exempt Jefferson Davis from amnesty because he was personally responsible for deaths of captured Union soldiers in Andersonville and Libby prisons. He might as well have thrown a bomb in an arsenal. Acrimonious debate followed, with unforseen consequences for "The Magnetic Man." He sat down amid a storm; the press accused him of reviving the bloody shirt. Davis did not help matters with sarcastic replies. But Blaine got his trouble's worth in popular support. The action surprised many on both sides of the aisle, for he was a convivial, popular, and usually moderate man. A few days later, a southern congressman noted Blaine on the Capitol steps. He nudged a companion, and said through clenched teeth: "Now there's Blaine, damn him! but I do love him." [36] Blaine did not press the point against Davis, and did not win the Republican nomination that summer, but he was in the public eye.

The southern congressman's remark illustrated the divided attitude of Blaine's whole generation. He was now fifty, at the peak of a career in politics that began when he was hardly more than a boy. He was born in Pennsylvania, and as something of a prodigy, entered Washington College near Pittsburgh at the age of thirteen. He got a reasonable amount of information, if not learning, from books, but lacked patience for systematic study. He taught briefly at the Western Military Institute in Georgetown, Kentucky, but disliked the South and moved to Pittsburgh to teach in an institute for the blind and study law. Before leaving, he married a sprightly, socializing, shrewd woman named Harriet Stanwood. In fact, he married her twice; once secretly in Kentucky, because neither wanted their parents to know, then later in Pittsburgh. It was an awkward story, the grist for many later gossip mills.

He went to Maine in 1854, to practice journalism and dabble in politics. He gained some influence, circulated with local lights, and sharpened skills at managing men for a better day in a larger arena. He was genial but not familiar, preferring groups to individuals, and exercised a remarkable spell over crowds. A gift for lucid explanation reflected an interest in English, the classics, and mathematics. A formidable memory made him a dreaded foe.

Like most of his family, Blaine was a Whig, and a great admirer of Henry Clay. He soon dominated the Republican party in Maine, in a period when that state had considerable influence in national affairs. From 1863 to 1876 he sat in the national House, and was so able a parliamentarian and politician that he served as Speaker from 1869 to 1875. In that capacity he gained a reputation for fairness in heated debates. His memory was a storehouse of precedents that expedited business. His eye was so quick that he tallied votes as he brought down the gavel, gave exact numbers, and then explained to the curious that he simply divided the members into groups of ten for faster counting.[37]

In 1876, he entered the upper house, and irritated many older senators with his sharp debating tactics. Innocent of senatorial decorum, Blaine frequently disputed their elaborate set-pieces intended for home consumption. "We had peace and good order in this body before he was transplanted from the other side of the Capitol," a colleague complained. "No place is big enough for him and anybody else. . . . If he desires to keep the country in a ferment, he ought to return to the other branch of Congress." [38] Blaine knew stage tricks, and used the dramatic pause at the right moment. Calmer men like Garfield distrusted his flash, but admitted he was brilliant. "On the whole, he is the completest gladiator in debate I know of." [39] He was the most compelling public figure of the day. Old Thad Stevens apparently first nicknamed him "magnetic," an adjective that fitted. Robert G. Ingersoll, adept at catching thunder in the rhetoric washing through politics, coined an enduring title while nominating him for president in 1876: "The Plumed Knight."

Blaine was one of those ambitious, energetic, nervous men whose daily lives had no point of rest. Few could imagine him asleep, and he seemed poised to run when sitting down. Friends said he was "brilliant," foes said he was merely showy. He entertained fresh thoughts and varied opinions, but was not really interested in ideas. Natural curiosity about life and shrewd insight into social forces made him a formidable analyst of the American party system. Like the true professional who sees politics as an art, he had no other serious interests. He was not reflective, read little, disliked travel, and devised no theory of government. A curious combination of tactician and strategist, he was too nervous to plot a battle in detail, but had the gift of seeing the heart of most issues. Blaine hated process and longed for conclusions. Unlike more successful but duller leaders, he would not plod through statistics to make a point. A man like Conkling charged his enemies; a thinker like Garfield weighed choices in the balance, and usually found himself wanting; aloof personalities like Hayes believed ideas swayed men, and played a waiting game. Blaine committed himself in bits and pieces to every fray, and consequently was on the defensive before the battle turned. Like most imaginative men, he lived in the future. Once committed to an ideal like tariff reciprocity, he visualized it finished and working, and lacked the patience to wait for slower men to organize the details.

His legislative record was barren, and his financial record suspect; opponents wondered at the power he exercised over so many men for so long. Personal vividness buoyed up his reputation, but he had great political gifts. He was a firm party regular without being rancorous.

If he lost a skirmish, he worked anyway. A persuasive, eloquent speaker, his presence in a campaign counted for much, placing many other politicians in his debt. Above all, he typified the "American" aspect of every issue in his time. He seemed to be like Grant, but with flair; a humble man at the top; an intense nationalist, yet taking a calm, correct view; a self-made man triumphing over "betters." No one who fought him in a campaign ever underestimated his skill or appeal.[40]

The petty details of his personal life filled daily papers, and he reigned over much of the public like a matinee idol. Part of his legend was the interesting combination of a notorious absentmindedness and a perfect memory. He regularly fired the gardener, then asked why he was not working. He came to the table trailing state papers, forgetting they were tucked in his hat or sleeve. Much of his adverse political reputation simply reflected sloppy work habits and poor communications.[41]

A memory for faces and facts he wished to recall balanced this irritating habit. He literally knew the voting pattern of every important county in the nation, and amazed visitors with his knoweldge of local conditions. Once introduced to him, a man was forever in his memory. In Maine, he talked to constituents about last year's crops, children in school, a prize bull in the pasture, or the wife's new dress. He received constituents and friends informally, with genuine personal interest in his tone, and captivating black eyes. "Had he been a woman, people would have rushed off to send expensive flowers," Mrs. Joseph B. Foraker said. Blaine spoke to everyone as an individual. He did not talk up or down. Among children, he was amusing, benevolent, but not patronizing. With young people, he seemed understanding and vigorous. Talking to older hands, he was shrewd, candid, and persuasive, never forgetting to stroke every man's *amour propre*. In a crowd of voters he was in tune with a dozen personal needs.[42] Fervent admirers welcomed the title "Blainiacs."

Of course, it was not all wine and roses. As Senator John J. Ingalls said drily: "To his extraordinary power of attracting friends, Blaine added an inexhaustible capacity for making enemies."[43] Observers remarked that men went insane over him in pairs, one for and one against. He had a bad habit of writing indiscreet notes, with admonitions no one followed: "Burn this letter." A loose view of money-making, which rather bored him, early blighted his presidential hopes. Questionable dealings with railroad bonds put Blaine on the defensive all his life after 1876. In that year, letters he took from a clerk named

Mulligan, allegedly showed he had used his position as Speaker of the House to promote railroad bonds, and caused a sensation. His dramatic, carefully staged rebuttal did not dispel doubts, and helped defeat his aspirations for the 1876 nomination. As Schurz snapped, he had "wallowed in spoils like a rhinocerous in an African pool." [44] It was an absurd charge, but it stuck.

A stubborn refusal to explain his expensive scale of living did not help. Blaine said only that knowledgeable friends invested his money. Mrs. Blaine had some assets; and like most people, he was always in debt. Beyond that he would not go. A whole generation of newsmen poured barrels of ink over acres of newspapers to prove either that he was crooked, or an innocent victim of political opponents. No one ever settled the issue. At best he was guilty of indiscretion—in effect, of being caught; at worst he had used inside knowledge to enhance stock values. He was not a criminal. The real problem was his inability to settle the issue though he discussed it openly. Doubt followed him like a shadow. The surprising thing was not the subject's interest, but that his public appeal continued.[45]

Blaine's tainted past was doubly unfortunate. It ruined his presidential hopes, but also cast suspicion on any fresh idea he espoused. If Blaine was for it, who must be against it? The charges made him a standing target for enemies in both parties. He developed new political attitudes in public, and worked valiantly to broaden Republican support in an industrializing social order. But he had only to mention tariff reciprocity, shipping subsidies, overseas trade, or voting rights to raise up a host of doubters.

Enemies added to this incorrect picture of corruption the suggestion of private dissipation. Hypochondria made him easy prey for the editorialists' pen. The family learned to expect a daily announcement that he was dying, and Mrs. Blaine spent much time soothing imaginary pains. He suffered from gout, had "nerves" that caused insomnia, and was generally on the move, but hints of decadence irritated him. "In some way gout is associated in the public mind with drinking and high living, of neither of which I am at all guilty," he complained.[46]

Blaine did not expect to climb the greasy pole. He compared himself to Henry Clay, talked often of "The Great Unknown," and affected an air of resignation. He did not hold grudges. "Life is too short for such things," he responded with a shrug, and seldom looked back. "Nothing is so weakening as regret," was a favorite maxim. And he appreciated publicity; "I don't mind being abused so long as I am not forgotten." [47]

By 1880, Blaine was acknowledged leader of the Republican "Half-

Breeds," and chief foe of the "Stalwarts." Neither was a cohesive movement; both reflected loyalty to a set of leaders and a general attitude, not a body of doctrine. The Stalwarts continued to talk about the South, avoiding new issues rising from industrialization. Conkling and Grant were their heroes. The Half-Breeds following Blaine were realistic. They knew the country was changing. Immigrants, new industries, growing cities, all demanded fresh political responses. Businessmen were not necessarily great social architects, but Half-Breeds favored a new party coalition resting on support from a growing middle class, the prosperous farmer, tariff-protected workers, and businessmen. They wished to raise *party* allegiance above *personal* loyalty, and unify divisive currents in society.

Blaine combined vigor and dash with a tendency to hesitate in crucial moments, and as 1880 opened, did not announce his political intentions. Speculation mounted in the press and among politicians. He was popular; nothing seemed to weaken his support in the West— the area beyond Pennsylvania in the minds of eastern leaders. He campaigned there against Greenbackism in the 1878 congressional elections, and the memory of his passage lingered. He could probably displace Sherman in Ohio, capture Border delegates, and dominate the Old Northwest and Plains states.[48]

Blaine faced a genuine dilemma. The wounds of 1876 still hurt, and he did not want to conduct the inevitable personal canvass, full of bitter charges and apologies. But he was sure Grant's nomination would wreck the party. If the General lost the election, Republicans would drift; if he won, men like Conkling would arrest any movement toward a broader coalition. Failure to contest Grant would leave Blaine's friends without a future; an open challenge might defeat the GOP with intra-party strife.

The personal factor was strong. Blaine opposed a third term for Grant as early as 1875, incurring his silent enmity, but Roscoe Conkling was the real foe. They started public life as friends, often dining out, exchanging visits, supporting each other's policies. But a clash was inevitable. Men of such temperaments, each ambitious for rule, mixed like oil and water. Tension flowed across their dinner tables and spoiled many literary quotations, as the Plumed Knight used his formidable memory to correct Lord Roscoe's sallies in verse. The breach came in 1866, in debate on a trivial bill. Conkling's pompous demeanor and rigidity irritated Blaine, who used the weapon sure to cut Lord Roscoe deepest—ridicule. In sharp, contemptuous tones, he referred to Conkling's "haughty disdain, his grandiloquent swell, his majestic, super-eminent, over-powering, turkey-gobbler strut." Cartoonists promptly gave Conkling a set of feathers. The suggestion of a mutual acquaintance that Conkling forget, if not forgive, produced one word: "Never." [49]

In 1880, Blaine weighed all these factors. He was a realist, and knew he could not win the nomination without a struggle that could make it an empty victory. Soon after Grant came home, Blaine spelled out the view for Whitelaw Reid. "I will never again fight an aggressive battle, horses cannot drag me into it, . . ." He appreciated the talk, and had few recriminations against personal enemies from 1876, counting "that as belonging to the Silurian epoch." The problem was clear: "If I should say publicly that I am not anxious to be nominated in '80, it would simply be taken as a piece of affectation." [50] He would rest "in the hands of his friends," openly challenging no other Republican, but allowing state organizations to gather enough votes for him to stop Grant. At a deadlocked convention, he would either accept a genuine draft or work for a compromise candidate pledged to his views.[51] By Valentine's Day, a "Blaine for President" headquarters opened in Washington, displaying portraits, loosing streamers in the breeze, offering buttons, fans, canes, umbrellas, and literature. The chieftain did not visit the rooms, and calmly rebuffed friends who urged a public assault on the Grant boom.[52] Ideally, he hoped Republicans like Sherman, who had no chance, would "clear the tracks," and that foolish independents would not dissipate strength in ceremonial resistance that could nominate Grant. Publicly, Blaine and Sherman kept their tempers; privately the Plumed Knight condemned the Secretary's shortsightedness.[53] April came, and Sherman showed no signs of abandoning the path to the White House.

John Sherman entered the contest with Hayes' approval and such help as he could muster. The President was "the Cinderella of his party," having rejected a second term. "I have had enough of it," he told the curious. But he was not disinterested in the contest's outcome. A great personal admirer of Grant, he was saddened at his old commander's presence in a ring of bosses. Hayes thought Conkling was "a corrupt and thoroughly rotten man," who would run Grant to thwart reform and change, but he felt Blaine's nomination would provoke a disastrous personal campaign. Logically, if unenthusiastically, he supported Sherman, but noted increasing discussion of Garfield.[54]

Sherman wore the mantle of his financial policies into the political arena with some hope of success. He would not "scramble" for the nomination, but in the summer of 1879 Garfield noted after a drive: "I think he is deeply committed to the hope of being nominated." [55] On paper, the Secretary had a good traditional base of support— federal patronage and influence in the South, whose delegates represented no votes on Election Day but helped nominate candidates. Sherman hoped to avoid the bloody shirt. "The true issue for 1880 is national supremacy in national matters, honest money and an honest dollar." [56] Though he made few speeches, his platform was clear. Fiscal soundness; moderation to the South, and acceptance of local rule if federal law prevailed; national aid to education; and tariff protection.[57]

His few speeches set no one afire, opened no wounds; the public saw little of Sherman on the stump. Management of his affairs passed to James A. Garfield, and if Sherman failed at the convention, he would support the "Sage of Mentor." It was a reasonable choice. Garfield was experienced, could manage Ohio's delegation, and had wide acquaintance among politicians. Sherman may have chosen him for personal as well as political reasons; together they might make one good politician. Sherman was cool and aloof; Garfield moved easily among people. The Secretary knew figures; Garfield knew books. Politics entered on both sides. Garfield was an organization man, wanting influence in a Sherman administration. Sherman wished to groom an heir, and genuinely liked his manager. If he noted ambitious men around Garfield, who did not discourage hints of "availability," he said nothing.

Sherman boldly but silently built his effort on Treasury patronage. His professed claim to be "utterly indifferent to the distribution of patronage," fooled nobody, and he cast a wide net across custom-houses and revenue offices around the country.[58] It was the only thing to do, but was self-defeating. Office-holders did not reflect changing desires in their constituency, and were far too optimistic about Sherman's chances. They reported what he wished to hear more often than the truth, and did not represent true popular support. Above all, they made Sherman the target of newspaper criticism. Grant had bosses; Sherman had an empire.

To add delegates from the South was equally logical and fatal. In the state conventions below the Potomac, Sherman's agents broadcast promises and "twelve-dollar lunches" to the faithful.[59] He quickly gained his maximum strength and suffered from a bad press. "What is the use of being for Sherman when no one else is for him?" a friend asked.[60] By convention time, the effort was exhausted. Sherman had performed the difficult and awkward feat of getting stuck half-way up the greasy pole. He rebuffed advice to transfer strength elsewhere; there was always a chance in a fragmented convention. But he would not obstruct the majority's will, and privately admitted defeat by assuring friends he would support whoever won.[61]

The Mugwumps had a favorite in Vermont's flinty senator, George Franklin Edmunds. He was the light that would not fail, the one candidate "on whom personally there does not rest the shadow of reproach." [62] Edmunds had played all sides of the street so long that such diverse men as George William Curtis and Ulysses S. Grant could call him both reformer and conservative. He merited the title: "The Stalwart Sweetheart of the Reformers." [63]

Edmunds supposedly represented the New England Conscience in a senatorial career that spanned the years 1866–91. Constitutional law was his specialty, even less likely to raise a crowd than Sherman's fiscal song. No baby's lips tenderly pressed his whiskered cheek. He played no sycophant to crowds. Instead, they heard reminders of duty, country, and integrity that brought a cynical smile to the politician's face and left the average voter disinterested. Edmunds boasted that he never asked patronage favors for anyone, which merely doubled the load of his venerable colleague, Justin S. Morrill. He worked to outlaw polygamy in Utah and fund the Union Pacific's debts, but left no mark on anything bearing upon public interests. Many a bill disappeared into his Senate Judiciary Committee, never to return.

Personally, he was not calculated to inspire much popular enthusiasm, but to men of like mind he "answered very well as a standard bearer, . . ." amid jumbled events in the spring of 1880. Even among friends Edmunds was stiff and reserved. He wrote letters in an elegant hand on stationery bordered with mourning black. His attitudes were purely negative. He could say "no" to both Republicans and Democrats, and did so often enough to seem constructive. A legalistic mind hardly answered the moment's needs, however. As a colleague noted: "He can see the knot hole in a barn door, but he can't see the door." Massachusetts' Senator George F. Hoar urged Edmunds only half-facetiously to stay in the race. "But, Edmunds, just think of the fun you would have vetoing bills." [64] He was a bitter, waspish debater. Many men bore the sting of an encounter on the Senate floor. But there were skeletons in his closet, and he admitted "something of a fondness" for spirits. President Hayes, his judgment perhaps warped through Temperance lenses, thought him a "confirmed—well, hard,

drinker." Charles Francis Adams, Jr., thought Edmunds once suggested a bribe in return for saving the Union Pacific, but did not press
the issue.[65] His lack of any national constituency revealed the political
ineptitude of the "reformers" pushing his cause.

And so the spring developed, bringing alternate rainy days and
sunny skies in both the weather and politics. The party conventions
promised to be exciting. Blaine, Sherman, Grant—the established men
—took the headlines. Edmunds and other favorite sons got a nod now
and then. Garfield went his way, with friends in all camps. The choice
depended partly on the opposition. And no man ever safely predicted
what Democrats might do.

If Republican hearts leaped up at the name of Ulysses S. Grant or
James G. Blaine, Democrats took cheer from Samuel J. Tilden. In the
years since 1876, he symbolized both the party's frustrations and hopes.
He was an unlikely figure to provoke such attitudes, a sober, grey man,
whose hallmark was a devious silence. Now sixty-four, he traced interest in politics almost to his birth in upstate New York. His father
was a merchant and postmaster in New Lebanon, with a flair for
political intrigue and a host of powerful friends. It was not unusual
for young Samuel to see Silas Wright, William L. Marcy, or Martin
Van Buren arrive for an evening's talk over a bottle of wine. The
young man learned the arts of manipulation and the values of silence.
He led an uneventful, repressed youth, fancying he was dying of various disorders, sampling patent nostrums in his father's store. He preferred books to the swimming hole, and nurtured a talent for epigrams
and dialectical argument. The family regularly indulged in paralyzing
debate over trivial issues, mistaking discussion for democracy. For
weeks they weighed the question as to whether he should attend Yale;
he went for one term, then left because he disliked the food and
climate.

Tilden studied law and kept a careful hand in the incredible factions
of New York Democratic politics. During the war he was publicly
neutral, but deplored Republican federalism and measures like the
draft. Taking Jefferson and Jackson as idols, and natural law as a text,
he always opposed government in the market place. Early loneliness
fortified a tendency to detached analysis and a love of convoluted
speculation.[66] Smothering any desire to comprehend the needs of ur-
banizing politics, he earned the contempt of city machine masters like
Tweed, who called him a spokesman of "the cheese-press, and hay-loft
democracy" of upstate New York.

Walking a careful circle around the edge of life, Tilden easily sang the virtues of yesteryear. "I have felt gloomily the decay of all my early ideals of my country, and engaged in the effort to restore them." [67] Like Grant, he used silence as a shield, and others mistook it for strength and wisdom. He never closed with a problem he could attack from afar, and approached men with an Ottoman sense of intrigue. He often kept important people like David B. Hill waiting for hours, only to say: "Hill, we must keep the bad men to the rear," or "We must elevate the standard. Thank you for coming. Goodbye." [68] In an empty hour, he might visit a friend in the newspaper world or some equally useful occupational area. Sitting on a chair's edge, "Whispering Sammy" swayed slightly in a black Prince Albert, voice thin and wavering, to discuss dogs, the wine cellar, or sheep at his estate "as if they must be sinister suggestions for the overthrow of the Republic." [69]

Tilden grew rich in corporation law, and at one time oversaw much of the railroad mileage west of the Hudson. He developed a ruthlessness in business he did not overtly carry into politics, earning the title "The Great Forecloser." He lived elegantly, and spent considerable sums on charity, but supported institutions more often than people. He could endow a library, but tell a clerk who asked about vacations: "Your vacation will begin at once, and continue indefinitely." [70] Money gratified few personal needs. Art, travel, the human parade, were all abstractions. Only a dry interest in nature, properly viewed from a windowsill or carriage, alleviated a chilly and cerebral character.

He prosecuted the Tweed Ring, and as a reform governor after 1874, attacked the "Canal Ring" and other nefarious groups, but was a latecomer to reform. Fear that Tammany's odious reputation would taint Democracy's national image and thwart his presidential ambitions brought Tilden into the fray. Most activists distrusted him as a wire-puller and phrasemaker. Blaine put it squarely: ". . . in the work of the reformer he did not forget the shrewd calculations of the partisan. He understood better than any other man the art of appropriating to himself the credit of events which would have come to pass without his agency, and of reforms already planned by his political opponents." [71] During the campaign of 1876, the civil service reformer Dorman B. Eaton scored Tilden. Noting that he did nothing for sanitation, charity, or labor, he concluded: "There never was a more preposterous claim set up than that of Tilden to be a reformer." [72]

Tilden's public image was a godsend for his party, however. He brought it some young men, and projected respectability that proffered an alliance between New York, the mid-Atlantic states, and South that would restore Democratic rule. The crisis of 1876 tarnished his reputation; many Democrats blamed his vacillation for losing the presidency. They found scant comfort in his private declaration: "I will never be a party to any course which will array my countrymen in civil war against each other." [73] But he remained the greatest Democrat, subject of newspaper speculation, and center of intrigue, dominating the New York Democracy, with powerful allies in newspaper offices and counting houses. As a martyr to compromise, he had a sentimental claim the party could not lightly ignore. To abandon him in 1880 might lend consent to the solution that raised Hayes and saved the Republicans.

Tilden's commanding prestige in the Democratic party symbolized its inherent weaknesses and dilemmas. It was little more than a collective grievance. The shocks of civil war and Reconstruction demolished it, and the components were useless without a central doctrine or figure. Tilden was both, the only major northern Democrat in most men's recollection. The rest of the party's support scattered over the expanding West, centered in cities with bosses who opposed Tilden, or rested stolidly in the South. The overriding concept of "local rule," remembrance of things past, and dislike of Republicans kept the party an entity, but this was self-defeating, since it meant a lack of focus and discipline. The only thing that might create order and purpose was a great leader, a commanding issue, or the prospect of spoils. Long absence from the presidency gave the Democrats none of these in 1880. They nursed local grudges, excusing inactivity with quotations from Jefferson and Jackson. The ideas of these two men had not fitted their own times. To bring them forward in a rapidly industrializing society as guides of conduct was an admission of political bankruptcy.

Given Tilden's record of evasion, the more he failed to act the more he looked like a candidate. On doctors' orders, he toured Europe early in 1877. That fall, he spoke to the Young Men's Democratic Club in New York, and occasionally dispatched letters full of epigrams and proverbs. In 1879, he testified before the Potter Committee. That summer he moved to "Greystone," an elaborate mansion in Yonkers, to escape the city's heat and oppressive callers. There he was a gentleman farmer, raising purebred livestock and experimenting with sheep, thus adding "Sage of Greystone" to the title roster. On Washington's Birthday, 1880, he wrote a public letter to the Democratic Association of Massachusetts, condemning militarism, third terms, and federalism. Early in 1880, the signs of spring included private surveys of his popularity, frequent newspaper interviews, and a steadily rising demand in the Democratic press that he run again to vindicate the "Crime of '76."

Not everyone mounted the bandwagon. Independent papers like the *Washington Post* noted that he represented "a lost cause," settled on March 5, 1877. The opposition was more personal. "Take away his quarrels and his grievance and there is nothing left of Mr. Tilden but a very commonplace railroad-wrecker and tax dodger." Even a gay blade and aging boy like Sam Ward thought it time to abandon "that old jack-in-the-box, S.J.T., with his fresh pot of money and his left foot in the grave." [74]

The nagging question of health disturbed Tilden's friends. A light stroke left him frail. He was addicted to water cures, cold baths, special diets, and electricity nostrums. "His intellect is unimpaired," Abram S. Hewitt admitted, "but his body is afflicted with infirmity which may compel him to decline to be a candidate." [75] Tilden laconically told a secretary: "It takes all my time to live." [76] Once more the opposition was less kind: "Great expectations go with the vice-presidency in the event of Tilden's nomination." [77] He granted enigmatic interviews, designed to renounce ambition and keep his name in print. To one reporter he said: "But I am out of politics. I have nothing more to do with it," then added his usual twist: "I am waiting. I am lying perfectly still and waiting." [78]

Tilden's greatest enemy was neither bad health nor the Republican party, but John Kelly, boss of Tammany Hall. "He hates you as the Devil hates holy water," Robert Roosevelt warned Tilden.[79] The boss himself offhandedly condemned both the Sage and the fraud issue in referring to "the old humbug of Cipher Alley." [80] The genteel avoided Kelly and all he represented. Little but the label "Democrat" allied him to Tilden. His short, square figure, close-lipped mouth, stern eyes, and quick steps denoted a powerful inner man. Determination and rustic origins marked his every aspect; he displayed a degree *summa cum laude* from the school of life. Born in 1822 of Irish immigrant parents, Kelly matured quickly in the streets of New York. At thirteen he was an apprentice soapstone cutter and came by his physique naturally. Newspaper work and politics attracted him, and in the 1850's he first opposed then joined Tammany Hall, slowly climbing the ladder of political office.

The death of his wife and two daughters turned him inward, and after a wandering European tour, he came home to take over an organization demoralized and reeling under public condemnation after

Tweed's fall. He changed the Hall from a personal fief at the mercy of snowballing corruption and internal division to a machine that ran on the grease of patronage and relief. "He found it a horde. He left it a political army." [81] Kelly typified the organization man with no philosophy, but he had a keen sense of belonging to people he could help. Whatever others thought of him, the men running his organization and their constituents obeyed his command. He was a rare phenomenon, a Democrat who could organize and deliver votes.

He would not deliver them to Tilden. Kelly distrusted tendencies even to verbal expressions of reform sentiment. City dislike of the country and upstate wire-pullers also animated Tammany opposition to "hayseeds" around Tilden. By March, Kelly was in open revolt. When the state convention endorsed Tilden in April, he threatened to leave the party if Tilden won. His men rallied around bitter slogans— "Tildenism is personalism, which is false to Democracy and dangerous to the Republic." On April 23, Kelly told the Tammany central committee that if Tilden won the nomination, he would campaign against him. [82] The Democrats seemed to repeat the Republican story in 1880. How strange that men compared Grant and Blaine to Tilden and Kelly. Were there any dark horses in the Democratic stable?

They tended to be grey rather than dark. Most possessed varying degrees of political "availability." The search for a suitable compromise between the "establishment" Tilden represented, and the "machine" Kelly commanded had twisted turns. It often savored of archeological digging. Veteran dealers wanted "the Old Ticket," of 1876, matching Thomas A. Hendricks of Indiana with Tilden. Hendricks' peculiar appeal in the Midwest lingered after a checkered career. He began life as a Douglas Democrat, sat in the Senate from 1863 to 1869, and symbolized northern discontent with the war effort. Critics called him a "Copperhead," and he opposed national abolition of slavery, wartime controls, and federalism. He voted for war measures, but trimmed to all sides of most questions, and expounded localism during Reconstruction. In 1872, he was elected governor of Indiana, and in December, after Horace Greeley's sudden death, received 42 of his 62 electoral votes as a compliment. An engaging personality, political craft, and love of spoils made him a good campaigner and balance weight for Tilden in 1876. But to bring him forward now only invited the redoubled charge that Democracy faced entirely backward, and existed largely to revive war issues.

The search for a compromise candidate settled for a moment on an even less likely figure, seventy-year-old Horatio Seymour, popular wartime governor of New York and the party's candidate against Grant in 1868. Tilden and his friends took the Seymour boom seriously. From the confines of a Mohawk Valley farm, "The Great Decliner" did little to inhibit its growth, and avoided explaining a past that resembled that of Hendricks. In March, he smiled through an interview, and said at last: "The quarrels among the Democrats are over old men, and it is the height of folly to continue them." [83] It was sensible advice, but he did not refer to his age. In June, he wobbled a little more, giving ear to suggestions of a draft, reportedly telling visitors "If it takes that shape, I will run if it kills me!" It no doubt would have, and he finally refused to be a candidate.[84]

Justice Stephen J. Field of the United States Supreme Court, late of California, had hopes. He represented conservatism, business, and the Far West—as enemies quickly pointed out. Rumors that Jay Gould was financing Field, and knowledge that a campaign from the Bench would not enthuse anyone, collapsed an organization that "was brought here in sections from Washington and set up on arrival." [85]

Delaware offered a more logical candidate than her size warranted in Senator Thomas Francis Bayard. Tracing a distinguished family of public servants to the beginnings of American history, "the imperious Bayard" had all of life's advantages. At fifty-two, he was strikingly handsome, bearing with ease the marks of wealth and aristocracy. Private tutors educated him for the law, and he practiced in Wilmington and briefly in Philadelphia, beginning at the top and rising. He entered the Senate in 1869 as a champion of states' rights, tariff reform, the gold dollar, and the ways of the Fathers. Lineage, an absolutely safe constituency, and self-confidence kept him clear of political machinations, but he was a good fighter in the senatorial club. "He was ambitious for station, but not for profit," an observer noted.[86] A Border spokesman for the South, he could also hope for support from some northern Democrats. Like most secondary party contenders, Bayard fancied Tilden's strength would fall to him if the New Yorker failed to run. But he disliked Tilden's devious ways, admitting privately: "The intimates of Mr. Tilden were not mine, and we were very antipathetic." [87]

His aloof personality posed a problem for aides. At best they could hold him up as a spokesman for integrity and fixed principles. "You are the first choice of the South," a supporter wrote, "but the fear is expressed that you are too respectable in character and too proud a statesman to receive the nomination of any body of politicians." [88]

His views were equally unattractive to politicians in bars and county courthouses. Most Democrats could applaud his stand on states' rights, though he did go to extremes. "I am in favor of reducing the functions and revenues of the Federal Government to a minimum consistent with absolute safety and competent strength to maintain itself against all comers," he wrote a friend, "and of restoring the powers of local self-government to the states wherever they have been unwisely absorbed by the centralizing currents of our time." [89]

Just as he had no idea of using government, he little understood the representative process. When Democrats began to favor greenbacks and easy money, he simply resigned from the powerful Senate Finance Committee rather than seek a compromise. In December, 1879, he offered a resolution ending legal-tender status for greenbacks. It failed but weakened his support in the West and South. More reasonable men urged him to "put a *silver lining*" on his currency views. "You must come to the consideration of the question with a little more fact and less theory," Augustus H. Garland of Arkansas gently counseled, "more understanding and less imagination, from the external to the internal, more of logic and less of poetry." [90] Others argued he could slight the South; it would follow any Democrat. He had vigorously fought Radical reconstruction, and in 1861 opposed coercing seceding states. As the *St. Louis Globe-Democrat* noted, that record had not thwarted many Democrats recently. Men like Seymour, McClellan, and Tilden rose to the top in the same situation.[91]

Bayard entered the contest in 1880 assuming he was Tilden's residual heir, no matter how little they had in common. By the winter of 1879, he outlined his views in the usual speeches and public letters, favoring a sound currency, low tariff, and non-coercion of the South.[92] For the rest, he would say nothing bad of any other candidate, and "take all my wounds *in front* (if I am to get any) and not be struck by a stray bullet while dodging." [93] Naturally, that did not preclude artful dealing. He hesitated to work with Republicans in New York City for national support in return for local help from Democrats. Not because it was dishonest; the opposition might be untrustworthy on delivery day. New York friends in finance and business floated his local boom with discreet speeches and the printed word. In February, 1880, he stooped to dealing with Kelly. Perry Belmont assured Bayard, after secret conferences, that Kelly would support him against Tilden for an unnamed price, probably the usual patronage and a nod from respectability in power.[94]

Bayard had little but a high-toned personality and negative record to recommend him. The Keystone State put forward a man of wider reknown in Samuel Jackson Randall. As Speaker of the national House since 1877, he was an inevitable presidential possibility. He had not reached that eminence without hard work. The son of a poor Philadelphia family, "Sam" Randall entered politics as an "American Whig," relentlessly supporting tariff protection but opposed to federalism. He controlled the only Democratic district in post-war Philadelphia, which elected him to Congress from 1862 until his death in 1890. It was a waterfront area of shops, wharves, small factories, warehouses, groggeries, and junk-yards, but its inhabitants were not surprised to see their elegant Representative threading through piles of rope at dockside, shaking hands with men in greasy overalls, or hoisting a glass of bad liquor in a waterfront dive. Randall genuinely loved his constituents, and had a fierce pride in the common man. He protected their interests with a shrewdness and vigor that boded ill for challengers. And he had security. It was no idle boast that "the devil can't beat me in my own district." [95]

Randall's appearance belied his origins. He cultivated the smooth approach, and dined out more often at the Union League Club than at waterfront bars. Cartoonists captured his personal tone, drawing him as a pharaoh, Roman senator, or magician in evening clothes. Everything about him spoke of connections to wealth and industrial power. His courtly manners, charm, and careful dress reflected the clubroom, and he radiated an aura of fine wines and good cigars. Despite a rather monotonous voice, his formal speeches savored of the Roman Senate, and he conducted private dealings behind a screen of reserved elegance. A perceptive newsman caught him in a fine snapshot, meeting constituents at a state convention: [96]

> Amid all the diverse greetings of diverse men, friends and admirers, secret enemies, the envious, the discontented, the disappointed, the defiant, the cringing, his face was like a mask, immobile, unchanged. Not a shadow of an emotion flitted across its fixed expression of formal courtesy, or swerved the straight glance that his bright, dark eye shot into the eye of every man who grasped his hand.

Randall headed a powerful bloc of northern Democrats who consistently voted for tariff protection. Representing industrial districts, producing both finished goods and raw materials, they were a major source of division in the national Democratic structure. Though favoring local autonomy, moderation to the South, and economy in government, they would not lower tariff schedules. They were individualists, believing in thrift, hard work, and competition, but within a home market closed to foreign goods.

Randall's reputation also rested on a hatred of government expendi-

ture. "The Brakeman," with a shrewd eye scanning every appropria-
tion bill for excess fat, was "a killer of jobs and lobbyists, as well as a
retrencher." Republicans condemned the "gospel of cheese-paring retrenchment. . . ," but he was "all-powerful" on the House Appropriations Committee. Frustrated opponents found him a hard man to
defeat. He never seemed to sleep or sweat, no matter how dull or
furious the debates. Cautious, even-tempered, patient, he outlasted
everyone. He once attended a House session for 46 hours and 25 minutes, engaging in 75 roll calls without any sign of fatigue or irritability.
A host of friends supported him from fondness and respect, as well as
for self-interest.[97]

Randall's political situation was deceptive. He was a well-known
Democrat from a northern industrial state, with a good press, strong
with labor and business, and in the party establishment, but his protectionism was the kiss of death. He could gain no Republican votes
to offset low-tariff Democrats he alienated in the South and West. He
was powerful in the congressional club, but essentially a state leader
unable to expand his following. His urban-industrial connections repelled rural-agrarian Democrats, yet he could not become a Republican because of views on local rule and economy. He remained secure,
accepting only part of the great changes that came over the America
of his youth. To friends and supporters he was the man who made
good, and looked back to help others. To enemies, he was in the
spider's web, amid "a great throng of Philadelphia politicians clothed
in silk hats and the Randallian air of mystery, and 'bet-yer-five-hun-
dred-dollar' confidence." [98]

In 1880, Randall thought he was Tilden's heir. Like Bayard, whom
he fought subtly but bitterly, he counted on quietly gathering the old
man's delegates. In the belt of states clouded with factory smoke and
familiar with shipping, stretching from Chicago to Boston, he laid
careful plans. Frequent trips to Greystone kept his presence vivid, and
Tilden led him on; yes, he was second choice, but who could say what
might happen? Wiser heads were shaken when Randall talked of New
York's delegates. "My belief is that Tilden wants the nomination himself," a former New York congressman wrote, "is working and spending his money for it, and that he would cheat Christ himself if he
thinks he could win." [99] But Randall labored, hoped, and stayed in
Tilden's camp, even though disturbing reports rose in the spring that
Pennsylvania might have a more "available" candidate at convention
time.

His name was Major General Winfield Scott Hancock, commanding the Department of the East, known to newspaper copyists as "Hancock the Superb." He fought in Mexico, served in Texas before the war, and made a reputation at Gettysburg, in the Wilderness, and at Spotsylvania. After the war, he attracted Democratic politicians with moderate military rule in Louisiana and Texas, finally leaving rather than enforce martial law. A campaign against Indians, culminating in his present command, illustrated both ability and connections. In the process, he remained aloof from politics, and symbolized the glories of nostalgic victories. Time was good to General Hancock. He wore most of the country's highest decorations, and filled premier military posts. He remained alive in men's memories, even though he had lost hair and gained weight since the salad days when he sat a horse like something from a David painting. He remained at the edges of partisanship, mentioned as a likely contender against Grant in 1868 and 1872, discussed in 1876, no stranger to circles that made candidates in 1880.

From the viewpoint of strict "availability" he had many assets. Lack of a public record was an advantage when greater men attempted to explain theirs. A Union general with support in the South also appealed to northern Democrats. He had no friends to defend, and no enemies to defeat except in memoirs. The Democrats could hardly have made a less controversial candidate from whole cloth. No matter that he knew no politics, that his utterances were a wilderness of clichés, that he had no concept of government. The call for him came first from Louisiana, illustrating the South's apparent trust of former soldiers over politicians. There was magic in the phrase: "Nominate Hancock, and the bloody shirt will be folded away." He also had strength in Pennsylvania, and could expect support from both Tilden and Kelly, if neither agreed on another candidate. He waited on Governor's Island in New York, noncommittal, empty. "I shall be relieved when the convention at Cincinnati has chosen its candidate for president," he wrote General Sherman, "and I shall feel a decided relief from future care and responsibility if I am not that person!" [100]

So the talk went around, and the mountains labored. The Democratic party's candidates naturally spoke for its component strengths, and reflected its weaknesses. Tilden, Hendricks, and Seymour, were the residue of faded glories, still compelling enough to stir men's attention. Randall represented the successful politician trapped in a body of thought unfitted to national appeal. Bayard was the safe man, removed from stress and the daily struggle for survival, insured but insulated in a placid constituency that kept him from grasping the nation's changing needs. Hancock symbolized the desire to win. There was no unity, focus, or center except yesterday's heroes. Memory. That was the key descriptive word. The Democratic party was a random collection of local interests and leaders.

While ruminating about his party's nominations, Horatio Seymour predicted the Republicans would choose "some new man whose relationships are as yet unknown." [101] He was partly right; the man more and more people considered a dark horse was not unknown, but his "relationships" were attractive. His name was James Abram Garfield, recognized for work in the House of Representatives between 1863 and 1880. During the disputed election, he was one of Hayes' closest advisers, and after failing to win the House speakership became the Republican floor leader. Along with other Ohio men, he was a familiar figure at the White House, but made no secret of often disagreeing with the President. Garfield was a party man, moderate on most issues, and a shrewd if often baffling manipulator in the process that kept Buckeye statesmen alive. In January of this presidential year, the Ohio legislature elected him to the Senate, and now, as he managed John Sherman's campaign, he waited to take his seat when Congress assembled.

Friends had long prophesied his entry into the White House. He could afford to wait and challenge no one openly. Youth, vigor, an attractive personality, and a widening circle of supporters would make it almost automatic. The general public knew him as a classic success story. Born in a log cabin, he worked hard after his father died. The Ohio frontier was not safe for a young widow with four children, but his mother stubbornly refused to farm them out to relatives. The young Garfield felled trees, taught school, and by adolescence was a man in all but years. In the process, he developed a handsome mien, tall, bearded, with broad shoulders, and a rather slow gait that made him seem wary. He did not revel in a drab upbringing; the veils of nostalgia and sentiment did not hide the steep places. "I lament sorely that I was born to poverty and allowed to catch up any or no chance habits of mind, body, morals, and manners," he recalled, "and in this chaos of childhood, seventeen years passed before I caught up any inspiration which was worthy of my manhood." [102]

He determined to succeed by the magic trail of education, attended Hiram College, worked his way through Williams College in the class of 1856, and developed a fondness for books and ideas. He taught in rustic country schools, with pupils squirming in their seats, then at

Hiram. He liked aphorisms about Mark Hopkins and his log, but did not over-value education, longing for a life that combined action and thought.* He got a chance when war came in 1861, and became a strong Republican. A deeply religious man and lay preacher, Garfield saw a moral crusade in the war to save the Union. "The sin of slavery is one of which it may be that without the shedding of blood there is no remission." [103] He skirmished in Kentucky and western Virginia, stood at Shiloh the second day, and worked on plans that led to Chickamauga, earning a reputation and general's stars as a planner more than a fighter.

Now forty-nine years old, he was young for political prominence, but typified the classic tendencies of his country and party. Garfield's politics were grey with compromise, but the personality stood out brightly. Many people distrusted him, but few disliked him. Unlike Blaine, he was serious, without flashes of temperament. He seldom spoke on a subject he had not studied, and the more he studied the less he spoke. He was sober, though not dull. Colleagues and friends recalled him as "one of the real jolly good fellows" in Washington. He took an occasional nip, played billiards, smoked, and did not leave the room when a dirty joke came up.[104] He knew city ways, but wore country airs. "There was a splendid rusticity in his simple nature," Senator Ingalls of Kansas wrote, "which breathed unmistakably of the generation of yeomen from whom he sprung." [105] It did not hurt to note that feet now shod in expensive shoes once walked the towpaths along Ohio's canals.

Work in education and a lifelong interest in scientific farming gained him a following among intellectuals. He maintained a farm at Mentor, Ohio, and away from legislation, studied seeds, fertilization, crop rotation, and stock breeding. Garfield was not a pedant, but a practical man increasing yield; neighbors called him the "Sage of Mentor." In Congress, he supported federal subsidies to publish the records of western exploration, wanted the government to print a medical history of the war, and helped Simon Newcomb get money for astronomical studies. He secured funds for the Coast and Geodetic Survey and the Smithsonian Institution, urged a central office to plan federal aid to education, and worked on new census procedures.[106]

Garfield was a strange bundle of contradictions; a public man, ambitious for the highest places, who would abandon a bill for a book on philosophy or farming. He was genial and attractive, but unsuited to

---

*He told a friend later: "You and I know that teaching is not the work in which a man can live and grow." (Caldwell, *James A. Garfield*, 22.)

speaking from tree stumps or railroad cars. "I love to deal with doc-trines and events," he said. "The contests of men about men I greatly dislike." [107] He shrank from the hurly-burly of politics. "I hate to be a spectacle that people go to see as to a dog-fight," he wrote his wife in 1877.[108] His survival in a state noted for political strife mystified ob-servers, but he was familiar at the Pension Bureau, and discreetly advertised every gain for his district. He opposed none he could persuade, and had friends willing to do the overt fighting. "I am a poor hater," he said laconically.[109] An era that loved a vigorous stance in public men had a divided opinion of him. Was he weak or shrewd, cunning or slow, patient or dull? Roscoe Conkling, who hated him, put it bluntly: "He has no sand." [110]

Doubtless he looked that way to men who thought of politics as a crusade or war. His own view was more prosaic, reflecting intellectual habits of solution and compromise. "To be an extreme man is doubt-less comfortable," he noted shrewdly. "It is painful to see too many sides to a subject." [111] His puzzling silences seemed like consent when they were merely reflection. To those who thought him weak, hesita-tion looked like indecision when it was only caution. Since he mentally analyzed the ramifications of action and ideas, words carried different meanings. "Consult" implied just that; but to a politician like Conk-ling, it meant "contest." To advocates of speedy action and undying loyalty, he was a trimmer. "But his will power was not equal to his personal magnetism," even John Sherman later said. "He easily changed his mind, and honestly veered from one impulse to another." [112] The parts of Garfield's personality seemed better than the whole man. He was a scholar who read widely, but was not really intellectual; a politician full of irritating quotations. In bitter contests, he was likely to read a book rather than lead a charge. Deeply ambitious for place and power, he let other men shoulder burdens.

Garfield was an able politician, however. In a famous remark at Lincoln's death in 1865, "God reigns, and the government at Washing-ton lives!" he characteristically spoke first of the Deity and then of politics. "It would be just like my perverse nature if I should ever see quiet life again, to be restless and long for turbulence," he admitted.[113] Study led him to a larger view of politics than that of opponents like Conkling. In that respect he resembled Blaine, but lacked his vigor. As the southern question subsided, he saw that economics would rise. The labor problem, depression, trusts and railroads, money-getting would now confront politicians. They must find an answer. Like Blaine, he wished to raise party loyalty to a stabilizing force among a people who loved politics, and did not hesitate to admit his bent for compromise. He favored moderate tariff protection, and would not alienate silver men while saving the gold standard. He worried less over expenditure than equalizing its burdens. Accepting new ideas, he objected to reformist cant and the restless desire for immediate perfection.[114]

Garfield's closeness to Sherman, Ohio origins, personality, and management of Hayes' legislative program made him a center of talk as the presidential sweepstakes began, but he had no formal boom. He managed Sherman's effort only after an understanding that he was the older man's heir. Years before, he declined Hayes' advice to run for governor as a steppingstone to the White House, lest this divide the Ohio party and alienate Sherman. He listened to people from Cleveland talk about 1880, and publicly remained noncommittal, yet was clearly available. "I agree with you," he wrote a friend in 1875, "that shoving for the place is not a very safe means to secure it." [115] Long before Grant returned home, he assumed the General would get the nod, but as 1880 developed, saw there might be a deadlock. He also understood that Blaine's men had a tenuous agreement with some managers to support Sherman if Grant became too threatening. But they lacked enthusiasm, and by the spring of 1880, clearly favored Garfield.

Many of Sherman's avowed champions felt the Secretary could not win, but Garfield could. The sentiment for Blaine in the Midwest and Plains states, Sherman's support from the South and office-holders, and the normal following for a dark horse could easily give him the nod if the convention deadlocked, and if he played a careful waiting game.[116]

At convention time, he still had not firmly organized much for Sherman, and refused to attack Grant in public.[117] He evaded talk of being the compromise choice,[118] and privately noted a trifle more formally: "This, I think, is the attitude I should take: I will not offer myself as a candidate nor decline if it is tendered me." [119] He was a proud man,* and realistic enough not to mortgage the future with obvious double-dealing. But he certainly read the newspaper reports: "A Garfield tide is rising in the west," and did nothing to discourage a boom.[120] It was a mark of his touch that it made so little noise.

---

*He must have agreed with his wife, who wrote him on June 4, 1880: "I begin to be half afraid that the convention will give you the nomination, and the place would be most unenviable with so many disappointed candidates. I don't want you to have the nomination merely because no one else can get it. I want you to have it when the whole country calls for you. . . . My ambition does not stop short of that." (Garfield LC)

He had no illusions about Sherman's candidacy. "While I do not think he has much of a chance, if any, of the nomination," he wrote, "I still think if we want to prevent Grant's nomination, we ought to give Ohio to Sherman." [121] It was not a bugle call, but he did thwart efforts to divide the delegation in his own district, lest he get the blame.[122] As the convention approached, he had not written a nominating speech for Sherman, which was unusual in one noted for attention to details. He dreaded the prospect of an obvious bitter fight, somewhat fearful of what people would say if he succeeded, and with a touch of guilt in the form of recurrent headaches and inability to concentrate.[123]

June brought unusual heat to Chicago, the GOP convention city, chosen because it seemed to neutralize everyone's desires. It was close to Ohio country for Sherman, but not entirely friendly. It was western enough to suit Blaine, and was in Grant's nostalgic Illinois territory, though his strength really centered in the East. The Republicans were obviously deadlocked. Each major candidate had followed out his stated plans, and reached the limit of strength. Grant was stalled at just over 300 delegates, Blaine at just under that number. Sherman counted about 100. The rest scattered, but belonged to stubborn favorite sons like Edmunds. It would be hard to find the necessary 379 votes.

The assembly was a baroque affair. Streets heading to the convention hall were choked with traffic and hucksters. On one corner, vendors shouted "Here's your Blaine lemonade"; on another, eager supporters passed out buttons, badges, canes, umbrellas, and other paraphenalia for a favorite son. Politicians had arrived before the formal opening on Wednesday, June 2, and already showed signs of wear. The faithful recounted stories of famous men, bleary-eyed from lack of sleep, and perhaps reeling from more than exhaustion, crossing hotel lobbies in the early hours. The more the deadlock tightened, the more manipulation, bargaining, and threats increased. Many ladies attended the sessions, adding picturesque color to men's work, but there were only 20,000 seats for the estimated 50,000 visitors. Red and white badges of men guarding the doors flashed importantly as they bent to examine cards and credentials. The "City of Conventions," had refurbished its chief exposition hall. The walls thrust out portraits of famous Republicans, and bunting ran up poles supporting galleries. State shields marched along moldings, and flowers dotted the speakers' stand. The great cavern, "one of the most splendid barns ever constructed," was not designed for oratory, and the thunder of noise threatened to obliterate whatever flashes of lightning men like Conkling commanded.[124] The oldest delegate was an 83-year-old veteran from New Hampshire; the youngest, a first-time voter from New York. In the galleries, Prince Leopold, son of Queen Victoria, watched the proceedings with interest.

Hotels bulged with candidates' headquarters. Sherman had a lavish suite, with tables of food and "drinkables," and conspicuous for Negro delegates, each with a faithful guide. Conkling stayed in lordly but surprisingly affable splendor at the Grand Pacific. He charmed pass-ers-by and the gawking faithful, lolling elegantly on a settee, still the ladies' darling. He took a few walks with calm ostentation, but may have had indigestion when Garfield and other managers said they would fight a unit rule.[125] Conkling knew he could not deliver the solid votes of New York, Pennsylvania, and Illinois for Grant. If he could compel unit voting, the first ballot would bring Grant within a handful of a majority, and a boom spirit or quick bargaining would take him over the top.

Conkling lost the war in the first day's battles, as Half-Breeds moved into key positions. Cameron failed to become Permanent Chair-man, surrendering that honor to Senator George F. Hoar of Massachu-setts, nominally an Edmunds man and acceptable to most factions. But more importantly, William E. Chandler, representing Blaine, chaired the Credentials Committee. Garfield headed the Committee on Rules, to construct a platform. In three hours, the enemy took the nomination machinery; Conkling could only appeal to the delegates for a unit rule.

In Galena, General Grant alternated between his porch and the telegraph desk. Like Conkling, he foresaw a bitter fight that might disrupt the party and make the honor distasteful or dangerous. Re-luctantly, at the advice of more moderate men than his chief manager, Grant passed on through his son a message that, if Conkling thought it best, he would withdraw if Blaine also left the race. This would avoid a confrontation, and allow the two major factions to choose a mutually acceptable man. On June 1, Blaine wired Chandler similar advice, concluding: ". . . I would rather smother personal resentment for the weal of the party." [126] Though Garfield warned Conkling he would fight the unit rule to the end, the New Yorker could not face dealing with either the Ohioan or the Man from Maine.[127] Garfield was attract-ing attention, both among the public and the delegates. Senator Cul-lom of Illinois told him: "James, if you will keep a level head, you will be nominated for the presidency by this convention before it is over." Garfield shook his head slowly. "No, I think not." [128]

Visitors knew little of these machinations, and thrilled at the sight of the assemblage. When New York's Stalwarts marched abreast down the street and through the door to their seats, flags fluttered and parasols waved. Not by accident did they give "three cheers and a tiger" for Grant while passing the Blaine headquarters. Conkling chose the more dramatic moment, waiting until most delegates were seated, then striding to his seat, shoulders back and curls flouncing.[129]

On Thursday, June 3, Conkling began a series of attacks that threw the gathering into noisy confusion. Contesting each disputed delegate in the hope of wearing out foes, he raised other delegations' ire. Most agreed with Benjamin Harrison of Indiana in condemning these "unnecessary delays." Such confusion and disorder reigned that even Conkling could not hear the discussion.[130] On Friday morning, June 4, he offered the major resolution, asking virtual ejection of delegates who would not agree in advance to support the convention choice. It was a foolish move, but Platt argued they must bind Hayes men who threatened to bolt. On the motion for a roll call, 716 voted aye, and 3 nay. Conkling then insisted these three, from West Virginia, "have forfeited their votes in this convention."

This was Garfield's moment. Carefully nudged forward and coached by friends, he rose to condemn the motion. In a brief, moderate speech, he spoke for most delegates: "Is every delegate here to have his Republicanism inquired into before this convention will allow him to vote?" * Conkling withdrew the motion, and passed a short note to Garfield's seat: "New York requests that Ohio's real candidate and dark horse come forward. We want him in our seats while we prepare our ballots." [131] There was no unit rule either.

That evening, acrimonious debate on disputed delegates from Illinois afforded a moment's release from tension. A speaker mentioned Grant and Blaine, and the hall erupted in cheers. On the floor, Conkling stood on a chair and waved a handkerchief at the galleries. Delirium raged, with Blaine men waving huge white plumes, Sherman's supporters throwing confetti and streamers, and spectators on the floor cheering and jeering. One young lady jumped on a railing to sing her allegiance, and a somewhat embarrassed Marshall Jewell held her ankles lest she fall on his open umbrella.[132]

The following morning, Garfield reported the platform, notable

---

*Garfield earlier wrote his wife: "If I win that fight [against the unit rule] it will likely embitter him [Conkling] and his followers against me. If I lose it, the convention will lose interest in me. So I am between two fires." (Smith, *Life and Letters of James Abram Garfield*, II, 967).

chiefly for endorsing the Hayes Administration and omitting civil service reform, with a murky straddle on almost everything else. J. M. Barker of Massachusetts offered an amendment, paraphrasing Hayes' famous promise that "reform in the civil service shall be thorough, radical, and complete." In the disorder that followed, one Webster Flanagan of Texas gained a sort of immortality by stating:

> Texas has had quite enough of the civil service. [*sic*] During the last four years, sir, out of 1,400 officeholders appointed by the President of the United States, 140 represented the Republican party. We are not here, sir, for the purpose of providing offices for the Democracy. There is one plank in the Democratic party that I have ever admired, and that is 'To the victors belong the spoils.' After we have won the race, as we will, we will give those who are entitled to positions office. What are we up here for? I mean that members of the Republican party are entitled to office, and if we are victorious we will have office.

He lost, and the convention adopted a tame amendment and the platform.[133]

Nominations were in order, and weary delegates stayed dutifully in place for the inevitable wash of oratory. Blaine was the first major name, presented in a dreary and ineffectual speech by James F. Joy of Michigan, who seemed not to know his candidate. Apologizing for taking up the convention's time, he catalogued Blaine's enemies, and then announced for "James S. Blaine." Shocked friends shouted: "G. you fool, G.!" and Joy retired from the platform.[134]

A perfunctory nomination for William Windom of Minnesota followed, and when the cheering subsided John A. Logan of Illinois named Grant in a single sentence that provoked more pandemonium. This was Conkling's cue. As the noise subsided to a tense hum of expectation, he mounted a reporters' table, and waited for complete silence. Tall, trim, with the famous curl much in evidence, he raised a clear voice to fill a moment any actor would prize with a brilliant opening:

> And when asked what state he hails from,
> Our sole reply shall be,
> He hails from Appomattox,
> And its famous apple tree.

The convention cheered for Grant, for all he had been and symbolized. If Conkling had conciliated delegates, or spoken last, he might have won, but the speech that followed showed him at his best and worst. To friends, it was a great set-piece. "It had the warmth of eulogy, the finish of a poem, the force and fire of a philippic." [135] To foes it was all sarcasm, final proof he must not control the nomination. He began with calls to stir personal and party loyalty. "The election before us is the Austerlitz of American politics. It will decide for many years whether the country shall be Republican or Cossack." Hailing Grant as the only man who could carry doubtful states, he swept aside past criticism:

> Vilified and reviled, ruthlessly aspersed by unnumbered presses, not in other lands but in his own, assaults upon him have seasoned and strengthened his hold upon the public heart. Calumny's ammunition has all been burned once—its force is spent—and the name of Grant will glitter a bright and imperishable star in the diadem of the Republic when those who have tried to tarnish it have moldered in forgotten graves; and when their memories and their epitaphs have vanished. utterly.

As for Blaine: "With him [Grant] as our leader, we shall have no defensive campaign. We shall have nothing to explain away. We shall have no apologies to make." Was the third term a threat? "Nobody now is really disquieted by a third term except those hopelessly longing for a first term, and their dupes and coadjutors." [136]

It was magnificent, and it was war; but it was not quite true, and unwise to say. He had alienated marginal support from almost all camps, condemned all opponents as fools, and canceled Grant's purely emotional appeal with unintentional reminders that Blaine was not the only man with a record to defend. Arrogance alienated many who might not have blocked Grant. "His sarcasm is all right in some places," an Illinois delegate snapped, "but out of place here." [137]

Seconding speeches followed, then Garfield put Sherman's name before the delegates in phrases that alternated between fire and smoke. A delegate called out "We want Garfield," and Garfield rebuked him. Talking more of the Republican party than Sherman, he concluded weakly: "I do not present him as a better Republican or a better man than thousands of others we honor; but I present him for your deliberate and favorable consideration." His allusions to tossing waves turned Conkling's lip: "The man makes me seasick!" But the consensus was plainer: "He has nominated himself." Sherman's friends agreed, and soon complained of "the ding-dong about Garfield" in the Ohio delegation and across the floor.[138] Speeches for Edmunds and favorite sons followed, and the convention adjourned.

Monday brought firm lines and taut nerves. A storm downed telegraph wires, giving floor managers full control of their votes. The first ballots showed an inflexible pattern; Grant hovered above 300, Blaine clung to about 280, Sherman rose and fell between 80 and 120. The rest scattered, with token votes for Garfield. While the balloting continued, Blaine was in the Senate, talking coolly to colleagues, reading telegrams, writing letters. Sherman was at the Treasury. Grant rocked on the porch in Galena. The convention adjourned over Conkling's objections after 28 fruitless tallies. Sometime during the confusion, Conkling revealed defeat in a simple act. He went to Senator Preston B. Plumb of Kansas, whose state followed Blaine, and handed him a sheet of paper. If Plumb would write down whatever he wanted as a reward for giving Kansas to Grant, Conkling and the General would sign the pledge. Plumb hesitated, then refused, saying he could not defy his state.[139] If Lord Roscoe had come to this, it was all over.

The deadlocked ballots continued the following day. That morning, according to Garfield's recollection, when he entered the hall a man at the door handed him a scriptural leaflet that proclaimed the verse: "The stone which the builders refused." [140] He protested feebly as his votes mounted, and let Hoar gavel him into silence.[141] He was tired of supporting Sherman, now doomed, and feared Grant would somehow win, but was afraid to make an open break. On the 35th ballot, he received 50 votes, and tension signaled a break. As the 36th ballot developed, state after state moved to Garfield. When Maine voted for him, Senator Jones of Nevada rushed to Conkling and implored him to stop the rush by casting New York for Blaine. Conkling declined, saying he could not poll the delegation in time. Jones fairly exploded. "Cast the vote and poll the delegation afterwards." Conkling angrily refused; the tally gave Garfield 399 votes and the nomination. Sherman, Blaine, and others wired immediate congratulations; Conkling, without apparent animosity, moved for unanimity. His lieutenants were sullen, seeing Blaine's fine hand and Garfield's perfidy in the victory, but the Ohioan won *before* either Sherman or Blaine personally released delegates and wired congratulations. His long-standing hidden strength as the second choice of a majority of the delegates was evident.[142]

Reflecting its relief at tension's end, the convention went wild. Men bore state standards toward Ohio's seats in a rush of color. Delegates tore strips of bunting from railings and pillars, trailing them excitedly in colored arcs. Flags waved in a sea of hats and handkerchiefs. Garfield sat white and silent amid protecting friends, then rose, pulled down his hat and made a hasty exit through a side door. Conkling looked composed but was stiff with fury.[143]

How to placate him? The obvious solution appeared. While the delegates howled, Garfield's friends hastened to New York's Levi P. Morton, and offered him the traditional olive branch, the vice-presidential nomination. Garfield wanted Morton, an able organizer and fund raiser, one of the "Old Guard" for Grant, with connections in business and society. Even in the hubbub, Conkling's attitude was clear when Morton asked advice. "If you think the ticket will be elected, if you think you will be happy in the association, accept." The Senator suggested that he seek other opinion in the recess that followed. For himself, Conkling was already saying bluntly: "I hope no friend of mine will accept it." [144] Morton got other advice, and then declined as the New York delegation caucused.

The Ohioans had another candidate, who might offset Conkling's hostility and carry New York, Chester A. Arthur. In the confusion, Arthur found his chief in a reporter's room off the platform, pacing up and down in frustration. Arthur stepped in and said quietly: "The Ohio men have offered me the vice-presidency." Conkling looked at him. "Well, sir, you should drop it as you would a red hot shoe from the forge." Arthur had expected this response and flushed slightly, but did not raise his voice. "I sought you to consult—" Conkling interrupted angrily: "What is there to consult about? This trickster of Mentor will be defeated before the country." Arthur let him subside, then continued: "The office of the vice-presidency is a greater honor than I ever dreamed of attaining. A barren nomination would be a great honor. In a calmer moment you will look at this differently." Conkling was adamant. "If you wish for my favor and my respect, you will contemptuously decline it." Arthur had the last word. "Senator Conkling, I shall accept the nomination and I shall carry with me the majority of the [New York] delegation." This last was too much. Lord Roscoe turned on his heel.[145]

Arthur could calmly defy Conkling because he understood his personality. Conkling was angry; nothing had worked out right. He believed the ticket would fail. Arthur also realized that if the Stalwarts deserted now, they would hurt themselves. Most of the New York organization wanted to win. To rebuff Garfield's peace feelers meant ostracism, whether the ticket won or lost. Arthur was too loyal to his party and state, and too shrewd to take that risk. He would pacify Conkling later; he had done it before. That night the convention consented and the delegates departed, surprised at the results of their labors.

Reactions were predictable. The press mistakenly dismissed Arthur as "Conkling's man Friday." [146] Sherman called his nomination "a ridiculous burlesque," and said later it was "the whim of Roscoe Conkling to strike at President Hayes." [147] Blaine was more temperate, referring to Arthur's "wide acquaintance with the public men of the country" and his "personal popularity." [148] The young Henry Cabot Lodge shrewdly noted: "No one will abandon Garfield on account of Arthur, and in New York the defeated machine will, instead of sulking, be brought to full play under the direction of the shrewdest political manager in the country." [149] The Mugwumps seethed. Godkin said that for Conkling to take Arthur's nomination as a consolation prize for failing with Grant was "very like taking a suit of old clothes in lieu of the English mission." But he thought Arthur could not do much as vice-president. "It is true General Garfield, if elected, may die during his term of office, but this is too unlikely a contingency to be worth making extraordinary contingency for." [150]

The chief contestants expressed various degrees of disappointment. "As a matter of course, I cannot deny the natural disappointment of one seeking an honor and failing to get it," Sherman wrote. "I was disappointed from the first ballot to the close." On the larger question of Garfield's veracity and honor, he hesitated. Then and later, he publicly insisted Garfield was loyal and true, but a tone of disbelief ran through his private correspondence. He was too good a politician to miss the intrigues around the man from Mentor, and too prudent to say anything. He preferred simply to move on. "As to the campaign of 1880," he wrote later, "I made so many mistakes in regard to it that I do not care to single out the one in your district." [151]

Conkling left in quiet rage. "This is my first and last national convention," he told a friend. General Grant was obviously distressed, but merely looked and sounded tired. He thanked Conkling on June 10. "Individually, I am much relieved at the result, having grown weary of constant abuse—always disagreeable, and doubly so when it comes from former professed friends." [152] Foes exulted in killing the third-term movement, but Chauncey Filley of Missouri had medals struck for the "Faithful 306" who balloted for Grant. They bore the legend: "The Old Guard for Ulysses S. Grant for President," and had Roscoe Conkling's signature. [153]

President Hayes thought the result "a blessed one," and did not refer to Arthur. [154] With the usual optimism, he noted "the unit rule (cornerstone of the boss system) abolished, Cameron crushed, the Administration endorsed, civil service reform endorsed, the triumvirs beaten, the eager, self-seeking candidates beaten, the office seeking the man!" [155] It was partly euphoria, but Garfield's selection was more

significant than contemporaries realized. Not that Republicans chose
a dark horse, but *this* one. He typified "the best impulses of the party,"
and could hope to make them into deeds.[156] He was midwestern, the
area Republicans must control for future success; self-made, the kind
of man they must enfold and raise to leadership; moderate, the tone to
win more interest groups. He was progressive in accepting change in a
dynamic society. He did his share of work for the prize; but life, not
Providence, first thrust him to attention. Sense, not accident, gave him
victory.

Garfield's nomination surprised the Democrats. They expected to
confront one of the GOP's major figures, and counted on fights among
Republicans to help their cause. Garfield's chances were unclear, but
his record and popular appeals seemed likely to smooth over factional
differences. His selection eliminated two Ohio Democrats, Henry B.
Payne, another alleged Tilden heir, and Allen G. Thurman. It seemed
logical to choose an eastern man from a doubtful state. While Garfield
restlessly surveyed his chances and calculated strategy toward Conkling, the opposition moved on Cincinnati, mopping brows and swat-
ting flies.

The most impressive thing about the assembling Democrats was
confusion. Tilden's indecision sustained hope among lesser favorites
who planned to pick up the pieces if he withdrew or failed of nomination. The papers presented extra pages about Justice Field, Hendricks,
Thurman, and the major contenders, but most talk centered on Tilden.
"Old hands admit that no convention was so chaotic and so hard to
form any reliable opinion about," wrote one of Bayard's managers.[157]
The delegates assembled in the Cincinnati Music Hall, redecorated
for the purpose. Its high ceiling afforded a clear view of the stage,
and room for flying vowels. Elegant chestnut paneling muted the walls,
and a huge organ behind the stage was ringed in a tangle of potted
plants and hothouse flowers. From wall to wall above the delegates'
heads stretched the word "Welcome" on a huge silken banner. A spear-
headed staff trailing a blue pennant marked seats for each delegation.
It was hot and stuffy. The delegates settled to business, grumbling
accord with one man's remark: "Heat, flies, and discomfort!" [158]

A question lingered, animating discussion in the small knots of men
who talked outside the hall and watched each other through cigar
smoke in hotel suites: What would Tilden do? The Sage kept the usual
silence, but his managers smiled at everyone and denied nothing
favorable to his cause. John Kelly arrived with his braves, all suitably

prepared for warfare against either Tilden or Republicans. While banners waved below him, and some jeers mingled with huzzahs, Kelly stood on a balcony of the Burnet House and told a crowd he would never support Tilden. He all but said he would try a third candidate, or stay at home.[159] A good many Democrats disliked his methods, but recognized his importance. Tilden's continued silence was also irritating and politically dangerous. If he were a candidate, observers bade him say so; if not, they urged him to decline. This pose of indifference had palled. "Mr. Tilden is incapable of doing the simplest thing without a mask." Western papers earlier predicted that the great question was "Who is Tilden's heir?" But he would keep the convention "stretched on the rack of doubt till the last possible moment." [160]

Tilden's health did not support talk of nomination. He undoubtedly wished a unanimous selection, which he could graciously decline, while dictating a successor. If he could not run a repeat performance of the fraud issue, others would do it for him. On Sunday, June 20, his brother Henry arrived in Cincinnati, bearing a letter from the Sage. At ten o'clock that morning, the New York delegation heard Daniel Manning read the text. It was a babble of aloof advice, recrimination over past ills, and tortured phraseology, all hinting at a desire for a second nomination. Manning, who knew Tilden well, took it at face value. He was not a candidate. The New Yorkers at the scene doubted the wisdom of trying for a unanimous nomination, only to have him turn it down. It might soothe his pride, but would hurt some feelings. Manning passed the letter to the press. In the confusion that followed, Tilden wired his brother: "Do nothing. Don't meddle." [161]

The Republican *New York Tribune* hopefully called the letter Tilden's "farewell address to the Democratic party." [162] Others styled it: "Letter of Withdrawal, or a Fresh Bid." [163] Experienced reporters thought Manning and others had miscalculated; Tilden wanted the letter read first to the New York delegation, then to the whole convention, to create a stampede. "It was a very cunning thing," William C. Whitney remarked. "If the convention was determined to nominate someone else, as appeared to be the case, then the result would go down in history as a consequence of Tilden's withdrawal. If in the reading of the letter in the convention it had had the effect intended, then history would say that the party refused to let him withdraw." [164] Tilden's apparent withdrawal scattered other contenders. Only Hancock could fill the vacuum and unify a campaign. He boasted few real friends, but had no genuine enemies. Tilden could accept him, assuming he would take "advice," and he made sure that no friends drifted toward Bayard, who seemed unmanageable.

Tilden's action encouraged lassitude among the delegates, and many spectators sipped cool drinks in the cafés around the hall rather than sit in the muggy galleries, at the mercy of mosquitos "thick enough to eat one alive."[165] William H. Barnum of Connecticut gaveled the crowd to order on June 22, and George Hoadly of Ohio keynoted the proceedings with a rambling discourse on Republican perfidies and the Crime of '76.[166] Mention of Tilden's name brought cheers and the usual waving of flags and handkerchiefs, but the tension was gone as delegates straggled out after transacting routine business.

The following day, nominations were in order, and one by one the party's statesmen named favorite sons. J. E. McElrath of California spoke for Field, cataloguing his juristic appeal amid catcalls and cries of "Time!" and "Cut it Off!" As one paper noted: "Neither the people nor the delegates cared to tax their minds in an attempt to analyze the greatness of Field's legal triumphs, which were not described in a popular or entertaining way."[167]

George Gray named Bayard, stressing three themes: He could carry the business interests, no mean feat for ever-unpredictable Democrats; the Delaware senator could harmonize South and North, a debatable proposition among Tilden men; he was a lofty spirit—they must not say he was "too good a man to receive the highest honors of the Democratic party."[168] Illinois offered William R. Morrison and tariff reform. Daniel W. Voorhees spoke for Thomas A. Hendricks. He would gather in the lost sheep of 1876, carry doubtful and important Indiana, and harmonize all sections. A perfunctory speech for Allen G. Thurman followed, interlarded with the glories of Buckeye life and frequent references to the common man.

Daniel Dougherty of Pennsylvania then presented Hancock, the speech most delegates waited to hear. "[He] will suppress every faction, and be alike acceptable to the North and to the South" was the theme. No one need defend him, since he lacked a record, though Dougherty did not quite put it that way. He was "the soldier statesman with a record as stainless as his sword," who could carry the South and the mid-Atlantic industrial states. Cheers wafted the bunting, and a bright litter of confetti, streamers, and buttons fell on the floor as Wade Hampton of South Carolina rose. He liked Hancock, as Union generals went, but Bayard was a better man. He knew something, was independent yet safe, and commanded a larger constituency than anyone else. It was a limping performance, designed to sustain

Bayard, mollify Tilden, and keep the ladder down on Hancock's bandwagon.[169] Other southerners favored Hancock.

The exhausted delegates balloted under a two-thirds rule, and after six hours of wearisome talk gave Bayard 153½, Hancock 171, and scattered the rest among favorite sons, with 492 votes necessary to nominate. Hancock and Bayard divided roughly the same constituency, the South and mid-Atlantic states. Favorite sons would make the choice, and their staying power was an open question. Still, there was talk of Tilden, and the next day Rufus Peckham of New York read his letter of withdrawal to the convention. Despite stubborn echoes, the cheering stopped, and Tilden wired privately: "My action was well considered and is irrevocable. No friends must be allowed to cast a doubt on my motives or sincerity." The charade was over.[170] New York switched to Randall, but several states passed while balloting continued. Amid confusion, states changed to Hancock, and New York finally joined the flood to give Hancock 705 votes on the last ballot to a stubborn 2 for Bayard, 1 for Tilden, and 30 for Hendricks, before unanimity reigned.

The galleries clacked endlessly during the proceedings, and most professionals thought they influenced the "mad stampede" toward Hancock. It was "a wild hurrah, and the men flocked like sheep towards the bell-wether after the first stampede," one of Bayard's men wrote.[171] Sam Ward said Hancock's nomination "was made by the galleries," pure and simple.[172] That was more true than usual in conventions, popular appeal changing the minds of doubtful delegates. And Hancock obviously had the crowd. Announcement of his selection brought ten thousand to their feet, cheering and waving whatever happened to be handy—in one case, a young lady. Singing "Should Auld Acquaintance be Forgot," to the combined efforts of a military brass band and the huge pipe organ, they wanted a hero. Hancock then won the politicians. Kelly announced Tammany's support. "Let past differences be banished from our midst forever." [173]

The rest was routine. Henry Watterson read the platform while no one listened. Their attention strayed for good reason. It radiated the usual condemnation of "centralization," talked of "Home rule, honest money, consisting of gold and silver, and paper convertible into coin on demand," favored a "free ballot" without mentioning Negroes, and opposed Chinese immigration "except for travel, education, and foreign commerce, and that even carefully guarded." The delegates unanimously adopted it, named William H. English of Indiana for vice-president and went home.[174] Mugwumps, already dissatisfied with

Garfield and the Republicans, found no comfort with Hancock. Godkin suggested wearily "that all the conventions have now begun to
treat the platform as a joke." [175]

Talk of Tilden's intentions filled the lull when the convention adjourned, and illustrated his hold on the Democrats. A friend and
member of his circle, Smith Weed, thought the convention would
never have nominated him. Randall and Bayard were angry at being
kept waiting; Kelly was intractable; the state favorite sons each claimed
the succession; and the galleries controlled the convention. Most of
all, "in the talk and action the old dictation of the South was prevalent, without the old intellect." [176] Tilden told friends privately that
he could have won with effort. Publicly, he reverted to the usual
cryptic statements. He "did not feel able to enter upon five years of
hard, exhausting labor." [177] Tilden may have hoped his New York
friends would hold him before the convention as a compromise candidate, much as Garfield's managers had done, but Manning and
others took his purported word, fortified with knowledge of his ill-
health and inability to campaign. Tilden's arcane utterances had not
served him well. Other contenders took small comfort. Wade Hampton
told Bayard the galleries named Hancock, but the Senator's friends
beat Tilden, "and for this at least I am delighted." [178] Randall's supporters nursed grievances quietly. "Our turn will come next," one
wrote him. "We are *young* and can afford to wait." [179]

Immediate reaction outside the party was ridicule. "[Does] anybody
know what Gen. Hancock thinks about the principles of finance, about
the tariff, civil service reform, interstate commerce or free ships?"
asked the *New York Times*, and got silence for its pains.[180] "General
Hancock represents no policy, no principle, no issue, nothing but the
party which nominated him. . . ," George William Curtis said. "He is
a worthy gentleman, whose life has been passed in the military service,
and whose election as President would be a leap in the dark." [181]
E. L. Godkin thought Generals should stay in their quarters. "They
could not be as good soldiers as they are if they were fit candidates for the Presidency. Not one of them ever enters the political
arena without losing much if not most of what makes him really
valuable to his country." [182] The nomination did not match the Democratic congressional pattern. "It is a peculiarly constituted party which
sends rebel brigadiers to Congress because of their rebellion, and
which nominates a Union General as its candidate for president because of his loyalty." [183]

This criticism had its place, and events to come would test the convention's wisdom. In one way Hancock was a substitute for Tilden, standing on the fraud issue and facing backwards. But in a larger sense, he represented an unconscious and hesitant effort to move forward. Any public man's appeal rises from a past record and future possibilities. Hancock fitted the party's confusion and frustration; devoid of political entanglements, possessing at least an element of nonpartisanship and "available" to all factions, he had a chance to orient the party toward moderation. It was a feeble step, but a beginning. His outstanding quality, ironically, was lack of identification with the prevailing Democratic nostalgic mood.

Both parties surprised the country, and themselves, in nominating relatively unknown quantities, but men who reflected a painfully emerging desire for party unity and a turn from the past. Each candidate must command loyalty from recent opponents, and discuss issues that represented a changing electorate's desires and needs. The Republicans faced a formidable challenge. They must defeat Hancock, and set their house in order. Sounds from New York indicated that would not be easy.

III

☆☆☆☆☆☆☆☆☆☆☆☆☆☆☆☆☆☆☆☆☆☆☆☆☆

Campaigns and Feuds: 1880–1881

☆☆☆☆☆☆☆☆☆☆☆☆☆☆☆☆☆☆☆☆☆☆☆☆☆

Congressman Garfield often drove in the countryside near Cleveland to greet constituents, satisfying an interest in nature with views of prosperous farms and crossroads villages straggling along the Lake Shore Railroad. He appreciated the smell of hay in summer, bright orange splashes of fall pumpkins stacked against fences, and the silence of snowbound winters. In the fall of 1876, he borrowed enough money to buy acreage near Mentor, northeast of Cleveland. Each summer when Congress adjourned, and during holidays, the family slowly established a prosperous homestead. Much of its success came from good farming methods, and he oversaw work in the fields, garden, and barn. The post office, squeezed into a corner of a country store, was half a mile away, and the railroad station still farther. In a few years, he had a modest but comfortable two story farmhouse—typical of the region—with outbuildings, and a reasonably sound dirt road.

Garfield was ready to go there after Chicago's hectic scenes, to rest and plan strategy, but he stopped off at Hiram College for commencement exercises, and to see friends. He looked worn and a little stooped. His handshake was firm, but he seemed depressed, telling one friend in Cleveland the nomination came eight years too soon. On June 11, he shook off reporters and the curious, borrowed a new team of horses, and set out across Geauga County for home. At the shady house in Mentor, his spirits rose and he looked better. He faced family greetings, and piles of papers, letters, and telegrams in the study, signaling how the two-week absence had transformed his life. Summer progressed, and filled the lull in politics after the convention adjourned. The pace of days became slow and hot. He wrote letters, read papers, took telegrams from messengers coming from town, and entertained a few friends. An old college friend named Corydon Fuller arrived. Garfield put on a battered hat, almost ran out to Fuller's team, and drove them along the lane, talking politics. He had not wanted the nomination; was willing to wait; hoped there were no ill-feelings; and was unsure of victory.[1]

He had reason to doubt the outcome. The air at Mentor was calm with summer's deceptive laziness, but politics was not. Blaine candidly doubted the ticket would win, but favored defeat with Garfield to victory with Grant. Hancock's nomination on June 22 forecast a hard fight. As Colonel Alexander McClure of Pennsylvania noted, "General Hancock . . . had a strong hold upon the people, and was a very popular and dangerous antagonist for Garfield." [2] Most of all, Blaine could fairly hear tension radiating from New York and Washington. The Stalwarts were angry. If they stayed in their tents temporarily, Garfield would stay on his farm permanently.

Under city lights, General Arthur faced a roisterous welcome. Though he was exhausted and took a slow train east for rest, crowds called him out on the observation platform at many stops. The people were both curious and eager, for no one had suggested before the convention met that he might fill this role. He shook so many hands that his fingers swelled, and he had to have a ring filed off. At Grand Central depot the train passed over a row of torpedoes equalling a vice-presidential salute. The surprised candidate stepped down, carrying his own bags, in the best tradition of democracy. Onlookers took over his bags and umbrella, and Arthur nodded toward a cab, waved goodbye, and clattered off home.[3] He would see Conkling; but would the Senator listen to him? Silence stretched all the way to Mentor.

Garfield quickly decided to remain on the homestead and let the party organization campaign. Tradition dictated that candidates refrain from speechmaking or anything more than ceremonial public appearances. All things considered, it would be an advantage now. In mid-June, he made a quick trip to Washington for routine office business, and to see a few party leaders. Intermediaries already reported that Conkling was aloof, fearful that if he cooperated, Garfield would treat him as Hayes did. He wanted assurances of post-election rewards, but Garfield said nothing publicly, increasing Conkling's contempt. In Washington, the candidate visited Blaine for "a full, long, and cordial talk." He left a card at Conkling's hotel, and the Senator returned the call, but Garfield was out. They missed contact. Sharp eyes saw Garfield riding with Secretary Schurz, and passed the information to Stalwarts.

Garfield's friends tried to get Arthur down from New York, but the vice-presidential candidate made his excuses. He was busy, but would come to Mentor later in the summer. Could Garfield visit New York? "This I am not inclined to do. I have made all reasonable personal advances for harmonious action." He returned to Ohio, promising to write a letter accepting the nomination to please both Blaine and Conkling, but would not open correspondence with the New Yorker. "He must do that, and will find me cordial, but I shall not begin again." [4] The trip was a small event in the busy days, but presaged future dealings in the Garfield-Blaine-Conkling triangle. It was a catalogue of half-starts, gestures, missed connections, and a growing sense of pride in the presidential contender. He still heard nothing from Conkling, and at month's end wrote Blaine: "In one quarter silence. The Oracles are dumb and seem not yet to have determined whether it shall be peace or war." [5]

Garfield might not run the risks of public speaking, but he took a firm hand in party organization. The National Committee would superintend affairs, and its composition required careful balance and attention to wounded pride. The group met on July 1, and Chandler, representing Blaine but keeping friends among the Stalwarts, thwarted Cameron's efforts to pack the organization with Grant followers. After consultation, they rejected Tom Platt as chairman, and chose Connecticut's former governor, Marshall Jewell. He merited the place, having a firm reputation for administrative and organizational skill, perfected in business, and as a diplomat and Postmaster-General for two years in Grant's Cabinet. A good, though partisan administrator, he earned the ire of spoilsmen. "Why, God-damn! he ran the Post-Office as though it was a factory," one of the old hands exclaimed. [6] Garfield approved Jewell, who balanced the factions. The election depended on Indiana, New York, and perhaps New Jersey, and Garfield wanted an experienced hand at the helm. But not so the Stalwarts. Jewell's name provoked John A. Logan, who said in effect that if Blaine's cohorts were in charge, they could fight without the Stalwarts. Chandler and others reluctantly consented to Stephen W. Dorsey, late a carpetbagger from Arkansas and one of Grant's circle, as national secretary. The moderates did extract a promise from Logan not to "crowd or annoy" Garfield, whatever that meant. [7]

During these preliminary skirmishes, the candidate tried to compose a letter of acceptance suitable to all concerned. This was a major ritual in the presidential sweepstakes. Since contenders did not visit the hustings, they spoke through printed words. The formal letter accepting the nomination was a major campaign document, with a general personal emphasis not in the party's platform. Millions of copies would flood the country; required reading at firesides and in editorial offices. This latter was just the problem, for the candidate's stand on civil service reform would rouse everyone's ire. If he was strong, Conkling might depart; if weak, the crucial Mugwumps might stay at home; if he straddled, both would sulk. Garfield did not like the prospect, and cared little for the way the plank was inserted at the convention. "You have seen how it was added," he wrote Blaine, "and you know what a wretched business it has been for years. No phase of it would stand the school-masterish examinations and the absurd attempt to get on without the aid of congressmen in making selections. I believe in party government, and that the spirit and doctrines of the Republican party should prevail in the executive departments. But I do not wish to do anything which will alienate the doctrinaires from our support." [8]

On July 10, he released the letter to the press. It was long and opaque, favoring moderate protection, sound money, a free ballot, pensions for veterans, and a new Chinese treaty. The statement on civil service reform urged partisan appointments based on merit, but lacked militancy. The impression lingered that he would reward Stalwarts if they worked on his terms. The reformers' response followed expectations. Curtis thought the statement "inadequate and disappointing." [9] Godkin noted: "It is a cruel disappointment to those independents who had hoped to find in it a trumpet call." [10] The objections angered Garfield, who privately spelled out his stand to a friend, Burke Hinsdale. He would have fixed terms for minor appointees like clerks; leave policy-making positions open to presidential appointment; draw up firm rules for dismissal and follow them. He wanted a partisan merit service. As part of his normal attention to detail, he asked Jewell for information on fund-raising among government employees —on a voluntary basis, of course.

Life at Mentor was not all paperwork. There were family evenings on the porch, the pleasant sound of slamming doors and childrens' feet punctuating the summer twilight. Garfield wanted to follow Reid's advice: "There is no place where you can do so much for your supporters and be so comfortable yourself, from now until November, as on your farm." [11] But like it or not, the candidate was soon making impromptu speeches. The faithful would not stay away. It made Garfield uneasy; he felt isolated, at the mercy of misquotation and human error, but he went through the motions. "I could not play dummy on

my own doorstep, when my yard was filled with voters from all parts
of the country, hurling speeches at me on all subjects." [12] In due
course, he shook hands with an assorted array: the Fisk Jubilee Sing-
ers, the Young Men's First Voters Garfield and Arthur Club, the Lincoln Club of Indianapolis. He heard a speech in German, and praised
the gifts callers left on the doorstep. His few set-speeches were innocuous. Late in the summer, he spoke to three GAR reunions in
Ohio, without startling listeners either with his subject or his rhetoric.

Both necessity and design produced a small, efficient staff to handle
mail and callers. A room in one of the outbuildings housed secretaries.
Garfield worked in a small study in the house, greeting visitors with a
bushy smile, taking dignitaries on a tour of the farm if time permitted.
He drove important visitors in the buggy, so nothing but passing winds
heard the conversation. Mrs. Garfield occasionally served semi-formal
lunches and dinners. When visitors stayed overnight, the boys slept
in the attic or on the porch. Garfield's routine farm work was a welcome relief from papers and callers, and he strolled through meadows,
or petted cattle when the study got too hot or telegrams brought bad
news. He often greeted arrivals with hay in his hair and blisters on
his hands, joking about the cost of hired help.

Money was a problem. Until September, few sources of funds
opened. The business community did not respond to Jewell's pleas,
and Garfield sent a steady barrage of suggestions to national headquarters. He asked Evarts and Sherman to discuss the matter discreetly with New York friends, avoiding any protruding Stalwart toes.
The name of "Mr. Rockafeller" came to Garfield's mind, and he wondered if they might tap him with pleasant results. Though he appeared
calm in his routine, Garfield closely watched every aspect of the campaign. He worried about Indiana, where corruption was notorious on
both sides of the political fence, and suggested careful organizing and
poll-watching. He was an able overseer, and played a large role in
managing the party's efforts.

Indiana, New Jersey, and the Pacific States were critical, but New
York dominated his thinking and planning. Summer wore on and still
little word came from "the oracles." Garfield quickly assured everyone
he held no grudges, and "wanted all Republicans, including the '306',
to consider themselves in full fellowship," as he told Joseph Medill of
the *Chicago Tribune*.[13] Blaine, convalescing from a gout attack at
White Sulphur Springs, tried to calm his fears. "I cannot believe that
New York parties will hold back from your cordial support. A little
time must be allowed for pouting and petting; but they cannot in the
end afford to scuttle a ship on which they are passengers." [14]

One man in New York seemed to do his part. Arthur assured Stalwart friends, including Grant's son, that "I was a Grant man and a third term man to the last; and whatever occurred there was no compensation for my disappointment." [15] He was already smoothing ruffled feathers, and writing a letter accepting the nomination. Conkling seemed ready to succumb to Arthur's famous tact. "Genl. Arthur's constant effort was to make everybody else happy—no wonder we all like him," he wrote Morton.[16] The old canards about his spoilsman's past appeared in the press, more from Republicans than Democrats.

His opposite number, William H. English, could not stand closer scrutiny than the New Yorker. As a wealthy Indiana businessman and typical midwestern Democrat, he had run his share of errands. Opponents refurbished an old tale that Arthur was a British subject, born in Canada during his preacher father's perambulations around upper New England, but the candidate did not reply and the charge died. On July 15, Arthur issued a letter of acceptance. Because of his safer secondary position, it was a more forceful and able document than Garfield's. While favoring conciliation toward the South, he strongly supported the free ballot and praised Hayes' vetoes of the Army bills in particular, and Executive firmness in general. On the civil service, he surprised Mugwumps, standing for merit appointments, established tenure of office, and a board to investigate both conduct and charges.[17]

While Arthur raised funds and established lines of communication, his chief in New York remained silent. The press speculated, and politicians whispered. The first problem was how to bring Garfield and Conkling together without wounding the pride or public stature of either.

Conkling took Garfield's silence for weakness, fortifying his image of him as a spineless "angle worm." The constant talk about a Blaine-dominated administration if Garfield won also irritated him. Most of Garfield's silence reflected his habits and Ohio upbringing, but the presidential nomination increased his public stature and feeling of self-importance. He hoped pressure in the party and public opinion would make the New Yorkers come to him, sparing his prestige. The study at Mentor echoed with conflicting advice. Whitelaw Reid hastily opposed a growing feeling in party circles that Garfield should visit New York. "In general, I don't believe in running after the malcontents," the publisher warned. "Let them run after you." The Stalwarts would not "throw away" New York, and only wished to bargain for offices and future influence.[18]

That was all very well for Reid; he did not have to win an election and control a party. "Wild Bill" Chandler gave different advice, though reluctantly. Shortly after the national committee meeting on July 1, he dined with Conkling and assorted friends at Manhattan Beach. The talk was frank. The Stalwarts wanted assurances that Garfield would not treat them in Hayes' "outrageous manner." Significantly, Chandler saw Conkling's weakening control of New York; he genuinely needed federal patronage and recognition to survive. Chandler was practical, urging Garfield to make Lord Roscoe *feel* important now; they could work out details later. "The state of New York is important, probably vital, and it is worthwhile, perhaps, to stoop a little to conquer much." [19] This came easily to Chandler—he was accustomed to dealing with Blaine and other Republicans who would not sacrifice the party for personal interest—but it was flawed advice for establishing relations with Conkling. It was better for Garfield to refuse him than assume he could later modify a tacit understanding.

Stephen Dorsey was more candid, presumably reflecting at least part of Conkling's attitude. "I believe that a discussion of thirty minutes with the persons named will settle for all time the doubt that exists in their minds. What we want is the state of New York, and we want to do whatever is necessary to secure it, [just] so it does not imply dishonor or indignity." He could not speak of specific requirements, but in general the Stalwarts wanted to know if Garfield would reward them, "or whether the 'Scratchers' and 'Independents' and 'featherheads' are to ride over the Republican party of this state as they have for the last four years." [20] The implication was clear; Garfield should come in person because Conkling did not trust him at a distance.

Garfield balked. He did not think Conkling wished to humiliate him, but feared the trip's effects on New York's independents, "who live between the lines of the two great parties." If he came, it should be at the invitation of the national committee, with all leaders present, especially Blaine and Sherman. Party harmony dictated a little bending, though it was "an unreasonable demand that so much effort should be made to conciliate one man." Consenting to the trip, he asked Blaine to "stand by me," and hoped it would clear the air. "Of one thing you may be sure," he promised. "There shall be no surrender to any unreasonable demand. I will do nothing to compromise myself or the noble men who stand up to the fight . . . I want to know how large a force C. has behind him, and just what the trouble is." If the Stalwarts preferred defeat to conciliation, "we ought to know it." [21]

The trip was a carefully planned but apparently impromptu speaking tour. Garfield drew a huge crowd at Buffalo, and made some twenty-five speeches at stops along the route, with good public response, following his private admonition: "Say but little, beyond thanks and an occasional remark on the localities through which we pass." At Albany, Governor Cornell, Arthur, and local politicos boarded the train to talk while rails clicked behind them. Chauncey Depew and Hamilton Fish appeared, and humor enlivened serious discussions. In New York, Garfield drove through enthusiastic crowds to the lavish Fifth Avenue Hotel, favorite meeting spot of eastern politicians. He spoke briefly, reviewed some small parades, shook hands, and retired to confer.[22]

An embarrassing silence followed. Senator Conkling would not be there, Dorsey explained apologetically. Garfield flushed, and looked angry. Blaine, Sherman, Morton, and Platt assuaged his irritation, but Lord Roscoe's absence was eloquent. Entrusting affairs to Platt and Morton, he disappeared—some said to a nephew's, where he was "not in;" others reported he left the city. To Platt and other friends, Conkling was blunt before departing. He did not "trust to Mr. Garfield's imperfect memory of a private conversation, . . ." Furthermore, George William Curtis would be there, and he could not bear the thought of meeting him. And there was Blaine.[23]

The faithful heard a good deal from the Magnetic Man in the hotel parlor before the conference began. He, Sherman, and Logan spoke of loyalty, which only magnified Conkling's important absence. Neither Platt nor Arthur quite calmed Garfield as he listened to professions of fealty, but he noted an important strain in their conversation: "I think his [Conkling's] men are showing zeal and enthusiasm, and will work whether he does or not." Then they got down to business. Platt was candid, wanting to avoid "four years more of an administration similar to that of Rutherford B. Hayes." Garfield promised to "consult" friends and left the distinct impression he would reward the faithful. Morton took the job of raising funds, with an independent finance committee to regulate expenditure. Platt and Arthur understood that if they cooperated and the ticket won, Morton could be Secretary of the Treasury, minister to a major power, or head of a banking syndicate to refinance part of the national debt. Arthur believed Garfield promised the New Yorkers control of state patronage.[24]

As the conference ended, discreet word passed that Garfield could visit Coney Island for "a pocket interview with my Lord Roscoe." He declined, remarking sourly that "if the presidency is to turn on that I do not want the office badly enough to go."[25] Garfield went home with Arthur's assurances of cooperation. Back at the farm he noted: "No trades, no shackles, and as well fitted for defeat or victory."[26] Some Mugwumps said he gave in to the machine. But others like Curtis thought the whole affair, staged in public, would increase the candidate's stature and made Conkling look childish. Moderates like Reid argued that "it turned all our way."[27]

Conkling made a grave mistake in avoiding Garfield. Conflicting beliefs as to what actually occured were the foundation of a long struggle between them. Garfield did not mortgage himself, but his promise to "consult," and apparent agreement to a Cabinet post for Morton, seemed otherwise to the Senator. Wisdom dictated a clear understanding. Conkling's behavior was also insulting. More importantly, it showed Garfield and Blaine divisions among New York's Stalwarts. Platt and Arthur spoke for Lord Roscoe, but they clearly wished to stay in the national party's fold. Garfield's patronage arrangements were not unusual or unique, but the circumstances made them seem so to Conkling. Garfield now believed he had done enough to placate intra-party opposition. After all, how many presidential candidates openly sought support from senators of their own party?

Repercussions and bitterness over the conference lingered for years, but its immediate effect was welcome to Garfield. The Stalwarts opened up shop. Their newspapers supported the ticket; Arthur and company stepped up organization work; funds unfroze. Platt and Arthur told Conkling bluntly that he must enter the campaign, like it or not. If they sulked and Garfield lost, Republicans everywhere would blame their pettiness; if they sulked and Garfield won, they would get nothing. By August, Conkling visited the headquarters in New York, and announced he was arranging personal affairs to take the stump. He could not begin, he explained, until September. It would take a month to withdraw from lucrative legal cases. He told friends it would cost him $18,000 in legal fees, and another $11,000 for expenses.[28]

Conkling's eye still narrowed at the mention of Garfield, and pressure from that quarter was not what had brought him into the fight. His lieutenants, and personal appeals from Grant turned the trick. "If you insist on my speaking for him," he told his old chief, "I shall carry him through."[29] Modesty was never his long suit. On September 17, he spoke at New York's Academy of Music, harvesting cheers for the Republican party. Observers chose to downgrade his faint praise for the ticket's head. This fresh interest in speechmaking raised some eyebrows. "Conkling's zeal in the canvass indicates that he has made a deal with the Republican candidate," Godkin said.[30]

Grant remained enigmatic. After the convention he nursed bruises in the Rocky Mountains, allegedly enjoying splendid views, rushing waters, and freedom from politics. He did not congratulate Garfield, and seemed oblivious to the party's dangers. But the days had long since passed when Grant did not know his own politics. His appeal to Conkling indicated a readiness to enter the canvass. By mid-August he was rallying reinforcements for a projected tour of the doubtful Midwest, culminating in a "monster rally" at Warren, Ohio. He would "gladly attend any meeting intended to further the success of the ticket headed by Garfield and Arthur," he wrote John Logan.[31]

In Illinois, Indiana, and Ohio, Lord Roscoe and the Savior of the Union made a splendid team. The faithful traveled dozens of miles over rough country roads to glimpse Grant and hear Conkling utter words like "cossack." Garfield remained at Mentor while the campaign train wound toward Warren, where the Boys in Blue had gathered for days. He presumed the party would visit him, but decided against meeting them at the rally to avoid the risks of a public confrontation. Besides, it was really Grant's show. In Warren, Conkling spoke for two hours and Grant for seven minutes, with equal effect. The converted needed inspiration, not salvation. Conkling did not refer to Garfield, and the candidate understood the omission. It soured him further: "Conkling is a singular compound of a very brilliant man and an exceedingly petulant spoiled child." He feared that both Grant and Conkling were more interested in 1884 than 1880.[32]

The Conkling-Grant party, with about fifteen local politicians, later stopped at Mentor en route to Cleveland. In all the mythology surrounding Conkling's relations with Garfield, this moment shone brightest in Stalwart minds. Convinced that without their help Garfield was doomed, they pictured him rushing from the porch in a light rain to greet Grant's carriage, embracing Conkling—something no man had ever done—and exclaiming: "Conkling! you have saved me! Whatever man can do for man, that will I do for you!" Ever suspicious, even in legend, Conkling avoided a private talk with Garfield, insisting a stenographer accompany them as Garfield beckoned him upstairs. Platt subsequently argued that Garfield told the Senator he would not interfere in New York politics, and make no appointments without senatorial courtesy. The dramatic scene in the yard was a fiction, but Garfield doubtless talked about patronage. The party stayed for coffee and a light meal; then after an hour's conversation, returned to the train station and their appointed rounds.[33]

The press manufactured a "Treaty of Mentor," redrawing the boundaries of politics; that too was a dangerous fiction. Back in New York, Conkling took counsel with allies. "Have you any faith in Garfield?" asked Platt. The Senator hesitated, then grimaced. "Not much, but we will try him out." [34] The intra-party pulling and hauling continued. Blaine, Reid, Chandler, and other Half-Breeds sustained Garfield with daily letters and much advice, warning that a day of reckoning lay ahead. The Stalwarts were sure they alone would elect the ticket. "Doubtless Garfield owes his nomination to Blaine," one crowed, "but he'll have to thank Conkling for his election." [35] John Hay wrote Reid that Conkling "really thinks he is the Saviour of the Situation, and makes no bones about it." Hay wrote Garfield condescending advice: "It will pay you to keep a cheap friend to drone continually in your ear, 'It was *you* who were nominated at Chicago and elected by the people'." [36] With this combination of friends and enemies, Garfield struggled to retain self-respect, and check his temper.

Conkling had some grand moments in the Midwest, unfamiliar country to an eastern magnifico, but Republicans there profited more from Grant's tour. He never strayed into the baroque style of Conkling's set-pieces. The brief utterance was his forte; hearers did not care that he lacked flourish. He appealed frankly to the soldier vote, condemned the prospect of southern rule, and said such unkind things about Hancock that the general demanded an explanation. Sometimes his train stopped at a Democratic town with a Hancock meeting in progress, but the crowd usually came over to see him. In New York, late in October, he stood with Arthur on a hotel balcony to watch a huge parade wind into the dark between midnight and 4 A.M. He desperately wanted the GOP to win, but politicking was still a trial: "I felt as if I could not bear the idea of the Democrats getting possession of the government," he wrote a friend, "and consented to preside at the Warren, Ohio meeting. It has caused me a world of trouble. Letters and dispatches, and committees, are after me day and night to go to this place and that, to some [of] which I have been compelled for my own peace of mind, to give my consent. I am glad it will all be over soon. I should not mind so much attending these meetings, only that as soon as I make my appearance, there is a universal shout for me to say something, and the people will not be quieted without it. Speaking before the public is a terrible trial for me, and being totally without verbal memory, I cannot prepare anything in advance to say." [37] In the stolid form that took the keys to a hundred cities, and accepted homage from reigning monarchs still lurked a man fearful of inadequacies.

The Democrats got off to a loud start, filling the air with cannon fire and skyrockets to celebrate Hancock's victory. Party leaders returning to summer homes spoke little and smothered disappointment. Like opponents, they had to organize and decide on tactics. Hancock's military status lent itself to ceremonial aloofness. He remained on Governor's Island throughout the contest, transacting normal business amid uniforms and a spartan tidiness. The ceremony notifying the candidate of his nomination was the first great set-piece of the campaign. On July 13, a gorgeously arrayed committee of party statesmen gathered at a New York hotel and then proceeded in a body to Governor's Island. While the chairman read the formal notification, the General stood at parade rest, and thanked them for their pains. He promised to issue a letter of acceptance soon, outlining his views. The group returned to New York, and the following day joined the Democratic National Committee and other dignitaries at Gramercy Park to testify loyalty to Samuel J. Tilden. The Sage heard them in customary silence, then recited his fidelity to states' rights and the Old Democracy. A "light collation," as the papers put it, followed, and the gentlemen dispersed on their separate ways to win the election.[38]

Party leaders divided on just what to do with Hancock. They could hardly camp on his doorstep to ward off trouble, yet knew his political inexperience might be embarrassing. "Do not let our danger be overconfidence," Speaker Randall warned him gently.[39] Others had sterner private advice. "Hancock ought to ask a six month leave of absence and then he should keep his eyes and ears open and his mouth shut," a constituent wrote Randall.[40]

That was easier said than done. Just as Garfield had to placate Conkling, Democratic leaders had to conciliate members of their coalition. Bayard's friends joined Kelly's to grumble about Hancock's identification with "the Tilden wing of the party."[41] Hancock visited Greystone and wrote Tilden for advice on the letter of acceptance. These were traditional and expected moves, but did not endear him to Kelly. Tilden shrewdly receded into the background, content to write letters to reform associations, using the excuse of a sore throat to avoid speaking.

On July 29, Hancock issued a letter of acceptance. It read well for an Army man, but held few surprises. He promised to enforce the Reconstruction Amendments, and opposed federal supervision of elections. "The bayonet is not a fit instrument for collecting the votes of freemen." On the civil service, he was vague. "Public office is a trust, not a bounty bestowed upon the holder." As the candidate of reunion, he appealed for sectional peace. For the rest, he accepted the party's platform as an adequate guide.[42] The following day, English, already building walls in Indiana, released his letter, equally pitched toward reconciliation, and even more vague on civil service reform. He opposed Chinese immigration, and promised to make Indiana Democratic. The press displayed some disappointment. The New York Times called the total performance "A farrago of bunsbyism . . . ," and asked Hancock to discuss real issues.[43] Most Democratic leaders preferred the General's own advice to say nothing and take advantage of Republican mistakes.

Bayard, however, started the campaign with a vengeance, telling a Wilmington audience that Garfield represented military rule. The bloody shirt snapped in the breeze, and Hancock had to deny charges that if elected he would pay pensions to Confederate veterans. His remoteness, contrary to expectations, did not unify the party's campaign. Local chieftains, true to Democratic form, devised separate campaigns without much focus. Senator William H. Barnum of Connecticut chaired the national committee, and as an experienced sniper in the political woods, coordinated fund-raising, propaganda, and speakers' schedules. But English in Indiana, Kelly in New York, and less well-known men in the mid-Atlantic states carried most of the organizational burden.

The campaign machinery worked behind the bluster of public statements and the gaudy color of parades and barbecues. Fund raising proved easier than some expected; Tilden and his friends alone produced nearly $200,000.* Small but wealthy Democratic enclaves in banking and other business circles in New York and Chicago responded well. Kelly raised considerable money in New York City, but solid-bloc voting was his chief contribution. Until fall, Democrats were far ahead of the Republicans, and observers predicted they would win by carrying the South, Indiana, New Jersey, New York, and California. Hancock wrote Bayard and English optimistic letters, especially about Indiana, which he thought would come their way because a "new generation" of men were at the front.[44]

Perhaps so, but they were using old methods. The trip across the river in southern Indiana was not very arduous, and both parties ferried loads of Negroes over on election eve. In all the confusion and

---

*On March 5, 1884, the New York Sun reported the Democratic National Treasurer's tally for 1880 as follows: Tilden, $51,500; W. H. Barnum, $40,000; W. L. Scott, $43,000; Henry B. Payne, $20,000; Oliver H. Payne, $31,000. He reported all bills paid, and $1,800 in free balance.

free spending, it was hard to say who had the edge, especially since some of the "colonists" voted several times. Dorsey hired Pinkerton detectives to watch Louisville and Cincinnati. W. W. Dudley, one of Indiana's smoothest Republican operators, warned Garfield the Democrats would import voters, repeat them, and then cry fraud if they lost. He could only suggest Republicans fight fire with fire. While all parties charged that Indiana was "plastered with two dollar billers," Garfield told his men in the field to watch each district and polling place on Election Day.[45] His chief consolation, as Indiana's October state election day approached, was the wry knowledge that corruptionists probably canceled each other's efforts, like a husband and wife belonging to different parties.

Republican managers had hoped for Tilden's nomination, and hated to abandon the "scandal materials" they had on the "Great Forecloser." They turned now to an easy and rather genial ridicule, treating Hancock as unworthy of serious attention. An editor called him "a good man weighing 250 pounds," the ultimate dismissal. Cartoonists drew him as a huge Trojan horse, swarming with corruptionists and old rebels eager to topple representative government. Labeled as "General Risk," "Fort Doubtful," "General Went Off Half-Cock," he marched across the pages of humor magazines and genteel monthlies. Mugwumps distrusted Garfield, but had no illusions about the Democrats.

Of course, swords like that cut two ways. President Hayes early assured Garfield "that his personal history as an ideal self-made man would be a most popular feature of the canvass." [46] The appealing slogan "From the Towpath to the White House" rose above the sound of marching feet. The Democrats did not quite see it that way, and waited in ambush for Garfield. He was "touched a little with the mud stick," as one old reporter noted.[47] The waspish Charles A. Dana editorialized that "when they fired cannon in City Hall Park over the nomination of Garfield yesterday, the smoke rose in the air in the form of rings." [48]

An era of free-wheeling journalism would not let old rumors lie, and charges that Garfield had profited from the Credit Mobilier floated again. Fences and outhouses bore "$329," the sum of money he allegedly made from the stock. The charge was doubtful; but like Blaine, he never fully explained the connection, and suspicion lingered. Indiscretion may be worse than guilt in voters' eyes. Before the campaign formally began, friends investigated old stories that Garfield had received a $5,000 legal fee from a street-paving company in Washington while in the House. The DeGolyer Company got a contract, partly through Garfield's efforts, and while the fee was not a bribe, it was at least sharp practice. Democrats devoted much space to the subject. Blaine took a certain malicious pleasure in noting this privately. "How funny the Republican moralists would not go for me in the convention because of my alleged connection with schemes," he remarked with amusement. "Now they are all busily engaged in defending Garfield from far worse charges than were made against me." [49] Garfield shrank from answering, wisely preferring not to seem apologetic, but there was a measure of truth in his remark "that the Democrats . . . dare not meet the issues raised . . . but are seeking to draw us off into personal controversy." [50]

Maine voted on September 13, and Blaine promised Garfield a handsome victory to rally the party in the "October states," Ohio and Indiana. The Plumed Knight was jolted; the Pine Tree State elected a Democratic governor with a narrow margin. He hastily wired a long explanation, claiming that Democrats spent an extra $100,000 and used colonists from Canada. In Mentor, Garfield analyzed the returns differently. He thought the voters turned against "Blaine and his autocracy." More significantly, he saw that Republicans lost votes in shipping towns and gained in manufacturing towns. That meant one thing to a practical politician: the tariff was involved. Hastily urging the eastern headquarters to pour tracts and speakers into the Midwest, stressing tariff protection, Garfield stayed calm. "It is the Bull Run of the contest—let us win at Appomattox." [51]

Blaine reached the same conclusion. A few days later, with the usual agitation and nervous energy, he burst into party headquarters waving hat and cane. Spying Dwight Sabin of Minnesota at work over papers, he shouted: "Sabin, you want to fold up the bloody shirt and lay it away. It's of no use to us. You want to shift the main issue to protection." As Sabin calmed him and retreated to the privacy of an office to avoid reporters, Blaine's voice rose: "Those foolish five words in the Democratic platform, 'A Tariff for Revenue Only,' give you the chance." [52]

The Plumed Knight was right; prosperity was just returning after the Panic of 1873; this was no time for even a threatened change. Industrialization had moved steadily westward along the Great Lakes. An appeal on the issue might carry Indiana, Ohio, and the Old Northwest, as well as New York and part of the doubtful mid-Atlantic states. Garfield had nineteen iron foundries in his district, and the business upturn now rested on protected industries like steel, wool, and materials for railroad expansion.

Garfield urged Sherman to prod the managers into quick action. In short order, huge quantities of pamphlets and leaflets, stressing the importance of protection to workers, went to the crucial states. Marshall Jewell thought the Maine defeat was a victory in disguise. He worried over lack of funds, which Garfield could not remedy, and now saw that prospects of Democratic "tariff tinkering" might save them. He quickly contacted Wharton Barker in Philadelphia, who reported growing success at fund-raising.* To Garfield, he predicted the Maine election would "open the purses, the pockets and the eyes" of the whole business community.[53]

Thanks to General Hancock, these blessings did not come singly, but as whole battalions. The Republicans had great fun with his empty record on public issues, especially the currency and protection. In a moment of genius, they got out a large book titled *Record of the Statesmanship and Achievements of General Winfield Scott Hancock*, elegantly bound, and consisting of blank pages, with the word "Finis" printed neatly at the end. Democratic managers were equally, though not humorously, concerned about their candidate's record. As the October elections approached, reports from the Midwest indicated growing concern over the party's tariff stand. The Republican platform declared for protection, their own for a revenue tariff. How explain this to voters with industrial jobs? Was it best to say nothing, or straddle? [54]

It bothered General Hancock, who now seemed restive in his quarters. Perhaps he saw the White House ahead; or maybe he was truthful in saying the time had come for honest discussion of new issues. On October 7, he received a reporter from the *Paterson Daily Guardian,* and talked about the tariff. If the newshawk realized he had a bombshell, no glimmer of malice crossed his face while he industriously wrote down the innocent candidate's words. The tariff was important, said the General, but it was largely talk, a matter of schedules which Congress worked out for local interests. He was not a free trader, and business need not fear a Hancock administration. The government had to raise money with duties, and a little incidental protection was alright. He then offered an unconscious bid for immortality: "The tariff question is a local question." [55]

A wave of laughter buoyed up Republicans, and sent angry doubts

*It is worth emphasizing here that contrary to the usual stereotype, the Republican party was not run by businessmen. Until September, campaign managers relied on assessing officeholders for most of their funds. Democrats realized more contributions from businessmen than Republicans. When business support did come to Garfield's war chest, it was for a legitimate principle, tariff protection.

through Democratic ranks. Shrewd newsmen took up the refrain, and Thomas Nast drew a famous cartoon, showing Hancock whispering to a companion: "Who is Tariff, and why is he for revenue only?" The General's efforts to explain the remark only muddled the issue, and one of Garfield's correspondents was right in calling this "one interview too many." [56] The Republicans carried Ohio and Indiana later in the month by safe, if not large, margins. Democratic politicians privately admitted the tariff argument made the margin. Tilden said later in a simple epitaph: "When I was running for president, all my friends tried to persuade me to write a letter on the tariff. I didn't." [57]

In the confusion, someone fired a last shot toward the Republican camp. On Wednesday morning, October 18, Joseph Hart, editor of the New York Truth, found on his desk a letter on House of Representatives' stationery and apparently in Garfield's hand. It was addressed to one H. L. Morey in Lynn, Massachusetts, a routine answer to a question on Garfield's views about Chinese immigration. Like Hayes, Garfield opposed limiting immigration unilaterally, and favored re-negotiating the Burlingame Treaty. The letter's text, dated January 23, 1880, said labor was a matter of the marketplace: an employer had the right to buy it as cheaply as he could. Hart knew he had a prize. The Chinese issue constantly agitated California, Oregon, and Nevada and could determine their electoral votes. Most labor unions and probably most workers everywhere opposed the Chinese. This might offset the protection argument in industrial states. He hastily asked respected men like Randall, Abram S. Hewitt, and Senator Barnum to verify the text. They knew Garfield's handwriting, and agreed the letter was genuine. Hart published it on October 20, and stood back.

The press reacted violently. Jewell telegraphed the text to Garfield, who said it was a forgery, but did not reply publicly. His delay reflected a dual desire "to answer all my accusers by silence," and fear that a secretary might have sent such a letter without his knowledge. A search of office records in Washington over the weekend relieved his mind. On Monday, national headquarters issued his statement branding the letter "a base forgery." Republican managers feared the effects in labor circles,* but Chauncey Filley was more realistic. It all showed how inept the Democrats were; they could not even time a forgery correctly. On election-eve, it might have caused trouble, but

---

*Hart conducted a post-election investigation, but never found the forger. He was most likely one of his reporters, or a local Democratic politician. On December 9, 1880, Hart wrote Garfield the details of the investigation, and apologized, saying he now believed the letter was false, but originally thought it genuine. (Garfield LC.)

with ten days to work in, the Republicans could explain it, and gain a sympathy vote. Even Charles Dana, no friend of Garfield's, editorialized: "If a party requires such infamous aids, that party, by whatsoever name it may be called, deserves to perish." [58]

So the contest closed as it began, with confusion and alarm. Republicans poured men and pamphlets into the Midwest until the polls closed. Democrats staged parades and counted heads in New York, the South, and Far West until November 2. A strange sense of calm reigned in Mentor. Garfield worked in the fields, bringing in beets and hay, after voting early on Election Day. He was quiet, perhaps resigned. Toward dusk he settled in the study, reading digests of early returns. About midnight, he seemed safely elected, and with congratulations all around, the family and campaign workers sat down to a late supper. He stayed up until 3 A.M., when Republicans claimed all northern states except New Jersey, and California and Nevada in the West. The staff closed the office and went to bed. [59]

At Governor's Island, the exhausted Hancock retired at 7 P.M., asking not to be awakened. The telegraph wires clattered results to a nervous Mrs. Hancock. Military orderlies and politicians came and went with scraps of paper. Night lengthened toward dawn. About 5 A.M., Hancock roused up and sleepily asked for results. "It has been a complete Waterloo for you," his wife replied. He turned over, said "That is all right, I can stand it," and fell asleep. Mrs. Hancock contented herself with a monumental understatement: "An extraordinarily balanced temperament, it then occured to me." [60]

When Hancock awoke, he began reading dispatches from New York reporting alleged voting frauds that cost him the state and the election. A prominent visitor said 5,000 ballots went into the Hudson River. Hancock thought "all the 'Bulldozing,' bribery, colonization, delays" lost the Empire State. [61] For a while, Kelly and Barnum talked loosely of contesting the returns, but Hancock would not face another disputed election, and their case was far from perfect. The candidate also noted bluntly that "blunders, jealousy, and selfishness" among Democrats in Brooklyn may have cost the victory. On November 8, he conceded defeat, believing he was counted out, but fearing disorders. Talk continued of widespread corruption, easy under lax state voting laws. Indiana saw more than its share of visiting statesmen. Arthur admitted at a post-election Delmonico dinner that the Hoosier State went Republican with some financial help. William E. Chandler protested vigorously that Indiana Democrats were not untainted, and that

Republican organization and poll-watching was more influential than outright purchase or colonization.[62]

Any glance at a map revealed the contest's most obvious result, a solid South and an equally solid North. Hancock received 155 electoral votes to Garfield's 214. The Republicans' popular plurality was razor-thin, something less than 40,000 votes in a total of 9,200,000 cast. But 78 per cent of the voters balloted, indicating the campaign's importance. Garfield carried no southern state, and Hancock won no northern state except New Jersey, by 2,000 votes with Greenbacker aid. The Republicans lost Nevada, received only 1 of California's 6 electoral votes, but retained Oregon. Without the Morey Letter, they would probably have won all the Far West. Garfield was bitter about the forgery, believing Republicans would have controlled the Senate, now evenly divided, without it.[63]

Blaine spoke for most observers in noting the obvious: "The salient and most serious fact of the presidential election was the absolute consolidation of the electoral vote of the south; . . ."[64] but that was very deceptive. The election's real significance was Republican victory. Not many men predicted it in 1878, when the Democrats captured Congress. Fewer still prophesied it when Garfield won nomination, heading a divided party and facing an apparently reviving Democracy. He won the presidency with a handful of popular votes, but the party captured the national House with 152 seats to 130 for the Democrats, and 11 scattered among independents. The Senate was deadlocked, but Arthur's casting vote as Vice-President, and judicious arrangements, could at least thwart the enemy. In most industrial states, Republicans both increased their margins of 1876, and gained House seats. They lost seats only in New York, California, and Nevada, and captured 6 in the Border states. They lost Delaware by 1,100 votes, California by 100 votes, New Jersey by 2,000, and Nevada by 900. In every populous and industrial state, they reduced the Democratic margins of 1876.

The welter of figures and confused talk of corruption obscured the election's most important result—the sudden importance of the tariff question. Blaine was right in saying it could solidify the North and West to beat a solid South. Protection now began a long dominance in national politics, and Republicans were far more adept at its use than were their opponents. They believed in it more strongly, and allied it to prosperity. As the key issue of the time, it was the foundation of a new coalition of farmers, workers, and businessmen. It was a credit to politicians like Garfield and Blaine to see this so clearly.

Hancock was partially correct in calling the tariff a local question, but the Republicans made it a national cause, representing a functioning system rather than parochial interests. The humor magazines were right in noting that "General Hancock is probably convinced by this time that the tariff, if a local issue at all, is a local issue affecting a very extensive locality." [65] Democrats did not overcome northern and western distrust of their motives and abilities. Their backward image remained, and analysts condemned their "purely negative attitude . . ." and lack of constructive spokesmen.[66]

Garfield accepted congratulations placidly at Mentor, settling for a winter of Cabinet-making and mollifying party chieftains. He adopted the usual stance of unworthiness, and sighed wearily at burdens ahead. As he told his diary, "there is a tone of sadness running through this triumph which I can hardly explain." [67]

Carl Schurz was predictably among the first to contact the President-elect, ending a letter of mixed congratulations and advice: "Your real troubles will now begin." [68] Cabinet-making was as elaborately political as in any European state, colorful and intricate like the peacock's mating dance. New presidents had to insure a reasonable level of administrative skill in subordinates, while rewarding political friends without allowing them dominance, and disappointing political rivals without making them enemies. Garfield would satisfy geography and politics. The greatest juggling feat was to remain independent and in charge while pacifying Blaine and Conkling.

Though tactfully in the background, Blaine was early on the scene with shrewd and accurate advice about party needs and desires. He approached Garfield with a curious combination of respect and condescension, liking the new President, but fearing his weakness. He spoke in such genial terms that Garfield chose not to notice it, and they were soon close. Whatever men said of Blaine, he was a shrewd observer. From the high mountain of political sagacity, he wrote Garfield an astute analysis of the party's structure, pregnant with warnings of what to avoid. First, he said, there was "the Blaine section," located in the West and strong in Congress. This was Garfield's for the asking. Second, there was "the Grant section, taking all the south practically, with the machine in New York, Pennsylvania, and Illinois—and having the aid of rule or ruin leaders." These were "all the desperate bad men of the party, bent on *loot* and booty, . . . These men are to be handled with skill, always remembering that they are harmless when out of power, and desperate when in possession of it." Last, "The third section is the reformers by profession, the 'unco good.' They are to be treated with respect, but they are the worst possible political advisers —upstarts, conceited, foolish, vain, without knowledge of measures, ignorant of men. . . . They are noisy but not numerous, pharisaical but not practical, ambitious but not wise, pretentious but not powerful!" They were Garfield's by default, but he must not tell them so.[69]

Garfield agreed at almost equal length, but differed on civil service reform. He intended to be a partisan, but like Hayes, he wanted competent Republicans in office, and hoped Congress would pass a reasonable law to cover lower ranks of the service. He dreaded the prospect of Washington teeming with place-hunters, and hoped to remove, "as far as possible, from Congress and the Executive, the endless annoyance that comes from the swarm of small office-seekers." [70] He stopped rumors that he would retain Schurz, and finally passed the reformers a portfolio by appointing Pennsylvania's independent, Wayne MacVeagh, Attorney-General. He filled the War Department with Robert Todd Lincoln, a safe bow to history, since the Great Emancipator's son had Stalwart friends and made a fortune from railroads. After late juggling, he chose a charming southerner, William H. Hunt, nominally of Louisiana, for the Navy Department. He was more than a consolation for the South, and became an efficient and vigorous Secretary during a brief tenure. The West got a representative in Samuel J. Kirkwood of Iowa, in the Interior post.

These were the final results of a long, intricate process that Garfield carried on in a muffled silence. The names interested the public at inauguration time, but the party's big guns and the press trained on the State and Treasury posts. Carriages of visiting politicians rutted the snow in Garfield's driveway. The President-elect greeted most of them with a smile, offering both external and internal warmth against Ohio's winter, but he talked little, taking a debatable advantage of Mentor's isolation. He might have done better in personal dealings in Washington, avoiding a good deal of the inevitable confusion that came from secondhand reports and a swarm of intermediaries among powerful men.

Blaine was the first major problem. He could take only one position, the State Department. The Conkling element would assume he was the power behind the throne, no matter how much Garfield protested or acted. But Garfield could not omit him for obvious political reasons. Would Blaine, as Secretary of State, abandon presidential ambitions? Late in November, the President-elect went to Washington to close his house and office. Hayes, Sherman, and Dorsey gave similar advice:

take Blaine into the Cabinet, but retain firm control. Garfield visited Blaine's home for a frank talk. Both men knew the problems involved without discussing them. Garfield feared the Administration would be a battleground for 1884; Blaine promised he would not seek the nomination. Garfield left uncommitted, but leaning strongly toward Blaine. His selection was politically wise, but Garfield also saw Blaine's gifts as an analyst, and charm as a friend.[71]

Blaine expressed private doubts about taking the post. It was not a steppingstone to the presidency, and might tie him to Garfield's policies, even if he did not like them. He never worked well in tandem. But the doubts were phantoms. The position would make him Garfield's heir. He could pursue a new line in foreign policy, and ideas were already stirring. He need not face a bitter contest for re-election in Maine. The social aspect of the office pleased his family. Naturally, he did not forget the Stalwart brethren; it was a commanding height in the intra-party wars. "I believe with you as president, and in your full confidence, I could do much to build up the party as a result of strong and wise policy," he wrote Garfield.[72] On December 20, Blaine secretly accepted the post with assurances of loyalty. A month later, Sherman offered Garfield a kindly warning: "If you can only restrain his famous activity and keep him from meddling with the other departments, you will have a brilliant secretary." [73]

Others thought not. When the appointment became common knowledge in January, Grant frowned, and Conkling, offering apparent peace feelers, was instantly suspicious, though not surprised. One other small obstacle to filling the important Treasury post loomed; would Sherman wish to stay? Garfield carefully evaded the subject— then Sherman said he wanted to return to the Senate. Garfield pressed Ohio friends to unite behind Sherman for the seat he had just resigned without occupying. He also wanted Sherman as an Administration leader.

That left the inevitable confrontation with the New Yorkers. Powerful midwestern interests warned Garfield against selecting an easterner for the Treasury. Republican inflationists might join Democrats on financial issues to wreck the Administration unless they were represented in the Cabinet. As Blaine reported after conferring with Sherman and other party lights: "He must be identified with an agricultural community, not a manufacturing or commercial community." [74] Garfield narrowed it to two choices: Senator William B. Allison of Iowa, friendly to both Stalwarts and Half-Breeds; and Senator William Windom of Minnesota, financially acceptable without being radical.

Intimations of these changes in Garfield's attitude unnerved the New Yorkers. On December 13, a delegation under Governor Cornell's charge visited Mentor, and said they recalled Garfield's promise of the Treasury post for Morton. The President-elect shook his head; he had listed a number of posts he would *consider* for Morton. It was impossible to choose a New York banker. He did not say the obvious, which Hayes and Mugwumps pressed upon him: the Treasury commanded great patronage, including customhouses. He could not live with a Secretary under Conkling's control. Cornell and his friends feared Blaine, without quite saying so, and did not think it wise to reward that element of the party without adequate compensation for their own. Garfield said rather angrily he "would not permit this four years to be used by anybody to secure the next [presidential term] for anybody." [75] They left, dissatisfied and confused.

Conkling remained aloof in New York and Washington, dealing with Garfield through intermediaries like Dorsey. Shortly after the Cornell delegation left, Dorsey sent a long letter to Mentor, detailing Conkling's attitude. He wished to be friends, but had a right to rewards equal to Blaine's. Dorsey added with either realism or naivete: "I think he sees as clearly as anyone can that he is out of the race, that General Grant is out, that Mr. Blaine is worse than out, and he is anxious to be in with those who are not out." [76] Garfield turned the letter over in his hands. For a while in January he thought of offering Conkling the Treasury. He would doubtless refuse, but the gesture might ease his suspicion. He sounded out friends. Alarms filled the air. Reid said no; Blaine was more blunt: "His appointment would act like strychnine upon your administration—first bring contortions, and then be followed by death." Besides, they could still bring Conkling around. Sherman firmly vetoed the idea, on the sensible grounds that Conkling knew nothing of finance and would use the Department's patronage to thwart the President. [77]

There was nothing to do but have a personal conference, and Garfield reluctantly invited Lord Roscoe to Mentor. On February 16, Conkling spent an afternoon with "this man Garfield," as he called him from afar. Rustic Mentor was not to his taste, but the Senator remained courteous and frank. If New York could not have the Treasury, Garfield should pass over the state. Talk of naming Morton to the Navy Department was vain, "when there is no navy." That would do for some other state. Garfield asked about Judge Charles J. Folger, a party regular. Conkling liked him, but thought he should not leave New York politics just now. The conversation continued, and the Senator grew restive at Garfield's "trifling and undecided manner." When the host suggested tea, his guest closed up, telling friends later: "Tea! tea! tea!" [78]

Conkling knew little more when he left than when he came. Garfield was impossible to pin down. But he was optimistic among friends, and seemed to think Garfield would reward the regulars. That was wishful thinking. Conkling never proposed to work on Garfield's terms, and Blaine was fundamentally right in thinking Conkling must either come to heel or leave public life. After every conference with an opponent, Conkling thought his views triumphed. The idea of being subordinate simply did not fit his personality.

Garfield did not increase his standing with Conkling in the following days. He immediately offered Folger the attorney-generalship, knowing the Senator's opposition, but hoping the organization would compel his support. Folger consulted friends and declined. Morton had practically deserted Conkling, writing in mid-January that he was available for almost anything. On February 26, Garfield tendered the Navy post, and Morton agreed by telegraph two days later. This set Conkling ablaze. A mutual friend gave the ailing Morton a dose of brandy and quinine, and hustled him to "the Morgue" as the faithful called Conkling's home. After a little conversation, Morton agreed to decline.[79]

Garfield left for Washington on February 28, sure his Cabinet was complete. Hayes greeted him at the White House, and prepared the last ceremonial dinners and receptions. The President took no part in the campaign that elected Garfield, preferring a western tour to the hustings. He remained outwardly calm and placid, despite four years of struggling with friends and foes. His departure prompted the usual eulogies. "Whatever his critics may say, he has given the country a very clean administration," Garfield noted, "and his party has not been handicapped in the late contest by any scandals caused by him." [80] There was some rudeness. Sectional conciliation had not dulled all the edges of criticism. "Mr. Hayes came in by a majority of one, and goes out by unanimous consent," a Democratic paper said.[81]

The city stirred with inaugural preparations. Famous men came and went, and the curious were already staking claims to choice vantage points along Pennsylvania Avenue and around the White House and Capitol. Garfield made his rounds, dreading the prospect. Immediate events were not reassuring. On March 2, Morton staged an apologetic interview; the President-elect must release him. Garfield was angry, and coldly said Morton must withdraw by letter. That afternoon, a messenger brought the document, and he named Hunt to the post.[82] The prospect of further dealing with Conkling loomed.

There were other cracks in the edifice of harmony. Allison accepted the Treasury post on the evening of March 3. At 8:30 the next morning he "broke down on my hands and absolutely declined the Treasury, partly for family reasons, but mainly from unwillingness to face the opposition of certain forces." [83] The "certain forces" were clearly New Yorkers; Allison would not jeopardize his standing in both Republican camps, or risk losing power in the Senate. Garfield quickly turned to Windom, despite Blaine's mild objections.

The Post Office Department awaited a new chief, and had produced a cloak-and-dagger drama worthy of a dime novel. Early in the morning of March 3, friends virtually smuggled Thomas L. James into Washington for a conference with Garfield. He arrived on Whitelaw Reid's doorstep, confused and demanding to know what was going on. Reid explained the emergency; Hunt would take the Navy, and Garfield needed an able man for Postmaster-General. James was noted for efficiency and political moderation, though close to Conkling's organization. Grant had appointed him Postmaster of New York City, where he did so well that Hayes reappointed him after he declined the Postmaster-General's post. Conkling had mentioned him during the visit to Mentor, though unenthusiastically, and Garfield obviously felt he would not oppose the appointment. They went first to Blaine's house, which did not escape notice, then to Garfield's rooms. The incoming President was so tired that his sense of humor returned, and he talked easily with James while friends looked for Thomas C. Platt. Garfield asked Platt if James would be acceptable to Conkling and the organization. Platt said yes, and Garfield won James' promise to support Administration policies.[84]

Once more they reckoned without Conkling. Hearing of the appointment from Platt, he and Arthur rushed to the Riggs House. While Garfield listened placidly and others sat mute, Lord Roscoe launched into a major speech, as if he were in the Senate. He did not object to James as such, he declared, but the place was not big enough for New York. And no one had consulted him; Platt could not ratify such matters. The ease with which Garfield and Blaine had won an important follower angered him. They left, and Garfield prepared for a final dinner with the Hayes' and old friends, first at the White House, then at Wormley's Hotel.

The Cabinet was barely complete, and so were the new chief magistrate's inaugural remarks. In mid-January, he still had not written an address, remarking wearily: "I have half a mind to make none. Those of the past, except Lincoln's, are dreary reading. Doubtless mine will be also." He was "jaded," and had "an unusual repugnance to writing." He wrote from scraps of paper and memory until the small hours of Inauguration Day, a tired man producing a tired document.[85]

The weather was bad, and under grey skies at noon, Garfield and Hayes rode to the Hill through bravely cheering crowds. Garfield watched Arthur take the oath in the Senate chamber, then proceeded with his party onto the East Front. He sat for a moment in one of General Washington's chairs, and saw his aged mother survey the proceedings before rising to take the oath. His speech was a collection of platitudes, offering the usual end to sectionalism if everyone obeyed federal laws. He supported gold and silver as currency, and promised to ask Congress for a civil service law of some description.

The city celebrated with the usual fireworks, but the weather chilled ardor. Things did not come alive until that night, when ladies showed their finery at an inaugural ball in the National Museum. Mrs. Garfield displayed winning ways, and wore a simple but elegant outfit without significant jewelry. Guests danced, and ate their way through a formidable ration: 1,500 pounds of turkey, 100 gallons of oysters, 50 hams, 250 gallons of coffee, and 1,500 cakes—not to mention ice cream, biscuits, and hors d'oeuvres. It was all a noisy and probably good beginning, but had tired overtones. "Hayes looked as sweet and lamb-like as possible," a politician noted, "but Garfield's face looked worn." [86]

The Garfield family had a good press, and people liked their rather homespun qualities. Reporters noted "a genial good-feeling in the air, . . ." marking the customary honeymoon between a new Administration and potential critics.[87] Most immediate attention focused on the boisterous children, their ages ranging from nine to eighteen. Distinguished guests learned to dodge bicycles hurtling down corridors, and servants once saw the President lead them in a circle around the East Room. He wrestled with the boys, and was not a firm disciplinarian.

Mrs. Lucretia Garfield, the "Crete" of her husband's letters and conversation, was his childhood sweetheart. She was still a handsome woman, with a touch of firmness. She superintended the household, and was an able hostess, though sometimes at a loss for words. Complaining justly about the shabbiness of the White House, she resorted to Mrs. Hayes' expedient of putting chairs and tables over worn spots in the carpets. Her husband could not afford extensive redecoration, and Congress stubbornly refused to renovate the decaying mansion. Clerks said Congress would act only when it collapsed on several important senators and representatives.

Garfield paid little attention to ceremonial details, but his predecessor's Temperance policy worried him. He did not share Hayes' belief, but did not want to abandon it and cause newspaper criticism. He wished the subject had never come up, as he told Sherman while asking advice. Sherman was an Ohio man too, and hesitated a moment before responding with a typical compromise. Serve your guests liquor as a necessary formality, he counseled, but announce that you remain temperate. Hayes privately hoped the Garfields would stay dry, but did not press the issue.[88] The First Family took Sherman's advice.

The President walked toward his office every morning to face ever-present office-seekers. He told friends privately that "a man elected to the presidency had no recourse but to go through bankruptcy." [89] Three days after inauguration, he complained that "The fountains of the population seem to have overflowed and Washington is inundated." [90] It was the same story day after day; congressmen and local politicians clamoring for post offices, consulships, clerkships, and favors. He told Colonel Ingersoll he would rather run an ice-house in hell than make the choices or spread disappointment. "My God!," he once shouted in exasperation, "what is there in this place that a man should ever want to get into it?" [91]

It was a wearisome business, and he made enemies with many choices. Usually the man he wanted most for a place would not take it; the men he wanted least had to have it. Sometimes he stubbornly chose someone he liked, trusted, or simply wished to reward. He sent General Lew Wallace as minister to Turkey because he enjoyed *Ben Hur*. Maybe Wallace could gather material for a sequel at The Porte. The duties were light, the atmosphere exotic, and nobody need be the wiser. Wallace did not write the book, but did not hurt the Turks, nor they him, and even got to know the Sultan.

Such trifles did not disturb Stalwarts. Customhouses interested them more than ministries in Turkey or consulships at Valparaiso. The whispering gallery of politics reported that Secretary Blaine advised Garfield more than the public realized. He usually came before formal Cabinet meetings, then left to re-enter with the other members, none the wiser. General Grant grew increasingly irritated as his recommendations disappeared into silence. He visited Garfield, and thought they had an understanding, but saw few results of it. "I will never again lend my aid to the support of a presidential candidate who has not strength enough to appear before a convention as a candidate," he soon wrote privately, "but gets in simply by the adherance of prominent candidates preferring any outsider to either of the candidates before the convention save their own." [92] His syntax was muddled, but the meaning was clear.

Blaine was genuinely fond of Garfield, but suspected his strength in the inevitable confrontation with the Stalwarts. Mugwumps and Half-Breed wirepullers like Whitelaw Reid fancied their daily letters would see the President through, but the confrontation with Conkling after James' appointment stiffened Garfield. He decided to deal with Conkling on his own terms. He would work for the party, not for New York; the Senator must give as well as receive. If he did not, the break would simply come.[93] The campaign and Cabinet-making clarified Garfield's attitude toward the party's future. Like Hayes, he saw the whole must rise above the parts. Conkling could either ride with him or walk alone.

The President would try at least to reward friends in New York without alienating Conkling. The man trapped in all the pulling and hauling was a highly respected local politician and lawyer, William H. Robertson, who earned the title "Judge" during tenure on the county bench in New York. He and Conkling were always cool, but when the Senator thwarted his gubernatorial ambitions in 1872, the Judge went into open rebellion. In 1880, he boldly opposed Conkling within the New York convention delegation, favoring first Blaine, then Garfield. Conkling now called him "my bitterest enemy in the state of New York . . ." and would flatly oppose rewarding him or his followers. Garfield knew Robertson led delegates to his standard on that famous 36th ballot, and that he must now recognize him. While assembling a Cabinet and enduring Conkling's bluster, Garfield remarked only half-jocularly that he "was tempted to appoint Judge Robertson himself, the very head and front of the anti-Conkling people," as Reid remembered.[94] He did not; but Robertson and friends deserved rewards.

That bothered Conkling, but he doubted Garfield would go that far. Blaine's ever-present shadow did infuriate him. Blaine offered to make up with Conkling; they could each rationalize it on the grounds of party harmony. Conkling refused. When emissaries said Blaine and Garfield wished to deal fairly with the New Yorkers, Lord Roscoe snapped: "Do you believe one word of that?" [95] Sure of his Cabinet post, Blaine took a quiet offensive against Conkling in New York. Harmony was impossible; the break must come. He shrewdly wished to make Conkling's own organization bring him to reason. The legislature would elect a United States Senator in January, 1881. Garfield assured Conkling it was none of his affair. Blaine said nothing publicly, as Conkling prepared the seat for Tom Platt.

Just after Christmas, Blaine conferred privately in New York with Chauncey Depew, Reid, and Robertson over how to beat Platt and choose a moderate senator. Reid journeyed to Albany to influence "our friends." On January 3, his *New York Tribune* carried a biting editorial "By Authority," announcing the new Administration would not let its New York friends go unnoticed. "The administration of President Garfield is to be an administration for the whole Republican party. It will foment no quarrels, but it will not permit its friends to be persecuted for their friendship." Reid admitted to Garfield that Blaine wrote the editorial, and thought they had a chance to beat Platt's candidacy. Less dazzling men than Blaine now counseled a firm confrontation with Conkling. Sherman argued that even if Garfield did not win the first battle, he could create public support, ultimately beat Conkling, and unify the party for constructive purposes.[96]

Tom Platt cut a curious figure in the developing crisis. As one of Conkling's ablest managers, he often spoke *in loco Roscoe*. He was clearly less enamored of the baronial manner than his chief; like Arthur, binding wounds was his specialty within the organization. Critics called him "Me Too," as an echo of Conkling's whims, but he did not shine with borrowed light alone. Shrewd, crafty, and quiet, he was an organization man interested in making wheels go around. He was patient, and watched the New York political scene like a cat at a mousehole. Some colleagues distrusted him, thinking he meant to "set up for himself," but many others, tired of Conkling's rule, urged him forward.

With or without Conkling's knowledge, he now dealt with the Half-Breeds. If they would not oppose his election, he would protect Robertson and the "loyal 17" from Conkling's vengeance. Reid thought this an ideal solution; let the machine bury its own dead. Conkling would not last forever, and Platt seemed manageable. If Conkling and Platt wished to secure the election and then renege, they played a good hand. But Blaine was still the enemy. "The art of Mr. Blaine was that he kept out of sight," an observer noted later, "and used men like Reid, Depew, Robertson and Hay to hold Garfield up to the assault on Mr. Conkling which he himself had planned." [97]

On January 16, 1881, the legislative party caucus nominated Platt. At an elegant dinner party, seated across from Mrs. Henry Adams, Conkling played his role to the hilt. The butler brought telegraphic dispatches of the balloting in Albany. There was a vote for Evarts. He held the paper aloft and sneered: "Evarts, one vote. A tear for the departing administration." [98] Two days later, Platt won the seat. Conkling continued in his public role and his weaknesses. He faced a problem familiar to successful men—he was divorced from reality. He did not see that Garfield would win the fight. Public opinion and other Republicans would combine with dissatisfied elements in his own following, in the name of a party harmony needed to meet new issues and satisfy a people restive with mere factionalism in both major parties. The great days were gone. As Tacitus said of Galba, he had a brilliant future behind him.

Garfield remained enigmatic to Conkling, but had already told friends his strategy: "I ought to be ready for a fight, but should not begin it." [99] On Sunday night, March 20, he talked with Conkling at the White House for nearly three hours. They worked out a slate of nominations acceptable to both sides. When the Senator asked about the customhouse, Garfield evaded. They would wait on that until another day. But he was firm about rewarding his friends. Conkling suggested they receive "foreign appointments." Garfield balked. "I said they did not deserve exile, but rather a place in the affairs of their own state. I will go as far as I can to keep the peace, but I will not abandon the N.Y. protestants." Without waiting for Platt's approval, Conkling asked the President to send in the appointments. On Monday, March 21, they went to the Senate. [100] The Mugwump press was furious. All of the appointees favored Conkling; the President was merely avoiding a crisis. The longer he put off the evil day, the worse it would be. More importantly, Blaine was angry. Though sick, he rose from bed on Tuesday night to talk with Garfield. When he left, a servant passed the news to Conkling.

The following day, Wednesday, March 23, a Senate clerk carried a special message to Vice-President Arthur. Conkling was writing a letter at his desk. Arthur opened the paper, paled slightly, and signaled the Senator. The reading clerk announced the President had removed Collector Merritt two years before his term expired, and nominated Judge William H. Robertson to replace him. Merritt would become consul at London. Grant's friend and biographer, Adam Badeau would leave the London consulate for Denmark, whose present occupant would go to Switzerland, whose consul would come home. It was musical chairs to put Robertson in New York's citadel of influence and patronage. Conkling turned pale, but did not look up. Arthur quietly shredded an envelope to pieces. Platt asked what it all meant. "I don't know," Conkling said absently. "All we ask is to be allowed to win in New York, and it is hard enough to do at best." [101]

In making the nominations, Garfield said: "This brings the contest to an early close, and fully recognizes the minority element." [102] The Mugwumps saw party politics. It did not help civil service reform to remove Merritt, give his job to a partisan, and shuffle European posts for political reasons. Garfield placed the specifics of civil service reform within the larger purpose of reorienting the Republican party. Conkling saw it with his usual narrowness. Garfield had violated the understood arrangement of March 20; and the President was ignoring senators and local organizations. "The nomination is the result, sir, of a perfidy without parallel," he told one inquirer. Robertson's bland public surprise, and Blaine's avowals of ignorance convinced none but the converted.[103]

In the weeks that followed, Garfield told visitors he did not need Conkling's consent to appoint the collector in New York. It was really a national office, since it dealt with most of the nation's imports. Senator Allison, in his favorite role as a go-between, told Garfield that Conkling resented the lack of attention to senatorial courtesy as much as the appointment. Were they to have four more years of Hayes? That would hurt the party more than any favoritism toward Stalwarts. Garfield stood firm. He had consulted the Stalwarts more than anyone else in the party; they remained suspicious and hostile. Nothing pleased them but full command, and he would not surrender. "He [Conkling] considers himself affronted because he was not consulted," Garfield wrote Reid. "It is a worrying struggle of two years or a decisive settlement of the question now." Like Hayes, he saw presidential and national party control at the heart of the matter. "It better be known, in the outset, whether the president is the head of the government, or the registering clerk of the senate." As for Platt's "extraordinary" views, the question of his being consulted was "wholly irrelevant, . . ." to Judge Robertson's merits for the office.[104]

The Half-Breeds became slightly hysterical. Blaine called for "a little more grape" from the *Tribune* and urged friends to write Garfield their support.[105] On March 27, Reid wrote John Hay they must beat Conkling. ". . . this is the turning point of [Garfield's] whole administration—the crisis of his fate." He shrewdly noted that a protracted struggle would disgust the public, and probably force Conkling's organization men to compromise. The President "has only to stand firm to succeed." Hay read the letter to Garfield, who nodded in agreement. "They may take [Robertson] out of the senate head-first or feet-first: I will never withdraw him." [106] The combination of Stalwart opposition and Half-Breed condescension stiffened Garfield for a pitched battle. There would be no *beau geste*.

The appointments were now embroiled in efforts to control the Senate, which the election and Cabinet selections left balanced. The Democrats first claimed control by dealing with two independents; Arthur's casting vote decided a number of issues. The key to the puzzle was Virginia's William Mahone, elected as a Readjuster, pledged to scaling down his state's reconstruction debts and instituting some economic and social reforms. Neither major party liked him; both needed his vote. As a railroad entrepreneur fond of comparing himself to Napoleon, he commanded a high price. His slight figure held a determined man, and he gained power and patronage late in the Conkling-Garfield feud, with large consequences for himself and the Republican party.

Moderate Republican senators wanted the party caucus to settle the appointment issue, smoothing over ruffled feelings after the event, but Conkling dominated the first gatherings with his old swagger. He talked to fellow senators about prerogatives, then silenced them with bombast. He told friends Garfield was a liar and coward. He said Garfield could send Robertson abroad, and he would hold his nose in the lobby while the Senate confirmed. Grant entered the picture in late April with a strong letter to Garfield. "I do claim, that I ought not to be humiliated by seeing my personal friends punished for no other offense than their friendship and support." The letter irritated Garfield. Who was Grant to command? In a calm answer, he touched the heart of the matter in terms the General had never understood. "I feel bound, as you did when President, to see to it that local quarrels for leadership shall not exclude from recognition men who represent any valuable element in the Republican party." [107]

Arthur and moderate senators tried to close the wounds Conkling opened. On the evening of April 14, the Vice-President vainly begged Garfield to withdraw Robertson for another post. He said candidly that the appointment would ruin Conkling's organization and throw the Empire State into confusion. Platt promised to confirm Robertson

for another post. Special senatorial committees tried to pacify Conkling, but he treated them to elaborate polemics. "Conkling raged and
roared like a bull of bashan for three mortal hours," Senator Henry L.
Dawes of Massachusetts told his wife after one such gathering. At
another, Lord Roscoe imperiously threatened to expose letters from
Garfield that would make him "bite the dust." The President smiled;
Conkling could print them if he liked. Dawes told the New Yorker
to let it pass; harmony must prevail. Conkling answered with the
truth: "Your medicine, Dawes, is much easier to prescribe than to
take." He could not survive capitulation. "I could not be elected a
delegate to a county convention in Oneida County." [108]

As the struggle continued, Conkling's position weakened, despite
his loud bluff. Early in May, T. B. Connery of the *New York Herald*
answered a social call from Conkling. Finding the Senator out, he
visited Arthur, who was both charming and frank. Echoing Conkling,
he said the Stalwarts would fight to the end, knowing that Blaine was
their real enemy. Arthur asked for the *Herald's* support, and Connery
hesitated. "Try a cigar," said the smiling Vice-President. "Perhaps a
puff will aid your meditations. Smoke while you meditate." Connery
hedged, and then Conkling came in, "looking quite serene and unconcerned." He started conversing calmly, but was soon denouncing
Blaine, Robertson, and Garfield. Connery left without committing
himself, but knew the visit's real significance. If Conkling was reduced
to seeking newspaper support, he was finished. [109]

On May 4, the Republicans gained Mahone's vote and control of
the Senate. Conkling urged them to confirm everyone but Robertson,
and adjourn. A day later, Garfield in effect settled the issue. He withdrew all pending appointments except Robertson's. He called senators
to the White House in a steady stream. Sherman was already managing the President's case in the upper house, thanks to frank conversations during afternoon drives. Garfield now revealed a talent for
persuasion and a forcefulness that surprised both friends and foes.
His years of intra-party compromising, knowledge of the men involved, and understanding of how both to persuade and press, reflected a growing sureness and purpose. Promises of patronage and
future influence alternately repelled and attracted haughty senators,
who knew the President was eroding their prerogatives, but appreciated many of his points. On May 9, the party caucus rejected the idea
of adjourning and carrying Robertson's nomination over until December. Garfield outmaneuvered foes, and on May 13, the game was
up. Administration leaders reported they could confirm with Democratic help. [110]

Tired, baffled, and disgusted, Conkling entertained a ceremonial solution. He would make a last effort to avoid utter humiliation. The day Robertson's name came in, Platt suggested they both resign immediately, and force the state legislature to re-elect them in a show of confidence. Only this would balk Garfield and avoid a dangerous protracted struggle. Conkling rebuked him then, but Platt's predictions were now facts, and the senior senator now consented, though without hoping to succeed.* On May 16, their resignations went to the governor in Albany. Arthur read the letters to an astonished Senate. After a moment of silence, senators scraped chairs together in small huddles, or disappeared into cloakrooms to speculate on what it all meant.

It really did not matter. Garfield's brilliant tactical move leaving Robertson's nomination alone before the Senate gave him every advantage. Party loyalty, public opinion, Executive pressures were at his disposal. The Stalwarts damned Blaine for the move, and it savored of his theatrics, but the President had considered it independently. His patience and quiet appeals to the public and Republican moderates won. Conkling overplayed his hand, and now looked both threatening and ridiculous. Constituents asked why the public business stalled over such matters, and the press shifted to Garfield. The resignations released a chorus of ridicule and resentment, two weapons Conkling could not combat. "He has acted the boy," a senator noted, "and is now trying to bully the Senate." [111] A newspaper solemnly reported that two orphans had resigned from an asylum because they got no molasses on their bread. Senator Dawes said Conkling was "a great big baby, boo-hooing because he can't have all the cake, and refusing to play any longer, [who now] runs home to his mother." [112] In this homely fashion, he saw the matter's crux. No man should refuse "to play" when the party's welfare was at stake. Lord Roscoe was now the emperor without his clothes.

Garfield dismissed the performance as "a very weak attempt at the heroic," and predicted a wave of public laughter.[113] Cartoonists drew Conkling as an exploding gas-bag, with a lesser balloon labeled "Me Too" trailing behind. Conkling walked editorial pages carrying his head under one arm. On May 18, the Senate confirmed Robertson, and adjourned two days later. "This is a great relief," Garfield noted. "The war of Conkling vs. the administration has passed the first state successfully for me." [114]

The next act was up to Conkling. He could seclude himself and

*This at least is Platt's story, in his *Autobiography*, 151ff. Other sources are less certain of Conkling's initial attitude toward the idea of resigning, though they generally agree on his inertia and listlessness during the struggle's last stages.

await the legislature's action. He listened to Arthur. The Vice-President did not resign, as some predicted, and now planned strategy in Washington. Lesser friends urged a trip to Albany; they could not afford to lose any margin of safety. The Senators' presence might save wavering legislators. Conkling opposed the idea; to canvass would seem weak. But he relented, and Arthur accompanied the dwindling band to Albany. The press rightly condemned the Vice-President's "open and active conspiring," and cartoonists pictured him as a hallboy polishing Stalwart shoes, work unworthy of his station.

The truth was that Conkling did not quite know what to do. How to escape the mess? He wished to exit somehow, telling friends he was tired of it all, and would just as soon make money practicing law as survive in a political world he no longer understood. How could they now control legislators he had dismissed with contempt for years, and who sensed his defeat? Once in Albany, he was quiet, courteous, undemanding. It was unlike him. He looked suddenly grey at the temples and rather listless. He was not even good for an old-style speech. Men he summoned came as independents, not lackeys. Lesser leaders suggested they elect him and Platt with the understanding the two would then resign and leave politics. They were obviously powerless at the beginning of an administration, and New York could not afford two senatorial ornaments.

Through May and into June, state politicians dickered and balloted. Garfield wisely remained silent. "I have fought the assumption of Mr. C. against my authority," he told his diary, "but I do not think it best to carry the fight into New York." [115] But he reminded correspondents elsewhere that "if our friends in N.Y. have the requisite sense and pluck, they can end his [Conkling's] hateful career as a politician." [116] Presidential aloofness did not keep Blaine from the fight, and Half-Breed friends established rival candidates. Godkin had unusual opportunities to score Stalwarts. "The performance is altogether the most singular one in American political history, because the chief actors in it are politicians of long experience and great repute for shrewdness, and nevertheless have blundered in their own to a degree which no 'theorist' or 'visionary' could have equalled." [117] As he watched the proceedings, Garfield concluded that Conkling had simply committed suicide in public.[118]

An endless fatuity now enfolded the Stalwarts. In the last week of June, respectable legislators in company of biased guides, climbed a ladder outside the door of Platt's hotel room, looked through the transom, and saw the ex-Senator in the arms of what gentry called "an unspeakable woman." The *Albany Argus*, a Tilden favorite, and the *New York World*, no friend of Republicanism, broke the story on July 2. Platt withdrew at once, to spare Conkling this further embarrassment.[119] Lord Roscoe watched the politicians come and go, and saw the tally sheets repeat deadlocked figures.

In Washington, Garfield was in good spirits. His wife was recovering from a severe fever, and his distractions seemed to lessen. Politically, he ignored Blaine's high-pitched advice to give all the Stalwarts a coup de grâce, and appointed several to office. He would ruin Conkling and his style of leadership, but would not crush Republicans willing to work in harmony. With victory over Conkling in sight, he felt like a trip. On the day Platt withdrew, he prepared to visit Williams College with his oldest sons.

Blaine and Garfield were now close friends and political confidants. Their qualities matched. The President offered stability to the Secretary's quick thinking, a restraining hand to his rashness. Some evenings they walked together through small parks around the White House, taking the air and escaping callers. On the evening of July 1, Garfield visited Blaine's house, jocularly remarking that he hoped the Premier could arise early enough to accompany him to Williams College. The President was taking Secretaries Windom, Hunt, and James, with members of their families. Mrs. Garfield rested at Elberon, N.J., still weak from fever, but it promised to be a good outing for all the busy men.

On July 2, the President rose early as usual, and did some handstands on an upstairs bed, to the delight of his younger sons. They wrestled on the floor and he chased them down the hall before he finished dressing and came downstairs. The office-seekers were there, and some were tired of waiting. Everyone appreciated the informality that let the President treat such men patiently, but the confusion also prompted warnings against assassination. Garfield never took such advice. The leader of a democracy could not afford isolation, and he was a fatalist. "Assassination can no more be guarded against than death by lightning," he told Sherman, "and it is not best to worry about either." [120]

On the morning of July 2, Garfield met Blaine and they drove to the railroad station. At 9:20, while walking toward the train, two shots rang out, and the President clutched his back and cried out: "Oh, my God!" For a moment, Blaine did not understand, but saw a man running away from them, and then realizing what had happened, chased him a few feet, waving his cane.° Charles J. Guiteau, the real assassin, stood calmly on the spot he had taken to shoot the President, and then let men pin him on the floor. Bystanders carried Garfield into a small waiting room. One bullet had grazed his arm, the other struck his back. He bled little, but looked deathly as he sank into shock. While awaiting medical assistance, the President remained conscious and reassured bystanders. "I don't think this is serious. I will live." [121]

The news flashed to the country almost as quickly as the tragedy occured. Conflicting reports had Garfield dead, wounded but dying, and only slightly injured. At Blaine's elegant home, a passer-by rang the bell and reported the garbled news. Mrs. Blaine and Mrs. Sherman hailed a passing cab and rushed to the White House, the former concerned for her husband's life. Pushing through crowds of hysterical and confused people, they saw the President lifted on a mattress, in the care of six strong men. As they carried him up the steps, he looked at the windows where clerks anxiously watched and waved with a smile. Once inside, Garfield asked Mrs. Blaine to attend his wife when she appeared. Lucretia Garfield arrived late that night in a hastily assembled train, passing through crossings at the amazing speed of sixty miles an hour. She took the news clamly, and Garfield reassured her in the upstairs bedroom. [122]

The Cabinet telegraphed officials throughout the country, but Vice-President Arthur heard the news from reporters as he landed in New York after a steamboat trip down the Hudson from Albany. He was stunned, and went to his friend Senator John P. Jones' home in Washington that night. The following day he appeared at the White House to offer condolences. When he entered the room where ranking officials surrounded Mrs. Garfield, cold silence flustered the usually urbane Arthur. He stood awkwardly at the threshold until someone came forward and shook his hand. He mumbled regrets to Mrs. Garfield, inquired of the President, listened to Cabinet members' advice, and returned to Jones' home. [123]

The coldness merely reflected public temper. Guiteau's motives were political; though clearly insane, he was a follower of Grant and Conkling. Bystanders recalled his saying "I am a Stalwart, and now Arthur is President," or words to that effect. The police discovered letters

°In later years, Blaine told members of his family that he believed Guiteau meant to kill him, and mistook Garfield for him because he had worn a hat similar to Blaine's. He even recalled the assassin saying at the time: "My God! I meant to shoot Blaine!" This seems very unlikely, and illustrates the divergent honest recollections that surround such events. (See Robert Cutler, *No Time for Rest* [Boston: Little, Brown and Co., 1966], 15.)

with similar sentiments on his person, with marked editorials from anti-Garfield newspapers. In Albany, the legislative struggle seemed "spiritless." Still shocked, Arthur said little, and Conkling nothing, but Stalwarts knew a lynch mob could easily dispatch them in Albany, New York, or Washington. Until the President's fate was settled, each remained in virtual seclusion. The press almost universally condemned the Stalwarts, not for inspiring Guiteau, but for creating a situation where such animosity reigned. Attacks on the spoils system increased, beginning a public demand to end office-seeking that produced men like Guiteau. As Garfield's life hung in the balance, some people thought it was a plot to elevate Arthur. That notion soon passed, but the prospect of his accession haunted political moderates.[124]

The President's condition remained uncertain, and physicians could not locate the bullet in his back. A strong constitution balanced fluctuating strength that kept him an invalid all summer, while raising expectations of his survival. In mid-July doctors reported he would recover unless massive infection occurred, but he was unable to transact any public business. Professional nurses replaced amateur help and a crude refrigeration device cooled the humid air in his room. The doctors looked puzzled, administered customary remedies, but hesitated to operate.

Politics went on in Albany, and the Cabinet transacted business in Washington. Garfield's secretary made a rubber stamp of his signature for routine mail; the President actually signed only one document during his illness—an extradition request. A weary Conkling called at the White House, subdued and courteous, but realizing that his future was closed, whatever happened to the President. He played out this final hand of cards. On July 16, the legislature chose Warner Miller for Platt's seat, and Garfield exclaimed "Thank God!" On July 22, they named Elbridge G. Lapham to replace Conkling, and he was out of public life. The President was magnanimous and offered to do anything reasonable for him, but Lord Roscoe only wanted silence.[125]

The public alternated between hope and despair for the President, as a hot summer enveloped the country. Daily bulletins were conflicting, but in mid-August, infection began to wear down his strength and will to resist. The doctors probed for the bullet, further weakening the patient. Antiseptic surroundings and total rest might have let Garfield recover, since the bullet only grazed the spinal column and missed vital organs. Blaine vainly tried to persuade physicians they were looking for the bullet in the wrong place, even demonstrating its path on a dummy. Garfield patiently endured it all, but sometimes asked despondently: "I wonder if all this fight against death is worth the little pinch of life I will get anyway?" [126] Daily papers carried his every saying, and intimate details of his physical decline. Many people like William E. Chandler shrank from such reportage, and urged Blaine and the Cabinet to restore decorum at the sick bed. The patient himself wearied of it. "I should think the people would be tired of having me dished up to them in this way." [127] On September 6, a special train took him to Elberon, New Jersey, for cool sea air and a change from noisy Washington. He stood the trip well, but doctors could not predict how long he would be incapacitated even if he recovered.

Vice-President Arthur passed the summer in his New York home on Lexington Avenue. He bore himself well, and received regular information from Attorney-General MacVeagh. Late in July, he wrote in his sprawling hand on black-bordered stationery, almost a plea to avoid the presidential responsibility. "My heart is full of deep anxiety. May God in his infinite goodness bring us safely out of this great peril; and my faith is strong that He will." [128] He would not visit Washington unless the Cabinet advised it, to avoid upsetting the patient or stirring a newspaper war.

Still they waited. Garfield seemed momentarily better at Elberon, and even sat up in bed, but on the afternoon of September 19 he sank in a spasm of pain that quickly led to a coma. At 10:35 P.M., after seventy-nine days of anxiety and suffering, he expired on the anniversary of Chickamauga. The Cabinet wired Arthur that Garfield was sinking, and the Vice-President paced nervously around his home. Toward midnight, a reporter rang the bell and told a servant the President had died. Arthur overheard, and called out: "Oh, no, it cannot be true. It cannot be. I have heard nothing." The reporter insisted and Arthur went on in tears: "I hope—My God, I do hope it is a mistake." He walked back to the study, facing silent friends. The bell rang again, and a messenger passed him an envelope. Its contents announced Garfield's death, and the Cabinet advised him to take the oath of office at once. Friends went out to find a judge, and someone looked up the oath's wording. Justice John R. Brady of the New York Supreme Court soon arrived and administered the oath. Arthur wrote out a proclamation calling Congress into special session to arrange the succession should he die en route to Washington, and mailed it to himself at the White House. On arrival, he destroyed it.[129]

In the capital, Arthur stayed with Jones, while friends arranged a formal, if simple inauguration before suitable government officials. On September 22, he went to the Vice-President's room in the Capitol, and repeated the oath for Chief Justice Waite. Former Presidents Grant and Hayes, General Sherman, Cabinet members, and ranking congressmen watched in silence. Arthur was pale, soberly dressed, and formal. A brief "inaugural address," reflected his best qualities of firm management, dispatch, and efficiency.[130]

The inevitable state funeral proceeded. On September 21, Garfield's body lay in state at the Capitol, while thousands passed in silent homage. The cortege entrained for Cleveland and the burial on September 23. Silent people lined the railroad tracks, and the Western Reserve's population crowded Cleveland for the ceremonies.* There was talk of a suitable tomb. Former President Hayes would direct a public subscription. Behind the scenes, politicians remarked that Conkling's destruction was Garfield's real monument.†

To his credit, Conkling retreated into silence. "The death of Garfield sealed the lips of Mr. Conkling," a colleague said. The ex-Senator told friends: "How can I speak into a grave? How can I battle with a shroud? Silence is a duty and a doom." [131] He fell easily into the chill silence of time. Though he became a familiar figure in the narrow circles of corporation law, Conkling remained out of politics. Of an evening, reporters and social diners-out sometimes saw him with a few friends in a quiet restaurant. The Hyperion curl turned gray, but he stood erect and walked firmly. His eyes no longer flashed much fire, and he curbed the famous tongue. Soon he was "a gorgeous reminiscence." [132]

Arthur entered the White House amid fears that Conkling would be the power behind the throne. There was loose talk he would get the Treasury post. In 1882, as a gesture, Arthur offered him a Supreme Court seat. Conkling declined, briefly reminding the President his talents were better suited to practicing than to weighing the law. A small but devoted band of "Oneida Stalwarts" in upstate New York waited for Blaine. As 1884 approached, Conkling's name appeared briefly in the presidential sweepstakes. He did not sneer; he had learned to smile a little at Fate. "Why, you might as well set a corpse

---

*Throughout Garfield's illness, Guiteau remained heavily guarded in Washington's jail. Despite his obvious insanity, the District authorities prosecuted him for murder in November. He was convicted and sentenced to death in January, 1882. Legal appeals failing, he was hanged on June 30, 1882.

†Mrs. Garfield retired to private life without commenting on the political aspects of her husband's death. In 1884, consoling Mrs. Blaine for her husband's defeat in the presidential election, which both attributed to Conkling's enmity, Mrs. Garfield said: "For you, personally, my dear friend, I cannot be sorry. The treacherous foe did not lurk in camp to help elect Mr. Blaine, and with his diabolic hatred then arm the assassin." (Mrs. Garfield to Mrs. Blaine, November 18, 1884, Blaine LC.)

up in a window to look at a funeral procession go by as to nominate me for the office of president of the United States." [133] To some he remained a great figure, if not a wise politician. The usual American feeling for the underdog took an ironic turn in his direction. Some men still praised his past. To one such he smiled: "Ah! there was a time sir, when that confession would have deeply moved me; but now I am impassive and have scarcely any longer, as the Declaration of Independence says, 'a decent regard for the opinions of mankind.' " [134] A few public occasions came his way, but Roscoe Conkling went from fame to power to obscurity almost in an instant, and the latter in good measure at his own wish.

His fall was a larger event in American politics than most commentators noted. There would be other political bosses, but he was the last of a type. Future leaders commanded larger and more varied constituencies, responding to human material needs through politics. Their strength reflected loyalty to an organization and a national party. The difference between Conkling and Platt, his heir, was striking. Platt had a firm sense of organizational loyalty, and never arrogantly demanded personal obedience from followers. The organization covered all. Men rose from the ranks, but did not forget them. It was a fundamental part of nationalizing American politics.

Garfield's tragic death obscured much of this. Arthur's accession as an apparent opponent complicated the change. The whole process thwarted Blaine, who stood to profit most from the transition. "Ifs" are always captivating in history. Shrewd analysts like William E. Chandler saw that if Garfield recovered, he could command loyalty and allegiance from public opinion and the party. He had made his point before the assassination; that event solidified emotions to his advantage. "This worship will make him all-powerful if he lives." [135] Garfield's youth, vigor, growing power as President, and appealing image among a people addicted to political men as symbols of deeper aspirations, might end the Republican party's minority status. But Garfield died. Opponents took an obviously interim command. They would drift, not consolidate. Both parties seemed tired, and the circumstances of Garfield's death tarnished politics. Conkling's fall was part of a larger process, the destruction of an older personal style to which parties could not safely return. Blaine and the Half-Breeds saw this, and began a strategic attack on that system. They won only a tactical victory. The great battles lay ahead. Guiteau's bullet killed more than a president.

IV

☆☆☆☆☆☆ ☆☆☆☆☆☆☆☆☆☆☆☆☆☆☆

Arthur

☆☆☆☆☆☆ ☆☆☆☆☆☆☆☆☆☆☆☆☆☆☆

The nation buried its martyred President, and did not quite know what to expect from a new Administration. The long death watch, Arthur's modesty, and Conkling's fall, softened public criticism of the Stalwarts. Harsh accusations turned to apprehension that a fresh political struggle might start at the beginning of a full presidential term. The public seemed tired, and might welcome an interim Administration, even of this length. But politicians were fearful. Nearly all had finally acquiesced in Garfield's anti-Stalwart crusade. Would Arthur take vengeance? "The strange revolution that brings Arthur into the presidential office tends to make a burlesque of political life," Sherman wrote Hayes, expressing a common feeling among Republican moderates tired of fighting to save their party.[1]

The press gingerly approached Arthur with the attitude, "give him a chance." Avoiding divisive problems, the papers speculated about the private man. They usually described him as "a magnificent specimen of manhood," for he stood six feet, wore elegant sideburns, dressed in high fashion, and exuded an air of weary experience.[2] He was now fifty-one, and boasted both of humble beginnings and of overcoming them. His father was a Scotch-Irish Baptist preacher, whose duties carried him around northern New England, where Chester was born in Fairfield, Vermont. The young Arthur displayed talents that later made him a political organizer. "When Chester was a boy," an old friend reminisced, "you might see him in the village street after a shower, watching boys building a mud dam across the rivulet in the roadway. Pretty soon, he would be ordering this one to bring stones, another sticks, and others sods and mud to finish the dam; and they would all do his bidding without question. But he took good care not to get any of the dirt on his hands."[3]

He looked at the world through slightly closed eyes, as if most things were comfortably out of focus. Perhaps it was fear, insecurity, or dislike of people. In any event, he soon preferred abstract management to participation in daily events. At Union College he studied the usual classics, mathematics, pure sciences, and ancient history. It was a duty, not a preference, and he often missed classes. He lacked the gift for attack and lucid argument, but easily assimilated information from other people, and presented it with a dry, almost bored comprehension that made him a good student on paper. He practiced law in New York City without attaining fame. Arthur took an interest in Abolition, and figured in several prominent legal cases dealing with runaway slaves, but he was never a firebrand, and gained no adverse publicity.[4]

A generation that savored titles called him "General Arthur," though he commanded figures instead of men, and mastered shipping schedules, not cavalry routes, during the war. He was an early Republican and displayed his talents in managing New York's war effort. In peacetime, he virtually disappeared in the state party's internal management. After 1867 he was increasingly important as Conkling's special pacifier, and fought effectively with brandy glass and cigars. He managed campaign funds, subordinate organizers, and a vital local organization with a larger ideal of undefined but attractive Republicanism. "As a politician, he was brainy, thorough, careful, and devoted to research and minutiae," noted a co-worker in the vineyards.[5]

Arthur gradually attracted attention from powerful men. In 1868, he worked for Grant, while solidifying Conkling's new organization. He brushed the Tweed Ring, but without lasting impression, and remained a steadfast Republican, dedicated to making wheels that went around. In 1871, he somewhat reluctantly accepted the collectorship of New York, and for seven years combined administrative skills and a personal honesty that made him avoid even the appearance of evil. "If I had misappropriated five cents, and on walking down-town saw two men talking on the street together, I would imagine they were talking of my dishonesty, and the very thought would drive me mad," he once confessed, revealing an inner desire for approval of others, even in a world he disliked.[6] Personal detachment created the skills of objectivity. As Mrs. Blaine saw, he had a knack for "seeming to do things, while never putting his hands or his mind near them."[7]

The public thought it knew him in 1881, having passed a summer of suspense over the succession, but it read the chaff of newspaper speculation and personal gossip, not solid analysis. Despite his familiar

name and debated activities, people did not know the inner man. His
manners were an effective defense against life. "His personal bearing
was princely and incomparable," Senator Ingalls of Kansas wrote, "and
no one left him after even the briefest interview without a sentiment
of personal regard." [8] He sometimes kept guests from the inland political seas to talk of local politics, elections, people; but his heart was
not much in it.

Years of inner-party work kept him from understanding anything
but the mechanics of politics. He never comprehended the appeals of
a personality the public calls its own. He was not the hail-fellow-well-
met, or good-old-boy politician any more than Conkling, though for
different reasons. "He was never effusive or demonstrative in his greetings," a reporter said, "but always quiet, genial, and cordial." [9] It was
the kind of greeting men did not quite trust, seeming contrived. Arthur
divided his public and private personalities, and remained enigmatic
to everyone. "Though 'one of the boys' when with 'the boys'," Tom
Platt said with frustration, "he never lost his poise. He possessed a
rare faculty of adapting himself to conditions, that made him a good
'mixer.' In that he was the antithesis of Conkling. Arthur was a
diplomat." [10]

He drew a mixed press. Unlike Garfield, he had no appealing family.
A widower, he lived with a teen-age daughter, Ellen, and a college-age
son, "Young Alan." "Nell" studied with private tutors, and the President repelled all attempts to exploit her in the press. Young Alan
followed his father's social footsteps without a sense of proportion,
wining and dining his way through life. Private tutors, piano lessons,
and French grammar did not make good newspaper gossip; nor did the
President's frosty manner when the subject of his children was mentioned by visiting reporters. He was no Garfield, either to exploit his
background or wear it naturally. That was part of his problem in
public relations. He came from humble folk, but preferred to forget
them. It was almost un-American. "The truth is, the president was not
a generally popular man," a White House servant recalled. "He was
always courteous in his official relations, with just a touch of distance."
Dealing with rustic politicos might revive a personal origin he preferred to forget. He was silent to criticism, and "took no trouble to
contradict rumors, or to ingratiate himself with those who had started
them." [11]

Arthur's placid elegance was out of touch with American politics.
He was certain to fail as a national party leader because he simply
did not know how to approach the task. He could not retain Blaine

and the astute Half-Breed managers who might have used him for more than political transition. Just as obviously, he could not lean on Stalwarts. He was a man without a party, lacking means to overcome the handicap in public estimation. He took refuge in stoicism. "This is the damnedest world," he once sighed after a wearisome hour of patronage talk.[12] Arthur liked the appearance of power more than its substance. He designed a presidential flag, enjoyed military trumpets, and was at his best on state occasions. The ceremony, station, and opulence fed his emotional nature. But though he would suggest many appealing and necessary things, he lacked the capacity to see them through into law. Critics thought this a strange weakness in a career politician, but the truth was simple: Arthur was less a politician than an organizer and administrator. He had no common touch, no saving interest in events beyond immediate hearing. He saw life, perhaps defensively, as an organizational chart, a game of chess without human pieces. Events fortified his detachment. He departed as he came, alone.

Arthur had held lucrative public offices, making a good deal of money which he invested wisely. He enjoyed spending it, and had a reputation for "high living." Mrs. Garfield took her time moving; he was not anxious to enter the Executive Mansion, having seen its rickety interior. Unlike Congress he did not cavil at refurbishing it, and used the six weeks after Garfield's death to renovate the building. Consulting leading decorators and architects, he made it livable in the reigning steamboat palace decor. He could not rebuild it, but whitened the sepulcher. While caretakers carted off twenty-four wagonloads of junk and memorabilia dating from John Adams, Arthur measured floors and climbed ladders to inspect ceilings. Using a cane to point, he brushed past painters, carpenters, and tile-setters to direct installation of carpeting, new ceiling moldings, potted plants, and an elegant billiard room in the basement. He chose paint for the walls, and ordered an ornate and expensive glass screen from Tiffany's to separate state rooms from cold winds and rambunctious callers. When he moved in on December 9, 1881, the old house looked better. Arthur rounded up a staff equal to the redecoration, versed in French cuisine and flower arrangement. There was no talk of Temperance.

The period of official mourning for Garfield passed, but Christmas holidays produced no glittering receptions or parties. Arthur did not entertain that first season. Not until March, 1882, did formal receptions and state dinners begin. They soon took on European style in both extent and taste, and visiting diplomats looked forward to social eve-

nings with the chief magistrate. Arthur sustained his reputation as a
"night person," and irritated waiting politicians accustomed to Hayes'
and Garfield's early hours. He usually rose at 10 A.M., ate a Conti-
nental breakfast while dressing with the aid of a valet, then went to the
office. Between noon and 2 P.M. he saw important people. The Cabinet met regularly on Tuesday and Friday. At noontime on Wednesday,
Thursday, and Saturday he saw humbler visitors, to offset an apparent
lack of democracy. With family and friends, he stood genially in the
receiving line, but clearly wished to be elsewhere. Luncheon was
light, but dinner was a different matter. He might scoop up a dozen
friends on a late drive, and sit them down to twelve courses, finishing
at 2 A.M. over brandy and cigars. His younger sister, Mrs. John Mc-
Elroy, was hostess during the winter months. Formal dinners and
state occasions might lengthen if he liked the company; if not, he
arranged an early end to avoid boredom. During the day, he carried
a set of dummy documents to rustle importantly when a visitor's appointment expired, or conversation lagged.[13]

He dressed in the era's highest fashion. Cutaways with colored
piping, ruffled shirts, fancy shoes, a forest of canes and an array of
hats filled the closets. He ordered clothes in large lots and kept a
valet busy the year around. The papers described a "Regal Retinue"
of servants, opposing politicians counted his apparel changes, and
Democrats sneered at his "lovely coats, charming vests, and angelic
trousers." [14]

Arthur's generation did not believe in exercise, and his sedentary
life added girth. The sumptuous dinners and fine wines did not help
the problem, and even summer's inevitable tour of the hot-springs
circuit did not tone up his step. He liked fishing, but wore his best
even in a sylvan setting, and soon lost a taste for the rod and reel
because he could not shake off reporters and sightseers. He picnicked
in Washington's parks, and outside the city, with friends and a few
politicians. But the chef's ingenuity at the picnic basket made the
outdoor fare little less spartan than what he served indoors. The
President's closest brush with exertion came in a carriage, swaying
pleasantly over city streets and suburban roads and laden with genial
friends and a suitable basket. Arthur never drove, leaving that to
better hands and eyes. The equippage fitted his taste and station, reflecting an English style in dark harness with silver tooling, deep green
lap rugs, polished coachwork, and fine chestnut horses.

The theater was a favorite amusement, and he usually entered
fashionably late, forcing the company to suspend action while the

orchestra played "Hail to the Chief." The public in Washington, New
York, and the watering places saw a good deal of him, but his sense
of privacy forbade cultivating newsmen. Rumors of free drinking and
visiting ladies filled gossip columns, and sometimes brought out his
temper. When a Temperance reformer asked if he drank, he snapped:
"Madam, I may be President of the United States, but my private life
is nobody's damned business." A friend described a mutual acquaintance in his cups, and Arthur said with a languid firmness that "no
gentleman ever sees another gentleman drunk." [15]

These bits and pieces formed a somewhat inaccurate public image.
He seemed more interested in play than politics, and it always surprised the press when he uttered a sound thought. He was neither
lazy nor ignorant, but keenly realized the situation's limitations. A
shrewd reporter noted the problem: Arthur was a new type in American politics, more interested in what he had become than where he
started life. He was "the 'city man,' the metropolitan gentleman, the
member of clubs, the type that is represented by the well-bred and
well-dressed New Yorker; the quiet man who wears a scarf and a pin
and prefers a sack coat to the long tailed frock coat that pervades
politics, and a derby hat to the slouch [hat] that seems to be regarded
in some quarters of this Union as something no statesman should be
without. This is a novel species of president." [16]

Hayes feared Arthur would inaugurate a reign of "liquor, snobbery,
and worse." [17] The "worse" was obviously women, and he was an ideal
catch. Hostesses made endless hopeful matches, and the papers re-
tailed news, usually fanciful, of every lady in his company. Mothers
with eligible daughters envisioned neighbors' envy from the East
Room. Mrs. Blaine reported that his levees smacked of Louis XIV;
and Mrs. Henry Adams referred to "our good King Arthur," receiving
pretty girls in the grandest manner: ". . . it was more like royalty than
anything I have ever seen." [18] True enough, the mail brought marriage
proposals, but the President did not answer them. There were rumors
of temporary arrangements, but he remained permanently unattached.°
Scandalmongers said he placed fresh flowers before a woman's picture

---

°Arthur did have at least one mysterious lady friend, a stranger who pelted
him with blunt but sometimes sagacious advice. Her name was Julia Sands, and
they apparently met at least once while he was President, at his suggestion. She
was fond of sending him such frank advice as: "What is there to admire in mediocrity? Why do you take such comfort in half measures? Does it never strike you that
there must be back of them only half a mind—a certain half-heartedness—in fact,
only half a man? Why do you not do what you do with your whole soul?—or have
you only half of one?" (Julia Sands to Arthur, May [?], 1882, Arthur LC.)

every morning, but retreated to silence at the news that it was his dead wife's portrait.

All this personal reporting made good copy for the Sunday supplements as the first winter under Arthur passed into an election year, but politicians were interested in more mundane things, like survival. Most important of all, how would he manage the Republican party? And who among his old friends would sit near the throne?

The almost universal response to Arthur's accession was an amazed: "Chet Arthur, President of the United States! Good God!"[19] More sober estimates simply outlined the situation's dilemmas. "However favorable and hopeful the general judgement of his own capacity and purpose may be," the *New York Times* observed, "it cannot be claimed that his personal merits brought him to the position of high responsibility which he has just assumed."[20] The Mugwumps were the most nervous observers. "The prevailing opinion seems to be that [the new Administration] will be Stalwart," Godkin noted, "or in other words, will be composed of persons who admire General Grant in politics as well as war, and think Mr. Conkling a very great man."[21]

Arthur heard the echoes of all this speculation, and his past seemed to confirm these predictions. He stayed with Senator Jones while the White House was remodeled. Conkling, Platt, and Cameron visited discreetly, and General Grant's carriage was not entirely absent from Jones' doorstep. Arthur's silence seemed to give consent, but he was a proud and able man, and meant to avoid consciously splitting the party. He had never truckled to Conkling, and did not think Grant was pure gold. His view of politics went beyond the customhouse, or Roscoe Conkling's whims.

Stalwarts actually thought Conkling would receive the long-coveted Treasury post when public opinion calmed down. They tried to remove Robertson and restore the old order in New York. Conkling went to Arthur's hotel when he visited New York early in the administration, and talked for five mortal hours. Reporters pressed him in the lobby, but Lord Roscoe displayed a dark face: "I bid you all good evening."[22] As the months lengthened, and Arthur did little to reward Conkling's friends and restore happy times, the ex-Senator said pungent things about his old colleague. "I have but one annoyance with the administration of President Arthur, and that is, that, in contrast with it, the administration of Hayes becomes respectable, if not heroic."[23] Arthur handled Conkling gingerly, giving him the ceremonial offer of a Supreme Court appointment, and occasionally doing a trifling favor for the "Oneida Stalwarts." But he agreed with early comment that if he was "advised or led by Senator Conkling," the Republican party would simply leave him.[24]

General Grant got even fewer favors. He told friends at first that Arthur often asked his advice on appointments. Arthur seldom took it, assuming deference would satisfy Grant. The President intended to build a following, and after a while Grant was as privately critical as Conkling. Tom Platt was somewhat sympathetic, but got few tidbits. Arthur began to lean toward other professionals, like William E. Chandler. In the end, Platt remarked sourly that "he did little or nothing as president to cure the sores from which the Republicans of his own state were smarting." The Stalwarts did not like to hear him say he "was morally bound to continue the policy of the former president." [25]

Arthur did not quite intend to do that. He disliked Mugwumps, and did not oppose competent partisanship. He suffered from a handicap common in the period, simple isolation from most of his party. He spent a lifetime in New York politics, and despite personal urbanity, remained provincial. It was hard for him to imagine the growing area west of Philadelphia, or the brawling politics of Iowa and Kansas. New York's factional fights occurred in a curious kind of local vacuum, and it was too late for Arthur to master the arts of popular appeal. Baby-kissing and county fairs were not his forte.

He tried to learn secondhand, entertaining men like Ohio's Governor Charles Foster; talking of an afternoon with Senator Sherman; reading newspaper clippings datelined in the Midwest. He assured everyone that a national picture and the whole party were his chief concerns, but he learned little from visitors and correspondents, and fell back on his own brand of machine politics. As Chauncey Depew said, old cohorts found that "while their leader was still their friend, he was president of the United States." [26] Privately, he told a trusted reporter that "the American people would never have chosen him if it had been thought that he would reach the presidency, and so it was for him to show that he was worthy. The only way was for him to be the president of the whole people and nobody's servant." [27] He quickly dispelled fears he was a Stalwart front man, and the public appreciated it, but he developed no sterner image, and seemed an awkward compromiser.

Everyone expected changes. He could not retain Garfield's advisers. "There may be no sudden changes, no hasty over-turnings, but when the new administration has put on its permanent character, it will not

be a continuation of that begun the 4th of March [1881]." [28] Congress
came into session in December, and faced Arthur's first annual message. It was a hodgepodge made up in the departments, offering information, not analysis; reassurance, not proposals. Lack of time
permitted little else, but Hayes thought this might be the new Administration's tone. Do nothing the people did not demand. With
prosperity returning and the party quiet for the moment, "this caution
is politically wise. We want to be let alone. King Log is not a bad
king sometimes." [29]

There were ill omens, of course. Few days passed without reports
of feuding between Secretary Blaine's friends and Arthur. Blaine enjoyed the State Department and all its unseen privileges. He had
ready access to Garfield, and the post traditionally carried great status
and political authority. His wife, who so lightly dismissed Arthur's
regal manner, was an inveterate hostess, combining good talk with
shrewd judgment. Ambitious for her husband, she saw the State portfolio as a way-station to the top.

The nation was building new quarters for its diplomatic services,
and a lavish structure rose slowly near the White House. Its profusion
of pillars, statuary, and windows would house the three great federal
services—State, Navy, and War—by mid-decade. The foreign service
was small, over-worked, and often unequal to its tasks. Compared
both to the country's needs and foreign counterparts, it was an amateur operation. The conduct of foreign policy was so basically political
in the United States, that Congress frowned on an expert service.
Blaine confronted the departmental apparatus with dismay and realism. Red tape, slowness, and verbose evasion irritated the Man from
Maine more than his predecessor. Evarts could concoct a joke; Blaine
detoured around officialdom, and only complicated matters. The bu-
reaucratic mind accepted present evils and avoided future possibilities.
Blaine's temperament was exactly opposite. He teemed with ideas,
some good, many dangerous or inexpedient; but the permanent staff
usually tried to bury them all.

Lack of trained and sympathetic subordinates hampered Blaine
more than rashness or official lethargy. Despite Executive pressures,
Congress refused to establish a diplomatic corps equipped to report
on trade, diplomacy, and attitudes abroad. The consular list was a
burying ground for political liabilities. Low pay, bad posts, and tedious
work made John Hay compare it to the Catholic Church, "fit only for
celibates." Public preference for action over negotiation, and suspicion

of anti-republican pomp, did not increase efficiency or accuracy. "The general idea of the diplomatic service is that it is a soft berth for wealthy young men who enjoy court society," Frank Carpenter wrote the folks at home.[30]

Blaine entered office with many disadvantages. Political enemies and a virulent opposition press would attack anything he did. Opponents loosely called him "Jingo Jim," and predicted a reign of nerves in the State Department.[31] Blaine was openly anti-British, and jealous of American prerogatives in the Western Hemisphere, but was neither rash nor ignorant. He had no detailed foreign policy, though both enemies and friends asserted otherwise, but his attitude of mind welcomed change. Coming from Maine, he had close knowledge of shipping and transportation that fortified a growing interest in world trade. He had traveled throughout the United States and knew the country's industrial complex needed foreign markets. He knew the public would credit gains in foreign policy to him and the Republican party. A reasonable nationalism abroad might coordinate with the party's growing nationalism at home and enlarge its appeal to a changing electorate. Blaine's foreign policy was no more political than his predecessors', however. He genuinely wished to increase world markets, stabilize the nations around the United States, and begin to assert American interests. In this, as in so many things, his enemies and personal flair combined to thwart good intentions. The irony was compounded, for only a man of his dash and public reputation could have opened the subject of foreign affairs to meaningful public debate. He could only hope to build for another day and other men.

As the party fight with Conkling brewed, simmered, and then boiled through the summer of 1881, he conducted foreign policy while not writing notes to Garfield. He moved first in Latin America, a traditional sphere of influence. Continuing Evarts' pressures on Britain to re-negotiate the Clayton-Bulwer Treaty, he firmly insisted that sooner or later the United States would build an Isthmian canal. The British delayed, and squabbling between Mexico and Central American neighbors made Blaine hesitate to press the issue, lest the United States become entangled in Latin conflicts.

By the fall of 1881, a newspaper war swirled around Blaine because of alleged intervention in Chilean affairs.[32] That long, mountain-spined nation on South America's western shore held a strange significance for American diplomats. Though small, it contained a relatively stable governing class that promised to make it important in Latin American affairs. Nitrate and guano resources supported a growing naval power, and invited attacks from other countries, which the Chileans used as pretexts to dominate neighbors. It was not incredible for American naval officers to suggest that Chilean warships might threaten a future canal, carry influence across the Pacific, or endanger California. The United States Navy ranked with China's and was not a force in world politics.

More important to a man of Blaine's temperament and background, Chile's developing wealth invited European exploitation. British and French companies supervised nitrate extraction. American capital could not compete, and it was easy to raise in Washington the bogey of Chile and South America dominated from London and Paris in the future. Blaine became embroiled in the War of the Pacific, a long running fight between Chile and Peru, largely because he feared European intervention on one side or the other. Incompetent subordinates on the scene sometimes distorted his view. Nature had not made South America a preserve of United States investment or authority, as the British insisted, but in general, Blaine's attitude toward this first Chilean crisis reflected a logical belief that the United States must assert influence in areas whose development and future power it might reasonably hope to guide.

This view of Latin America produced a comprehensive policy that foes labelled "jingoism," and friends called "Pan-Americanism." By mid-summer, 1881, Blaine wanted to call a conference of American states to establish a system to arbitrate disputes in the area. He wished to prevent rivalries among small Latin countries that would invite European exploitation or intervention, perpetuate political instability, and retard economic growth. The proposed organization would mature in years of trial and error, but Blaine obviously wished to make the United States tacitly dominant, and avoid armed intervention in Latin America.

The stability and order this system produced would steadily enlarge the whole region's material wealth, make it dependent on United States goods while establishing its own industrialism, and avoid European domination. It would also balance the power relations among all the Latin American nations and the United States, and ease cultural and social exchange. The proposal symptomized Blaine's growing interest in world markets for American goods, but it reflected the general attitude of his generation even more. Like so many proposals to cope with change and uneven development, the idea seemed radical but was inherently conservative. It bespoke a profound belief in material well-being over moral rhetoric, favoring orderly development within a stabilized and clearly defined *system*. To the United States, the proposal was eminently sound, but Latin American republics opposed it as a step toward "Yankee imperialism." Blaine's reliance on materialism overlooked nationalism, bound to wreck any proposal based on intricate balances of power among nations.

Blaine had suspended his activities during much of Garfield's illness, and hesitated to place the idea before Arthur after September. Increasing frustration in dealing with individual Latin American states and the desire to leave a record if he resigned from the Cabinet, impelled him to gain Arthur's approval. The President consented, and on November 29, 1881, Blaine issued the formal invitations for a Pan-American Congress to meet later at a specified date. Arthur knew little, if anything, about the plan, but it raised doubts. It was modest, but who knew where it might lead? It required congressional cooperation, and might open dangerous debates. Sooner or later, it would involve abstruse subjects like the tariff and diplomatic service, armaments, and trade. Was it not too large a start? He privately concluded the Administration should begin piecemeal and work toward a general idea, not the reverse. A phlegmatic nature like Arthur's shrank from a challenge that Blaine welcomed.

Politics naturally entered in. Secretary Windom's voluntary departure from the Treasury on October 27 signaled a revamped Administration, and it was only a matter of time until Blaine left. When the congressional session began in December, friends tiptoed around dormant animosities. "Congress is in session," Mrs. Blaine wrote her daughter, "so we are daily expecting your father's head to roll in the basket."[33] Arthur baffled Blaine. He remained courteous and cooperative; nothing indicated he wanted the Secretary to resign. But "He never asked me to stay—how can I remain?" Blaine told John Watson Foster.[34] On December 12, Blaine resigned, and Arthur made Frederick T. Frelinghuysen his successor. The change suited Blaine's enemies, already clouding the scene with vituperation aimed to thwart a presidential bid in 1884. "The more we learn of Mr. Blaine's performance during his occupation of the State Department," Charles Dana said, "the less we see for regretting that his tenure of office was brief."[35] Frelinghuysen, scion of a New Jersey dynasty, suited "conservatives." The *Springfield Republican* said: "Mr. Frelinghuysen is understood to hold that the American eagle should not strain his naturally fine voice by shrill and prolonged screaming on small occasions."[36] The new Secretary told friends that Blaine wanted war with Chile, and the Arthur Administration would have none of it. Godkin welcomed Frelinghuysen as a dull but safe choice; he had no "sensational tend-encies." [37]

Loss of power was a bitter pill, but the success of his ideas would console Blaine. By January, however, Arthur was retreating. The State Department did not press the Pan-American issue, and the White House said nothing. Blaine was upset, but adopted "the patient dignity of perfect silence." [38] On February 3, he broke the tense calm with a remarkable open letter, asking the President to explain his intentions. He warned that abandoning the conference would invite European powers to enter Latin America. Border disputes and internal conflicts threatened fresh wars and rivalries among the southern republics. Blaine had sent the invitations with Arthur's consent, and the matter could easily become bipartisan. The proposal was a bold and neces-sary beginning to secure America's future in the hemisphere: [39]

> I do not say, Mr. President, that the holding of a Peace Congress will necessarily change the currents of trade, but it will bring us into kindly relations with all the American nations; it will promote the reign of law and order; it will increase production and consumption; it will stimulate the demand for articles which American manufacturers can furnish with profit. It will, at all events, be a friendly and auspicious beginning in the direction of American influence and American trade in a large field which we have hitherto neglected, and which has been practically monopolized by our commercial rivals in Europe.

The Administration did not reply. Frelinghuysen remarked at a dinner party that "Blaine may quarrel with me if he likes but I shall not with him." [40] On April 18, Arthur tossed the problem to Congress, asking its considered opinion on a complicated subject he said he had not understood when first agreeing with Blaine. The move added little to his stature, but was a backhanded way of spreading responsibility for withdrawing the commitment. Between April 24 and 27, Blaine testified before a House committee investigating the Chilean problem, and heatedly argued with Democrat Perry Belmont and others. Words like "ass," "poltroon," "servile parrot," "pygmy," and "a presumptuous little cur" filled the air. The subject, perhaps to Arthur's relief, sank in a mire of accusation and recrimination. Blaine rightly insisted he did nothing without Garfield's and Arthur's knowledge and consent, and aired his views in an editorial signed "Hickory" in the *New York Tribune*.

By summer, the issue was dead, and Blaine defeated. Inertia tri-umphed over vigor; caution thwarted imagination. Blaine made only a feeble precedent. He was the only man able to explain such an idea to the American people; irony, events, and his own personality thwarted the work. Latin American governments greeted Arthur's action with quiet relief; they did not favor growing American power. Arthur was not an "isolationist." He would not give Blaine a winning issue, but he sought to avoid entanglements in Latin America. He hesitated to found an international organization whose weak members could collectively out-vote the United States. Nor did he want to alienate Great Britain, while trying to revise the Clayton-Bulwer Treaty. Like Blaine, he favored commercial expansion, but preferred separate dealings to a general system. At the end of his term, he presented a group of treaties to the Senate, and was rewarded with silence for the effort. Neither attitude on Pan-Americanism won the day.[41]

Blaine was in an emotional slump and seemed indifferent. Politics was not alluring. He started writing memoirs, and entertained little. Opponents avidly hoped he would leave public life; friends eagerly awaited his book, *Twenty Years of Congress*. Both were disappointed. He was not retiring, and the memoirs were too bland for sustained reading or serious controversy. The disappointments rankled. Early in the summer of 1882 he and Mrs. Blaine drove past the State Department building. He looked out of the carriage with an attitude of resentment and longing. "Here I fully expected to raise my Ebenezer [monument] for eight years!" [42]

The predictably shallow press coverage depicted Blaine's foreign policy as a round in the factional struggle between Stalwart and Half-Breed. The public never mastered any details of far-away Guatemala or tiny Honduras, or even Mexico and Chile. But it whetted an appetite for the sensational with morsels from a burgeoning scandal called the "Star Route Frauds." The stars were asterisks in government contracts, standing for the words "certainty, celerity, and security." The Post Office Department granted special contracts for sparsely populated areas, arranging for mail delivery by horseback, wagon, and stagecoach in four-year agreements supervised from the Second Assistant's office. Congress was generous with mail subsidies, assuming that population growth would repay the initial government investment. Supervision was lax, and the law gave the Second Assistant wide discretion. He could even let contracts on lowest bona fide bids, then change payment totals. Thomas J. Brady, incumbent in charge, was doing that when Garfield assumed office. He had enriched a group of contractors and politicians for carrying mail across deserts and mountains in boots and hatbands. The ring assumed immunity because unnamed but important persons participated.

People first blamed the scandal on Arthur; it seemed logical in a Stalwart. But it dated from Hayes' administration, and Garfield's advisers warned him early to expect trouble. In February, 1881, Blaine wrote him that Stephen W. Dorsey would threaten exposures if he did not receive recognition. Blaine prepared the new President for a shock, noting that "in my judgement, there are cunning preparations being made by a small cabal to steal half a million a year during your administration." [43] William E. Chandler suspected that unless Garfield acted quickly, he would inherit "the prize of the Star routes." [44] In April, 1881, postal inspectors and lawyers put the case before Garfield. Attorney-General MacVeagh and Postmaster-General James were candid. Important men were involved. The Administration would have to prosecute Brady, Stephen Dorsey and his brother, and powerful local politicians. Garfield paced the floor a moment, then agreed. "Go ahead regardless of where or whom you hit. I direct you not only to probe this ulcer to the bottom, but to cut it out." [45]

The discoveries were interesting reading to the lawyers who prepared a case for a District grand jury. "The revelations these papers make would indeed seem to us most extraordinary but that we have grown familiar with such things," MacVeagh wrote James. "Mark Twain, I am sure, would never have invented them." [46] Garfield's assassination delayed matters, but Arthur encouraged the prosecutions. MacVeagh wished to resign after Garfield's death, and Arthur vainly tried to retain him, fearing his departure would weaken the case. He appointed Benjamin Harris Brewster as Attorney-General, saying: "I will give you all the help I can. You can come to me whenever you wish to, and I will do all I can to aid you." [47]

The inevitable mud-pie brawl followed. Brady published letters from Garfield asking about Post Office assessments during the campaign of 1880, and threatened to open secret letter-files. The cases dragged through 1882 and into 1883, taking up in bad taste where Guiteau's trial stopped. After months of debate, exposure, and recrimination, the juries convicted only two lesser postal workers; major defendants went free. Failure to convict reflected bad management and confused law more than lack of vigor from either the President or his agents. Even the *Nation* laid the blame on "an utterly incompetent jury." [48] Inevitably, the outcome hurt Arthur's image.

Star Route frauds, a confused foreign policy, Cabinet shuffling, breaks with Stalwarts, and apparent public apathy both helped and hindered Arthur's first months. He appreciated the calm to smooth the transition, but wished for better publicity. Star Routes got more headlines than quiet improvements in the Post Office, and the public seemed indifferent to a reduction of letter postage to two cents an ounce. The President remained distant. Blaine's departure, and Cabinet changes helped confuse the issue, but in 1882, the Arthur Administration seemed lackluster.

The President surprised some with occasional forthright stands for his prerogative. Congress passed a bill restricting Chinese immigration for twenty years, though the new treaty Hayes had negotiated assumed less drastic American controls. Arthur vetoed the measure on April 4, 1882, with an able message. He pointed out that such harshness might jeopardize American interests and citizens in China. It was also unfair to Chinese expectations, and would set a bad precedent. He did not wish to hurt the slowly growing commerce with China. A trifle overstated in 1882, it was a good thing to remember. Congress irritably sustained the veto, then passed an Act restricting immigration for ten years, which he signed.

That brought him a little applause, but a later veto caused a storm. The high-toned press called the annual rivers-and-harbors appropriations bill "the great divide." [49] To some, every dollar spent on internal improvements was a contractors' swindle, and the term "pork" meant more than breakfast bacon. Appropriations for river and harbor improvements increased steadily in the 1870's, partly out of congressional demands, but largely from need. In the absence of large-scale federal spending, these appropriations made reasonable economic sense, and usually went to areas without other funds.

In a fit of efficiency, and with an eye on the congressional election campaign, Arthur vetoed a modest $18,000,000 bill on August 1, 1882, and got some good press coverage for a moment. The *Cincinnati Inquirer* said the bill was "like a jack-pot, with everyone in." [50] Godkin, always lamenting government expenditure, pulled out the stops. "No appropriations bill was ever more wanton in its lavishness. No veto message ever was clearer and more irrefutable in point of argument." [51] Arthur might smile at Mugwump praise, but Congress was angry, and overrode. The President probably expected it and was no doubt grandstanding anyway, as Senator Hoar charged.[52] Well he might, for the party was in deep trouble as the congressional campaign developed.

A mid-term election was always a trial, but that of 1882 had the ingredients of disaster for the Administration. Arthur lacked popular appeal. Blaine's Half-Breeds were lukewarm, feeling, as Stalwarts had once noted, that defeat for the other side might be a tonic. The Stalwarts were divided and bickering in their last strongholds. No great issue seemed to separate the parties, and prosperity made it easier for men of divided loyalties to cast protest votes in local contests they would not risk in a presidential ballot. By summer, capital papers reported truthfully that Republicans were "deeply alarmed at their political prospects." [53]

Arthur used the only methods he knew, and persuaded Secretary of the Treasury Charles J. Folger, formerly a New York organization man, to run for governor in the Empire State. The President's managers fought Governor Cornell's partisans for the nomination, and Folger felt the chill breezes of defeat even before being selected. "You have no idea of the bitterness in this region towards all Stalwarts and persons supposed to be in harmony with the administration," he reported from upstate. "Old personal friends and clients of mine declare that they will not vote for me, if nominated; not, they say, that they dislike me but those behind me. . . . 'Gould and Conkling,' 'Gould and Conkling'—that is the cry and it seems to set men mad." [54] On September 20, the state convention in Saratoga chose Folger on the second ballot by a mere 17 votes out of nearly 500 cast. Cries of "Presidential bossism," and "Federal interference" filled the air. And for once, Democrats had an attractive, if unknown, candidate. "The Burly Buffalonian" named Grover Cleveland kept his own machine connections out of sight, and campaigned on honest government and independence of character.

Arthur further tarnished his public image by releasing federal Treasury agents from normal duties to campaign for Folger. Funds tightened as party contributors waited for the next move. New York, traditional source of campaign funds, would not even pay her own debts. The first week in October brought loud complaints from the moderate Republican press, and suggestions that Folger should withdraw, two weeks after his nomination. Nearly everyone blamed Administration forces for "the scrape into which they have got themselves and the Republican party." [55]

New York drew national attention as a test case for the President and his methods, to the delight of Democratic opposition. "There is no excuse for any abuse of Republican leaders by the Democratic press," the *Washington Post* opined. "The rival factions of the Republican party are daubing each other quite enough to satisfy all reasonable requirements." [56] Folger wearily made the rounds, but could not answer critics. "Eternal wrath attend the man who invented the terms *Half-Breed* (whatever that may mean) and *Stalwartism* (whatsoever that may mean), for the Democracy owes its good fortune and successes to that infamous invention . . . ," he wrote a friend.[57]

The Democrats mounted an unusually coherent national campaign, and had some astute backstage managers like Arthur P. Gorman in Maryland, and the men around Samuel J. Randall in Pennsylvania. They wrote each other about money and voting lists, sparing the Jacksonian rhetoric. Be unseen and unheard was their motto. The Democracy pushed hard in the Midwest and Border states, and stood to gain several southern seats because of congressional reapportionment after 1880. The outcome satisfied even optimistic Democrats. Papers headlined it "A Democratic Cyclone." [58] Two hundred Democrats would face 119 Republicans in the national House, though the GOP controlled the Senate with 4 votes. Republicans managed to gain 6 votes in the South over their 1880 totals, but it was a pittance compared to their losses. Of 57 Republican chairmen in the House, only 23 won re-election. In New York, Democrats gained 9 seats; in Ohio, 8; in Pennsylvania, 7; and 2 each in Connecticut, Illinois, Iowa, and Massachusetts. Michigan and Missouri returned 6 more Democrats than in 1880. Texas and Wisconsin each added 4 new Democrats.

Republicans staged bitter intra-party quarrels in New York, Pennsylvania, and Ohio, where Half-Breeds contested for leadership. The Chinese issue cost them California. Many Republicans stayed home or voted Democratic in local contests, out of disgust with drift and indecision on the national scene. Reid's *New York Tribune* headlined its coverage of the debacle "A Crushing Administration Defeat," trying to divorce Arthur from the party. "The people serve notice upon Mr. Arthur that they will not tolerate his attempts to build up a faction at the expense of the party . . . ," it said, echoing Blaine.[59] More independent sheets were less gentle. "The Republican party's message to President Arthur reads something like this: 'Mind your own business, which is not that of interfering in the local politics of your own or any other state. Cease trying to be a ward politician and the Executive of the nation at the same time." [60] The *Tribune* again echoed the Half-Breeds: ". . . this result makes President Arthur an absolute impossibility as a future candidate." [61]

Most of the criticism was set in type before the campaign ended, and reflected a settlement of old scores, but Arthur was heavy-handed in the contest, illustrating the dangers of maturing inside a personal organization. With his usual languor, he attributed the results to public apathy. He learned an expensive lesson in the art of presidential absence from local campaigns. New York's election results hurt badly. Democrats in his home state would control the House delegation, and elected Grover Cleveland by 200,000 votes.

The results did not noticeably bother Blaine. He worked on his book, entertained a few close friends, and was elaborately disinterested in the canvass except as an intellectual pursuit. He spoke in Maine, which his men carried easily in mid-September, but did not travel or issue manifestos. He sounded more liberal in a few speeches at home, favoring fixed terms for office-holders, with removal only for just cause. The election results seemed to prove the public preferred his view of party politics to Arthur's, and that Republicans needed a commanding national figure. "Mr. Blaine appears with new prestige, and is more than ever the Idol of the Republican party," a paper noted after the Maine victory.[62]

It was a bad season for the Stalwarts. Their remaining pillars, like General Grant, did not welcome the new Congress. A short session loomed, between December and March, but few expected anything of it. After Christmas, Mrs. Henry Adams noted in passing: "Congress is like a pack of whipped boys this winter." [63] Perhaps; but they were hardly inactive.

Republicans now treated the country to a rare political spectacle, an active lame-duck session of Congress. Both to make up for apparent lack of purpose during the canvass, and to establish a record for 1884, the GOP passed several major laws in a busy winter. The first and most politically hazardous was the long-predicted civil service reform. President Grant had surprised friends and foes by cooperating with an advisory civil service commission after 1871. This mountain produced mice of information and suggestions for future action, and Grant soon turned from the chilly reformers. Even his temporary allegiance developed some public support, however, and illustrated the growing weariness of politicians dealing with patronage. They could not ignore the danger of alienating support in making choices, and increasing appointments consumed the time of both President and Congress.

Hayes had taken a step forward, though his battles for change involved partisanship as much as reform. Garfield was equally tentative. Both men realized the Republican party must get the credit for establishing a comprehensive system. Garfield wavered on the subject, loathing crowds of place-hunters, yet shrinking from a frontal attack on the problem. He could tell his diary in a kind of internal monologue: "In some way the civil service must be regulated by law, or the president can never devote his time to administration." [64]

His assassination did not make civil service reform either easier or inevitable, but helped crystallize diverse groups favoring change. His death let public opinion demand comprehensive action in the name of a cause they understood in human terms. Reformers capitalized on Garfield's death, not shrinking from imaginary deathbed colloquies, and delirious ravings against the spoils system. Guiteau's performance at his trial did not impede their progress. As the President lingered during the summer of 1881, special conventions boosted reform. In August, Curtis pronounced a militant benediction over the old-fashioned spoils system: "We have laid our hands on the barbaric palace of patronage and have begun to write upon its walls, 'Mene, Mene.' Nor do I believe the work will end until they are laid in the dust." [65] A flood of petitions went to Congress, numerous state party conventions endorsed reform in the spring of 1882, and Congress debated various bills.

Arthur seemed confused and uncertain; his party was divided. Public interest peaked after Garfield's death, then declined. Both parties fighting congressional campaigns in 1882 resorted to assessments and promises of future rewards. Republican defeat in November heartened Mugwumps. The Administration could now favor reform on purely political, if not intellectual, grounds. It would be part of a victory platform for 1884, and protect Republican officeholders in case of defeat. Behind these partisan concerns was the growing conviction that things must change; the government deserved better personnel.

Arthur's annual message of December 4, 1882, was forthright, indicating his shift to reform. Familiarity with office-seekers bred contempt, and he suggested "discreet legislation" to protect himself and Congress, and opposed assessments. Mugwumps were fulsome with praise. ". . . we must do President Arthur the justice to say that he does not hesitate in the least," Godkin reported. "He takes the reform bull by the horns in the most manful fashion." [66]

Attention turned from Arthur to Senator George H. Pendleton. Few expected an Ohio Democrat to espouse civil service reform, and Pendleton was more noted for cravats and manners than ideas. He was a big man, with an elegant beard and ready smile, noted for hospitality and quiet shrewdness, meriting the title "Gentleman

George." Politics and ideals ran through the Democratic attitude toward reform. Pendleton warned fellow Democrats that independents who favored them in 1882 could make the difference in 1884's presidential contest. If the Democracy avoided the civil service question, they might never return from the wilderness. This ironically squared with Republican desires to gain political capital. Schurz had warned Garfield: "The Republican party cannot afford to let this movement pass to the credit of the Democrats." [67] At the same time, most reformers believed Pendleton was sincere and welcomed bipartisan action.

Debates in and out of Congress during 1882 and early 1883 summarized the attitudes of politicians and public. The usual opposition to permanent presidential appointment arose, and some commentators envisaged an all-powerful executive sustained on the Army's bayonets, the Navy's ships, and the civil service's pens. The *New York Sun* voiced old fears of an independent service. "The proposition that men shall be appointed to office as the result of examinations in book learning and that they shall remain in office during life, is a proposition that ought to be speedily broken down and turned out," Dana warned readers. "We don't want an aristocracy of office-holders in this country." [68] The examples of Prussia and England automatically offended patriots. A much more important fear sustained some opposition to reform. At a time when few men had more than grammarschool learning, they logically assumed written examinations would produce an establishment of socially conservative rulers. The West and South feared eastern domination in the civil service. Most Democrats preferred to win the election of 1884, clean out Republicans, then enact a law to protect new appointees.

When Congress reconvened in December, the debate centered in the Senate after the House easily passed Pendleton's measure. The Senate covered the subject well, but produced nothing new on either side. In the process, numerous significant amendments relieved much apprehension among politicians, and established a flexible outline for a future service. Republican Senator Hawley warned colleagues: ". . . the public sentiment has come to absolutely demand it; the necessities of the case demand it; for with the growth of the country to 55,000,000 of people, and the growth of the list of appointees up to more than 100,000, it is quite obvious that in a short time this business of peddling patronage will absolutely crush every executive department." Others like Senator Hoar praised the measure's tendencies toward efficiency and expanded services.[69]

On January 16, after amendment and full debate, the law establishing a Civil Service Commission passed both houses. The House finally approved 155 to 47, with 87 members absent; the Senate by 38 to 5, with 33 absent. It was clearly a Republican measure, and Senator Joseph Brown of Georgia suggested the title "a bill to perpetuate in office the Republicans who now control the patronage of the government." [70] The GOP favored the bill with a few exceptions in the South and Old Northwest. Southern Democrats almost solidly opposed it, perhaps attesting to the absence of a propaganda movement there, and hope of future spoils. New England voted solidly for the bill, suggesting Mugwump influence, and a tacit assumption that the section would continue its influence through established political power and education. Urban representatives favored the measure more openly than rural counterparts.

The Pendleton Act established a permanent Civil Service Commission of three members, whom the President appointed with the Senate's consent. The so-called "classified" service consisted largely of Washington clerks, personnel of customhouses with fifty or more employees, and certain members of the Post Office Department. The president might regulate coverage by proclamation. In 1885 the Act covered some 10 per cent of the federal service—about 15,000 people. The President had unusual discretion, reflecting a wise decision not to codify details. Senator Dawes was correct in labeling the act permissive; it "presupposes a friendly president." [71] No executive was likely to abandon or sharply modify an establishment that grew with necessity. Most intelligent people admitted the Commission allocated positions better than a haphazard spoils system, insured higher quality of personnel, and established the basis of future federal expertise and power.

The law's framers produced a compromise, carefully retaining the American attitudes necessary to make the system work. Both entrance to and promotion within the service rested on merit examinations, character references, and ability, but did not exclude any substantial class of citizens. As Dorman B. Eaton remarked: "This bill assumes that every citizen has an equal claim to be appointed if he has equal capacity [to the task]." [72] The law provided tenure on merit, mollifying fears of an aristocratic bureaucracy. The Commission allotted positions in proportion to state populations, and Pendleton accepted an amendment that permitted entrance to the service at any level, avoiding a hierarchy.

Mugwumps expressed their usual combination of disappointment and relief, but the bill's enactment reflected the power of a dedicated and knowledgeable minority. They used all the arts of propaganda and political force available, countering the politicians' too-easy dismissal of them as "visionaries." Arthur took the law seriously, and named Dorman B. Eaton first chairman of the Commission. The new body toured the country in the late spring of 1883, gathering information and shrewdly interviewing people it would deal with. It soon leaked the first ground rules of examinations to the press, and most hopeful applicants took heart. The reformers wanted little more now than a knowledge of arithmetic, bookkeeping, American history and geography, and acceptable language skills. Six months after the law passed, most commentators quietly agreed that it was a success. The debate that swirled so long around the apparently dull issue of civil service reform was not dead, but reformers were on the way to total victory, though grumbling at every rest stop about confusions and delays attending political success in democracies.

In the complicated and tortuous American political system, landmark legislation is seldom radical and usually not even new. Its importance is in its adoption. It generally comes at the *end* of prolonged public discussion, and reflects a consensus. Because such laws are final in the basic ideas they institute, and expandable in the programs they enact, they provoke bitter contests. Like most of the era's methods to control growth and adapt change, civil service reform was conservative in immediate objectives and radical in long-term results. It established an expert and vital federal service. Mugwumps grumbled about the slow forward motion, but no one could now return to simple spoilsmanship.

Weary congressmen who turned from civil service reform found an even more abstruse problem close at hand. The tariff schedules must be revised to offset an unusual problem—a growing surplus revenue threatening to upset returning prosperity by keeping investment money in government vaults. That was an unwelcome prospect, but the idea of a full-dress tariff debate with political implications made strong congressmen reluctant to get up in the morning.

The existing protective system dated from the war, whose Morrill Act of 1861 aimed to produce revenue and close the home market for war-stimulated heavy industry. During the conflict, protection did not foster monopolies or raise prices. It did produce gold exchange for the government and helped develop a booming consumer market, but insatiable war demands drew in foreign goods as prices rose above tariff rates. When peace came, large sectors of business, agriculture, and labor opposed reduction, hoping to protect the home market during a period of transition to lower price and production levels. Significantly, western areas producing raw materials like wool, hides, ores, and lumber opposed downward revision. The rising currency debate, and eternal southern question obscured halting efforts to revive the long pre-war tariff debate. This confusion aided protectionists. By the time discussion began, formidable blocs of political support joined their cause.*

Protection was largely a Republican doctrine, fitting an industrial-urban constituency. A number of influential and shrewd spokesmen made the subject a specialty, and tirelessly repeated its virtues for decades. People like John Sherman and William McKinley of Ohio; William D. "Pig Iron" Kelley of Pennsylvania; and Justin S. Morrill of Vermont were familiar in nearly every federal election campaign between 1870 and 1900. They shared the common background of rising from humble origins to power, and developed an amazing rapport with varied constituencies. It was a work of political genius to devise a political argument appealing to industry, labor, and some agriculture. Despite inevitable splits in these groups, the protectionists steadily extended a dominant political coalition resting on the tariff question.

Their arguments were potent, simple, and at least as sensible as their opponents' rhetoric. The tariff protected mature establishments and fostered "infant industries" while the developing American economy could not meet foreign competition because of high wages. Like the rest of the argument, this drew both labor and capital into protection's ranks. The tariff closed the home market, permitting agriculture to feed, clothe, and otherwise supply an expanding population. The whole system, like so much else in the period, aimed to stabilize economic transition and maintain a steady wage and price level. A closed market also raised and kept American capital within the system for reinvestment and plant expansion, in a steady cycle of profits and job development. This curtailed reliance on foreign capital, and diversified industry for future security.[73]

The idea's symbolic value was also a great political asset. It seemed logical to immediate needs, had a historic past, and looked to an unknown future it could stabilize. It dated from the Republic's begin-

---

*I am not concerned here with the economic or fiscal effects of tariff protection, but with the issue's political ramifications and its role in stabilizing and developing political parties.

nings, and was associated with great names like Alexander Hamilton, Henry Clay, and Abraham Lincoln. It fed the idea of nationalism, answering the needs of emotion and the pocketbook at the same time. As spokesmen like McKinley tirelessly repeated, Republicans stood for a national system, not a mere arrangement of schedules. Men from areas with factory chimneys, railroad tracks, and specialized farms allied their belief in national government with material self-interest to benefit both business and labor. They matured in the hard times of the 1850's and the booming war economy of the 1860's, when protection seemed to aid industrial expansion. They logically and sincerely believed that westward expansion, increasing technology, and growing population would sustain a protected home market. The United States was a secondary industrial power, but its varied resources would make it a world economic power with government assistance.

Like their opponents, protectionists over-stated the case. General Hancock was essentially correct in noting the tariff's local nature, but he ignored the effective way Republicans collected local interests into a national appeal. The party's fundamental unity on the issue was the secret of its success for a generation. Many, if not most, intelligent Republicans favored gradual reduction after 1877, but congressional lobbying did not permit either scientific management or delegation of authority to an impartial commission. The question before men like Sherman, McKinley, and Garfield, was either to accept an excessive rate or abandon a system. They chose to save the system. Even Senator Morrill, a fanatical protectionist, admitted this. "The great error of those who favor a protective tariff is that they sometimes ask too much . . . ." [74] Realists like Thomas B. Reed simply went down the line for protection, noting "the only place you can pass a perfectly balanced tariff is in your mind: Congress certainly will never pass one." [75] Rutherford B. Hayes, seldom identified with the subject, and therefore calmer about it than friends, sounded a moderate but realistic note in 1873: [76]

> The practical question and the theoretical may be and usually are very different. My leanings are to the free trade side. But in this country the protective policy was adopted in the first legislation of Congress in Washington's time, and has been generally adhered to ever since. Large investments of capital, and the employment of a great number of people depend upon it. We cannot, and probably ought not to suddenly abandon it.

The business community did not totally favor protection. Men engaged in shipping and importing obviously favored lower rates than those selling in the home market. Manufacturers of some goods favored free or cheap raw materials, and posed serious problems within both parties. A Massachusetts woolen or leather manufacturer might be Republican on everything but tariff schedules on these items. He lobbied for lower duties on leather and wool against fellow-Republican producers from Ohio, Pennsylvania, and the Far West. Statesmen of compromise kept these dissidents in the party with persuasion and other rewards, but this dangerous gap in the protectionist argument widened as the 1880's developed.

Tariff proponents were fond of calling all enemies "free traders," though a mere handful of ideologues preached that absolute doctrine in college classrooms and editorial offices. But it was a powerful answer to challenges of reform. It was especially appealing to workers, who usually saw the first downward step from protection as the beginning of general reduction. "Reduce the tariff, and labor is the first to suffer," William McKinley proclaimed, while representing a polyglot Ohio district enamored of protection.[77]

Critics said manufacturers merely added the difference between cost and the tariff schedule to the price of goods, raising prices to consumers; that they hoarded profits for distribution or reinvestment. McKinley had an easy answer. After reciting columns of figures to prove American wages outranked those of Europe, he proclaimed: "We do not want fifty cent labor." It was hard to answer his rhetorical question: "When prices were the lowest, did you not have the least money to buy with?" After 1880, as the issue began to dominate national politics and force intra-party reorganization, national election returns indicated that labor accepted most of these arguments.[78]

The idea that tariffs created trusts entered the great debate rather late. Columns of figures and hours of rhetoric could "prove" either side of the question. Protectionists noted that monopolies in oil and rails did not depend on protection. McKinley and others hoped that within a closed home market competition would reign, keeping prices and productivity at a level consumers could absorb. "We have few, if any, manufacturing monopolies in the United States today," he said in 1882. "They cannot long exist with an unrestricted home competition such as we have. They feel the spur of competition from thirty-seven states, and extortion and monopoly cannot survive the sharp contest among our own capitalists and enterprising citizens."[79]

Protection gained political support as industrialism moved west. By the 1880's, when states around the Great Lakes either manufactured goods or produced raw materials, protection's appeal broadened the

Republican electorate, which already leaned to the GOP because of its use of federal power to develop new territories. Mere chance did not make the area a battleground during that decade. Specialized farming increased rapidly, involving truck crops, dairy products, beef and mutton, and fruits and vegetables to feed city populations. Prosperous farmers there and in the settled East liked the "home market idea" better than their counterparts on dry western plains or in the cotton-bound South.[80] These elements naturally feared immediate competition from cheap Canadian wheat, livestock feed, and beef.

American politicians also excluded cheap Nova Scotian coal, fish from the Grand Banks, and lumber and wool from western Canada. Farther south, Mexico offered a similar threat with cheap ores, hides, beef, and some wool. Tariff protection was thus as important to many farmers and raw material producers all over the country as it was to manufacturers and workers. Their political power, material interest, and emotional attachment to Americanism helped make the tariff a legitimate and vital subject of political discussion.

Democrats historically favored lower tariffs. High rates increased prices, they argued, without raising wages. Protection was sectional, favoring manufacturing over agricultural areas. Farmers sold in a free market and bought in a closed system. It fostered monopolies, and restricted necessary foreign importations of goods the United States could not produce. It made other countries retaliate against American exports, and often hurt the farmer in the world market. This was an attractive rhetorical argument, fortifying Democratic localism and distrust of government intervention. Its faults were negativism, the inability to help producers against foreign competition, and an embarrassing admission that protection had apparently worked, but should now end.

The Democracy's own ranks split dangerously on the issue, seeming to prove the protectionist argument. Democrats from industrial and some raw material districts favored the tariff. Samuel J. Randall led them brilliantly, and forestalled any serious revision for over a decade. "Randall and his Forty Thieves," were targets of Democratic criticism and a major source of party division. Republicans tirelessly scored Democratic provincialism, noting that their reform bills penalized manufacturing interests and favored select agricultural products.

The Republicans reaped an important psychological benefit from protection; it symbolized prosperity in the public mind, often in ironic ways. Spokesmen argued cogently that protection fostered the good years in an economically insecure generation. In periodic depressions, they argued with equal vehemence and greater effect that it was no time for "tariff tinkering." Illinois' low tariff advocate, Representative William R. Morrison, was right in noting: "The trouble with the tariff question is that the Republicans have the advantage on catch words, and the people as a rule do not understand the question, and it is too hard a study for them." [81] He failed to explain why millions of people avidly read tracts on the subject, and attended three- and four-hour speeches on the highly involved issue. He did not account for Republican discipline, organization, and propaganda in using the issue; or explain why a Democratic cry of "low taxes" took so long to affect people.

The tariff question's persistence and dominance in national politics was not accidental. It combined the virtues of local and national appeal. While the country moved awkwardly to an industrial economy, insecure and apprehensive, protection linked the past and future. It was the foundation of the Republican party's nationalism, and its members used the issue skilfully and honestly to widen their appeal, solidify gains, and maintain momentum. In practical ways, it was potent for both parties. A protectionist could favor the total system, and the specific tariff rates on items his area produced, having the best of two worlds. A tariff reformer could oppose the total system, but accept its application to what his area produced. As the 1880's opened, this issue clearly reflected a new urban-industrial constituency. Both parties must utilize it politically. It was a basic factor in making Republicans the dominant national party, and in reshaping the Democracy around the new issue of tariff reform, and all it symbolized.

Despite a few efforts to lower rates in the 1870's, tariff reform had failed. Garfield was a moderate protectionist, but the issue did not dominate his brief administration. Late in 1880, the economist David A. Wells wrote a friend that "tariff reform is the deadest of all things." [82] Arthur seemed unlikely to approach the complicated and dangerous subject in 1882, but surplus government revenue,* and complaints from businessmen about inequities and imbalances in the schedules presaged some kind of change. Congress could reduce the surplus without seeking lower tariff rates, but every method was politically dangerous. It might follow the protectionist argument, and reduce or abolish excise taxes on liquor, tobacco, and luxuries. This, however, angered

---

*It is important to note a fact dealing with the surplus which most general accounts ignore: The Treasury maintained a surplus in gold of at least $100,000,000 for redemption purposes throughout the period.

Temperance supporters and opponents of "a free chaw of tobaccer." The Treasury could enter the market and redeem outstanding government bonds before they reached maturity, but this forced their cost above par, and increased interest burdens. Politicians could reduce or juggle selected tariff rates, which merely invited a protracted and doubtful struggle. Republicans favored a surplus to spend on public works and pensions, and even suggested a refund to the states for educational and welfare needs.* This naturally produced cries of federal oppression, pork-barreling, and high taxation for the consumer. By January, 1882, with Treasury warnings hanging over their heads, congressmen knew that tariff revision "has really taken a strong hold upon the public mind." [83]

Arthur surprisingly favored an expert commission to furnish Congress with information and recommendations. His interest reflected a background in customhouse duties that let him see the virtues of export-import trade. But he was hardly a free trader, and did not propose to disrupt the party. Like the businessmen he increasingly represented, he wanted to "clean up" tariff schedules and reduce inequities. Congress did not welcome the struggle, but as Senator Morrill said wearily: "I suppose that if the Bible has to be revised from time to time, the tariff may have to be." [84]

The idea of a commission appealed to proponents of both change and delay, and was not new. Joseph Wharton of Pennsylvania's Industrial League proposed one in 1878; in 1880 Senator William Eaton of Connecticut suggested an impartial group to supply Congress with accurate information. In May, 1882, the Republican Congress established a commission, assuming the President would fill it with protectionists. He did not disappoint them, though the body was reasonably talented and distinguished.† For most of the summer, it toured the country, heard 604 witnesses during 78 days of hearings in 29 areas, and

---

*A modern economist might argue that the amount of possible tariff reduction would not have benefitted the whole economy as much as *careful* expenditure of the surplus on public works and pensions, if these funds could be channeled to the poorest sectors of the population, and most isolated parts of the country. The money was thus spent at once, re-entering the economy with an inflationary effect.

†After a good deal of searching, Arthur appointed John L. Hayes, managing agent of the National Wool Manufacturers Association, as chairman. He balanced this with a wool grower, Austin M. Garland of Illinois. Duncan F. Kenner of Louisiana spoke for sugar and the South; Henry W. Oliver of Pennsylvania for iron; Jacob Ambler of Ohio was a moderate; William H. McMahon of the New York Custom House had fiscal knowledge; Robert P. Porter of the Census Bureau had skill; and John W. H. Underwood of Georgia and Alexander R. Boteler of West Virginia spoke for geography.

produced 2,625 pages of testimony. As Congress assembled in regular session after the Republican defeat in November, it released a surprisingly moderate report, favoring an expanded free list, lower duties on major items, and a new administrative system. Even Mugwumps, traditional anti-protectionists, were pleased. "The report of the Tariff Commission . . . is a much more impressive document than was generally looked for," Godkin admitted.[85] In his annual message of December 4, 1882, Arthur insisted the party was pledged to revision: "The present tariff system is in many respects unjust. It makes unequal distributions both of its burdens and its benefits." Papers in some Republican areas were equally firm. "The Republican party can do nothing more dangerous to Republican success in 1884 than to neglect tariff reform, or to pretend to reduce the tariff, and not do it." [86]

Congress hastened to do the latter, all parties cooperating. Both houses produced revenue measures, and quarreled over the constitutionality of Senate action. The Senate tended to represent manufacturing interests, while the House helped raw material producers. Within the Republican Party, men like Sherman, speaking for midwestern raw materials, nearly came to blows with eastern senators touting industrial interests. Among Democrats, low rates on sugar, cotton, hides, coal, and iron ores, did not seem attractive in a New South undergoing industrial expansion. Lobbyists for conflicting interests infested Washington, and prolonged the struggle until business elements raised a familiar refrain against "unsettling business conditions with tariff talk." [87]

In March, 1883, neither house seemed able to compromise, and threatened to end without even a new measure. Thomas B. Reed, beginning his House career as a parliamentarian and sharp-tongued debater, devised a rule that crossed the gap, and by strict party votes, a bill passed as the session ended. It satisfied no one, and earned the contemptuous title "Mongrel Tariff." Excuses for accepting it bordered on rationalization, and it reduced rates haphazardly by decimal points. It was the best either party could do. "I shall vote 'yea', . . . because it will reduce taxation . . . ," a Kansas representative admitted, "and in the next session I shall endeavor to bring down pig-iron, lumber, woolens, and other things. I only take this measure because the present law is worse [and] therefore I will swallow this infamous and nauseous dose." [88]

Outwardly, the Act did not enhance the Republican party's or the Administration's prestige with the voters, but it followed a familiar pattern of awkward compromise that avoided political disruption. The Republicans were willing to obey the dictates of national party harmony, and smothered resentment between manufacturers and raw materials producers. However inadequate as a tariff, the measure showed the Republican coalition's flexibility, and revealed intra-party cooperation useful for other battles in the tariff wars.

Democrats could not say as much. The debates opened old wounds and cut new ones, as the party discovered a divided allegiance reflecting not only geography, but constituency. Randall's group would not accept serious reduction, and small enclaves in the South illustrated the growing appeals of protection in new industrial areas. Democrats like New York's Abram S. Hewitt warned that the party's fissure must heal. Morrison was "disheartened and disgusted with our own folks." When debate finished, Hewitt angrily told Randall: "I consider you have broken from the Democratic party. You had better join with the Republicans!" It was not a happy beginning for a Democratic crusade against protection, but most congressmen were too tired to plot further strategy. Senator James B. Beck of Kentucky simply went home and slept fourteen hours.[89]

Congress adjourned with a mixed record. The dog days of summer would bring reflection on next year's presidential campaign. Arthur won some laurels for suggestions, not results. The Republicans were a minority congressional party again, and if Democrats produced a reasonable candidate, they might capture all the citadels of power. It was a strange season, combining lassitude and foreboding, mixing dread with excitement.

As 1883 closed, attention inevitably turned to the presidential question. The President was in a strange position. His calm demeanor, moderate recommendations on many issues, and apparent abandonment of the Stalwarts produced a brighter public image. He was better at urging than acting, however, and his term seemed an interlude between unknown quantities. Even the *Nation* offered faint praise; but General Grant was more accurate in saying the Administration "has seemed to me to be a sort of *ad interim* one." [90] If Arthur did good things, friends had to explain his motives. If he was inactive, critics called it his normal attitude. "Whenever Arthur did a creditable thing, people would say, 'He is after all a better man that we thought he was,'" Carl Schurz later wrote.[91] To hold a man better than you thought him is not a clarion call for battle. "Arthur has given us a good administration," Frank Carpenter said, "but it has been negatively rather than positively good. He has done well, in other words, by not doing anything bad." [92]

As a matter of pride, Arthur sought the nomination in 1884, but had few illusions. He told friends he would not fight too hard. His health was poor, and a bitter fight would be unseemly. At first, he relied on the record and public good will. Postage reduction was supposedly a great boon. Every citizen who licked a stamp would praise Arthur for a penny saved. The party even put out a pamphlet titled "The Great Postal Triumph." [93]

Such trifles did not capture presidential nominations, and Arthur turned to the only constituencies he knew: business, the South, and office-holders. Garfield had not developed a southern policy, and entered office less optimistic than Hayes. He doubted the Republicans could raise the status of the Negro, or break the growing segregation barrier. He also suspected radical white elements in states like Virginia, talking of debt repudiation and agrarian reforms. Necessity drove Arthur, unfamiliar with the South, to simple expedients. In 1881, William E. Chandler became Secretary of the Navy, later accepting command of the President's convention boom.

Time had mellowed the fiery Chandler's view of southern matters. The master of bloody shirt oratory and honest champion of Negro rights was now interested in gaining delegates. He and Arthur turned first to Virginia, where they dealt with William Mahone and the Readjusters. They simply overlooked Republican opposition to Mahone's reduction of state debts. Party leaders had managed him with patronage in the Senate during the Garfield-Conkling feud, and Chandler assumed more taffy would control him. They hoped to win the state delegation for Arthur, and equally important, carry several congressional seats in districts where Republicans divided almost evenly with Democrats. Chandler gave Mahone virtual control of Post Office, Navy Yard, and judicial appointments in Virginia. This produced Republican opposition to lily-white southern organizations, and dealings with mavericks and radicals. In January, 1883, the President firmly scotched talk in the national committee about reducing southern representation at the coming convention.

Arthur's relations with the Negro begged many questions. He lacked experience, and disliked aiding people who obviously could not help him. He knew many Negroes felt the party had deserted them, and confessed he was "constantly bored by these so-called southern Republicans, who excel in office-begging." The present southern Republican parties were failures; a new arrangement, trying to unite businessmen and dissatisfied groups might succeed. "I have made up my mind that a permanently defeated Republican party is of little value in any state, north or south," he said candidly, "and that if any respectable body of men wages war on the Bourbon Democracy, with reasonable prospects of success, it should be sustained." [94]

Chandler candidly answered complaints from those reluctant to ratify an all-white Republican party. The Secretary thought Republicans could win marginal states only by splitting the Democrats. This involved political cooperation with state radical elements without endorsing their programs. Republicans could not otherwise likely win the national House either in 1882 or 1884. What else could they do when "straight Republican, carpetbag, negro governments" had failed miserably? The existing system made the southern party a closed, ceremonial club for a handful of patronage brokers. [95]

The idea of uniting business elements, both North and South, around Arthur was not illogical; cold-blooded politicians would not shrink from temporary deals in national elections with local dissidents. But the policy produced a strange new Republicanism. Arthur's agents cooperated with debt-repudiationists in Virginia, a State-Credit Party in Tennessee that opposed repudiation, a Greenback-Independent fusion ticket in Alabama, Liberal Democrats and Greenbackers in Arkansas, and questionable elements in South Carolina, apparently bent on nothing but plunder. Federal appointments helped gloss over this new movement. [96] In the West, Arthur's Secretary of the Interior, Henry Moore Teller of Colorado, influenced delegates. And in the Navy Yards of Brooklyn, New York, and the South, Chandler fed adherants with jobs and contracts. As the convention assembled in 1884, Arthur's men claimed 163 delegates from former Confederate states. Of course, the method had drawbacks. Mugwumps expressed displeasure, though the President expected nothing from them anyway. "It [Arthur's boom] will represent merely the custom-house, postoffices, and other government positions in the south, and will be as thoroughly mercenary a brigade as it would be possible to get together anywhere," Godkin remarked. [97]

Arthur's northern organization centered inevitably in New York City, despite Stalwart aloofness. Conkling would not cooperate, and Grant was openly hostile, but the President had a following among business men. His fiscal soundness and caution appealed especially to merchants and bankers. They were unusually vocal, but not overly influential, and could not overcome the public notion that Arthur's candidacy had "a flavor of Wall Street about it." Merchant groups in upstate New York also held conventions, adopted resolutions, provided some funds, and pledged their loyalty to him. But even here the President did not command full support. Manufacturing interests feared his divided tariff stand. Midwestern business groups, like most other Republicans, favored Blaine, both for his record and popularity. If the tariff dominated the coming campaign, as most commentators expected, the area would be a battleground.[98] By late spring, the President's effort was stalled. He could make a respectable showing, but nothing more. Perhaps that was all he ever wanted to do.

These quadrennial rites of spring produced some familiar but illogical names. As Arthur's boom stabilized, and support for Blaine seemed strangely unfocused, the Sherman brothers drew undue press attention. The General, in comfortable retirement in St. Louis, was not openly receptive; he once referred to politics as "that school of scandal and abuse." He pushed his brother John, and was also a friend of Blaine. Veterans' groups and some Republicans who wanted to avoid a defensive fight with Blaine, urged his cooperation, but for the moment Sherman remained opposed. "Why should I, at sixty-five years of age, with a reasonable provision for life, not a dollar of debt, and with the universal respect of my neighbors and countrymen, embark in the questionable game of politics?" he asked his brother.[99]

In late May, the mail brought a typical "Strictly and Absolutely Confidential" letter in Blaine's scrawled handwriting. He urged the General to accept the call; he could unify the party; friends would do the trick without a canvass. "You can no more refuse than you could have refused to obey an order when you were a lieutenant in the army." [100] That was a long time ago, and Sherman had learned to disobey. He ignored Blaine's injunction not to reply and burn the letter. An apparently firm denial followed. He noted the fate of Grant, Hayes, Garfield, and other generals in the White House, "and am warned— not encouraged by their sad experiences." [101] Why Blaine bothered to write remained a mystery. There was no real demand for Sherman, and the Plumed Knight was on the way to victory. Perhaps he offered a circuitous peace feeler to John Sherman—or had cold feet at the last minute, dreading a campaign. But Sherman's disavowals of presidential ambitions had a hollow ring. Late in the game he congratulated Blaine as a "fellow candidate," and suggested he would have taken the nod in a deadlocked convention.[102]

In genial moments, the nervous General was likely to put off political talk. "I am not a statesman; my brother John is. If any Sherman is to be nominated, he is the man." [103] Senator Sherman had that old feeling again, as 1884 rolled around, but the disappointment of 1880 still weighed heavily. Comfortably back in the Senate, he was not too sure the party could win. "A nomination is far from being equivalent to an election," he wrote his brother. "The chances are for the Democrats but for their proverbial blundering. . . . I would gladly take [the nomination] as an honorable closing of thirty years of political life, but I will neither ask for it, scheme for it, nor have I the faintest hope of getting it." [104] His remarks had the ring of realism. The business element most favorable to him seemed wedded to Arthur. His relations with the independents were never good. Blaine gathered the genuine popular support. Sherman hoped only to be second choice for everyone, a compromise candidate like Garfield in 1880. Blaine's managers feared that a concerted movement crying "Anything to beat Blaine" would settle on Sherman, but it was an outside chance. The Ohioan forbade lieutenants to fight Blaine openly, lest the Man from Maine ruin his hopes for 1888. It was getting to be a familiar story for "Uncle Jawn." A friend noted: "As in 1880, he was the phantom across Sherman's path to the White House." [105]

Tremors of alarm naturally ran through the Blaine camp when Garfield died. The grand plan had failed, and the enemy was now in charge. Or so it seemed. In October, 1881, newspapers began discussing exile for Half-Breeds, a turn of the screw emanating from Conkling. Blaine talked about party harmony and leaders sacrificing themselves for the common good, so why not make him practice it? Whitelaw Reid gave Blaine counsel that fortified his own thinking. He must not let Arthur make him minister to England, as gossip suggested. "To go quietly to Augusta, take care of your health, have a good time and take your fair share in political campaigns, as they come along, is to garner and increase [your] force. You are . . . the residuary legatee of [Garfield's] popularity. You ought to be and can be chosen at the next election, as his successor. To that end, Augusta is worth a thousand Londons." [106]

Blaine resigned in December, his diplomatic plans first in suspension and then a shambles, but he remained unusually calm, refusing to open any major breach in the party. A few political appearances sparked popular demonstrations, but he did not invite acclaim. In Washington, he wrote his memoirs, and despite a few brief flurries over the Chilean matter, did not criticize Arthur openly. In 1882, he assured friends he did not "wish to pose for an hour as a presidential candidate." [107] Mrs. Blaine told relatives that "Father" wanted to be Secretary of State again, but had no presidential ambitions.[108]

By 1884 the opposition press condemned him to a strange obscurity by repeatedly analyzing his eloquent silence. He had never disappeared from public view and needed no publicity to keep his name alive. "His admirers are more numerous than those of any other man . . . ," an opposing paper admitted early in 1884.[109] In March, the publishers released the first volume of *Twenty Years in Congress*, a bland summary of his earlier career. The *Nation* called it "Blaine's Bid For The Presidency," in large letters, and sneered at Republicans who "go into raptures over its beauties of diction and breadth of view." [110] The book sparked a fresh outburst of nervous opposition to Blaine. Cartoons filled the papers; rumors of new Mulligan letters excited editors; and Mugwumps began talking of public morality and duties young men owed their country. Blaine spoke in more liberal tones after 1881, favoring modest civil service reform, distributing the surplus, warning the party to accept a firm tariff program. Reformers dismissed it all as the homage vice paid to virtue.

If Blaine was the avid office-seeker his enemies described, he conducted a strange canvass for the presidential nomination in 1884. His near-seclusion savored more of Sherman's tactics than those peculiar to the Plumed Knight. He was sincere in protesting against *seeking* the nomination, but he would not have to do anything if he simply capitalized on a growing reputation as the people's candidate against Stalwart bosses. Blaine did not relish the prospect of a bitter campaign that might hurt the party and his own fortunes. There was something in his nervous personality that made him draw back at crucial moments, and he had tasted fame enough to know its evanescent quality. Now, in 1884, he would not actively seek the nomination, but leave his affairs in the hands of astute men.

Stephen Benton Elkins was chief among these, with a growing reputation for political management. His name was unfamiliar to the public, but men in banking, railroads, and mining easily recognized "Steve." Born in Ohio, maturing in Missouri, sweeping through the raw but profitable post-war West, he amassed a fortune in rails and mining, operating chiefly from Santa Fe and Denver. Not satisfied with this geographical spread, he widened an empire from New York. Marriage to the daughter of Senator Henry Gassaway Davis, conservative Democrat of West Virginia, aided his penetration of that area's coal, timber, and railroad resources. He added political contacts in both parties to a fortune he spent lavishly but well. Now in his mid-forties, Elkins was a busy figure in Blaine's camp, and dominated a group of talented subordinates who managed the Plumed Knight's career with the same forceful tact that made him rich and powerful.

A round, innocent face made Elkins look like an aging baby, but he was one of a shrewd, tough breed of managers preferring organization and the soft-sell to personal pressure in dealing with others. Though ambitious for office, he truly liked Blaine and the attitude he symbolized. He admired the Republican party even more, and saw that only a national figure preaching a national issue, sustained on a firm organization, could save the GOP from Arthur's languor and Stalwart designs.

By April, Elkins and other friends were assuring reporters and commentators that Blaine would not scramble for the nomination, but would certainly take it if offered. In short, he would avoid opening breaches in the party's unity before a critical contest. Elkins laughingly told callers that Blaine would pay $10,000 for each word he uttered publicly about politics. In effect, "Blaine was being carried into the convention backwards by these friends." These spokesmen shrewdly added that "the machine elements of the Republican party" beat Blaine in 1876 and 1880; the people would not let them do it in 1884.[111] This latter point roused Blaine. At a Washington's Birthday dinner, he told Senator Ingalls he would let the nomination go. "But I don't intend that man in the White House shall have it!" And strolling around Lafayette Park with former Secretary of the Treasury George S. Boutwell, he emphasized his dislike of Arthur, with a cold glance toward the White House. That was the central theme in his private dealings: the Stalwarts must not revive.[112]

Roscoe Conkling kept silent, but General Grant was more irritable. Blaine had tried the soft touch in dealing with Grant, but to no avail. "I never had at any time the slightest malice against the General," he wrote Elkins in 1883, "and never did a thing respecting him that I am not glad to have the light shine on fully and openly." [113] But Grant decided to oppose Blaine, with or without Conkling's open support. A small but influential Stalwart legion would support a candidate if the General made the first move. In late March, the *New York World* printed a "scoop" interview with Grant. The General looked up from his cigar long enough to announce support for Illinois' legendary Stalwart, Senator John A. Logan. He explained that Blaine was unsafe, would cause a defensive campaign, and was too controversial for the party's good. He did not expect Conkling to help, since he was doing so well financially. Between puffs he suggested the tariff would dominate the campaign, while the southern question receded.[114]

The idea drew headlines. John A. Logan was an "available" choice for a man like Grant. A bitter-end Stalwart in 1880, he was a popular figure among the nation's Boys in Blue. Originally a Douglas Demo-

crat from downstate Illinois, Logan fought through the war to emerge
a Radical Republican. He was familiar at GAR encampments, an organization he helped found. No one but Grant had suggested he might
enter the White House, except to ask a favor from a better occupant.
In crudely political terms he had some assets. The stories about him
were legendary, ranging from alleged battlefield prowess to the meaning of the long black hair and bristling mustache that won the Indian-
like title "Black Eagle." He was not noted for patience. In the Senate,
he often raised his voice for reasons other than acoustics. Many an
experienced frontiersman added to his vocabulary after hearing Logan.
And more than once he wrestled with a spirited horse for the privilege
of a morning ride. He believed in the appeals of reason, but also liked
more substantial things like pensions, internal improvements, and Republican victories. He was rough, but with a likable heartiness that
appealed to many.

Mugwumps howled, and even professionals smiled derisively. The
Stalwarts were obviously making straw men for bargaining. But Illinois Republicans took Logan seriously; before Grant announced his
allegiance, there was a Logan boom in the Prairie State. Of course, it
had weak foundations. As a prominent newspaper owner reported to
Illinois' other senator, Shelby Cullom: "Logan's boom is growing, but
it is simply because there is nothing to get in the way, and it is the
same fellows all the time that are blowing and halooing." [115]

Blaine's managers did not take Logan seriously; if worse came to
worst, they would enfold him. But New York worried them. Stalwart
strength could tip that state to the Democrats, either for spite or reward. Blaine could not carry it without an arrangement, either with
Stalwarts or independents, and neither group wanted him. Throughout the spring, his managers conducted a discreet guerilla war in
New York, trying to thwart Arthur overtly and Conkling covertly. The
state convention revealed that the President controlled only about half
the national delegates, with the rest for Blaine or unannounced. It was
a reasonable victory at that stage, but did not indicate he could win
the state's electoral votes. [116]

Elkins and his band acquired help from a surprising source, Thomas
C. Platt. The people wanted Blaine, he argued; it was "his turn" for
the nomination. Resistance was futile; cooperation might be fruitful.
Besides, there was the state organization to think about. Platt visited
his old chief, Roscoe Conkling, and said he would support Blaine.
Roscoe glared. "Well, Senator Platt, you are about to do what I could
not bring myself to do. You know what Blaine did to us." Platt ex-

plained that it was the best way to beat Arthur, and thwart a thin but distressing Edmunds boom. Conkling nodded, and returned to the silence that had replaced his verbosity. Platt never missed a bandwagon; there would be future rewards, come victory or defeat. He played his part well and faithfully throughout the convention and campaign.[117]

As May approached, Blaine was clearly the popular choice. In Pennsylvania his name opposed the Cameron machine, and "Elegant Don" hastily returned from a European tour to join the parade. Sherman assured Blaine's men they could have his votes if they needed them. Convention after convention in the Midwest endorsed the Plumed Knight in a genuine show of popular enthusiasm. The *Washington Post* said this came from his status as Garfield's heir, charisma, and the simple cry: "The leaders are all against him." [118] As Frank Carpenter put it in his widely syndicated column: "The Republicans of the rank and file of the party from all the states were for Blaine. The politicians were for Arthur, and the conservatives for the dark-horse candidate." [119]

The *New York World*, always reluctant to boost a Republican, had to admit the idea's validity. "The whole Republican people seem suddenly to find out that they want Blaine! They shout for him in their district conventions. They vote for him in colleges and cars. They instruct delegates for him. In Pennsylvania his name smashes the Cameron machine. In New York, it runs the Arthur machine off the tracks onto a switch. Everywhere, it gives custom-houses and post-offices a black eye." [120] It was an ironic theme compared to Blaine's past news coverage, but he relished it in silence. As the boom rolled over opposition, he seemed to hesitate, and kept asking people to keep him from being nominated. "I would not turn my hand over for it." With the convention only weeks away, he began a quiet movement for General Sherman, telling incredulous friends: "We can name a ticket that would carry every northern state—General Sherman and Robert Lincoln. That ticket would elect itself. It would be irresistable." [121] Surely he was joking; this momentary hesitation would give way to reason. Especially since the Democrats, who started so well in controlling Congress, now seemed confused and disorganized.

The light snows that blanketed Washington in December, 1883, did not dampen the ardor of arriving Democratic congressmen. This regular session of the congress elected in 1882, had a majority of 80 in the House for their party. They would elect a Speaker, chair committees, and discuss national problems as the presidential canvass approached. The lack of commanding national Democrats gave congressmen and editors a good deal of authority. Men like Randall, John G. Carlisle, William R. Morrison, and Henry Watterson intended to use it for themselves and the party. The Treasury surplus remained, and inconclusive debates around the Mongrel Tariff hardly closed the issue of reduction, but Mugwump observers like Carl Schurz doubted the ever-disorganized Democrats could do anything serious about it. Considering their past record, they would waste the surplus, and do something foolish about protection. They had not debated the tariff question in years, and perhaps forgot how divided the party was on the issue.

The elections of 1882 had produced a scattering of fresh faces in the Democratic House, and acute listeners could hear rising editorial criticism of Democratic failure to touch new issues. Constituents began to write congressmen about economics rather than history. They also adopted a stiffening attitude toward the obstructive protectionist Democrats. "Let Randall and all the 'old-men-afraid-of-their-constituents' take care of themselves," a Nebraskan wrote.[122] This, and similar remarks, indicated an attitude that might either carry the party upward or split it permanently. Men higher in politics than farmers or editors saw that Democratic protectionism could not survive during the debates of 1883. "I shall not be dictated to!" Randall told Abram S. Hewitt in the spring of 1883. But the New Yorker wagged a finger under the Pennsylvanian's nose and thundered: "You will find your days numbered next December in the Democratic caucus."[123]

The Democrats' struggle for the Speaker's post revealed the party's inherent problems. Randall represented eastern protectionists, with the comforting precedent of previous success in the position, but a formidable newcomer, backed by an increasing number of southern and western spokesmen, challenged the smooth Philadelphian. John Griffin Carlisle of Kentucky entered the House in 1877, and mastered the arts of both parliamentary delay and expedition. His friends did not cavil at calling Randall's followers "stuffed shirts," arguing the time had come to unify the party with or without the easterners. One of Carlisle's supporters spoke with a fervor that warned of coming battles: "I am for Carlisle against the world, the flesh and the devil."[124] The Democratic caucus elected Carlisle speaker, and a bitterly disappointed Randall began employing tactics of frustration and delay that marked his inevitable end as a major factor in the national party. He hovered over the important Appropriations Committee chairmanship, watching expenditures with a legendary knife handy; but other crucial posts went to reformers.

Fears of a tariff debate on the eve of a presidential contest unnerved eastern Democrats. Many of them, even in Randall's group,
accepted select revision, but knew a general debate would force both
reformers and conservatives to defend present positions. Protectionists
also dreaded "southern domination," which Carlisle's election seemed
to presage. The loose alliance between East and South might give way
to western pressures on more divisive issues than the tariff. After the
holidays, returning congressmen reported growing demands for tariff
reform in the Mississippi Valley. More easterners admitted they could
only delay, and vote with the Republicans if reduction was too erratic
or sweeping.[125]

The agitation was more than a temporary problem, and illustrated
the growing conviction in some Democratic quarters that the party
must reorient its constituency. The Republicans were clearly triumphing in the industrial-urban sector, and Democrats could make an
equally potent national appeal by reversing the tariff argument. As
Henry Watterson counseled: Talk about prices, trusts, eastern domination, and weak markets for western produce. This made sense as an
escape "from the bloody shirt as an issue." [126] If they talked economic
problems, the North would abandon efforts to regulate southern affairs, and go on the defensive for protection. The surprising fervor
that tariff reform produced illustrated its potential to expand the Democratic party's appeal. For the first time, leading men argued that if
reform failed now, they would pursue it to success at future national
conventions, no matter how long it took. As Watterson soon noted,
Randall and his followers could support reduction or "pack up their
gripsacks and go over to the Republicans." [127]

Protectionist Democrats confronted the mounting Treasury surplus
with a variety of schemes to avoid tariff reduction and soothe longings
for public expenditure. By January, 1884, pending bills suggested
spending the money on public education, rivers and harbors, federal
buildings, state claims, and bounties to Mexican War veterans. The
new chairman of the Ways and Means Committee wanted none of it,
and Illinois' crusty William Rawls Morrison was not a man to take
lightly. "Horizontal Bill" had passed through the school of hard knocks
without polishing any edges. He grew up near Waterloo, Illinois, and
absorbed frontier politics around the family tavern. As a private in
the Mexican War, he satisfied part of an adventurous urge later fulfilled in the California gold rush. Back in Illinois, he was a Douglas
Democrat in local affairs, fought as a volunteer colonel during the
war, and entered the House in 1873, after one wartime term. He represented midwestern agrarians who bought goods in a protected mar-

ket they now thought did not benefit them in return, and disliked
federal intervention in the economy. He often adopted a sleepy look
behind greying whiskers, and while listening to protectionist arguments, would drawl slowly: "I think I've heard that before." [128] Morrison believed protection raised prices and penalized the non-industrial
sector, but he also had no love for Randall, who dropped him from
important committee appointments in 1877 because of reform views.

Morrison faced a hopeless task. The party dared not open general
hearings on the subject just before a presidential convention. Leaders
knew a Republican President and Senate would kill serious revision.
They hoped for moderate reduction to symbolize changing attitudes,
but had no comprehensive plan. The Republicans expected an attack
in the form of horizontal reduction in a bill Morrison reported on
March 11, 1884. It lowered most schedules 20 per cent; put salt, coal,
and lumber on the free list; and limited maximum rates on cotton
goods to 40 per cent; woolens to 60 per cent; metals to 50 per cent;
but stipulated that no rates should fall below those of 1861. This was
the most reasonable plan reformers could concoct, and had some Republican precedent from the 1870's. The opposition in both parties
ridiculed it as a hodgepodge, illustrating dangerous confusion among
reformers. Mugwumps disliked its erratic nature, arguing "It is merely
a reduction of a protective tariff." [129] Many Democrats disliked both
the measure and its sponsor. "The Morrison bill is like Bill Morrison, a
very much overrated affair," a St. Louis paper acidly noted. "It also
resembles the Morrison [presidential] boom and Yankee beans in
being composed chiefly of wind." [130]

Randall got conflicting advice from constituents and from friends in
the South. Many wished to avoid voting, to refuse to discuss the matter, and wait for another day. Others wanted stern opposition, fearing
reformist control of the national party. A banker's panic in May frightened some tariff moderates, who warned against "tinkering." From
Richmond, a friend wrote Randall some realistic, if hedging, advice.
"Theoretically, many of us are for a revenue tariff, pure and simple.
But practically, we are for harmonizing all interests in the defense of
liberty." [131] Midwestern protectionists like Ohio's Henry B. Payne,
condemned Morrison and the reformers as "demented, conceited, desperate schemers." [132] On April 15, Morrison won House consent to
later consideration by only two votes, 140–138. The Republicans let
an Ohio protectionist Democrat, George L. Converse move to kill the
bill on May 6, with a vote of 159–155. Forty-one Democrats joined all
the Republicans. The razor-thin victory presaged Randall's coming

decline; southern and midwestern Democrats, who had supported him in the past, now voted in effect for party unity on the issue. The former Speaker's votes came largely from New Jersey, Pennsylvania, and California. From this time forward, reformers gave Randall no quarter and asked none. Cartoonists drew him as Benedict Arnold, skulking into the Republican camp. His hate mail increased, and papers condemned "the deliberate treachery and time-serving timidity" of protectionist Democrats.[133] The tariff's power to unify and revive the Democracy was clear after the vote.

The bill's defeat, however narrow, was a mixed victory for Republicans. They beat revision with party unity, and showed to their own satisfaction the confusion and disorder among the Democrats which made them unfit for national rule. Republicans assumed an air of tolerance; Democrats had a few good ideas on tariff reform, but the paving stones of good intentions led only in one direction. Privately, intellectual reformers like the Massachusetts Mugwumps around Edward Atkinson, agreed. "There is something the matter with the Democratic side," Theodore Lyman wrote. "There are some able and very many honest men over there, but they have no unity of action, nor ruling ideas." [134] The important thing was how the debate affected the presidential problem. Morrison admitted before the defeat, "there is too much tariff in the presidential contest for the Democratic candidate to succeed this year." [135] Still, they might make it, if they could find a candidate.

V

☆☆☆☆☆☆ ☆☆☆☆☆☆☆☆☆☆☆☆☆☆☆☆

The Democracy Revives—Barely

☆☆☆☆☆☆ ☆☆☆☆☆☆☆☆☆☆☆☆☆☆☆☆

A pleasant, curved driveway led to "Greystone," Samuel J. Tilden's castellated mansion in Yonkers. The visitor who swayed along in a carriage saw immaculate grounds, where prize sheep nibbled grass under carefully cultivated trees, and grooms exercised purebred horses. He was not likely to see Tilden when he alighted at the portico, walked into the large entrance hall, and gave the butler his hat. "The Governor," was probably stretched out on a sofa, listening to a secretary or niece read aloud. In the spring of 1884, Tilden was seventy, in failing health, and publicly disinterested in political office. He drove around the grounds in a specially built carriage with soft springs, and passed days reminiscing or reading, when not tending his investments. He almost never appeared in public.

These rituals fitted an apparent retirement, but the Democracy would not let him go. Hancock's defeat in 1880 enhanced Tilden's political stature. That margin was so thin that many thought he could have won, and might do so in 1884. As the new year opened, papers noted with a kind of awe, "The hold of Mr. Tilden upon the Democrats is remarkable." [1] Just after Washington's Birthday, people who feared his candidacy would revive old issues warned against choosing St. Louis for the national convention. That city evoked memories of 1876, and might help Tilden's men. The Sage read books and watched sheep, apparently aloof and disinterested, but this attitude merely fed speculation on his intentions. By March, more and more papers commented on "The mysterious, vague and undefined candidacy of Mr. Tilden." [2] The sheer amount of press coverage, dwarfing discussion of

186

all other contenders, symbolized both Tilden's appeal in the party and its lack of national leaders.*

This was not unnatural. The tariff debates of 1884, Republican movement to Blaine, and weakness in the Democratic coalition highlighted the drawing power of a symbolic figure. "If Mr. Tilden would accept the nomination, that would relieve the Democracy of all jealousy and heart-burning—all controversy between rival candidates, all difficulty in the convention or after the convention," Melville Fuller of Chicago wrote William H. Barnum in 1883.[3] Congressional debates revealed deeper splits than most Democrats expected, and the chorus for Tilden rose. "He will subordinate the tariff issue, on which the party is divided, to the issue of reform, on which the party is united."[4] Just what "reform" meant, no one said. Tilden's men were good at generalizing, and weak on specifics. His persistent appeal rested only on nostalgia, and the desire to avoid issues.[5]

Party professionals were divided. They wanted victory, saying frankly that 1884 might be their last chance. If Blaine won, the Republicans might solidify forever. But most Democratic politicians did not want Tilden. His supporters were old; younger men cheered "reform" rather than Tilden. He was a convenient and usable symbol, but unmanageable as a candidate or president. Past experience on that score unsettled many leaders, who disliked the Sage's foggy utterances and slippery innuendoes. The problem of health also remained a factor. Tilden suffered from the effects of a stroke, and had "nervous palsy," though his mind was sound. Friends and physicians supplied nostrums, and he tried prevailing cures, ranging from cold baths and special diets to electrical massage, but age forbade any extensive improvement. Clark Howell, of the *Atlanta Constitution,* a strong Tilden organ, visited him in February. As he waited in the library, the old man tottered toward Howell, shook his hand, and seeing pity in the visitor's eyes, said candidly: "My boy, don't you see it is impossible?" They talked of the party's prospects, and Tilden betrayed a sense of humor. Noting Hendricks' desire for the Old Ticket in 1884, the Sage laughed: ". . . and I do not wonder, considering my weakness!"[6]

In mid-March, the disappointed Howell said Tilden was not available, whatever that meant, and other papers printed copious docu-

---

*The press coverage of Tilden between January and July, 1884, is remarkable. No New York paper devoted much attention to another candidate, and papers in the Midwest and South repeated this pattern. Cleveland was not generally mentioned until convention-eve, and then chiefly as a vice-presidential candidate or possible dark horse. Cleveland's managers appreciated this press attitude, since it allowed them to work backstage without attracting opposition.

mentation from Tilden's friends and former associates. Other Democrats were not so sure. Bayard reported what everyone inside the party hierarchy knew; Tilden's "literary bureau" discreetly supplied newspaper copy and arranged interviews.[7] The usual fog closed in, summarized in a neat scene Tilden staged for a *New York Sun* reporter. He met the young man standing before a roaring fireplace, cheerful and composed, making witty asides to a secretary. He seemed candid about politics. "I do not want the nomination and cannot take it. No, I cannot give up the peace and quiet which I enjoy here for four years of toil and strife." The caller noted the luxurious library and mentally agreed there was something in the remark. After a discreet interval, he rose to go. As he turned, Tilden remarked that his health was sound. To prove it, he vigorously raised and dropped both arms, then stamped first on one foot and then the other.[8]

Like the man biting the proverbial dog, this was news, and sparked fresh discussion of Tilden's intentions. A month later, Senator Benjamin Harrison of Indiana thought he would take the nomination. The health issue did not alter Harrison's analysis, especially in view of Tilden's arcane personality. "At the White House, being feeble and sickly, he could refuse to see anyone but the doctor and nurse." That would be an advantage in dealing with both friends and foes. "The Democrats would kill a well man in six months." [9] And many Democrats scored those busy dusting off Tilden. His few pompous speeches, couched in epigrams and platitudes, irritated independents. "What the people want are issues that can be seen and felt and grappled with—issues with relations to which the attitudes of the parties are clearly defined," the *Washington Post* remarked.[10] In April, the *New York Times*, dreading the prospect of Blaine's victory, cut through the rising Tilden talk: "No great party was ever so reduced to desperate straits as the Democratic party of today." [11]

Still the chorus rose. Observers did not know what to make of the Tilden boom. Was it serious, or a device for someone else? Was the Sage merely seeking the usual nomination he could refuse, then to dictate another's selection? Tilden was opaque, but friends were more firm. They wanted a complimentary nomination, as in 1880. Tilden's real hope, negative in design but positive in purpose, was more fruitful. His ambivalence prevented favorite-son booms that would disrupt the party; and indecision increased his influence on an heir. Despite all the talk, that heir's name was uncertain, and favorite sons continued to walk softly around the Democratic camp.

For the state candidates, 1884 repeated the uncertainties of 1880, when Hancock's nomination surprised local overlords living on false security in safe constituencies. Samuel J. Randall claimed support in 1884 because of strategic Pennsylvania and the protectionists he commanded in the South and West. On all other questions he was a standard Democrat, with the small added hope of appealing to urban-industrial voters. His reputation as "the watch-dog of the Treasury" preceded him into battle, and his basic philosophy appealed to old-line Democrats: "If there be one evil greater than another today in this country, it is that we have too much legislation." [12] Randall's men hoped to counteract the increasing southern image Democrats gained from their congressional work, and he had some appeal as a compromise candidate between Tilden and midwestern contenders. But his defeat for the Speaker's office in 1883 ended his presidential aspirations, though he remained stubbornly optimistic.

For the moment, he curried Tilden's favor, assuming like other favorite sons that the old man's support would fall to him. He would win the nomination if possible, but protect the tariff plank, and go with the winner. He lacked organization, however, and did not quite know which way to turn, while Tilden kept matters suspended. Aides complained of "a total lack of concert of action among your friends. It is pretty much a 'go as you please' affair." [13] In March, an emissary saw Tilden, who "said substantially that he would not be a candidate, and that he would not accept the nomination even if it were made by acclamation." But he discussed every contender except Randall, leaving grains of doubt in the guest's mind. By May and June, Tilden was still noncommittal, saying that he liked Randall, but the people must choose.[14]

Senator Bayard wanted lightning to strike, but hesitated to raise any rods. His reputation persisted; he was "too clean and too cold to get the nomination." [15] He appealed south of Mason and Dixon's line, but what about the rest of the country? Would he survive a campaign against Blaine, or die by contrast? He remained passive, assuming like Randall that he was Tilden's heir. As in 1880, he dealt with August Belmont and John Kelly in New York. Kelly refused to take Tilden seriously, but unlike other professionals, saw at once that Tilden had an equally offensive protégé in Grover Cleveland. The New York City machine was willing to deal with Bayard, assuming that Belmont and rich friends financed the effort. By June, as professionals awoke to Cleveland's subterranean movement, it was too late. Bayard's agents

decided after a New York conference that his "chance is only toler-
able, owing largely to the fact that the country is disposed to go for
whoever New York asks for." [16]

A host of local boomlets arose in Tilden's shadow, without seriously
affecting party unity. Talk of Tilden revived interest in Hendricks,
though the two no longer spoke. Indiana's aging spoilsman still appealed as "the living tail of the old ticket of 1876. . . ." and people
seriously thought he could win the nomination on the hope of carrying
the Midwest, and rewarding deserving Democrats.[17] The Republicans
were unkind, frequently referring to age and debility. "Hendricks
Resurrected," Reid's paper headlined. "A Professional Candidate." [18]
Events caught Hendricks conveniently in Europe, but upon his return
he suggested a dislike for civil service reform, opposed a tariff debate,
and thought the party was defrauded in 1876.

This made most observers yawn, but mention of other names made
them rub their eyes. In New York, sober men talked of Roswell Petti-
bone Flower as a compromise choice. Flower was rich from mercantile and banking interests and maintained a perpetual gubernatorial
boom, but had served in the House unnoticed. His elegance was a
dubious distinction, though the anti-Cleveland *Sun* often compared
him favorably to "our obese governor." [19] Flower took the matter seriously, lining up business friends and some officeholders. He entertained
lavishly in New York, and elegant guests like William C. Whitney sat
through pompous disquisitions from above the salt about duty, country, and efficient government. "The real amusing part of the dinner to
me," Whitney wrote his wife in 1883, "was to discover that Flower is
a candidate for *the presidency*." [20] Flower's bandwagon had no wheels,
and the men on it cheered perpetually from the same spot. "There
can't be much in it," the editor of the *Buffalo Express* wrote Cleveland.
It alternately amused and irritated Mugwumps. Republican sheets
merely reported "A small boom for the Flower barrel," assuming that
without his money there would be no noise.[21]

Farther west, Ohio groomed two contenders. The conservative protectionist Henry B. Payne, posed as a "safe" candidate for the South,
mid-Atlantic states, and Midwest. His connections to Tilden let him
join the crowd of death-watchers around the Sage's political fortunes,
but he obviously lacked a serious constituency. Buckeyes offered a
more impressive figure in Allen Granberry Thurman, "the old Roman,"
and "Knight of the Red Bandana," an alleged favorite of workingmen
and tillers of the soil. Though born in Virginia, he grew up in Ohio,
as a Douglas Democrat opposed to secession but disliking federal

authority. During the war he was moderate and in peacetime fought Rutherford B. Hayes for the governorship. Failing at that, he entered the United States Senate for two terms, 1869–81, because of Ohio's amazing politics, and made a reputation for thrift and moderate states' rights, symbolizing the average man at the top. Whipping a red bandana from his pocket to wipe his brow, Thurman seemed both common and colorful, and might be a compromise candidate.

Some surprising names appeared. California persistently suggested Stephen J. Field, and the lofty jurist had pamphlets circulated and gave interviews. Rumor said Conkling would desert Blaine for Field, though just what strength this added was a mystery. Nearly every Democratic governor and senator got news coverage in the background, while men speculated about Tilden in the foreground. Someone even asked plaintively: "What is the matter with Hancock for another nomination?" a question that was answered with thunderous silence.[22]

Outside their immediate preserve, Democrats could consider the unlikely but not altogether unlovable figure of Benjamin Franklin Butler of Massachusetts. Few men boasted as varied or puzzling a career. Born in the tough seafaring environs of Deerfield, New Hampshire, he was associated with life's underdogs and outcasts. He taught while working through law school, and established a lucrative practice in Lowell, Massachusetts, combining a flair for money-making with a desire to help the poor. He served as a Democrat in the state legislature, but raised volunteer troops at the war's outbreak and relieved Annapolis, Baltimore, and Washington in the conflict's first months. As military governor of New Orleans, he ordered southern belles to restrain expression of their open dislike of Union soldiers or be labeled "women of the streets." A prominent Radical Republican in the House, he managed the impeachment of Andrew Johnson, and popularized the term "bloody shirt" by waving one to emphasize Negro rights. In 1878, he went back to the House as a Greenbacker, and in 1882, after several expensive defeats, became Democratic governor of Massachusetts. Now in 1884, he openly sought the party's presidential nomination, claiming support of workers, farmers, and immigrants.

Butler was stout and bald, with drooping mustache and eyes not quite in line. The *Boston Pilot* once called him "an amiable kleptomaniac," and he seldom rebutted stories alleging he stole silver spoons and other rebel property. "Old Cock-Eye" was a bundle of contradictions. He affected to dislike public acclaim while avidly courting it.

He seemed a mere political corsair, but as governor won support from Wendell Phillips, Clara Barton, Susan B. Anthony, and blue-bloods who would not let him cross their thresholds. He opposed land grants to railroads, threatening to take his own share from the Boston Common, but wanted tariff protection for American goods. Respectable society ostracized Butler, but many of the poor loved him. "What public man in America has ever undergone such a swish of filthy abuse as General Butler . . . and his enemies are our enemies," an Irish paper wrote. Butler counted all publicity of equal value. Cartoonists drew him as "the Widow Butler," because he said he did not seek office like a coy maiden, but as a widow who knew her way around. Opponents fought him because he symbolized the dangerous whimsical element in radicalism, rather than for his diffuse programs. And he was always good copy. "If there comes a time when there is an absolute dearth of news," Murat Halstead once told a friend, "when you can't think of anything to make an interesting letter, there is always one thing you can do, and that is to pitch into Ben Butler." [23]

The "Widow" wanted the Democratic nomination or a separate ticket in 1884. His electoral votes would bring a high price if a disputed election went to the House. He flirted with Boss Kelly, who seemed receptive, and spent some money on quiet popularity polls. Butler's agents toured the Midwest, sounding workers and farmers, but came back discouraged. True, many a farmer leaning on a dung fork agreed he would raise temperatures among the money bags. Workers said he would foil smoother political operators. But the General's agents in the Midwest followed in the wake of men preaching the merits of a newcomer, Grover Cleveland.

Few people outside New York knew Stephen Grover Cleveland. At best they recalled his election as governor in 1882, but attributed that more to Stalwart foolishness than Democratic virtue. His biography made dull reading, as he readily admitted. Born in 1837 in Caldwell, New Jersey, the son of a Presbyterian minister, he passed through the hard times common to many successful politicians. He matured in upstate New York, and centered his life on Buffalo. His father died early, and "Grove" and his brothers worked at odd-jobs to support the family. The young Cleveland taught at the New York Institute for the Blind, then turned to an arid technical law that suited a taste for facts. In his student rooms, a plaque bore allegorical figures of Life, Duty, and Death. "If I have any coat of arms and emblem, it is that." [24] Study did not suit his taste or broaden his horizon. "I think I floundered through four books of the Aeneid," he once said drily, in recalling school days.[25]

Responsibilities fortified a repressed personality, giving him an early veneer of "maturity." He moved in a small group of rowdy masculine friends, and favored the piano-roll and beer stein to the parlor or opera house. He seemed unconcerned about mankind's good opinion, but resented an apparently indifferent world. When a group of law associates snubbed him, he remarked firmly: "Some day I will be better remembered." [26] He was more interested in financial security and emotional safety than public acclaim. Corporation law involving impersonal papers and briefs rather than a courtroom's intimacy made Cleveland modestly wealthy before he entered politics.

Fortunately for his development, he settled in Buffalo. He would not have mastered the unsettled life farther west; in the East, his dullness would have obscured any personal abilities. He showed little inclination to swerve from the road to security. Chauncey Depew of the New York Central Railroad offered him a handsome retainer. Cleveland thought about it, and then summed up his aims: "I have a very definite plan of life, and have decided how much work I can do without impairing my health, and how much additional responsibility I can assume. I have accumulated about seventy-five thousand dollars, and my practice yields me an income which is sufficient for my wants and a prudent addition for my old age to my capital. No amount of money whatsoever would tempt me to add to or increase my present work." [27]

Just as he refused to leave the comfortable security of law practice, he did not broaden his mind with reading. Speculation disturbed his equipoise; he liked certainties. Told of biblical revisionism, he stirred uneasily. "The Bible is good enough for me, just the old book under which I was brought up. I do not want notes, or criticisms, or explanations about authorship or origins, or even cross-references. I do not need, or understand them, and they confuse me." Behind the stolid facade also lurked hints of both romanticism and belief that mankind was depraved, rising from youthful Presbyterianism and a cramped course in the school of life. He once remarked on a splendid sunset: "It is too good for us [mankind]. . . . It is something we don't deserve." [28]

Cleveland moved into an eventless middle-age, unmarried, revealing no private personality fundamentally different from public attitudes. He grew fat from beer, heavy food, and lack of exercise. Nieces and nephews called him "Uncle Jumbo," after Barnum's famous circus elephant and he accepted the criticism within the family. He could display a ponderous humor, but preferred others' jokes, and laughed in unison with friends at the local tavern after a hard day's work. If he did finally relax, he could display "a pervasive atmosphere of rotund jollity," but reverted easily to a serious demeanor.[29]

He resented the political whiggery of "better" lawyers, but also thought government activity threatened individualism. He dabbled idly in local politics before the war, but party work bored him. During the war he hired a substitute, after agreeing with his brothers to support their mother and sister. He later favored Bayard over Tilden, perhaps disliking the latter's talk of "reform." In 1880, he worked for Hancock, and gained some recognition in local Democratic circles.

Cleveland brought no formal philosophy to politics and government, but his natural attitudes created a rhetoric that fitted neatly with prevailing Democratic ideals. Individualism made him prize small government, and he always believed in negative laws. They might regulate, but not promote through favoritism, the total society where individual competition reigned. Men working under natural law would produce social benefits without risking freedom.[30] He talked of "obligations," and attracted some young men to the Democrats, but he spoke more of "duty" than new purpose. His fatalism forbade planning, and a sense of mankind's limitations made him suspect reformers who talked either of equality or charity. He was not callous, but would have every man his own master. Nothing came higher than freedom of motion. A man of talent moved up; a man without talent could not claim society's help.

In calling for honesty, retrenchment, and administrative reform, Cleveland differed little from other Democrats, but he disliked criticism, and tolerated only men who followed his decisions without question. In time, he became frankly pompous. "It is no credit to me to do right," he once told friends. "I am never under any temptation to do wrong!"[31] But how he decided "right" baffled those trying to bring him to their view. Cynicism triumphed in some circles. "The Lord is very kind to Cleveland," L. Q. C. Lamar once remarked. "He always tells him to do the thing he wants to do."[32] Bluntness was his weapon, and supporters called it honesty. "Probably he never wilfully deceived a human being in his life," William Allen White recalled. "But he deserves no special credit, for with his heavy mental and moral equipment, deception was a jugglery he would hardly have tried. Cleveland might throw the hammer or put the shot, but he could never work a shell-game on man or woman."[33]

Cleveland dealt poorly with men personally, preferring the abstract "public." * He entered national politics without experience in group management, fruitful compromise, or molding public opinion. These were abstractions to him, manipulated like checkers on a board. He always thought it enough to sound a clarion call and take a stand; good men would follow a good example. This attitude was fatal to a disorderly Democratic party composed of jealous, semi-independent barons; but Cleveland came by it honestly. He never once overtly sought an office, dealt with antagonists on purely human terms, or explained motives to critics. He was fortunate in having shrewd managers who organized, threatened, and cajoled supporters because they needed him for victory. He never learned the virtues of placating opponents for larger ideals than immediate personal loyalty. Despite the tireless work of shrewd press agents, Cleveland was never popular, and remained a figurehead rather than a person to voters.[34]

Cleveland easily might have become a congressman or judge, but in 1870 ran for sheriff of Erie County. Comrades of the ward hall and horse trough touted the place as a step to higher office, with a lucrative salary based on fees. It was a distasteful job in a brawling port city, but Cleveland was efficient, even tripping the hangman's lever for two capital offenders, a task other sheriffs left to deputies. This became part of a legend of honesty and responsibility. He was lucky, earning credit for negative achievements in a Democratic party desperate for new "respectable" talent. He attracted the attention of upstate machine leaders because of calm honesty, apparent quality, and efficiency. The men now gathering around him came and went silently, breaking the routine with an occasional guffaw or joke, smoking bad cigars and smelling faintly of the grape and stein. He was one of them, but stood apart, using their skills without publicly acknowledging the debt. They realized the party must widen its upstate enclaves of power, and saw in Cleveland a convenient symbol of honesty in government. In 1881, he won the mayoralty of Buffalo, and gained a reputation for negative honesty that suited Democratic Warwicks. As the "Veto Mayor" he appealed to "retrench and reform" elements without forgetting the loaves and fishes.

Arthur's gamble on Folger in 1882 was their chance for success. Cleveland wanted the governorship badly, and worked for the nomination with a group of managers in newspaper circles connected to Til-

---

*A recent biographer has put this well: "Cleveland possessed the personal qualities to command but not to lead." (Horace S. Merrill, *Bourbon Leader: Grover Cleveland and the Democratic Party* [Boston: Little, Brown and Co., 1957], 123.)

den. Daniel Manning, Daniel S. Lamont, Edgar Apgar, David B. Hill, and finally William C. Whitney formed a coterie that silently carried Cleveland to the top. A diverse group in taste, sharing a desire to win and a basic love of political dealing, they were ideal managers for Cleveland.

In 1882, as the state convention prepared to choose Folger's opponent, the elegant Whitney hurried to Manning's hotel room, interrupted his conversation with a stranger, and announced firmly: "The man who can defeat the Republicans worst is that buxom Buffalonian, Grover Cleveland. You upstate Democrats want to unite with the New York [City] Democracy on Cleveland, and we'll not only elect him governor this fall, but president a little later. I have never met him, but I know he's all right." Manning then introduced his guest, Grover Cleveland.[35] The vignette illustrated Cleveland's chief quality, a lack of publicity that made him acceptable to party factions. The legend was growing; he would soon be a full-blown symbol. Whitelaw Reid's paper admitted the shrewdness of his selection. "The nomination of Mayor Cleveland for governor . . . means hard work for the Republicans. Mr. Cleveland is young, able, and has a clean record."[36]

As Governor of New York, he rapidly enlarged a reputation for forthright administration, and became so intractable that opponents discussed "His Obstinacy," and "the Veto Governor." He shrewdly put men demanding favors on the defensive; they had to explain their case to a watchful and silent executive. His familiar remark "I don't know that I fully understand you" unnerved them. It was also irritating. He reprimanded elements of his own party, laying foundations for an important factor in national crusades: "Grover Cleveland has shown himself what we took him on trust to be last fall—bigger and better than his party." Every ringing veto enlarged his public aura of honesty and independence from bread-and-butter Democrats. In vetoing a bill, he said: "Of all the defective and shabby legislation which has been presented to me, this is the worst and the most inexcusable."[37]

True; but as the French say, all that is true is not good to tell. Tilden was suspicious, yet knew Cleveland was an attractive candidate. The Sage summed him up neatly: "Oh, he is the kind of man who would rather do something badly for himself than have somebody else do it well."[38] Tilden did not support Cleveland openly, and for all anyone knew, wanted the nomination himself in 1884. He did not say so, but realized that Bayard, Randall, or southerners could not be his heirs. It was best to start fresh; a man with a recent record, even if negative, had many advantages. On the other hand, Tammany Hall hated

Cleveland. In 1883, because he distrusted the City element and disliked their easy assumptions of rights and influence, he conducted a guerilla war against the Hall's minions and prerogatives. The old conflict between "hayseeds" and "city-slickers" flared into new bitterness. Tammany did not mind the Governor's talk about "honesty," "duty," and "The People." As Bourke Cockran, leading lieutenant of the Tammany braves, said bluntly, they had heard it before. They objected to "his plan of governing without reference to the party which puts him in office." [39] They also suspected talk of retrenchment and reform. These clichés unnerved men who needed street contracts, padded payrolls, and generous relief funds.

Cleveland was no sooner elected governor than opposition papers noted that his mere presence in Albany made him a logical Democratic presidential aspirant. To the last moment, Cleveland maintained an elaborate disinterest in further political heights, but did not fool anyone working for him. He knew Tammany's growing opposition was a blessing, increasing his claims to genteel reform habits. He saw that Tilden's strength could only come his way. And he let everyone imagine he would "take advice" in office.

His affairs passed quietly to the Democratic party's only really astute managers. Daniel Manning was their chief, working closely with Cleveland's personal friend, Daniel S. Lamont. The stout, taciturn Manning was the obverse of rural success, the classic city boy who made good. After a poverty-ridden youth in a large family, he became a page in the state Assembly at Albany. He was a paper-boy, then worked on the *Albany Argus* as a messenger, copy-boy, compositor, and finally a legislative reporter. Journalism was an excellent school of politics. He committed to memory all the tiny facts that cumulatively became insight into managing individual politicians and organizing a party. His quiet, careful reporting earned friends in county and ward politics, and after 1877 he managed the state Democratic organization with Tilden's blessing.

Lamont's career was similar, and he became Cleveland's private secretary with the honorific title "Colonel," an encomium not limited to the South. If anything, he was quieter than Manning, and seemed to disappear into the paneling while listening to others. William Collins Whitney brought color to the group, but never overplayed his hand. The son of a wealthy New England Democratic family, he sported a Yale education and connections in northeastern establishments. He helped Tilden attack the Tweed Ring, but had contacts in the city machine, and understood Kelly better than anyone in the upstate group. A patron of the arts, he regularly toured Europe, and lived lavishly in several town-houses and on the spa circuit. His own fortune came from city traction systems and shrewd stock dealings. His greatest political assets were an amazing skill at organizing campaigns, and a personal charm that managed diverse interests.

Cleveland and all these aides had the combined assets of one able candidate who might fill the Democracy's vacuum of national leadership. By 1884, the Governor had a small reputation for "reform" that attracted independent voters who could determine the election's result. It was their kind of reform, emphasizing efficiency rather than innovation, but some critics noted the men around Cleveland and questioned the reputation. Charles Dana called him "our obese governor," and "the stuffed prophet." Still others thought him a machine product of Whitney, Manning, and Lamont. But, as the papers kept repeating, he was safe, better than his party.

As 1884 approached, Manning and Lamont traveled to the Midwest, and Greystone. Cleveland was quiet, avoiding controversy outside New York. Seeming to be the ideal bipartisan candidate, he was not connected to southerners, was removed from western agrarians, acceptable to Tildenites and almost welcomed Tammany's distrust as a badge of gentility. He did his duty, watched the press, and let others work. When friends raised a picnic toast, "Here's to Governor Cleveland, our next president," he frowned slightly. "What are you talking about? I've never had a thought of such a thing." [40] The crotchety New York Sun called such talk "Nonsense run wild." [41] With the new year, occasional politicians hinted at "the springing of a candidate, as yet unnamed, upon the Democratic convention." [42] Others around Tammany sneered: "And who is Grover Cleveland?" [43]

Manning had a simple but effective strategy. He would keep Cleveland quiet and let other contenders wear out. They were familiar faces with enemies and weaknesses; the New Yorker would acquire their strength by default. He would strengthen the County Democracy, respectable non-New York City elements hostile to Kelly's braves, with funds and organizational talent. Outside New York, Manning would quietly canvass the Midwest and Border states, hoping to make Cleveland second choice of most delegations. Finally, he would persuade Tilden to step aside, still assuming he could control a Cleveland administration. Manning would try to avoid a split with Tammany, but if it came, independent Republicans might make the difference in electoral votes.

Manning did not become Cleveland's manager-in-chief without a small struggle. Mutual friends early suggested the new Governor call on him and deal with pro-Tilden forces. Cleveland balked; not only from pride, but because he wished to state his independence. The Tilden people came to him, thus fortifying allegiance to his cause. Manning was a calm and invisible link between the camps, anxious not to advertise his new wares. While he worked with the enlarging County Democracy, he cautioned friends against publicity. "It is possible that you [newspaper] boys will arouse a sentiment that will be troublesome to us. Cleveland is not yet a candidate and Tilden is not yet out of the way." [44] Some independent voters in marginal states that could give Cleveland victory watched this subterranean action with the practiced eyes of professional reformer-politicians. The public knew little of Cleveland, but these men had seen the machine's inside and knew how it worked. After Blaine's nomination, the Governor in Albany had the best chance among wavering Republicans. [45]

Of course, every mention of an independent Democracy rallying around Cleveland enraged Tammany. Cleveland had done nothing for the working-class, or immigrant groups like the Irish. He vetoed a bill providing lower commuter fares because it seemed to violate a contract clause, opposed state aid to Catholic charitable institutions, and rebuffed Kelly's demands for recognition and patronage. He was as weak in city labor circles as he seemed strong with aloof independents. As one labor paper said, he "watched like a lynx for every bill in the interests of the working classes, that he might put his foot upon it." [46] Cleveland's aides tried to negotiate with Kelly. Firm assurances about patronage and recognition might soften Kelly's fears that Cleveland in the White House would reward only a section of the party, but Cleveland's heavy-handed manner precluded harmony. The Hall invited him to attend a meeting to condemn the "Crime of '76," and pledge fealty to Democracy, but he did not even acknowledge the message. [47] Talk of independent voters and empty "reform" crusades rankled Kelly. He wanted to carry the traditional blocs; as a spokesman once said: "For one Republican gained, we would lose twenty Democrats." [48]

Kelly openly favored Ben Butler, with some approval from labor and immigrant groups. The first week in July, he announced bluntly: ". . . I would regard Cleveland's nomination very much in the light of party suicide, and hope it will not be done. It would kill us. The laboring people are not with him, and cannot be made to support him. . . . I will not lift a hand for him." [49] He knew that Blaine, run-

ning on a pro-Irish past, an "American" foreign policy, and tariff protection, would carry New York. Kelly's talk only enhanced Cleveland's
chances. A man with "Boss Kelly" and the "Widow Butler" against
him gained many friends.

Manning's agents in the Midwest fulfilled their general plan. The
favorite-son strength in Ohio, the Border, Illinois and Plains states was
shaky. With a little help and discreet promises, it would go for Cleveland after the first ballot. Business leaders like Henry Villard and
James J. Hill in the Old Northwest favored him; and western Democrats preferred an apparently liberal New Yorker to a southerner.

Tilden's attitude was still the great question mark. The Sage kept
supporters guessing. By May, the papers belatedly noted the obvious;
Tilden's followers could choose another man. A month before the convention, Tilden's aides let Randall down easily. He would not be the
heir. The Sage would dictate no successor, but a forthcoming letter of
withdrawal "will have a tendency to promote the chances of Cleveland
. . . in our state convention." A secretary admitted Tilden had been
silent "to keep the party together." [50] The tactics of stalling favorite
sons just short of real strength worked well. It allowed a dark horse
to win, and kept everybody confused enough to stifle opposition.

Manning now made his move with Tilden. The second week in
June, he appeared at Greystone to say that Cleveland would have "a
thoroughly Tilden administration." The Sage finished his usual letter
of withdrawal, and authorized Manning to inform delegates that "while
I could not assume to dictate to the Democratic party, my judgement
was in favor of nominating Mr. Cleveland." [51] On June 10, the press
carried Tilden's letter which dimly outlined reasons for not assuming
a fresh burden. Poor health dominated the argument, but as Thomas
F. Grady of Tammany Hall remarked: "Tilden's physical infirmities
floated the excuse [for his withdrawal], but Manning's political necessities suggested the physical infirmities." [52] Upstate newspapers killed
the Flower boom, attacked Kelly, and increased propaganda for Cleveland as the man to unite New York and the whole party. At the state
convention in Saratoga on June 18, Manning astutely let Tammany
vote against Cleveland, but kept the whole delegation under a unit
rule. Cleveland stayed out of the headlines, an unknown but respectable harmonizer who would not forget his friends.

Mugwumps and reformers had opposed machine politicians enough
to know how to launch their own boom. As it became clear that Blaine
could win the GOP nomination with the blessing of most Republican

leaders and a clear majority of Republican voters, reformers and independents diverted attention to their perpetual straw man, George F.
Edmunds. Their fundamental argument was not original. A Blaine
candidacy would be a "prolonged defense." [53] He would be a whet-
stone for every dissident's knife. Younger Republicans like Henry
Cabot Lodge and Theodore Roosevelt joined older Mugwumps, despite mutual dislike, to argue that Edmunds could carry New York
and crucial mid-Atlantic states. On just what platform they did not say.

Edmunds maintained a "sphinx-like silence," but later told Senator
Morrill in his usual high-toned rhetoric: ". . . I could not in any case
court popularity by saying or doing anything that I would not say
and do were the office of senator a life [tenure] one." [54] Busy, self-
important men like Roosevelt carefully planned demonstrations on
convention-eve, and told each other in daily letters that "reform"
would beat Blaine at the last moment. Neither their work nor Edmunds' silence prevented some acid newspaper criticism. The *Washington Post* called him "a professional tool of the corporations and in
no respect a representative of the people." [55] The *New York World*
lit into the independents and Edmunds. "All the pharisees support
Mr. Edmunds. But they support him on pretenses that are hypocritical.
Their real object is to beat Blaine, *whom they cannot control,* and as
they hate Arthur they fall back with much pious snivelling on Edmunds." [56] Dana condemned the "hollow-eyed and weary Independents and kickers who . . . nursed [the Edmunds boom]. It was a select
and particularly small boom, yet, as Mr. Webster said of Dartmouth
College, there were those who loved it." [57]

As delegates went to Chicago for the Republican national convention, Blaine closed his campaign for the nomination. A month earlier,
he instructed Elkins not to pressure delegates beyond the boundaries
of party unity. "I never want it [the nomination] unless it be the un-
bought, unbiased will of the nominating power." He warned against
spending money. *"I enjoin this upon you with special emphasis."* On
May 22, he authorized Elkins to act in his behalf on all matters.[58]
Blaine stayed in Washington, seemingly nonchalant, but when the convention opened, he left for Augusta to avoid embarrassing President
Arthur when nominated. Observers predicted a Blaine victory within
six ballots, but the President kept calm. One of his cabinet members
said with a puzzled air: "I do not believe he feels as much concern in
[*sic*] the result at Chicago as we do." [59]

The delegates gathered with a rush early in June, as Blaine's enthusiastic partisans predicted victory, punctuating yells and toasts with flag-waving and energetic last-minute efforts among doubtful brethren. They pressed white plumes, buttons, literature, canes, and special hats on everyone. Both galleries and the floor were Maine's territory, but Mugwumps staged final efforts to beat "The Man." On Monday, June 2, they heard Curtis praise Edmunds as one whose record sparkled like a clear mountain stream. Roosevelt myopically mounted a rickety chair, waved a "nobby" straw hat, and shouted.

The convention opened on Tuesday, June 3, and Mugwumps won a brief victory in electing a Negro delegate, John R. Lynch of Mississippi, as temporary chairman, over Blaine's friend Powell Clayton of Arkansas. A restless convention heard debate on the proposed unit rule, aimed to prevent a Mugwump bolt. Curtis announced: "A Republican and a free man will I go out of this convention." The California delegate making the motion withdrew it, and Curtis remained pure.[60] The next day, William McKinley, a Blaine supporter, reported a platform with few surprises. It favored civil service reform, and promised that tariff protection would dominate the campaign.

The assembled multitude came to cheer for Blaine, and got their chance on the evening of June 5, when nominations were in order. Dreary speakers put forward Joseph R. Hawley and John Logan. Then the famous "Blind Orator," Judge William H. West of Ohio, named Blaine in a stirring example of spread-eagle oratory, appealing to young voters and all those favoring change. "Nominate him, and the shouts of September victory in Maine will be re-echoed back by the thunders of the October victory in Ohio," West proclaimed. "Nominate him and the camp-fires and beacon-lights will illuminate the continent from the Golden Gate to Cleopatra's Needle." When he finished, the crowd raised a roar that fluttered the gas-lights. Confetti made a blizzard in the air, and a forest of white plumes waved on the floor and in the galleries. Ladies shook parasols and chanted "Blaine! Blaine! The Man From Maine!" while escorts threw hats, streamers, and pieces of bunting. They drowned out the brass band, and subsiding with weariness, started up again when someone made a cuckoo sound. A young lady in white sang repeatedly: "God Bless Jim Blaine!"

The independents were disgusted. Andrew D. White thought it was shocking; Roosevelt said it was uncouth; and Godkin later condemned "a mass meeting of maniacs." [61] When order returned, a New York businessman nominated Arthur with a bow to efficiency, safety, and economy in government. Ohio's Joseph B. Foraker named Sherman, with the usual apologies and a cut at Blaine: ". . . we want a man who is distinguished, not so much for the brilliancy of his genius as for that other, safer, better, and more assuring quality, the brilliancy of common sense." Amid these *non sequiturs*, Foraker mentioned Blaine and set off another demonstration, which he almost joined.[62] John D. Long of Massachusetts spoke for Edmunds, and the convention adjourned.

The next day, tense but subdued delegates gathered to vote. On the first ballot—with 411 votes necessary to win—Blaine commanded 334 delegates, to 278 for Arthur and 93 for Edmunds, with the rest scattered. On the second call, Blaine gained 5, Arthur lost 2, and others remained stationary. The third tally showed a rise for Blaine to 375, and in the confusion his enemies tried to adjourn. McKinley and others helped beat the motion, then chose Blaine on a fourth ballot. While the cheering raged, Arthur congratulated Blaine by telegram.

It was different on the convention floor. Carl Schurz solemnly looked at his pocket watch: "From this hour dates the death of the Republican party." [63] Curtis watched happy delegates with an air of disgust. "The sad and kindly face of Lincoln, whose portrait hung in the hall, seemed to watch the proceedings of the convention with an air of earnest solicitude and apprehension; and it had disappeared from its place before the nomination was made." [64] The selection that night of John A. Logan as Blaine's running mate satisfied the rank and file, and further alienated Mugwumps already talking of a bolt if the Democrats named a respectable candidate.

Professionals did not deny "the overwhelming popular demand for Blaine." He was the people's choice; good organization only confirmed the fact. That also proved to Mugwumps how gullible people were in a democracy where personality counted. Cynics like Tom Reed agreed, from another angle. Henry Cabot Lodge encountered him on the street after the convention. Reed disliked humanity in general, and successful people like Blaine in particular, and always had a ready tongue. "Well, it is a great comfort to think that the wicked politicians were not allowed to pick the candidate, and that the nomination was made by the people," he drawled in an amused, high-pitched voice.[65] Arthur was the most disappointed rival. "Like the Arabs, we quietly folded our tents and silently stole away," a manager wrote him.[66]

It was comforting to say, like Tom Platt, that it was "Blaine's turn," but the Plumed Knight represented more than a spin of Fortune's wheel. He symbolized change, embodied success, spoke for vitality. He stood for a unified party, a dynamic foreign policy, workable civil service reform, the unifying doctrine of tariff protection, and federal activity. Blaine conducted his canvass for the nomination without bitterness, and attracted able managers who tried to retain party unity while advancing his fortunes. Blaine doubted final success; the "great Unknown" might beat him yet. But he was the people's choice, and deserved the laurels.

Blaine's selection had a mixed effect on the Democrats, scheduled to convene early in July. They could try to cover weaknesses with a personal campaign against him, but he was genuinely popular. They were still divided and confused. The *New York Times* noted at convention time that some nineteen Democratic leaders thought they had a chance for the nomination.[67] None commanded a truly national constituency. Somehow the party must organize its disparate forces around a man or cause.

Manning and his deputies arrived in Chicago early, to tie loose ends and persuade wavering brethren. General Butler, coming later, got a loud, if mixed reception. Passing through a crush, he went to a Palmer House balcony, and addressed applauding pilgrims in the usual forthright manner. After much confusion and many epigrams, he discovered he was standing in a window of Manning's suite, under an immense picture of Cleveland. He withdrew without signs of embarrassment, and made the rounds to shake hands and suggest deals. Southern Democrats recalled his New Orleans days. "We may be willing to eat crow," one spat, "but we'll be damned if we'll eat turkey buzzard." Kelly and his braves arrived in Indian costumes, complete with war paint, feathered headresses, and tomahawks. The County Democracy marched in more sedate outfits, looking grim. They were not averse, despite gentility, to fist-fights with City opponents.[68]

The convention opened on Tuesday, July 8, in Chicago's Exposition Hall. A lowering sky occasionally broke into patches of blue, and shafts of sunlight brightened rippled bunting. Only some fifty people sat on the platform and had a good view of the galleries. Huge pictures of Washington, Jackson, and Jefferson faced the assemblage. The outcome remained doubtful, with nearly every candidate's intentions obscure, but it was a fine time for cheering. Allen G. Thurman led in the Ohio delegation and a supporter cried: "The California delegation, after travelling twenty-five hundred miles, catches its first glimpse of Paradise in the person of Allen G. Thurman." On that first exciting day, every mention of Tilden's name evoked applause, and the prospect of gathering some independent Republican sheaves stirred the professionals.[69]

A long list of nominating speeches consumed the second day, and displayed the party's bent for confusion and delay. Bayard, Hendricks, Thurman, Carlisle, had their moments as the clocked dragged its rounds. After Carlisle's nomination, Mayor Carter Harrison of Chicago rose to voice an almost universal sentiment. "On behalf of ten thousand hungry and five thousand thirsty people, I move that the convention adjourn until seven o'clock this evening." He apparently felt that half the crowd were Prohibitionists. His motion failed, and the noisy delegates heard New York's Daniel N. Lockwood name Cleveland. Insisting that Cleveland alone could carry New York, Lockwood praised "his honor, his integrity, his wisdom, and his Democracy." As the cheering and jeering subsided, Tammany moved. Thomas F. Grady indicted Cleveland as anti-labor, anti-immigrant, and unpopular in New York City. As he labored on, a delegate shouted "Why don't you speak for Blaine?" Bourke Cockran, famed for a silver throat, continued the attack. In the confusion, a Missouri delegate voiced a general feeling: "I simply want to know whether this is a session of the New York delegation at Albany, or whether we are here for the purpose of attending to business in the City of Chicago. We are tired of this thing." Edgar Apgar compared Cleveland to Tilden, and the convention finally adjourned.[70]

Most delegates fidgeted through the next day's speeches for George Hoadly of Ohio, and Samuel J. Randall, but Wisconsin's fiery "old warhorse," General Edward S. Bragg, walked to the platform amid expectant tension. He spoke for the western element that increasingly favored Cleveland. Irritated at Tammany's attacks, he planned to answer charge for charge, no matter "party harmony." He began a blood-and-thunder oration that soon had spectators cheering and rival delegates making threats. He was acrid, sarcastic, and demagogic. Speaking for young westerners, he cried out in a famous phrase: "They love him, gentlemen, and they respect him, not only for himself, for his character, for his integrity and judgement and iron will, but they love him most for the enemies he has made." Through the pandemonium, Grady shouted: "On behalf of his enemies, I accept your statement!" Bragg then arraigned the Hall for hypocrisy. "Wherever the thin disguise can be breached, you will find it covering nothing but personal grievances, disappointed ambition, or the cutting-off of access to the flesh-pots to those who desire to fatten upon them." Tammany leaders spoke of labor, but had smooth hands. "Yes; their labor has been upon the crank of the machine; their study has been political chicane in the midnight conclave." A leather-lunged gallery dweller pierced the disorder with: "Give them a little more grape,

Captain Bragg!" Ignoring the loss of rank, General Bragg finished with a warning and admonition. "The party wants some new life. They have followed old leaders to death. . . . Let our old war-horses be retired with honor." [71] After more talk, the conclave adjourned until the evening session.

Reformers like Morrison and Watterson wanted the tariff plank to be a bugle call for the present campaign and future organization. They hit a stone wall, as men around Randall defeated serious revisionism. After fifty hours of debate in the Resolutions Committee, they got a modestly defined "tariff for revenue only." The platform "emitted no more than a squawk" on the subject.[72] As the convention heard the rambling, obscure document—straddling on silver, protection, and civil service reform—word passed that General Butler would offer a substitute platform favoring cheap money, opposing civil service reform, and supporting a selective protective tariff. In May, both the Anti-Monopoly Party and Greenback Party named him for president. Now he apparently thought like Cinderella's sisters; he could wear the Democratic shoe.

The clerk offered Butler's substitute platform and the General prepared thirty minutes of his own inimitable oratory. Amid mingled cheers and boos, he swayed slightly on the platform, immaculate in a frock coat with pansies in the buttonhole. He spoke "in his customary jerky, forceful way, gesticulating freely, and facing the audience at the right, the left and in front of him." In a few minutes, Butler delighted spoilsmen and disgusted reformers. Reaching civil service reform, he looked at the portrait of George Washington and raised a wavering finger. "And he could not have passed examination for a clerkship. . . . His early education had been neglected. And in his will, written by his own hand, he spells 'clothes' 'c-l-o-a-t-h-e-s.'" He insisted everyone had a right to office as long as he could keep it. The convention alternated between amusement and embarrassment, then voted Butler down.[73]

After adopting the regular platform, the delegates balloted for president. The first tally, with 547 necessary to win, gave Cleveland 392 votes, largely from the Midwest, with some from New England and the Border states. Bayard followed, with 170 from the South. Thurman had 88; Randall, 78; the rest were scattered. A second ballot might either make or break Cleveland, but Manning urged adjournment to strengthen his lines. It was a gamble, but it paid off, for the irritable delegates were in no mood for open pressure.[74]

The galleries emptied, and worn-out enthusiasts sought sleep, but hollow-eyed leaders talked through clouds of smoke and surrounded by a litter of bottles and sandwich wrappers, about the next day's chances. Manning held his men firm, and renewed contacts in favorite-son delegations. Cleveland's opponents had a last trump card that said volumes of the party's straits; they prepared to "holler for Hendricks." Assuming he could totter onstage, Hendricks was to emerge from a small room near the platform at a crucial moment during the second ballot. His clique would cry for "the Old Ticket," and stampede delegates into redeeming the past. Manning heard of the plot, and warned his men to sit on their hands. The whole scene would have been pathetic and quaint, except it had a chance to succeed.[75] About noon the next day, when the clerk called Illinois, a vote was cast for Hendricks, initiating an immense demonstration in the galleries as the old man entered. The Chair abandoned the gavel while spectators cheered. But only about a fourth of the delegates joined the demonstration. After the shouting died, Daniel W. Voorhees cast Indiana's votes for Hendricks, but Illinois gave 38 votes to Cleveland. Randall released Pennsylvania for patronage, and her vote began the avalanche that chose Cleveland on a revised second ballot.[76] Hendricks got his reward later that evening, as the vice-presidential tail to a second ticket.

In Albany, Cleveland feigned indifference. Townsfolk gathered around the capitol grounds, and at telegraph billboards throughout the city, were ready to cheer the news. Sounds of cannon fire penetrated the Governor's office and Lamont looked up. "They are firing a salute, Governor, for your nomination." Cleveland was bland. "Do you think so?" After fiddling with papers, he said calmly: "Well, anyhow, we'll finish up this work." Lamont shortly got the official telegraph news. "Is that so, Dan?" Cleveland noted. "By Jove, that is something isn't it?" He shook hands all around, dispatched the news to the governor's mansion, and prepared for the inevitable citizen's demonstration. That night, a torchlight parade passed in review; dawn revealed trampled grass, ripped picket fencing, and a litter of garbage. He was on his way.[77]

Cleveland's managers talked of "reform," and pictured the candidate as a harmonizer, but opponents thought otherwise. "The work of the machine is done," Dana's *Sun* reported. They gave Whitney, Manning, and other New Yorkers high marks, but thought Cleveland's negative record would lose labor and immigrant votes.[78] Bayard's men were bitter, reporting "it was and will be useless to work against any such a combination of strong, active and experienced men as those who appeared in behalf of Cleveland." They saw Tilden's fine hand, and credited Cleveland's victory to the idea he could carry New York.[79] Others thought the choice a mere straddle. Cleveland lacked a national record, was an indifferent campaigner, and could not carry industrial states. J. Sterling Morton argued that "principles, character and a lofty mind [Bayard's] were put aside for supposed availability, record-lessness and mediocrity." [80]

Republicans did not quite know what to think. As an unknown quantity, Cleveland might be either weak or strong with the crucial independents. They took the path of least resistance at first, noting that he was "a small man everywhere but on the hay scales." [81] Democrats had qualms, while publicly retaining a discreet silence. What would Tammany do? The sachems talked volubly of rest, with sly hints about supporting Butler. "The golden-tongued ex-Senator Grady was as dumb as an oyster, and the silver-tongued Bourke Cockran said that if he wished to talk he could not do so clearly until he had taken a Turkish bath," the *Sun* reported. There was hope, of course. A lesser spokesman noted wearily: "I suppose we'll fall into line. We won't spend our last dollar for the ticket, as we would have done for any other candidate." [82] In other words, a little dealing could make a lot of difference.

Cleveland's nomination surprised the public. The press usually mentioned him as a vice-presidential candidate before the convention met. His selection did not reflect any clarion call for reform; nor was he the people's choice. He won with astute management, by seeming to be Tilden's heir and acceptable to independents, and because party opponents fragmented his opposition. He symbolized a certain new-ness, without challenging the party's reigning negativism. As an un-familiar man, with able managers, he offered a chance for a unified, empty campaign. All this could spell victory, if the Democrats con-centrated on Blaine's past, and avoided discussing their own future.

Between the two nominations, independent Republicans went into a flurry of activity. Throughout the spring, their spokesmen warned against Blaine's selection, but leading party figures pooh-poohed a bolt. Party allegiance was a fundamental fact of life; not even reform-ers and intellectuals changed it lightly. Independents now wanted to purify politics without accepting changes in American society which an emerging national party system could manage. They wished to take the Republican party back to an imagined Eden, and did not want to join in the Democratic coalition. Cleveland's nomination saved them. They could vote for a man, not a party. Anyone who understood the Republican party saw the ironic aspects of the situation. Blaine did

more than anyone else to mold the party to new issues, and widen its
constituency. He appealed to the young, to many workers and farmers, minority groups and businessmen. But the very "reform" element
that should have profited from his beginnings in a new kind of politics
made him seem a front for spoilsmen, the tool of interests more vivid
in their imaginations than in reality.

The independents, soon rewarded with the capitalized title "Mugwumps", started building a paper movement with the nervous zeal
and sense of accomplishment common to intellectuals unaccustomed to
political activity. The day after Blaine's nomination, a formative group
gathered in Boston, ready to sing hosannas of reform, and pleased at
the idea of using their vote to win the election. Men like Moorefield
Storey, Richard Henry Dana, and John Quincy Adams in Boston;
Curtis, Godkin, and Schurz in New York, filled the press with an-
nouncements of withdrawal. In Boston, "All was excitement, and everybody was on fire. Not a man in the room wished to support Blaine." [83]
Shuttling between The Hub and New York, dissidents formed a "Committee of 100," with allies in the press, some financial circles, and the
professions. Curtis hesitated to join because he thought the bolt might
affect sales of *Harper's Weekly.* Charles F. Adams, Jr., warned friends
that leaving the GOP would make them "what the Italians call *fores-
tieri,* or dwellers in the woods." If the Democrats lost, where would
they go? Curtis devised a candid answer. "When the only argument
is that we [Republicans] are not so bad as the other fellow, it is time
to call a halt." [84]

Schurz quickly became the most vocal and ubiquitous critic of
Blaine. Their antagonism was hardly new. While in Hayes' Cabinet,
Schurz thought Blaine weak on civil service reform. He dismissed his
support of Garfield against the Stalwarts as an effort to dominate a
weak Administration. Late in 1883 and early in 1884, he mounted a
guerilla war against Blaine's nomination in the genteel press, and lectured on the evils of spoilsmanship. Blaine had long since returned
the sentiment, calling the Liberal Republicans of 1872 "political recu-
sants and self-seekers." [85] Intermediaries like Missouri's respected ex-
Senator John B. Henderson now tried to heal the breach. ". . . I do
believe that if Blaine be elected, he will give us a good administration. . . . If he has been a Prince Hal in days gone by, when responsibility comes he will be a Henry V. The Falstaffs who have followed
him that thrift might follow fawning, will not be recognized in shaping
his policies, nor be suffered to bring odium upon his administration."
Schurz hardly read the letter before answering. "I cannot look upon
Mr. Blaine as a mere jolly Prince Hal, who has lived through his years

of indiscretion and of whom the presidency will certainly make a new man." [86]

The Mugwumps soon made their influence clear. Important newspapers announced they would not support Blaine, including several in New York, where Republicans needed every vote. Only dislike of Blaine united them. "Some strange novelties appear," Senator Bayard wrote Senator Henry G. Davis, "and to find *Harper's Weekly,* the *New York Times,* the [*New York*] *Evening Post,* the *New York Herald,* etc., all aiding the Democratic nominee is enough to make a man stare." [87] They got a mixed reception among Democrats. Senator Vance of North Carolina thought mugwumpery was "a kind of sickly, sentimental, Sunday-school, 'Goody-two-shoes' party, which appears desirous of ruling the world not as God has made it but as they would have it." [88] Democratic city machine managers did not trust Mugwumps. Richard Croker of Tammany once remarked: "All your high principles will not induce a Mugwump to take more than a fitful interest in an occasional election." [89] Democratic ward-workers feared a national administration would reward local Mugwumps more than those who organized immigrants and sweaty workers. The Curtis-Schurz group did not enhance their image among the unwashed by saying of Cleveland, "He is strong, not because of his party, but despite it." [90]

The Mugwumps lived on momentum and outrage between the nominations. Had the Democrats chosen anyone but Cleveland or Bayard, they might have stolen away like the Arabs. But, by rote, they argued that Cleveland stood for civil service reform and leaned in the right direction. They cited his public letters during the campaign of 1882, and the already popular phrase "A Public Office is a Public Trust" * as evidence of things not quite seen. The Republican press warned that civil service reform would come after Democrats filled the offices. In October, Curtis frankly asked Cleveland to state his views, and just before the election he answered to the Mugwumps' satisfaction: "I am, of course, a Democrat, attached to the principles of the party; and if elected, I desire to remain true to that organization. But I do not think partisan zeal should lead to the 'arbitrary dismissal for party or political reasons.'" [91]

To potential power in the press and the influential middle class, Mugwumps added an irritating self-righteousness. "We have not left the party," one proclaimed loftily, "it is fairer to say that the party has

---

*One of Cleveland's campaign subordinates actually coined the famous phrase. (See McElroy, *Grover Cleveland,* I, 87.) In 1880, General Hancock used a similar expression in his letter of acceptance. "Public office is a trust, not a bounty bestowed upon the holder." (*New York Times,* July 31, 1880.)

left us." [92] Some regulars thought the bolters had listened to each other too long; "the Independents were themselves the 'authors of nine-tenths of all the scandals, and the only believers of the other tenth.' " [93] Most Republicans preferred the sharp weapon of ridicule. "Mr. George William Curtis and Mr. Carl Schurz are supposed to be riding side-ways," one noted, "because there is not one among them [the Mug-wumps] masculine enough to ride astraddle." [94] Cartoonists parodied "Wise Men of the East," who "addressed long letters to the mugwump press over their signatures. These names are invariably parted in the middle or else spelled out in full, as for instance, Thomas Wentworth Higginson, F. Winthrop White, James Freeman Clarke." [95] Masters of doggerel had a field day: [96]

> Oh, we are the salt of the earth,
>   and the pick of the people too;
> We're all of us men of worth,
>   and vastly better than you!
>
> *Chorus*
> Sing hey! the political flirts!
>   The dainty, delicious few!
> There's Captain Beecher and Corporal Schurz,
>   And Captain Codman too!
>
> The majority's sure to be wrong,
>   we are the moral few—
> But they're 'coming it' awfully strong,
>   and that makes us awfully blue!
>
> Sing ho! the political flirts!
>   the moral, immaculate few!
> There's Curtis and Godkin and Corporal Schurz,
>   and the Boston 'Tizer' too!

In July, a pro-Blaine Irish-American rally in New York heard the prin-cipal speaker bitterly indict Mugwumps. "If I ever go to heaven and meet them there, I hope God will let me camp on the outside." [97] Blaine would not comment publicly, and privately feigned noncha-lance. "Oh, they have re-enacted the moral law and the Ten Com-mandments for a platform," he had once said, "and have demanded an angel of light for president." [98]

As everyone predicted, New York became a major battleground. The independents fought regular Republicans. The Irish fought each other. Germans and Catholics wavered over local issues like parochial aid to schools and Temperance. Tammany sulked and was rude about Cleve-land. It was hard to say who was ahead as the campaign started, but the Mugwumps made the most noise. As the courtly Bayard said with surprise: "The Independents attack him [Blaine] with a bitterness quite unknown to the Democrats." [99] It seemed odd. Some of his best friends were Independents.

While Republicans quarreled, Democrats seemed passive. After Cleveland's nomination Randall suggested the party stay quiet until fall, organize and raise funds, pacify its branches, and keep the candidates quiet. Cleveland would "grow on the people," and they could avoid "a hurrah campaign" while Blaine exhausted himself. The stolid Cleveland remained in Albany, planning few if any speeches, writing a letter of acceptance. He made a few ceremonial appearances, as when he accepted the nomination on July 29 at the executive mansion in Albany. Hendricks rested at the Grand Union Hotel in Saratoga Springs, preparing for an onslaught in crucial Indiana.

Boss Kelly hung between passivity and hostility. When reporters early asked if he would support Cleveland, he snapped: "I cannot tell you." When they pressed the issue, he pointed to the door. [100] Complaining of sore throats, the braves left for home. A few papers, notably the *Sun,* could not take Cleveland and endorsed Butler, now a dangerous undecided factor for both parties. Kelly's full cooperation could offset Butler's gains among workers hostile to Cleveland. Independents did not worry the braves as much as the Democratic candidate. "Cleveland is no Democrat," Kelly reportedly said. "If elected, he will prove a traitor to his party." [101] As the fall campaign season developed, Cleveland privately kept an air of impartial independence. "I had rather be beaten in this race than to truckle to Butler or Kelly. . . ." he wrote Lamont, threading a passage between camps. "But I cannot forget that a stiff upper lip may be the best means of bringing about a united action." [102]

This shrewd stance had worked before. By September, Kelly knew Blaine might carry the Irish wards, and once in office could easily keep them Republican in national elections, whatever they did in local affairs. The City organization was discovering it had no real independence in national affairs outside the party. If they worked and won, they could claim rewards; if they sulked and the ticket lost, they would get the blame. On September 6, Kelly met with chieftains to hear grievances against the national ticket. Workers and the Irish found Blaine attractive. Who could trust elegant City men, or rural upstaters around Cleveland? It looked like "Old Tilden" again. Kelly was grim, then laid down the law. They would cooperate, however listlessly, and assume that victory meant more pies than defeat. On September 12, the Hall endorsed the national ticket. [103]

Outside New York, Democrats were at last developing a few leaders who nearly matched the Republicans in organizational ability. Only nominally attached to the party's past, they liked the political game as well as power. Maryland was recognizing the talents and claims of Arthur Pue Gorman, who combined business and local politics with a taste for national influence that took him to the Senate in 1881. At his "Chesapeake Dinners," Gorman planned strategy with the wine glass and soft touch rather than epigrams or self-righteousness. Enemies said he was slippery and deceitful, but he was only skilled in using both hands independently. His talents shone largely because he had so few competitors. In a party of petty chieftains and aloof rhetoricians, "the Gorman of legend was a great politician, a wizard of his craft, a magician, a man who could do miracles." [104]

Gorman, like Republican counterparts, understood that parties had to be national. The old quadrennial system of jerry-building must go. He represented more than Borgia manners and "nobby" clothes. As a Marylander with both rural and urban supporters, he knew the appeal of traditional Democracy that called Republicans a "rich and respectable" enemy, but he leavened this with fresh attitudes. Jeffersonian rhetoric would not carry Baltimore. He did not mouth the golden lies of a "Lost Cause." He organized, rewarded able lieutenants, and managed diverse and exotic groups. The sounds from Italian, Hungarian, Polish, and Jewish immigrants, shipping and manufacturing interests, railroad traffic that moved East and South, showed him mutual interests among business, labor, and specialized farming. He guarded them with tariff protection and a stable currency, and was Democratic because he disliked federalism. But he seldom explained his philosophy. He loved the flowers of political success, and would dig in the dirt that made them grow, provided he wore gloves.

William C. Whitney turned to similar tasks in New York, branching discreetly into Connecticut, New Jersey, and further west. Like Gorman, he saw that a new Democracy had to start in the North; only organization could build a party. They would worry about making it run after victory. He saw Cleveland as a manageable symbol, but would worry about that later, too. For now, he organized the National Committee's fund drive, gathered aides, and directed affairs from New York City and Chicago. Wealthy business associates and social friends raised nearly half a million dollars, principally from New York.

The Democrats did not quite know what to emphasize. A tariff assault would reveal intra-party weaknesses. They could not openly campaign for spoils with Mugwumps as the battle's spearpoints. Localism would not swing doubtful states. The currency question was dormant. Fate soon took the question from the managers' hands. At the nominating convention, Cleveland's opponents whispered about the Governor's "woman trouble." [105] He referred vaguely to "my woman scrape" among friends, and his managers apparently understood there was a skeleton in the closet. Tammany sachems discussed the problem openly before the nomination, but had divided views after the fact. Then the *Buffalo Telegraph*, on July 21, printed the story that Cleveland and one Maria Halpin had produced an illegitimate child in his earlier days. Cleveland had acknowledged responsibility, and paid for the child's care in an orphanage. The scandal quickly filled the nation's press.[106] In Buffalo, some ministers preached against vaguely delicious lewdness, and the story ballooned to encompass most Democratic leaders. In the first confusion, Cleveland told friends the tale was true. He directed personal wrath against people who apologetically said he was not guilty, but only trying to protect the reputation of a dead law partner, Oscar Folsom, who, unlike Cleveland, had to think of a family.

Democrats blamed Republicans for the sordid exposure, which seemed a logical response to the Mulligan Letters. As with most such incidents, the perpetrators remained unknown, though the effects were clear and sudden. Independents busy holding up Cleveland as a paragon of virtue were despondent. Opportunists like Kelly and Hendricks suggested Cleveland withdraw. As Henry Ward Beecher said with political realism, "any clean man will be better than a spavined man for the race. Cleveland, if debauched, and held to by the Independents, will elect Blaine, by such a majority as will tread the Independent movement hopelessly under foot." [107] Some Mugwumps and Democrats hastily urged Cleveland to explain the whole business. Americans liked underdogs in politics, and candor might even strengthen him. He wrote a memo to this effect, but wiser heads vetoed an open discussion. Better silence and aloofness while others explained. The candidate shrewdly said only: "Whatever you do, tell the truth." In private, he noted "the policy of not cringing was not only necessary but the only way." [108]

Interest in Cleveland's post-puberty activities was understandably high, and various newsmen, ministers, and politicians undertook private investigations. A group of impartial clergymen was the most influential, reporting the story was true, but noting that Cleveland honestly accepted responsibility and supported the child. Cleveland assured friends like Mrs. Beecher that he was not a gross debauchee, frequenting Buffalo's bawdy houses and rum shops in youth, or maintaining a harem in the governor's mansion now, as the sensational press hinted. But the Democrats were defensive. Grinning and confident men chanted:

> Blaine, Blaine, James G. Blaine,
> Continental Liar From the State of Maine!
> Burn this letter!

They now met the wry chant "Ma, Ma, where's my Pa?" with a rather weak self-assurance: "Going to the White House, ha! ha! ha!"

The explanations, hesitation and embarrassment put Mugwumps off guard. They now saw their exposed position. If the scandal beat Cleveland, Republicans would repudiate them with vengeance; but they could hardly tout Cleveland as a spotless reformer. Weary demoralization spread through their ranks.* "This reply to his friends to 'tell the truth' I thought very noble in him, and felt that it would add another star to his diadem," a supporter wrote. "But I now fear that the truth bears with crushing weight upon him and upon us all." The scandal left "a strong and unpleasant suspicion on the mind, and takes away that whole-souled devotion to the cause which we felt before these disclosures were made public. We then felt that we had in every sense of the word a clean character and a clean record, public and private. Now I fear it has resolved itself into a choice of two evils." [109]

But some independents had a sense of humor. One of Curtis' guests spoke pragmatically: ". . . we should elect Mr. Cleveland to the public office he is so admirably qualified to fill, and remand Mr. Blaine to the private life which he is so eminently fitted to adorn." [110] Mugwumps agreed, and used miles of newsprint to explain the differences between private and public morality. John Hay and other practical men found argument fruitless. The bolters merely "shut their eyes and screamed praises." [111] Gorman was more knowledgeable than the rest. Democrats had time both to explain the scandals, and curry a sympathy vote. "I do not believe they [the scandals] will control a single vote." [112]

Equally unsavory missiles rained down on Blaine's camp. Fresh

---

*Women did not vote in this era. They tend to be more affected by questions of personal morality in public officeholders than men, and might have voted against Cleveland. As it was, the scandals probably did not hurt him. The influence of wives on husband's voting habits in this era was probably low, and many men might laughingly sympathize with the luckless candidate.

Mulligan Letters—some authentic—appeared weekly; all the old charges reappeared. On August 8, the Democratic *Indianapolis Sentinel* printed a supposed exposé of Blaine's irregular marriage, suggesting he went to the preacher only because Miss Stanwood was pregnant. The candidate instructed Indianapolis attorney Benjamin Harrison to sue, and explained that he married Miss Stanwood twice because they wished to keep the wedding secret from their families, and because his job depended on being single. In mid-September, the angry Blaine told Harrison not to bring the suit to trial and thus feed the flames, but to drag it out quietly and drop it after the election. Cleveland never forgave Buffalo, and Blaine never forgave Indianapolis, but the latter gained a good impression of Benjamin Harrison. To his credit, Cleveland avoided the subject. "I am glad you wrote as you did in regard to the Blaine scandal," he told Lamont. "I am very sorry it was printed and I hope it will die out at once." [113] A smut broker offered Manning and Lamont damaging letters about Blaine. Manning hesitated, but finally stated the proposition to Cleveland. The candidate listened, took the papers, told Manning to pay the man, and pulled a wastebasket closer to his knee. Tearing the sheets to small pieces, he remarked acidly: "The other side can have a monopoly of all the dirt in this campaign." [114]

This attitude did not carry over to the press. Cartoonists abounded because of circulation wars, and perfected their wares with new technical processes and vivid imaginations that impressed rustic readers more than print. *Harper's Weekly* paraded Nast's vicious anti-Blaine cartoons throughout the campaign. *Puck,* a comic weekly, ran yards of doggerel to prove Blaine was wallowing in spoils like Carl Schurz's celebrated rhinocerous in an African pool. Frederick Opper's pen showed a pious Blaine at the piano: [115]

> I know not what the way may be—
>   I know not how I'll get that seat.
> I'll have to use chicanery—
>   I'll have to lie and bribe and cheat.
> It may not be an easy task
>   To cover up my tatooed skin—
> And 'magnetism' will not mask
>   the dirty jobs that I've been in.

Opposition papers charged that Blaine was anti-Catholic, though his mother belonged to that faith and a sister was a nun. Reporters escorted physicians to the Plumed Knight's meetings, who said he was dying of Bright's Disease, palsy, leprosy, insanity, and other ailments.

Joseph Pulitzer, climbing the slippery steps of sensational journalism, accused Blaine of being a Know-Nothing, anti-immigrant, and the greatest public menace since Catiline. When vandals chiseled out dates on the tombstone of a Blaine child who died in infancy, foes suggested it was part of a plot to cover an irregular marriage. They also said Blaine let weeds cover his mother's grave because she was Catholic.[116]

Mixed in these attacks, tinged with a prurient edge that made many voters redden with embarrassed delight, ran equally empty charges against Cleveland's public record. Opponents said he hired a convict substitute during the war to evade service. The party platform proposed some kind of tariff reduction, and demagogues in blue argued this was a justification for ending pensions, even after Cleveland publicly stated that he favored them. But his most bitter critics occupied Dana's *New York Sun,* and when it came to the petty, cruel, and vicious, nothing was new under the *Sun.* Its editorials suggested Cleveland enjoyed hanging two criminals while sheriff, and was "a coarse debauchee who might bring his harlots to the White House." [117] No wonder such diverse elements as General Butler and *The Nation* condemned the whole campaign. Cleveland bore the assaults in stoic but angry silence, suffering wounds that never healed, and increasing his distaste for people. He had "blue" days, "wishing that the presidential nomination were in ———, or on some other shoulders than mine." [118]

The scandals were distasteful and shocking, but a cold-blooded man could assure the Democrats they were a blessing, however foul the disguise. The public and press raked over personalities and ignored issues. Blaine ran a more defensive campaign than even enemies predicted. His efforts to discuss the tariff disappeared in echoes of slander. Democrats avoided major questions, and did not state what they would do in office. In a perverse way, scandals unified the party and covered its weaknesses more than a serious campaign.

Behind the sound and fury, a solid organization formed in both camps as cooler fall weather arrived. The Republicans raised some funds among businessmen for a tariff battle; Democrats spread speakers and literature with unusual skill in the Midwest and mid-Atlantic states. Hendricks invaded Indiana in August with a host of old warhorses, speaking to enthusiastic crowds as a vivid, if lame, reminder of past glories. He even survived a train wreck that shook up younger men. Tactful criticism from New York did not soften his appeals for easy money, pork, and a turnover in the civil service. Taking as his motto, "an honest and sturdy partisanship," Hendricks made up for Cleveland's silence. In numerous interviews, he left the impression that Cleveland was a nonentity. If only the party had chosen him, Butler's votes would come their way. And why all the talk about "reform?" It was a Democratic year, if they did not rock the boat or forget friends after victory.[119]

Cleveland's silence covered an unwillingness to risk the campaign trail's exposure, and hesitancy about dealing with other Democrats, notably Tilden. He wrote a letter of acceptance, endorsing the party's platform and suitably moderate on civil service reform, then dispatched a copy to Greystone. Tilden took the paper and asked: "Colonel, is this subject to change or amendment in any way?" Lamont answered: "Not a single word," and stood uneasily while the Sage read without apparent reaction.[120] This man Cleveland might not be so manageable after all. Late in the campaign season, Cleveland spoke in New York at national guard encampments and a few county fairs, then moved downstate for last-minute appearances. In mid-October, he arrived in New York City for a huge meeting at the Academy of Music. He shook hands until his fingers hurt, spoke to a cheering crowd alive with flags and banners, and reviewed a brilliant torchlight parade up Fifth Avenue. In Brooklyn, he faced boisterous Democrats holding up banners and throwing confetti.

The applause did not change his stolid appearance, and he seldom smiled. The *Sun* punctured his visit downstate with a series of interviews with workers who called him "a monopolist" who had vetoed a Mechanics' Lien bill, the Five Cent Fare bill, and other pro-labor laws. The *Sun* insisted men in overalls would support Butler. Cleveland's silence indicated "that he has no ideas on any of the burning political questions of the day." He could only "prate heavily about the benefits of good government, and office being a public trust." [121] The *Sun's* bias was well known, but Cleveland never went beyond clichés. He avoided the tariff, spoke in generalities of civil service reform, and talked of duty and responsibility. He seemed ready to prove Abram S. Hewitt's remark: "Cleveland is the greatest master of platitude since Washington." [122]

Actually, he was pursuing wise tactics, allowing others to cover disturbing gaps in the party's unity. There was little enough to say. He had no public attitude on protection beyond the platform's straddle, and could not define the civil service problem until it confronted him. He was probably a gold standard man, but would not raise that dangerous question. There was safety in silence, success in dullness. The campaign was colorful enough. General Butler started where the scandals stopped.

"The Beast," as southerners still called Butler, shrouded his intentions in mystery. Critics laughed at his pronouncements about labor and the downtrodden. He was a spoilsman neither pure nor simple, they said, and would go to the highest bidder. Some thought he could not decide to be "a fly on the wheel," or a "jackass among chickens." [123] Bayard was wary; he might take Democratic money and shift the election to Blaine. Bayard thought the party should "put him to death . . ." but did not say how.[124] The General was in an excellent bargaining position. His appeal to rag-tag labor elements in the mid-Atlantic states could decide the election. Cleveland's agents offered him a share of New England's patronage, or the attorney-general's portfolio, to campaign for the Democratic ticket. Republicans were less certain. Butler frankly told William E. Chandler he wanted to throw the election into the House, thus raising his price enormously. Blaine was suspicious and uncertain. "The Butler problem is difficult," he wrote Elkins. "It is difficult to tell what the gains and losses would be by his staying out or his going in. One course would hurt in some states, and help in others, and *vice-versa*. The whole problem is this, *viz:* If Butler runs he will get 250,000 votes, more or less—less probably. If he does not run who will get the majority of these votes? I think I would, and hence would gain by his staying out." [125]

Blaine's intuition was sound, assuming protection was the major issue with workers. But he hesitated, and let managers subsidize Butler's ceremonial campaign among eastern Democrats. Late in July, Chandler's good ship *Tallapoosa* visited Portsmouth Navy Yard to welcome survivors of the ill-fated Greeley Arctic expedition. Pundits noted Butler on board, and speculated about a "Tallapoosa Treaty" that would bring him into the fray against Cleveland. Butler denied making such a "treaty" aboard the *Tallapoosa,* but did not deny working for the Republicans. In fact, he received about $5,000 weekly from Chandler to divert Democrats in New York, New Jersey, and Connecticut.[126] He also campaigned in the Midwest, taking votes from Blaine, and lending credence to belief that he worked both sides of the street to send the contest to the House. After the election, Wayne MacVeagh told a friend the Republicans would not have rewarded Butler and were merely using him.[127]

Whatever the final arrangement, Butler had a good time on the hustings, and ignored charges that he was "a side-show for Blaine." [128]

He described utopia to audiences in the doubtful states, and his shrill voice, bald dome, and drooping eye became familiar to cartoonists. Despite his absurdity, thousands heard him. "He appears before mechanics in a slouch hat and before farmers in a broad-rimmed panama, and receives at fashionable hotels in the spotless attire of a man of the world," the *New York Times* commented. "Everywhere, his burly form, bald head, grim visage, and general air of carrying all before him are immensely diverting. He is the General Boum of the campaign." [129]

He won some support from local newspapers, and got national publicity through the crotchety *New York Sun*, which could not abide Cleveland's dull pomposity. Dana lost 50 per cent of his circulation, but argued that Butler alone was attacking trusts and speaking for the poor, though a tone of weary resignation dulled the paper's conviction. In the last stages of the New York "sideshow," Butler outdid himself, traveling in a lavish private car for fifteen people, with nickel fittings, lush upholstery, a stained glass ceiling, and potted palms. At some stops, Democrats rained tin spoons on the platform, while Republicans beat tin plates—a reminder of the silver he allegedly stole during the war. He gave up the railroad car, but went on in less ornate vehicles, thoroughly confusing everyone. And as if Butler and scrofulous comment on personal scandals were not enough, Prohibitionists further confounded the outcome with a dangerous fourth ticket.

The post-war generation took Temperance reform seriously, and the movement had some able leaders and small power enclaves in the Midwest and South. Cheap liquor of varying quality made "Demon Rum" a widespread household threat. Temperance was so strong that neither protectionists nor tariff reformers would remove the excise taxes from spirits and confront the cry "Free Whiskey!" from the Dry press and pulpit. As the *New York Sun* noted, Prohibition was "a power that cannot be laughed at." [130] It had never figured prominently in a national campaign, but was now dangerous to both major parties. Both party conventions heard Temperance memorials and speeches from leading figures like Miss Frances E. Willard. The Republican politicos were heavy-handed with a petition asking for an anti-liquor plank. "Kick it under the table," someone said, and janitors found the roll of paper covered with tobacco juice and heel prints after a Resolutions Committee session ended.[131] Blaine said the issue belonged in state and local politics rather than a national canvass, which further angered Drys.

On July 23–24, the National Prohibition Party met in Pittsburgh, to

name former Kansas governor John P. St. John for president, and
William Daniel of Maryland for vice-president. St. John was a gadfly
and some of the press enjoyed parody: [132]

> There was an apostle of St. John
> Of doubtful apostolic mien;
> With swagger and rant and intolerable cant
> His demeanor wasn't fit to be seen.

> He invited the crowds his hobbies to ride
> And urged the last one to hop on,
> But they quickly declined, and preferred to hop on
> This equestrian apostle John Petered St. John.

Ridicule usually fortifies solemn reformers, and St. John spoke loudly
about the virtues of a dry mouth and pure heart. Republicans saw
him as a double threat; their voters tended to favor Temperance, as
part of "respectability," and he might easily become a "throw away"
refuge for those who could not support any other candidate. Republican managers apparently tried to buy St. John, and might have nullified him, but easy success in Ohio's fall election let them mistakenly
drop the idea. St. John decided to stump New York in the campaign's
closing weeks, making forty speeches instead of the three he originally
scheduled. As Election Day approached, the spectacle of Butler and
St. John unnerved Chandler. "The St. John movement is now gathering the sore-heads and dis-satisfied Republicans who dare not go for
a man of Cleveland's character," he wrote Reid.[133] To combat all this,
Blaine's managers planned a bold step. He would travel the campaign
trail, discuss real issues, and combat confusion, even if it meant risking
more confusion.

Blaine was in Augusta, Maine, receiving a few delegations of politicians and supporters, and hesitated to enter the campaign lest he
rouse more personal attacks. But as scandals developed in July and
August, and the Democrats avoided issues, he was more receptive to
a tour. It was almost unprecedented, but seemed logical to his temperament. He was not the kind of nominee to rock on a front porch until
Election Day.

The vice-presidential candidate traditionally carried the greater public burden, but Logan and Blaine were uncomfortable soul-mates.
Pundits rearranged a popular ditty, parodying "Black Jack's" bad
grammar, and Blaine's coolness: [134]

> We never speak as we pass by
> Me to Jim Blaine nor him to I.

But Logan wanted to win, and a Stalwart past enhanced his appeal to GAR units in the Midwest. He had a "skyrockety temperament," but that only enthused the veterans. Amid exploding fireworks and popping corks, he wound a trail across the Midwest and Old Northwest, surrounded by garish pomp. In Madison, he reviewed a line of eighty one-armed veterans, each holding a flaming torch in his remaining hand, and pledged undying fealty to Republicanism. Mugwumps treated Logan with contempt. His letter of acceptance dwelled on the southern question, rebel rule, and pensions. "There is a pastoral simplicity in General Logan's letter of acceptance [that is] almost touching," Godkin sighed. The *New York Times* was more brusque: "It is impossible to seriously discuss Gen. Logan's letter of acceptance, and we do not feel like ridiculing it." [135]

The soldier vote did not worry Blaine as much as the ever-doubtful Irish, especially in crucial New York City, Brooklyn, New Jersey, and Connecticut. Blaine started the canvass with much Irish support. His twisting of the British lion's tail as Secretary of State, his family background, and the Irish propensity to follow a dashing leader helped him. "I guess your Donegal and Londonderry blood will carry you through," Thomas Ewing wrote him in late August.[136] William C. Whitney said Irish sentiment was not "so much against Cleveland as in favor of Mr. Blaine," but it might become Democratic.[137] Both parties wooed the Irish, Republicans promising a cabinet post and local patronage; Democrats offering the same, with heavier emphasis. Democrats brought Charles Parnell's mother to New York, and she openly favored Cleveland.* Both parties staged elaborate clambakes, parades, outings in the park, and newspaper coverage of every conceivable Irish accomplishment.[138]

The New York race was so close that any of the four odd groups could control the election's outcome: Butler, the Irish, Prohibitionists, and upstate Stalwarts. Lord Roscoe still practiced law in New York, and traveled periodically to Utica or Washington, but said nothing of politics in his "proud retirement." In the spring of 1884, he secretly opposed Blaine's nomination, feeding unsigned editorials and letters to the *New York World*, rehashing Blaine's past and warning that his candidacy would wreck the party. After the convention, he adopted a "cold and indifferent neutrality" in public, but his few hundred friends upstate could make or break Blaine if the Irish or prohibitionist Republicans deserted in large numbers.[139]

---

*This is ironic precedent for Republican use of the celebrated Sackville-West incident against Cleveland in 1888.

Blaine, as usual, wished to forget the past, not only because it was to his advantage; it seemed foolishly personal. "Can Conkling be induced to speak for us?" he asked Elkins. "It would be an immense thing for us. How can he be induced to do it?" [140] He should have known better, but in due course a delegation of Republicans called on the ex-Senator, and suggested that he think of the party. Would he campaign for Blaine? This was the kind of moment great actors await for a lifetime. Lord Roscoe savored gall on his tongue as he rose, smiled beatifically, and delivered the ultimate thrust: "Gentlemen, you have been mis-informed. I have given up criminal law." [141]

Early in September, Conkling traveled upstate, gathering old friends to his car at every stop. In Utica, he held no interviews, released no statements, and rested from legal briefs. On October 24, the *Utica Daily Press* printed a comprehensive indictment of Blaine, over the signatures of 146 Oneida County Stalwarts. Conkling's name was absent, but analysts assigned him authorship. It certainly represented his views and attitude. The committee's fundamental dislike of Blaine rested on a lesson they learned well during the fight with Garfield: he would not let any single party faction control him. They disliked his unpredictability, not any alleged corruption. Conkling did not campaign, and expected a Democratic victory, but did not openly aid Cleveland. [142]

Blaine's part in the early campaign rested on literature rather than speechmaking. Campaign weather did not really begin until September, except in the "fall states." On Saturday, June 21, the stiffly attired Committee of Notification arrived in Augusta, saw the sights in the morning, then walked arm-in-arm by pairs from the Augusta House to the Blaine mansion. The candidate heard out his distinguished guests, read his acceptance, and entertained the group to luncheon.

The formal letter followed on July 15, and was a disappointment. Instead of clarion calls, he dwelt heavily on trade statistics, the tariff question, and future Latin American trade and development. He deliberately tried to raise serious issues, and divert attention from his personality. He favored a fixed standard and tenure for the civil service, international bi-metallism, an end to the southern question, and renewed efforts to industrialize the area with northern assistance and capital. It was sound, but very dull. It made sense, but smelled of the scholar's lamp, and contained no spirited swordplay, such as Blaine usually preferred. The opposition professed incredulity. "Is this Blaine's letter?" asked the *New York Times*. "Can it be that Blaine—bold, dashing, magnetic Blaine of Maine, has put forth these four columns of safe and stale platitudes, of dull and sleepy maunderings about census figures and the balance of trade, about the public lands and the Mormon question?" [143] George William Curtis thought it "very different from the restless air of the State Department under Mr. Blaine." [144] Godkin dismissed the letter as "a collection of platitudes drawn out to the utmost limits of verbosity." He then noted its significance: "It is clear that Mr. Blaine desires to turn the campaign into a tariff battle." [145]

This was the plan exactly. Though Blaine was his "own platform," he wished to spread protection's appeal to the Midwest. While he worked in Augusta, national, state, and local committees distributed millions of pamphlets, and put hundreds of orators on the stump to sing the tariff's praises. Republican strategy was simple and time-honored; they would carry Maine handsomely in mid-September; blanket Ohio in mid-October; then on to Indiana, and back to New York for a grand finale. Despite his distaste for details, Blaine watched closely. "I would advise that you keep a steady flow in editorial columns on tariff protection—*wages*, especially *wages*," he wrote Reid. "The opposition dread this. They want to keep up a howl about Mulligan and confine the discussion to that kind of *hog-wash*. . . . The tariff, as you are treating [it], with short, sharp illustrations quite steadily, will drive them mad." [146]

Blaine was receptive to the idea of a midwestern tour. It was risky, but because of the noisy scandals, seemed worth a try. Murat Halstead warned that touring was "a killing business for a presidential candidate." [147] But after the Maine election on September 8, Blaine prepared to visit lower New England, New York, the Border and Ohio Valley, go up to Wisconsin and Michigan, and then back to New York for the last week. With his son Walker, and aides like Maine's Joseph Manley, he left on September 17, and after speeches in the route's main cities, arrived to a prodigous welcome in New York. On September 19, General Grant hobbled into his hotel suite on crutches, complaining of gout and newspaper criticism. Unlike Conkling, he endorsed Blaine and party unity. Blaine spoke to a crowd of 10,000 and reviewed the inevitable parade, punctuated with much drum-thumping and huzzahing.[148]

The party then moved west into territory Blaine knew better than most eastern Republicans. He understood and liked the region's varied population, mixed economy, and boisterous enthusiasm, and the Midwest returned his affection and regard. Emphasizing tariff protection, expanding world trade, and political nationalism, he aimed much of his argument at the industrializing upper south. Tennessee, Alabama, Virginia, West Virginia, and Georgia, especially, had risen a small distance under the "New South" idea. If the area abandoned politics for industry, it could rejoin the Union in every way. Blaine had some hope of at least electing a few congressmen there. His refusal to revive bloody-shirt tactics made some old Republicans condemn a "soothing feast of taffy," but warnings of southern rule seldom dominated the speeches.[149]

The pilgrims came to see and hear Blaine. He steadily talked tariff, with a good response in these industrializing states. The crowds amazed observers. "Hosts of one hundred thousand were not unusual," a reporter wrote. "Acres upon acres of people would pack in together and wait with stolid patience for hours simply to see him. At his presence, a cry would go up so wild in its frenzy of enthusiasm as to be always thrilling." [150] Ohio was especially exciting. Blaine called on Mrs. Garfield and visited Hayes in Fremont. He toured iron foundries and machine shops in the state's "Smoky Triangle" around Cleveland and was charming, personal, vivid, with something in his conversation that every worker could remember. In Toledo, he vigorously attacked Democrats for parochialism and stubborn silence on leading issues. Democratic victory would give "to the narrowing dogma of states rights the precedence in that grand march which has been made and which could be made only under the banner of broad nationality." He left the Buckeye State in "a fury of affection," and entered Indiana and Illinois for repeat performances. Logan prepared the Windy City to do her best, and hosts of people cheered as Blaine rode through packed streets. At night, he and Logan spoke from a hotel balcony, and a river of humanity bearing guttering torches passed below, chanting in "one solemn, heavy voice." [151]

Democrats condemned the whole tour as unfitting a presidential candidate. ". . . the Republican candidate is dragged around the country by a mob of low politicians and put on exhibition like a two-headed girl or a prize ox," a humor magazine intoned.[152] The group doubled back from the Old Northwest toward New York, an exhausted but spirited Blaine noting that he traveled nearly six weeks and made some 400 speeches. The immediate results were encouraging. Maine and Vermont gave him heavy majorities in September. Ohio followed suit by 32,000 votes in mid-October. At the same time he lost West Virginia by a mere 4,300 votes, a form of encouragement in the "Border Wars."

As the car clicked eastward, Blaine thought about "the New York problem." His instincts preferred returning to Augusta, but insistent voices from New York urged him to return for a last dazzling display. Elkins, Reid, and Chandler, though divided in what to do and say, wanted him to raise money in the timid business community. Contrary to reports, the national committee was broke, having over-spent on midwestern contests. It could not promise any last-minute effort in New York; the candidate's presence might make the difference. The Democrats were well financed. Tilden, Whitney, Gorman, and Barnum wrung the East Coast dry.[153] Blaine hesitated. The contest had so many variables that it might be worth the chance. He could stop in New York and try to offset the Mugwump defection by publicizing connections with respectable middle-class elements like the clergy and professionals. He could speak to the Irish. And he might raise funds for last-minute work against Tammany. On October 24, from Indiana, he wrote William M. Evarts and others that he would speak to a group of wealthy supporters at a lavish banquet at Delmonico's Restaurant.

Blaine entered New York near Jamestown, and local party dignitaries met the train. Andrew Sloan Draper of the state committee urged him to avoid New York City. It was too dangerous; the smallest slip might shift the whole state. He should cross upstate New York and go over the mountains to Maine. Blaine showed marks of the exhausting tour, but explained why the New York managers needed him, and boarded a special train for the City.

An exhausting schedule awaited him. On Wednesday, October 29, he faced three major events; greetings to a large delegation of ministers, reviewing yet another parade, and dinner at Delmonico's. After suitable conferences with managers, he would go north to Augusta. At 10 A.M. that Wednesday, he walked downstairs from a hotel suite to a lobby filled with ministers. Reporters and politicians looked on the reception as a chore. No preacher was likely to say anything valuable. The easy cynicism that comes with political reporting made newshawks dull-witted. The room was stuffy, and few people knew the group's spokesman, Reverend Samuel D. Burchard, pastor of Murray Hill Presbyterian Church, hastily chosen to replace the scheduled speaker, now delayed in Philadelphia. Blaine looked tired and pale, but stood impassively on the upper steps as Burchard spoke. His paean to Republicanism and respectability contained one impressive passage: "We are Republicans and don't propose to leave our party and identify ourselves with the party whose antecedents have been rum, Romanism and rebellion. We are loyal to our flag, we are loyal to you."

Blaine answered routinely.* He returned to his rooms after greeting the ministers, to spend the afternoon with campaign planners and review an ornate parade. The idle, curious, and trapped bystanders drifted away. Reporters straightened their derbys, lit cigars, and strolled off to file what they could make from the speeches.† They were frankly disinterested. As one recalled: "A clergyman's speech, however, seemed to us the last thing to be followed closely for a sensation: it was assumed to be non-explosive." [154]

Frank Mack of the Associated Press covered the gathering with two trained stenographers as a routine part of his work. He noted the excited and well-dressed ladies in the crowd awaiting Blaine's arrival, and heard the rush of cheers that greeted Blaine's cheerful smile and jolly wave. Burchard rustled forward self-importantly, and read his remarks. Mack listened closely, and after the "three R's," nudged his companion. "Did you get that?" The stenographer did not stop writing. "Bet your life—the old fool." When the crowd broke up, several ministers spoke excitedly to Blaine, who asked to see the reporters' copy. When Mack said the AP dispatch was already gone, Blaine looked apprehensive, but wearily turned away. He later saw Mack and passed off the whole incident with "a compound of wan smile and far regret." [155]

Arthur P. Gorman and a friend drove past the hotel as the clergymen gathered. He was frankly "blue." Polls showed Blaine would carry New York City and win the election. "I do not know that we would have done better with another candidate," he said as they neared headquarters. "It has been a scandalous campaign, with credit to nobody on either side." But he professed hope, and started to shuffle papers at a desk. "I shall keep up my whistling until I have passed the graveyard."

The sound of hurrying footsteps preceded a breathless stenographer into the room. He waved a paper at Gorman, and blurted out the news of "Rum, Romanism, and Rebellion." Gorman listened, then said with a puzzled air: "Surely, Blaine met this remark?" The messenger shook his head, and Gorman wheeled into action. "Write that out!" he snapped, and excitement suddenly filled the room. "This sentence must

---

*In 1876, Garfield privately made a similar remark to a friend: ". . . we are defeated by the combined power of rebellion, Catholicism, and whiskey, a trinity very hard to conquer." (See Caldwell, *James A. Garfield*, 251–52.)

†A curious legend persists that the remark affected no one present, and was overlooked by *all* the press. In fact, the next morning's *New York World* had full coverage and a scathing attack, as did other papers, though few outside New York City seriously noted the event.

be in every daily newspaper in the country tomorrow, no matter how, no matter what it costs. . . . If anything will elect Cleveland, these words will do it. It is amazing that a man so quick witted as Blaine, accustomed to think on his feet and to meet surprising changes in debate, should not have corrected the thing on the spot. It is too late now. He cannot deal with it at all. The advantages are now with us." [156] Presses ran through the weekend, printing handbills and wall posters advertising the remark. On Sunday, November 4, two days before the election, many Catholic clergymen denounced the implied bigotry from their pulpits.

The obscure Doctor Burchard was immortal; epithets and ridicule rained on him from all quarters. Dana called him "a Silurian or early Paleozoic bigot." [157] More composed critics merely said he was politically ignorant.* Blaine finished the day without challenging the alliteration, but by the weekend he was the center of a newspaper storm. On Saturday, November 1, he denounced the "unfortunate remark of another man," and disavowed its contents. "I am sure that I am the last man in the United States who would make a disrespectful allusion to another man's religion . . . for though Protestant by conviction myself, and connected with a Protestant church, I should esteem myself of all men the most degraded if, under any pressure or under any temptation, I could, in any presence, make a disrespectful allusion to that ancient faith in which my mother lived and died." [158] It was a forceful and honest statement, but no one could gauge its effect. As his train passed through New Haven, leaflets detailing "The Three R's" showered down from overpasses and tenements.[159]

So the incident passed into legend, as Blaine repeatedly told fellow politicians that he had not heard Burchard's remark. He assumed Burchard would deal in platitudes, and was thinking of something to say after he finished. Despite the bright crust of legend on the story, Blaine may have rationalized away a failure of nerve common in emergencies. At least once he told a friend, Justice Harlan, that Burchard's remark "went through him like a knife." He knew its significance, but trusted no one else heard it, and delayed answering, hoping it would not catch fire.[160] Otherwise, why had he asked newsmen what they proposed to file on the meeting, seeming "apprehensive" when

*On December 9, 1887, Burchard met President Cleveland at a formal White House reception, and caused some merriment. He told friends he had no political sense, but came to appreciate Cleveland's administration. (See Richard D. Harlan, "The Phrase That Beat Blaine," *The Outlook Magazine*, 126 [December 8, 1920], 649–50; *Washington Post*, December 10, 1887.)

they said the story was already gone? As Gorman noted, it was incredible that so astute a man could miss or ignore the comment. Pro-
ceeding through that "Black Wednesday's" rounds, he thought of "the
Great Unknown" that always produced the unexpected.

Parades consumed much of Wednesday afternoon, and Blaine waved
from a vantage point, with frequent asides to guests. He seemed
energetic, though weary and eager to rest in Augusta. When the last
units bearing banners and signs marched past, the candidate and party
returned to their rooms for a brief rest, and to prepare for the evening's
speech. Blaine was eager to leave New York City. He did not predict
the contest's outcome; he only wanted it to end. Some friends like
Elkins and Evarts warned against speaking to a lavish assembly of
businessmen; the opposition press was sure to depict it as a banquet of
money kings, indifferent to the sorrows of the poor.[161] But once more,
the party's need for funds compelled Blaine to counter his better
judgment. At the appointed hour, he arrived at Delmonico's famous
restaurant. The dining room boasted fresh flowers, elaborate bunting,
special covers for each place, and a French menu and wine list. Some
of the nation's richest men attended, with a scattering of clergymen,
lawyers, editors, and jurists. Blaine praised material success in the
speech, but talked more of America's opportunities and resources, and
spoke of foreign trade. The audience seemed surprised that a man of
his "magnetic" reputation discussed such a dull subject, and failed to
comprehend the argument. In a discreet bid for funds, Blaine emphasized dangers to tariff protection in a Democratic victory.[162]

The speech was a reasoned and logical argument, but politically
unwise. It did not really matter; the opposition press would distort
everything he said or did. Had he walked on water, they would have
said Jay Gould held him up. The next day's press reported the banquet
like something from the last days of the Roman Empire. Wine allegedly poured across expensive waistcoats, and exotic food passed
down superfluous gullets amid gross luxury. Joseph Pulitzer's cartoonists had cut plates before the event for a cartoon showing a ragamuffin
worker's family, pleading for crumbs from this decadent table, with
the headlines "Mammon's Homage," and "Belshazzar Blaine and the
Money Kings." The issue sold out, and special reprints went to Democratic headquarters.[163] The dinner's adverse publicity may not have
cost many votes; probably not as many as Burchard's slip. But to the
distress of Elkins and other managers, it produced no funds. Business-

men were not going to contribute, refusing to believe Blaine could lose.* Once more, they were more sluggish and less organized than political counterparts.

The days between Thursday and Monday, when the party left for Augusta, were a jumble of controversy, weariness, and speechmaking. For weeks, New York's pavements had shaken under the assaults of increasingly elaborate and imaginative human advertising. The Blaine marchers were spectacular. One of their parades featured hundreds of men in white papier-mâché suits of armor, complete with tall plumes and swords. When it rained, marchers donned suitably embossed capes and high hats, adding a touch of the debonair to the charmingly absurd.[164]

During this last campaign weekend, Cleveland spoke on public duty and the future's promise. On Saturday, he reviewed an immense parade of well-drilled marchers. Some carried signs saying "Tell The Truth," or "A Public Office is a Public Trust." But they usually focused on Blaine. Fifteen-hundred nattily dressed Democratic lawyers passed in serried ranks, carrying tall sticks with symbolic letters attached. They struck matches to sheets of paper, chanting: [165]

> Blaine, Blaine, James G. Blaine,
> Continental Liar from the State of Maine!
> Burn this letter!
> Burn this letter!

Blaine had his share of the display. As the train left for Augusta, he heard the echoes of poetic bursts like: [166]

> See the rockets looming 'Blaine!'
> Hear the cannon booming 'Blaine!'
> Men and women praying 'Blaine!'
> And the stars are saying 'Blaine!'

On election-eve in Augusta, he retired with a rather curt "Good night, gentlemen," to guests and reporters who nervously eyed special telegraph instruments. He was not sanguine. "If I carry New York by only a thousand votes, they will surely count me out." [167] Mrs. Blaine remained awake, nervous as returns clacked in. First reports were en-

---

*After the election, Blaine wrote William Walter Phelps, friend and Republican Congressman from New Jersey: "Our special misfortune was the loss of both New Jersey and Connecticut. . . . I class them both as preventable accidents. I was not sustained in the canvass by many who had personally a far greater stake than I. They are likely to have leisure for reflection and for a cool calculation of the small sums they were asked in vain to contribute." (See Hamilton, *James G. Blaine*, 589–90.)

couraging; they would obviously carry most of the Midwest and Far West. But fluctuations in close states like Connecticut, New Jersey, Indiana, and above all, New York, unnerved the family. Mrs. Blaine retired, but a restless and sinister murmer of voices rose up through the ceiling of the room below, and pacing footsteps kept her awake.[168]

In Albany, a downpour washed out most premature enthusiasm. Messengers who brought news to Cleveland's office dripped water on the floor, and breathed excitement. He was fidgety, working over routine papers, smoking heavily, talking to aides about fishing. Fallen telegraph lines increased fears that Republicans would report fraudulent tallies. By midnight, New York's determining vote was clearly in doubt. Lamont and others wired Democrats in each county to watch the count. The following day, with the outcome uncertain, rumors swept New York that Jay Gould, who controlled the telegraph, would falsify returns. Ugly crowds gathered downtown, shouting "Hang Jay Gould!" and hanging effigies to lampposts. From national headquarters, Gorman authorized a statement against the alleged plot, and helped Whitney raise money for a recount.[169]

Cleveland was firm. "I believe I have been elected president, and nothing but grossest fraud can keep me out of it, and that we will not permit." [170] The *Washington Post* and other papers warned "There will be no 'visiting statesmen' this time to meddle with the official count in New York." [171] As the recount began, happy Democrats chanted victory slogans: [172]

> Hurrah for Maria! Hurrah for the kid!
> I voted for Cleveland,
> And damned glad I did!

In the South, the prospect of Democratic victory unsettled Negroes. Some fled north; others took to the woods. Cleveland publicly denied his administration would be anti-Negro, but "Many a former slave has spent the past three nights on his knees." A better spirit prevailed in Atlanta, where jubilant crowds burned bloody shirts to symbolize the end of sectionalism. Newspapers did not say who furnished the blood.[173]

The recount began on November 11, and Blaine was not optimistic. Republicans could not "unquestionably" prove fraud. He did not wish to enter the presidency with a doubtful title. "I have not the slightest desire to win by technical exclusion of votes, or technical gain of votes," he wrote Elkins. "All I want is a fair count. I shall be perfectly content whatever the result." [174] The final tally gave New York's electoral votes and the presidency to Cleveland by fewer than 1,200 ballots. William E. Chandler wrote two expressive words in his little pocket diary: "Great Scott!" but thought the count was fair. "If we had only had a thousand *more* votes in New York. It was a lack of votes, not a theft of votes, that lost the state to Blaine." [175]

Cleveland won with 219 electoral votes, to 182 for Blaine, and a national plurality of about 30,000 votes. He carried all the South, Indiana, New York, Connecticut, and New Jersey. The national House would be Democratic, 182–140; Republicans controlled the Senate, 41–34. Democrats gained House seats in Illinois, Iowa, Kentucky, Michigan, North Carolina, and Virginia, but declined from their sweep of 1882. A bitter campaign had not produced a Democratic mandate.

Mrs. Blaine was shocked as her husband conceded defeat to disappointed neighbors. "It is all a horror to me," she wrote. "I was absolutely certain of the election." [176] Blaine radiated the fatalistic attitude common to defeated office-seekers. "Steve, it was all planned for the best," he told Elkins, "and no one could have foreseen what has occured." [177] He seemed glad it was over, whatever the result. "The whole campaign was a disaster to me, personally, physically, pecuniarily. I ought to have obeyed what was really a strong instinct against running. . . . It was the wrong year, and gave my enemies their coveted opportunity." [178]

Men debated the importance of various lines in the tangled web. Reid thought it was fraud, pure and simple, but most venom centered on Reverend Burchard, whose remark supposedly caused at least 1,200 defections among the Irish. "I should have carried New York by 10,000 if the weather had been clear on election day, and Dr. Burchard had been doing missionary work in Asia Minor, or Cochin China," Blaine supposedly told friends.[179] Off-hand, most agreed and damned the pious minister's infamous utterance. Logan thought the Delmonico dinner was a major cause of Irish defections. "If Blaine had eaten a few more swell dinners, and had a few more ministers call on him, we should not have carried a northern state," he remarked acidly.[180] This was simplistic. Carl Schurz noted how many Irish voted for Blaine despite "Black Wednesday." Cleveland ran behind Hancock's record of 1880 in some Irish wards in New York, Brooklyn, and Boston. He won the governorship in 1882 by nearly 200,000 votes, but captured the state two years later by 1,200.[181] Blaine argued that in a combination of disarrayed elements, the Irish vote made the difference, but did not necessarily cause defeat.

Mugwump defectors were numerous enough to shift New York, and liked to say so; they expected recognition from Cleveland. But the opposite end of New York City's social spectrum, the Negro community, could have given the election to Cleveland by staying home, or voting Democratic from disgust with the Republican drift to lily-white parties in the South, and toward economic issues in the North that did not seem relevant to colored people.[182] Somewhere in the middle of this range, the Temperance people claimed the victory. St. John said he elected Cleveland, and expected recognition. Republicans like Senator Plumb of Kansas and former Governor Cornell of New York, blamed the Drys. St. John won 25,000 votes in New York, but many Temperance voters reportedly balloted for Cleveland. "Mr. Blaine thinks it was rain that beat him in New York," a newsman said, "The St. John people take another cold water view." [183]

Analysts threshed this mixture of chaff and wheat, but the professionals were more interested in Stalwart voting. Roscoe Conkling never announced his preferences, but the upstate Stalwart vote declined enough to give Cleveland the state. If Conkling had instructed followers to vote or campaign for Blaine, he could have made him president. While the vote was in doubt, he answered a query from the Democratic State Committee, saying only that a recount should be fair and impartial. A few days after the election, the New York Sun gave him credit for apparently beating Blaine. "It was a handful of unforgiving Stalwarts that did it." At month's end, the Washington Post suggested Democrats "chip in and elect Mr. Conkling as a Republican Senator." Of course, there was satisfaction on both sides. It was a death gasp for Conkling, however costly. He would have no power after this, which delighted many.[184]

The Reverend Doctor Burchard and his three rolling R's were a colorful incident in American political history, and an ideal scapegoat to rationalize away defeat, but in the strictest political sense, he did not defeat Blaine. The Irish vote in 1884 was an uncertain quantity, liable to shift either way. Both parties campaigned with that in mind. The Stalwarts were not usually uncertain. As party men, they should have voted for the ticket if not the man, and elected Blaine. They could not do this, attesting once more to their narrowness. Conkling had his revenge.*

Every pundit had *the* explanation. Confusion made it easy to combine the odd elements to explain Blaine's defeat. The youthful Theodore Roosevelt, who supported Blaine while many friends bolted, told reporters that "A combination of untowardness did it. If the Conkling

---

*It was his last great moment. Conkling died in April, 1888, after over-exerting himself walking home through the great blizzard that engulfed the city.

wing of the Stalwarts had been true; if Burchard's terrible alliteration had not been sprung; if that 'soap' dinner at Delmonico's had not come off; and if the Prohibitionists had been as honest as they claimed, Blaine would have won." [185] After a while, people like Thomas Nast tired of the discussion, and welcomed signs that said: [186]

THE WORLD SAYS THE INDEPENDENTS DID IT
THE TRIBUNE SAYS THE STALWARTS DID IT
THE SUN SAYS BURCHARD DID IT
BLAINE SAYS ST. JOHN DID IT
THEODORE ROOSEVELT SAYS IT WAS THE SOFT SOAP
    DINNER
WE SAY BLAINE'S CHARACTER DID IT
BUT WE DON'T CARE WHAT DID IT
IT'S DONE

The election of 1884 passed into history without much analysis. It was too colorful, close, and full of improbabilities to promote much detachment. In the discussion about Burchard, Stalwarts, and cold water, commentators overlooked several fundamental facts. Democratic politicians conceded that behind the facade of mud and tinsel, the tariff question dominated the canvass. And they admitted the Republicans had the best organizations and arguments on that score.[187] Republican victories in House contests illustrated both Blaine's personal popularity and protection's appeal. The GOP gained 5 seats over the 1882 totals in California; 1 each in Connecticut and Tennessee; 2 each in Massachusetts, Missouri, Ohio, and Virginia; and 4 each in Wisconsin, Pennsylvania, and New York. Blaine won nearly 400,000 more popular votes than Garfield received in 1880. General Butler got over 200,000 votes, likely taking them from Blaine rather than Cleveland because of his tariff record. Most of St. John's votes represented rural Republicans, in the states from Kansas to New York. It was impossible to say who would have won without any minor candidates.

Thus Blaine's defeat was not so striking as his near-victory. He did very well, despite a smoke screen around his public life, the party's even balance in critical states, and lack of funds. His dramatic tour influenced the outcome, and set a pattern for the future. Blaine symbolized party organization, the appeal of nationalism, and tariff protection, and his popular image brought him within sight of the great prize. The contest announced that old issues were dying. Economics would replace talk of rebel rule and carpetbaggers. An urban-industrial constituency was forming around the Republican party, but a successful Cleveland administration might conceivably reorganize

Democrats around a new power base. The election was not a mandate for anything but a certain change of tempo, if that. Cleveland won by insignificant pluralities in swing states, not from popular demand. But there was ironic cheer in this for Democrats. If Blaine's defeat was a personal loss, Cleveland's election was a *party victory*. If Democrats could win a national contest with an unknown candidate, without discussing serious issues, while retaining splinter groups, they were apparently learning skills of organization and coming to represent something more than the past.

Democrats celebrated in the red glare of bonfires, and amid sounds of feasting. Their direction was uncertain, but there was at least a path. Others were apprehensive, not so much about Cleveland as about those around him. Hayes feared "the turning back of the hands of the clock in the southern business and in the reform of the civil service." [188] Others were more personal. "The lecherous beast goes into the White House, with the venomous Copperheads," a Blaine supporter wrote.[189] Blaine was calm, outwardly fatalistic, awaiting better days. Cleveland said little, but privately nursed a bitterness that time would not erase. "I intend to cultivate the Christian virtue of charity toward all men except the dirty class that defiled themselves with filthy scandal." A tone of self-pity and willing sacrifice increased. "I look upon the four years next to come as a dreadful self-inflicted penance for the good of my country." [190] It was reverse modesty. Like one of Bayard's friends, he knew that "thinking, sober, earnest men feel that, even in success, the battle is but half fought. The Democratic party has now almost as great a problem to solve as before." [191]

President Rutherford B. Hayes. (Hayes Memorial Library.)

Senator John Sherman of Ohio, author of the Sherman Antitrust Act. (Ohio Historical Society Library.)

Senator Roscoe Conkling of New York, who resigned in protest against President Garfield's policies. (Library of Congress.)

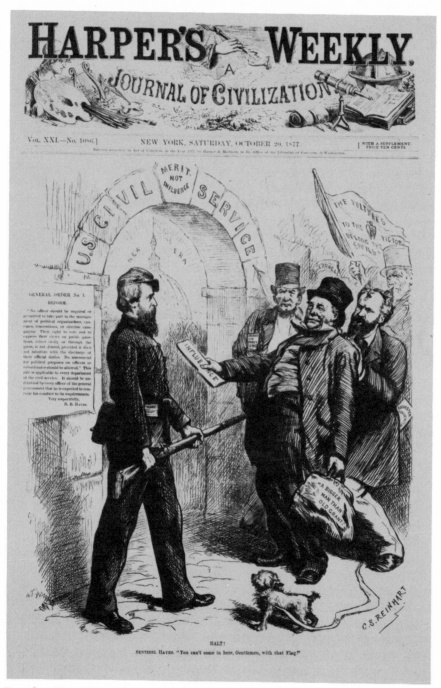

President Hayes defends Fort Civil Service from the Spoilsmen. (*Harper's Weekly,* Oct. 20, 1877.)

"Saved from Its Friend?" The Democratic Party laments President Hayes' supposed acquisition of sympathy from the New South. (*Harper's Weekly*, Oct. 20, 1877.)

Destruction of Union Depot during the Railway Strike of 1877 in Pittsburgh. (*Harper's Weekly*, Aug. 11, 1877.)

"The Lightning Speed of Honesty." The country protests congressional slowness in the session of 1877–79. (*Harper's Weekly*, Nov. 24, 1877.)

Samuel J. Tilden, Dec. 4, 1874. He won the popular vote but lost the election. (Library of Congress.)

"The Tilden Vampire" survives politically by killing other candidates. (*Harper's Weekly,* Sept. 23, 1879.)

A view of the GOP National Convention at Chicago, June 2, 1880. General James A. Garfield (right center) is speaking. (Library of Congress.)

A brooding President, Ulysses S. Grant. (Library of Congress.)

"Hancock the Superb," a popular campaign portrait of General Winfield Scott Hancock. (*Harper's Weekly,* July 10, 1880.)

President James Abram Garfield, c. 1880. (Library of Congress.)

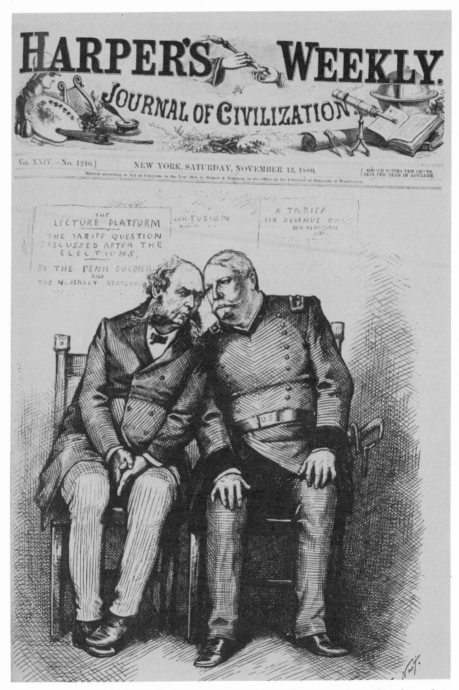

"Who is Tariff, and why is he for revenue only?" A famous cartoon that figured in
General Hancock's defeat in 1880. (*Harper's Weekly,* Nov. 13, 1880.)

Roscoe Conkling as "Marius among the Ruins." (*Frank Leslie's Illustrated Weekly,* Oct. 22, 1881.)

A formal portrait of President Chester Alan Arthur. (Library of Congress.)

President Arthur roughing it. (Library of Congress.)

A POPULAR MELODY APPLIED.

We never speak as we pass by,
Altho' a tear bedims her eye; * * *

The spell is past, the dream is o'er,
And tho' we meet, we love no more!

Puck commemorates President Arthur's break with Roscoe Conkling. (*Puck*, May 30, 1883.)

Senator William E. Chandler of New Hampshire. (Library of Congress.)

"Gentleman George" Pendleton, of Civil Service Reform fame. (*Harper's Weekly*, Feb. 22, 1879.)

President Grover Cleveland. (Library of Congress.)

Senator James Gillespie Blaine, "the Man from Maine." (Library of Congress.)

A flattering portrait of General Benjamin Franklin Butler, candidate for the presidency, 1884. (Library of Congress.)

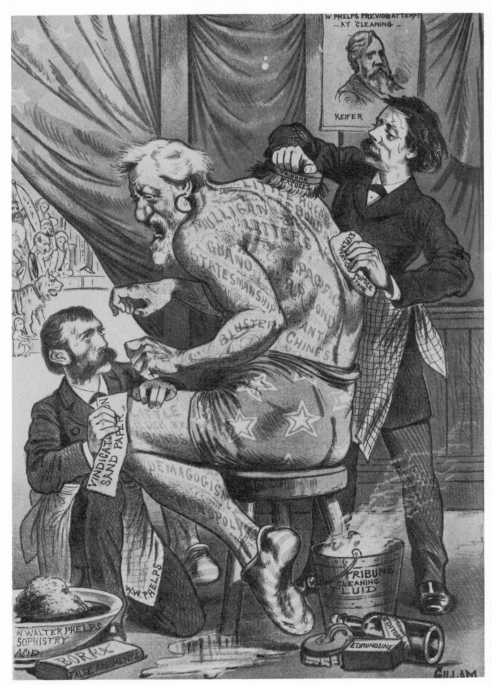

"Love's Labor's Lost." Whitelaw Reid and Walter Phelps try to erase Blaine's record. (*Puck*, May 7, 1884.)

Belshazzar Blaine and the Money Kings. (*New York World*, Oct. 30, 1884.)

☆☆☆☆☆☆☆☆☆☆☆☆☆☆☆☆☆☆☆☆☆☆☆

Part Two
1885–1892

☆☆☆☆☆ ☆☆☆☆☆☆☆☆☆☆☆☆☆☆☆☆☆

VI

☆☆☆☆☆☆ ☆☆☆☆☆☆☆☆☆☆☆☆☆☆☆☆

Spoilsmen and Reformers:
1885–1887

☆☆☆☆☆☆ ☆☆☆☆☆☆☆☆☆☆☆☆☆☆☆☆

Governor Cleveland preferred the calm of paperwork to trains, receptions, and hotel life. As winter closed on the nation in 1884, he made a Cabinet via the mails, apparently indifferent to both the fears and desires of many lesser Democrats. Filling the great portfolios of State, Navy, or War did not occupy his first thoughts. He needed a household staff, and especially wanted quiet, efficient "Dan" Lamont as private secretary and go-between with other leaders. Lamont did not relish the task, fearing Washington's confusing glamor. For a time, he actually refused, drawing wry grimaces from his chief. Finally, Cleveland appealed to personal attachment. "Well, Dan, if you won't go, I won't, that's all." [1] Lamont "went." In time, opponents called him "The power behind the throne," but Lamont knew his place. His soft manner and shrewdness helped the blunt Cleveland. As a newsman said: "Lamont also owned a big lump of diplomacy, and knew how to manage men and affairs." [2]

Choosing a private secretary did not inspire the press or party. As Cabinet-making proceeded, attention turned to Greystone. What was Tilden's relation to the new administration? Mugwumps feared the Sage would dominate the inexperienced President, but counted without Cleveland's firm sense of prerogative. He did not seek Tilden's counsel, and by inauguration-time the Sage knew Cleveland would be independent. Tilden suggested men for Cabinet posts, urged Cleveland to oppose free silver, and wanted federal money for seacoast defenses and other worthy local projects. But he declined to advise unless Cleveland asked. He was not surprised when the President calmly ignored him. "Men in power generally have their plans, and take views which they prefer to the wishes of those who have ceased to have power." [3]

Tilden's friends would get rewards, despite nervous fears that Cleveland would ignore them. The first scare came with newspaper talk that Bayard would fill the Treasury portfolio. Randall hastily warned Tilden: "That means the end of your friends." [4] Party regulars wanted a partisan in that post, so rich in patronage, with many lines across the country on which to build an organization. Many also wanted a protectionist Secretary. They finally agreed on the unlikely figure of Daniel Manning. He would represent Tilden, use patronage for the party and Administration, and had no dangerous theories. Manning balked. He knew nothing of the post, and always preferred dim backgrounds to the light of public office. He would also stand between the Cleveland and Tilden camps, and had juggled those affairs long enough to feel the strain. Tilden pressed him to take the office, promising to give sound fiscal advice. "Unless he accepts the Treasury," Tilden wrote, "I am not mistaken in the belief that the veterans will have no true and reliable friend among the advisers of Mr. Cleveland." [5] Manning finally agreed, and Mugwumps condemned the appointment as an obvious reward to machine politicians.

The State Department went to a man independents rated more highly. Tilden was less concerned over State than departments with domestic patronage. Cleveland was not talkative about his intentions, and had no past connections with Bayard, but the Delaware Senator was an obvious contender, especially when Tilden voiced no opposition. He told Randall not to fight the choice. "He will make a bigger fool of himself there than anywhere else," the Sage remarked dourly.[6] Cleveland considered Bayard's connections with Tammany, and weighed the possible effects of his alleged pro-British attitude on the Irish element. But he basically liked Bayard, who was more competent for the task than any other Democrat. The choice helped pacify Mugwumps. Godkin praised the selection for fitness, and as a repudiation of Blaine.[7]

Cleveland developed a genuine fondness for William C. Whitney, though midwesterners disliked his elegance, and southerners suspected his financial interests. Cleveland encouraged the softening-up newspaper talk that made Whitney a candidate for the Treasury, Attorney-Generalship, or Navy Department. Legal experience in many complicated fields fitted him for the legal post, but his interest in party management made the Navy Department more likely. Ruthless energy, efficient partisanship, and modest interest in a new fleet made him an effective Secretary. Cleveland also wanted him in the official family to help entertain; the bachelor President would not follow Arthur's pattern of regal levees and all-day picnics. The Whitneys were rich and had good taste. He thought nothing of ordering 200 gallons of terrapin and 80 cases of champagne for a luncheon to Navy subordinates. Though Whitney seemed brusque and machine-like behind a pince-nez, he could be warm and genial, and Cleveland let the Secretary quietly absorb details of party management and patronage.[8]

The South's large demands posed some danger. That region boasted a surfeit of "eligible" men, most of whom had both political liabilities and powerful claims. Northern correspondents warned Cleveland to proceed with caution if he meant to give a southerner the Interior post, since it oversaw the Pension Bureau. Men who once wore blue would not like an Administration that let men formerly in grey handle veterans' affairs. Most early advisers pushed the fortunes of Georgia's John B. Gordon, Rebel general and United States Senator,[9] but despite his standing as the Lost Cause incarnate, Gordon was an incompetent administrator, and had moved too often between the halls of government and railroad offices to suit most Democrats. Cleveland settled on a less controversial man, Mississippi's Lucius Quintus Cincinnatus Lamar. Though he had drafted Mississippi's ordinance of secession, Lamar was less identified with the war than "rebel brigadiers," and talked freely of New South industrialization and sectional harmony. He matured in the law and philosophy; the self-made man with a southern accent, and a shrewd opportunist combining the advantages of Old and New Souths. In appearance, he embodied courtly nostalgia for plantation days, and his rhetoric exuded the honeysuckle of harmony and reunion. Like most Bourbons, he spoke of the past and worked for the present and future. He turned elegant Jeffersonian phrases, upheld southern culture, and spoke softly of laissez-faire economics. He also sat on the boards of flourishing railroads and investment concerns. Age had not dimmed his eyesight when it came to finding a path to the public trough.

The South's electoral votes could claim more than one Cabinet seat, and Cleveland passed the Attorney-General's portfolio to Arkansas' Augustus H. Garland. A native of Tennessee, with roots in the Whig party and the old Bell Democracy, Garland opposed secession, but went with the tide after Fort Sumter, like most southern moderates. He sat in the Confederate Congress, and after the war figured in the celebrated Supreme Court case *ex parte Garland*. He was chosen United States Senator in 1867, but not seated, and practiced law in Little Rock until elected governor in 1874. As a senator after 1877, he fought state debt repudiation, and sought internal improvements for the South.

The Mugwumps awaited their reward with apprehension. Republican predictions might come true; Cleveland seemed uninterested in the independent voters who fancied they made him president. There was loose talk of making Schurz a Cabinet member, or sending independents to diplomatic exile, but Cleveland could not afford to irritate eastern machine Democrats with such overt plums. Instead, he straddled, and named a Brahmin to the War Department, Massachusetts' William Crowninshield Endicott. A product of the Salem Latin School and Harvard, married to a Peabody, "Judge" Endicott was a patrician with enough Mugwump leanings to satisfy Cleveland. He had been a Whig, then a Democrat, and earned his title on the state supreme court after several unsuccessful attempts at the governorship. Kelly and his ilk opposed the choice; they would have precious little to say if they visited the War Department during Endicott's management. But he was better in their eyes than a genuine reformer. And the War office was not as rich in patronage as other, more accessible departments. The city managers did not expect a Cabinet seat, but they would demand lesser offices when the time came.

In the "West" of eastern imaginations, only Indiana and Missouri had voted for Cleveland; it was Blaine country. As the Administration took on a southern-eastern tone, Allen G. Thurman complained that "honest Democrats of Ohio" had no friends but Bayard.[10] The whole area was *terra incognita* to Cleveland, who once innocently said that he moved west to Buffalo, much to the amusement of Nevada's Senator William M. Stewart. He also distrusted the "Granger element" there. Casting about, he found Wisconsin's William Freeman Vilas. As a low tariff gold Democrat with suitable corporate connections, Vilas would help build a new party in the Midwest with patronage. He had a Union war record, New England background, and was a good judge of political currents in the turbulent Northwest.[11] On inauguration-eve, Cleveland offered him the Postmaster-General's office.

Cleveland later noted: "I have a first rate cabinet, but after all the best things have to be worked out alone."[12] The sentiment was not universal, on either count. The strange variety of his advisers prompted the press to fabricate a letter to the President from a lady: "Please send me scraps of your cravat and your cabinet to make a block in my crazy quilt."[13] Theodore Roosevelt called it "the Apotheosis of the Unknown." Blaine suggested the Senate not confirm some of the nominees, because they favored free trade and were old rebels.[14] The group somewhat resembled Hayes', reflecting a divided party and a relatively unknown executive's desire to be independent. None of the members would offer Cleveland advice he did not wish to hear. Politically, no appointment except the southerners fully paid debts, or built for the future. Bayard was almost politically independent; Vilas did not really speak for the West; Manning represented Tilden; Endicott symbolized good intentions; Whitney was a party manager and personal friend. No one represented agriculture, labor, or immigrants.

These first selections illustrated Cleveland's parochial background and few contacts with the party's sources of strength. His friendships perpetuated each other in the same mold. He took advice from a small circle, the press he read, and random selections from the mail. His almost painful isolation from the party, and from social, economic, and political changes beyond the Hudson put him at great disadvantage in vitalizing the Democratic party. He might well vent a few secret doubts. ". . . I know that I am honest and sincere in that desire to do well," he wrote his brother, "but the question is whether I know enough to accomplish what I desire." [15]

March 4, 1885, was almost spring-like, with only a touch of winter's chill. Democrats flooded into Washington, determined to give their first president since Buchanan a boisterous welcome, and perhaps to seek a job. Fireworks, rebel yells, and an occasional wild shot announced the southern brethren, and many from all states walked on rubber legs through the last hours of Republican rule. The new President did not cut a handsome figure, and many Democrats wondered about his policies. "The Democrats have come here to look over the man they have elected, rather than to honor him," Frank Carpenter wrote.[16]

But for the moment, a carnival atmosphere reigned, and the departing Arthur passed the succession on in style. "King Arthur" left as he came, an enigma to everyone, but the good will signalling a change of the guard saw him "generally respected, alike by friend and foe." [17] He tactfully left most of the waving to his successor as they drove up Pennsylvania Avenue, through crowds of people just a little rough around the edges in manners. Vendors of noise-makers, ice-cream, buttons, and flags moved among those awaiting Cleveland's speech. After proper ceremonies inside the Capitol, the party emerged to cheers and huzzahs at the East Front. Cleveland spoke from memory, holding brevity a virtue. His rather high, clipped tones carried reasonably well, and the faithful heard him promise the usual sectional accord, peace in foreign affairs, and impartial government at home. He favored less government, and said that "civil service reform should be in good faith enforced." The people could expect no sudden departures from their new executive.[18]

Later that night, the lavish Pension Building hosted an inaugural ball, alive with the colors of uniforms, fine dresses, and decorations. The absence of a First Lady did not dampen anyone's spirits. People watched Cleveland for a hint of personality. Months had passed since the election, and he remained unknown. Were all those gamy stories true? It seemed incredible, if not unlikely, to the ladies watching him work through introductions—shaking hands firmly but without emotion, nodding to old friends, and apparently disinterested in making new ones with display. It was a festive time for triumphant Democrats, and despite warnings from Republicans, the country gave the new Administration a honeymoon. Observers knew that behind inaugural music a tense party awaited the spoils of victory, and millions, of all political persuasions, felt a trifle sad at the revelry. The nation was in the last stages of a long deathwatch for its greatest hero, General Grant.

As Arthur assumed political independence, Grant had moved steadily into the shadows of retirement. He unwisely committed his finances to relatives and friends in stock speculation and doubtful investments. The sharp "bankers' panic" of May, 1884, combined with mismanagement to topple his firm, Grant and Ward, leaving him penniless, an object of public charity and sympathy. Friends helped, but the story was all too familiar. "There is much sympathy for the General," a comrade wrote General Sherman, "but it is mingled with much fault finding." [19] While trying to aid him, others noted with exasperation that "He seems to be a perfect child in financial matters." [20] That, of course, was part of his popular legend; the common man fallen among city slickers.

Friends like Mark Twain suggested he write some memoirs. The General thought it was a joke until the first few articles succeeded, and critics praised his spare, lucid style, devoid of the bitterness and calumny that swirled around his career. While he wrote, further tragedy brought him national attention. In the winter of 1884, he complained of hoarseness, and doctors diagnosed terminal throat cancer. In a race with time, he produced his war memoirs as an estate for the impoverished family. For months he daily faced a pencil and pad, until by the spring of 1885 he finished a two-volume narrative of war-time experiences.

The qualities of patience and stoicism that made him a popular idol raised his last days from morbid spectacle to humble grandeur. By the summer of 1885, he could not speak, and jotted down messages for friends and daily reports to the doctor. In fitful rest, memories and reflections mixed with reality, and though the public did not read these scraps, they revealed a sensitive nature armored in public silence. He received famous men, satisfying most with a scrap of paper and thin smile. He wearied quickly, and they left when decorum permitted. He did not expect the miraculous cure the doctors and family thought possible. "The fact is," he scribbled, "I think I am a verb instead of a personal pronoun. A verb is anything that signifies to be, to do, or to suffer. I signify all three." [21] A note of dry humor sometimes entered the little diary. "I talked a good deal with my pencil," he told himself.[22] In reflective moments, his career seemed awesome in retrospect, and he would leave life puzzled: [23]

> If I live long enough, I will become a sort of specialist in the use of certain medicines, if not in the treatment of diseases. It seems that one man's destiny in this world is quite as much a mystery as it is likely to be in the next. I never thought of acquiring rank in the profession I was allocated for; yet it came with two grades higher prefixed to the rank of general for me. I certainly never had ambition or taste for political life; yet I was twice president of the United States. If anyone had suggested the idea of my becoming an author, as they frequently did, I was not sure whether they were making sport of me or not. I have now written a book which is in the hands of the manufacturers.

Political friends introduced measures to restore his permanent military rank with a lifetime salary, but partisanship delayed until it was only a gesture. On March 4, 1885, the House passed the necessary legislation, while President Arthur waited impatiently to sign it as his last official act. The announcement brought a gust of cheers, attesting an almost universal hope of easing the General's last days. On July 23, 1885, Grant died at Mount McGregor. Politics was suspended for a splendid state funeral, and he ultimately rested in an ornate tomb at the edge of Manhattan, far from the scenes of youth or places of conquest in manhood. In death as in life, he seemed misplaced. Grant occupied a unique position in people's affection and regard. They easily forgave his weaknesses and remembered his strengths, for he typified in both the common men from whom he rose. His fault was not in doing wrong, but in not knowing the right things to do. Opinions of his place in history varied, but his hold as a personality on the people he represented had few equals in history. Perhaps a political opponent, Samuel S. Cox, wrote the best brief obituary. "Modest as a man, great as a general, noble as a patriot, General Grant has a place in the hearts of his countrymen which hate, nor malice, nor envy can ever reach." [24]

President Cleveland generated a good deal of public curiosity among the thousands of office-seekers and visitors who crowded Washington. The sight of a Democrat in the White House seemed to rival P. T. Barnum's circus in popular imaginations, and the party's faithful thought they had special rights. "For years we have been praying for a President of the Democratic faith," a southern lady told a staff member, "and I do not see why he will not see us today. Why, *he is our own president,* and we must see him! Is this the reception we are to expect after waiting for so many years?" [25]

The staff called Cleveland "the Mahdi" because of his impassive demeanor, and those who met him saw a large but undistinguished figure. Several days a week he stood in the receiving line with Cabinet officers and their ladies, shaking visitors' hands. "I got a pleasant smile from a large mouth, eyes small and swollen," a visiting society woman recalled, "a plain face but it is a strong one and a good head." [26] Public receptions had their hazards. One elderly gentleman worked up to the President, looked him over and announced firmly: "I've voted for lots of presidents in my time, but I ain't never seen one before. Well, you're a whopper!" [27] Cleveland was sensitive about his weight, but did not rebut criticism, or try to disguise his contours. He cared little for clothes until his marriage, when Mrs. Cleveland ordered a new wardrobe. A woman commented on his appearance during an informal train ride: "Well, if I had fifty thousand dollars a year, I wouldn't dress like that." [28]

Cleveland lived a bachelor existence amid office-seekers and politicians, and often longed for Buffalo days with maudlin sentimentality. His taste in food and drink was plain, and he did not appreciate Arthur's quasi-regal legacy. He often kept friends late when not working, for a glass of whiskey and a cigar, talking jovially if they did not mention business. Sometimes he exchanged meals with the servants and wrote an old friend, Wilson Bissell: "I must go to dinner. I wish it was to eat a pickled herring, Swiss cheese, and a chop at Louis' instead of the French stuff I shall find." [29] Ugly rumors circulated about his drinking habits, but while he was not a Temperance zealot, Cleveland cared for liquor only as a social lubricant. He once urged Vilas to visit despite a cold, offering to cure the malady with appropriate tonic. He left formal entertainments to staff planners and his sister Rose, the mistress of the White House. Mrs. Whitney put his entertainments to shame, and added musicales and art shows to her repertoire. The Secretary's household staff often set a lavish table, complete with ships molded in ice and sherbet floating in seas of punch.

Cleveland did not enjoy riding or walking, and seemed to thrive on a sedentary existence behind a paper-littered table. When he did drive, an escort usually followed. Despite Garfield's recent assassination, opponents criticized security precautions. "When Cleveland would ride, an armed, booted, spurred detective with a foolish revolver on his foolish hip, swung to his foolish saddle, and clattered foolishly behind."[30] More often, the President simply slipped out for an hour's squirrel shooting in Maryland. Fishing was his greatest passion, and it was a brave man who started a conversation while a grim chief executive awaited his prey under a broad straw hat, in an old coat fit for a janitor or a woodcutter. He kept his lines in the White House basement, and often took down a favorite shotgun, "Death and Destruction," to check its oil and grip.

His love of detail made leisure hours few and far between these first hectic months. The Cabinet met on Tuesday and Friday, and he was pleasant with subordinates, though not jovial like Hayes. He heard their troubles, but did not interfere unless they asked. He listened to advice, but usually did not take it against his inclinations. Though usually courteous, he could easily roast a laggard clerk, and draw a deadly aim on newspaper reporters or tiresome politicians. "Mr. Cleveland had no oil in his store-room," a newshawk recalled, "but instead, boxing-gloves, mauls, and sledge-hammers."[31]

The inability to delegate work was a great weakness, and he spent endless hours over trivia. Late at night, aides saw his hands and profile reflected in a shiny desk surface; and he often sat calmly over papers until dawn during congressional sessions. While he worked, important people waited, and often left irritated, thinking him indifferent to their problems or suggestions. He thought eighteen-hour days set good examples for subordinates, but they were really a way to avoid people. He had a bad habit of mixing indirect criticism with grudging praise. After an endless session, he told a secretary: "Well, I guess we'll quit and call it half a day." But he also hired the young George B. Cortelyou as a stenographer, though he was a Republican. "I don't care anything about your politics," Cleveland said irritably, "all I want is somebody that is honest and competent to do my work." It was a dull existence, but he did not openly complain. "Grover Cleveland is the only president in our history who seems to need no amusements whatever," Frank Carpenter wrote. People supposed it hurt his health, but Cleveland seldom strained himself. "He is a healthy man, and is more careful of himself than the public is led to believe by the newspapers," Lamont said.[32]

Cleveland rarely spoke publicly, preferring to send a formal letter to a party gathering. He replied to most personal mail by hand, later answered the telephone, and sometimes opened the door when the bell rang as he was passing. His speeches sounded better in print than spoken, but neither performance was distinguished. Size gave him a certain platform presence, but he lacked the practiced orator's tone and flourish. "He was not blessed with imagination, but was a matter-of-fact man," Missouri's Champ Clark said.[33] "No, I have no style," Cleveland agreed, with a shrug. "I simply say what is in my mind and seems to be necessary at the time, and say it in my blundering way, and that is all there is to it." [34] With a touch of innocent pride, he developed a doubtful gift for polysyllabic words. He informed Congress it ought not to notice a law that had "fallen into innocuous desuetude," and critics called the gesture a ponderous attempt at archaic sophistication.[35] Others praised his rude candor as honesty, and the unwillingness of a strong mind to flatter.

That was all part of the legend, but his unconscious effrontery sometimes seemed planned. He almost cultivated bad relations with the press, a residue of distaste for 1884's scandals, and a natural dislike of personal display. But the man who would be President and party leader has no private life. He sometimes thoughtlessly called officials to late-night conferences when they were entertaining guests or resting from overwork, and never fostered the human touch that would have added political strength. He avoided crowds when he vacationed, and even used unmarked exits to escape well-wishers. He traveled too often with "the kid-gloved and gold-headed cane Democracy," fortifying the notion that he knew little about the rustic constituents who made him president.[36]

Cleveland enjoyed the presidency when his authoritarian personality governed, but the necessity to compromise, advertise, or curry favor brought out his inflexibility and dislike of advice. He alternately liked and loathed the office, but unlike professional politicians, could not start afresh each day. Sentimentality occasionally triumphed, and he would tell a visitor: "Sometimes I wake at night and rub my eyes and wonder if it is not all a dream." [37] But in those first few months he had little time for sleeping or dreaming. Office-seekers were literally coming in the windows.

Cleveland found the whole prospect of filling offices distasteful. He disliked people, objected to "dealing," and did not quite know what to do with patronage. He condemned "the din of party strife," and promised efficient reform, but had no real plan. Nothing reasonable would pacify either Mugwumps or hungry professionals; he assumed wrongly that he could strike a popular middle course. A few days after the election he said, "henceforth I must have no friends," which seemed a strange sentiment to them. He could be jovial and easygoing with callers, swapping stories and passing cigars, until they mentioned the visit's purpose. Then he became "a monumental icicle." [38]

Ideally, Cleveland had to do several things with patronage if the party was to grow. He must first create a body of men, especially in the North and West, loyal to him as a national leader, and to the Democracy as a cause. He must avoid strengthening local bosses, while satisfying their minimal demands, and attaching them to the whole party. And he must develop a body of doctrine and group of programs for future national success. But Cleveland saw patronage as a way of avoiding factional fights by creating an element loyal to him, and alienated almost everyone. He vaguely thought officeholders should favor the government over their party—a sound enough doctrine—but loyalty to Cleveland became the acid-test of fitness.

Lack of contacts among Democrats, and unwillingness to travel penalized him in the crucial distribution of offices. He did not know who offered sound or accurate advice, or proposed honest names, outside his immediate circle. He told Ignatius Donnelley of Minnesota that he hardly knew where to turn for information on western appointments, and admitted that his glaring errors of appointment in that region reflected genuine ignorance.[39] Critics said he usually avoided well-known spoilsmen for lesser-known spoilsmen. "Cleveland appeared to delight in digging up and inducting into his places statesmen who had studiously and successfully hidden their talents in a napkin until he turned his flashlight upon them," Champ Clark wrote.[40] This was doubly unfortunate. He often chose inept men, and seemed to build "a presidential party" against established leaders. "The Democratic party isn't in power," Vice-President Hendricks said after a White House call. "Grover Cleveland is making a party of his own." [41]

The Mugwumps were first in line, clamoring for the double reward of receiving office and advising the President. They were in a hurry because the long drought sharpened Democratic appetites. "It is no exaggeration to say that those calling themselves Democrats were then [in 1885] simply ravenous for spoils," an Adams recalled.[42] Leading independents raised their own hopes by repeating endlessly that Cleveland "has no such thing as a 'clean sweep' in his mind."[43] Curtis hastily telegraphed Washington: "I beg the president to remember Charles Sumner's advice to Stanton—'Stick.'"[44] Cleveland could not help repelling both the manner and advice. "May I say that I want to do just the right thing, and at the same time gratify a host of kind friends and good men of whom you are an honored representative?" he wrote the carping Schurz. "I take up my burden every morning and carry it as well as I can till night, and frequently up-hill."[45]

Schurz was the most voluble Mugwump adviser, taking hours of the President's time to explain civil service reform as if he were a school-master with a distinguished but dull pupil. Schurz outlined the new Administration's three general alternatives. It could return "to the old practices of the spoils system"; it might "strike out boldly and con-sistently in the line of reform, aiming straight at a non-partisan service"; or worst of all, it would "go forward in the line of reform far enough to disgust some of the old party . . . but not far enough to inspire the reform elements outside of the party." He did not help matters with supercilious reminders that "there is more trust in you than in the party." Cleveland kept his temper, but said Schurz was "a hard master."[46]

Cleveland stubbornly resisted Mugwump control. It would alienate more powerful Democratic leaders, but he also disliked their dogma-tism. He would not be their creature, or an agent of local bosses. Cleve-land was neither a liberal nor a conservative, but an individualist, acutely conscious of prerogatives. Like any public man, he wanted to stay in office, and knew established leaders could help him more than independents. The question was how to control the leaders and create personal support. In short order, he referred to "these fool friends of civil service reform."[47] But he did not want an open break; in 1888, they might hold the balance of power again. He spent hours explaining the search for a middle way.

Men like Secretary Bayard, with contacts in Congress and among independents, patiently reminded people that Cleveland's party would not support sudden changes, and a brusque tone entered the President's dealings with Mugwumps. He too could wield the chalk and map-pointer. "A reasonable toleration for old prejudices, a graceful recogni-tion of every aid, a sensible utilization of every instrumentality that promises assistance, and a constant effort to demonstrate the advantages of the new order of things," he reminded Dorman B. Eaton, "are the means by which this reform movement will in the future be farther advanced, the opposition of incorrigible spoilsmen rendered ineffectual, and the cause placed upon a sure foundation." In the meantime, reformers should avoid "supercilious self-righteousness," and "carping criticism," and not "demand complete and immediate perfection." [48]

Cleveland intended to reward the faithful within reasonable limits. ". . . I have no sympathy with the intolerant people who, without the least appreciation of the meaning of party work and service superciliously affect to despise all those who apply for office as they would those guilty of flagrant misdemeanor." [49] He was more realistic than independents in facing the onslaught, knowing the desperation of his party after twenty-five lean years. As many influential leaders reminded him, "Democracy is the poor and ignorant party of this country—the great barefooted, unwashed, dirty-socked party," and the genteel element could not expect a hat-in-hand attitude.[50] "The people I have to deal with—that is, the people of the country—are not perhaps just what I wish they were," Cleveland told a friend, "and they perhaps have ideas which are not useful or correct, but their ideas to a very great extent must be met or my efforts to do good must miscarry." [51]

For every epistle from Carl Schurz, the President received a dozen urging rewards for the faithful, like the delightfully outraged note from a Shelbyville, Indiana, newspaper publisher: "The western people desire a *change* in the offices. What are we here for? Surely not to keep Republicans in office. *Turn the rascals out!* Your greatest point is your firmness. So with one blow, make a *clean* sweep. To keep the offices filled with Republicans, we could all have voted for Jim and Jack." [52] Local Democrats warned Cleveland against ignoring voters who elected him; moderates counseled impatient reformers to forbear while the Democrats raised some dust.

Of the 125,000 non-military federal offices, some 96,000 were under Post Office Department jurisdiction. Most appointments were fourth-class postmasterships in small towns, paying less than $1,000 a year, but wielding great local influence. "The fate of the party and the administration lies in the crossroads post-offices," Frank Carpenter reported.[53] Tilden urged Manning to influence fresh appointments of postmasters. "They act as agents and canvassers for the newspapers of their party, and as local organizers. The immense power of this influence is now wholly on the side of the Republicans." [54] An auditor in the Post Office Department explained that the local postmaster was often a storekeeper, and might easily wrap goods in a Democratic newspaper while complaining shrewdly of the high cost of Republican living. "Each country post office is the center of news, and around its stove each winter night assembles a convention wherein the political opinions of the mature are strengthened or modified, and those of the young are formed." [55]

Vilas' carriage often stood in the White House driveway late at night, as he "made postmasters" with Cleveland. The two men pored over letters of recommendation, investigators' reports, and politicians' demands. Cleveland liked Vilas, and they often fished together, with a bundle of departmental papers on shore awaiting their pleasure. If the White House got oppressive, the President might take a drive, reading appointment papers in the breeze. Late in April, 1885, Cleveland let Vilas define rules for suspension or refusal to reappoint Post Office employees. "Offensive partisanship" was a basic criterion for dismissal, but the term covered a multitude of theoretical sins. The postmaster could not speak, organize, write or use his office for political activity. The President would rely on advice from congressmen and local Democrats, and need not show cause to remove incumbents.

Reformers objected bitterly to the wholesale replacements that followed, and especially at the policy of not stating grounds for removal. Cleveland defended his position with appeals to familiar facts. Time and personnel were limited; everyone knew how bitter the campaign of 1884 was, and his files bulged with accounts of the lowest kind of partisanship. He contentedly insisted that "By far the greater number of suspensions . . . were made on account of gross and indecent partisan conduct on the part of the incumbents." [56] Politics did not prevent occasional clemency or graciousness. He kept Joseph Manley as postmaster of Augusta, and dismissed one in Mississippi who villified Blaine in 1884. In the annual message of 1885, Cleveland argued forcefully that much of the complaining reflected incompetence in men he replaced, and perfectionism in those who urged more speed.

Everything he did toward reform provoked reactions in political sectors he needed to win. The city machine bosses raved against independents who lectured them in the press; and the President seemed intent on building his own party. They were frank. "Politics are impossible without the spoils," Richard Croker of Tammany once noted. "It is all very well to argue that it ought not to be so. But we have to deal with men as they are, and with things as they are." The always strained relations between Cleveland and Tammany did not improve as the Hall's emissaries arrived in Washington for payments. After a few weeks of cold interviews, and grudging victories, the City men adopted a rude humor. "He never did anything for his friends," one remarked of Cleveland, "and as we are not his friends, perhaps he may do something for us." The President's flirtation with independents in East Coast cities angered organizers of immigrant groups. They would not stand by idly while rewards passed to "respectable" hands, threatening their local rule more than Cleveland realized.[57]

The Administration's eastern orientation also nettled midwesterners who wished to build a stronger party both to thwart radical agrarian tendencies, and steal Republican thunder. "We are New Yorked to disgrace and death; and mugwumped to a state of idiocy," Nebraska's J. Sterling Morton wrote. "The President has a big belly. His brains are not proportioned to it." [58] Cleveland silently nursed grudges, but spoke out occasionally. "Why, Mr. President, I should like to see you move more expeditiously in advancing the principles of the Democracy," one politico said unctuously. Cleveland stirred irritably. "Ah, I suppose you mean that I should appoint two horse thieves a day instead of one!" [59] And behind all his troubles with "practical" men, droned a Mugwump chorus. "[The] President seems to think that he has to stoop down for the purpose of lifting up his party to his level," Schurz wrote Bayard. "I have seen that sort of thing before. The danger is that he who thus stoops down may not be able to quite straighten up again himself." [60]

The months passed, and Democrats filled the offices despite assorted criticism from right and left. Late in the term, Republican Senator Eugene Hale of Maine told colleagues that Cleveland had filled over 42,000 of 55,000 appointive offices available. Long before that, Cleveland joined predecessors in wondering why he ever wanted to be president. ". . . the d———d everlasting clatter for offices continues to some extent," he wrote friends, "and makes me feel like resigning, and *HELL* is to pay generally." [61]

As if these party troubles were not enough, the Republican Senate attacked. Denying the President's right to remove officials without public and adequate cause, some senators rumbled about reviving the Tenure of Office Act, or refusing to confirm appointments. Officious senators like Edmunds demanded papers and the testimony of executive officers. "I shall not submit to improper dictation," Cleveland said early in the struggle, and forbade subordinates to release documents or testify without his consent.[62] Congressmen could examine departmental files, and Cleveland instructed subordinates to furnish information whenever feasible, but not to answer *demands*. The public generally sided with presidential independence that seemed to connote more action than did senatorial delay and obstruction. In a series of explanatory messages, Cleveland took high ground. "The pledges I have made were to the people, . . . I am not responsible to the Senate, and I am unwilling to submit my actions and official conduct to them for judgment." [63] Cleveland knew "the spoils system is involved in my controversy with the Senate," and would not accept senatorial dictation any more than did Hayes or Garfield. Unlike them, he faced the opposition party, and did not undertake the double burden of resisting encroachments from his own followers. Mugwumps irritated him more than ever as the contest brewed, and he finally suggested that "as the man [asked] of God when he was fighting the bear: 'If you can't help me, don't help the bear!' " [64] The Senate failed, and Cleveland remained independent, though he was characteristically more concerned with defending his prerogative than in expanding presidential power.

Cleveland actually saw fewer office-seekers than his immediate predecessors, but they were no less distasteful for their relative invisibility. He thought he did well, all things considered. "You know the things in which I yielded," he once told a friend, "but no one save myself can ever know the things which I resisted." [65] He failed to use patronage to good political effect, however. Another man with a conciliatory manner and shrewder insight into people would have done better. Cleveland mistook diffuse newspaper praise of rhetorical flourishes for support. He logically sought a middle way, but identified it with himself, not the Democratic party, offending those who otherwise might grudgingly accept disappointing acts. He seldom reflected on this, except to complain about ingratitude, and had no serious plan to construct a national party with patronage. Also, he did not advance civil service reform as Mugwumps defined it. The appointment power was part of the executive's ability to build or weaken his political following. Cleveland might have smoothed over many inevitable mistakes with a more genial and public personality, better information, and wider advice. By 1886, he had quarreled with his party, Mugwumps, and the Senate. And GAR veterans were increasingly hostile to this first Democratic administration since the war.

Federal generosity to Union veterans did not lessen as the war faded into memory. In 1876, the government spent about one-tenth of its budget on compensation to veterans; in 1886, the total rose to one-fourth. The increase reflected the political power of various organizations, especially the Grand Army of the Republic. Cleveland did not intend to curtail pensions, or veterans' preference for government employment.* He asked only for good taste. During the campaign of 1884, he answered ugly stories of his staying at home to make money during the war with silence. In forming his Administration, he carefully included men close to veterans' organizations. William F. Vilas and General Bragg would especially represent veterans. None of his advisers considered curtailing pensions or paying ex-Confederate soldiers.

The "soldier vote" seemed solidly Republican to idle observers, but Democrats like Bragg and Vilas had fought for the Union. Veteran's status did not determine a man's vote, though the threat of a "southern" Administration that might shrink benefits undoubtedly added heat if not light to post-war elections. Critics of northern veterans' organizations conveniently forgot the South's great over-representation in Congress. Men who condemned the "bloody shirt" in Republican politics easily ignored the same, more intense phenomenon in the South. But local politicians and pension agents working for special individual legislation raised the cost of benefits after the war. Opponents charged that aging Boys in Blue would not be happy until they reached "the bottom of Uncle Sam's strongbox." [66]

The question was a blind spot for many honest and able public men. Intelligent people like Hayes, Benjamin Harrison, and Garfield bitterly opposed any reduction in pensions. They easily unfurled the flag and defended rascals to the tune of patriotism, not merely for political advantage, but because they disliked southern ideas and feared succeeding generations would forget the war's full meaning and cost. If economics entered the problem, most Republicans agreed with Wisconsin's Senator Philetus Sawyer. Why worry about a surplus, when you could spend it on good works among veterans and on internal improvements? It was more feasible than minutely lowering tariff taxation, with its political and economic risks. The funds also went to the neediest level of society. "The money will get into circulation and come back into the Treasury very soon," Sawyer remarked, "so go ahead and do what you think is right in the premise, and there will be no trouble." [67]

Cleveland was bound to take another view. Such bounty seemed charity to him. In the summer of 1886, he began vetoing private pension bills for undemonstrated need. Congress handled thousands of such measures each session, the fruit of lobbyists' efforts. They were seldom large, but formed a backlog of paperwork. Cleveland began submitting

---

*The same system, of course, roughly applies today. Veterans receive preference in federal employment, and have gained many added benefits like housing finance, medical care, and tax exemptions from both local and national government.

each private bill to the Pension Bureau's tests, and found that a high percentage were fraudulent or had misty origins. Night after night, he read the covering papers, writing vetoes to show the country his sense of duty and desire to reduce government expenditures.

He revealed a rare sense of humor in killing special bills. "The ingenuity developed in the constant and persistent attacks upon the public Treasury by those claiming pensions, and the increase of those already granted, is exhibited in bold relief by this attempt to include sore eyes among the results of diarrhea." He noted a flood of measures compensating men for hernias supposedly incurred on bad saddles. "The number of instances in which those of our soldiers who rode horses during the war were injured by being thrown forward upon their saddles indicate that those saddles were very dangerous contrivances." He objected to a widow's plea for compensation after her deaf husband drowned because he could not hear a ferryboat. He lost his hearing in the Army, and the government should pay. "How he could have saved his life if he had heard the warning is not stated," Cleveland noted heavily.[68]

Republicans generally condemned the President's "flippant, sneery language." Senators Blair and Logan called the performance "silly" and "impertinent," a grandstand play for press coverage and the cheese-parers' vote. Hasty Mugwump defense of Cleveland did not disabuse good Republican heads of this idea. Cleveland obviously wished to codify the pension laws, eliminate special agents, and remove the issue from politics. As usual, he attacked without explanation, and in a manner that put him on the defensive in dealing with Congressmen and much of the press. More importantly, it fortified his image of personal pettiness, and inability to delegate details. It was all very well, critics noted, to write one or two vetoes to make a point, but no president should spend a career checking each measure. Machine opponents saw it as string-saving. "Cleveland delighted in the little," a Tammany brave said later, "and would labor pantingly at the windlass of small things. It was this bent of the infinitesimal that led him to put in hours darkly arranging a reason to shatter some old woman's pension with the bludgeon of his veto." [69] For the moment, he had some satisfaction, especially in vetoing the Dependent Pension Bill of 1887 that offered assistance to almost everyone with a military record.

Much of the press and some veterans supported Cleveland's veto of the "Pauper Pension Bill," but between June, 1886, and the summer of 1887, an endless series of colorful and politically dangerous incidents flowed from the question. In April, 1887, as part of routine paperwork, the President endorsed Adjutant General Richard C. Drum's idea of returning southern battle flags that Union forces captured during the war. They were moldering in an attic, and it would be a nice ceremonial gesture. Southern authorities would presumably return Union flags. Secretary Endicott agreed, and the Adjutant General's office announced the transfer.

Cleveland's action, whatever the proposal's merits, illustrated his political inexperience. No midwestern Democrat, attuned to the devious uses of demagoguery, would have touched such an idea unless the southerners moved first, but to Cleveland, it was a reasonable, routine matter. Public reaction surprised him. Lucias Fairchild, national commander in chief of the GAR exploded. Called "The Empty Sleeve" because he lost an arm at Gettysburg, Fairchild was a power in Wisconsin politics and a usually moderate organizer among veterans. He had crossed the bloody chasm to receive ceremonial decorations from southern organizations, but like so many men of his generation, he only grudgingly surrendered the war's glorious memories. On the evening of June 14, as he entered the Alexander Hamilton Post Number 182 in Harlem, a bystander described the President's order. Suddenly shaking with fury, he uttered a famous directive: "May God palsy the hand that wrote the order! May God palsy the brain that conceived it! And may God palsy the tongue that dictated it!" During the next few days, he expanded the theme on an eastern speaking tour, while Cleveland drew fire from all quarters of the country.[70]

Governor Joseph Benson "Fire Alarm Joe" Foraker of Ohio, a spread-eagle demagogue, answered a correspondent with an equally famous telegram: "No rebel flags will be returned while I am governor." Sensing political damage, Cleveland and advisers decided they required congressional consent to exchange such property. The President withdrew the order with a terse explanation, though Foraker insisted he "sneaked like a whipped spaniel." The angry Cleveland blamed subordinates for unwittingly creating the incident. Its political effects varied. Rude polls showed the battle flag incident occupied more newspaper space than any other item during the summer of 1887. They also revealed fresh sentiment in the Border and Upper South for the President that might help defeat the few Republican congressmen tenaciously holding seats there.[71]

The struggle continued through the summer, as veterans' organizations overplayed their hands and created sympathy for Cleveland. In June, 1887, John G. Carlisle and others urged him to visit the Midwest. The presidential campaign was a year away. The party had some latent strength in the Midwest which a visit might bring to the polling place. He accepted the invitation of St Louis' Mayor David Francis to address a "monster rally" of some 200,000 people to celebrate the national encampment of the GAR. After the battle flags incident, Francis timorously suggested the President would not be safe, and Cleveland retreated to the loftiest heights of non-partisanship and presidential grandeur. While denying any personal fears, he refused to subject his office to insult. On July 2, he sent a waspish message to a veterans' reunion in Gettysburg, condemning men who "trafficked in sectional hate." [72] Secretary Whitney was more earthy and shrewd. "Let the solicitude for his personal safety grow. . . ." he wrote Lamont, sensing a developing disgust with demagogues.[73]

Veterans' organizations apparently entertained any kind or degree of foolishness. In August, a reunion in Wheeling outdid everyone for rudeness. A newspaper editor hung from his window along the line of march a large banner proclaiming: "God Bless Our President, Commander-in-Chief of Our Army and Navy." The first units, one including former President Hayes, passed under it without incident. Later marchers, however, stopped at the sign, walked around it, trailing flags in the gutter, jeered, and almost provoked a riot. This was too much. In September, the GAR encampment opposed a general pension bill, and refused to censure Cleveland. Most veterans were disgusted with blatant leaders, and cared little about the tempest. They might be unlettered, but they recognized bad manners. Seasoned commentators saw that the President gained politically. The Cleveland luck was holding. And public attention on his newly married state offset much adverse publicity.

Like his predecessor, Cleveland called on the family ladies for White House entertainment and planning. His younger sister Rose was hostess much of the year, but she had enough of her brother's traits to gain a mixed reaction from guests and the press. She liked precision and order, had literary ambitions, and was also "a rather sharp-tongued young lady, with a predisposition to Woman's Rights." But she stood in the receiving line and innocently confessed to relieving the tedium by silently conjugating Greek verbs. Her slender volume entitled *George Eliot's Poetry and Other Studies* went through twelve printings in a year, earning some $25,000.

The President's matrimonial intentions, if any, captured public fancy. "The gossip about the President marrying springs up with every new girl to whom he pays a compliment," Frank Carpenter noted.[74] Soon after the election, some papers speculated on his intentions toward Miss Frances Folsom, daughter of a former law partner, and for a time his ward. A good many years separated them, and Cleveland had little time for courting, but a *sub rosa* romance developed. In 1886 the White House announced a June wedding. "The good people of the country will, I am sure, be satisfied to have their President behave on such an occasion like anyone else," Cleveland wrote his sister, "and dispense with all nonsense and flummery." [75]

The White House needed a woman's touch, and its staff welcomed Miss Folsom on her wedding day. The President's friends and well-wishers flooded the mansion with gifts; diamonds were a major motif. Hopes for a calm ceremony vanished in the rush of guests and newspaper reporting, though Cleveland tried to take it all in stride. He worked steadily all morning until the ceremony began. The nation devoured every tidbit of news around the event, and marriage did smooth some of Cleveland's edges. He also dressed better, displayed less temper, and took to matrimony with the eagerness common to elderly bachelors who finally capitulate.

He professed amazement at the public interest. Sightseers gawked at the newlyweds until he ordered the park behind the White House closed. "Frankie" Cleveland drew special correspondents and Sunday fashion editors in droves, but the President resented most of the publicity. Inevitably, Mrs. Cleveland's picture appeared on cigars, patent medicine, underwear, candy, and corsets, until a Democrat introduced a House bill to prohibit such advertising. It died, but publicity declined as the couple settled into matrimonial routine. In time, five children surrounded the aging father, and some Americans saw their president carry his own grip off the train when visiting in-laws. Mrs. Cleveland played no part in politics, but tried to raise the children without publicity, and immediately took charge of White House social events. Like most First Ladies, she wished to sustain her husband, not participate in his work.

Cleveland naturally disliked newspaper sensationalism. Cheap sheets printed a flow of lies ranging from wife-beating to Mrs. Cleveland's alleged pro-English feelings. He grew touchy about allusions to his weight and good-looks, but could not stop the cartoonists' pens. Respectable opinion joined his pleas for privacy, and condemned "special reporters" who followed celebrities. "Surrounding himself with pickets, putting himself behind walls, landing on a desert isle, plunging into jungles, or going up in a balloon, will avail nothing against the enterprising reporter," warned Godkin.[76] Cleveland despised reporters, with unhappy political consequences, and often referred publicly to "the lying press," and "those ghouls of the press." [77] He tried, without much success, to differentiate between newsmen and publishers. "I believe a large majority of reporters are decent and honorable men, who would prefer to do clean and respectable work," he said in a later interview.[78] He never overcame a dislike for the fourth estate, however, and once answered a bright reporter's leading question with growling firmness. "That, sir, is a matter of too great importance to discuss in a five-minute interview, now rapidly drawing to a close." [79]

The First Family gained sympathy as sensationalists fed a thin but lurid stream of gossip. Mrs. Cleveland's natural desire to shelter the children led to rumors they were sub-normal or deformed, the result of their father's early debauchery. The old canards that he was a drunkard and beat his wife made the rounds, and finally prompted Mrs. Cleveland, on the advice of political managers, to public disavowals. On the eve of her husband's renomination, she denied such lies in a letter released to the press. "I can wish the women of our country no greater blessing than that their homes and lives may be as happy, and their husbands may be as kind, attentive, considerate and affectionate as mine." [80] Cleveland seldom commented publicly on such matters, but thanked friends who did. He was especially grateful to Mrs. Whitney, who firmly scotched any lies within her reach. "Somehow it has seemed to me that people don't know how wicked and malicious they are, and I have wondered why the whole world did not indignantly stamp upon them," he said. "I did not know how mean politics make men and women." [81] Somehow, it all fitted his view of both humanity and politics as a form of strife for place and power, in which the best man did not always win, or savor victory when achieved.

Cleveland's lack of contact with political currents and leaders beyond the Hudson was a major disadvantage in broadening the party's electoral base. Propagandizing was a large part of any president's political role, but Cleveland preferred speaking in print and through Eastern friends on western errands to taking the stump. He also distrusted western tendencies to "soft" money, corporate regulation, and free trade. By mid-term, however, politicians in both parties finally faced the problem of federal regulation of railroads.*

*The development and regulation of American railroads remains the most widely discussed and controversial single problem in Gilded Age historiography, illustrating not only the subject's importance, but historians' tendency to focus on issues that can be cast in right/wrong molds. The literature on the subject is immense, and I can only discuss here the outlines of regulation's immediate effects on politics, especially on the Democratic party.

Railroad development, speculation, and consolidation provoked both hostility and support for all the steam engine symbolized. Most western communities welcomed the railroad, to raise property values, increase population, and unify markets. But enthusiasm sparked over-building and waste. Inevitably, after the fact, it was easy to proclaim all railroad interests "The Octopus" and all farmers embattled yeomen defending freedom and competition. Most people involved in the struggle wanted to save and extend competition, but offered varied plans to avoid monopoly or government control. Railroad interests faced several directions. Constructive investors and managers opposed the free pass, wanted standardized taxation, and hoped to avoid demagogic opponents in local politics. But many businessmen dreaded any legislative battle. A minority clung to the laissez-faire doctrines they conveniently overlooked when seeking federal subsidies. Few, however, agreed with the owner who remarked of pending laws: "God governs the world, I think, by general, and not by special legislation." [82] More businessmen frankly wanted to replace rate wars, bad building, and political jobbery with enlightened consolidation. "The struggle for existence and survival of the fittest is a pretty theory," George Perkins remarked, "but it is also a law of nature that even the fittest must live as they go along." [83]

Much of the railroads' bad reputation was a compound of tangible faults and intangible emotions. It was difficult to grasp the chicanery of invisible trusts or the alleged advantages of tariff reform, but almost anyone could fancy oppression in a train's smoke, hear evil in its lonely whistle, and wish to control the iron road it traveled across former public domain. Demagogues and sensational newspapers made every railroad agent a plutocrat. The railroad was a tangible symbol of conspiracy to the agrarian who already suspected the sleek cities it served, distant men it allegedly enriched, and people like himself whom it left behind.

Its influence was often baleful, and in sparsely populated, over-taxed western states, the lines wielded inordinate influence. Men who took favors were "working on the railroad," and its support was a mixed blessing for politicians with poor constituents. "Being a cattle thief don't disqualify a man for anything he may want in this state," a Nevadan commented. "Really, . . . it adds to a man's standing in the community—[but] being connected with a railroad is what *lays a fellow out*." [84] By the mid-1880's, vague but often bitter public hostility to railroads symbolized most of the discontent in America between rich and poor, farmer and businessman, city and countryside. The "Granger Laws" of the early 1870's controlled some intra-state traffic, and when

Wisconsin's supreme court sustained regulation, the governor ordered a
100-gun salute.

The problem was not simple, however, and its solution must enfold
conflicting desires within each major group involved. Farmers were
important in advertising needed regulation, but not all agrarians favored
severity. Eastern farmers, selling in nearby urban markets, disliked
western farmers who undersold them in basic products like wheat because of lower transportation costs and larger yields. Railroad owners
caught in the growing competition of a trunk-line system rapidly filling
the area from Boston to Chicago, wanted stable rates and accepted the
principle of national regulation for their own and the country's good.
When Cleveland took office, a leading business journal summed up the
confusion surrounding a decade's talk of how to meet the problem: [85]

> Thus the curious spectacle is presented of friend and opponent alike
> pleading for redress at the hands of the government. The mercantile
> community asks that violent fluctuations in rates be done away with,
> that drawbacks and rebates be made impossible, that no more be
> charged for a long haul than short one, that discrimination be abol-
> ished, that diversion of freight be no longer permitted, and that various
> other grievances, real or imaginary, be attended to. The railroads, too,
> now look to the government to help them out of their difficulties. . . .
> In a word, merchants want to be protected against the railroads, the
> railroads want to be protected against themselves, and investors
> against both. And they all cry for the same soothing syrup—legisla-
> tive enactment.

The West resented eastern domination; the East thought long hauls
and expanding markets favored the West. Rural areas disliked city rule,
and urban planners distrusted agrarian politics. Investors generally favored an expert commission, with legal redress, patterned somewhat on
the Civil Service Commission. Agrarians demanded simple legal prohi-
bitions, with the right to sue for damages, testifying to American faith
in simple laws. Most railroad owners accepted inevitable regulation.
For every man who talked the virtues of free enterprise and an open
marketplace, several others pointed out evils of over-expansion, jerry-
building, and rate wars. If regulation must come, let the national government devise a single system for interstate traffic, now involving
three-fourths of the nation's rail shipments. Uniformity would follow in
safety devices, equipment, and schedules. It might also remove railroads
from state politics; a welcome prospect to men in private cars, in fields,
and behind mercantile desks.

Precedent for regulation grew with the lines. New Hampshire had
a state agency in 1844. Four states regulated traffic in some fashion in

1860. By 1897, twenty-eight states would oversee railroads. But means and powers varied widely. Some state bodies were mere tokens. Others, like that of Massachusetts, investigated, publicized, and recommended to the legislature, but enforced few restraints. Foreign precedents were weak, since no other country combined America's problems and size. Attempts at federal regulation met ennui and stubborn resistance from scattered, contradictory sources. Many Democrats opposed federalism. Reformers had no comprehensive plan suitable to all sections of the country, since railroad stability and importance varied widely. Poor economic expertise compounded confusion and eased the task of demagogues, who clouded the issue with moral rhetoric. But the Supreme Court's open hints that Congress needed to enact a comprehensive law helped move thinking people toward a national plan during Cleveland's term.

Senator Shelby M. Cullom of Illinois, known largely for a fancied resemblance to Lincoln, headed a congressional group favoring a mixed commission. Representative John H. Reagan of Texas, with friends in both the mercantile and agrarian communities, initially tended toward strict prohibitory laws. He wished to outlaw pooling, rebates, drawbacks, free passes, and rate discriminations. The third, and least significant group, opposed regulation and clung to a nonexistent free market. Most politicians knew compromise must prevail, especially since reformers trod unmarked legal ground. Reagan was a colorful figure in rustic politics, "the Old Roman" to constituents, and a handy man with a crowd on the subject of railroad regulation, "federalism," and monopolies. He began a crusade in the early 1870's, urging simple prohibitory legislation against railroad excesses. He feared a commission would favor businessmen, and distrusted experts, feeling, in good Jacksonian tradition, that every man was his own economist. He had some support from eastern chambers of commerce and mercantile shipping interests, but spoke largely for western and southern farmers. He had little luck with his bills in the Senate, though the House was more amenable to his oratory.[86]

The commission idea moved toward triumph in 1885, when a Senate committee under Cullom's direction began to take testimony and codify recommendations for a full-scale congressional debate.* Cleveland was "keenly interested," though he showed little concrete understanding of the issue.[87] The committee toured the nation's principal

---

*The other members were Orville H. Platt of Connecticut, Warner Miller of New York, Arthur P. Gorman of Maryland, and Isham G. Harris of Tennessee. The last two were Democrats.

cities. Some witnesses in the Plains states opposed a commission. "The people want no board of railroad commissioners," one Granger snapped. "They want just and wholesome laws, with well-defined provisions for enforcing them. . . . The people prefer to trust the courts * rather than a commission." [88] Senator Charles H. Van Wyck of Nebraska, with strong Populist tendencies, condemned the whole notion. "Annexing a commission with large salaries and little power is not what the people are demanding." [89]

Cullom staged the debate in the winter of 1886–87. He argued that a commission would shelter small shippers and individuals who could not easily sue corporations. "Pygmies do not invite giants to combat," Representative J. H. Rowell of Illinois noted trenchantly. The mere existence of a commission would dampen corporate immorality. The body could avoid expensive suits with out-of-court settlements beneficial to small litigants. If the agency could not settle a case, it would in effect argue it before federal courts by allowing a suit. The commission would create precedent that no law could codify, and gather information for future recommendations.[90]

After full debate, a law of February 4, 1887, established a commission of five members, hopefully non-partisan. Though some commentators lapsed into the usual newspaper cynicism, it was a constructive and logical compromise. It regulated only interstate commerce, and required "reasonable and just" charges, but did not fix rates. It prohibited pooling, rebates, drawbacks, and excessive short-haul charges on the same line. Railroads had to post rates, and the commission could investigate almost all aspects of the business, though its instructions were not binding as court orders. It could institute equity suits, and require annual inspection of records.

Cleveland doubted much of its intent and power, but signed the law. He named Michigan's distinguished jurist, Thomas M. Cooley, as chairman, but did less well in choosing others. William R. Morrison, defeated in the elections of 1886, was the most controversial selection, and made Cullom explode. "Colonel Morrison knows nothing about the subject. If you are going to appoint broken-down politicians who have been defeated at home, as a sort of salve for the sores caused by their defeat, we might as well repeal the law." [91] Cleveland appreciated the

---

*Most historians argue that conservative federal courts thwarted the drive toward regulation, in concert with a weak commission. This does not square with the contemporary feeling among many liberals that the courts were a better enforcement agency than a commission. A simple lack of expert advice was probably most important in blunting the edge of attacks on monopoly through regulation, either with commissions or laws.

commission largely because, as he told Cooley, "you fellows are the only men I ever appointed to office who never gave me any trouble." [92]

This first attempt at federal regulation of industry had flaws, but like all political compromises, made a reasonable beginning. Fear of government in all quarters, hazy legal precedents, and political necessity made its powers uncertain. One newspaper commentator summed up a problem which antitrust legislation never surmounted: "The law forbids pooling, but it cannot prevent conferring, which practically is exactly the same thing." [93] Moderates thought the commission would expand its power as the legal foundation grew, and presumed its mere existence would warn railroads against excesses. In the broadest sense, the law's significance was recognition of consolidation's tangential evils. Prior to 1887, government promoted railroad development; hereafter it would regulate. Like most laws in this time of change, it incorporated as much expertise as society offered on a dangerous political subject. Its importance was its existence. Most significantly, Republicans passed the law after full publicity, and justly earned more political credit than the Administration. The President seemed indifferent; the subject was dull and unreal to him, and he saw it on legalistic grounds. More provocative things occupied him as the party drifted uncertainly towards a reelection campaign.

Cleveland was briefly more interested in the silver question than railroad regulation, but brought little theory to either subject. The men who made him president favored gold, reflecting east-coast business affiliations. But Tilden, a strong advocate of "safe" currency, did not oppose silver coinage if the currency adjusted "under a free system. . . . I am willing to take all that the business of the country can absorb; it is impossible to do anything more. To force the quantity of the currency above its natural level is as idle an attempt as was Dame Partington's effort with her mop to keep back the Atlantic Ocean." [94] It took little persuasion to solidify Cleveland's dislike of inflation, and westerners repeated old noises against a president of their own party. "He learns his financial theories from Wall Street," a Missouri editor insisted, "the leeches that suck the blood of the honest yeomanry of the west, like vampires." [95]

The President wanted to avoid the subject. He saw political danger, whatever its economic bases. But he did remark: "Whenever I see a Bland dollar, I am reminded of the aphorism about the cloud with the silver lining. It is 80 percent silver and 20 percent mist." [96] The short, sharp panic of 1884 sent chilling ripples through an over-extended western economy, raising old demands for monetary inflation. Just before Cleveland's inauguration, Abram S. Hewitt and prominent Democrats urged him to end rumors that he favored silver. A firm statement would bolster confidence, and thwart a congressional attack on gold. Despite warnings from western congressmen, Cleveland let Manton Marble, former editor of the *New York World* and friend of Tilden, write a letter which Cleveland sent to Democratic congressmen, denying any desire to "help silver." At about the same time, the House defeated an attempt to end silver coinage, notifying Cleveland the issue was merely dormant. He earned some praise from Tilden. "Your silver letter is absolutely perfect," the old man wrote. "It is the only silver thing I know of that transmutes itself into gold." [97]

The whole problem troubled Cleveland. He knew the sharp debates the Bland-Allison Act provoked, and did not want to open old wounds. He settled at once on the usual gesture—a special agent to examine chances for international bi-metalism at a fixed ratio. In the summer and fall of 1885, Marble toured Europe, seeming to talk for silver but working for gold, even phrasing replies from leading foreign officials and bankers to his own letters.[98] He naturally reported failure, and Cleveland duly sent the reports to Congress. In December, he disavowed silver in the annual message, ascribing sluggish business conditions to fear of inflation. Westerners like Morrison insisted Congress would continue silver coinage, and discreetly attacked Cleveland. "The President has seen fit to ally himself with a faction of the party, not one fifth of it, [and] on the uppermost public questions—tariff and taxes—to slap in the face the other four fifths." [99] Secretary Manning noted passion around the issue. "A majority of the representatives from the West and South are actually mad as wild Texas steers on this silver dollar business. As we pass each other in the streets, they seem to sneer and hiss through their teeth the words 'gold bug' and look as if they would like to spit upon me." He urged caution; let the issue lie rather than act against silver.[100] Republicans would help Democrats in the Senate defeat inflationary measures and "the House is by no means ready to go it alone for free coinage of silver." [101]

For the moment, Democrats avoided the issue. Charles Fairchild, Manning's successor in the Treasury, wanted to spend the surplus on government bonds. Friends in both houses of Congress agreed; it was no time to rock the boat. But Cleveland stood publicly against a major sector of his party on the issue that moved them most. He needed some other cause to unite the party for its coming contest.

The "off-year"congressional elections of 1886 involved no earth-shaking issues or lurid personalities, and were a kind of Administration victory. The Democrats lost only 12 seats, retaining the House and narrowing Republican Senate control to 2 votes. The results revealed indifference, or apparent approval of the President. Republicans, however, gained over their 1884 totals in the Midwest, continuing a drumfire for the tariff, warning that a southern-agrarian party would sooner or later move against protection and its urban-industrial constituency.

Those who stopped to reflect on the effect of two years of power on the national Democratic party had some qualms. Authority seemed to sober the Democrats, and Cleveland would not launch any crusades, but the Democratic philosophy and structure remained unshaken. In time-honored American fashion, it was a coalition of mutually conflicting interests that baffled many observers. Partisans like Maine's wryly humorous Tom Reed relied on wit to dispatch enemies. He once said the Democratic party was the organized incompetence of the country, "struggling with their own inertia and mistaking it for the Constitution." To those like him who recalled the party's role before and after the war, it remained "a hopeless assortment of discordant differences, as incapable of positive action as it is capable of infinite clamor." [102]

Its structure mystified many. In the North, city machines resting on ethnic groups and "the poor" remained staunch Democrats, while their rural cousins, as in New York, either opposed them with the same label, or voted Republican. In the South, men with few ties and no common interests all wore the label for obvious historical reasons, and because the party opposed federal authority and kept the Negro "in his place." In the West, which southerners helped populate, many men were Democrats to avoid national authority and practice loosely defined individualism. This jumble of localism did not produce national figures. Suspicion of central direction kept Democrats from using organizational talent, when every man and his following wished to go separate ways. A national Democratic leader could only hope to define parallel paths for jealously independent followers.

Many strands went into the fabric of Democracy. Some northern workers voted Democratic because Republicans were pro-Negro. They distrusted nationalism that threatened local rule in a "little Ireland" or "little Italy." Republicans also favored federal spending, alienating insecure economic groups who liked taxation that fell on the fixed property of their "betters." Some immigrant groups like Scandinavians and Germans, accustomed to nationalism, tended to be Republican.

But the Irish typified ethnic groups who fled governmental authority and did not want to meet it in a new home.

Whatever its variations among sections or interest groups, the Democratic party stood for localism and the self-help myth in many perverse ways. Preaching the Jeffersonian concept of "home rule," its leaders hewed to the concept of small government in both Alabama and Brooklyn. Southerners naturally feared national government that aided Negro rights. Machine bosses did not want it in their baronies. Philosophical speculators in the Tilden mold used opposition to "federalism" to cover cracks in their own unity. Politicians sought federal expenditures, but without guidelines or regulations. No Republican believed as fervently in self-help and the market place as Tilden, Cleveland, Bayard—or even John Kelly, in an ironic way. Much of this came from war-time experience, when honest critics despised regulations against free speech, high taxation, and obvious waste. Centralism was a new phenomenon in American political life; the country had always avoided it except in war-time. Republicans by the mid-1880's were gaining slowly but steadily in the urban constituency that accepted tariff protection and nationalism. The worker sensed interconnections in society, economics, and politics; the farmer protected an apparent freedom from man-made laws while struggling with nature's regulations.

National Democratic leaders continued Tildenesque discussions of government's evils. William E. Russell, governor of Massachusetts, close friend of Cleveland, and a bright new party light, sounded distressingly like ante-bellum southerners. "To it [the Democratic party], government is a power to protect and encourage men to make the most of themselves, and not something for men to make the most out of." [103] To people like this, government protected a market place where talent made its own rewards. It could not foster or create virtue. In a parallel line ran fears of taxation and spending, and diverse interests lauded Cleveland's economies. A Missouri newspaper praised in magnificently mixed metaphors his vetoes of "money-grabbing bills, oozing out at every pore with fermenting slush and jobbery." [104] Beatrice Webb saw the fundamental differences that divided the parties near the century's end: [105]

> The Democrat represented the faith in the responsibility of the individual; each individual being like a 'little dynamo working automatically for the good of the community.' The Republican, on the other hand, represented a faith in centralized power, in the capacity of the few who are in authority at the centre of the state or the municipality to regulate the many and manage the affairs.

Politicians cut corners on philosophy, but differing allegiances to basic tenets of individual action and distrust of government were a matter of style, not substance. Kelly and Croker had their views while looking out on teeming sidewalks and seething slums. Men like Cleveland, Tilden, and Senator Bayard were more arid or bucolic, while contemplating papers or sheep. Bayard represented the old-style Democratic leader, who set the party's general tone while missing its leadership. In 1891, out of office, he visited the bustling Great Lakes area, then wrote Cleveland's friend Don M. Dickinson of Michigan a dazzling vision of individualism: [106]

> I can still shut my eyes and see the stately procession of majestic vessels, freighted with the native products of the vast Mid-west, moving noiselessly along the pathways of beneficient exchanges. What a lesson is here against governmental interference! How wisely the well-instructed spirit of self-interest works in self-directed channels, and is developed by natural competition without fear of contact with malificent statutes!

These wondrous vessels passed federally supported lighthouses in dangerous channels, and often asked assistance from the Coast Guard. They unloaded goods at wharves and docks built with federal subsidies or local taxes, and sold cargoes in a protected market. In this particular instance, commercial traffic moved in an area of the country which generous and wise federal policy developed with land laws, railroad subsidies, and tariff protection.

Dislike of federal control, and the conflicting desire for national economic support cost Democrats a great deal. In the 1880's, New Hampshire's Republican Senator Henry W. Blair repeatedly sought federal aid to education with a formula based on illiteracy that would give southern states desperately needed money. He managed bills through one house of Congress four times in the decade, but never got a law passed. Strange combinations defeated the measure because it was allegedly unconstitutional, threatened federal interference in local affairs, or avoided tariff reduction by spending surplus revenue.[107] Local leaders eager for school funds squirmed under the lash of doctrine, but surrendered to fears of "bayonet rule." The *Shreveport Times* proclaimed that federal aid was "humiliating" and was "squinting too much in the direction of centralization." [108] Northerners like Governor Russell paraphrased these arguments. "National gifts do not come without national control. I think that any state that is looking longingly to the Treasury of the United States to help it in education might well quote the lines of the old poet, 'I fear the Greeks, even when they come bearing gifts.'" [109] Of course, wise men south of the Potomac understood the real reasons behind oratory. ". . . race prejudice at the South and a fear that the education of the negroes would make them less easily manipulated in elections had more influence in the adverse action [against the Blair education bills] than constitutional scruples," Jabez Curry wrote a friend.[110]

This serious split between past rhetoric and present needs, reality and philosophy, weakened the Democratic party. As industrialization advanced, northern voters saw less reason to support a party talking of local rule, while markets expanded beyond city boundaries and state borders. "It is quixotic to undertake a conflict of ideas on behalf of Jeffersonian principles—a tilt against a windmill—when there is no one to take up the gage of battle," a hardworking politician wrote Samuel J. Randall, "no one to witness, and no one interested in the result." [111] In the 1880's, as industrialization triumphed, Republicans organized local interests into constructive national causes, and despite temporary setbacks, laid the foundation of legitimate issues for a long rule in national affairs.

Cleveland symbolized the least realistic aspects of this philosophical debate. In 1887, he sternly vetoed a bill granting free seed to drought-striken Texans. "Federal aid in such cases encourages the expectation of paternal care on the part of the government, and weakens the sturdiness of our national character, while it prevents the indulgence among our people of that kindly sentiment and conduct which strengthens the bonds of a common brotherhood." [112] It was hard to imagine a Republican president curtailing seed distribution, especially since his party had established the program. Cleveland saw his office as purely executive, and had poor relations with Congress. His distaste for personal confrontation and political management made him avoid the normal give-and-take of national politics. "I did not come here to legislate," he once said, in an astonishingly parochial view of his office. He saw a constitutional division between legislative and executive functions that simply did not exist. His contemptuous remark, "I have a Congress on my hands," did not ease the strain with sensitive congressmen. An able publicist and group manager might have overcome this conflicting philosophy in daily political dealings simply by avoiding its practice, but Cleveland lacked the desire to move beyond his limitations. He vaguely saw that "In the scheme of our national government, the presidency is preeminently the people's office," but used it negatively.[113] He thought it enough to enunciate a truth, and wait for mankind to accept it.

Cleveland was in a strange position as the campaign of 1888 approached. People thought well of him, but he did little to expand his party's thin victory margins of 1884. He remained a figure, not a man. He had alienated party elements like Tammany, but gained some new support. As a northerner, he fulfilled one important promise; the South gained a modicum of respectability in a loose and wary coalition. Southerners would vote for him, and, in the larger arena, his caution and inaction calmed fears of a dangerous Democratic supremacy in national power. "The superstition that a Democratic president will absolutely ruin the country is effectually dispelled, . . ." Schurz wrote him in 1886.[114] Cleveland's term was a strange interlude in American politics, certainly so in view of the alarms that accompanied his inauguration. His dullness was safety.

Whatever the public image, Cleveland's party stature was weak. Professionals found him obtuse and exasperating. For every bit of ground he gained, he lost good will in sectors that might defeat him. Patronage and rhetoric build parties only in clever hands. A suitable issue was the only real hope for re-election. Study, beliefs, and talents took him toward revenue reform. It would put Republicans on the defensive, and only a dwindling minority of Democrats opposed tariff reduction. The issue was intangible and over-arching, yet propaganda could make it real in terms of prices and taxation. With proper management, the subject would carry itself, and Cleveland need not campaign. In the spring of 1887, advisers convinced him that tariff reform would cover the party's weaknesses, and win him a second term. It was not an especially courageous choice. It was one of Cleveland's few astute political decisions.

In the pleasant Thanksgiving season that followed victory in 1884, many politicians sought Cleveland's ideas on patronage, silver, and the tariff. He was understandably cautious on all scores, but told visitors he wanted "a reform of the tariff on conservative lines, . . ." [115] No New Yorker was likely to please tariff reformers in the Midwest and South, but in the early summer of 1886, Cleveland made at least a token effort to soothe unrest among western representatives. "Horizontal Bill" Morrison brought a revenue reduction bill to the House floor, tailored for the farm vote, and reflecting party needs in congressional elections. The President agreed to urge bickering Democrats to vote for modest reduction, knowing a Republican Senate would defeat it. He failed miserably, especially since most of the men he conferred with disliked his stand against silver. "This kind of missionary effort does not seem to be in his line," a paper noted, as protectionist Democrats combined with House Republicans to beat the bill, 157–140, on June 17.[116] Morrison lost his seat that November, along with several other tariff reformers like Frank Hurd in Ohio. Leadership in the crusade passed by default to Cleveland. Efforts to revive Morrison's bill in December's lame-duck session failed, and Cleveland "expressed himself very intensely as to his disappointment." [117]

The vacuum of congressional leadership after 1886 further disorganized the diffuse sentiment around tariff reform, convincing Cleveland's advisers he could use it as a unifying party issue. The westerners were clearly angry. Old resentment toward the East now had the added weight of dollars and cents, as the industrial sector outstripped the farm community in income and threatened their political power. Democrats in Border states thought tariff reform would combat the Republicanism that followed industry. Public opinion was confused, but many western leaders saw that it could crystallize quickly around a leader. "I anticipate the result of the obstructions thrown in the way of tariff reform will not unlikely be, sooner or later, the election of a congress unmistakably devoted to it," Vilas wrote David A. Wells, "and that we shall have our reformation in a flood." [118] The Democratic protectionist minority would fall if it continued to thwart modest reduction.

The midwestern economic system radiating out of Chicago resented dependence on New York-Boston-Philadelphia banking and commercial control. Expanding farm production in the Mississippi Valley disturbed some leaders of public opinion. How much wheat, corn, and meat could the United States absorb? How long could farmers buy expensive goods to support labor's wages, and sell surpluses in a world market? An increasing number of editors, teachers, businessmen, and younger political leaders in the area favored free raw materials and lower duties on finished goods. They also saw tariff reform as a way of seeming "new," and avoiding both the currency question so popular in the West and the race question in the South. New Democratic leaders in states like New York and Pennsylvania used the issue to attack established party figures like Randall.* Eastern Mugwumps joined the crusade. Tariff reform was one of their oldest shibboleths. They disliked surplus revenue that tempted venal politicians, and free spending that encouraged federalism. New Englanders in declining industries like tex-

---

*This simple desire for power in younger people impatient with elders and entrenched rulers even in their own party, stands out in studying the rise of both protection in the 1870's, and tariff reform in the 1880's. It is certainly true of the silver crusade that followed, and may be a major, if prosaic, explanation for the cyclical recurrence of "reform" movements in American history.

tiles, leather, and ship-building wanted free raw materials and larger foreign trade. They created propaganda organizations like the National Tariff Reform League to spread their gospel and unite Democrats.[119]

Stubborn pockets of resistance remained in the party. Western farmers did not unite behind tariff reduction, and many still liked the home market idea. They disliked the degree and kind of protection, not the principle, and were increasingly cautious about the tariff as industrialism created the cities they fed. Areas producing wool, hides, lumber, sugar, flax, and ores were protectionist. Any Democratic plan to lower the tariff must account for this practical sentiment. Nor was labor united for a reform crusade. Republicans had perfected an organized appeal to workers, stressing the dangers of reform during prosperous times. Former Governor George Hoadly, protectionist Ohio Democrat, warned Cleveland to "go slow." "You have both the manufacturer and the Knights of Labor to be afraid of." He urged the President to wait until after the election. He could then slowly educate the people if they re-elected him. If the Republicans won, they would hang themselves with excessive rates.[120]

And of course, there was Samuel J. Randall. Though ill, and with dwindling congressional strength, the former Speaker remained a power. Ties of loyalty, affection, and self-interest drew protectionist Democrats to him. "The protectionists, with the help they get from Randall, are in the majority," Morrison warned.[121] Many southerners also doubted the wisdom of a tariff crusade. "I would repeal the tobacco tax entirely if it could be done, take the tax off distilled fruits," a Border Democrat counseled, while favoring the "ideal" of low tariffs. "Then touch [the] tariff gently and in such a manner as to interfere as little as possible with all manufacturing interests now in operation." [122] Protectionists exploited this ambivalence, still hoping to win southern industrial areas. Pennsylvania's James M. Swank, planning a propaganda war, urged an end to the bloody shirt. The GOP should "press the tariff issue upon our southern brethren." [123] Republicans favored spending the surplus on public works, education, the diplomatic service, and naval defenses. The Democrats, however, had an appealing cry in "lower taxes!"

The President's views were uncertain as summer came on in 1887. Carl Schurz told of seeing him shortly after his election to talk about reform questions, including the tariff. Cleveland listened, then leaned forward wearily. "I am ashamed to say it, but the truth is I know nothing about the tariff. . . . Will you tell me how to go about it to learn?" [124] He may have exaggerated for effect, but the subject was not

a large one in his repertoire. Like most New York politicians, he hesitated to touch the issue. As Congress adjourned in the spring of 1887,
Cleveland moved steadily into the reformers' camp, however, largely
as a moderating influence between low-tariff southerners and more
cautious mid-Atlantic and western spokesmen. Press leaks reported he
was considering a special session of Congress; other reports said Fairchild and his staff were writing a bill for the regular winter session.
The Treasury stopped buying bonds and let the surplus grow, to reinforce the point about excessive taxation. The President asked vacationing congressmen and officials to see the folks at home and report
accordingly.

Reports from Carlisle, Whitney, and others came in with summer's
heat. Midwesterners found the issue alluring; southerners were eager
for the fight; eastern protectionists were sullen, indicating a sense of
coming trouble and possible defeat. Between September 30 and October 22, Cleveland toured the Midwest and Old Northwest with elaborate calm. It was "a social trip and everyday-kind-of-visit-to-the-
people. . . ." he told friends. He drew large crowds, but talked in
platitudes. In November, off-year state elections in the region seemed
to favor reform Democrats.[125] That fall, Cleveland conferred with
Carlisle and a select group of advisers at "Oak View," his home outside
Washington, but kept plans secret. Randall knew something was afoot,
and made noises about suitable compromises. Why not revise internal
revenue taxes, lower duties on selected necessities, and reform customs
administration? Cleveland was not receptive to emissaries, and Randall
underwrote his point with a trip to Atlanta's Piedmont Exposition,
stressing the protection theme in an industrial South. The smooth
Philadelphian laughed at talk of party discord, but symbolized its
presence.

On December 6, the President startled Congress with an annual
message dealing entirely with the tariff. It was brief, forceful, and a
clear call for all revenue reformers to sink mutual differences and join
in a general crusade. Cleveland recited the history of high taxation, but
avoided any detailed tariff debate. He thought the surplus invited
"schemes of public plunder," and preferred reduction to spending.
Public works produced "demoralization," and were wasteful. He characteristically opposed depositing Treasury funds in banks since it
would create "too close a relationship between the operations of the
government Treasury and the business of the country and too extensive
a commingling of their money, thus fostering an unnatural reliance in
private business upon public funds." He forthrightly condemned "our

present tariff laws," as "the vicious, inequitable, and illogical source of unnecessary taxation." In almost the same breath, he opposed "dwelling upon the theories of protection and free trade. This savors too much of bandying epithets. It is a condition which confronts us, not a theory." Carefully avoiding any plan for reduction lest he offend Congress, and assuring all that he opposed drastic changes, he suggested administrative reform, an expanded free list, and lower duties on raw materials, hopefully to improve foreign trade.[126]

The message had tremendous effect. Newspapers nearly burst with discussion, and congressmen hastily outlined positions. They had expected reform, but not this dramatic coup. The *Washington Post* wondered why Cleveland had not personally appeared before Congress "in state" to emphasize the point.[127] Democrats distributed the speech as a pamphlet, and discussion spread out from Washington. Reformers literally cheered, and looked forward to the coming campaign. Whatever the battle's outcome, Cleveland had offered his party unity on both an issue and a personality. He hoped to harmonize all factions, but if opposition developed, his agents would fight Randall's followers. Tom Reed saw the move's astuteness, and wondered who suggested it. After all the adverse publicity around the battle flags order, and his pension vetoes, this was a wise political stroke.[128]

Godkin praised the message for creating "a live political issue to take the place of the dead and decaying controversies of the past." [129] Many ranking Democrats were less sure. They had advised Cleveland to wait a year before raising the subject, and now feared he went too fast for public education. The protectionists would have nine months and a presidential campaign to make their always attractive propaganda even more appealing to workers, and who could say what Democrats would do once confronted with a bill in Congress? Republicans could defeat a reform measure in the Senate, and an endless debate would work against change. Randall made that point to friends. After hearing the message, he said to a colleague: "Well, he means to force the fighting and he will not be disappointed." [130] His supporters wrote encouragement, mixed with vituperation. "The message of Mr. Cleveland leaves the Democratic party no alternative but to commit itself to a system of permanent internal taxation and the destruction of our industries, or throw him overboard," a Georgian said.[131]

The opposition professed to welcome "Grover Cleveland's formal declaration of war against the industrial system of America." [132] Cleveland forced all protectionists into a total defense of the system. He made "protection the overshadowing issue; it dwarfs and dismisses all other questions, it clears away all cowardly evasions and juggling subterfuges. . . ." a Philadelphia paper insisted.[133] Cleveland did not exactly welcome the battle, but stubbornness fortified him for the contest. "If every other man in the country abandons this issue, I shall stick to it," he told Carlisle.[134] Not many Democrats understood the tariff's fiscal complexities or effects, but they saw it as a unifying issue that promised "reform." It might also draw sectional party elements together, and not only give Cleveland a second term, but create a longer lease of party life. Secretary Whitney cared little for the details. He preferred delaying on the issue, but if the President thought otherwise, they would fight it out now. It sounded good, and the present tariff was probably unjust. "Further than that—it looks as though it was a winning issue." [135] Cleveland thought so too.

VII

The Tariff Wars: 1888

In 1886, James G. Blaine turned from writing memoirs to building an elaborate "cottage" at Bar Harbor, giving it his wife's maiden name, "Stanwood." Here he showed visiting statesmen around the gardens, and discussed cabbages and kings while rambling through the adjacent countryside or along the seashore. Friends explained these activities as signs of retirement. A year later, he and his family visited Europe, spending early summer in London during the lavish celebrations of Queen Victoria's Golden Jubilee. He was a well-known and popular visitor, though some Britons suspected his foreign policy and pro-Irish tastes. He and Mrs. Blaine got along easily in English society. Its duchesses and politicians found him as intriguing as did their American counterparts. In July, they went north as a guest of Andrew Carnegie at a Scottish castle. Weeks passed in coaching parties, countryside tours, and dinners with guests from many countries. He discussed politics with a detached vigor that baffled people who could not decide if he wanted a political future or not. It seemed his for the asking; newspapers in America still brimmed with discussions of his personal life.

That fall, he visited Ireland, making friends in his family's country. The route went back to England, then to the Continent, where he took the waters at Homburg with a large part of Europe's nobility and overworked politicians. The "cure" did not improve his gout, but added to his fund of stories. Lesser German towns, then Vienna and Budapest, hosted the entourage, and he planned future trips to Italy. In November, the family went to Paris for the usual gallery tours, salons with French politicians and social figures, and to be near the opulent American colony at Christmas. Paris papers carried President Cleveland's annual message, and Blaine shook the pages irritably as he read the call for tariff reduction. But he saw a large political opportunity for the Republican party, and gladly received George W. Smalley, the *New York Tribune*'s London correspondent.

Would Mr. Blaine care to answer the President's challenge? As titular head of the party, and leading exponent of tariff protection, he certainly would. While Smalley and a stenographer took notes, Blaine outlined the Republican answer to the Democratic crusade. He noted first how the British press liked the message, a calm thrust at what protectionists labeled "English free trade doctrines," but he genuinely feared reduction would unsettle prosperous business, shrink the farmer's home market, and the worker's wages. He favored foreign trade through reciprocal agreements rather than general reduction. That reminded him of the farmer who tried to drain a swamp by digging a ditch to the river, with results "that need not be told." But what about the chronic surplus? Spend it on public works, education, coastal defenses, and shipping subsidies to encourage foreign trade. Excessive taxation was not the problem; Democratic reluctance to foster national economic development was the issue. He would reduce the surplus by repealing internal revenue taxes on tobacco, and use revenue from whiskey taxes to build a navy. Distributing the rest to the states would reduce local property taxes. The politics in the issue was another matter. "It will bring the country where it ought to be brought, to a full and fair contest on the question of protection." [1]

On December 8, the *Tribune* carried Blaine's "Paris Letter." John Hay praised it lavishly as "the clear blast of the trumpet, declaring battle and bringing the fighting men into well-ordered ranks. You have given us our platform for next year." [2] Of course, opinion was not uniform. Democrats and independents condemned Blaine's refusal to discuss trusts, high prices allegedly due to protection, the farmers' growing restiveness, and his easy solutions for the surplus. The *New York Times* said free tobacco was a bid for "the quid vote." The *New York Herald* dismissed excise tax reduction. "A free 'chaw' for the poor man, but after that he must pay the monopolists' price for everything." [3]

Most Republicans followed Blaine's lead, but Democrats waited in nervous tension on their own protectionists. Randall was firm. "A conservative course of action will secure the desired legislation; a radical course will not." [4] Privately, he knew the effect of Cleveland's message on voters outside protectionist territory. Henry Grady wrote him with candor. "It is hard to stand up against it [Cleveland's message]. The people have an idea that 'Cleveland knows what he is about,' and the reliance on his common sense is great." Randall vowed "to stand as firmly as I can" against serious reduction,[5] but Pennsylvania and the nation were in for a surprise. Randall's poor health, attacks from younger Democrats, and firm presidential opposition weakened his organization. In Harrisburg, on January 18, opposing Democrats behind William L. Scott ended Randall's rule of the state party. The reformers were right. A national issue could make a national party, if it incorporated new faces and astute propaganda.[6]

Speaker Carlisle would deal no more with Randall, especially since he was obviously declining. When Congress met, he named Texas' revenue reformer Roger Q. Mills to chair the Ways and Means Committee that would draft a tariff bill. The Texan had secretly worked on a measure for months, indicating planning behind the President's attack on protection. Mills was a formidable opponent, with a bristling yet generous manner, and seniority enough to know the written and unwritten rules in the House. The "Colonel" was not honorific. Mills early advocated secession, and suffered severe wounds while serving in the Confederate Army. From 1873 to 1892, he represented a district in Texas around Corsicana, not noted for generosity toward industrialists or easterners. A quick tongue and opposition to federalism made him an outstanding "Confederate Brigadier," and fervent opponent of the tariff. He condemned "free poker and a taxed Bible," noting that he could not remove duties on books, or take playing cards off the free list. He left dinner parties rather than sit with industrial lobbyists.[7]

Mills outlined a tariff bill before Congress met, and in December and January worked with select Democrats to refine schedules and plan strategy. He avoided public hearings that would air protectionist arguments, and faced the charge of writing "a dark lantern bill." The committee reflected his bias and intentions, speaking for agrarian interests. Party moderates like William L. Wilson of West Virginia urged caution during conferences trying to square reformers' hopes with reality's possibilities. The Republican Senate would not pass a reform bill, and everyone knew the President's party was merely firing opening shots in a long war. But reform would probably follow Cleveland's re-election on the issue. Wilson and others did not want a bill that "will startle and alarm the public and array an excited and alarmed sentiment against us." Randall was more blunt. He heard the Committee members with open contempt. When one finished a small set-speech, he said: "There are just two points in what has been said to be noticed, and the rest is bosh." Later that evening, he referred to Mills' "one horse committee," and prepared to go down with his ship.[8]

On April 2, the "Mills bill" appeared. It added wool, salt, lumber, coal, bricks, paper, lime, raw flax and jute, tin plates, and cotton ties to the free list. Woolens and cotton faced an *ad valorem* duty of 40 per cent. The bill lowered rates on iron and sugar, and though the average change of seven per cent was not large, each decrease had symbolic importance. As Republicans predicted, it was a sectional measure, without serious over-all reduction. The bill was politically weak. It favored the South, whose support the Democrats did not need to win, with light reductions on pig iron, coal, sugar, rice, and cotton. It antagonized midwesterners by lowering duties on wool, copper ore, flax and hemp, lumber, and salt. The measure would win few friends in New England with lower rates on finished crockery, woolens, glass, and metal products. It would shrink the surplus a mere $50,000,000. Mills had fulfilled the hopes of many Southern Democrats, who argued frankly that "We want such a revision of the tariff as will most thoroughly benefit our own section." [9]

The President opposed any drastic reductions, and most realistic Democrats and independents only wanted a reasonable start, but many thought the measure "a compromise in which reform gets a thin slice and protection the rest." [10] Henry Watterson would reluctantly take it and build for the future. It was "protective, though not protectionist, in its character." [11] Like most reformers handling national questions, low-tariff advocates fell back on piecemeal apology. It was hard to answer jibes from the other side. "If 30 percent is outrageous on Republican epsom salts, why is 55 percent any less so on Democratic castor oil," asked a Wisconsin Republican, carefully choosing items for maximum effect.[12]

House debate began on April 17, with the desired political results. Congressmen and editors who had avoided the subject, found its public appeal surprising. Millions of Americans apparently discussed rates on cotton ties, raw wool, and crockery. Long before the presidential campaign started, party managers reported a "pamphlet famine." Congressmen franked tons of reading material to constituents as House debates consumed attention in the press. Cleveland at last perceived the political power in a cry for lower taxes. "I fear it will be fatal to ignore or antagonize what appears to me to be an increasing sentiment in favor of the President's action on tax questions," a Pennsylvanian warned.[13]

In the House, able oratory and bitter words illustrated the issue's appeal. Leading young Republicans like William McKinley helped older hands like "Pig Iron" Kelley, and gained a national reputation for future wars. McKinley made a series of impressive speeches on the tariff's relevance to wages, and despite Mills' clever answers, gained attention in a Midwest that would need campaigners like him in the fall. The House discussed the bill for 240 hours, in 151 separate speeches, consuming 51 days of regular time—and enough print to fill twenty volumes of dictionary size. Mail trains left Washington daily, freighted with pamphlets, reports, and correspondence for the countryside. Contrary to cynical predictions, public interest did not lag. And the President used a little oil instead of sand, for once. "On the Democratic side the club of patronage was wielded unblushingly for the bill," an opposition paper later reported.[14] The country was aroused, and the battle's outcome mattered. The Mills bill would not ruin the nation, but Republicans shrewdly advertised it as a bad beginning, with all the faults of agrarian sectionalism. The coming presidential contest would be as heated as the present debates. Cleveland closed his party's ranks, and had no serious rivals for its nomination. But Republicans were less certain.[15] The leading question remained: Was James G. Blaine "available"?

Blaine built his cottage at Bar Harbor, and traveled, but as 1888 arrived, the old charisma roused faithful followers. Occasional rude voices reminded his partisans of the past. He had lost, and in a scurrilous campaign that buried issues and blurred the party's image. It would happen again, with a greater vengeance. The aging Roscoe Conkling said "Blaine can be nominated by acclamation . . . and be defeated in the same manner." If the Republican party had no better choice, he argued, "it had better die and be decently buried." Men of like mind sneered at talk of a comeback for "the Plumed Possum of the Kennebec." [16] But the bright echoes of public clamor lingered. In 1886, critics accused Blaine of leaking portions of his memoirs to a congenial press, to whet appetites and ease criticism. In the same year, he toured protectionist areas in Pennsylvania and other doubtful states to help local candidates. Friends and family said "his whole visit was a royal progress." It was not quite that splendid, but the affection was there. Crowds were already chanting:

> Blaine, Blaine, the man from Maine,
> We had him once, we'll have him again.

In the spring of 1887, his head-cold rated front page discussion. Reporters trailed him in Europe like spies in a Balkan war, donning servants' costumes, bribing grooms and butlers for gossip from the coach and table. He denied availability, but critics thought otherwise: [17]

> His mind is big, his conscience plastic,
> His principles are most elastic
> He hints that office is despised,
> But we think he's willing to be surprised.

The professionals were as confused as the public. "It still looks to a calm outsider . . . as if the Plumed Knight can get the nomination if he wishes it, . . ." former President Hayes wrote his daughter at Christmastime.[18] Former Senator Benjamin Harrison, practicing law in Indianapolis amid soft footfalls in his own political preserve, agreed, unless "he concludes that the opposition in his own party is so strong as to make a second defeat probable. . . . In that event (within limits), he and his friends will be able to name the candidate. He will want a man who can probably win and who will be very friendly." [19] Blaine could be quiet and let aggressive managers build a boom as they did in 1880. Without the Presidency's natural cohesion, the party was unfocused and drifting, coalescing around local favorites. When they ran their limit, he might stage a dramatic coup, as Senator Plumb of Kansas predicted. "He may come back from Europe next June, have a great throng to meet him and make a speech that will fire the heart, etc." [20] People divided on Blaine's intentions but most agreed that "beyond all doubt [he is] the most popular man in either party." [21]

Before going abroad, Blaine assured allies he would not seek renomination. "In the first place and *radically*," he told Reid, "*I do not feel that I want the office—conceding the election.*" He dreaded the prospect of a personal canvass. He would consider only a unanimous nomination, but might treat even that as a gesture, and decline. "Above all, I abhor the idea of becoming a chronic candidate, a sort of 'Tichborne' claimant for the presidency." [22] There was no reason to think the party would choose him unanimously; if nothing else, Sherman and Edmunds would stand up and be counted. His cousin and biographer, Mary Abigail Dodge, seemed equally firm. "I do not think that you or any friend of Mr. Blaine's would wish him to enter a scramble, or a struggle, or even an effort for the nomination," she wrote Elkins.[23] Blaine said another campaign would kill him, but analysts discounted this as the usual hypochondria. Conflicting reports encouraged supporters. "His health is not a matter to be taken into account any more than yours or mine, so far as I know," Miss Dodge also wrote Elkins.[24] Cleveland's tariff message and the "Paris Letter" dramatically increased talk of Blaine's candidacy. Andrew Carnegie kept a private cable code for political news, and let people believe Blaine was only hesitant.

Blaine sincerely wished to avoid a contest. His trip to Europe was an attempt to avoid the question, but he was a prisoner of his popularity. His attitude toward a unanimous courtesy nomination was more hypothetical. He knew that was impossible, but could not withdraw flatly and irritate followers who might have future influence. And he wanted to help name a successor; a grateful legatee would grant the State portfolio for which Blaine still cherished a hope. On January 25, he wrote B. F. Jones, chairman of the national committee, that his name would "not be presented" at the convention. This "Florence Letter" did not end speculation, however, and he sent later withdrawals to Jones and Maine's Joseph Manley. He also entertained ubiquitous reporters. Late in February, T. C. Crawford of the *New York World* interviewed him in Florence. Blaine had a cold, the result of viewing Alpine scenery from an observation deck, but obviously enjoyed the plush hotel suite's red and gold decor. He looked well, and laughed easily, admitting the various withdrawals sounded like entries in the sweepstakes, but insisted he was sincere. He would campaign for the nominee, and serve the party, but genuinely did not want renomination.[25]

These interviews and the "Florence Letter" relieved opponents and chagrined friends. A day later, he answered further queries with "an emphatic negative," surprised at the talk's persistence. Significantly, he sent his withdrawal to Jones, not to Elkins or Reid. Jones published it; the professionals would have held it and urged him to be silent. He could do little more but flatly refuse any further honors from his party, though privately he did say: "My Florence letter was, in my own mind, a formal and final withdrawal from the presidency." [26] Blaine also knew that speculation on his intentions tended to keep the party unified before the convention met.

As favorite sons displayed familiar wares, hungry gossips made meals of every morsel, and dinner parties revolved around discussions of Blaine's desires. Washington, the world's largest whispering gallery, echoed to speculation. Some critics thought he feigned indifference. "It certainly seems needful for Mr. Blaine to use a great many words to say he will not under any circumstances take the nomination," said the *New York Times*.[27] "Blaine is the man in the bushes," the *Atlanta Constitution* unkindly insisted.[28] Professionals thought he would let favorite sons exhaust their strength, then accept renomination on the theme of party unity, or dictate the choice. The Plumed Knight's friends at home did not disabuse people of either notion. Robert Ingersoll talked with Blaine, and thought his declinations sincere, but "the friends of Blaine are going to make all they can out of the corpse." [29] Elkins remained the leading "friend," a man who had the necessary contacts from 1884, and Blaine's complete confidence. With proper attention, he could center the diffuse Blaine sentiment on a harmony candidate and collect rewards for his chief, himself, and a host of allies.

As even Godkin admitted, the feeling for Blaine was "clearly spontaneous, and widespread." [30] He could not transfer the personal affection, but he could take political power to another man. Who would be the heir? "The tendency, I think, is towards a western candidate for president," Blaine told Levi Morton.[31] In a tariff battle, the party should choose a midwestern candidate and Blaine saw Benjamin Harrison as the most likely victor. The Hoosier's friends were already quietly building a boom, and dealing with Elkins. He played a careful waiting game, insisting Blaine was out of the running, but hinting that the man who got his strength must prove he could win, and promise to reward the faithful. Harrison watched the scene coolly, believing Blaine wanted a "draft." [32] Harrison was notoriously calm at such times. Other favorite sons were more nervous.

In January, as the jockeying started, Senator Sherman took his usual lofty ground. "If it comes," he told Wharton Barker, "I will accept it as a duty and if it goes to someone more worthy I will not be a mugwump." [33] The junketing B. F. Jones, feeding reports to Elkins, thought otherwise. Sherman and Harrison both had "the presidential fever in the severest form" and Sherman suspected Blaine of playing possum.[34] As usual, the Ohio Senator seemed to have a good chance, coming from the right state, with a national reputation on the tariff question. But he had not altered the "Ohio Icicle" image of earlier years. Sherman stayed in Washington throughout the spring, watching tariff legislation and continuing his justly earned reputation for responsible caution. In April, the Ohio state convention endorsed him, but divisions remained. Governor Foraker was lukewarm; William McKinley, though now loyal, had followed Blaine in 1884. Many delegates frankly said the slightest tremor would send them to Blaine. Sherman knew he was second in most Buckeye hearts, but started a boom after agents assured him Blaine was not a candidate.

Sherman naturally turned South, the great hunting preserve for lesser Republicans. His followers there were "mostly old time politicians and wise owls," with Negro delegates open to persuasion. "If his barrel is rolled industriously and skilfully in the south, he can pick up lots of delegates," a paper admitted.[35] In mid-spring, he and aides toured the section, appealing with tariff protection to newly industrialized areas, and refusing to reopen the "southern question." But he did not draw the color line. When a Birmingham hotel owner refused to serve Negroes, Sherman took other lodgings. McKinley and Foraker followed in his wake, talking of nationalism and an integrated economy, but he had trouble holding colored delegates, and did not arouse any new enthusiasm.

It was much the same elsewhere. In New York, Sherman talked to bankers and businessmen, but Tom Platt and other leaders warily avoided commitments, waiting to see how the majority went. "I think his friends are discouraged," Elkins reported in March.[36] He faced a mixed reception west of Ohio. ". . . the friends of bimetallism concentrated their efforts to defeat John Sherman . . ." Nevada's Senator Stewart recalled. Agents reported frankly that "the whole atmosphere at Chicago will be anti-Sherman" when the convention met.[37] Elkins said bluntly: "He has no real claim on Blaine's friends. This word has been passed around." [38] Age dictated that 1888 would be Sherman's last chance at the nomination. He clung tenaciously to the hope of victory, but never had a serious chance. At most he might be a ceremonial harmony candidate, and apparently agreed to pool his votes with Senator Allison's, if it seemed that either could succeed. He knew that men in his own camp favored William McKinley, who had youth, vigor, and personal charm. McKinley was loyal, but it was not a comforting thought.

The contest produced some strange names. Michigan's political dabbler, Russell Alger, believed he could grasp the glittering prize. He was now fifty-two, rich from lumber and railroad investments in the Old Northwest, and a party gadfly. He flooded the mails with alternating requests for support and assurances of victory, counted heads at routine GAR reunions, and thought he could "carry the country by storm." "I wish I had you in my office an hour," he wrote Foraker. "I would prove to you, *that I am going to be nominated.*" Foraker wrote on the letter, "Sick people are always going to get well, and candidates are always going to get elected, you know," and filed it.[39] Alger went through all the coy rituals common to isolated favorite sons, but appealed only to a few businessmen and Boys in Blue. Other midwesterners thought him the candidate of money, pure and simple. Sherman accused him of outrageous bargaining for colored delegates, before and during the convention. Alger's profuse and tortured explanations neither warmed Sherman nor cleared his own record. "I regret to say that the evidence shows the results are largely due to the barrel," Mark Hanna reported after surveying Alger's paper empire.[40]

It was a good year for midwesterners, as the parallel candidacies of Benjamin Harrison and Walter Q. Gresham proved. The latter had a strange career. Despite ambivalent views on slavery, he was an early Republican in Indiana. When war came, he raised a volunteer unit, entering as a private and emerging as a major general. After the war, he gained a small reputation for bipartisanship among Mugwumps and purists, but covered ambition with a thin veneer of weary resignation. In 1880, Harrison defeated him for a Senate seat, but Gresham went on to serve Arthur as Postmaster-General, with an interim term in the Treasury Department. In 1884, the President made him a circuit judge of the Chicago district, where Gresham earned an anti-railroad reputation that stood well with some labor groups, but alienated many party leaders.

Blaine would have none of him. "He is a disciple of Ingersoll in religion, and he has been a demagogue and iconoclast on the bench." [41] Gresham's managers pushed him as a compromise between party leaders and independents. Matthew Quay was vague; Tom Platt was severe. "I must say their [Mugwumps] advocacy of Judge Gresham is what weighs him down more than any other one thing, and causes the entire party to look on him with suspicion since it is a notorious fact that they are already committed, bound, and pledged to the support of the Democratic candidate." [42] Harrison's agents did not wish to divide Indiana's loyalties, and offered an "arrangement," but the Gresham men refused. It was play-acting; Gresham never had a chance. Realists noted the obvious early in the game. "The Gresham boom in Indiana has shrivelled like the beautiful 'She.' " [43]

Farther west, in the Plains states critical to GOP success, stood Iowa's Senator William B. Allison. Iowans saw the values of seniority and Allison knew the virtues of silence. Friends explained his dullness as "innate modesty," but he had no popular following. However, Allison was an ideal intra-party compromise selection, lacking serious enemies in the leadership, and boasting a long congressional record of constructive conservatism. Cleveland fully expected to face Allison in the campaign. He could easily slip into place as everyone's second choice. Allison tried to be calm about his chances. His little boom grew quietly, and if lightning struck, so much the better. If not, he would be a lifetime senator. [44]

In the East, New York hesitantly offered Chauncey M. Depew. He was a standard fixture in the Empire State party, and despite railroad attachments, was considered moderate by most factions. When an intraparty crisis loomed, both Platt and opponents were likely to dust off

Depew while seeking a better man. Business wealth made him suspect outside an elite circle, and he typified the elegant eastern city man, damnable in western eyes. The public knew him as an after-dinner spread-eagle wit, fashionable at banquets and patriotic holidays. "He changed his calendar so as to make the Fourth of July embrace 365 days," John P. Altgeld said, "leaving but six hours for the remainder of the year—and then started for the White House." [45] This was a little unjust, but only in its clear focus. Depew now represented a local organization demanding recognition from a winner not yet in sight. Platt would use him to hold New York's convention votes and bargain with the victor. No one took Depew seriously, despite elaborate eastern newspaper coverage. During the convention, an opponent put his picture in a store window, with titles reading at the top, "The Grangers' Choice," and at the bottom, "The Workingman's Friend." The kind of laughter his witty speeches provoked ushered him off the political stage.[46]

Most prominent Republicans smiled at reporters, and explained their lack of intentions as spring developed the political lists. The abundance of old and new favorites illustrated how failure to hold the presidency could fragment a national party. Newspapers discussed a long list of Republican candidates, and suggested geography might be important. Indianapolis was near the center of the area Republicans must carry to win.

Benjamin Harrison's home on North Delaware Street in Indianapolis typified his personality and success. It was solid but not garish, and comfortable but not especially cheerful. The grounds were neat, and friends were welcome to call for conversation or social talk, but the idle curious went elsewhere. "Little Ben" was familiar on the streets and in legal circles, but talked only when he had something to say, and then said it well. He was not a back-slapper, and his reputation rested on intellect, integrity, and precise familiarity with the law and politics. The people of his state knew and respected him, and did not think talk of his political future surprising.

He was not the dark horse he seemed at first glance. The family name dated from the Hoosier state's beginnings, and was famous in the nation's history books. A Harrison in Indiana was like a Roosevelt in New York or a Bayard in Delaware, but he did not live on the family name, and had talents of his own. He was born near Cincinnati in 1833, and studied with private tutors before entering Miami University. After graduation in 1852, he read law, and practiced in Indianapolis. As an original Republican, he was early in the ranks both to save the Union and free the slaves. He fought with Sherman around Atlanta, and gained a reputation for lucid presentation of facts, stern but fair discipline, and careful organization. At the war's end, few men loved him, but a good many respected his skills.

In peacetime he fought Copperheads in Indiana, and though a Radical on reconstruction, built a career on nationalism embracing tariff protection, sound currency, and fair veterans' benefits. In 1876, the bucolic demagogue "Blue Jeans" Williams narrowly beat him for the governorship, but in 1881 he began a Senate term that brought national prominence. In that office Harrison worked hard to make western territories states, favored railroad regulation, generous land laws, fair dealings with Indians, and internal improvements. Indiana's ever-shifting politics denied him a second term, but his name was familiar to Republican powers when he returned to law practice. That reputation rested on his geographical situation, constructive conservatism, and abilities at persuading crowds. This last was the oddest aspect of his character, for he was clearly "a stranger to the art of popularizing himself." [47] Men already said he could charm a crowd of twenty thousand—and persuade them to vote Republican—but he could make them all enemies with a personal handshake. This baffled most people who dealt with him, though William Allen White of Kansas saw the problem's origin: "Nothing succeeds like a well-ordered inferiority complex, pushing a good brain and a kindly heart to a high goal." [48]

Harrison inclined toward ideas and rules rather than people. Upbringing told him that law governed life; good ideas triumphed in a system of automatic progress. What need had he for tiresome personal persuasion? His proper role was to lead, to clarify what others hazily thought. They would listen, weigh evidence, and follow truth. He had faith in human intellect and good intentions, which always surprised powerful men who thought otherwise. It seemed strange that one with experience in law and politics had such an idealistic view of humanity.

Much of Harrison's destiny flowed from Indiana's tangled politics, economics, and social structure. Like neighboring Ohio, she was varied in aims, and doubtful in politics. In presidential elections the state invited the lures of money, organization, and propaganda. "There has been more money spent in Indiana, to carry that infernal state, than almost any other in the Union," Shelby Cullom once said. [49] Lying on the great Border, Indiana reflected America's confused transitional status. She had large cities, and a network of small towns; old settlers and many immigrants. Wets and Drys, Catholics and Protestants, farmers and workers, northerners and southerners, vied to control the state.

Harrison lived calmly in this cauldron without altering any principles. The law, said Edmund Burke, sharpens the mind by narrowing it. Though a trifle unjust to Harrison, if not to lawyers, the maxim was part of law's appeal to him. He liked legal discipline and precision. The profession spilled easily into politics, and he never altered a basic Republicanism. He believed in the party's nationalism, and was an earnest and sincere advocate of tariff protection, free and equal suffrage, Negro rights, and federal support for economic expansion with workable safeguards for individualism.

A warm personality was not among Harrison's political assets. He liked truth when most men savored flattery. A belligerent attitude fostered the view that "when sitting, [he] appeared to be a big man, and when standing a small one;" and he was "Mr. Harrison, the man who never laughs. . . ." to most callers.[50] Friends who recognized his talents tried to soften this exterior. His friend John New once arranged a speaking engagement, then cautiously urged him to "warm up" with the crowd: ". . . for God's sake be a human being down there. Mix around a little with the boys after the meeting." Harrison later confessed failure. "John, I tried it, but I failed. I'll never try it again. I must be myself."[51] Hayes liked to tell of the mutual friend who introduced Harrison with a backhanded compliment: "Don't think he *means* to insult you; it is his way."[52]

Most observers admitted he was "very sincere and true in all his relations, public and private."[53] Harrison sometimes wrote a brief apology, blaming his curtness on overwork. "Perhaps I am too wilful, too judicial. . . ." he admitted to Elkins.[54] He was a "loner," disliking trivial company, somewhat fearful of his impression, admitting he "could find company no doubt, but I am not a good hand at doing it."[55] Despite belligerence, he hated infighting. "I haven't a good stomach for a 'row' . . . ," he told a friend. "There are many things in political life exceedingly distasteful to me. . . . I find it only possible many times to do second or third best instead of the first, as I would like."[56]

This personality equipped him more for administration than politics. A man of high intentions and wide views, he seemed narrow and dour to important Republicans on less lofty heights. Candor unnerved men who liked to deal, and he never learned to soften blows with padded gloves. He dealt in ice when better politicians used fog. A hard worker, he was unable to delegate authority, and overwork sharpened his natural tendencies to favor contempt over praise as a goad. Like so many successful men, he thought good examples could right the world. These traits were not clear in 1888 to those who expected rewards for making him president. His lack of personal magnetism was an advantage. The party intended to emphasize an issue—tariff protection—and needed a candidate to explain it to the masses. The campaign of 1884 had been "personal" enough for most Republicans.

Harrison's position and connections made him a presidential possibility when he entered the Senate. In 1884, midwesterners talked loosely of using him to frustrate Blaine, but the Hoosier knew better. He could not win, and would not make enemies. As 1888 approached, talk of his candidacy rose again. He did not overtly encourage it, but was available. In the meantime, he would arrange quiet newspaper coverage, talk in a few clubs, and "confer" with friends. While public talk of Blaine continued, muffled drums in the jungle of manipulation said Harrison was the man to watch.

Two friends spoke for Harrison. The state attorney-general, Louis T. Michener, had contacts in midwestern newspaper circles. He disregarded his mentor's frostiness, and though he never taught Harrison to unbend, admired his talents. Eugene Gano Hay, equally knowledgeable in the newspaper and legal worlds so important to political candidates, sharpened local contacts in sister states. Michener planted newspaper articles stressing Harrison's opposition to Chinese immigration, but respect for treaty rights, his pro-western work as a senator, and general anti-trust attitude. The *Indianapolis Journal* went to every potential GOP delegate. Michener's letters and literature stressed Harrison's nationalism and acceptability to most of the party. It was all informal, of course, and without the candidate's blessing or opposition. "We cannot organize a regular bureau for General Harrison, and get him puffed in the Chicago and New York papers. . . ." he wrote Hay. "He would never consent to it, and such fulsome flattery is so foreign to his nature that I believe it would hurt him." [57]

Harrison was not entirely inactive. On Washington's Birthday, he delivered a distinguished speech before the Michigan Club in Detroit. Many leading Republicans from the Old Northwest attended, and liked the little man, so much more forceful on the platform than socially after dinner. "I am a dead statesman, but I am a living and a rejuvenated Republican, . . ." he assured them. In late March, the Marquette Club in Chicago heard him stress free ballots, just pensions, and tariff protection. As usual, he impressed important people. Scattered speeches in Indiana did not hurt the cause. [58]

While backing out of the nomination, Blaine showed his usual astuteness in analyzing possible successors. He disliked Sherman's dullness, and knew he was "not in sympathy with *our friends*." Gresham was impossible. Allison was personally acceptable, but his moderate tariff record "would destroy the effort of the party to make a campaign for protection." The rest were nonentities, except Harrison. "The one more remaining, who in my judgement can make the best run is Ben Harrison. I could give many reasons but forbear." He posted the letter, "strictly confidential" as usual, to Elkins.[59] The attitude was not surprising. In 1884, he had retained Harrison as the best lawyer in Indiana to prosecute men spreading tales about his marriage. In 1886, he urged a second Senate term for Harrison, and followed his fortunes closely. Blaine knew Harrison could carry the Midwest, and presumed he would reward him handsomely. He wanted another try at the State Department.

Harrison's men took Blaine's "Florence Letter" at its word, and asked for Elkins' support. The General would do nothing to alienate Blaine's followers. Many still hoped the Plumed Knight would face a draft, and welcomed time to analyze the situation. "My friends have regarded me as an obstructionist rather than a promoter," Harrison assured him.[60] Elkins was surprisingly candid, if he meant to stage a coup for Blaine. He agreed Blaine was loath to face another personal campaign that might defeat the party. As for an heir: "A great many quiet influences are working in your behalf," he assured Harrison. "At the proper time, this will be a very important factor. . . . In a quiet way, word is being passed around to the Blaine men that you are the choice of a great many of them. . . . I am inclined to think that next to Blaine, you are the strongest candidate; and that you have more elements of strength than any others." [61] As things developed, Elkins urged Michener of "the necessity of the General [Harrison] and his near friends always having a kind word for Blaine." [62] By April, Elkins discounted all other favorite sons. "Harrison is bound to be nominated [if Blaine is not], and it is the wisest and safest thing to do." [63] Michener said that "no good friend of Mr. Blaine's will have any occasion to regret it, and I do not use this language lightly, for I understand its full import, and mean to be understood in that light." [64]

The pieces gradually found places. By convention time, party lights knew that despite the superficial hubbub around people like Alger and Depew, only Harrison could head the ticket if Blaine was truly not available. He could carry Indiana and New York, and focus attention on the tariff question. Platt understood the game, and pledged his cohorts to Depew, but seemed willing to support Harrison. The men around "Little Ben" gained confidence as convention time approached. "Harrison is going to be the nominee," Michener wrote. "We are making no blow, doing no bragging, telling no lies, and are working quietly and diligently." [65] It helped to know, for once, what the Democrats would do.

The President's tariff reform message generally closed Democratic ranks behind him, but a few critics complained as the reaction solidified early in 1888. Some feared he could not carry New York. "How can the prestige of 1047 [votes in 1884] answer as a rallying cry for his nomination at St. Louis?" Would he face another contest as "the Beast of Buffalo," his personal past blotting out the unifying theme of reform? Opponents had a slogan: "The Republican Prayer: Renominate Cleveland." [66] William Henry Smith was generally right in telling Hayes, "nobody cares for Cleveland. He is a necessity to the Democratic party, and has no personal hold on the hearts of the people." But he added significantly: "He is a rallying point—nothing more." [67] In a contest emphasizing issues on both sides, that was enough. By now, other Democratic lights were dead or superannuated, and in the usual fashion, an incumbent president produced no real successor. "Besides, who else have they?" a Republican paper asked in discussing Cleveland.[68]

Some thought they had David Bennett Hill, seeking re-election as governor of New York. He was Cleveland's opposite in temperament. Where the President raised a trumpet call for reform, Hill bent to the machine's crank. Cleveland dropped horseshoes on opponents, but Hill preferred pillows. He started his career in Elmira, became one of Tilden's youthful aides, and was lieutenant-governor with Cleveland. He succeeded to the governorship, then won it in his own right in 1885, and was "cooperative" when it came to patronage and home rule in the wards. Hill would hardly challenge the national Administration, but obviously wanted to build for the future as Cleveland's heir and bargain with the President's agents for the present. Cleveland's managers took him seriously enough to soothe critics. Tammany got fresh attention and a few offices. Secretary Whitney interrupted a crusade against waste in the Navy long enough to add workers and let fresh contracts in Brooklyn, Norfolk, and Boston. Don M. Dickinson of Michigan, the new Postmaster-General, sweetened pills with suitable appointments. In the process, Hill thought he laid a base for future operations, and ignored the Mugwumps, Republicans, and humorists who lampooned his pretensions. "He has no more chance to be either nominated or elected the next president than he has to succeed Pope Leo in the Vatican, . . ." a Philadelphia sheet snapped. Humor magazines were even less kind: [69]

> He has aspirations lofty, but he isn't very deep;
> His ways are most transparent, and his methods very cheap;
> He would like to lease the White House, but he'd never fill the bill;
> His chances? Small potatoes, and not many to the Hill.

In the first week of June, Democrats streamed toward St. Louis with all the paraphernalia common to national conventions. California delegates wore flame-colored suits, poured a hundred cases of local wine for guests, and threw twenty-dollar gold pieces with delightful abandon. Randall's men came in blue suits, with white hats, gloves, and canes, and stubbornly talked about protection. The Colorado delegation gave the chairman a solid silver gavel, but party leaders did not take the hint. Southerners punctuated their progress with rebel yells, and stronger vintages than wine. It was an unusual Democratic convention. Victory seemed in the air; "reform" dominated. The convention hall reflected a style best called High Cuckoo Clock, worthy of the carpenter's trade and draper's art. Its exterior was a cascade of balconies, cupolas, dormered windows, and statuary depicting the rise of liberty and expansion of the Republic. Inside, bunting hung from long galleries along a narrow hall that ended in a raised platform, in front of an immense painting of the Capitol building.

The first day passed in routine business, but on Wednesday, June 5, the keynote speaker voiced a tone of moderation on all questions that dominated the President's thoughts. After more speeches, Daniel Dougherty of New York named Cleveland, and cheering men and women filled the aisles. Large artificial yellow eagles on poles flapped cloth wings. State banners moved toward the platform, and behind the stage, the painting of the Capitol opened in the center to reveal Cleveland's reassuring features in more than life size. Seconding speeches, and a unanimous nomination followed.[70]

The third day produced squabbling over the platform and a running-mate. Cleveland warned against any large promises for tariff reform, and dispatched Gorman with an amended copy of a platform plank emphasizing adequate protection for American labor.[71] Watterson and other radicals defended this moderation rather lamely, and the party took its medicine. Governor Isaac P. Grey of Indiana was Cleveland's most logical running-mate. He was young, an experienced midwestern reformer, and might carry Indiana. But for reasons best known to

himself, probably to avoid Indiana factions, Cleveland wanted Allen
G. Thurman. A California delegate named the Old Roman in a bravura
performance.[72] Thurman's name would stir souls

> . . . wherever it is mentioned, from the British line to California, and
> from where the stormy Atlantic breaks against the beetling cliffs of our
> Eastern shores—from the wave-washed rocks of Massachusetts to
> where the Pacific laves the golden sands of California. Allen G. Thur-
> man! What an epitome of America's civil history is in that name! His
> character and life are well known to every man, woman and child in
> this land, and the reverence and respect in which he is held as a fire-
> side god ensures his triumphant election. His public record will be a
> more enduring monument to his name than tables of stone or brass.
> History will write his name in letters of fire among the list of America's
> illustrious sons.

California wines were obviously potent. Common sense and political
necessity gave way to emotion and presidential desires, as delegates
broke out thousands of red bandanas to flutter for Thurman.

Cleveland could hardly have made a poorer choice. Thurman was
old and infirm, and the President intended to stay in the White House.
That meant no national figure would campaign. The Administration
owed him nothing. Vice-President Hendricks had died in 1885, and
Thurman was about the same age. It was not comforting to have
Democrats explain that a new law insured the succession. General
Bragg of Wisconsin said "You have nominated a pocket handkerchief!"
William H. Barnum of the National Committee had called Thurman a
"corpse," but was silent after the selection. "Mr. Thurman is seventy-
five years old," *Judge* reported. "They'll resurrect Andrew Jackson
next." And a few men like Ohio's George Hoadly warned Cleveland
that Thurman's selection was "a serious mistake," that would "deter,
and not in any degree, attract" votes and enthusiasm.[73]

But criticism died in the cheering, and enthusiastic delegates went
home with furled banners and high hopes. Republicans seemed in worse
condition. They still had the "Blaine problem," and if he did not run,
other GOP candidates seemed small beside Cleveland in more ways
than one. Democrats appreciated the confused serenade *Puck* gave
their opposition: [74]

> Bouncing Benjy Harrison
> Is summoning his garrison.
> Five-million-dollar Alger
> Jumps like facial neuralger.
> The forces of McKinley
> Are gathering somewhat thinly.

His friends may win for Gresham
If t'other folks don't thresh 'em.
Those who will go for Allison
On others breathe a malison.
There's 'honest' old John Sherman
Would like to balance Thurman.
And even Chaunce Depew
Thinks he can get there too.

Intentionally or not, Ben Harrison's name led all the rest.

As Democrats left St. Louis, Republicans converged on Chicago. Managers established lavish hotel quarters, circulated among delegates, and arranged various entertainments for supporters until the proceedings started. "Alger came down with his *crowd* and his *ducats*," a Sherman man reported.[75] And the gathering had its humorous incidents. Senator Allison got unsolicited support from a neurotic lady determined to make him president. For months she had pestered him with letters and advice, trying to be a go-between for cloak-and-dagger work, dutifully reporting conversations she heard while seated behind potted palms.[76]

As the leading contestant, Sherman was most nervous. McKinley, Mark Hanna, Foraker, and Ohio congressional leaders arrived early to end rumors of disaffection in his camp. McKinley predicted Sherman would get 360 votes on the first ballot. Asked about a second choice, "the Major" answered firmly: "An Ohio man has no second choice." [77] Sherman expected a grand play from Blaine's followers, but did not know how to avoid it. "My theory is that Blaine is a candidate, has been from the beginning, and will be until defeated. . . ." he wrote Hanna.[78] He had some reason to believe it, even at the end of a private wire in Washington. Delegation after delegation made it clear the rank and file wanted Blaine, whatever the badges on their lapels said. Mike DeYoung of California, unloaded the usual flashy group pledged to "Blaine or Bust!" Enthusiasm for the Man from Maine was an electric current under the discussion. Two of his sons attended the convention, privately opposing their father's nomination for health reasons. But Elkins was much in evidence, and no one knew his real intentions.[79]

The proceedings started on Tuesday, June 19, when delegates heard Temporary Chairman John M. Thurston of Nebraska eulogize Blaine. Thunderous cheers greeted his praise of "the gallant leader, that chevalier of American politics, the glory of Republicanism and the nightmare of Democracy, our Henry of Navarre. . . . We cannot place him at the head of the ticket, but we can make him commander-in-chief of the forces in the field, where he will be invincible. And although James G. Blaine may not be our president, yet he remains our uncrowned king, wielding the baton of acknowledged leadership, . . . the greatest living American, and the worthy object of our undying love." [80] It was a bit strong, even for convention oratory, and managers of other candidates shifted nervously while applause raged.

Wednesday passed in routine matters, and on Thursday, William McKinley reported the platform to enthusiastic hearers. The Republican party, he warned, would not surrender any significant portion of protection "at the joint behest of the whiskey trust and the agents of foreign manufacturers." The document bitterly denounced southern suppression of the ballot, favored bimetallism, and promised to continue civil service reform. But all these stood in the shade of tariff protection.

Reaction was mixed. "Pig Iron" Kelley allegedly raised his hands in supplication. "Lord, now lettest thou thy servant depart in peace, for mine eyes have seen the glory of the Republican party." [81] E. L. Godkin disagreed: "Protection is the Frankenstein of the Republican party." [82] But another Mugwump, George William Curtis, saw the real symbolism in a tariff campaign. The Republican party had moved from the war's residue of moral questions to economic issues, centering on protection. He feared the party might succeed only too well with this new direction.[83] Many Republicans thought the tariff plank too radical, but had no alternative. Most cared little about civil service reform; it was institutionalized, and hardly a moving cause. But western silverites feared the currency question would disappear. Senator Stewart and others thought they had firm assurances from all candidates, especially Harrison, not to oppose a congressional move to expand the currency if the party won.

With the platform adopted, the convention settled to the long task of hearing nominating speeches. Harrison's name came early in a calm, reasoned speech from ex-Governor Albert G. Porter, stressing his appeal to business and labor, and Indiana's importance. Of the remaining favorite sons, only Sherman drew many cheers, and they strained a little en route to the ceiling. The convention adjourned at dinner-time, to ballot the next day. Ohio's managers continued to hear distressing rumors that more delegates favored McKinley than Sherman. The Major's appearance on the floor always created "a prolonged hum of applause." Reporters said "It was plain that Mr. McKinley was very near to the hearts of a great many delegates." [84] If the convention wanted a genuine draftee, he seemed logical as the midwestern heir of

Sherman, having a distinguished tariff record, youth, and no enemies. Every protest of his loyalty increased his availability among delegates wanting to avoid the usual dull compromise.

Balloting began on Friday, and the first roll call gave Sherman 229 votes, with 416 necessary to win. Gresham followed with 107; Depew, 99; Alger, 84; Harrison, 85; Allison, 72; Blaine, 35; and the rest scattered. Sherman's strength came from the South, Ohio, and some midwestern enclaves. A second ballot underlined the deadlock, and amid great confusion a third seemed to indicate no progress. The professionals knew otherwise. At its end, Depew rose to withdraw and personally support Harrison. He did not know the Indianan, but recognized his political assets, and explained them to the New York delegation at dinner after the convention adjourned. Over the usual gourmet fare, Depew candidly told Platt and others to follow Harrison, and the Empire State group began a shift to Harrison that marked his growing appeal.[85]

On Saturday, as the fourth ballot proceeded, Connecticut cast votes for McKinley, and the Ohioan risked a demonstration to insist he was not a candidate. Climbing on a rickety chair he waited, in a hum of speculation and scattered applause, pale but with a firm voice, to insist on his loyalty to Sherman. He would not be a Garfield. He had ambitions, but justly resented "imputation upon his integrity or purpose," as a friend wired Sherman.[86] The speech silenced supporters, but did not dampen their ardor, or detract from his reputation. The ballot's results showed Harrison's increasing appeal, as he moved to second place behind Sherman, with 216 votes to the Ohioan's 235. A fifth tally produced similar results, and weary delegates adjourned briefly for rest and fresh air. They had barely assembled late that afternoon, when the Chair entertained a motion to adjourn until Monday. Political dealings would obviously mar the Sabbath calm.

Hanna warned Sherman that Ohio's delegation was breaking up; and Foraker said they had stood by him long enough. He urged a shift to Blaine, obviously eyeing the vice-presidential slot. Hanna asked Sherman to let Ohio name McKinley. Murat Halstead agreed. "Can we afford to lose the opportunity of securing a nomination for the state? Give us the word and we believe we can pull McKinley through." This was the only way to stop a break to Blaine, which they all expected.[87] In the week-end's confusion, Sherman kept a single resolve. This would be the last chance, and he intended to stay in the race. He blamed Blaine for the deadlock. "His course has been deceptive and I think dishonorable."[88] In Sunday's debates, Sherman's managers did not move many delegates. "Sherman won't do; he is too cold," one said. "Why, he is a red hot stove compared to Harrison," answered an Ohioan.[89]

Sunday's real news came from Scotland, not Chicago. Carnegie at last dispelled all doubts; Blaine would not accept a nomination. "Earnestly request all friends to respect my Paris letter," he cabled the Maine delegation.[90] Elkins took the cue, and Harrison's managers were not averse to final arrangements, but did not care to report all the details to their chief in Indianapolis. Before the convention met, Michener suggested to Harrison that Pennsylvania's Matthew S. Quay was "rather practical," and would join their column only with assurances of post-election favors in writing. He actually drafted a letter for Harrison to send Quay, but a chilly silence fell on the arrangements, and Quay did not mount the bandwagon. Harrison warned followers not to "bargain," and said he would not "be bound by any promise," express or implied, either during the campaign or later if election should follow nomination." [91]

Men in all camps thought Platt was "the largest factor in the nominating problem." [92] Now, on this placid Sunday, he took a drive with Elkins where the wind had no ears. Depew and others already underscored the obvious; Harrison's votes came from doubtful states, where tariff protection would win. He was the man. That was all very well, but Tom Platt wanted firm assurances; he would not re-enact Conkling's role with Garfield. Since 1880, he had built the New York organization with fresh bricks, and badly needed the mortar of patronage. He liked Elkins, and understood his role as a link between Blaine and Harrison. Elkins swore ever afterwards that he made no bargains, but Platt stepped from the carriage convinced that a successful Harrison administration would make him Secretary of the Treasury. Platt conveniently overlooked New York's earlier shift to Harrison, and falsely believed he nominated the Indianan. That night, weary men returned from Indianapolis, where they talked briefly with Harrison. They too thought him amenable to distribution of rewards and punishments.[93]

Monday brought an air of tension. Michener and W. W. Dudley answered a polite summons from the Sherman men, and heard Charles Foster offer Cabinet seats if they would follow the Ohioan. The Hoosiers smiled and declined, knowing a different story would soon unfold. The seventh ballot—amid noise, distracting cries for order, and weariness—made Harrison the leader, with 279 votes to Sherman's 230. Allison withdrew, and a small group of leaders hastily convened below the New York standard, including Platt, Depew, Quay, and

Iowa's David B. Henderson. When they scattered, wise heads nodded: "That settles it." As the eighth ballot proceeded, Harrison moved toward the prize and spectators fell into a strange calm. Emmons Blaine left the platform; in the galleries, his brother Walker rose quietly from Mrs. Platt's side and disappeared. When Tennessee made Harrison the nominee, scattered cheers broke out, but exhaustion and anti-climax kept most delegates in their seats. The usual seconding speeches followed, stressing party harmony. That night, Levi P. Morton, in a strange replay of 1880's missed opportunity, joined Harrison as the vice-presidential candidate. The ticket needed his financial connections and organizational skill, and New York's support.[94]

Special wires took the good news to Indianapolis. Neighbors gathered on Harrison's lawn to cheer and call for a speech. The candidate betrayed little emotion as he waved to arriving tourists running down the street from all directions. Factory whistles blew, trolley bells clanged, and firecrackers punctuated the proceedings. Closer to home, the picket fence quickly disappeared under the onslaught of souvenir hunters, and Harrison even patted a baby on the head. Secretaries inside the house hastily assembled material for a speech, but the candidate gave an effective impromptu address that set the tone of things to come.

By Monday, after four days of bargaining, uncertainty, and elaborate discussion, most delegates and political observers in Chicago expected the choice. They saw at once that Harrison might carry the doubtful states, was Blaine's heir, and had wider appeal than any other local favorite. But his talents and obvious "availability" submerged in discussions of Blaine. "The nomination was made by orders from the top of Carnegie's coach," Charles Dana insisted, and most insiders realized that Elkins passed the succession to Indiana. Blaine called the result "the close of my personal aspirations for the presidency," and added for good measure: "The nomination never attracted me except in '76." He congratulated Elkins on a job well done. "I rejoice in Harrison's nomination. It would have been a huge blunder to nominate me." [95] Sherman was bitter, blaming Alger for buying votes, Platt for making "a corrupt bargain" with Harrison's managers, and Blaine for double-dealing.[96] Harrison quickly began talking unity, and in classic fashion, downgraded his own skills. "I do not flatter myself that anything in my person or record contributed in any degree to bringing about this state of things," he told Reid, "but negative qualities may be useful as well as positive." [97]

Harrison's selection illustrated the Republican party's cohesion and discipline, although critics falsely called him the creature of bosses.

But the way he triumphed was also fruitful of later dissension. Though he made no bargains, managers had let powerful men like Platt think otherwise. Harrison lacked the charm or talent for manuever to offset inevitable friction within the party. As a spokesman of great issues, a constructive nationalist, and vigorous campaigner, Harrison was the best available Republican in 1888. As a party harmonizer and leader of individual men, he was unsuccessful. The problem was ironic; he saw the whole better than its parts. But he filled the GOP's present need—a candidate to focus a larger effort without threatening it. His motto was simple. Let every man blend into the party.

On June 26, a friend in New York's legal circles wrote Lamont some candid advice. "A word to the wise. Don't make any mistake. There will be no 'walk over.' Your opponents are disciplined, skilful, hungry and desperate. . . . *This is gilt edged counsel.* Lay it to heart." [98] In the relaxed days following the convention, this seemed sound but a little premature. That very day, however, President Cleveland went through the traditional ritual of accepting renomination. An elegant delegation, representing the states and territories, gathered at "Grass-lands," one of Whitney's homes, for the usual collation, then proceeded to the White House. Cleveland received them in the East Room, and could not resist some personal remarks. "I knew then [in 1884] something of the bitterness of partisan obstruction; but I did not know how bitter, how reckless, and how shameless it could be." [99] The delegation stood through expected remarks on the tariff and exhortations to the faithful, and departed for a tour of Mount Vernon.

The President did not intend to campaign, and routine political management fell to Lamont, Whitney, and trusted personal aides. The National Committee stood behind the aging figurehead of Connecticut's Senator William H. Barnum. But its real powers were Gorman and Calvin S. Brice, Ohio railroad magnate and industrialist. Neither man was a logical choice, for both were protectionists, and ranked low in the estimation of independent voters. Cleveland chose Brice to raise funds in the business community, and Gorman to spend the money, and failed on both counts. Critics scored the former as "a corporate magnate," and the latter as "an embodiment of the boodle idea in politics." [100] George F. Parker, Cleveland's secretary and aide, thought Brice "a clear-headed, busy, thorough-going man." [101] Cleveland was uncritical during the campaign, but later called Brice "selfish and cold-blooded." [102]

The whole Democratic organization reflected the old party curse of disunity, localism, and indecision. "If Gorman and I could handle this campaign," Whitney wrote his wife, "we would win 'hands down'; but we would kick out of the way a lot of 'Southern brigadiers'—and *some* cabinet officers." [103] Lack of money and trained organizers intensified inability to satisfy "an unprecedented demand for speeches" and pamphlets. Orders from state organizations in the Midwest for 500,000 leaflets were not unusual, and national headquarters could not buy or ship enough throughout the campaign.[104] Various sectional and local problems thwarted a unified campaign. "There will be no campaign worth talking about in this section [the South]," the *Atlanta Constitution* promised with relief.[105]

Party leaders disagreed on where to focus the effort. Some warned that only victory in the Old Northwest and Ohio Valley would save Cleveland, and proposed a network of speakers and blizzard of literature out of Chicago. Brice disagreed, arguing that "all our means and thoughts should be given to New York, New Jersey, Connecticut and Indiana." [106] If Cleveland had begun the crusade a year earlier, an intense propaganda effort might have carried a few states with mixed economies, but by fall they were Republican. New York City, as usual, posed a great problem. An intense fight between Tammany and the County Democracy over the mayoralty threatened both state and national tickets. Cleveland's advisers warned that Hill might drag his feet in the presidential fight rather than risk the governorship. In October, one of the President's close friends said national headquarters had "a sort of amateurish air," and radiated indifference. ". . . they have washed fully as much as they will hang out." [107]

Firm presidential leadership might have overcome this confusion and lassitude, but Cleveland wanted only a rhetorical crusade. Always an inept campaigner, he now resented demands on his time. He would not tour, or even make a few ceremonial set-speeches. He rejected a bid to address a national farmer's organization because it interfered with his summer vacation. He was momentarily disfranchised, and could not even vote in November. It seemed undignified now to say anything but a few epigrams about duty, country, and what men must do to be saved politically. The letter of acceptance of September 8 was a diffuse and labored effort that opposed trusts without offering a remedy, promised reasonable pensions, vaguely wanted more civil service reform, and criticized tariff protection. "Unnecessary taxation is unjust taxation." Still, he was not radical. "We have entered upon no crusade of free trade." The Democrats would adjust schedules with "the utmost care for established interests and enterprise, [and] a jealous regard for the interests of American labor." [108] Trapped in apology, he said nothing Republicans were not saying to better advantage.

His refusal to humanize issues left local managers at wits' ends. "Frankie Clubs" in honor of Mrs. Cleveland sprang up spontaneously, and might have added color if not light to the proceedings, but Cleveland opposed them as undignified. Thurman toured, but fulfilled prophecies about his debility. He spoke to large crowds in the Midwest, where he was already familiar. But at a colorful mass meeting in Madison Square Garden, he tottered onstage to announce he could not speak, and left an embarrassing vacuum in the proceedings. Even in August, before "campaign weather" set in, Republicans were drilling and marching. One of their efforts in New York showed the gulf between the two parties when it came to presenting a case. "I watched the Blaine procession here last night, from beginning to end," a friend wrote Lamont: [109]

> There were about 15,000 men in line, and who came very largely from Brooklyn and New Jersey. It was a respectable but by no means enthusiastic parade. These people, however, have got a complete start on us in our campaign. It is perfectly useless for our managers to rely on either Tammany Hall or the County Democracy conducting a national canvass and educating the people in this city. They are going to respectively conduct each its own canvass, and in the meantime the work of the Republican propaganda is not being counterbalanced by any work on our side.

The President went his way, checking fishing tackle, reading correspondence, leaving details to Lamont and Whitney. He seemed not to realize that the Republicans were far ahead on the road to victory.

Early in the campaign, a shrewd reporter noted the source of Republican energy: "Defeat had brought unity." [110] Blaine's failure in 1884 shocked the GOP, and four years later, Republicans intended to win with unity and organization from ward to nation. They also knew, as an independent paper said in June, that "old time methods of campaigning are obsolete. [This] will be a campaign of argument, not of brag and bluster." [111] The usual color would predominate, but the early "pamphlet famine" indicated intense public interest in facts.

Harrison did not wish to dominate the campaign machinery, but insured full national representation on the committees, to avoid eastern domination. Matthew S. Quay occupied the national chairmanship, and Jacob Sloat Fassett of New York was treasurer; John C. New, Harrison's close friend, headed the Executive Committee; Michener was a smooth go-between for the candidate and managers. Harrison wanted to avoid a constellation of local bosses and state interests, as Senator Plumb counseled, but knew intrusion would create friction. "It has seemed to me from the beginning that the only proper course for me was to stand loyally by our organization and to urge all friends to do the same," he told Wharton Barker.[112] Necessity left no choice; he would deal with the leaders after victory.

New York's Tom Platt was a powerful, though not lordly, chieftain. Patience and talent for the devious brought him success in the New York organization after Conkling's fall in 1881. Piece by piece, he arranged a formidable state party resting on careful discipline, consultation among local leaders, and willingness to be Republicans rather than obstructive individuals. His appearance was deceptive. To most he seemed a chipper cynic, wearing an air of boyish dissipation. As a youth, he was dreamy and ineffectual, and in middle-age liked the theater and music hall. But he subordinated diverse tastes to a need for power and identification with a system. He had no faith in man's perfectibility, but believed parties could create comfort and security. He blended carefully into the larger scene, but held the reins tightly. "He must be smarter than he looks!" was a remark common to men who later regretted it.[113]

"The Machiavelli of Tioga County" learned a great lesson from Lord Roscoe's fall: No man rises far above the organization. Spreading responsibility, he consulted subordinates and ruled through consent. Even when he did not take advice, he *seemed* to want it. Platt was essentially a harmonizer of diverse views, judging the time to strike, how to organize, and what to emphasize. "He had no sympathy with graft or grafters," a trusted lieutenant said, "but he did not affect to believe that everybody was a knave." Control of the nominating procedure, influence in the state legislature, careful application of federal patronage, and contacts among newspapermen were the foundation of his success. He accepted human nature, and disciplined those who threatened the organization. He was hardly a saint, though not the boodler enemies depicted, and simple tastes typified Lord Bryce's acute observation: "The aim of a boss is not so much fame as power, and power not so much over the conduct of affairs as over persons." Passersby at the Fifth Avenue Hotel often saw him with cronies, exchanging stories and lighting cigars in the "Amen corner." The talk was frank, and when the "Easy Boss" made a point, everyone nodded a silent amen; the organization had spoken. Unlike Conkling, he was patient and tolerant. "Because Platt played the game for love and not for money, he was not prone to cherish long animosities or to pursue bitter revenges," an observer recalled.[114]

His success mystified "respectable" Republicans, but Theodore Roosevelt, always a realist, knew the origins of Platt's appeal. "In the country districts his machine included the majority of the best citizens, the leading and substantial citizens, among the inhabitants. Some of his strongest and most efficient lieutenants were disinterested men of high character." This reflected Platt's appeal to *party* loyalty, rejection of personal grandeur, and acceptable policies. The opposition also helped. "Very many of Mr. Platt's opponents really disliked him and his methods for esthetic rather than for moral reasons," Roosevelt noted, "and the bulk of the people half-consciously felt this and refused to submit to their leadership." Platt's enemies at best "usually put up some rather inefficient, well-meaning person, who bathed every day, and didn't steal." But they were politically ignorant, and unwilling to touch the voting masses.[115]

Like most Republicans, Platt rested a state-wide lead on small towns, farmers, and upstate cities. The premier urban boss sat in Philadelphia, in the person of Matthew Stanley Quay. He rose from the ranks of Don Cameron's machine as "a lieutenant of rare efficiency," making "no visible effort to advance himself or magnify his own importance."[116] In time, he justly earned the reputation for a velvet glove, and always preferred chloroform to grapeshot in dispatching opponents. Like Platt, he did not seem willful or aggressive, wearing an air of shrewd laziness, looking for the main chance from the corner of an eye. Drooping eyelids and mustaches created a faintly oriental air. He seemed indolent, indifferent, amused, and ruthless all at the same time. Proud of a trace of Indian blood, Quay surprised those who thought him a mere machine master by standing firmly for minority rights, bitterly opposing various projected land swindles and raids on the few remaining tribal rights.

Now a senator, he moved easily in the circles of power. Men disagreed with him, but Quay had many redeeming virtues. He read widely and well, and knew ancient languages. As an amateur in heraldry, he delighted in correcting snobs who discussed lineage. Indifferent to criticism, he carried few personal grudges, and often asked cartoonists for autographed originals of hostile artwork. He believed fervently in tariff protection, and organized his followers brilliantly. Ward by ward, county by county, he studied the Keystone State, knew local leaders, read newspapers, remembered statistics. State patronage, personal favors, and emphasis on party loyalty made him supreme. "He was very reticent; like Bismarck, he knew how to keep silent in fifteen different languages." [117] But properly angered, he could "raise a fiery cross" and engulf enemies with speakers and literature. He preferred civilized dealing, but if men insisted, he opened private files—"Quay's Coffins." Like Platt, he expected loyalty, even when a man did not get his price. There would be other times and places. One bolter asked Quay why he opposed his candidacy. "You taught me all the politics I ever knew," the man protested. Quay smiled. "That's true, but I didn't teach you all *I* know." Platt paid him the highest compliment. "I'd like to have been Matt Quay's office boy for just about six months." He was best known in 1888 to eastern leaders, but Sherman and Michener assured Harrison he was the man to be in charge.[118]

Opponents pictured Platt and Quay as baronial knights, ruling polyglot empires with rods of iron, and holding national administrations to ransom. They were not plaster saints, and accepted men as they found them; nor were they philosophers or egalitarians. They defined Republicanism as a national doctrine that promised rewards to many groups, stable economic growth, emotional satisfaction, and personal power. But they were organization men, a necessary phase in nationalizing politics, linking ideals to people they organized. They accepted the burgeoning industrial system. Rightly or wrongly, good or bad, true or false, it was real. They were optimistic enough to think politics could spread its benefits to people they better understood and represented than occasional silk-stocking reformers or states-rights Democrats. They gave the immigrant and new city dweller a sense of belonging to a powerful organization and a good cause. They offered secure Americans stability, orderly growth, and success within a national system. They also had the good sense not to be pretentious about long-term motives, or pompous about origins. This, too, satisfied a varied constituency preferring reality to rhetoric.

To supplement Platt and Quay, a special businessmen's committee sat under the direction of Philadelphia's department store magnate, John Wanamaker. He accepted the task reluctantly, for a puritanical nature rebelled at some of Quay's methods. He was a high Republican, but disliked the dirt where Quay planted flowers. The crisis was too great for personal animosity, however. With his usual efficiency and vigor, Wanamaker brusquely tapped wealthy friends for more than $200,000, mostly for literature that poured westward from Pittsburgh and Chicago. By fall, private polls predicted victory, so he bet a third of the money on Harrison's victory, making a 30 per cent profit to distribute among campaign committees and workers. He downgraded the flashy campaign. "They [Democrats] were not beaten in November, nor in October, but long before that." While Wanamaker canvassed friends, Iowa's James S. Clarkson, formerly Allison's manager, quietly canvassed industrialists. He reported a total fund of $3,300,000, with very little wasted.[119]

This organization, duplicated on every level, explained Harrison's running start. It did not rest on bribery or coercion, but on propaganda. The men in charge used the printed and spoken word and did not shrink from big things, but they never overlooked details. Issues moved men, candidates captivated them, but organization made them vote and counted the ballots. The Platts, Quays, Clarksons, and Micheners financed private polls to determine expense outlays; put men in charge of literature who knew where to mail; arranged for poll-watching; assigned wards and counties to trusted aides. They spent less money on buying voters than on informing those open to their arguments. While Democrats worried over presidential dignity and mollified local leaders, Republicans acted. And General Harrison was moving with the best of them.

Harrison did not intend to campaign like Blaine in 1884. "I have a great risk of meeting a fool at home, but the candidate who travels cannot escape him." [120] At first he hoped not to speak at all beyond the usual ceremonial duties, feeling that this would further emphasize party loyalty. "My desire is to have a Republican campaign, and not a personal one. . . ." [121] He turned public attention to issues, hoping to avoid 1884's scandals or methods, and to "encamp on the high plains of principles, and not in the low swamps of personal defamation or detraction." [122] But he could hardly frighten off eager pilgrims crowding about the doorstep. And they would come to hear him, pay respects, and simply gawk.

He began speaking in a clipped, forceful style, talking in a few paragraphs of the tariff, Negro rights, and party differences. The crowds liked it, but Quay and the managers grew nervous. Four years earlier, three innocent R's allegedly cost them the White House. Impromptu speeches afforded endless chances for foot-in-mouth disease. "Shut up General Harrison," Quay told friends. But the public response was so great, and the speeches looked so good as pamphlets, that Quay changed his mind. "Keep at it," he wired the candidate, "you're making votes." By August, he told Michener: "If Harrison has the strength to do that [keep talking], we could safely close these headquarters and he would elect himself." [123]

It was a demanding role, and Harrison surprised everyone but friends with his success. He offset a chilly personality with an impressive presence, dignity, and clear, concise style. He had no taste for bombast, and never talked down to an audience. Leading hearers into a lucid, pithy argument, he linked facts to homely similes and unornamented logic. Only William McKinley ever equaled him in this kind of effective campaigning that combined the human touch and basic issues.

The speeches and audiences epitomized the comfortable vulgarity of American politics. On July 4, the formal Notification Day, Harrison reviewed the Tippencanoe Club of Marion County, Indiana, composed of men who had voted for William Henry Harrison. Despite ages ranging from 75 to 101, they marched in review through a rainstorm. In following weeks, the General faced diverse groups like a Colored Men's Travelling Club, the Republican White Hat Club of Ohio, the Porter Flambeau Club, and an Indianapolis Railroad Club. On September 8, the astonished candidate looked out a window to see a horde of well-organized girls, aged seven to fifteen, led by a young man astride a properly obsequious pony, with a drum and fife corps of eight boys. They milled on the lawn until Harrison appeared, did some fancy drills, and waited for a response. He could only say he loved children, and hoped their parents would vote right. September and October were crowded. "The delegations here begin upon me now with a rush," he wrote Alger, "and I suppose the country will have to endure a daily speech from me for several weeks." [124] Just before election, he reviewed a huge parade of business clubs, whose chief ornament was a large bull wearing a white cloth. A man in green sat astride, holding the legend: "John Bull Rides the Democratic Party and We Ride John Bull." [125]

The delegations left a bright array of gifts, including a 500-pound lump of iron ore from Vermillion Range miners. A small silver-mounted plush chair symbolized the presidential seat. "A highly polished horse shoe," from an immigrant English steelworker brought good luck. Watermelons, eagles, crochet work, gavels, canes, local farm produce, filled the house. What the staff could not eat or use went to local charities. The Harrison and Morton Railroad Club of Terre Haute offered the campaign's highlight, approaching the General's home with an artificial locomotive that belched real smoke and fire, whistling and ringing bells. Between July 7 and October 25, Harrison spoke eighty times, to 300,000 people who followed in the wake of such appearances. He impressed old hands. "To speak day after day as he has done to different phases of humanity, varying his short addresses so that no vein of sameness runs through them, never dropping a stitch in his logic to be picked up by his adversaries in unravelling the force of his expressions, leaving nothing for his partisans to explain—why, it is marvelous!" [126]

Behind this effort, newsmen wrote stories from special rooms in the house. The General had cool relations with reporters, and even the brashest shrank from a confrontation, lest he join Lot's wife in salty rigidity. Harrison took only one brief fishing trip to Lake Erie late in August, but even then spoke from the train in Ohio and Indiana. "I am quite tired of hearing my own voice," he wrote Morton, "and if there was a party pledged to the prohibition of public speaking, I would join it." [127] He told a group in mid-September that "even at home, when I sit down at the table with my family, I have some apprehensions lest someone may propose a toast and insist that I shall respond." [128] It seemed an unfair distribution of labor, but the managers were equally busy emphasizing tariff protection.

On July 21, with Mrs. Cleveland and distinguished guests in the galleries, the House passed the Mills bill, 162–149. Only four Democrats opposed the measure, but others reluctantly favored it under presidential and party pressure. They felt a twinge of guilt at "going back on Sam Randall," especially since the Pennsylvanian was dying of cancer. The bill ended protectionist Democracy, and symbolized a new-found party discipline. It showed clearly that if the party lost the issue this year, it might use it again in 1892 to better effect. As wise men predicted, the tariff was a party unifier.

The bill went to the Senate Finance Committee, safely in Republican hands. A special sub-committee with a Republican majority framed a "Senate Substitute," reported on October 8. "There is no danger of passing the Mills bill," Sherman assured David Harpster, wool lobbyist.[129] The Republican caucus decided to keep Congress in session until election-eve, to avoid passing a bill that might weaken the party, and to provide a national forum for discussion. They substituted lower sugar duties, eliminated tobacco taxes, put some luxuries on the free list, and promised a $70,000,000 revenue reduction. The Senate heard learned disquisitions on nails, birdcages, and sulphur until October 20, as Cullom noted, "for home consumption." [130]

Harrison and other speakers emphasized dangers in beginning wholesale revision, and fear of deflation among workers and farmers serving urban areas. Harrison foresaw "a feast of cheapness," and counseled listeners not to forget "that the spectre of low wages will also attend the feast." [131] His heavy emphasis on labor's benefits from protection somewhat offset a doubtful reputation with workers. He had refused to violate treaty rights in the anti-Chinese agitation, was a corporation lawyer, and had what the Midwest called an "aristocratic" background. There was grumbling that manufacturers coerced men into singing Republican tunes, though in Pennsylvania, New Jersey, and Connecticut many unions openly supported Harrison in Democratic districts.[132]

As the campaign progressed, wavering newspapers went over to protection; some, like the *Chicago Tribune*, doubted Democratic intentions. Others candidly feared lower duties on their section's products. The Republican party and its tariff stand remained powerful factors in the Old Northwest, especially among Germans, Norwegians, and Swedes. Public interest in the subject amazed even veteran campaigners. "The demand for tariff literature is phenomenal," William McKinley wrote Morton, urging the National Committee to dispatch every pamphlet it could find to the Midwest. "In sixty days there will be no time for reading; it will be 'parade and pyrotechnics.'" [133]

Well-financed private groups supplemented the GOP campaign, with a headstart on both parties. The American Iron and Steel Association, the American Protective Tariff League, the Industrial League, and many local Home Market Clubs more than offset reform counterparts. James M. Swank, Wharton Barker, and other Pennsylvania industrialists distributed millions of pamphlets, carefully postmarked from Minneapolis, Chicago, Milwaukee, Des Moines, and other western cities, to avoid an eastern tinge. Protectionists' efforts taxed credulity. They even trained parrots to say "tariff is a tax" in parades to ridicule Democratic opponents. The *Nation* lampooned the whole effort: [134]

> Protection, O protection, the joyful sound proclaim
> Till each remotest nation has heard the Tariff's name!

Democrats found it hard to answer the protectionist argument. "Lifelong Democrats say to me, we cannot support a party who advocates free trade," an upstate New Yorker wrote Lamont. "We need protection. . . ." [135] It helped little to explain that reform was not free trade. Farmers producing raw materials did not want foreign competition, but favored lower duties on finished goods. Industrial workers disliked farmers, and wanted cheap food with high duties on what they produced. ". . . in certain iron industries, the employees look with some fear on the Mills Bill," a Buffalo lawyer wrote Lamont. "Every laborer and workingman engaged in the iron industry have confidence in Mr. Randall." [136] Harrison's formal letter of acceptance, dated September 11, shone beside Cleveland's effort, and sharply underlined these fears among workers and farmers. "The Mills bill is only a step, but it is a step toward an object that the leaders of Democratic thought and legislation have clearly in mind." He favored "sound money," civil service reform, admission of western territories, and arraigned Democratic frauds in southern voting. But he returned to protection: "We do not offer a fixed schedule, but a principle." [137]

Incessant firing in the tariff war drowned out all other issues, much to the discomfort of the Mugwumps, and anti-southern demagogues like Foraker. Harrison's stand on Negro rights was clear. He had always championed a universal free ballot, and supported federal aid to education with a national agency to coordinate the program. On the local level, he wanted equal accommodations in public services. He would not compromise on the issue during the campaign, though he did not arraign the South, treating the whole question as a national problem requiring national solutions.

Mugwumps had no home in the storm. Cleveland disappointed them, and at best they argued he was better than either party. Godkin admitted tariff reform was paramount, and Curtis said he would split the ticket—for Cleveland and against Hill. Democratic regulars did not really care. "Civil service reform is not in the platform because the Democratic party is tired of playing wet-nurse to a sham and a fraud," the *Atlanta Constitution* trumpeted. "If the Mugwumps desire an honest and economical administration of the government, they will have to take Grover Cleveland as a Democrat, pure and simple." [138] Harrison's letter of acceptance urged "a friendly interpretation" for the existing law, to be "faithfully and vigorously enforced." In state politics, he had favored merit appointments to offices requiring special skills, and in 1882 voiced a complaint more common than politicians admitted. "My brief experience at Washington has led me often to utter the wish with an emphasis that I do not often use that I might be forever relieved of any connection with the distribution of public patronage." [139]

The campaign devoured money on both sides, and Republicans had advantages in the business community, though Democrats were not poor. Charges of corruption filled the air in "swing states" like Indiana, New York, and Connecticut. Quay exploited the New York situation by subsidizing Irish speakers, and got the small Union Labor party in New York to vote for Harrison in return for Republican aid in local contests. A "Harrison and Hill" movement rose in the Empire State, as many disgruntled Democrats preferred "Brains" Harrison to "Beef" Cleveland. But Hill remained as loyal as circumstances permitted, urging fellow workers to "pull straight for the whole ticket." He stumped outside New York, paid his own expenses, and praised Cleveland. All to no avail; the President did not endorse him, and remained suspicious.[140]

Indiana posed the usual problems. Republican agents wanted to "put the manufacturers of Pennsylvania under [sic] the fire and fry the fat out of them," with a good portion of the renderings earmarked for the Hoosier State. Indianans were no strangers to the persuasions of money and patronage. A large pro-southern population from across the Ohio River, disgruntled Greenbackers, and Prohibitionists made up the usual combination that threatened regular parties, though most registered voters were Republican. William H. English promised the state to Cleveland, with proper help. George F. Parker, one of the President's secretaries, did not object, urging only that outsiders be unobtrusive.[141]

But Harrison's friend and supporter, W. W. Dudley, became the center of the loudest storm in Indiana.* If Dudley had a motto, it was "Vote early and often." He was familiar in circles that counted "persuasion" more salutary than propaganda, and did not shrink from the two-dollar bill that took "floaters" to the voting booth. As treasurer of the National Committee, he oversaw collection and expenditure, with a special eye on his native state. Late in October, Democrats gleefully reprinted a circular letter he supposedly wrote on how to make Indiana "safe." It was standard fare, familiar to both major parties for decades, but caused a commotion. Dudley urged field workers to make the Democrats pay highly for voters to exhaust their resources. Republicans should also prevent frauds in the ballot boxes. He wanted every Republican at the polls, and every suspicious voter challenged. But his conclusion really sparked condemnation. "Divide the floaters into blocks of five and put a trusted man with the necessary funds in charge of these five and make him responsible that none get away and that all vote our ticket." [142] "Blocks of Five Dudley" thus entered the history books.

The letter was typed on National Committee stationery, postmarked New York, October 24, but it contained numerous misspellings, and Dudley's son denied the signature was genuine. Dudley cried fraud, and sued newspapers printing the text. Harrison was uncertain, but refused to exonerate Dudley. Thereafter, they did not speak, though offending newspapers printed minute retractions when Dudley agreed

---

*It is impossible to determine the extent or influence of outright corruption in Indiana in 1888, or any other year. Both parties were culpable, and probably canceled each other's efforts. The Republicans did not necessarily have more money, but had more familiar and logical arguments for the doubtful voter, and better "agents."

to drop the suits. Michener remembered receiving such a letter, but thought it normal. A Democratic mail clerk had stolen a copy, which said something of the opposition's methods. If the letter was a forgery, its sentiments were true enough, and the crime lay in getting publicity. Purchased voters probably did not swing the state; no one could accurately determine the letter's effect on events. It all seemed customary to men in the field.[143]

Party organization and the tariff issue drowned out most individual voices. True to Harrison's wishes, men blended into a common effort. But one could not; and he was coming from Scotland in time to join the fray.

Even as delegates left Chicago after choosing Harrison, many Republicans chanted: [144]

> We'll vote this year for Tippecanoe
> And for James G. Blaine in '92.

Leisure unsettled the Plumed Knight, but he was uncertain about returning during the contest. If he came home, he must campaign. A tour might offend Harrison. But most managers wanted him in the fight. On August 10, his steamer, "The City of New York," nosed toward a Manhattan dock, where the ever-faithful had gathered for days. Tugs gaily decorated with flags, pictures, and bunting fussed noisily around the ship, spraying water and firing small cannon. On shore, brass bands played and thousands of people rustled nervously with banners and placards, ready for the inevitable parades. Blaine waved cheerfully, making witty asides to friends and family. "Blaine, Blaine, James G. Blaine," drifted across the water, mingling with cheers and whistles in disorderly homage to the most popular American. That night he faced an immense torchlight parade.

Harrison wanted Blaine in the campaign, but knew he might suffer by comparison. Victory would revive the "Blaine problem," and men around him already suggested the premier Cabinet portfolio for the Plumed Knight. But Harrison never hinted at friction or jealousy during the fight, speaking of "that matchless defender of Republican principles—James G. Blaine." [145] Managers carefully timed Blaine's entrance into the campaign for maximum effect in the "fall states" and on the whole country. In mid-September, he spoke in New York and then moved west; according to the critics, "like an untamed whirlwind, with mass meetings, processions, torchlights, blue-lights, Roman candles, and a delegation from Congress to play on the cymbals, the psaltery and the hand organ. . . ." [146] Maybe so, but huge audiences welcomed him, especially when he climaxed the tour with an elaborate visit to Harrison on October 11.

Most of the Midwest seemed to be there, in a sea of people with forests of signs. Every special unit west of Pennsylvania had to be in a parade that filled the morning. That afternoon, Blaine spoke to 30,000 at the State Fair Exposition grounds, and again that night celebrated protection's virtues before 6,000 selected guests at Tomlinson's Hall. Blaine made only one *faux pas,* failing to condemn trusts. His argument that they were inevitable, and not connected with the tariff, drew adverse publicity. "Mr. Blaine's view is certainly a flippant one, to call it by no harsher name," the *Chicago Tribune* remarked.[147]

Blaine's frenzied reception, Harrison's effective speeches, and clock-like Republican organization worried Democrats. They were clearly losing, as advisers told the President. Republicans entwined appealing protectionist arguments with the anti-English sentiment below the surface of American life. A sharp blow against that might offset the tariff's appeal, and Harrison's growing popularity.

Stanley Matthews once remarked, "there was not a codfish on the banks that had not been subject to arbitration." [148] The influence of domestic politics on foreign relations, and American impatience with diplomacy, haunted the endless controversy over fishing rights in Canadian waters. Since Independence, and more recently after the war, several administrations tried to settle the question to home advantage. But competition among fishermen, American and Canadian pride, and adverse money settlements made the United States particularly irritable about the subject by 1888. The question of duties on Canadian produce entering the United States, and business on trunk lines into Canada complicated matters. Cleveland wanted to negotiate a new treaty that would avoid the frequent brawls among fishing fleets off the Grand Banks, guarantee American fishing rights, and please Irish elements who saw any dealing with England as traitorous.

Early in 1888, Alvee A. Adee, the most permanent fixture in the State Department, wrote Secretary Bayard the bald truth. "I fear the love of our Irish cousins for us depends largely on the chances of our squabbling with England." [149] In August, Irish friends warned Cleveland of the pro-English label fast appearing on Democratic arguments. "We are seriously behind in our campaign work. The dark spots are the manufacturing centers," Patrick Collins said. "If the working people ever get 'Free Trade' into their heads, it will take a surgical operation to get it out." He suggested the Administration create an anti-English incident, like a ship seizure, to solidify wavering districts that might determine New York's electoral vote.[150] Whitney wanted Cleveland to challenge the Republican Senate, which would not ratify a treaty that helped Democrats. "I want him to take the aggressive on the fishery question," he told his wife, "and after they [the Senate] reject the treaty, retaliate! I am sick of all this talk about an 'English' party." [151]

Moderate Republican senators like Wisconsin's John Coit Spooner, wanted to amend the new treaty with Canada rather than defeat it. They would thus delay, or get credit for it. But the senatorial caucus rejected the idea on July 14. August 23 brought a special message from Cleveland, asking Congress to grant him rights to suspend by proclamation the passage of goods in bond across the Canadian border. "The President has done just what I expected him to do," Spooner said. "He has run up the American flag. The Democrats think it will knock out the tariff issue, and it is their trump card." [152] On September 8, the House passed the necessary legislation, which died in the Senate. Lurid talk drowned out essentials, as English papers said the message "dished the Republican party." Canadians thought it "electioneering claptrap," and Democrats hoped to nullify protection's appeal.[153]

Republicans made the retaliation message a boomerang. The surprise originated in the unlikely locale of Pomona, California, then a lovely town nestled in orange groves. California, like all thinly settled western states with "colonial" economies, favored protection. Westerners wanted high rates on wool, food products, hides, and ores, and also liked Harrison's pro-western senatorial record. Cleveland gained some votes with a blatant anti-Chinese law in September, but the Republicans could clearly carry all the West with a little aid.

A Pomona citrus grower planned to give that help. George Osgoodby, of American birth but English parentage, was excessively loyal to his country and the GOP. He listened to bitter debates among his cronies at the corner grocery store, and decided to act. Posing as an English citizen named Charles F. Murchison, he wrote the British minister to the United States on September 4, asking which party the British government favored. Sir Lionel Sackville-West, never noted for intelligence, in effect told Osgoodby to vote for Cleveland. The orange grower received the reply about September 13, and did not quite know what to do. He had wanted all along to use any politically damaging results, but now feared the vengeance of local Democrats. His lawyer passed the letter on to Harrison Gray Otis, publisher of the *Los Angeles Times*, who printed it late in October.[154]

The indolent Sackville-West was an ideal dupe. Loose personal morals made him distasteful to some American officials, though he mixed well with congressmen. "The Americans thoroughly understand him, and tell him all sorts of things they don't [tell] to anyone else," Cecil Spring-Rice, a legation secretary, wrote home. "They have a common taste for whiskey, poker, and business." [155] Sir Lionel now spread his bountiful fatuity before the enraged Administration. A Democratic reporter called on him after missing Bayard at the State Department, and the Minister explained jovially that it was all true. He had a right to his views, expressed them in a private letter, and did not see that it was anyone else's business. The newspapers would attack him, would they? "Indeed! Well, let them come on. I read the papers, you know, and I shall enjoy it greatly, I assure you." [156] To a *Tribune* reporter, he was even more incredible. "Of course, I understand that both the action of the Senate and the President's letter of retaliation were for political effect. In a general election it is but natural that every point should be seized upon by both parties which would have an effect upon the voters." [157]

The next day, Cleveland polished the table with his fist, as the Cabinet discussed the problem. Bayard emerged to tell newsmen the government would not countenance "foreign interference," and condemned the "Murchison Letter" as a Republican trick.[158] Sackville-West hastily agreed, in two notes to the Secretary. "It is clear to me now that the whole affair was a trick to make use of me, and I repeat again my disclaimer of any thought or intention of meddling in domestic politics, when I wrote the letter which has been published." He called daily at the State Department to protest innocence, and Bayard suggested that silence was the best refuge. Sackville's repeated newspaper interviews angered Cleveland as much as the original letter. "Lord Sackville allowed himself to be drawn into the snare," Bayard told reporters. "It would seem to me that he had lived in America long enough to imbibe at least a little of our Yankee smartness." [159]

Politicians flooded Cleveland with complaints. He must dismiss Sackville, and Bayard too if possible, to erase the Administration's English tag. The Irish were furious, responding to Blaine's jibes about doubtful Americanism with cheers. A Midwestern sheet proclaimed: "Queen Victoria keeps a pet dog named Cleveland." [160] Republicans chanted "Sack, Sack, Sackville-West," and marchers held signs reading: "No frigid North, no torrid South, no temperate East, *no Sackville-West*." [161] Cleveland called the Minister "a wretched marplot" and wanted the British government to recall him gracefully. On Sunday afternoon, October 28, he promised Irish-American politicians to dismiss him if necessary.[162]

Bayard's efforts to secure Sackville-West's recall were fruitless.

Edward J. Phelps, American minister in London, reported that normal Foreign Office slowness combined with reluctance to destroy the Minister's career. Bayard knew delay was fatal, and on Cleveland's instructions handed Sackville-West his passports on October 30. Phelps soon left the London legation to a *chargé d'affaires,* and the British did not replace Sackville-West until Cleveland left office. Bayard denounced the Republican "plot" in campaign speeches, and told reporters, "to save my life, I cannot make up my mind whether the British Minister was more rascal or more fool." [163]

And so another colorful incident passed into American political history. Critics labeled it a plot to beat Cleveland by avoiding issues, but anti-English feeling reflected the tariff argument. Cold-blooded politicians thought it part of the game. To Republicans, it was welcome payment for the Morey Forgery of 1880, and Democratic importation of Irish leaders in 1884. Cleveland's retaliation message and anti-Chinese stand were blatantly political. The two "letters" probably canceled each other, but were an excellent rationalization for defeat if Cleveland lost on the tariff issue.

The last days of campaigning were an orgy of parading, and tub-thumping. There was no rest for Harrison, though Cleveland remained silent at his White House desk. A Harrison-Morton Glee Club serenaded the Republican candidate, while last-minute parades unwound in most of the country's cities. A steel-ribbed ball 14 feet in diameter, and 42 feet in circumferance, and weighing 1,000 pounds, was rolled from Cumberland, Maryland, to Indianapolis, then added 5,000 miles of travel throughout the Midwest. On Tuesday, November 6, Harrison rose early to vote in a nearby livery stable, returning home to wait beside special telegraph wires. He doubtless agreed silently with Terence V. Powderly: "I am so glad this damn campaign is over; if it lasted another month, I believe every man, woman and child in the country would be stark, staring mad." [164] Despite thin margins in some crucial states, Harrison's election was clear almost from the first returns. Cleveland accepted the results stoically, but Indianapolis went wild, and for an awful moment threatened to put Harrison through the speech-making ordeal again for thank-you appearances. A light rain fell at Spiegel Grove on November 9, when returns indicated firm Republican victory. Former President Hayes heard a newsboy shouting "All about the election of General Harrison!" and rushed half-dressed from the house to buy a paper. While mist covered his bare head and beard, he nodded: "How good. How good." [165]

It was a clearer victory than most observers expected. Harrison carried all western and northern states except Connecticut and New Jersey, where Prohibition Party tickets received almost exactly enough votes to give the states to Cleveland. Harrison received 233 electoral votes to the President's 168. Cleveland compiled a popular lead over Harrison of about three-fourths of one per cent in the whole nation, but it was fictitious, coming from increased Southern votes. Harrison carried the major industrial and raw material areas, losing Connecticut only by about 400 votes, Virginia by 1,500, and West Virginia by 500. The House went Republican, with 173 members to 156 Democrats, and the Senate remained in GOP hands, 47–37. Republicans added House seats in border states, but lost a few midwestern states where Temperance and local issues were important. They gained slightly in Delaware, Maryland, West Virginia, and Kentucky over the 1886 totals, but declined a little in Tennessee, Missouri, and Arkansas. But the Great Border seemed within reach to many Republicans eager to gain House seats if not electoral votes, and this was significant to men planning laws for the coming Republican Congress.

New York drew an unusual share of attention, for Hill won the governorship by 19,000 votes, though the state went to Harrison. Charges of treason filled the papers and Cleveland's correspondence, but despite the usual "dealing" for local offices with national votes, Hill did not lose New York for Cleveland. He campaigned hard, widely, and well, praising the Administration. Lamont told Cleveland that without Hill the margin of loss would have been greater. Hill had everything to lose for his own supposed future as a national leader by defeating Cleveland, but he was a realist, and knew the charge would linger indefinitely as a convenient rationalization. "It is one of the penalties of politics that no man must succeed at the expense of his associates on a party ticket," he told Alton Parker, "whether this success comes with or without his procurement or knowledge." [166] Though he refused to exonerate Hill publicly, Cleveland did not think treachery lost New York, and admitted that the tariff and Republican organization probably carried the state.[167]

That was the consensus, even among Democratic newspapers. Charges of cheating, the impact of Sackville-West's literary productions, and Temperance votes did not figure as prominently as discussions of the tariff issue. ". . . the tariff agitation [did] the most serious work against Mr. Cleveland," an independent Washington paper admitted.[168] Western Democrats were especially critical. "Had Cleveland's tariff reform message been dated December, 1886, instead of

1887, we should win victory everywhere," J. Sterling Morton of Nebraska wrote in September. "The people would have become educated before this time, but the term of school has been too short for teaching economics to 60,000,000 people. . . . He taught economics a year too early or a year too soon." [169] The *New York World*, which seldom had a good word for Republicans, blamed defeat on Cleveland, not the party. He was wrong in "precipitating the tariff issue on the perilous edge of a presidential campaign. . . ." And Democrats were not responsible for Cleveland's "obnoxious personal acts or characteristics." [170]

The criticism was sound, for Cleveland *lost* the election just as surely as Harrison won. Only a bold, personal campaign could have counteracted the brilliant Republican effort, and Cleveland remained stolidly out of the limelight. The whole contest proved again that issues enthuse, but tactics and organization win. Charles Dana was a little too gleeful, but essentially correct: [171]

> What's the matter with the Democracy?
> It's beaten.
> Who beat it?
> Grover Cleveland.

Cleveland took refuge in that fabled haven, the long-run. "It is better to be defeated battling for an honest principle than to win by a cowardly subterfuge," he told a reporter in the kind of interview he should have given during the canvass. In private, he edged this conviction with bitterness. "Perhaps I made a mistake from the party standpoint; but damn it, it was right. I have at least that satisfaction." And he roasted independents for dragging their feet. Most people were simply relieved the contest was over, and appreciated a southern suggestion for a six-year presidential term, adding two years between raucous campaigns.[172]

Republicans were well-financed, and disappointed Mugwumps said "money was used in this election with a profusion never before known on American soil." [173] But Republicans used funds to advertise tariff protection and the party's nationalism, and although industrialists provided most of the money, the GOP did not speak merely for business. It could never have won an election with a monolithic constituency. All observers agreed that millions of people read closely the pamphlets that filled the mails, and listened attentively to speakers who discussed protection. The tariff was one of the most vital and meaningful issues in American political history, reflecting the material self-interest of workers, farmers, and businessmen. It also appealed to all the emotions and security around political nationalism. Harrison's election outlined the party's new urban-industrial constituency. Careful legislation, continued popularization, and an effective presidential leader could solidify that constituency, and make the party truly national. Republican use of new techniques, careful planning of expenditure of money and men, and party discipline brought success. That was the great lesson of 1888. "To one Democratic speech, the Republicans made ten," a defeated Democrat noted sadly, "and their organization and activity in that respect was wonderful." [174]

Winning all three branches of the federal government made Republicans dangerously over-confident. The people voted for protection, *not a higher tariff*, and clearly wanted taxation reduced. In this moment of narrow but exhilarating victory, the party had dangerous internal problems, as a post-election confrontation between Quay and Harrison illustrated. Quay expected the President-elect's "fervent and grateful congratulations." Instead, Harrison remarked calmly that "Providence has given us the victory." Quay swallowed his surprise, and later snorted to friends, "Providence hadn't a damned thing to do with it." Nor had he received any firm assurances about proper rewards. He stirred uneasily, saying "Harrison would never learn how close a number of men were compelled to approach the gates of the penitentiary to make him president, where he could return thanks to the Almighty for his promotion." [175] The remarks were much overdrawn in the moment's heat, perhaps even apocryphal. Still, the scene could have happened. Both Quay and Harrison were like that.

VIII

The Billion-Dollar Congress:
1889–1891

Republican Senator Joseph R. Hawley of Connecticut took time from Christmas festivities to send President-elect Harrison some wry cheer: ". . . choosing a cabinet is like dying—it is something that nobody can do for you." [1] Senator Sherman knew the coming Republican Congress must enact a record for the party's future, and urged Harrison to recognize congressional interests even at the expense of the traditional power blocs in state organizations. He understood the dangers of a misstep in the cabinet-making quadrille, however, and could not forbear a rare trace of humor: "You should feel like a gallant young gentleman entering upon life with a world of girls about him, free to choose—to propose, but not to dispose." [2]

Harrison needed the humor, though he seldom returned the favor. He remained in Indianapolis through the winter, in traditional style, building an administration away from the confusion and alarums in Washington. He began to baffle men who thought him a cipher, or front for a "Blaine administration." A few like Smith M. Weed had predicted otherwise. "And as I look upon it," he wrote Whitney, "Harrison is a pretty cool, deliberate fellow, and will be very apt to be an independent president and to have his own way; and I think, give the country a pretty good government." [3] That sense of "independence" took various forms in Harrison's mind. He was no pedant, dividing constitutional prerogatives into neat compartments for Congress, the Executive and the courts. But he was intensely aware of his administrative role, and knew politics well enough to dislike interfering in congressional matters.

He saw the Cabinet as a kind of Privy Council, subordinate and deriving power from his consent. However much they reflected political power when appointed, the members became presidential advisers, not clashing chieftains. He wished to satisfy the party, but would not seek artificial harmony over the Administration's total good. He added to this firm view and dour personality a sudden interest in secrecy that made him send secretaries to various parts of town to mail inquiring letters in plain brown envelopes, avoiding curious reporters.[4]

The press teemed with speculation over Blaine's future. Harrison heard the loose and cynical talk about becoming a front-man, and being two small for "grandfather's hat." Much of it was Democratic spite, but it would irritate any man. And Blaine *was* a problem. Harrison insisted later "there was no day after the election that he would not have been chosen if I had been called to act then." But it was not quite that simple. He distrusted Blaine's rashness, and wondered how well they could work together. He worried about Blaine's health, and his notorious weakness as an administrator; the kind of looseness that irritated his precise nature, and might cause trouble in foreign relations. Would Blaine conduct a "safe" foreign policy? And would he avoid politics? His past, however constructive and valuable, was not an altogether comforting guide.[5]

December passed without a public decision, and Blaine alternated between nervous doubts about Harrison, and fear that he might not enter the new State Department building. The President-elect said he would not announce the Cabinet formally until it was completed, acting only after Congress counted the electoral votes in December. Such niceties of protocol bordered on evasion or absurd etiquette to warm-blooded souls like Elkins and Blaine. Harrison was sincere, and realized he could not exclude Blaine. But a little waiting might make the heart grow fonder.

Blaine let Harrison know through proper emissaries that he was available. "I notice that some of my 'friends' are quick to announce that I have retired *from political life*," he wrote Reid before the election. "That travels somewhat beyond the record, and there may be time and opportunity to correct it." [6] When the polls closed, he urged Elkins to deny any idea he did not want a Cabinet seat. Walker Blaine spoke to important senators like Hawley and asked powerful editors to raise a cry for his father. Blaine understood the predicament, however nervous it made him, and wanted to avoid irritating the touchy Harrison. He refused to suggest names for the Cabinet and would not intrigue for the War portfolio Elkins wanted so badly.[7]

To a man of Blaine's temperament, the waiting seemed endless. Days passed, with nothing to tell friends. Behind the scenes, others urged

Harrison to decide. "In view of all the public and private circumstances of the situation," one wrote, "he feels that not to be appointed to the Department of State would be to disgrace him before the country." [8] More to the point, Senator Hale of Maine warned of the general consequences. "But the live men of the party who do the fighting in the rank and file, aside from hundreds of its active leaders, expect now that Mr. Blaine will be called to his old place." [9] New Year's came and went. "I have heard *nothing from nobody* about nothing," Blaine wrote Alger.[10] Courtesy wore a little thin. When the subject came up among knowledgeable visitors, he snapped: "I am going into that cabinet, or I'll know the reason why." [11]

By mid-January, Harrison was through shuffling papers, and thought Blaine had waited long enough to understand presidential authority. "You and I want to be happy in Washington," he allegedly told a friend. "It will not be as pleasant for us with Blaine out as with Blaine in. So we had better take him in." [12] On January 17, he offered Blaine the State portfolio with a rather scolding letter, writing of loyalty and patience. Blaine answered at once, promising to be the good subordinate. He was especially interested in Latin American affairs, and improving the foreign service, but would do nothing without presidential approval. There was no hope of keeping it a secret, despite Harrison's early high-toned pronouncements. The press boiled with rumors, and it was best to answer the more lurid talk. Reaction was typical. ". . . we have hoped that he [Harrison] would not call such a trickster to his councils," Godkin announced imperiously, to no one's surprise.[13] "First and foremost, James G. Blaine will be the premier of the Harrison administration," the *Chicago Tribune* remarked, in a backhanded compliment to the new president, "and the mugwumps can put that in their pipes and smoke it." [14]

The long tension ended, but the affair illustrated Harrison's method of operation, and boded ill for future dealings with party leaders. Blaine was in fact a good subordinate; he now had little to do with party management, and could afford refuge in foreign relations. The situation was not so simple for Tom Platt, expecting the Treasury post. The Easy Boss met a freezing silence as he lifted his begging bowl. Harrison always denied that any "arrangements" produced his nomination. Labeling all deals "absolutely false," he stubbornly insisted, "when I was elected, I was absolutely without any obligation or promise as to any official act or appointment—as thoroughly so as if I had been born that day." He thought Platt should return to the Senate, "from which he had so foolishly resigned," and "until after the election, I had no thought or suspicion even that Mr. Platt wanted any place under my administration." [15]

Platt did not remember it that way, recalling what he thought was a firm promise from Elkins during their carriage ride the Sunday before Harrison's nomination. Elkins now sounded as muffled as an echo from a fog bank, remembering what suited him as he tried to retain Harrison's good will. Platt blustered about having it in writing, but did not produce any texts. Like most easterners, he was surprised at Harrison's stubbornness. It sounded like Garfield all over, without the latter's charm. Morton went to Indianapolis at Christmas-time, but was none the wiser. "The president-elect was all ears and no tongue," Platt told Alger.[16] Harrison would not deal openly with Platt, fearing newspaper repercussions and further misunderstandings. He did not choose Platt, and thought the Treasury, as usual, should go to the West to avoid outcries against eastern financial domination.

The problem seemed insoluble, as both Platt and Harrison insisted on alleged rights. Harrison condemned the other side's "obstinacy," and repeated his basic theme like a slogan on a blackboard. ". . . I cannot allow my liberty of choice to be unduly restricted," he kept telling Elkins. "As I said to you before the convention, it is my purpose to treat all the states fairly—to please them if I can—but not to allow my administration to be used to put *down* anybody." [17] He talked with New York's Senator Frank Hiscock to avoid confronting Platt, but the message was the same. Morton actually suggested Platt for the Navy, and Warner Miller for Agriculture, which made Harrison slightly incredulous. As inauguration approached with no New York appointment, Harrison seemed inclined to accept Platt's half-challenge, so reminiscent of Conkling: No New Yorker but Platt should enter the Cabinet.

A lull in the tension shifted Harrison's gaze west, where he spotted William Windom of Minnesota, who had served as Secretary of the Treasury for Garfield. He thought also of Allison and McKinley, but lacked patience to make up the former's vacillating mind and believed the latter was too young. Windom now practiced law in New York but his origins and past Granger connections made him a good risk.[18] The news embittered Platt. "I am frank to admit that one of the most poignant disappointments of my life was my failure to become at some time Secretary of the Treasury," he recalled in old age.[19] He had no serious relations with Harrison until very late in the term, when ironically, Blaine built a rickety bridge between them. Years later, he quietly admitted that Harrison had never really offered him the post; it was all a misunderstanding, due to the devious communications so common to political dealings. And while he never liked Harrison, he reluctantly admitted he was a good president.

Still, New York remained. It was all very well to think that passing over her claims would bring harmony, but wise men knew better. Despite a frosty exterior, Harrison tried to avoid political recriminations, while insisting that men honor both his office and nationalism. "They [New Yorkers] will find me kind and reasonable," he insisted. "The hard things they have said, some of which have come to me, have provoked no heat on my part—nor are [they] in any way responsible for the difficulty." [20] But he did not solve the problem until later. After arriving in Washington, he talked with Elihu Root and other "respectable" Republicans, who urged a compromise appointment from Brooklyn, General Benjamin Franklin Tracy, as Secretary of the Navy. An able administrator, he had some of the vision a "New Navy" needed. Of course, he was not well known to Platt. Party workers could not explain the puzzling appointment, "unless President Harrison took him because he lived near the Brooklyn Navy Yard," as one told reporters.[21]

That left Matt Quay among the moguls to pacify. His ambitions were a little less certain to the men who sent Harrison information. He enjoyed the victory, and would probably be satisfied with state patronage, but Pennsylvania could well demand John Wanamaker's recognition. Harrison hesitated; the appointment might look like a reward for big business and displease Quay. But Clarkson, Michener, and others sustained Wanamaker's ability. In January, Harrison asked the Philadelphian to visit Indianapolis, and offered him the Navy post. Wanamaker refused, since that department's purchases might create a conflict of interest with his business. He impressed Harrison, who offered him the Postmaster-General's office after Clarkson politely refused it.

Joseph Pulitzer was already conducting a blatant campaign in the New York World to discredit Wanamaker, but produced only noise. Wanamaker did not entirely satisfy Quay, and later fought him in state politics, but was an able cabinet minister. He personified the businessman's desire for efficiency, cheapness of cost, and stable profits that benefitted both customers and stockholders. An indefatigable worker, he often startled Washington milkmen by arriving home as they delivered bottles. His technical innovations greatly improved the Department, and he finally recommended government ownership of the telephone and telegraph system. Though he improved delivery, and lowered mail service's cost, Congress would not follow his recommendations to expand parcel post service. "There are five insurmountable obstacles," he told a caller, "first, there is the American Express Company; second, the United States Express Company; third, the Adams Express Company; fourth, the Wells-Fargo Express Company; and fifth, the Southern Express Company." [22]

The remainder of the Cabinet provoked less criticism among politicians. Redfield Proctor of Vermont spoke for New England in the War Department. John W. Noble of Iowa represented the Plains states in Interior. William H. H. Miller of Indiana filled the Attorney-General's post, largely to counsel Harrison as a friend. In the new Agriculture Department, Wisconsin's Jeremiah "Uncle Jerry" Rusk calmly worked through technical problems to help farmers, and tried to stimulate foreign trade. Research bureaus, printed bulletins, and field agents helped spread the new science of farming.

Harrison did not like Cabinet-making. "I said to a friend today that if all of the cabinet officers could have been found in Alaska, it would have promoted harmony in the party in the states," he told Blaine.[23] Mistakes were inevitable, but he held to one central principle, vital for any personal success or national party unity, "that a cabinet selection from a state did not mean the crowning of a boss, and should not put any barrier between me and my other friends." [24] Harrison's selections were better than his predecessor's, and his ideal of national party representation was vital, but he lacked the ability to pacify disappointed men. He could not resist explaining too much, telling men why they should repent—always unwelcome advice. Harrison was a strange political figure on the American scene. He understood national goals for both his party and country, but could not stoop even slightly to make others see. He prized candor, forgetting that silence and white lies could often disperse dark problems.

Valentine's Day brought no respite, and Mrs. Harrison continued packing for the trip east. Relatives, friends, and politicians came and went in a steady stream through the parlor and study. On February 25, with the usual panoply, the party left for Washington. The President-elect spoke briefly in Indiana, and welcomed Governor Foraker aboard near the Ohio border. The Buckeye First Lady recalled the amusing spectacle of Harrison trying to tame a grandson, the celebrated "Baby McKee." While the infant crawled over the "black but entirely submissive thundercloud," Harrison talked of Indian troubles, the tariff, western statehood, and politics.[25]

In Washington, the President-elect finished making last-minute Cabinet selections while the Clevelands packed at the White House. Mrs.

Cleveland did not retire until 3 A.M. on Sunday, after trying to fit cumbersome mementoes into awkward boxes for shipment to New York. The out-going President worked over last papers. Monday offered intermittent cold rain, and a soggy parade route. Bunting flapped miserably along Pennsylvania Avenue, and people huddled under umbrellas. "Rain all day!" John A. Kasson complained. Horse's hooves splashed in the water, taking elegant carriages toward Capitol Hill. Cleveland borrowed an umbrella from Secretary Fairchild, saying jovially: "We are honest folk, and will return it." A sea of black umbrellas greeted the official party at the Capitol, and commentators speculated on the "Harrison hoo-doo" * that supposedly gave the new president's grandfather a fatal chill on a similar inaugural day.[26]

Cleveland showed no emotion as his successor urged the South to join the protective system. "Mill fires were lighted at the funeral pyre of slavery," he said. "The sectional element has happily been eliminated from the tariff discussion." That was news to the departing Congress. Harrison urged good foreign relations, expanded trade, a free ballot and honest count, and opposition to trusts. He had a crust for civil service reformers. "Honorable party service will certainly not be esteemed by me a disqualification for public office, but it will in no case be allowed to serve as a shield of official negligence, incompetency, or delinquency." The crowd dispersed to shelter and internal warmth, and Harrison drove to his new home. The Clevelands were ready to leave for New York and a comfortable law practice. Many observers thought Cleveland finished, and he did not seem to care. "I am glad I am free," he told a steward. But Mrs. Cleveland made a different remark. "Now, Jerry," she told an aged servant, "I want you to take good care of all the furniture and ornaments in the house, and not let any of them get lost or broken, for I want to find everything just as it is now, when we come back. . . . We are coming back just four years from today." [27]

Changing the guard did not alter Washington's social tone. The Harrisons seemed no more interested in "high society" than the Clevelands. Physically, the White House was a cut below the Indianapolis home. Congress still refused to renovate it, though the staff installed electricity, one of the era's new wonders. The Harrisons feared it would shock them, and sometimes left the lights on until a butler turned the

---

*Mrs. Harrison allegedly later told Mrs. Foraker that her husband took no chances of a chill, and under his formal clothes wore a full sewed chamois suit. She did not say who sewed him into it. (See Foraker, *I Would Live It Again*, 135.)

switch. A staff of ten, including four messengers, ran the establishment, but many physical arrangements were awkward. Men bearing potted plants from the conservatory often crossed in front of visitors, and the fancy Marine Band was so big it deafened guests. Out of public view, domestic infelicity reigned among the staff until Cleveland's chef quit because of overwork and a low budget. That pleased the President's secretary, for power passed to a Negro cook, "whose ability in cooking real wholesome and appetizing United States eats is still recalled." [28]

The President avoided newspapermen, but inevitably became a subject for their pens. He rose early and strolled around the White House gardens or in Lafayette Park, inspected the stables, or looked in shop windows along Pennsylvania Avenue if there was no crowd. He prayed with the family, ate breakfast, then started a long day's work. He bought fancy equippage, but seldom rode. He disliked policemen, and often slipped away from guards. Many a tourist noted him on the streets, usually in a tightly buttoned Prince Albert, with brown kid gloves and furled umbrella. He seldom spoke to passers-by, and they took the hint.

Harrison was a hard-working executive, attentive to detail, and usually acted only with full information. He absorbed information on new styles of penmanship in the departments, development of naval armor plate, filing methods in the Pension Bureau, and personnel procedures. He made the White House a well-regulated office, and kept copies of correspondence, filed letters received, and learned to dictate.[29] Harrison took just pride in this precision, but it was an unfortunate trait. He never learned to delegate authority, and sharpened his temper with overwork. Furthermore, he would not use the helpful excuse of ignorance when dangerous matters arose among politicians, and disliked delays that might have solved problems. He rarely lauded an overworked staff, which remained efficient and loyal. "In his contempt for flattery, he seldom indulged in praise," John W. Foster recalled.[30] And he had a temper. Elijah Halford, his private secretary, once told reporters the secret to greeting Harrison. "When I see him in the morning and he greets me with, 'Halford, how are you today?' I sit down by his desk for a pleasant talk about matters. When he greets me with 'Good Morning, Mr. Halford,' I bolt the door and wait until after lunch for the talk." [31]

There were moments of relaxation and humor. On vacation, he was relaxed and genial with the family, enjoying privacy in the forest's silence, where every prospect pleased and only the newsman was vile. He played with "Baby McKee," threw rocks across the water, over-ate from a picnic basket, and enjoyed all the things common to mortals. "The critics who accused Benjamin Harrison of being 'an iceberg' should have seen him romping with the children of the family," a guest recalled.[32] His friend John New once pictured the President in attitudes politicians found hard to believe. "When he's on a fishing trip, Ben takes his drink of whiskey in the morning, just like anyone else. He chews tobacco from a plug he carries in his hip pocket, spits on his worm for luck, and cusses when the fish gets away." [33] The press compensated for the older Harrisons' dullness with elaborate attention to "Baby McKee." For want of anything significant, doggerel laureates penned odes to the grandson by the seashore:

> What are the wild waves saying,
>   Baby McKee;
> Down by the white sands playing,
>   Baby McKee?
>
> They are saying in a liquid, tender
>   Monotone,
> Why in thunder can't they let a poor
>   Kid alone,
> Down by the white sands playing,
>   Baby McKee.

Popular sheets had a shorter version, illustrating the Baby, Wanamaker's teaching Sunday school, and Vice-President Morton's vintages: [34]

> The baby rules the White House,
> Levi runs the bar,
> Wanny runs the Sunday School,
> And dammit, here we are!

Caroline Harrison, "Carrie" to her husband, had little taste for Washington's glitter and did not play the role of salon hostess, so dear to Mrs. Blaine. A quiet, somewhat nervous and withdrawn woman, she preferred painting chinaware as gifts for friends to formal receptions and state dinners. Like the President, she enjoyed vacations away from politics, and disliked publicity.[35]

A shrewder politician would have sighed often about the burdens that accompanied office, but deception was foreign to Harrison's whole nature. He could not play any role but himself. Stories of his brusqueness were soon legion. He seldom invited anyone to take a chair during an interview, lest they stay too long. An obvious air of impatience covered his conversation. He valued papers more than politicians, and did not cavil at saying so. He once greeted Foraker, watch in hand, motioned to a huge pile of reports, and announced: "I've got all these papers to look after, and I'm going fishing at two o'clock." He snapped the watch case, and waited stonily for the Ohioan to state his business.[36] Acutely conscious of his own station, he seemed oblivious of other men's vanities. "If a man travelled three thousand miles across the country to say something to President Harrison," Senator Hoar noted, "he would find himself broken in upon two minutes after the conversation began with a lecture in which the views in opposition to his were vigorously, and sometimes roughly, set forth."[37] Unlike William Mc-Kinley, he could not seem to listen; unlike Blaine, he could not tactfully confound a man with his own arguments. It was an unhappy trait, and made lasting enemies. One Senator called him "the hitching post;" Platt said he was "a marble statue." Lemuel Quigg, a cog in the Empire State organization, was more earthy, saying Harrison was "a purely intellectual being, and had no bowels."[38]

Blaine was strangely patient in dealing with Harrison. The President gained his respect, and he appreciated the order and neatness he lacked. "He is a man with whom nothing is gained by argument or urgency at the wrong time," he warned Elkins. "I have learned that lesson well. He is a very true and sincere man."[39] The strangest aspect of this chilly man was his reception among the people. He remained a compelling set-speaker, spurning florid rhetoric for appeals to reason that were unusually moving. Like Hayes, he traveled widely, telling people things they did not always wish to hear, drawing large crowds and earning much newspaper praise. But he could not secure his best programs partly because he would not fully delegate management, or meet everyone as an equal.

The train bearing Harrison to his inaugural carried trunks of letters from office-seekers and congressmen. Like Garfield, he faced crowds of place-hunters each morning. Civil service reform seemed not to blunt the edge of need or avarice. Senator Manderson of Nebraska said his own list of office-seekers was "a directory of the state."[40] Harrison and politicians of both parties knew that civil service reform as an organized movement was dead. Cleveland's wavering course and final realistic submission to patronage claims was the coup de grâce. Gadflies like Godkin, Eaton, and Schurz were aging and out of office, repeating stale arguments to dwindling audiences. But the new President sincerely favored reasonable adherance to reform.

His inability to deal gracefully with other powers confounded good intentions, however. He rejected Illinois Senator Farwell's advice to distribute appointments among congressmen by state population. Senator Quay brought the President a long list of deserving Republicans, but politely refused to sustain their claims with anything but his own recommendation. Harrison denounced him for trying to foist hacks on the Administration, and strengthen his state machine at national expense. Quay was not surprised. Like Platt, he only came out of courtesy. Life with Harrison was largely a gesture. The President posted hours for office-seekers and their congressional friends, and stubbornly refused to be rushed. ". . . I have a desire to please our party friends in these selections," he told Senator Cullom. "But I cannot escape the responsibility for the appointments, and must therefore insist upon full information about the persons presented, and upon my ultimate right, in all kindness to everybody, to decide upon what must be done. It would be very gratifying to me if the responsibility were placed upon someone else." [41]

His method raised the whole touchy question of who actually ruled, Executive or Congress? As a former senator, he understood the lordly manner especially common to members of the upper house. Recent history was strewn with the good intentions of presidents who avoided consultation and flattery. Sherman counseled caution; the Administration must have no policy which the party and Congress did not espouse. If Harrison could not gain that support, abandon the idea for the moment. And Senator Hoar knew that senators looked down on presidents. "The most eminent senators . . . would have received as a personal affront a private message from the White House expressing a desire that they should not adopt any course in the discharge of their legislative duties that they did not approve." They visited the President to give advice, not take it.[42]

Talk that Blaine or anyone else dominated him irritated Harrison. "There is no Kitchen Cabinet, and there will not be," he told Elkins. "All my friends shall have equal access and their fair influence." [43] His methods, not the choices, made bad feelings and wounded pride inevitable, and Harrison was not one to smoothe on the balm of Gilead. "I had but two enemies in Maine," Tom Reed once sighed, "one of them Harrison pardoned out of the penitentiary, and the other he appointed collector of Portland." [44] The President's hard answers never softened wrath. "God Almighty's overcoat would not make a vest for Harrison," Elkins said angrily after waiting months for personal recognition.[45] Harrison got little credit when he did relent. "I suppose he treated me about as well in the way of patronage as he did any other senator," Cullom recalled, "but whenever he did anything for me it was done so ungraciously that the concession tended to anger rather than please." [46]

Harrison privately understood this weakness, but could not change his personality. Despite chilly dealings with major state and congressional leaders, he did not make Cleveland's mistake of trying to build a "presidential" faction over their heads. In most instances, he took advice from congressional delegations and trusted advisers. Given time to investigate nominations, he generally chose capable Republicans acceptable to most local leaders, however distasteful to semi-independent powers like Platt and Quay. In this as in so many things, his gruff manner hid a genuine and realistic desire not to weaken national party unity, but his personality and methods often thwarted these constructive intentions.

"Headsman" Clarkson started decapitating Democratic postmasters in a spasm of partisanship that sickened Mugwumps. He had the merit of candor. "By what right does the professional moralist sneer at politics?" he asked in a magazine article.[47] "If [the people] are taught to consider that there is not only public but personal advantage to be gained, they will work, and for working they will be rewarded," he wrote Michener.[48] Following Cleveland's example, he dismissed postmasters for "notorious partisanship" without showing cause, and relished cries of "Go to it, Clarkson!" from fellow spoilsmen. He did not seriously hurt the mail service before leaving office, but attracted bad publicity, and Harrison should have repudiated him.

The endless pension question was also embarrassing. James "Corporal" Tanner of Indiana became Commissioner of Pensions, with a compelling cry: "I will drive a six-mule team through the Treasury," and "God help the surplus!" [49] From March to September, he rampaged through the office, allowing doubtful claims, and even permitting the staff to raise their salaries. Harrison finally accepted a forced resignation with relief. The Dependent Pensions Bill of June, 1890, simplified the whole procedure by recognizing claims from virtually everyone connected with the Union war effort. Eligibility for a pension required only a veteran's physical disability, whatever its origin, a record of 90 days of service, and honorable discharge. The pension list swelled and costs rose, but as Tanner remarked, the surplus disappeared into needy hands. The policy was politically unwise, and invited continuous Democratic attacks against Republican spending. Harrison admitted Tanner was a bad appointment, but stubbornly defended increased pensions. Like most veterans, he thought a good cause could not command too high a reward.*

Office-seekers and politicians consumed Harrison's time and patience, but the public expected larger things. A generation's questions loomed up for settlement: silver, protection, the trusts. Blaine urged a special session. The party could pass the tariff bill in 1889, and counteract adverse propaganda before the congressional elections of 1890, but Harrison feared "it would bring a strain upon us before we get our cables out." He preferred to dispense offices, plan legislation, and give the country a respite from politics. By September, Blaine was resigned to a long regular session, probably stretching into the summer of 1890, fruitful of party warfare and public disgust with a wrangling Congress.[50]

The Republicans had only a slight working margin in the House. "Their majority is very small," the *Nation* noted, "and they can scarcely adopt a measure that will not make it smaller." [51] But a thin margin is often a good ruler; no good party member can leave the fold. The new Speaker would have to rule firmly, with an eye on the whole party program. Three leading Republicans sought the gavel: Joseph G. Cannon of Illinois, William McKinley of Ohio, and Thomas B. Reed of Maine, the most familiar candidate. While Congress gathered in late November, friends organized their causes. Henry Cabot Lodge and a group of New Englanders worked for Reed, while Mark Hanna and Ohio men pushed McKinley. On November 30, the party caucus chose Reed to oppose John G. Carlisle. McKinley lost no friends, and in retrospect could thank his lucky stars for missing the coveted place. As the Administration floor leader and Chairman of the Ways and Means Committee, he avoided the bitterest public battles, and framed a tariff act that made his name a household word. McKinley, now forty-seven, was an able representative of a varied district that helped him understand industrial America. He was the leading champion of protection, making it a national doctrine symbolizing material progress and political stability. Justly famous for personal charm and a legendary ability

---

*Former President Hayes revealed again this attitude on the pension question. "The rich, the well-to-do, and those who depend mainly on them, are strangely blind as a class to what is due—in short, to justice to the Union soldier. Bonds for money lent the government in paper, worth thirty-five to sixty-five cents on the dollar, are paid in gold at their face value, with gold interest at highly remunerative rates. *That* national obligation, I, with you and the rich people, insisted upon because it was just. But the men paid twenty or thirty cents a day for life and uncounted sacrifices are said to make a 'raid on the Treasury' if they ask that promises be kept." (See Hayes to R. M. Hatfield, March 22, 1889, Hayes HML.)

to manage men toward a constructive compromise, he obviously had a bright future. But he lacked the iron will necessary to tame the unruly House, and Reed was a better choice for the Fifty-first Congress. McKinley, for all his genuine talents, was "too amiable, too sweet-tempered, too reluctant to encourage innovation [in rules]," as Cannon said.[52]

The session opened on December 2, amid the traditional blaze of flowers, with visiting ladies in fine dress filling the galleries. Hubbub on the floor subsided as McKinley and Carlisle escorted Reed to the chair after the formal election, his man-mountain shape dwarfing the escort and much of the furniture. As he firmly dropped the gavel for order, representatives of both parties knew they could expect "discipline."

Weak men did not approach Tom Reed, and strong men came gingerly. He literally loomed over the proceedings, filling a chair with nearly 300 pounds, and standing in debate at 6 feet 3 inches, in size 12 shoes. Fond of the table and no stranger to the liquor cabinet, he did not state precise dimensions to the idly curious. "No gentleman ever weighed over two hundred pounds," he once told an inquirer.[53] Mark Twain saw him win twenty-three successive poker pots; and he swore when Fate thwarted him, either in finding a shoe lace or losing on a pet bill. A famous and corrosive wit preceded him in daily combat. Like McKinley, but for different reasons, he enjoyed the rough-and-tumble House, calling the Senate "a place where good Representatives went when they died." His tart tongue was famous. "Everybody enjoys Reed's sarcastic comments and keen wit," McKinley once remarked, "except the fellow who is the subject of the satire." [54]

He came honestly to success. Born in Portland, Maine, in 1839, he worked through school, graduating from Bowdoin with honors in 1860. Restless before repression settled in, he briefly visited the California gold fields, taught school, then practiced law in Maine. From April, 1864, to the war's end, he was a Navy paymaster, but never let it go to his head. "Tell them I kept a grocery on a gunboat down in Louisiana in wartime" he told a man inquiring about his war record.[55] Entering Congress in 1877, he rapidly gained a well-deserved reputation for parliamentary skill. Unable to follow the new America emerging from the War with Spain, he abdicated in 1899, practicing law until his death in 1902.

Reed was a bitter partisan, with no respect for Democrats, and no great regard for humanity in general. A high-pitched Maine drawl made his remarks more infuriating than calm blasphemy. "Oh, the gentleman from Texas is safe," he once told Harley Kilgore. "His district is Democratic, naturally. The common-school system does not prevail there." [56] He practiced for years on calm retorts to toss at hecklers. "Having imbedded that fly in the liquid amber of my remarks," he said of one member who interrupted a speech, "I will proceed." [57] At a public address packed with Democrats, he noted that a candid snapshot of everyone in the Democratic party would show them doing some "mean, low-lived, and contemptible thing." He heard the resulting jeers and hisses with equanimity, then remarked: "There, I told you so." [58] He said Democrats never opened their mouths without subtracting from the sum of human knowledge, but he was most noted for personal sarcasm that embodied less philosophy than hostility. He coined the remark that a statesman is a dead politician. Asked what to say in a colleague's obituary, he answered drily: "Anything but the truth." [59] His words usually bore uncomfortable reminders of basic truths, with "a tiny drop of poison that entered into the victim's veins, and forever destroyed his peace of mind." [60] He took men as they were, and hoped to make them behave within the existing system. "One, with God, is always a majority," he noted presciently, "but many a martyr has been burned at the stake while the votes were being counted." [61]

Any idealism in him had long since evaporated under the hot glare of public life. He typified the materialist, seeing politics as a strife of interests, and security as man's basic drive. Preferring to perfect old systems rather than introduce new ones, he covered fear of change with a humorous pessimism. He accepted representative government, but did not gild its weaknesses. "We have got to do what the resources of the country and, above all, what the sentiment of the country will support and sustain." [62]

From every new proposal, he asked the password of practicality; good things rose from experience, not sudden inspiration. "This human nature of ours is queerly made up," he reminded reformers. "A man cares infinitely more for a little thing which is present than for a great thing afar off, and as he thinks, contingent. A man will be set wild by sand in his shoes and give no thought to the question of a final place of punishment for the wicked." [63] Believing fervently in tariff protection, internal improvements, and business stability, he defended his party even as it moved slowly. ". . . there are so many people in the world who have to be got into line to make any movement practicable that I am always afraid to undertake too large a program, or to try too much at one time," he wrote Wharton Barker. "The Republican party on the whole represents about that desire for progress, and that element of conservatism which seem to me to embody the most practical thing we can take hold of." [64]

Reed harbored futile presidential ambitions. He never rose above sectionalism, and could not hope to unify the GOP in any national campaign. He was a good top sergeant, not a field marshal. Lacking sensitivity to change, he never mastered the arts of compromise or persuasion, and believed in two-party government—Ins and Outs. He thought things were best when Republicans ruled and Democrats watched them, a view he could afford from a safe constituency.

He was well suited, however, to devise new House rules. Democrats thought the opposition liked laws too much. "They must either legislate or talk," Joe Bailey of Texas said, "so we let them talk." [65] Reed returned the favor. "The right of the minority is to draw its salaries, and its function is to make a quorum." [66] That was just the fine and dangerous point, for obstructive Democrats refused to answer the roll call, made a point of no quorum, and demanded adjournment to avoid any hellish Republican action. Speaker Carlisle was willingly helpless before the tactic, but Reed knew his party had to act. Gossip in the cloak rooms said he would force new rules on the House after the holiday recess. He discussed the problem with aides like McKinley and Cannon, and each gathered precedents for the struggle.

It came on January 29, with debate on a contested seat. Democrats cried "No quorum!" and expected the House to adjourn. Reed signaled his lieutenants, who moved to their desks. With a white face but firm hand, he raised the gavel, and directed the clerk to record as present the names he called. A moment of incredulity gave way to pandemonium, as shouting Democrats surged into the aisles. To the charge that he could not count a member present, Reed replied calmly: "The Chair is making a statement of fact that the gentleman from Kentucky is present. Does he deny it?" In days to come, he continued the tactic, until a fellow wit asked: "Say, Tom, did you count a hat?" McKinley tried to soothe members, and Reed got his rules by a strict party vote on February 14.[67] He formed a junta on the Rules Committee. After making strategy, they usually called in Benton McMillan of Tennessee, representing the Democrats. "Mack," Reed would say, idly passing a piece of paper to his genial foe, "here is an outrage McKinley, Cannon and myself are about to perpetrate. You will have time to prepare your screams and usual denunciations." [68] Oblivious to cries of "Tyrant!" and savoring the title "Czar Reed," he held a tight rein, passing a flood of legislation. "The school of Jefferson for the time being has been retired by the people," Representative Cutcheon of Michigan said frankly,

"and the school of Hamilton and Washington is placed in control." [69]
The everlasting tariff question was the first major problem.

William McKinley lived in a cramped hotel suite at the Ebbitt House.
Though he spent much time with an invalid wife, "Little Mac" often
paced the sidewalk smoking a cigar, talking to passers-by, or conferring
with more important people in the lobby. As chairman of Ways and
Means, he must manage a tariff measure, with the satisfaction of knowing it would advertise his influence and talents with the name "Mc-
Kinley bill." He was genial and approachable, with a shrewd sense of
tariff politics. He hoped to counteract the higher rates many powerful
Republicans espoused with a nationally oriented measure, extending
industrial protection's favors to the West and South, and to the farmer
in general. He wanted to avoid Mills' "dark lantern bill," and held hearings that produced a fat volume of testimony from hundreds of witnesses. Night after night, he and fellow committee members like Robert
La Follette went to the Ebbitt, spreading papers on the floor to get a
view of the whole task. Charges that he interviewed only industrialists
favoring protection irritated McKinley, but the bill naturally leaned
toward business interests. As the *Washington Post* noted with some
exaggeration, "not a farmer has turned up." [70]

The discussion and planning produced the usual rate increases,
though few were as important or high as critics making political capital
charged. Wool rates topped those of 1883. Duties on iron and steel
generally equalled those of the Mills bill, and were sometimes less. As
spring arrived, McKinley incorporated several features with both
political and economic overtones. Since most of the revenue surplus
came from sugar importation, the measure put raw sugar on the free
list, and kept a small duty on refined sugar to benefit southern cane
growers and refiners. He included a full agricultural schedule, to close
the home market for truck produce, cereals, and meats imported from
Canada and Mexico. Two items produced sharp debate. To compensate
domestic sugar growers, the Treasury would pay a bounty of two cents
a pound on home production from July 1, 1891 to July 1, 1905. The
canning industry imported large quantities of tin plate, and McKinley
hoped to foster a new American industry by raising that duty above
two cents a pound until 1896. The bill reduced tobacco taxes, and
fulfilled the party's pledge to eliminate the surplus and maintain protection.

The bill's merits vanished in a flood of abuse and misrepresentation
even before McKinley reported the measure on April 16. The wisdom of

earlier suggestions for an extra session was now clear. The Senate was deadlocked over trust legislation, free silver, and an election law. The longer the struggle persisted, the more likely rates were to rise. Exhaustion and frustration would compel Republicans to pass a law they did not like, suitable for Democratic target practice in the fall elections. Reed favored throttling debate since Democrats wanted to stall proceedings, but former President Cleveland gave the best political advice. Democrats should let the bill pass, avoid stating their own views, and talk in generalities about trusts, prices, and reform.[71] Opponents were already allying the farmer against McKinley's bill. The agricultural schedules, they argued, were useless. It was like the boy who said: "Jim, if you will give me your big red apple, I will show you my sore toe." [72] The opposition press steadily drummed the idea that tariff protection would repay those who gave "fat" for Harrison in 1888. "I should not suppose that such a fiction was seriously believed anywhere." Connecticut's Senator Platt insisted vainly.[73]

If increasing rates and the volume of criticism unnerved McKinley, they outraged Blaine. He was having a good time in his old office. ". . . how Mr. Blaine enjoys the return to the State Department," his wife wrote.[74] Despite a little frost in his beard and growing goutiness, the charming Blaine kept staff and callers busy checking out ideas and restraining his eagerness. He even developed a mild crush on Mrs. Henry Cabot Lodge, writing poems on calling cards when he missed her: [75]

> My dear lady of Boston,
> I have once more lost on—
> The hope of a fair afternoon!
> I shall wait then in sorrow,
> For the brighter tomorrow
> Which cannot for me come too soon!

Representative Lodge and Mrs. Blaine ignored the harmless flirtation of their respective mates, but President Harrison still suspected Blaine's political ambitions, and complained that he did most of the work which newspapers credited to Blaine. Mrs. Blaine kept chilly diplomatic relations with the White House, noting drily: "The duties [of the State Department] are interesting, but Mr. Harrison is of such a nature, you do not feel yourself at all at liberty to enjoy yourself." [76]

Both Harrison and Blaine wanted some lower tariff rates in McKinley's bill. In 1888, Harrison promised to work for international trade under the protective system, especially south of the Mexican border. Both he and Blaine avoided serious reciprocity discussions with

Canada, since that involved anti-English feeling, with little prospect
for success. They also knew that outraged European countries might
retaliate with their own tariffs. But how to avoid an intra-party fight
over Blaine's cherished reciprocity idea? He wanted the House to lead,
and let him escape sensitive politicians. At McKinley's invitation, he
explained the plan to Ways and Means Committee members on February 10. Free sugar would give Latin American producers open access
to a lucrative American market without any corresponding favors for
exports south. Why not require reciprocity from these countries on
some goods? This would begin gradual, selected downward revision
within the protective system, increasing overseas markets and decreas-
ing political dangers. Blaine's usual animation enlivened the statistics
in his remarks. McKinley listened attentively and asked many questions. He was intrigued, but colleagues were silent. They gave Blaine a
hard time, and his nervousness did not help the explanation. It seemed
so sensible and modest a beginning; he could not understand their
torpor. But as ultra-protectionists began to chant, reciprocity was "the
thin edge of tariff reform."

Blaine failed, and walked slowly downstairs, despairing of understanding. Congressmen were so obtuse. On April 10, he wrote McKinley
an open letter protesting against taking hides from the free list. Manufacturers imported large quantities from South America; the party
would gain fewer votes from cattlemen than from people who bought
shoes. "Such movements as this for protection will protect the Republican party into a speedy retirement." [77] McKinley consented, and hides
remained free. Like Blaine, he had second thoughts about protection,
and wanted overseas markets for America's steadily increasing production of both industrial and agricultural products.

Reciprocity, as Blaine said, was an excellent beginning for flexible
downward revision, expandable as events required. It would appeal to
farmers, and prove Republican claims of framing a far-sighted measure.
Blaine was entertaining a new Pan-American Congress. A reciprocity
clause in the new tariff bill at this highly symbolic moment might lay
the groundwork for future commerce. As Blaine's circle noted, "Mr.
McKinley [was] one of the earliest converts to reciprocity." And he
"frequently consulted" John Watson Foster and other experts in the
State Department, asking sharp questions about foreign trade and
taking away volumes of statistics.[78]

But for now, he could not break resistance, and on April 16, reported
the bill without a reciprocity clause. Blaine was busy, but would return
to battle with the Senate. House debate started on May 7, and ended
on May 21, with the measure's passage by a strict party vote of 164-

142. Unanimity among both parties was noticeable. Reed ignored lurid charges of gagging the House. They had other business to transact, like Representative Lodge's election law. Let the Democrats howl.

Harrison's discussion of the tariff in 1888 did not excite southerners as much as frequent allusions to "a free ballot," which forecast Republican interest in another effort to help the Negro. "The Republican party has always stood for election reforms," Harrison told audiences. "No measure tending to secure the ballot box against fraud has ever been opposed by its representatives." [79] He wanted a federal election law to lessen corruption everywhere. ". . . I have treated the question as a national, and not a sectional one, for these vile southern methods are spreading their contagion, like the yellow fever, into our northern states. . . ." he wrote Reid. "I would not be willing myself to purchase the presidency by a compact of silence upon this question." [80] He emphasized the subject in the inaugural address, and in the annual message of December, 1889.

Harrison was impatient with the dreams of slow material uplift around internal improvements and patronage. His precise nature rebelled at open southern defiance of the Constitution in suppressing and coercing Negro voters. The hope of uniting tariff protection and a free ballot to improve southern Republicanism combined with disgust at these methods to drive him and many influential Republicans to formulation of new election laws. Violence at the polls in 1888 and 1889 stiffened their resolve. They also worried at a sudden upsurge of national interest in a nostalgic view of an "Old South," where every home had magnolias, and slaves sang happily in the fields. Jefferson Davis was becoming a twilight hero. Stephen Foster's songs invaded the North. Elaborate conclaves reminded southern veterans of a "Lost Cause."

Political reality naturally joined this worrisome fear of a South revived in the old pattern with added political power. Republicans knew that Negro ballots would add enough southern House seats to end their minority status, especially if industrialism and the appeals of tariff protection increased. Reed, as usual, was blunt. "Why should they [Democrats] poll their ignorance, and we not poll ours?" [81] Northern Democrats, like Governor Russell of Massachusetts, called GOP protestations about ballot frauds "the wail of bitter disappointment." [82] But cries from lonely Republican outposts in the South stirred northern brethren. "To be a Republican in active politics in the South is to be a foolish martyr," a Georgian wrote Sherman.[83]

In December, 1889, Senators Hoar of Massachusetts and Spooner of

Wisconsin canvassed colleagues, and drafted an elections bill which they introduced in April. But they passed leadership on it to the House, where Henry Cabot Lodge wished to originate the measure from his special committee on elections.[84] He seemed a strange leader for such a crusade, with his social connections and Puritan lineage. "His getting on in life is all the more creditable to him because he has labored under the handicap of not having been a rail-splitter, canal boy, tanner or merry ploughman," a newsman wrote.[85] Thin but voluminous writings earned him the title "Scholar in Politics," but Chauncey Depew said his mind, like New England's soil, was intrinsically barren but highly cultivated. Lodge stood between the younger generation who wanted to tie Negro rights to industrial nationalism, and older men who still responded to wartime rhetoric. He was also a shrewd politician, not overlooking party gain from southern votes, and said he did not care if the law put a federal soldier at every polling place in his own district.

Lodge avoided any serious prospect of military rule in the bill, relying on legal remedies rather than penalties or federal force. When 100 registered voters in a city or district of 20,000 or more petitioned the federal circuit court, a bipartisan board would canvass alleged irregularities. The board's majority decision in disputed contests certified a House candidate, and if he appealed, the circuit court decided. Other provisions touched jury selection, and ultimate federal enforcement. The House passed the measure on July 2, after heated debate. Southerners understood the implications: If the federal government could take this step, with aroused public support, it might enforce the Fifteenth Amendment and close loopholes in state voting laws.

Lodge received many illiterate threatening letters, and much of the press condemned the "Force Bill." "The South stood one reconstruction," a southern paper said angrily. "It remains to be seen whether it will meekly submit to another." [86] Bayard and Gorman threatened an endless filibuster, talking windily of separated powers under the Constitution. Reaction among northern Negroes was generally favorable, but prosperous southern Negroes wanted to be left alone. Southern congressmen and officials said whites would have a blood bath to avoid Negro domination. "I will not vote to make a negro my ruler. . . ." a southerner said flatly. "I was a white man before I was a Republican." [87]

More than the South opposed the bill. City machine bosses did not want federal inspectors in their wards. In the West, holders of pocket boroughs like Nevada's Senator Stewart, objected for similar reasons. The Farmers' Alliance thought it would strengthen the Republicans, and were uncertain about the color question. City Mugwumps suspected popular suffrage, and made a strange alliance with bosses and conservative labor leaders like Terence Powderly, who feared any possible use of troops. Southerners threatened to boycott northern goods, and some of the business community urged the bill's sponsors to go slow. That made Senator Hoar shake with rage. ". . . rather than have constitutional government overthrown and be governed by minorities for the sake of protecting their southern investments, the people of Massachusetts would prefer to have their factories burned and live on codfish and 50 cents a day." [88]

These strains mingled with the voices of men who never quite abandoned the Negro. "A Republican can believe in tariff reduction or even free trade and yet properly adhere to the party," William E. Chandler wrote Reed. "But he cannot fail to advocate the Fifteenth Amendment and all proper laws to supplement it and to enforce it and yet be a Republican. His only proper place is with the Negro-baiting, Republican-killing Democracy." [89] The measure appealed to "the conscientious Republican element." [90] As usual, Senator Sherman combined realism and idealism in answering an opponent: [91]

> I appreciate as fully as you do the importance of maintaining and encouraging the good will, harmony and reciprocity now existing between the North and the South, and dislike to vote for any measure that may, in the opinion of men like yourself, tend to renew sectional excitement and controversy. But what can we do? Here it is alleged and apparently admitted that more than a million of lawful voters are substantially disfranchised by the Democratic party where their votes would change the result; that not only are they denied political rights, but the political power awarded to them is used against them; that in this way gross inequality of representation in Congress is made in favor of the South, so that the vote of one Democrat in the South is equal to two or three Republicans in the North. Now is it strange that we should feel this is an injustice that ought not to be inflicted by the South or tolerated by the North; that we ought if possible to secure a free and fair election of members of Congress, so that all citizens may have an equal vote, and have their votes counted?

Filibustering stalled the Senate, and it was foolish to think there would be cloture. Republicans like Edmunds, who saw the constitution through a keyhole, refused to change procedure for any measure. Vice-President Morton would not bend the rules of recognition, even to please Harrison and party leaders. The tariff bill foundered, and Senator Quay led the way out of the confusion. After heated caucus debates, he persuaded the Senate to pass over the measure until the short session in December. Spooner condemned "the almighty dollar" that put tariffs above civil rights, but Hoar secured pledges from all

Republican senators but one to consider the bill later.[92] "It will probably give us a tariff bill," Senator O. H. Platt said, "but acquired at what a sacrifice!" [93]

Nevada's silver-haired silverite, William M. Stewart, took time from analyzing an alleged international gold conspiracy against silver to hatch one of his own. Southern family ties fortified his dislike of federal interference in state affairs, and he easily adopted an air of vacuous good intentions. "The best remedy for the [Negro] question is time, . . ." And he conjured up visions of doomsday. "Whenever the federal government obtains control of state elections, as contemplated by the bill, the alternative is presented of monarchy or revolution." [94] He kept western senators available, and watched the calendar. On January 5, 1891, before a friendly presiding officer, Stewart moved to displace the Lodge bill for a free coinage measure. The silver Republicans sustained him, and at month's end, western senators defeated a final attempt to save the bill.

Spooner was outraged. "I am too angry to write. . . . We are fallen upon bad times for the party. The Confederacy and the western mining camps are in legislative supremacy. Think of it—Nevada, barely a respectable county, furnished two senators to betray the Republican party and the rights of citizenship for silver. . . . We are punished for making too easy the pathway of rotten boroughs into the Union." [95] Lodge was equally angry, and Harrison simply abandoned the struggle, but one of Sherman's correspondents saw the debacle's real significance. "This is but another sign that *the inevitable is coming,* and that the people are more interested in the money matters than in election bills." [96]

It was sad but true, and the Republican party's last great effort to insure Negro voting passed into history. The silverites defeated the measure, sacrificing national good to the white metal.* The Lodge measure was a sincere effort for a free ballot. It was tinged with politics, but non-partisan bills are very rare. Negro votes would help Republicans, but would also aid Negroes caught in the closing vise of segregation. The measure was national, and might have improved voting habits everywhere. Its provisions threatened local authority only when it was corrupt. The debates and narrow defeat further illustrated fundamental differences between Republicans and Demo-

---

*This point merits emphasis, since many historians criticize the whole Republican party for first introducing a sham measure, then for defeating it. (See Meier, *Negro Thought,* 22; Woodward, *Origins of the New South,* 255 and 322.) It is also worth noting that in 1894, the Cleveland Administration passed a blanket act repealing all existing federal laws dealing with election supervision.

crats in the continuing quarrel over federalism. And it pained men of good will to recall how close they came to victory.

The Senate had not heard the last from silver advocates. Before Congress assembled, Michener and other party leaders warned of rising sentiment for inflation among farmers in the Plains states, and nearly everyone in the Rocky Mountain area. Republicans must meet the challenge or "they will break our party in 1890." [97] Silver's champions held the balance of power in the upper house, and would scuttle any measure to prove their point. Silverites talked endlessly about eastern plutocracy but no group in American history ever benefitted more from congressional over-representation, except farmers. Western senators from half a dozen states whose populations did not equal one large eastern city gave the world lessons in the power of pocket boroughs in fights for special legislation. Nevada's William M. Stewart, and Colorado's Henry M. Teller led a van of men with tenure and secure seats. Their power increased when the "Omnibus States" of North and South Dakota, Montana, and Washington entered the Union in 1889, followed by Idaho and Wyoming in 1890. Harrison supported federal development of western territories, and early admission of states, but finally remarked: "I wish this free coinage of senators would stop." [98]

Opponents too easily labeled the silver bloc "Bonanza Kings," bent solely on raising the price of metal they mined. In the 1870's, silver mining was confined largely to Nevada and Colorado, but by 1890, subsidiary discoveries all over the West made it that section's "major crop," somewhat comparable to cotton in the South. Increased production lowered its price, and descending agricultural income began to incline indebted farmers to silver inflation. Reed dismissed the talk as transitory, but Stewart promised him otherwise. "Speaker Reed is mistaken; the excitement of the West is not temporary. It will last as long as contraction continues, and the people will have relief or know the reason why." [99] Times were not too hard, but restless farmers might easily drift to silver inflation in a real depression. As the nation moved into industrial urbanization, agrarians resented minority status on the edge of progress. In that broad sense, the rising demand to "do something for silver" reflected a larger constituency than mine owners.

There was no easy political solution. The Bland-Allison Act had not materially eased the currency problem, and politicians hesitated to enact even larger subsidies. The world's great powers remained firmly based on gold, and a series of international conferences did not secure bimetallism. No major nation would support silver, and all only wanted to give the subject a first-class funeral with elaborate public display. Most silverites spurned international negotiations, and organized propaganda agencies and held national conventions to promote unilateral action by the mid-1880's. A thin but vocal network of local organizations culminated in agencies like the National Bimetallic Coinage Association, with headquarters in Washington and easy access to Capitol Hill. Newspapers, pamphlets, speakers, preached the white metal's virtues. Stewart feared tariff protection would override silver in national politics, and in 1888 urged friends to "build fires in the rear." To underscore their point, silverites convened in St. Louis before Congress met in 1889, loudly threatening to kill other legislation unless they got free coinage. Stewart urged Harrison to purchase the maximum amount of silver under the Bland-Allison Act, while Congress wrote a new law. Nevada's Francis Newlands soon warned the President that "agitation on this subject will be directed in the congressional elections against every man who fails to support the bimetallic principle." As if to anticipate the flood, in 1888 the Treasury finished a new vault 89 feet long, 51 feet wide, and nearly 12 feet high.[100]

Westerners thought Harrison would sign a free silver bill. But while the President favored bimetallism, he warned Congress against free coinage in the annual message of December, 1889. In January, he frankly told westerners he opposed an "unsound" measure. Like Platt, they were misinformed about his earlier intentions.[101] He favored Secretary Windom's plan to purchase all American silver at its market price with paper currency, redeemable in silver at the same rate. If Congress contrived a better variation, he would consider it with his usual fairness.

By spring, all hopes of a short session disappeared into legislative wheels that ground over the tariff, free silver, election bills, and antitrust measures. Congressional tempers mounted, and public patience grew thin. Silver was the key; no other law could pass the Senate before its adherants were satisfied. Opinion was hard to judge. Opponents argued against another subsidy, condemning "Bonanza Kings" who might speculate on silver's price at the Treasury's expense. The business community seemed uncertain, wishing, like politicians, to avoid the problem's deeper implications, but willing to accept a workable amount of new currency backed by gold. Lodge and Senator Orville Platt spoke for moderate Republicans in noting that free coinage would pass both houses, if its adherants knew that Harrison would not use the veto. The question was silver or paper, and Republicans should get credit for the best solution.[102] To emphasize their point, silver senators passed a free coinage measure on June 17, and continued to delay the tariff. A month later, Reed enforced discipline, and McKinley used persuasion to beat the measure in the House with a strict party vote.

In the Senate, powerful men attended quiet conferences, leaving the floor to those who liked debate. Sherman, Allison, Aldrich, Orville Platt, all preferred reason and persuasion. Silverites kept the Finance Committee from reporting a tariff measure until June 18, after the free coinage bill passed the Senate. Sherman undertook a compromise, re-calling Mark Hanna's report of business opinion. "Pass the McKinley tariff bill and a conservative silver bill and we are all right this fall." [103] The silverites were more candid; they would attach a rider to the tariff, and the majority could have both or neither.

The resulting Sherman Act required the Treasury to buy 4,500,000 ounces of silver a month—the estimated American production—at market value. Treasury notes issued in payment were redeemable "in coin," and the Bland-Allison Act was repealed. Since the plan dealt in ounces, the Treasury paid less subsidy if the market price fell. The law did not threaten the gold standard for the moment, but laid up future trouble with the word "coin." The Treasury Notes became the ninth form of circulating United States currency. Reaction was mixed. Most silverites expected to compromise, and as Senator Teller said, would take "the next best thing" to free coinage. When the news reached Stewart, he said forcefully: "Good! and good will be the verdict of the country." [104]

Most observers were tired enough to accept any apparently reasonable law. Few expected the "Janus Faced" compromise to last. "Of course, the settlement is only provisional," Dana's *Sun* insisted. "The silver issue is scotched, not killed." [105] In the welter of pressure and need for haste, it was the best law possible. But like all predecessors, it only postponed the evil day when, as President Hayes had predicted, all disaffected elements would rally to silver in a final battle to determine who ruled America. In the meantime, exhausted congressmen still had to survive a tariff debate and an antitrust crusade before they rested.

Rutherford B. Hayes enjoyed retirement in Fremont, and spent most days reading or talking with old friends like William Henry Smith. Though avoiding public controversy, he did not "rust" in idleness, and served as a trustee for several educational and philanthropic institutions. If anything, age made him more radical, and he committed many heresies to his diary and private conversations. In the Christmas season of 1887, he discussed the trust problem with Smith, and condemned unregulated big business. "The governmental policy should be to prevent accumulation of vast fortunes, and monopolies . . . should be held firmly in the grip of the people. . . . Shall the will of monopolies take the place of the government of the people?" [106] He could not answer the rhetorical question, but the words reflected a growing uneasiness among Americans. Popular weeklies, and many newspapers, ran an increasing number of articles on the "trust problem," arguing that business served a larger social body than shareholders.

It was not a new issue. Regulatory legislation virtually followed the rails that now unified markets. Hostility and fear toward "natural monopolies" like railroads, canals, roads, and utilities spilled easily into the arena of private business. Technology, larger investments and profits, new products, and a better informed public combined to make business regulation a major political problem. An era and people concerned with order, efficiency and growth naturally liked what most corporations produced. Nostalgia for small businessmen overlooked their high prices, uncertain deliveries, and narrow range of stock, but a people believing that individual effort created the industrial system was bound to dislike its end product, an impersonal if efficient corporation. And teachers, ministers, and lawyers stressed the theme of declining individualism and eroding social morality.[107]

The usual desire to explain shortcomings with a conspiracy entered the debate. The corner grocer in Lawrence, Kansas, or Chicopee Falls, Massachusetts, or southside Chicago, monopolized his immediate market, but was at least a person. And he could always blame prices on distant producers and distributers. His shrug of the shoulders or calm explanation was more eloquent than miles of statistics and tons of documents. No significant number of Americans ever believed in equality, but paid homage to *equal opportunity* in the marketplace. It bewildered many that competition ended in trusts and a system that prized stability over competition outside its own established rules. By 1890, most Americans blamed impersonal corporations for high prices, closed markets, and ruined competitors, but they did not wish to destroy efficient or productive bigness, seeking instead to retain its economic advantages while avoiding social excesses.[108]

The sudden increase in combinations during the 1880's upset many people, especially since they controlled so many products in daily living. In the confused city markets now dominating national business, gas, coal, ice, sugar, whiskey, and a host of other personal items seemed monopolized. By 1890, thirteen states regulated combinations. Both

Presidents Cleveland and Harrison condemned them. Each session of Congress produced bills, petitions, and talk aimed at regulating trusts and restoring opportunities for personal initiative. These protests came most forcefully from agrarians, who resented monopolistic control of warehouses, grain elevators, and processing systems, as well as transportation and manufacturing agencies. Trustification was a world-wide phenomenon, but took on moralistic overtones in America because it challenged so many basic social assumptions.[109]

Not everyone wanted an antitrust crusade. Many businessmen obviously accepted the dictum that "where combination was possible, competition was impossible." Some organized labor, in the pangs of slow and uncertain growth, also suspected anti-monopoly laws that might apply to unions. Many leaders like Samuel Gompers frankly wished to share at the businessman's pie counter, and saw more wages and better working conditions in standardized production than in a chaos of small units. They would accept trusts if owners recognized the closed shop.[110] Convenient and moving rhetoric covered uncertainties with moralism instead of analysis. "Like the cat, they walk in quest of prey with velvet feet," James B. Weaver told Populist friends, "and like the assassin, they lie in wait and spring upon you without warning. The corporations never make public their purpose. They hold no public meetings. Their plans are laid in the counting room, around the lunch table, and in the secret meetings of their directors away from the public." [111]

How to regulate business without threatening productivity? Genuine lack of legal knowledge, historic precedent, and economic information hampered plans that avoided mere negativism. Some politicians and lawyers, like Senator Spooner, doubted Congress could regulate anything but commerce. Control of production was a state and local matter. That, of course, proved impossible; if states passed stringent laws, corporations simply moved headquarters to more lenient states.[112] But by Harrison's inauguration, the issue was bipartisan, reflecting in traditional manner a consensus for action. The departing Cleveland put a shot in the target, and a month after taking office, Harrison sat through a scorching sermon on the duties of rich and poor from the Episcopal Bishop of New York as part of the Constitutional Centennial.

When Congress convened that winter, antitrust bills filled the hoppers, with "plenty more in the brains of statesmen seeking popularity." [113] Sherman offered his own first draft to the upper house on December 4, 1889. After he wrangled with Edmunds over proper assignment, the measure passed through the Judiciary Committee and under many pencils before facing debate. Sherman criticized the Judiciary Committee's substitute, but it was generally clear. The Ohioan had the satisfaction of gaining credit for its passage. The final bill declared illegal every "contract, combination in the form of trust or otherwise, or conspiracy, in restraint of trade or commerce. . . ." and prescribed punishment. It empowered federal courts and district attorneys to institute suits, and awarded triple damages to successful plaintiffs. Sherman defended its verbal generality. "All we, as lawmakers, can do is declare general principles." He vigorously denied the law was antibusiness: [114]

> The bill does not seek to cripple combinations of capital and labor, the formation of partnerships or of corporations, but only to prevent and control combinations made with a view to prevent competition, or for the restraint of trade, or to increase the profits of the producers at the cost of the consumer. It is the unlawful combination, tested by the rules of common law and human experience, that is aimed at by this bill, and not the lawful and useful combination.

He exempted labor from the law. ". . . combinations of workingmen to promote their interests, promote their welfare, and to increase their pay, if you please, to get their fair share in the division of production, are not affected in the slightest degree, nor can they be included in the words or intent of the bill." Nearly every speaker echoed these views.[115]

Harrison signed the measure on June 26, after full congressional debate and newspaper coverage. It was hard to see realistically how the measure could be more severe. Businessmen accepted the inevitable; some welcomed regulation and a definition of government attitude. "A very severe bill," the *Wall Street Journal* noted.[116] The law was not a sham, and the Republican party intended its enforcement. The problem's complexity defied exact statutory definition, but time would create precedent for a middle way. The act illustrated quick American response to industrial combination. After barely a generation of development, the national government regulated railroads and combinations, something no other industrial power attempted.* In 1890, the law went as far as most people desired.

---

*Subsequent failure to enforce the act rigorously during the 1890's should not detract from its framers' honest intentions. Other events soon swept aside public interest in a national antitrust crusade. No body of precedent, and more important, no group of trained and aggressive lawyers quickly developed to interpret the act. The Justice Department was handicapped by small staff and low budgets. Both Presidents Cleveland and McKinley became too preoccupied with other matters to initiate any sweeping attack, but the latter promised to pursue the subject during a second term if re-elected in 1900. It remains fashionable in texts and general accounts to dismiss the law as "ceremonial," ignoring the fact that all laws are ceremonial in symbolizing a public urge to do something tangible about a problem.

Like the ICC Act of 1887, the Sherman Law justly redounded to
Republican political credit. GOP leaders took the initiative, framed an
honest and widely accepted measure, and publicized their action. They
needed that publicity, for the session seemed stalled in an unusually
hot summer, with Congressional elections fast approaching. The Senate
faced one more hurdle, the tariff bill.

Tariff struggles were hardly new to ranking senators, but every
revenue measure taxed the patience and parliamentary skill of leaders
in both parties. Like the silver question, the tariff was a magic rock
that gushed oratory and dissension for every man who struck it. "The
contest over a revision of the tariff brings to light a selfish strife which
is not far from disgusting," Spooner said wearily before McKinley's bill
came to the upper house.[117] It arrived on May 23, and went to the
imperious Senate Finance Committee, where Vermont's venerable
Justin Smith Morrill occupied the chair. Some of the nation's landmark
legislation bore his name, and he was a fierce protectionist; but Morrill
was eighty years old, and passed formal management to Allison. The
experienced and tactful Iowan had helped to frame the "Senate Substitute" that scuttled the Mills bill, but now asked the chairman to let
Rhode Island's Nelson W. Aldrich take the McKinley bill in hand. Both
men feared the political impact of rising schedules and hoped to lower
many rates, though the upper house was usually more protectionist
than its counterpart across the Capitol.

Aldrich had only entered the Senate in 1881, but was already a ranking member of its inner circle, and a formidable expert on revenue
measures. He was self-made, successful in business and politics. He
mixed the two for profit, but genuinely believed the protective system
aided his working-class constituents. Suave, elegant in attire and
manners, Aldrich avoided "the farce of mixing in the mock debates." [118]
He liked to pay debts with terrapin suppers and make deals while sail-
ing. Though enemies said he represented ruthless business, Aldrich
started life with the desire to write, had artistic tastes, and carefully
repressed a hidden strain of melancholy that threatened his equanimity.
He was cool but soft, demanding but genial. "Most people don't know
what they want," he remarked often, proposing to explain their best
interests, and almost always winning.[119]

His first major problem was a fellow Republican, for Secretary Blaine
insisted on explaining reciprocity to the skeptical Finance Committee.
He arrived in June, hat in hand, and properly calm. The Senators endured his discussion, but coolly declined to open the subject very
much. They would consider some kind of reciprocity, but would not

let the President usurp their prerogatives. Blaine rose to go, and knocked his silk hat off the table. By design or accident, he picked it up in pieces, and Washington soon buzzed that he "smashed his hat on the McKinley bill." In leaving, he warned: "Pass this bill, and in 1892 there will not be a man in all the party so beggared as to accept your nomination for the presidency." [120]

Blaine was not out of ammunition. His usual charm fortified McKinley's own growing desire for reciprocity. The smooth Ohioan visited elders in Senate corridors with calm explanations and appeals to political reason. Even Harrison stooped enough to entertain doubtful brethren at the punch bowl.[121] On June 19, Harrison sent the Senate a special message, with Blaine's recommendations, and on the same day Senator Eugene Hale of Maine introduced a draft reciprocity clause from Blaine's pen. It was a wide-ranging proposal, allowing the President to open Latin American markets for a variety of American machinery, raw materials, and food products in return for tariff concessions.

Blaine again revealed his perception of world trends, and an ability to grasp changing opportunities. Like McKinley, he knew the partisan press was already discussing higher prices allegedly to follow a new tariff. Reciprocity thus fitted economic and political reality. It would open new markets, and dull the notion that protection worked only for a select few. He genuinely believed America must help develop economic unity and political stability in the hemisphere, to everyone's advantage. However valid, his arguments fell before stern opposition from powerful orthodox protectionists. Men like Morrill and Orville Platt had thwarted presidential efforts to negotiate reciprocity treaties for a decade. ". . . there is no telling, if we should enter upon such a policy, where it would end," Platt insisted.[122] Tom Reed condemned dealing with "a lot of dagoes," and snorted that reciprocity was "commerce on paper." It was better to build a wall of fire around the home market.[123]

Blaine patiently explained that he was not abandoning protection. Indeed, reciprocity might save it. Individual arrangements in an expanding system would gradually develop new markets. "We are a very rich nation," he wrote in an open letter to the mayor of Augusta, "but not rich enough to trade on this unequal basis." [124] Another open letter explained the source of Democratic opposition. "They know and feel that with a system of reciprocity established and growing, their policy of free trade receives a serious blow. . . . The enactment of reciprocity is the safeguard of protection. The defeat of reciprocity is the opportunity of free trade." [125] And he calmed those who feared that a struggle for markets meant international quarrels. "Our great demand now is expansion," he told an enthusiastic audience in Maine. "I mean expansion of trade with countries where we can find profitable exchanges. We are not seeking annexation of territory." [126]

Blaine argued that the tariff bill would not "open a market for another bushel of wheat or another barrel of pork." But agrarian critics of protection thought there was no demand for foodstuffs in Latin America, which exported them to Europe. Senator George G. Vest of Missouri, famous largely for his soliloquoy "Dog as Man's Best Friend," roared. "All this talk of reciprocity and pan-American conventions and brass bands and terrapin and champagne is the merest froth and rot." [127] Blaine used his personal appeal well, however, and by late summer a rising chorus demanded reciprocity. "It captivates the businessman with the appearance of a shrewd trade in it," a friend wrote Sherman. "It appears to employ the duties not merely as a means of protection, but [as] a means of bargain for the extension of our own trade." [128] A western representative admitted the attraction of both reciprocity and Blaine. "Blaine's plan has run like a prairie fire all over my district." [129]

This was the kind of diplomacy most Americans liked, without bargaining and with the upper hand. ". . . there will be a reciprocity section of some kind," an Ohioan predicted.[130] The final version did not please Blaine, but at least it was a beginning. Opponents called it "reciprocity with a club," for it empowered the President to institute regular tariff duties on certain Latin American goods if those countries did not lower rates on American imports. Blaine's hope of including machinery, textiles, and leather goods died aborning. Congressional fear of executive agreements, and protectionist suspicion were the main obstacles to Blaine's constructive and farsighted plan.

The Senate opened the tariff debate on July 7, and the measure's nearly 500 amendments promised an endless struggle. Complications with free silver and the Lodge bill made Aldrich predict a working Christmas. The windy silverites, filling pages with dull speeches on the gold conspiracy and the virtues of currency inflation, were the chief problem. Their numbers were "a very decided advantage in tariff legislation," when it came to bargaining for silver.[131] Not that they loved protection less, but the cause of the white metal more. Few men praised the tariff more than Stewart, eager for high rates on wool, hides, ore, and lumber. But as he warned, "there will be no tariff legislation this session unless a silver bill is passed." [132]

Aldrich considered invoking cloture, but it was impossible when he could not keep a quorum, and men like Edmunds opposed changing the sacred rules of free debate. Aldrich fell ill, no doubt of disgust, and Allison managed the bill, while rates climbed amid rolling logs. The hot summer wore on as the Senate endured discourses on nails, sulphur, and alcohol used in the arts. The House was not much more comfortable. Reed placidly surveyed its disorder, but donned a cotton shirt with a waist sash, resembling "an honest rutabaga wound in a black ribbon." Even the impeccable McKinley shed his waistcoat and talked to reporters with thumbs in galluses, "a veritable Napoleon in undress." In an effort to cool off, Democratic members resorted to special lemonade, famous for rye content. Several Republicans crossed party lines to sing its praises.

The fruitless debate angered businessmen, irritated the public, and played into Democratic hands. "Mills continue to fail and the Senate does about as much in a week as a set of men in business would do in half an hour," a correspondent angrily warned Sherman. "You are killing the Republican party as fast as you can." [133] Another was unusually candid. "Just look at the Senate, please. There it sits, day after day, like a great big nincompoop or a knot on a log, unable to move or do anything." [134]

The knot finally loosened in September, and a blue-ribbon conference committee settled details between the two versions. Inevitably, Sherman was involved, to his distaste. "I have been hard at work for a week or more on this tariff conference committee," he wrote William Henry Smith: [135]

> I trust I will not live long enough to have any connection with another. While I believe thoroughly in the doctrine of protection to American industry, I must confess the application of it to a particular measure is accompanied with so much selfishness and greed that it always sickens me of the task, and derogates from the great benefit of the public policy of such laws.

Harrison signed the bill on October 1, and weary congressmen dispersed to campaign. The law satisfied most Republicans, including the silverites, but the Democrats, already publicizing each minor upward revision, predicted a GOP debacle. The cry of "high tariff means high prices" was gaining ground, especially when allied to free spending during the "Billion-Dollar Congress."

No American tariff ever suffered such misrepresentation as the McKinley Act. Most upward revisions were slight and selective. It solved the surplus revenue problem with free sugar—a household commodity —and lower excise taxes. But the free sugar provision did not take effect before the elections. The law came during industrial expansion that reflected Republican interest in a business-labor constituency. Four features marked the outer limits of protection: a bounty for domestic sugar, protection to foster an infant tin industry, a full agricultural schedule, and reciprocity. Whatever its merits or demerits, the law was a political blunder. Few tariff schedules truly deserved increase, and the Republicans should merely have fulfilled their 1888 pledges to reduce the surplus and stabilize rates. Politics, however, dictated otherwise, as McKinley freely admitted in explaining the bill's faults.

Despite its weakness, the tariff reciprocity adopted was a momentous event.* In the largest sense, the movement to formal reciprocity grew from a generation's halting efforts to enter world markets. No man contributed more to that ideal than James G. Blaine, coming to the position after practical observation and with acute political intuition. A growing body of important Republicans like McKinley and Harrison were determined to expand this reciprocity system. They saw that America's future must be global, resting on commercial supremacy. They wanted commerce to aid American internal production and external safety, and optimistically believed that material progress brought political stability, with constructive American dominance in the hemisphere. It was a logical assumption, but only essentially disruptive means could start the process, and like any expanding force, commercial development acquired its own dynamic. It risked confrontation with other powers engaged in similar expansion, and above all, unwittingly helped develop a nationalism that liked dangerous political action rather than slow economic growth. Reciprocity was logical, rational, and, like all grand designs, ironically risky.

The clamor of debate ended, and congressmen reflected little upon the long-term meaning of the session's work. Republicans had every right to expect a sweeping mandate. They had fulfilled campaign pledges in one of the most productive sessions in American history. They revised the tariff, reduced the surplus, lowered taxes, moved against trusts, tried to stabilize elections with federal law, and aided silver. But wise men never counted votes until they were in the ballot box.

*The law also refunded 99 per cent of duties collected on raw materials imported, then exported as finished goods for foreign markets.

In July, Ohio's Charles Foster assured Sherman the party had nothing to fear. "With the passage of the tariff bill and the election law we will be in good shape." [136] But further west, Clarkson felt a bad mood among farmers, and warned Allison he could not educate anyone without money; the state organization was "very poor, practically bankrupt." [137] Farmers were restless across the Mississippi, where falling prices and rising mortgages angered normally Republican voters. "There is an ugly outlook," a man wrote Sherman. "The 'Farmers' Alliance' wants to cut a day in two, and the free coinage men are ripe for revolt." [138] In that "wonderful, picknicking, speechmaking Alliance summer of 1890," a host of strange figures captivated prairie provinces with invective against the industrial East and an extravagant Congress.[139] A movement gaining the label "populism" was pulling discontented Midwestern elements into a threatening phalanx, either to overwhelm an older party or make a new one. "I never seen the time before but what I could soothe the boys down and make them feel good," a Dakota politician wrote, "but seemingly this fall they are not to be 'comforted.'" [140] Blaine dutifully campaigned in the Ohio Valley. He spoke for McKinley, waging a desperate fight against Democrats determined to make him protection's scapegoat, but the Plumed Knight privately expected an opposition sweep.

And no wonder. Few congressional elections produced so much lurid oratory or misrepresentation. The tariff bore the brunt of the battle. In New York, Tammany displayed an excellent example of how local prejudice often counted more than national interests or mere accuracy. "There is two bills before the country," a brave told a huddle of immigrants, "the Mills bill and the McKinley bill. The Mills bill is for free trade with everything free; the McKinley bill is for protection with nothing free. Do you want everything free or do you want to pay for everything?" Abandoning economics for ethnic cant, the speaker then sang the praises of his native Ireland as compared to his local enemy's native Italy.[141] Democrats dispatched an army of peddlers to sell household goods at "pre-McKinley prices," predicting tinware would rise so much that farmers would drink from gourds.* Importers brought in large quantities of goods, before the new tariff rates went into effect. Many people who had sustained protection in the past now accepted

---

*The Populists were always uncertain tariff reformers, and after 1890 a few admitted privately that the McKinley Act had not raised prices. "I do not know of a single article that is higher than it was a year ago," a Granger wrote in Texas. Of course, it was less politic to say so from the stump, or tail-end of a wagon. (See J. H. Brigham to A. J. Rose, September 4, 1891, Rose papers, Texas History Collection.)

the proposition that high rates meant high prices, with ominous political results for Republicans.

McKinley patiently explained his tariff law in a bitter personal campaign. He faced a new district which a Democratic legislature had gerrymandered against him by 3,000 votes. On Election Day, he went down to defeat, but by only 300 votes, indicating his popularity. He was certainly not the only man to lose a seat. When the shouting died, a mere 88 Republicans would face 231 Democrats and 14 Populists in the new House, though the GOP kept the Senate by counting doubtful silverites. The Midwest was a slaughterhouse. In Kansas, Republicans lost 5 seats; 7 in Illinois, 6 in Michigan, 4 in Missouri, 3 in Nebraska, 9 in Ohio, and all the marginal gains of 1888. New York dumped 8 incumbent Republicans, Pennsylvania lost 3, and Massachusetts retired 5. It was much the same everywhere else, except in safe seats like Reed's in Maine. Agrarians captured nearly two House seats for every one safe Republican incumbent in the Midwest, and Democrats made impressive gains in northern cities. "Well! I find it a trifle difficult to put the thing into words!" Reed said. "It looks just for the moment as if this was a world made mostly for cowards and laggards and sneaks." [142]

Reed blamed the debacle on misrepresentation about tariff rates. "Every woman who went to a store and tried to buy went home to complain, and a wild unrest filled the public mind. The wonder is that we got any votes at all." [143] That was true enough, but the electorate also momentarily condemned Republican spending, the "Billion-Dollar Congress," and Harrison's icy administration. Reed's remark that this was a billion-dollar country availed nothing when men combined these complaints with agrarian unrest, the election bill, and bitter local issues.* The Administration purchased bonds with surplus revenue, unhappily depleting the Treasury while reducing taxes, but as Lodge said, "The sting of the present defeat lies in the fact that the Republican party never since the war deserved so well." [144] And it did sting. After the election several lame ducks, including McKinley, Thomas H. Carter of Montana, and Joseph G. Cannon of Illinois, discussed their future. Wreathed in cigar smoke and gesturing expansively, McKinley declared his defeat a personal blessing. He could earn some money at law practice, rest from the rigors of public life, and see the family. Cannon voiced a proverbial candor. "That's what I tell all the boys, but, Mack, don't let's lie to one another." [145]

---

*Depth research in local politics for 1890 might show that issues like public spending, parochial schools, and Temperance were as influential as the traditionally accepted agrarian unrest. Federal spending was especially important.

The election catalyzed many divergent forces, but farm discontent was most obvious. Alliance agents claimed state and local victories in the South, along the Border, and in the western plains. The threatened radicalism let a New York paper oppose formation of more new western states, "until we can civilize Kansas." [146] Republicans were in confused rout. "You cannot get ten of them together without finding wide disagreements as to tariff, election bill, and every other Republican measure or principle," an old friend told Harrison.[147] President Leonidas L. Polk of the Southern Farmers' Alliance was firm. "If the Democrats of the Fifty-second Congress do not manifest a willingness to grant our demands, a third party is inevitable. . . . [We] are determined to gain the ends [we] are striving for, and will smash any party that opposes them." [148]

The results mixed apprehension with hope. The Administration inevitably acquired an interim quality. Americans had fervently debated domestic issues, and vigorously passed laws. They also learned some lessons in foreign policy.

As he left office, Secretary Bayard shared with many observers a certain apprehension about his successor. The country seemed interested in domestic affairs, but Blaine's charisma might let him expand Americans' horizons. Bayard talked himself into calmness. ". . . I am compelled to think him a very enfeebled man, and am inclined to expect a much less 'aggressive policy' than he started out with in 1881." [149] Though he was not an isolationist, Bayard was cautious, and knew the limitations of his post. A few years earlier, no diplomat could afford boldness in directing American affairs overseas. A major maritime power without a navy carried little weight among those who enforced European diplomacy with fleets and bases. In 1880, a naval officer reported the American Navy ranked below China's in world lists, resembling an oriental paper fort, with suitably bellicose but impotent dragons painted on the walls to frighten off aggressors. Massachusetts Congressmen John D. Long said it was "an alphabet of floating washtubs." [150] Oscar Wilde's Canterville Ghost commiserated with the American lady who complained that her country had no ancient ruins or exotic curiosities. "No ruins! No curiosities! You have your navy and your manners!" [151]

Despite its coastlines and overseas trade, the United States was not a major power in merchantmen or modern warships. Ships were expensive, and without colonies to protect or sea lanes to patrol, seemed ornamental to economy-minded congressmen. Except, of course, for

Navy Yards that became centers of jobbery. It was more politically profitable to repair useless vessels than build new ones. Workmen and contractors voted, and all parties kept them busy in key states like New York, Massachusetts, Virginia, and California. But poor technology, disinterest in new ideas, an ossified officer corps, and lack of equipment were equally to blame. Not until the late 1880's did a body of thought, methods of teaching, and new skills in naval architecture and steel manufacturing make a modern navy feasible. The officer corps was backward, reflecting an ancient interest in social caste and formal entertainments. An anonymous observer complained to Secretary Chandler, after seeing an American warship entertain visitors in the harbor of Nice, about "the sole apparent purpose of giving a series of dancing parties." [152]

A few ranking officials and politicians attacked the problem piecemeal in Arthur's administration. They saw the Navy as part of commercial expansion in a dawning era of international competition for spheres of influence. They were not jingoists or imperialists, but realized that no other country would respect American rights if she brought nothing to bear but moral suasion. Agrarians, heavily over-represented in Congress, opposed naval expenditures because they dissipated the Treasury surplus without reducing the tariff. A navy seemed useless to men whose states had no coastline, and it helped Republicans. Southern Democrats did not all fit this mold, however, generally favoring a modest outward attitude. The country's inability to defend its sealanes or coastlines unsettled many people. "What do the nations of the earth care about your moral power after you leave your own shores?" Senator Charles Jones of Florida asked in 1884. "All that they respect when the emergency arises is a decent display of public force." [153] Representative J. C. Burrows of Michigan was more to the point. "We never dare be out after dark as a nation, and we never lose sight of land unless it is in a foreign ship." [154]

Change depended a good deal on the Secretary of the Navy. He could influence congressmen and accept new ideas and technical innovations, or use the office as a pork barrel. Garfield and Arthur improved the service with active secretaries. The fleet's decrepitude shocked William H. Hunt in 1881, and he inventoried both ills and virtues as a basis for future growth. He noted sarcastically that Chileans could ravage the West Coast, Brazilians the Gulf Coast, and Austrians the East Coast without meeting shore fire or an active American fleet. He chose talented subordinates during a brief tenure, lobbied with suspicious congressmen, and passed on a legacy of action to William E.

Chandler, his successor when Arthur entered office. Critics expected nothing but spoilsmanship from the partisan Chandler, but as a New Hampshire man, familiar with both water and politics, he wanted a modern fleet. The mere technological problems of steam and new armor plating nearly foiled him, and Democrats gleefully embroiled every step in bitter controversy, but when he left office, Congress had authorized a small fleet of steel-protected, steam-driven warships.

William C. Whitney energized the post like a dynamo. He was an efficiency reformer, more interested in costs than ideas, and used his power for partisan advantage, exposing Republican waste and creating Democratic spoils. The record was mixed, though Whitney reduced costs, applied some new technology, upgraded the working staff, and systematized routine business. He saw the Navy as a business, and found even Bayard's modest expansionism alarming.[155] While politicians reduced costs and improved men and equipment, a few officers and thinkers popularized fresh ideas. After 1884, the Naval War College in Newport, Rhode Island, expanded education for a new generation of officers, under the fresh influence of Admiral Stephen B. Luce and Captain Alfred T. Mahan. The latter's plans to combine naval power and commercial expansion met the era's needs, appealed to national pride, and captured the imagination of many powerful people.

President Harrison was among these. For a Hoosier, he displayed surprising interest in sea lanes, and wanted an able administrator for the Navy portfolio. "I regard it as one of the most important in my cabinet," he told Elkins, "and I shall want a man of the highest integrity and of the best administrative ability." [156] He found in Benjamin F. Tracy of Brooklyn a good combination of reasonable partisanship and constructive nationalism. His annual reports were models of clarity and foresight. With Harrison's support, he firmly repelled boarding parties of spoilsmen, including Senators Platt and Quay. He wanted steel vessels, mounting accurate large-bore rifles, manned by trained crews under skilled officers. By the end of his term, the United States ranked seventh in world fleets. Hard training and good technical education began to replace social etiquette and lassitude in the service. An able administrator, Tracy commanded devotion from equally talented subordinates and did much to renovate both ships and men; but he had a larger purpose than a new fleet. "The sea will be the future seat of empire," he said in 1891, "and we shall rule it as certainly as the sun doth rise! To a preeminent rank among nations, colonies are of the greatest help." [157]

A latent urge for territorial expansion paralleled the rise of naval power, and caused some apprehension. All parties agreed on defending the Monroe Doctrine, and renegotiating the Clayton-Bulwer Treaty for an American Isthmian canal. But increasing interest in Pacific affairs warned of future challenges beyond the West Coast. Romantic Samoa symbolized the competition among major European powers for oriental footholds. The United States did not have the means or desire to challenge European control of the islands, but served diplomatic notice of a developing Asian policy. Bayard and Cleveland were not territorial expansionists, but gradually realized the importance of eastern commerce.

Just as Europeans suspected American intentions in the Western Hemisphere, the United States suspected European activities in the Pacific. Bayard wanted a multi-power settlement in Samoa, which came in time, but warned that Hawaii was an American frontier. The weak Hawaiian monarchy would fall someday, and the United States would not let the islands go to other hands. Blaine and Harrison shared these general attitudes, but wanted to avoid annexation if diplomacy and trade developed informal ties among nations. Harrison's patriotism was more intense than Blaine's. Both envisioned future annexation of Cuba and Puerto Rico—neither wished territorial expansion at the moment—but the needs of commerce, imbalances of world political power, and a rising nationalism that reflected domestic consolidation on all levels, made an American world role inevitable. The question was not when, but how; not a matter of substance, but of style.[158]

Naval theorists, politicians, commercial expansionists, did not create a body of public opinion overnight. The nation was not ready for bold new ventures abroad. But a growing number of influential men, as in all great movements, gave these attitudes momentum. That focus initiated a new outward look, but in a larger sense they reflected it, for no great movement is imposed on people. It grows from their experience. Some critics thought American interest in the Pacific forced and unnecessary, but the same needs and desires that took Americans to the Pacific shoreline inevitably roused interest in what lay beyond the water's edge. It was not merely a romantic urge, but a combination of business, strategy, defense, and a frank desire for world recognition.

Blaine thus resumed his Latin American diplomacy in a more congenial atmosphere than in 1881. It now seemed more than a mere extension of party politics; he gained support for the ideas, if not the details, of pan-Americanism. He wished to reconcile the Monroe Doctrine with hemispheric reality, and unite the area with ties of commerce and material common sense. Members of both parties urged such cooperation in the late 1880's, and in May, 1888, Cleveland allowed a bill authorizing an international congress to become law without his signature. In July, Bayard sent formal invitations to Mexico, Haiti, Santo Domingo, and fifteen other southern republics. They responded hesitantly, fearing "Yankee domination," but delegates gathered at the State Department in October, 1889. After touring much of the eastern United States with luxurious accommodations that irritated the Democratic press, they sat in Washington from mid-November to April, 1890.

Harrison chose four manufacturers and two merchants for the ten-man American delegation, revealing his interest in trade. The agenda included mundane things like patent regulations, port fees, a customs union, transportation and communication systems, and Blaine's cherished general arbitration plan for inter-American disputes. Harrison supported Blaine strongly, despite their growing coolness. The Secretary's ability to include a reciprocity plan in the McKinley Tariff impressed some delegates, though they grumbled at its negative manner. Latin American nationalism and the sheer complexity of the problems prevented any general agreements, but Blaine made an important beginning in simply opening questions to debate. He took the initiative, knowing the United States must offset its adverse image in Latin America with constructive and patient action.[159] But, as so often in the past, he no sooner made his point than unforeseen events seemed to belie American good intentions or constructive labors. The troublesome Chilean problem revived as if to haunt him.

The Navy boasted new ships and fresh ideas, but the same old sailors ran the machinery. American seamen did not differ from those of any other country or era. When their ships docked in foreign ports, they naturally sought a change of scenery. In October, 1891, sailors on shore leave from American ships in Valparaiso offended local sensibilities by brawling in the red-light district. Authorities rescued a group from a mob that killed a sailor, seriously injured another who later died, and hurt four more. On October 20, four days after the riot, Secretary Tracy cabled for a full explanation. Two days later, officers answered that the sailors were justified in resisting a mob, and were being held with undue severity in a Chilean jail.[160]

The incident hardly merited front-page coverage, but the ever-confused Chilean political situation, and misrepresentation of the American minister, led to harsh words that created an international problem. "Jingo Jim" Blaine quickly emerged as harmony's spokesman. He wanted no disruption of slowly developing pan-Americanism. "We have nothing to worry about from Blaine," a Chilean said on October 30.[161] They had much to worry about from Harrison, however, who inflated the incident in the annual message of December 8. For the next two months war seemed imminent, despite European amazement, Chile's obvious weakness, and American unreadiness. The Chileans offended Harrison's patriotism, but he also suspected European designs on Chile's valuable mineral deposits. The French, Germans, and British used "Yankee imperialism" to cover efforts to dominate Latin American trade and investment. British warships regularly visited Chile's long coastline. Britain had refitted her navy, and advised armed forces in other countries. For that matter, Chile's small, but modern fleet could ravage California, incredible as it seemed.

Harrison grew restive as the Chileans procrastinated. "It does not seem to me fair that we should be requested to send the sailors of the *Baltimore* who were assaulted in Valparaiso before a secret tribunal where we can have no assurance that their statements will be correctly interpreted or recorded, and where we are not allowed to be represented." [162] Harrison was unperturbed at world opinion, and cared nothing for Chile's alleged underdog status in the row. He seemed eager to make Latin America and the European powers respect American naval rights. When Blaine urged delay, Harrison retorted: "Mr. Secretary, that insult was to the uniform of the United States sailors." [163]

Through December and into January, saber-rattling thwarted diplomacy. Some Democrats told Harrison they would not make war a party issue, and the country seemed ready to follow his lead. Harrison was firm, while Blaine "changes his mind every five minutes," according to Elkins, now Secretary of War. As the crisis peaked in late January, 1892, and Chile accepted an American ultimatum, Blaine urged magnanimity and careful attention to Latin pride. "I have relied on Chile's good sense for reparation and I believe we will get it more easily that way than by arbitration," he wrote Harrison. "We can afford to be very generous in our language and thus make a friend of Chile—if that is possible." [164]

Arbitration ended the issue by summer, but it fortified growing anti-Americanism south of the border. "Now that Chile has escaped United States intervention by the policy of conciliation, it must build toward future strength by cementing its bonds with Europe," the Chilean minister to Berlin noted. "The future of South America lies with Europe." [165] The crisis stirred predictable Jingo comment in the United States. "No power, great or small, will venture in the future to insult

our flag, assail our uniform or defy our citizenship," a Democratic paper
reported. "We have made peace secure forever, so far as human vision
can forsee, by showing that we can be ready at any time for war." [166]
Brave words, but not quite realistic on any score. Powers, large or
small, would always resent American influence, and great nations, as
Blaine noted, should rely more on rational development than emotional
posturing. As one critic noted sharply: "We do not need a steam hammer to crack nuts." [167]

The incident illustrated a permanent difficulty in dealing with Latin
America. Nations perpetually in transition or threatened chaos created
endless political and social factions that might one day rule. In a sense,
whatever the United States did was diplomatically wrong, including
inaction. Blaine's answer was wisest, if slowest, and despite his touchy
national pride, President Harrison was fully committed to the idea of
widening trade.

Secretary of State Evarts, for all his surface wit and apparent in-
dolence, was interested in the technicalities of commerce and consular
reports. Before issuing men their diplomatic commissions, he often
lectured them gracefully on what to note. They must not think statistics
dull; personal observations on local economy, government, and customs
would enliven the special papers he gave congressmen, sent to President Hayes, and issued as monthly newsletters. He filed massive quantities of information for successors, and made some good changes in the
diplomatic service and permanent department staff. Every successor
followed this example, largely because each new Secretary understood
his widening powers and responsibilities. Arthur's Administration
negotiated several important reciprocity treaties with Latin American
countries, but hostile protectionist Republicans joined Democrats to
defeat them. Each passing year increased knowledge, and small but
continuous changes in personnel, procedure, and communication slowly
widened into an institutional approach.

Harrison agreed with Blaine's objectives, however much their methods differed. He promptly negotiated ten reciprocity treaties under the
McKinley Act; with Spain, Austria, Germany, and Great Britain for
her American possessions, and with several Latin American nations.
The President also knew the power of public persuasion, and in the
spring of 1891, crossed the country to speak of many things, but largely
of foreign trade. His party, including family and ranking officials, lived
in a comfortable private train, and passed through almost every major
city in the South and West. He was at his best speaking briefly and with

vigor to enthusiastic crowds. Mrs. Harrison told her little diary that Memphis was "certainly the dirtiest city I ever saw," and found Little Rock "muddy and disagreeable." But her husband did not neglect local politicians, and impressed many with his lucid, vigorous speeches.[168]

Like Blaine, he paid special attention to Latin American trade, and told suspicious southern Democrats to open their ports, with suitable federal aid. In Texas, he discussed a ship channel for Houston, breakwaters for Galveston, and forecast widening markets for southern goods and added profits in shipping northern products.[169] He lived to see modest gains. Between 1880 and 1901, the national government spent large sums on port facilities and levee improvements for river shipping. Gulf ports increased exports by nearly 100 per cent, while the national level rose 65 per cent.

It was hard to develop congressional support and public sentiment for critical tangential help, like subsidies for merchant shipping, however. Most Republicans, especially Blaine and Harrison, favored building a new merchant marine with federal aid, like other maritime powers. But persistent effort produced only modest help from a suspicious Congress. Rural politicians opposed funds for allegedly rich ship owners and manufacturers. Southerners distrusted yet another federal spending program, even when it benefitted them. And early experiments with trade and mail service to Brazil were unprofitable. The nation would not support steady, long-term assistance. But Blaine's secretary remembered seeing him tell an oblivious grandchild all about extending South American trade. "Only, Congress will never give us the subsidy for it." [170]

Congress was not inclined to give them anything after 1891. Republicans were in a strange position. Unity, hard work, and national programs gave them the government in 1888. They enacted campaign pledges, but in a way that produced discontent and made them a minority congressional party again. Democrats were learning to advertise, symbolize, and enlarge their programs. For all his abilities, Harrison was not a successful national Republican symbol. As usual, Blaine's position was uncertain. Was he a candidate for 1892? In any event, age dictated an early end to his career, and the party had no successors of equal vitality.

To precise, logical men like Harrison, the nation's mood was curious. Prosperity was fairly sound, but people were restless. The Democrats in effect controlled Congress, but merely harassed opponents, awaiting 1892. Republicans had no more domestic programs to offer. The administration's foreign policy mixed realism and reflex, far-sightedness and the old piecemeal solutions. The country would not sustain a plan, and its merits disappeared in partisan abuse. Blaine could not enact enough of his program to help the Republican image. He talked eloquently and honestly of shipping subsidies, tariff reciprocity, and hemispheric solidarity as a grand plan for orderly material growth, but Democrats were already talking about 1892, and many farmers seemed strangely ripe for revolt.

IX

☆☆☆☆☆☆ ☆☆☆☆☆☆ ☆☆☆☆☆☆☆☆☆☆

The Restless Farmers

☆☆☆☆☆☆ ☆☆☆☆☆☆ ☆☆☆☆☆☆☆☆☆☆

The elections of 1890 startled Republican politicians. Even admitting that many local issues helped unseat GOP representatives, keen observers in the South and the area beyond the Mississippi knew that farmers were "restless." Agrarians played a strange role in American history and in the balanced political struggles of the 1880's. Most were conservative in wanting material success. They doubted any easy social progress, given that cranky phenomenon philosophers labeled "human nature." The farm voter was erratic. His immediate material self-interest did not always parallel that of the whole nation, and over-representation in Congress made him a constant irritant to both major parties.

James S. Clarkson of Iowa knew this better than most men. As editor of the *Des Moines Register,* an original Republican, and a fierce partisan, he carefully analyzed voter sentiment. Iowa seemed likely to go Democratic when Hell went Methodist, as Jonathan Dolliver once said, but the farmer also liked panaceas that seemed to belie his historical stereotype of shrewd, suspicious conservatism. Iowa was "the golden buckle on the corn belt," producing quantities of staples like corn, wheat, swine, and feeds whose prices were set in distant cities by men who "farmed the farmer." Now, in 1891, when the post-election dust settled, Clarkson worried about President Harrison's re-election. He was on the edge of Harrison's circle, but organized in local affairs like any good Republican. Like other experienced workers, he saw the dangers in any farmers' uprising. It might unite South and West in a fitful threat to both major parties. It would also disrupt the growing but precarious Republican coalition of worker-businessman-farmer.*

---

*I cannot recapitulate the history of Populism in this chapter, but hope instead merely to outline basic ideas that animated the movement, and show what it looked like in the context of national politics. I will discuss Populist politics in later chap-

Clarkson did not quite know how to meet this unrest. In the immediate past, most agrarians adopted a national party tone, responding to the GOP's nationalistic program of land division, internal improvements, tariff protection, and a growing home market. But Republican policies seemed to ignore farm debts, over-production of staple crops, and lack of new dynamic farm programs. Agrarian resentment rose as politicians paid more attention to urban workers than farmers. Railroads were not a complete blessing, after all. Business seemed to move inexorably and logically into trusts that allegedly raised the price of things farmers bought, without corresponding benefit in the price of what they sold.

Politicians hoped to combat this feeling with more organization that brought farmers into local affairs, and to discuss national issues. Clarkson wrote Harrison of his ideas, admitting they reflected a view of farm life in the round. Man was basically gregarious. If he relieved tensions and aired grievances, he was manageable and happy. "The Farmers' Alliance is in itself more the product of social hunger than political thought or action," he told the President. "The farm neighborhood has little social life, has none of the secret societies, nothing of clubs, scarcely a church sociable. We propose to put a Republican club into every farm neighborhood possible, as soon as we can, and make it a social and literary as well as political force. . . . Just as the Farmers' Alliance utilized the social hunger of the average farm neighborhood, we will utilize the social force and intellectual hunger of every farm community, and every town and city as well, where we can apply it." [1] His attitude reflected myth, reality, and a frank desire to avoid political dissension.

It was not an illogical notion. The nation was familiar with the "Granger movement," rising from the Patrons of Husbandry and similar farm organizations after the war. Though they gained national recognition while fighting for railroad regulation, the societies emphasized social and educational activities that buttressed the nation's oldest myth—the sanctity of rural life. The movement grew during the 1870's, but declined along with prosperity in the 1880's. In the mid-1870's, forty-four states had the Grange or similar organizations. Many towns on Kansas prairies or in Vermont hills centered on a Grange Hall, where Sunday afternoon picnics and week-night dances or initiations into the order heightened rural drabness. On holidays, at wed-

---

ters. I should emphasize that I do not mean the terms "farmer" or "agrarian" to include *all* farmers, but to apply generally to those who were discontented with the system in the early 1890's. Less than a majority of the farmers embraced what we loosely call "Populism."

dings, and fairs, families appeared with baskets and watermelons, home-made pies and displays of needlework to hear speeches and discuss current events, leaving when food was "conspicuously absent."[2]

All this had a certain already nostalgic charm, and found a ready market in print for city folk to read. The farmer of the 1880's seemed able to afford neighborly attachments without abandoning the sharp bargain or profit. Regional and National Grange headquarters supported local efforts to improve rural prosperity, with pamphlets, books, and newspapers extolling the virtues of new planting methods, modern machinery, and market information. But rural reading perpetuated the basic national philosophy of self-help. The increasing desire to glorify and preserve the small independent farmer had roots deep in American life, but also signaled his passing. An age of collectivized "business farming" was at hand. The Granger movement was essentially reactionary, trying to segregate the farmer from society, raising his standard of living without contamination from alleged city vices and industrial development.[3] Grangers saw the farmer as the last individualist, comfortable on land that produced daily needs, with a profit for luxuries.

Many farmers, especially in the South, feared the glamorous appeals of education that widened youth's horizons to include the city, business, or a non-agricultural career. Agrarians often suspected higher education as a pillar of the caste system they opposed in economics and politics. Favoring "technical education" that embraced technology useful in the field and corral, they opposed the "frills" of languages, history, or pure science. Larger school grants also meant higher taxes on farm property.[4] This was especially true in an already poor South, and among those who preferred to strike tangible enemies like railroads, which represented a larger pattern of national development that threatened to leave the farmer out of the national feast of plenty.

Behind the pleasantly romantic and nostalgic popular view of agrarian life loomed a steadily increasing variety of genuine economic problems. In 1885, a New York paper warned that "Future storms will come not from the South, but from the West."[5] As the age of eager subsidy for transportation passed, farmers away from cities and towns increasingly grumbled at excessive government support to industry, without apparent aid to agriculture.[6] Discontented western agrarians drifted in spirit toward distressed southerners, threatening connections that politicians of both major parties had laid between the East Coast and the land beyond Pennsylvania.[7] Southern farmers stirred uneasily within the Democratic party. Some openly suggested a new West-South alliance, cooperation between farmers and workers on the theme of hard work and low pay, and some recognition of mutual interests between poor whites and Negroes.

Events baffled the farmer. He worked hard, produced more, and received a declining share of the national income. Cotton, wheat, corn, and meat products poured from the plains and mountains, flooding the home market and seeking outlets abroad. A multitude of individual producers faced inflexible marketing arrangements that profited middlemen and made each year's income uncertain, no matter the cost of production, or expectations that accompanied it to the grain elevator or cattle buyer's stockade. Science improved fertilizer, and the farmer grew more for a lower price. Machinery lightened daily toil, but increased borrowing and the temptation to plant more land fed a cycle of over-production. Twenty years after the depression of the 1870's, the farmers' price for corn and cotton was halved. In 1894, they received less for 23 million acres of cotton than for 9 million in 1873. Competition from India and Egypt tightened the export trade. The price of silver, a staple crop in the Far West, also fell. In 1872, an ounce sold for \$1.32; in 1884, for \$1.11; and it brought \$0.63 in 1894. With a long tradition favoring currency inflation to reduce mortgage debt, the distressed farmer was bound to embrace silver. It might also grant him the larger prosperity he thought an unmindful nation and impersonal economy lavished on those who worked more often with columns of figures than plow-mules or wheat combines.

Rural rhetoric sounded increasingly radical, in a tradition of vivid stump oratory, and often incorporated biblical colorations of apocalypse. As the groundswell of discontent rose with the approaching 1890's, few agrarian interests looked toward socialism, however. They would grant individualism a still larger role through government regulation of the market place. Like most Americans, they wished to even out life's inequalities of opportunity, not destroy the prevailing system. Railroad control, currency inflation, price supports, would reduce "special privilege" in the existing economy.[8] Competition had not raised debts or reduced income; unseen workings of a system still open to regulation produced discomfort. They blended faith in material well-being and belief in man's rationality; people who made the economy could also remove its flaws. "All we demand is a just measure of the profits realized over our labor in connection with capital," Senator William A. Peffer of Kansas said.[9] Retrospective critics thought the whole agrarian problem was "not the stirrings of red revolution, but merely a struggle between small and large capitalists."[10]

By the late 1880's a variety of organizations offered solutions, blending into what the press called "The Alliance Movement." The National

Farmers' Alliance founded in 1880 fought railroad discrimination, mortgage combines, interest rates, and low prices. Further south, in Lampasas County, Texas, a movement that became the "Southern Alliance" grew rapidly. By 1886 it absorbed fragmentary groups and, to nervous politicians, seemed ready to join with northern agencies in a new national party. But the various alliances grew slowly, often proposing different solutions to similar problems. Leonidas LaFayette Polk of North Carolina illustrated the changes, style, and rationale in many farm groups. A compelling speaker, with an engaging personality and the patience to explore new ideas, Polk was a genial small-town booster with visions and ambitions. He dabbled in real estate, taught Sunday School, defended southern mythology. But he also traveled tirelessly among neighbors with the good news of scientific farming and cooperation. In 1877, he became the state's first agricultural commissioner, pushing scientific training and practical mechanization, trying to unify agriculture. In the mid-1880's, his voice reached beyond North Carolina in the farm press. At decade's end, he was president of the national Farmers' Alliance.[11]

Polk accepted political action, first working with farm clubs that pressured the state legislature for special programs. He also urged cooperation among farmers to keep the blessings of individualism and gain the advantages of collective buying and selling. He could second the increasing number of voices who told farmers to unite in the pattern of business and labor. If bigness and efficiency produced stability and profits, let the farmers consolidate. "It is the duty of the farmers to organize in this day of combination," Major Mann Page of Virginia counseled.[12] Further north, a Michigan Grange newspaper offered similar advice. "We note the success of united effort, and as each class labors for its own interests, unless the agricultural class meets combination with combination, they will be overwhelmed in the conflict." [13] Before 1892, farm spokesmen steered a careful course between their constituents' immediate needs and the chance of alienating other interest groups. They asked, in effect, for equal economic rights in the existing system. "Grant to agriculture the same privileges and benefits that are given to manufacturers, banks, railroads, and other great factors which enter into production and distribution," a farm journal said in 1891. "When this is done, and the farmer has his rights, the country will retain its people and the cities will not be crowded as they are at present." [14]

These national spokesmen, and a thousand local leaders, turned enthusiastically to cooperative societies which mushroomed in the 1880's among many interest groups, including organized labor.[15] Co-ops seemed a logical and workable solution to many agrarian demands. Farmers could pool capital to buy seed, fertilizer, equipment, and other goods at reduced prices. They could market produce through cooperatives at higher prices than as individual sellers, and might also break monopolies in ginning, retailing, processing, and perhaps even transportation. Some cooperatives succeeded, when talented men were in charge, but the total experiment failed. Few men had the capital, business talent, information, or time to be both businessmen and farmers. Nor could they create a competing market within the existing system. Co-ops also alienated local merchants and the middle class, whose help farmers needed for larger goals. But the co-ops illustrated most farmers' belief in regulated competition, and aimed at higher individual profits, not collective socialism.[16]

Some thought the answer to weaknesses that defeated co-ops was a broadly based subsidy program. Charles Macune of Texas presented the "Sub-Treasury Plan" at the December, 1889, meeting of the Southern Alliance in St. Louis. It seemed captivatingly simple. The national government would establish a sub-treasury, warehouses, and grain elevators in every county that offered for sale in a given year at least $500,000 worth of non-perishable staple commodities like cotton, tobacco, wheat, corn, sugar, oats, barley, rice, and wool. The government would issue on deposit a legal tender loan at 1 per cent interest, equalling 80 per cent of the current market value. The sub-treasury would sell unredeemed products a year later at public auction.[17] The plan aroused controversy among reformers, and opponents used it to ridicule all agrarian ideas. It was class legislation and would circulate yet another unstable form of currency. The government would be receiver for huge farm surpluses, and prices would inevitably fall as they entered the market. Farmers would use the income to grow more staples, increasing the market glut. Much of the criticism was sound; some was unfair. But political opponents bludgeoned Populists with the idea's implications, even though few agrarians sustained the plan.*

---

*Historians still commonly see price supports passed after 1933 as evidence of Populist farsightedness in meeting the "farm problem." This generalization is partly true, since the government raised farm income through such subsidy schemes and storage plans, but the subsidy program has not saved the small farmer, who increasingly left agriculture for industrial jobs. Subsidies have enriched people storing surpluses, and perhaps unwittingly aided in "collectivizing" farming. The farm problem's solution seems to be fewer farmers. Historically, the federal subsidy program may be merely a stopgap that cushioned the end of individual farming. As world food supplies dwindle in the future, the government may subsidize large "business farms" to produce more staples, and more efficiently than the old individual farmer system.

The farm organizers made slow progress. They crossed long distances in dilapidated buggies or on weary horses to leave pamphlets at lonely farmhouses. Having contacts with a larger world, they fortified hopes for the future and enlivened the present. They often drew large crowds, but left too little permanent legacy. In the West, they confronted the hard facts that farmers could not afford time or money for a permanent organization. In the South, they faced Democratic charges that agrarian unrest would bring Negro rule. Such a widespread collection of individualists seldom agreed on concerted actions or views. In 1891, the Alliances boasted 35,000 speakers and organizers, but most were part-time amateurs lacking central direction. Lack of funds, poor leadership, and local antagonism from vested interests frustrated even the best intentions.

Many farm leaders avoided politics, fearing they could not defeat established national parties—even poor men did not lightly abandon old allegiances, West or South—but by the 1890's, the whole agrarian effort moved toward a national political crusade. The appeals of party politics might unify a farm movement where preachment failed. Political pressure won some local victories, and concerted action in national contests might return higher dividends. "We don't want a farmers' party," Polk said in 1888, "but we do want to see the farmers of this country take sufficient interest in political matters and political action to keep a strict eye on all that their party does." [18] He was more candid a year later: "Plainly, we will not consent to give indefinite support to men who are . . . unfriendly to our interests. . . . If this be party treason, make the most of it." [19] A few veterans of other reform crusades, like Ignatius Donnelley, noted candidly that non-political Granger organizations were like guns "that will do everything but shoot." [20]

No wonder old hands like James S. Clarkson and Democratic counterparts saw trouble. Powerful journalists might call discontented agrarians "hogs in the parlor" of polite society, but the farmers had power.[21] If they built an organization for all disaffected groups, American politics might take a new turn.* Clarkson did not have the answer in 1890, but he knew that many farmers would now ask why their share of the American dream had not quite come true.

---

*The Populists never overcame a reputation for attracting cranks. Macune admitted the problem in running his own organization. "It attracted all the discontented, it appealed to all who were not entirely satisfied with existing conditions, and it repelled none because it made no expression upon details or methods about which there might be different opinions." (See Macune, "The Farmers' Alliance," 9–10, THC.)

The rapidly developing and profitable western expansion of agriculture during the mid-1880's well illustrated how much the farmer believed in that dream. Thousands of families moved onto the apparently rich plains of Dakota, Kansas, and Nebraska after the war, eager to take up public land or buy cheaply from railroads that often overemphasized the area's soil and climate. The national and world market for wheat, corn, and swine seemed firm, and with adequate rainfall and mild winters farmers could extol the virtues of a new-found Promised Land. Most were "easterners" and wished to reproduce the settled communities they left behind. They liked square corners in fields, and pleasant streets in towns they visited on weekends and market day. Confidence in the future produced false security. Debt seemed a weapon against hard times, and in a land of far horizons and immense fields, a boom spirit became the accepted tone. Prosperous farmers of specialized crops, or those in the eastern plains where rain was more predictable, frowned at rumors of agrarian radicalism. It gave the West a bad name, and frightened investment capital. It was wiser to emphasize profits for farmer, money-lender, merchant, and town dweller. This produced a smug rhetoric. "Nothing causes the Nebraska farmer more dismay than to return from town after spending a few hours there, and find that his farm has been converted into a thriving city with street cars and electric lights during his absence," the *Nebraska State Journal* assured smiling readers in 1887.[22]

This web of plans and monotone of optimism brought eager capital from the East. Though the farmer complained of high interest rates and mortgage combines, he seldom condemned the investment system. Many eastern firms poured funds into marginal investments, failed with a resounding crash in the mid-1890's, and hardly fulfilled the "Shylock" portrait so common among bewildered clients.[23] In the new Plains and Mountain states, eagerness for forced economic growth and acceptability in eastern eyes produced shaky grandiose schemes. Every likely spot became a town, surveyed with numbered lots assessed at a hundred times their value. Each river bend would produce a teeming port. All flat terrain was ideal for railroad tracks. River junctions grew on paper into great cities, controlling the commerce of whole regions, with rail-heads, wharves, grain elevators, and subsidiary industries.[24] It was all in the grandest American style, and produced just enough to warrant further indebtedness and louder talk. When the crash inevitably came, ruined men naturally found scapegoats east of the Mississippi River.[25]

Appeals to caution seemed unreal in an area outside the main currents of business life. It was like a separate country, and developed "a fever of speculation in real estate which affected the whole population, destroyed all true sense of wealth, created an enormous volume of fictitious wealth, infected with its poison all the veins and arteries of business, and swelled the cities to abnormal proportions."[26] In weak agrarian economies, all the pieces fitted a circle. Men with marginal railroad stock invested more capital and hope in equally uncertain cattle or land schemes to develop the railroad's present business and future growth. In small communities, where people knew each other, the banker often extended credit to doubtful risks that would have gone begging in the East's less personal money marts.[27] Economic softness in one sector endangered subsidiary business, and there was no diversified system to absorb depression's shock.

However genuine and pressing the problems of daily economic life became as prosperity thinned in the late 1880's, much of the farmers' discontent reflected a growing disenchantment with ideals that carried them west. The higher the goals, the harder the fall. The rains did not come on time; someone should have said so. Mortgage rates were higher on dry plains than in eastern Iowa or Kansas; somebody was at fault. Freight rates on Kansas wheat varied from those on Minnesota wheat. It all produced unusual bitterness. "The man who had followed the advice of Horace Greeley and gone west in the early seventies, after losing his Indiana or Ohio farm in the panic of 1873, was in sore straits," a Kansan recalled.[28] In the ruthless country of the "Old Southwest," where climate was erratic, distances vast, and life barren, broken men expressed their despair. In the drought year of 1886, travelers in Blanco County, Texas, read the writing on an abandoned farmhouse floor: "250 miles to the nearest post office; 100 miles to wood; 20 miles to water; 6 inches to hell. God bless our home! Gone to live with the wife's folks."[29]

Many farmers had realized just enough affluence to deepen that hostility into a desire for revenge. Advertising, new forms of communication, better transportation, made them want luxuries undreamed of twenty years earlier. Apparent prosperity sent them into debt for a new barn, fresh house paint, a piano, magazines that touted other pleasures. Luxuries even came to the table—meats processed in distant cities, fresh fruits and vegetables shipped in new refrigerated cars, goods preserved in sugar that sweetened the diet and symbolized luxury. On terrain suited to mechanization, the farmer accepted costly chattel mortgages for reapers, new plows, and combines.[30] No one could blame him; and no one dared warn him.

A natural desire for more acreage often increased indebtedness. Many marginal farmers hoped to supplement incomes with real estate speculation. As part-time developers, they were especially prone to risky ventures, and their hopes lay buried in the wreckage of shattered booms.[31] Of course, it was not easy to accept personal responsibility or live with poverty. Western propaganda encouraged eastern capital in the 1880's, and agrarians logically condemned money-lenders when the crash came. Mortgage companies often extended credit rather than repossess valueless farms. Eastern lenders were not generally more exhorbitant than local agents, but it was easier to think otherwise. That interest rates actually declined during the period made no impression on farmers who had to produce more staples to pay stationary debts. High rates on chattel loans, secured with property that was usually either a necessity like machinery, or a symbolic luxury like a piano, especially embittered debtors. Hostility toward mortgage companies, railroads, and processors coalesced into a view of an integrated economy as a conspiracy that seemed to drain the farmer to other men's advantage.[32]

There was an apparently endless cycle of high debts and low prices. A Populist speaker summed up the dilemma: "We went to work and plowed and planted; the rains fell, the sun shone, nature smiled, and we raised the big crop they told us to; and what came of it? Eight cent corn, ten cent oats, two cent beef and no price at all for butter and eggs—that's what came of it. Then the politicians said we suffered from over-production."[33] It seemed pointless for the farmer "to make two spears of grass grow where one grew before. . . . Now he is struggling hopelessly with the question how to get as much for two spears of grass as he used to get for one."[34] The process fed a politically dangerous resentment: "The farmer fed all other men and lived himself upon scraps."[35]

Reality belied the picture of bucolic bliss where everyone laughed while tossing hay, no barnyard ever smelled, and the day's jolly labor ended with a song-fest of happy rustics around an old oaken bucket. Immediate problems were harsh and pressing, but the long range looked no better. The farmer now seemed fixed in place as a subsidiary agent who fed industry and commerce. He thought himself the nation's mainstay, the source of its values and prevailing attitudes, but he occupied a minority economic status. The system that lightened labor and increased productivity extended his reach but not his grasp. A prosperous economy generated great rewards, but any weakness penalized men on its edges. Clinging firmly to the virtues of individualism, the farmer grew suspicious of an impersonal system.[36]

Few people could accept the obvious answer: an agricultural system without the small independent farmer. "The logical conclusion from the evidence offered, is that the troubles of the farmer are due to the fact that there are altogether too many farms, too many cattle and swine, too many bushels of corn, wheat, rye, oats, barley, buckwheat, and potatoes," a reporter noted in 1890, "too many tons of hay, and too great a production of nearly all other farm products for the number of consumers." [37] The quickest way to emphasize the point was to feed the stove an ear of corn. "And if while we sat around such a fire watching the year's crop go up the chimney," Vernon Parrington recalled, "the talk sometimes became bitter . . . who will wonder?" [38]

Like so many other national problems, agrarian unrest was sharpest in the South. The war's legacy of destruction and stagnation remained virtually untouched in hills and along rivers, despite a few glittering showcase city sections. The magic indexes of railroad construction, bank deposits, and port shipping, did not hide the starker realities of cheap cotton, share-cropping, crop liens, and a standard of living for both white men and Negroes not far above that of European peasants. A narrow tax base resting on real property increased the independent farmer's burden, and made him hostile to public expenditure. Intangible city wealth, corporation income, and outside capital remained relatively untouched, thereby increasing resentment toward "foreign" domination and exacerbating historic tensions between city and country, farmer and businessman.[39] Debts seemed greater because of their proximity. The country storekeeper was a part-time banker, and the landowner "shared" his cropper's incomes. Various credit systems functioned "after the manner of a huge pawnshop," as men traded future progress for future debts, hoping to gain present prosperity.[40] Isolation, ignorance, and arid one-party politics heightened tensions in southern life. The section would predictably raise radical spokesmen, venting feelings in the bitter remark: "The basest fraud on earth is agriculture. No wonder Cain killed his brother. He was a tiller of the ground." [41]

The agricultural decline of the late 1880's swept away thousands of marginal, speculative farmers in the West, and depressed prices in the South. The stubborn, established farmers remained, ready to demand political solutions for economic problems and perhaps to create a national crusade. After 1890, talk of a "Peoples' Party" met greater response. Most farmers in the West did not leave traditional party attachments, yet there were enough discontented agrarians, as the elections of 1890 showed dramatically, to turn many areas away from Republican allegiance. The farmer likely to accept another party was more heavily in debt than his Republican neighbors. He had genuine economic grievances, and leaned toward political action in the classic American mold. If laws might produce debt relief, raise prices, and bring governmental support, he would vote for those realistic, material self-interests.[42] This indebted farmer was not yet typical, but he could be the catalyst for other dissatisfied elements. Cattlemen, sheep-herders, professional reformers, some immigrant groups, could create a catch-all party, unusually powerful in the era's balanced politics.[43]

Above all, agrarian spokesmen had appealing rhetoric. Their situation typified a growing unrest among many Americans who liked the fruits of cohesive economics, but feared declining individualism.[44] Few farmers looked back to a lost Eden, or forward to a socialist commonwealth. They wanted the existing system, with larger, protected advantages. They were more sure of anxieties than remedies, however. In 1891, a Kansas farmer combined immediate material problems with emotional distress in a letter that summed up the foundations of a farm revolt: [45]

> At the age of 52 years, after a long life of toil, economy and self-denial, I find myself and family virtually paupers. With hundreds of cattle, hundreds of hogs, scores of good horses, and a farm that rewarded the toil of our hands with 16,000 bushels of golden corn, we are poorer by many dollars than we were years ago. What once seemed a neat little fortune and a house of refuge for our declining years, by a few turns of the monopolistic crank, has been rendered valueless.

It was exaggerated, but symptomized much. "A neat little fortune," and "turns of the monopolistic crank" revealed personal motivation and a temptation to blame frustration on unseen forces.

Farmers were not united in discontent, and appeals to join third parties went unnoticed in agricultural areas near cities and towns. Those who saw railroad tracks leading to nearby cities that consumed their products complained less than men in Kansas or Alabama. The eastern farmer serving urban populations with dairy products, truck crops, poultry, and fruits had surprisingly little in common with western and southern counterparts. The small, cozy, rich farms of Delaware, Connecticut, Pennsylvania, or Maryland differed sharply from risk-farming in Dakota or Nebraska. The writer, politician, or businessman vacationing in upstate New York, central Ohio, or Wisconsin, seeing prosperous dairy herds, varied fruit and vegetable crops, could hardly imagine the grinding poverty of Georgia's cotton belt.

The genteel press still depicted eastern farms with neat buildings and bucolic occupants, in an unrealistic view of happy yeomanry. But the settled farmer near cities anywhere, close to markets, with a light debt burden and varied crops, did distrust his western and southern brethren. Their talk of monopoly was not persuasive when the industrial system consumed his products. Backcountry farmers disliked railroads, but dwellers near cities wanted more service, and were less inclined to harsh regulation.[46] Eastern farmers disliked long-haul freight advantages that western producers enjoyed, and often blamed Plains states' problems on bad weather and over-speculation. The established farmer near cities also suspected currency inflation. He liked tariff protection that closed the home market and eliminated Mexican and Canadian imports.[47]

As western competition in corn, wheat, and beef overwhelmed eastern farmers, states like New York and Pennsylvania established agricultural experiment stations to help diversify agriculture. Sorghum, beet sugar, vintage grapes, fruits, and poultry sustained eastern farm income as the huge western tracts made eastern wheat and corn production unprofitable.[48] In states like Illinois and Ohio, whose farms served industrial populations, agrarian discontent never matured into viable political movements. Larger populations, better soil and climate, diversified crops, and disinterest in currency manipulation thwarted radicalism.[49]

This in turn fortified western views of sinful cities that corrupted the young and made good farmers serve a bad system. The city's lure for youth disturbed older agrarians everywhere, who complained that the "brightest boys want to leave the farm."[50] Economic distress merely intensified Granger distrust of formal education that put classics and pure science above "practical" skills, and turned honest yeomen into dudes and city-slickers.[51] More tangible factors increased this emotional conflict between town and country. Whole counties bore the cost of city government, but reaped few benefits. Banks often favored urban investment, further curtailing farm credit.

State and federal funds often went for city or commercial improvements—there were no customhouses in the countryside. River and harbor appropriations did not immediately help dirt farmers, and hymns of praise to sturdy rustics, free from city temptations and business vices, created little affection between countryside and town square. Farm organizations underlined this hostility by excluding merchants, professionals, stockholders in corporations, and even business clerks. Populist leaders hoped to unite disaffected urban elements and agrarians, ignoring the ancient hostility between the two groups.[52] Few insults carried greater sting than to call a city dweller a "hick," or a farmer a "dude." This clash of emotions and differing economic self-interests always thwarted any unity between workers and farmers. Few political dreams had such long life with so little substance.

These attitudes intensified older sectional suspicions. The East symbolized oppression to men who borrowed from its bankers, paid railroads with offices in New York and Boston, elected politicians who moved in its circles. The feeling worked both ways. As the western land boom collapsed, the Northeast sharpened old suspicions of western stability and big talk,[53] but most of the hostility came from prairies and southern hills. Agrarian politicians vented hatred of established seats of power in lurid talk of exploitation and revenge. The East had education and cunning. If the tributary West and South rose, it would have to accord them a role in national development and tastes. If not, then let the newer areas seize power.[54] Demagogues like South Carolina's Ben Tillman raged against "the bond-holding, blood-sucking East." [55] Midwest agrarians welcomed a new politics based on western interests and attitudes. "All this will deprive New York of her imperial power," an Indianan trumpeted. "National results and politics can no longer be dictated by politicians in New York City, and in the next national election, the east will look to the west instead of the west looking to the east." [56]

This attitude sharply reflected western and southern resentment at being "left behind" in national wealth and power. "It [unrest] results from an earnest conviction that we are not receiving from our capital invested and our labor applied, a fair share of this accumulating wealth of the nation," a farm journal insisted.[57] An alternating attraction and revulsion for city life ran through all this talk, as farmers hoped to be independent yet enjoy the fruits of an industrial system possible only with urban populations. "The tendency is away from the farm and away from the rural districts," James B. Weaver lamented in 1887, "the trend is toward the city, where the needy congregate and where crime becomes organized and where the Republic is stabbed." [58] Trips to cities and towns often fortified agrarian distrust of urban values and peoples, but as agriculture moved inexorably to a minority status in American economic life, a host of varied adherants sang its praises.[59]

Human agents of an impersonal economic system and "dangerous" cities fared poorly at agrarian hands. Isolation bred the ironic twins of neighborliness and suspicion of human nature. Men who worked long hours in hot fields or herded cattle and sheep in freezing weather naturally both envied and disliked soft-handed salesmen, mortgage agents, and "drummers" who purveyed the good tidings of how things were done in the respectable East. Middlemen living off commissions, riding in fancy rigs, traveling in first-class coaches, and sitting in elegant offices angered farmers. The drummers' flashy clothes and glad-handing manner enhanced rural fears of city contamination, but mixed them with a subconscious longing for bright lights and a taste of forbidden fruits. Their easy travel and alleged profits lent credence to charges that some men farmed farmers, and did very well at it.[60]

This view also affected attitudes toward intellectuals and experts. Ben Tillman's venom was not typical, but his general feeling represented that of southern dirt farmers. The "One-Eyed Plowboy" saw well enough to reach fame and power by extolling his constituents' virtues. In their imaginations he was powerful and wise, but not above them. "I am simply a clodhopper, like you are," he told listeners, while calling the public school system "an abominable humbug." He flayed Charleston; thought the state university a den of aristocratic agnostics; and labeled The Citadel a "military dude factory."[61] It was an unhappy agrarian legacy in areas that needed expertise, education, and acceptance of broad social change.

These and other ideas agitated the farm communities' edges. Tied to immediate economic grievances, they contained the makings of political action. It was useless to praise the whole economic system when a major part endured both real and fancied grievances that touched men's ideals and goals in life. To tell angry men they were in a period of economic transition was folly. They would know the reason why. If there must be a fall, someone should provide a cushion. As the 1890's arrived, they proposed to gain it through politics.

Things focused among discontented farmers in the hot summer of 1890. Off-year elections were notoriously faction-ridden and often pivoted on whimsical local issues and personalities, but angry farmers in Plains states and the South showed their power in local contests by attacking candidates of both regular parties. "The farmers seem like unto ripe fruit," an Alliance organizer noted earlier, "you can gather them by a gentle shake of the bush." Other observers detected a feeling that might broaden into an agrarian crusade. "The idea seems to have obtained in the minds of thousands of farmers that every man's hand is against them, and hence, there is a kind of war spirit pervading their entire being."[62]

The arid Plains states, riddled with so many divisions among farmers themselves, at the mercy of climate and staple crop prices, produced the most colorful campaigns. In June, 1890, Kansas farmers organized the first major People's Party, and began talk of a national third party movement for the presidential contest in 1892. Populist speakers swept up and down the plains like whirlwinds, raising political dust and creating awesome noise. This kind of radicalism was hardly new, but the crowds such speakers drew surprised Republican leaders. Nearly every country schoolhouse shook to cheers and applause from local farmers hearing one of their number or an imported speaker excoriate the evil East, oppressive railroads, and high interest rates. A business-man on weekend rounds might hear lusty voices in songs about earthly rewards coming from a clapboard church. A row of tattered backsides projected from windowsills, and horses stamped restlessly in the yard, nervous amid strange surroundings and odd sounds.[63]

Nearly every candidate for Congress or local office in the Plains states faced a barrage of questions and heckling as he explained the tariff, sound money, or the general virtues of Republicanism or the Democracy. Populists drew the biggest crowds, however, peppering speeches with verbal grapeshot at financial interests supposedly domi-nating "old parties." "It was a fanaticism like the Crusades," a con-temporary recalled, "a season of shibboleths and fetishes and slogans. Reason slept, and the passions—jealousy, covetousness, hatred—ran amuck. . . . Far into the night, their voices rose, praising the people's will as though it were God's will, and cursing wealth for all its iniquity." [64] The talk became therapy, as people aired long-repressed grievances and hostilities, and women were suddenly vocal.[65] Hus-bands discussed high costs of machinery and low crop prices; wives pointed to expensive but desirable luxuries and better homes, things that went unrealized at market-time. Behind these voiced grievances was a colorful host of weekly newspapers, drilling into isolated read-ers' minds lessons in daily economics, and a catalogue of promises unfulfilled and hopes gone sour.[66]

The voters read and talked, but took greatest pleasure in the oratory a handful of vivid leaders poured out like lava from long dormant volcanoes. Mary E. Lease, "a large woman, bronzed by sun and wind, with a powerful voice and an eloquence which never failed to capture the crowd" climbed to temporary fame. Hard experience with sun and grasshoppers qualified her to discuss a brand of economics and view of life that appealed to those from a similar pattern. She was a strong-willed woman, bitter at the world, and sure of her nostrums' healing powers. Critics ridiculed her as "Patrick Henry in Petticoats," and

"The Kansas Pythoness." She had simple answers. "You may call me an anarchist, a socialist or a communist, I care not, but I hold to the theory that if one man has not enough to eat three times a day and another man has $25,000,000, that last man has something that belongs to the first." [67] The cause needed more than her train fare, and excited crowds often filled her laundry basket with loose change, and in better times, a rain of silver dollars.[68] She was not learned, but seemed sensible, touching in bright stereotypes the humdrum events that made up a million hidden lives. She enjoyed her role. "Mrs. Lease . . . was sometimes a bit of a demagogue and was not without a letch for money and the fleshpots thereunto pertaining. . . ." noted the critical bourgeois, William Allen White.[69] There was truth in *Judge's* assertion that like most reformers, she wanted place and power. "Mary Lease will never consent to be saved unless she leads the heavenly band." [70]

Ignatius Donnelley, a masculine counterpart handier with the pen than the tongue, moved toward prominence in the developing Populist movement. His checkered career in Minnesota and national politics reflected alternating urges for respectability and domination of a crusade. As a member of the national House from 1863 to 1869, he gained a taste for office and power that his radical talk never quite covered. Flirting with nearly every anti-monopoly and agrarian splinter group in the Old Northwest, Donnelley touched the bases of Greenbackism, farmer-labor groups, and orthodox Republicanism without losing a nervous personality. Short, pugnacious, looking like a belligerent child, he "had grown old in the service of fiat money." [71] He dabbled in real estate, believed in the lost continent of Atlantis, "proved" Francis Bacon wrote Shakespeare's plays, and printed his delusions of apocalyptic punishment and utopian salvation as novels. Like most radicals, he thought to reform the world, but only revolted against his origins. He also enjoyed the role. "For my part, I rather like this walking on volcanoes," he once said in a revealing insight.[72]

That was true of many men now taking the lead in Populism, as 1890 passed into history. The respectable James B. Weaver of Iowa, watched the world from behind a set of whiskers with a calm glance worthy of an establishment politico. But as Greenback candidate for president in 1880, and ally of various splinter reform groups, he was a natural Populist leader to combine moderation and energy. William A. "Whiskers" Peffer won the waspish John J. Ingalls' Senate seat in 1890 to represent Kansas as the first Populist member of the upper house. His beard reached the beltline, and his shaggy figure and clipped oratory enlivened national debates. Jerry Simpson, "Sockless

Socrates of the Prairies," represented a Kansas House district after 1890, and despite the ridiculous nickname was shrewd enough not to despise those who lacked socks. These and other leaders were not all of Populism, and most rose to the crusade's top through writing and speaking, but they symptomized a restless urge for change, and liked to live in the shadows of tall words and big promises. They did not represent a majority of the nation's farmers, however, and were not the only active reformers. Intense believers in labor rights, railroad regulation, and state control of schools equaled the Populists in numbers and reforms, if not volume of words. But Populists were the most important of these groups. With suitable leadership and an appealing central issue, they had the best chance to control agrarian states.[73] And state control could widen into national influence.

Life was inevitably harder for reformers in the South. Any threat to Democratic rule raised the bogey of "Negro domination," but in poverty-stricken areas like interior Georgia, men like Tom Watson were desperate enough to risk life and limb to escape the strangling grasp of a sterile one-party rule reproducing the past. In most of the South, Populism appealed to fundamental human needs, but conflicted with old emotions around the Democratic party. The "fluence men" of both parties vied for inebriated and frightened colored voters. In rough-and-tumble areas like East Texas, a few Populist leaders built local machines by candidly adopting adversaries' methods. They herded Negroes to the polls, threatened and persuaded white neighbors, and defiantly challenged existing authority.

A guerilla war raged between southern Democracy and Populism. Western agrarians used the ammunition of speeches, but in the South, both sides used real bullets, nightriders, and the torch. Ballot boxes vanished in mysterious fires, or in the sluggish currents of hidden bayous. Negroes stayed indoors, or voted with people most likely to survive—usually Democrats. Poor leadership, lack of time and money, and a long tradition of violence hampered every southern Populist move toward success on any level.[74]

As Populism gained momentum with scattered but impressive election victories in 1890, nervous opponents used the time-honored weapon of ridicule. Cranks, professional reformers, the drifters and bummers of politics found a ready haven in Populism. Even sincere agrarians admitted the movement became "an asylum for all the cranks in the universe." [75] Grover Cleveland feared agrarians would make Democracy "a sort of political Cave of Adullam to which would resort 'everyone that was in distress, and everyone that was in debt, and everyone that was discontented.' " [76] Democratic Governor James S. Hogg of Texas ridiculed the movement in effective rural language. It threatened states rights, white rule, and Democracy, he said. Above all, its members were incompetent malcontents. Populist spending proposals, including funds to promote rain-making, totaled an alleged $35,000,000,000. "Such fellows could not drive a wagon and team without running over every stump within range of the road. They could not operate a windmill without bursting every joint of the machinery. Many of them could not set a mousetrap. Yet they go around telling you how to run the government." [77] Populism never escaped this stereotype of crankiness. It was a major factor in defeating the agrarian crusade in a nation seldom radical in hard times, and that always demanded political respectability.

By mid-summer, 1890, the agrarians were making their point. "Whether they will be able to improve the condition of the farmers or not, the Alliance members will have the satisfaction of having caused almost a panic in the Democratic party of the South and the Republican party of the West," the New York Sun prophesied.[78] In December, 1890, the Southern Alliance, Colored Farmers' Alliance, and other groups gathered at Ocala, Florida, to plan political action. Demands included free coinage, an expanded government banking system, tariff reform, a graduated income tax, and more railroad regulation. In May, 1891, a national Populist movement began to form with a convention in Cincinnati. A gathering in St. Louis in February, 1892, formally organized the Peoples' Party.

The program rising from these organizational moves blended belief in individualism and equal opportunity with controls on competition. Men fearful of business influence in government assumed that a powerful government would remain personal and modest in functions. Populists saw government as a negative force to restrain enemies, and a positive element to subsidize their livelihood. The general tone was humanitarian, but with an edge that unsettled many sympathizers and outraged opponents. "I claim it is the business of the government to make it possible for me to live and sustain the life of my family," Governor Lorenzo D. Lewelling of Kansas said in 1894.[79]

Despite its exotic rhetoric and windmill style, Populism was not a national force in 1890. Nor did the People's Party represent a majority of farmers. Western agrarians supported Republicans pledged to reform policies more often than separate tickets. Southern farmers feared the race question enough to follow Democrats who promised attention to their ideas. In the areas of its widest appeal, Populism competed

with other reformist splinter groups.[80] Agrarian victories in 1890 did
not unduly alarm regular politicians since the voters hardly threatened
the system. Only an issue and leaders overriding these conflicting
local demands could disturb national politics. Of course, some people
thought free silver might be the unifying theme for discontented
voters, if prosperity did not continue.

Agrarian distress rested on material self-interest. Increasing production did not bring higher prices. Expansion based on credit produced
higher interest rates, especially for critical short-term borrowing. The
economy favored the industrial worker and business community, as
farmers profitably serving cities readily agreed. Marginal farmers
caught in snares of debt and fears of being left behind in national
development naturally sought debt relief and price increases for their
crops. Most men, whatever their occupation or status, went through
life indebted. They worried over home mortgages, future expenses,
monthly bills, and unexpected costs. Pious exhortations about frugality
and self-denial seldom altered the normal human proclivity to spend
all income. Pride magnified debt in a thousand petty irritants. To owe
the local bank was not disgraceful or unusual, but for an individual
to have to say he could not pay his bills was humiliating and compounded hostility. For every debt collected under duress, a local creditor overextended loans to a neighbor in temporary distress. For every
grocery or doctor bill refused extension, many others quietly disappeared as "bad debts" or silent charity. These were the normal acts of
communities where men dealt in human terms. In a unifying economy,
with large investment necessarily in the hands of central agents, it was
easier to blame poverty on mysterious combines and distant conspir-
ators than to admit bad personal judgement.

Rural debt was especially poignant. The farmer saw himself as
thrifty, independent, and personally free. Illustrious names like Jefferson and Jackson supported these beliefs. In large measure, men farmed
to avoid the complications of city life. This exposed the marginal
farmer to the sharp symbolism of declining status. He registered debt
not merely as mortgages, or in columns of figures. A new bonnet for
his wife, a comfortable retirement, a suit of clothes or trip to the fair,
luxuries like candy or coffee were the apparent differences between
success and failure, not merely in farming but in life. The ability to
buy these things and savor this status seemed threatened in the con-
solidating economy of the 1880's, and money took on diverse symbolic

meanings to a people who thought debt shameful. City dwellers and businessmen often used checks and intangible figures, but the rural population thought of "hard cash." They saw increasingly little of it, and the silver dollar became a symbol.

Like urban dwellers paying home mortgages, farmers expected to retire debts on land and houses. Rates on standard mortgages were bad enough, varying naturally from county to county and according to the lender's belief in ability to pay, but borrowers felt the pinch of debt more in chattel mortgages for short term notes, where rates were erratic and excessive. A year's credit to buy new machinery or horses carried rates in Kansas of 40–375 per cent, and many counties were mortgaged to full assessed valuation.[81] Farmers bitterly disliked special fees, commissions, and discounts in tight money markets. The mortgage company was usually reluctant to repossess a homestead or acreage, but movable property was at the mercy of an interest deadline. A man watching agents drive his horses to auction or repossessing a reaper naturally liked the idea of paying debts with depreciated dollars.[82]

In the South, crop liens perpetuated the plantation economy without much system. Merchants and local banks would not extend credit on land they did not want, taking as collateral the area's only negotiable commodity, a future crop. A weak banking system and dependence on one basic product perpetuated the debt cycle, and rooted farmers in poverty. With all its immediate significance and symbolic value, debt inevitably focused farm discontent. "The underlying causes of the unrest pervading the industrial and agricultural classes in the two decades leading up to the Populist Uprising may be summed up in one word, INTEREST," wrote one who was there.[83]

Hostility easily created human scapegoats. How did the middleman earn commissions? His soft hands and smooth words revealed a status and invisible power the debtor naturally resented as he hooked harness traces, or greased a tractor's wheels. "The average land owner and farmer, though exercising the most consummate skill and practising the most rigid economy, cannot hope to achieve fortune in a lifetime," Leonidas Polk wrote in 1891. "The speculator in 'futures' and the manipulator of stocks, with no knowledge of frugality and without legitimate skill, achieve fortune in a day." [84] This resentment focused on the "millionaires" which an excited press discussed and magnified with a mixture of contempt and envy. Populist agitators led in a new anthem: [85]

> There are ninety and nine who live and die
>   In want, and hunger, and cold,
> That one may live in luxury,
>   And be wrapped in a silken fold.
> The ninety and nine in hovels bare.
> The one in a palace with riches rare.

This view widened steadily into a fear of national or universal catastrophe. "If the present strained relations between wealth owners and wealth producers continue much longer, they will ripen into fruitful disaster," James B. Weaver warned. Believing the basic economic and political system sound, Populists naturally attacked agents who turned it from supposedly automatic progress for everyone to benefit a few. ". . . a bold and aggressive plutocracy has usurped the government, and is using it as a policeman to enforce its insolent decrees," Weaver declared.[86]

Most people use the idea of a conspiracy to explain baffling things in their world. It orders apparent chaos, removes personal responsibility, and magnifies self-importance by increasing the power of unjust adversaries. Invisibility is a kind of opulence that feeds starved emotions. "Conspiracy" fortified the momentum of Populism's crusade. To fight mortgage rates was one thing. To free mankind from the grip of a "money monster" was a more compelling rationalization for both frustration and economic grievances. How well it savored of biblical dramas familiar to rural audiences: "We must expect to be confronted by a vast and splendidly equipped army of extortionists, userers and oppressors marshalled from every nation under heaven," Weaver said.[87] It was hardly a new or uniquely American view, but Populists added a dark grandeur to its appeal.[88] It simplified things to discuss "the invisible government, whose throne room was Wall Street, [that] controlled the visible government in nation and state, in spite of statesmen's warnings and popular protests." [89]

An added ingredient of archaic patriotism extended the view. As the world's leading banker and richest power, Britain must be involved. "Wall Street has become the western extension of Threadneedle and Lombard Streets," Weaver trumpeted, "and the wealthy classes of England and America have been brought into touch. They are no longer twain, but one, and have restored to Great Britain all the dominion she desires over her long lost [American] colonies." [90] Frequent attacks against absentee ownership and foreign investment filled Populist pronunciamentos and platforms, with Britain the chief culprit.[91]

At least a ragged edge of bigotry circled the conspiracy thesis common to Populism's spokesmen, if not its rank and file. Jewish merchants sometimes endured ridicule and persecution. Their special connections, both in fact and fancy, with the "Money Power" made them suspect to agrarians. They were non-producers, rare enough among farmers to seem sinister, and they represented a historic scapegoat. The agrarians' public spokesmen like William Jennings Bryan contended that this represented a dislike of monopolistic wealth, not racial or social bigotry, but it fitted neatly with a prevalent human urge to escape personal responsibility by blaming weaknesses on agents of a larger process.[92]

These attitudes were efforts to order and comprehend economic distress. Just as Populism offered nothing radical outside the American mainstream, it differed from other reformist movements only in degree of response to hardship. Orthodox explanations of cyclical hard times did not pacify the marginal farmer. "There is something besides over-production that has caused [hard times]," Leonidas Polk argued. "I believe that it is not God's fault that we are in this bad condition. Congress could give us a bill in forty-eight hours that would relieve us, but Wall Street says nay."[93] A historic American belief in the virtues of simple legislation, the values of agrarian life, and the force of conspiracy combined to make currency manipulation a compelling issue for debtors. "There is more potentiality for evil in the country today, in the present condition of the silver question, than there is in the tariff question," Boston's elegant Edward Atkinson warned in 1882.[94]

The increased value of investments in silver mining, its solid constituency in the Far West, and over-representation in national politics, made silver a logical and politically dangerous rallying issue. Its ties to other mineral investments and already well-organized propaganda agencies like the National Bimetallic Union gave it tactical appeal to agrarian leaders.[95] Though Populists committed to deeper reforms of American life protested against shallow currency manipulation, free coinage would almost inevitably sweep all before it in a depression. It had in the 1870's, and there was no reason to doubt it could do so again.

An expanded volume of currency, resting on tangible silver dollars rather than fiat paper money, promised to raise prices and reduce mortgage debts.[96] Debtors wished to repay debts with the kind of dollars they borrowed. William J. Bryan later summarized the argument's attractive logic:[97]

The mortgage remains nominally the same, though the debt has actually become twice as great. Will [the farmer] be deceived by the cry of 'honest dollar'? If he should loan a Nebraska neighbor a hog weighing 100 pounds and the next spring demand in return a hog weighing 200 pounds, he would be called dishonest, even though he contended that he was only demanding one hog—just the number he loaned. Society has become accustomed to some very nice distinctions. The poor man is called a Socialist if he believes that the wealth of the rich should be divided among the poor, but the rich man is called a financier if he devises a plan by which the pittance of the poor man can be converted to his use. The poor man who takes property by force is called a thief, but the creditor who can by legislation make a debtor pay a dollar twice as large as he borrowed is lauded as the friend of sound currency.

That the creditor extended funds on shaky collateral, naturally escaped notice, and few spokesmen recalled how often the farmer borrowed money as a capitalist rather than an underdog.

The problem was real in human terms, however, and in usual American fashion, distressed farmers wanted government action. Silverites argued that adequate government recognition would stabilize the white metal's price, and regulate the purchasing power of all dollars.[98] They ignored gold's presence as the world's standard of value. References to this often let patriotism draw an unbalanced picture of America as a world power. "Standing among the nations of the world as a giant among pygmies," Richard P. Bland argued, "why should we ask the aid or advice of baby England, baby Germany, or Lilliputian France, in establishing for ourselves a bimetallic system?"[99] It was easier to hark back to American history, when in good times gold, silver, and paper remained reasonably stable, forgetting the flight of gold in periods of doubt and depression.[100] By 1890, free silver had national appeal. It did not appear suddenly. Its complexities and debatable merits as a cure-all disappeared in compelling slogans. High school boys abandoned afternoon baseball for pamphlets on the money question. In poverty-stricken Alabama, a hill family heard of its blessings, and equating free silver with free lunch, dispatched a runner with a bucket to gather their share.[101]

The Populist crusade enfolded its members. Like all earnest men devoted to ideals and in the grip of need, they fancied themselves alone in a hostile world. The sunburned farmer who watched his income dwindle on the hot plains of Kansas or Iowa, and the despairing tenant in the brooding South, believed that they alone sensed the impending crisis, but many intelligent men in business and politics had long sensed growing frustrations and imbalances in the system. Their hands were clean, they wore fine clothes, and spoke grammatically, but they were no less disturbed for being well-off or in responsible places. The mid-1880's produced a wave of speculation on the triumphing industrial system. Books, articles, novels, government reports, and laws reflected this concern and interest, but the symptoms were easier to see than the malady. "I may be wrong, but from my point of view it appears that machinery is constantly making capital more independent of labor," a New York manufacturer wrote a newspaper friend in 1885. "[And] that while labor has shared in the benefits of the great forces that now control the world, its wants, owing to the march of education, have increased much faster. There was a time when ignorance was bliss and men were content to be the slaves of capital. Now men are generally educated to the belief that they are the equals of others in the natural rights; and yet they find the opportunities to employ those natural rights for their own benefit greatly abridged." [102] William Henry Smith agreed, writing Rutherford B. Hayes: "The future of no party is assured. The great question of the relations of capital to labor, that is now at our doors, must be met. Woe betide the party or the man that trifle with it." [103]

But what to do? Laws did not control corporations that sharpened tensions between capital and labor. The American people did not want to dispense with bigness—they wished only to make it respond to personal demands—but the country had no tradition of government intervention to enforce economic decrees, or body of men sufficiently bipartisan to establish the art. A sense of impending crisis grew with industrialization. Senator Orville H. Platt of Connecticut, a constructive conservative, offered little but warnings and sincere hand-wringing: [104]

> I believe future politics are to turn on measures affecting 'industrial independence.' We can't shut our eyes to what is called socialism, vaguely, and we all ought to be socialists in the best and true meaning of the term. The character and condition of our laboring classes, and how they can be best advanced in those respects, is the burning question both in politics and ethics. It demands attention and it will compel attention, and it is very likely to be a dangerous question. It requires honest study and honest treatment. Politicians and statesmen had better meet it wisely. The country is full of discontent, and the great need of men who from the standpoint of sympathy with the common people can so gain their confidence as to head them wisely.

Most men connected with business were not shortsighted materialists or bloated bondholders, but they were committed to a system that produced both speculation and solid economic building, and did not know how to correct evils without threatening virtues. Wharton Barker, successful Pennsylvania businessman, disliked the "aggression of concentrated capital." He could only predict "the conflict between capital and the working classes has become irresistable." [105]

Men with a sharp sense of life's just rewards, both to the famous and obscure, like Hayes and William McKinley, worried over the problem. Years of managing Ohio politics broadened their view without eroding their humanity. They believed in laws, but knew that individual human response was the key to any long-term stability in society. "My point is that free government cannot long endure if property is largely in a few hands, and large masses of people are unable to earn homes, education, and a support in old age," Hayes said.[106] McKinley often publicly condemned the "mad spirit for gain and riches which is so prevalent in American society . . . by gambling in stocks, speculation in wheat, by 'corners' and 'margins.'" [107]

It all had an ironic side in 1890. No economy had ever produced so much material wealth for so many people, but every increase in well-being prompted cries for more security, social balance, and luxuries that denoted success. Labor enjoyed greater privileges than ever before; agriculture seemed integrated into the economy except for some soft spots; but the whole production process baffled politicians who tried to even out its impact. Senator Cullom praised the Sherman Anti-Trust Act, but knew it would not reach any root cause of consolidation. A law could not arrest the tendency of life itself. "We are in a rather peculiar situation politically in this country just now," he wrote Wharton Barker in 1891, "and while much of the dissatisfaction and restlessness of the people is not founded in reason, yet there is ground for very considerable complaint. The inevitable tendency seems to be for the big fish to swallow up the little ones. There is no doubt about the fact that the aggressions of capital have been very great, and nothing is accomplished, apparently, that puts a check upon it, or has so far. And while the prices of manufactured articles are not increased by the concentration of capital above what they were when more people were proprietors of business institutions, yet, after all, I think it is unfortunate for the country that the control of the business of the country is concentrated in so few people." [108] He saw that crucial ethical and moral considerations, weighing both man's highest and lowest aspirations, would enter any national debate on the system's merits and weaknesses.

Republicans and Democrats felt the time's curious changes. They were uncertain of law's efficacy, not quite convinced that men who made the system could always control it with government, yet their ambivalence was less compelling and less politically useful than simple commitment, as Populists were proving. As 1892 approached, leaders in both parties knew that farmers had genuine needs, and reflected deep discontents. But there was no real third party threat. In good American fashion, everyone would wait for the next election.

The inauguration of Grover Cleveland, March 4, 1885. (From G. F. Howe, *Chester A. Arthur.*)

Thomas F. Bayard, Secretary of State (1885–89) and first Ambassador to Great Britain. (Library of Congress.)

William C. Whitney, Secretary of the Navy, 1885–89. (Library of Congress.)

Secretary of War Daniel S. Lamont, 1897. (Library of Congress.)

William R. Morrison of Illinois, Democratic tariff reformer. (Library of Congress.)

Samuel J. Randall, Democratic Speaker of the House. (Library of Congress.)

Allen G. Thurman, "The Old Roman," Grover Cleveland's running-mate in 1888. (*New York Daily Graphic,* June 8, 1888.)

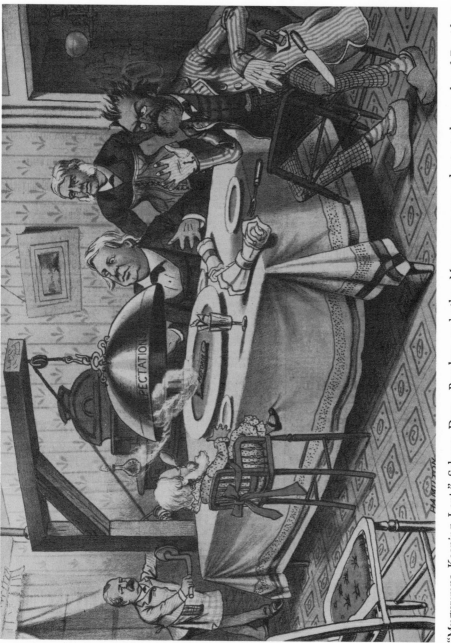

"Mugwumps Keeping Lent." Schurz; Dana, Beecher, and other Mugwumps are aghast at the results of President Cleveland's reforms. (*Judge*, March 11, 1885.)

Roger Q. Mills doses the overweight "Infant Industries" with his tariff reform medi-cine. (*Puck*, April 11, 1888.)

An anti-tariff cartoon. (*Puck*, June 27, 1888.)

"Marse Henry" Watterson, influential editor of the *Louisville Courier-Journal*. (Library of Congress.)

Stephen B. Elkins, Secretary of War, 1891–93. (West Virginia University Library.)

Matthew Stanley Quay, political boss and senator from Pennsylvania. (Library of Congress.)

Thomas Collier Platt, "The Easy Boss." (Library of Congress.)

A campaign picture of Benjamin Harrison, 1888. (Library of Congress.)

Senator Nelson W. Aldrich of Rhode Island, tariff and currency expert. (Library of Congress.)

VOL. 14 NO. 351 JULY 7, 1888. PRICE 10 CENTS.

Judge

Entered at the Post Office at New York as Second-Class Matter, Copyright 1887 by the Judge Publishing Co.

"The Hour has Come, the Man is Here." American labor and Columbia want Benjamin Harrison in 1888. (*Judge*, July 7, 1888.)

"Putting His Foot in it." Minister Lord Sackville-West is caught in the bear-trap of American politics by the "Murchison Letter." (*New York Daily Graphic,* Oct. 26, 1888.)

President Benjamin Harrison's rainy Inauguration, March 4, 1889. (Library of Congress.)

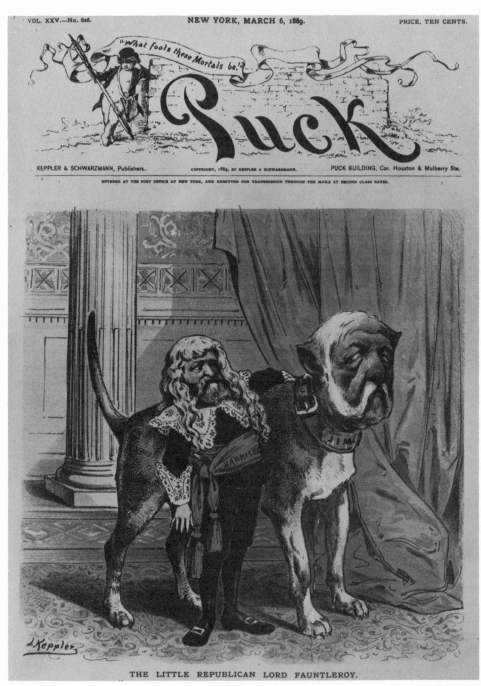

VOL. XXV.—No. 626.   NEW YORK, MARCH 6, 1889.   PRICE, TEN CENTS.

KEPPLER & SCHWARZMANN, Publishers.   COPYRIGHT, 1889, BY KEPPLER & SCHWARZMANN.   PUCK BUILDING, Cor. Houston & Mulberry Sts.

ENTERED AT THE POST OFFICE AT NEW YORK, AND ADMITTED FOR TRANSMISSION THROUGH THE MAILS AT SECOND CLASS RATES.

"What fools these Mortals be."

THE LITTLE REPUBLICAN LORD FAUNTLEROY.

"He is going to try to please and reconcile everybody, bless his little heart!" James G. Blaine is President Harrison's watchdog and manager in a Democratic cartoon. (*Puck,* March 6, 1889.)

"The Amazing Growth of the Pension Pig"—a Democratic view. (*Puck*, March 14, 1888.)

Senator William B. Allison of
Iowa, co-author of the Bland-
Allison Act of 1878. (Library
of Congress.)

"Czar" Thomas Brackett Reed
1897. He caused a furor over hi
rules to expedite legislation. (Li
brary of Congress.)

Congressman William McKinley of Ohio. (Library of Congress.)

☆☆☆☆☆☆ ☆☆☆☆☆☆☆☆☆☆☆☆☆☆☆☆☆☆

Part Three
1892‒1896

☆☆☆☆☆☆☆☆☆☆☆☆☆☆☆☆☆☆☆☆☆☆☆☆

X

☆☆☆☆☆ ☆☆☆☆☆ ☆☆☆☆☆☆☆☆

"Grover, Grover, Four More Years"

☆☆☆☆☆☆☆☆☆☆☆☆☆☆☆☆☆☆☆

President Harrison, like most of his predecessors, had mixed feelings about living in the White House. He preferred administration to political manipulation, and never mastered the art of oiling wheels. Expecting everyone to understand the limitations of his office, he had scant patience with complainers. Like Mrs. Harrison, he disliked "the circus aspect" around the country's first family. Even his evening walks were a chore, and he seldom talked much to accompanying confidants. In a close-fitting Prince Albert, with an erect stance, and dead-level look, Harrison resembled a pouter-pigeon on parade in LaFayette Square or Dupont Circle. Returning to the White House, he would nod curtly at the historic columns: "There is my jail." [1]

Perhaps. But it was worth a struggle. As he remarked privately, no Harrison ever ran from a fight. Pride, "availability," and belief in his Administration's programs forced Harrison to make some crucial decisions early in 1892. He may not have wanted a second term, but the succession seemed clear; Blaine apparently would take a draft. The Secretary's age and health seemed to make him less available than in 1888, but many hinted otherwise. He was over sixty, increasingly ill with gout, nervous headaches, and complications from a case of Bright's Disease. He seldom arrived at the State Department on time, and after the Pan-American Conference, the President and departmental staff increasingly conducted foreign affairs. Newsmen did not help matters. Arriving late one morning, Blaine waved to a crowd of reporters, lounging in the hall with cynical informality. One remarked candidly: "If you had not appeared today, we were going to give you a typhoid fever." The Secretary only smiled, but said another time: "I know nothing about my health until I read the New York papers." [2]

395

Blaine was weary. Time was not kind to a man of his temperament, and nothing deflected Fate's remorseless toll upon his children. Walker Blaine died of pneumonia on January 15, 1890. The parents had hardly absorbed the shock when daughter Alice died on February 2, 1890. These blows compounded Blaine's fatalism, and produced a growing lassitude that seemed out of character. His hair whitened and he grew forgetful, as if preoccupied with interior sounds. In May, 1891, he collapsed at Andrew Carnegie's, and stayed in bed several weeks. Mrs. Blaine wrote his letters, read at the bedside, and cautioned politicians not to exaggerate one way or the other. Spring became summer, with some improvement, but little verve. Magnetism had run its course. The President was gracious, sending flowers and keeping in touch about major decisions. But he was human, and everyone knew a steady stream of clandestine reports from mutual acquaintances advised him of Blaine's health and alleged intentions.

The news was conflicting. The press varied talk of Blaine's recovery with speculation about his death. The Secretary resumed his duties in 1891, but inevitably, there was friction with his chief. ". . . no unpleasant word was ever exchanged between me and him when we were face to face," Harrison insisted, no doubt correctly.[3] But Blaine's absence meant more work for Harrison, and he could not safely spare time from other duties. The alternative was Blaine's resignation, and that might be political dynamite. Still, it rankled for the press to laud Blaine's every suggestion, and report his habits minute by minute, as if any president he served was merely an invisible prop. "Mr. Blaine's illness just at this time throws upon me a good deal of responsibility," Harrison wrote Senator Allison in May, "with the disadvantage of not being perfectly informed as to what has been done."[4] He even asked mutual acquaintances like Murat Halstead to suggest that Blaine acknowledge his extra work. It would ease tension and give due credit. Blaine praised Harrison, but not too loudly; the press did not find it interesting.

Frequent visitors from Washington, obviously checking on his health, irritated Blaine. Secretary of War Redfield Proctor reported to the President in detail. "He came downstairs to see me, and was bright and pleasant as usual, but I was surprised to see so much evidence of sickness." Blaine seemed acute, wanting information from the seats of power, sending regards to Harrison. He would be well soon, he promised; Maine's clear air was doing wonders. But Proctor noted a different undercurrent. "It seemed to me that he made an effort to appear brisk and well, and that this was marked enough to be of itself an indication of weakness."[5] Other reports were equally conflicting. Blaine praised Harrison and the Administration's policies, skirted politics, and said he would soon return to Washington. One news-hawk thought the performance a little strained, like an aging prima donna reaching unsteadily for a high note. John Bassett Moore made the trip, and found Blaine nursing a gouty foot. He rose cordially, with a twinkle in his eyes. "You see, I am not dead yet."[6]

In the winter, Blaine helped calm the Chilean crisis, read reports, and entertained, but curious moments still punctuated relations with Harrison. During a Cabinet meeting in the spring of 1892, he suddenly left the room without a word. After an awkward moment, Elkins, now Secretary of War, hurried outside to find Blaine in near-shock, talking loosely of respect for Harrison, protesting this was the end of every-thing. Blaine recovered but it all seemed an act. "He dons a jaunty hat and walks briskly along where he may be seen," Colonel Alexander McClure noted, "and then returns home in a state of collapse."[7] Be-hind the comic-opera manipulations, and outside the situation's true pathos, a nagging chorus of critics and friends alternately urged Blaine to retire, or make a final trip up the political mountain. Godkin insisted renomination was "incredible and impossible," but powerful friends alienated from Harrison disagreed.[8]

One thing had not changed; Blaine's public following was large and vocal. If he dropped a hint in Maine, it echoed in Seattle. "People are like sheep," Michener reported to Harrison's secretary in August, 1891, "and just about this time they are nearly all jumping over the fence into Blaine's fields."[9] After Christmas, "Corporal" Tanner told Senator Cullom not to raise his hopes as a favorite son. "However, we must accept the inevitable. The people are wild for Blaine."[10] The under-ground feeling intensified by New Year's. ". . . the country is for Blaine and reciprocity, and will not be restrained," William Henry Smith told a friend.[11] One politico recounted a frank conversation with Blaine. ". . . he would return to his work; would be loyal to the President; would not be a candidate, but would accept if the convention saw fit to tender the nomination in such a way as to make it complimentary, and show the nomination to be in accord with the wishes of the party." Michener's brigade did not know what to think, but wanted Blaine either to spurn or seek the nomination.[12]

As usual in times of crisis, Blaine dithered, apparently wanting a ceremonial nomination. Nelson Dingley of Maine brought him Christ-mas cheer. Blaine seemed energetic, warming himself at the fire, re-peating the latest stories. Politics? He really had none at the moment.

He wanted to stay in State. "You can be nominated if you say the word," Dingley said. Blaine shrugged. "But I do not desire to embarrass my friends. I cannot announce that I am a candidate and still remain in the cabinet of President Harrison. On the other hand, if I refuse to yield to the pressure brought to bear on me, I shall be charged with deserting my friends." No, he would not seek a nomination; yes, he would accept a "draft." [13] A little later, Senator Plumb of Kansas told friends Blaine "would run if he had to carry his coffin on his back." [14] At the same time, Blaine disavowed presidential aspirations to Reid, but thought the *Tribune* could say there was nothing wrong with a Cabinet officer accepting a nomination that by-passed his chief. [15]

Harrison did not see it that way. He dreaded a re-election campaign, and with a suitable heir, might stand aside. But he disliked Blaine's conniving friends, whatever their hero's real attitude. His advisers told a similar tale. Blaine was still popular west of Pennsylvania. Harrison, they regretted to report, was not. The Administration was sound and clean, but uninspiring. They did not say it in so many words, but any hope that Blaine might run weakened Harrison's chances for renomination, let alone re-election. The Far West liked the Plumed Knight; he could win, and might increase silver's influence in national politics. Grumbling farmers in the Mississippi Valley agreed. Clarkson and others thought Blaine could dull the Alliance appeal, and avoid a Republican massacre.

But like Harrison, Blaine had his pride. He knew that many ambitious men curried his favor merely to thwart Harrison, hoping to control the party behind a sick candidate. A few friends told him the truth. He should not be a straw man for anyone. In February, he seemed to take their advice, denying any further presidential ambitions in an open letter to Clarkson. "I am not a candidate for the presidency and my name will not go before the Republican national convention for the nomination. I make this announcement in due season. To those who have tendered me their support I owe sincere thanks and am most grateful for their confidence. They will, I am sure, make earnest efforts in the approaching contest, which is rendered especially important by reason of the industrial and financial policy of the government being at stake." It seemed firm, and most independent and opposition papers accepted the statement at face value. Insiders noted a tinge of bitterness in the whole affair, and thought Blaine would decline, after misleading many friends. [16]

It was a hard choice, but Blaine was sincere—for the moment. He did not want to challenge Harrison, but knew this was his last chance for even a complimentary nomination. He could not remain Secretary of State indefinitely, and the greater prize might be worth a last gamble. The debacle better illustrated Blaine's hesitance than any dark designs. He hated to disappoint friends, and did not know how to meet divided advice. It was still early. Friends said the party could not live without him, and would not survive with Harrison, but the President was not an avowed candidate. There were a few other contenders, old and new.

As usual, there was Senator Sherman, though he had no illusions. The defeat of 1888 stung him deeply, since it ended any serious presidential possibilities. "I do not want the nomination, but assume that Harrison will receive it and make the contest," he wrote in mid-May. "I am inclined to think that Blaine occupies very much my position." [17] He doubted Harrison could carry New York, and assumed he would be a respectable sacrifice. Sherman was too tired to struggle much. "I am not a candidate for President, and am in one respect like the rebels were down South, [and] want to be let alone." [18]

In silencing discussion of his own merits, Sherman turned attention to Ohio's Governor William McKinley, both his and Blaine's "residuary legatee." [19] The party needed younger men, familiar with the burgeoning yet discontented West. McKinley filled that bill and steadily amassed popularity and political credit. "McKinley talk" worried Harrison as much as the "Blaine problem." Emissaries visited Columbus to discuss matters with the genial Buckeye who easily won the governorship in 1891. Nothing seemed to keep him down, and he was already gathering talented men for a presidential boom. But McKinley had a fine sense of timing, and 1892 might not be his year. The President's agents thought he was at most a dark horse, but remembered the "peculiar McKinley applause" that rippled across the convention in 1888. He was a man to watch.[20]

McKinley's position resembled Blaine's. He was obviously popular, and public denial of ambitions might thwart future work. Silence lent consent to other men's talk and hopes. He cared little enough for Harrison. Like most congressmen, he bore the marks of dealing with the icy President. He was content to be Sherman's heir in Ohio, and if possible, Blaine's in the nation. His friend Mark Hanna, with a genius for organization and attracting talented aides, wanted to advertise his merits. If Harrison wished another nomination, he should have it; if not, McKinley would await the call. Hanna was more enthusiastic than the Governor, sensing better prospects for victory with McKinley than ever with Sherman. He genuinely liked and respected "the Major," whose soft-spoken personal dealings so well complemented his own desire to win. He was frank with Sherman, reporting that McKinley "has had a feeling that the lightning might strike." Hanna and friends "had done a little work in that direction." [21]

The Governor entertained distinguished visitors that spring, including Michigan's ever-hopeful Russell Alger. McKinley said he was not interested himself, preferring 1896, when Harrison's chill and the Blaine fervor had passed. It looked like a Democratic year anyway.[22] McKinley was sincere, but as Hanna said, it paid to advertise. They might as well softly announce for 1896 now. There was no denying that "aggressive forces among younger Republicans wanted William McKinley." [23] If the convention deadlocked, "McKinley can be nominated easily," Hanna soon assured Sherman.[24] Harrison's friends were equally aware of the Ohioan's popularity. "McKinley is the favorite of the dark horse brigade," one wired him on convention-eve.[25]

Newspaper talk that "a majority of Republicans" favored Harrison irked Tom Reed, who said "the people have no idea of the actual condition of revolt which exists." He wanted no more of Harrison; the party could not "live four years more in a dripping cave." Exhortations to mount the President's slowly moving bandwagon brought a snort: "I never ride in an ice-cart." [26] Reed hardly typified general party opinion, but put in tart language the hidden thoughts of many powerful men. Midwestern states that went for protection in 1888 seemed wobbly. The Far West, traditionally Republican, and especially favorable to Harrison in 1888, was restless. Silver leaders nursed grievances, and resented eastern power. Of course, no one knew quite what to do about it. Russell Alger's private car heated western rails, and he confirmed the dissatisfaction.[27]

The Far West did not elect presidents. Harrison and the party were more secure there than eastern leaders surmised. Western love of protection and federal aid might override desire for still more silver legislation in a tariff-reform campaign. Tom Platt was more significant than any westerner, and in the winter of 1891, the Easy Boss wanted no more of Harrison. Unsure of Blaine's intentions, or the likelihood of a McKinley draft, he stayed aloof.[28] Like everyone else, he had no plan, but talked with Foraker about a temporary alliance on Sherman. He did not trust McKinley, who had a mind of his own, and the bosses could dump Sherman for someone better in a deadlocked convention.[29] Harrison was "a good, strong, wise president," Platt said, who could not win re-election. The President's arrogance, coldness, and isolation from the party's rank and file spelled defeat,[30] but Platt and other state leaders drifted, to Harrison's advantage. Their opposition might help renominate him, standing ironically in the limelight as an underdog. It might all turn out as Senator Orville Platt predicted. Noting that Harrison "has made Quay his enemy because he would not be controlled by him," he thought Harrison "has been an able, clean and safe President. These are the qualities the people look for in a president." [31] By mid-spring, despite presidential silence, Harrison was obviously seeking renomination. But he must settle the nagging "Blaine problem."

Harrison tried not to dismiss Blaine; the Plumed Knight's followers might combine sympathy and outrage for a genuine draft. However, as the President frankly told his secretary in March, whether Blaine stayed or went he was "a disturber and an unfriendly critic." [32] That was rationalization, for Blaine was not a critic. Harrison tried indirection and tact. Maybe newspaper talk would shame the Secretary into disavowing his followers. But Blaine remained silent, perhaps fearing a grand gesture would lose both the State portfolio and his followers. His every move attracted speculation. Late in May, he visited New York to see an oculist. Or so he insisted to newsmen. His listless appearance shocked veteran reporters. Quick smiles and repeated protestations of good health seemed forced, though the old charm was intact. "Did you ever before interview a dead man?" one reporter later asked a colleague. Chauncey Depew asked point-blank if Blaine was a candidate. Blaine seemed candid. He thought Harrison could not win renomination or re-election, but he was not a candidate, and could not face a canvass. "It would kill me." Depew believed him, and went to work for Harrison.[33]

The President's advisers thought "it was plain that his enemies had determined to rally upon Mr. Blaine and the Secretary had agreed to such use of his name." [34] Early in June, Harrison settled the matter, dispatching Elkins to urge Blaine either to announce his candidacy or resign. A nature like Blaine's could only rebel. At 1 p.m. on June 4, three days before the convention met, the President received his curt, formal resignation. Harrison read the letter, telling Halford with relief: "Well, the crisis has come." He sat down and penned an equally perfunctory acceptance, and Halford delivered it to the Blaine mansion at 1:30. In the stillness, Halford heard Blaine say in the dining room: "Well, I am no longer Secretary of State." [35]

A fever of speculation spread over Washington. Why had Blaine resigned so suddenly and curtly? Was he now a full-fledged candidate? Most superficial observers blamed Mrs. Blaine, whose dislike of the presidential couple was all too clear. The President, so the story ran, also refused her several patronage favors. The social wars had triumphed over good taste and political sense. But this was hardly true. The situation was intolerable to Harrison, and he called Blaine's intentions to account. Both men were discourteous, but neither was hasty or trivial.

The instant Blaine resigned, red and white lapel badges advertised "The Peoples' Choice." His picture rolled down the fronts of headquarters in a dozen cities. Eager supporters circulated pamphlets, placards, and posters. With the convention at hand, enthusiasm might carry Blaine to the top. He did not expect a triumph. It was all over. "The truth is, I do not want that office," he had told a relative. "When the American people choose a President they require him to remain awake four years. I have come to a time in life when I need my sleep." [36] And many people now thought he played friends false. "The Plumed Knight carries a broken lance," Harry New shrewdly said.[37] Blaine was sorry to leave State, but life had become wearisome. If friends wanted to manufacture a boom, he would not interfere, but he had no illusions about success.

Blaine's agents met a group of hardened regulars in their last-minute surge toward success. On May 23, before Blaine resigned, Harrison placed Michener in charge of a renomination campaign. That night, he and a handful of tight-lipped, professional aides met in a hotel suite, blocked out a plan, and began to discharge the President's commission. As "The Twelve Apostles," they became familiar figures at the national convention, scheduled to meet in Minneapolis on June 7. Michener contacted every potential delegate or alternate in reach. A sudden flood of mail advertised the President's achievements and the dangers of a revived Democracy. Cabinet members and a few friends contributed funds to Harrison's small but efficient personal organization.[38]

The President was not idle. Earlier in the spring, he entertained McKinley and other midwestern leaders with unusual cordiality. He even tried to smooth Tom Platt's hurt feelings indirectly, offering to make Chauncey Depew Secretary of State. The surprised New Yorker declined, fearing his railroad holdings would embarrass the Administration during the campaign. Depew was already telling reporters that "whoever runs for president on the Republican ticket will succeed or fail upon the record of the Harrison administration." That meant the President's renomination.[39] Harrison did not limit himself to uncongenial personal dealing. In May, he toured Pennsylvania and western New York, "a brilliant raid into the heart of the enemy's country," Dana said in the *Sun*. The President drew large crowds, treating attentive listeners to his customary lucid discussion of protection, bimetallism, and local issues. Dana's paper added a thoughtful postscript to the persistent Harrison puzzle: [40]

> It is a singular psychological quality that enables this gentleman, who cannot discourse privately to an audience of one, two, or half a dozen individuals without chilling their very gizzards, and who is not strong in rhetoric addressed to great and important audiences, to charm the hearts of such citizens as gather by scores or hundreds at country railroad stations to see the second-term train go by.

As the convention date arrived, with Blaine's bright image almost hanging in the air, Harrison could count on success, barring an unforseen accident. Quick action, lack of other leaders, and vigor avoided humiliation from his own party. "When we arrived at the convention," South Dakota's Republican Senator Richard F. Pettigrew recalled, "we found everything cut and dried for Harrison's renomination." [41] Re-election was another matter, especially since the Democrats seemed united and determined to win.

Tourists on Madison Avenue in New York, often saw the heavy figure of former President Cleveland at a handsome residence at Number 816. It was a four story row house with exterior red brickwork and brownstone trim, expensive but not garish, with a curved arch above the door and ornamented window frames. Inside, simple furnishings reflected the family's tastes, and the cries of young children punctuated routine existence. The attractive Mrs. Cleveland shopped like other housewives, did charity work, and occasionally entertained politicians. Cleveland departed on an exact schedule almost every weekday morning for the gilt-edged law firm of Bangs, Stetson, Tracy and MacVeagh on Broad Street. The duties were lucrative, but not taxing. His old bent for impersonal dealings served the firm well, and he refereed important cases, not arguing in court. The family alternated city existence with trips to the Adirondacks, and summers at Buzzard's Bay.

Cleveland left office with the usual disclaimers of future ambition, and many people wanted to agree. Henry Watterson thought New York would cut him down to size. "Cleveland in New York reminds one of a stone thrown into a river," Marse Henry predicted. "There

is a 'plunk,' a splash, and then silence." [42] Cleveland lent credence to
this attitude in the first months of what he called civilian life, seeming
to care little for vanished pomp or power. In reminiscing, he more
often said "When I was in Washington," than "When I was President." [43] He was not "social," but occasionally took his wife and friends
to the theater, sitting in comfortable obscurity behind the drapery of
a private box. Even this aroused sniping from unreconstructed foes
like Charles Dana. The *Sun* enlivened its pages in the spring of 1890
with a running discussion of Cleveland's weight, and he made the mistake of replying. The *Washington Post* covered Cleveland's theater
appearances, noting that he preferred an orchestra seat to a box, but
"is altogether too big and fat to occupy one with comfort." [44]

Cleveland was never widely popular, and no stream of pilgrims
darkened his existence, but familiar party leaders visited his offices
and home. There were not so many Democratic leaders that he went
unnoticed. His attitude toward renomination seemed ambivalent. On
December 12, 1889, he spoke in Boston. "The tariff reform, of course,
is ours, and we don't propose to be robbed of it under any pretense
whatever." It sounded like a bid for 1892, though he privately discounted a political future. He was happy with a growing family, he
told aides; he made a good deal of money with little effort, and liked
the work. "Besides, I feel somehow that I made a creditable showing
during my first term, all things considered, and I might lose whatever
of character and reputation are already gained in it." [45] The elections
of 1890, apparently turning on the tariff question, highlighted a growing Democratic desire for Cleveland's return. On November 13, he
spoke at a banquet honoring Allen G. Thurman. In December, he
addressed the New York Reform Club on tariff reduction, setting the
pace and issue for any "boom." He carefully judged the merits of each
request to speak in terms of its origin. In January, 1891, he spoke at
Jackson Day exercises and to the Young Men's Democratic Association
in Philadelphia. In February, as he rode in General Sherman's funeral
cortege, brazen cries of "Grover, Grover, Four More Years!" came
from the crowds.

A gulf still yawned between him and congressmen. Cleveland talked
gingerly of moderate tariff reform, and a vague impulse to change, but
the Congress elected in 1890 was discussing silver. "What are they
thinking about?" he exclaimed irritably.[46] Advisers counseled silence.
Any anti-silver statement would alienate convention votes from the
Midwest and South. Many Senate Democrats voted for a free coinage
bill in January, 1891, that outraged Cleveland. Consulting with Fair-

child, Whitney, Lamont, and other friends, he wrote a terse, biting letter to E. Ellery Anderson of the New York Reform Club, condemning the party's movement toward inflation. Warnings that it would affect his chances for renomination produced the old stubbornness: "Damn the nomination. I will say what I think is right." On February 10, 1891, the Reform Club cheered his short letter. "It surely cannot be necessary for me to make a formal expression of my agreement with those who believe that the greatest peril would be invited by the adoption of the scheme, embraced in the measure now pending in Congress, for the unlimited coinage of silver at our mints." He roundly condemned "the dangerous and reckless experiment of free, unlimited, and independent silver coinage." [47]

Most friends overlooked Cleveland's careful qualifications; he would take bimetallism as a political expedient. He really wanted a campaign for tariff reform, a much less divisive issue. His fan mail increased after the anti-silver stand, but he overlooked its rather genteel origins. Not many farmers sent congratulations. Cleveland subsided after making the point, and told Governor Russell of Massachusetts to emphasize tariff reform. Lamont warned against further outbursts; he must not seem "the representative of the ultra-anti-silver sentiment." Both Cleveland and his friends rather nervously wanted to agree with Wisconsin's General Edward S. Bragg; " 'Cleveland and the tariff' will be the next battle cry, and 'unlimited silver coinage' at the present ratio will soon be recognized as a 'fallacious bubble.' " [48] It was a comforting thought, true or false.

As usual, Cleveland did not mount a public campaign. Friends would run the machine, while he wrote letters and spoke to select audiences. He refused to enter the congressional elections of 1890, and state contests in 1891. "I have never been a stump speaker," he truthfully told a friend, "and do not think I should be a success in that role." [49] But he read the papers, and resented attacks from fellow Democrats. "I am quite tame and harmless; and I do not see why so many Democratic senators need exhaust themselves in admonitions to the people who profess the Democratic faith." [50] The backstage campaign did not stifle his advice. He urged Lamont to pay property taxes for "our poor voters" in Massachusetts, register all the faithful, and spread the usual blizzard of literature. [51]

His pretensions irritated much of the eastern press. Whitelaw Reid's *Tribune* naturally scored efforts to make him the peoples' champion. "It is fair to say of Mr. Cleveland's administration that it is to be remembered for nothing except its war on the Union veterans, its complete absorption of the civil service, and its half-hatched Mills bill." [52] The independent press hesitated, but had no other leader. Critics like Dana laid down a steady barrage against "Old Perpetual." The *Sun* elaborately analyzed a Cleveland letter to a reform group and another to the Capital Laundry. Lavishly praising the laundry list's style and content, the waspish paper accused Mugwumps and sexless independents of automatically falling down to worship "The Stuffed Prophet." [53]

Through 1890 and 1891, Cleveland's boomlet grew slowly. He was the party's natural center, however much he disagreed with its edges. No southerner could command a nomination; the Midwest had no national figures; and no one else represented a unifying issue like tariff reform. He spoke just enough to make his presence felt without palling on the faithful or the unpersuaded. The Republicans won in 1888 with superb organization; Democrats must copy that success in 1892. "Those who propose to juggle with the question of tariff reform will never again find their intended dupes asleep and uninformed," he wrote the Tariff Reform Club of Hagerstown, Maryland. [54] "Nothing can excuse the Democratic party if, at this time, it permits the neglect or subordination of the question of tariff reform," he warned a similar group in Montclair, New Jersey. [55] The National Association of Democratic Clubs with headquarters in Washington, began to campaign systematically for Cleveland in the spring of 1891. Friends like William L. Wilson toured the country to preach tariff reform, stress Cleveland's stature, and attack Republican programs.

Still, the nagging silver question would not down. Congress debated the subject in the spring of 1892 and the Senate daily threatened to pass free coinage bills. "At this rate some of us will be bringing up the rear, to the music of tariff reform," Cleveland wrote Whitney, "while the main army is being slaughtered amid the shouting for honest money." He could not control Congress, but hoped no "sensible man supposes for a moment that we can elect a president upon a platform advocating free coinage." [56] He repeated the same idea to critics of his anti-silver statements. "If by platform declaration or the action of the Democratic House it is demonstrated that our party is wedded to, or willing to assume free coinage of silver, I believe we are beaten before we fairly start," he wrote Alabama's Hilary Herbert. [57]

His movement toward the nomination seemed both obvious and halting. Speeches and letters affected the converted, but did not move the doubtful. Critics like Dana condemned "the elephantine economist of the Mugwumps," and "the same old corpulent Cobden." [58] But commentators saw little alternative to a third Cleveland campaign except David B. Hill, and his prospects varied from a chance of success one day to ridiculous pretension another.

David Bennett Hill came a long way with few apparent advantages. Havana, New York, his birthplace in 1843, offered few facilities to broaden horizons beyond common schooling. Local politics and newspaper work filled out his knowledge of men, a common pattern in upstate circles. After the war, he dabbled in local affairs, became one of Tilden's aides, and served in the state Democratic organization and legislature. In 1882, he became mayor of Elmira, but resigned to be Cleveland's lieutenant governor. He succeeded Cleveland, and won election in 1885, and 1888. As governor, he mixed reform interest and administrative efficiency with machine politics, supporting better criminal laws, shorter hours for state employees, conservation and agricultural experimentation. But he tolerated nothing that threatened the party's precarious state organization, and succeeded in briefly wedding New York City to the rural elements by loosening the collar on Tammany's tiger, and spoon-feeding it patronage. Legend said he gained his famous motto as a newsboy, refusing to sell a Republican paper with the stout assertion: "No, sir; I will not sell you that paper. I am a Democrat." [59]

To the uninitiated, he resembled Casper Milquetoast at the helm. He was of medium height, with a bald pate, heavy mustache, and expressionless stare. Like his mentor, Samuel J. Tilden, he seldom committed himself to anything. Yet as James M. Cox noted, a slight figure "was rescued from insignificance by his penetrating glance and shrewd look." [60] He was amiable, but a fierce fighter when defending the party organization that replaced family life in his personal affections.

Hill's philosophy was no larger than Cleveland's. He liked the game of politics, and preferred the oil can to a philosopher's quill. As one who scrambled to the top, he touted individualism, and accepted reigning Democratic ideals of negative government. "People should not be educated to the belief that the government is powerful enough to override the laws of trade and supply and demand, prevent overproduction of crops or guarantee favorable results to every business venture," he said in 1890. "The people must support themselves, and their measure of prosperity must depend on their own industry. It should be understood that success in life does not depend on governmental measures." [61] The professional organizer like Hill did not trust the red lights of political camp meetings, or loud huzzahs along parade routes. They had their place, but the wise man counted ballots.

The machine became his idol. "Hill studied politics as some study for orders in a church," a City critic noted. The calmness that made him a successful planner repelled warm-blooded men. "His atmosphere is bright but cold, as if the sun glanced on an ice field." [62]

Hill ignored criticism as the homage failure paid success. He knew almost every Democratic leader in the state, and spent most of each day in "pipe-laying" for the faithful in courthouse squares and along city streets. Lack of philosophy and belief in patronage strengthened his ties to regulars who despised Cleveland's personalism. "A diamond has no arteries," one defender said, in explaining both Hill's coolness and appeal to machine workers. "We love him for the *friends* he has made," another said. And in New York's bitter politics, partisans easily rallied to his persuasive slogan: "None but Democrats on guard." [63] As governor, Hill opposed changes that threatened Tammany, and pushed just enough reform laws to gain a modest reputation with some ethnic and labor groups. In rural areas, he successfully walked a tightrope over the chasms of Temperance politics and local school questions, while favoring protection and bimetallism. Opponents called him "a peanut politician," but his hold on New York's Democracy steadily increased.

In January, 1891, the legislature made him a United States Senator for the term beginning on March 4, but he would not leave the governorship. Despite genteel disapproval, he remained in the governor's mansion until January, 1892, in effect filling New York's two highest offices. Hill symbolized the successful spoilsman, confounding men who thought abstract issues should dominate politics. Age did not cost E. L. Godkin any spleen; he called Hill "a cheap wire-puller," "a political highwayman," one living "a busy lifetime of political crime." Hill was "the worst man a political party in America has ever offered for popular suffrage," whose popularity proved the truth of Mugwump suspicions about free and easy voting. [64]

It was partly true, partly hyperbole, and largely threatening to Cleveland. Hill aimed at higher things when Cleveland became President, supporting him loyally in 1888 in hope of succeeding to leadership in 1892. In the congressional elections of 1890, he toured the South and Midwest, gaining friends among politicians and speaking to good crowds. His activity contrasted well against Cleveland's passivity. On most national issues he was moderate, saying little about local matters. The strategy was clear. Major portions of the South, Midwest, and New York could easily produce enough delegates for the nomination. It all made Cleveland "blue." "I do not think there is any use in mincing matters," he wrote Lamont in 1890. "Mr. Hill and his friends would never permit me to carry the state of New York." [65]

He felt otherwise after the congressional elections indicated a Democratic trend. "Hill and his friends are bent on his nomination for the presidency, and failing in that they are determined that it shall not come towards me," he wrote Wilson Bissell. "You know how I feel about this matter as a personal question; but if I have pulled any chestnuts out of the fire, I want those who take them to keep a civil tongue in their heads; and further than this, I don't want to see my hard work wasted and the old party fall back to shiftiness and cheap expediency." [66] Hill alarmed Cleveland's forces by brazenly invading their camp, capturing newspapers, buying off local leaders, casting the net of "regularity." "The glittering bauble of the vice-presidency has been suggested to *me* by an 'influential New York politician,' and on a ticket with Hill!" Michigan's Don Dickinson incredulously wrote Charles Fairchild.[67] Both had been in Cleveland's Cabinet, and responded by helping shift the convention from New York City to Chicago, though Hill said: "Everything passed off in the meeting of the National Committee just as I desired." [68]

In February, word circulated that the state committee would convene an early convention to bind New York's slate to Hill. The *World* printed a one word warning: "Don't." Republican papers suggested Hill went too far in planning a rigged "Snowshoe Convention" in Albany. "Governor Hill began by saying 'I am a Democrat'," a Philadelphia GOP sheet noted. "His party in his state is likely to end by saying 'I am Hill.' " [69] Cleveland's friends quietly arranged to contrast his probity with Hill's maneuvering, and Dickinson staged a Washington's Birthday speech for him at the University of Michigan. The intertwined themes of political idealism and the responsibilities of citizenship showed to better effect than Hill's work. ". . . it was the only mean trick I ever played on you," Dickinson coyly wrote Cleveland years after the event.[70] Cleveland was not that unwitting, however. Dana decried the set-piece as "a last attempt to rally the faithful around the colossal convexity of Grover Cleveland," but the former President's boom went into high gear.[71]

Cleveland now frankly sought the nomination, hoping to divert the party from radicalism, and desiring re-election. A group of "Anti-Snappers" formed a slate of delegates to contest Hill's men at the national convention. Reprints of Cleveland's speeches, and capsules of his record went through the mail. Friends increased contributions to a small but efficient literary bureau. And no one asked or gave quarter in the New York party. By mid-March, a Chicago paper re-marked of the state's bloody war: [72]

> Christians have burned each other, quite persuaded
> That all the apostles would have done as they did.

Hill's campaign had the merit of candor. In March, he swung around the southern circle, capitalizing on agrarian discontent with Cleveland's anti-silver stand, and promising future rewards to new supporters. His themes were simple. He would accept reasonable tariff reform, stand pat on bimetallism, divide the spoils, and carry New York. "There was a clatter, a din, a clash, a scent of brilliant political coup, and pell-mell the professional editors and the professional politicians took seats in the Hill bandwagon," a Georgian noted.[73] Hill made his point among the hotel bar-room and courthouse lawn set, but could not shake the spoilsman image. Few southerners believed he could win nationally; and Cleveland's agents were busy with admonitions about rocking the boat. "Senator Hill has not been able to make clear to us that he believes anything in particular," a Mississippian noted as the convention gathered. "He seems to have no grasp of principles and his idea of a national politician is a man skilful in obtaining political success by offices, contracts and the parcelling-out of places and dignities." [74] That much did not shock southerners; it was simply more logical to go with Cleveland, and hope for the best.

Cleveland's most vocal and colorful southern critic was Henry Watterson of the *Louisville Courier-Journal*. Piercing eyes, heavy white brows, and shaggy locks made him resemble an outraged Mark Twain. He was an old-fashioned defender of the South's cherished institutions, and few opponents bested him. He disliked Cleveland's pomposity and shifting attitudes on tariff reform. "Mr. Cleveland is no longer a possibility," he argued in February. "His selection, if such a thing were under the circumstances conceivable, would be an act of deliberate suicide." [75] By May, Watterson bluntly told the Kentucky state convention to avoid New York altogether. ". . . it seems that if we go there for a nominee, we shall walk through a slaughter-house into an open grave." A compromise was in order, as he said in a purple style familiar to his readers: "We do not gather grapes from thistles, nor pluck the flower of love from brands blazing with the fires of hate and strife." [76] It sounded good in Kentucky, but like everyone else, Watterson had no real alternative to Hill or Cleveland. He supported John G. Carlisle, and when the Kentuckian's brief boom evaporated, switched to Iowa's Governor Horace Boies. Cleveland never forgot nor forgave, privately revealing a talent for invective he kept out of public statements.[77]

The former President continued his rounds with little public fuss and much private attention to details. He still used the familiar exalted tone to avoid a personal campaign. ". . . I cannot bring myself to regard a candidacy for the place as something to be won by personal strife and active self-assertion," he told General Bragg in March.[78] The *New York Herald* said his alleged desire for private life was "simply the figment of an overworked imagination, and a bit of amusing hyperbole."[79] Talk of agrarian discontent and a third party left him unruffled. As he told Charles S. Hamlin, "if the South wanted to have a Force Bill, and acted so foolishly as to desert the Democratic party, why let them try the experiment."[80]

It was not very likely, in any event. His organizers and friends had the nomination almost secured by June. Since January, the faithful George F. Parker and other quiet men had communicated from New York to the prairies and piedmont. Cleveland cooperated languidly. "Well, I received this the other day," he would say, passing a letter to Parker. "I don't know the man, but he may be of use to you." Parker often used the correspondent to form a local club or relay useful information. The organization acquired muscle tone in mid-May, when Whitney arrived, and "the Cleveland army now had a commander."[81] The former Navy Secretary admired Cleveland, and wished equally to avoid agrarian domination and Hill. "I shall soon be back," he had promised Cleveland in 1889, "and I mean to organize a working machine to throw stones at the wicked."[82] The elegant, precise Whitney spent his own money freely, and stenographers, clerks, private telephone wires, printing contracts for pamphlets, and personal conferences enlivened his progress.

New York remained a special problem, but Charles Fairchild and other loyal Clevelandites worked against Hill and Tammany in February. They collected substantial funds from City Democrats in banking and commerce, established outposts in Brooklyn, and paid agents to trail Hill's caravan. It was the usual touchy situation, for Tammany seemed intractable. Appeals to party unity and national victory did not move the braves, who still thought one term of Cleveland enough. As usual, local matters obsessed them. "I believe that if Thomas Jefferson himself could be the candidate of the party this year or any other year," Fairchild said, "he would be traded for a mayor or an alderman should it be thought necessary to do so in order to elect the latter."[83]

An anti-Hill convention in Syracuse chose a contesting slate of delegates on May 31, denounced the McKinley Tariff, approved bimetallism amid appeals for party unity, and endorsed Cleveland as the man to carry New York. Tammany retaliated with increased printed and verbal attacks on Cleveland, and pledged a convention fight. The Tammany train went to Chicago a week early, leaving a trail of anti-Cleveland speeches. It was all rather pointless. Hill and Tammany only enhanced Cleveland's stature with non-New Yorkers, and seemed merely spiteful in threatening the chance of national victory over local issues. One by one, the major state conventions endorsed Cleveland throughout the spring, until by national convention-time he seemed the only serious contender.

But over-confidence did not pay, and Cleveland wanted first-hand reports from field agents. Early in June Whitney arranged a secret conference with political managers worthy of a Dead-eye Dick novel. On June 9, the chosen few registered under false names in various New York hotels. At 11 A.M. under a rainy sky they gathered at Whitney's town house on West 57th Street, to report strategy and analyze the future. Dickinson, Vilas, William F. Harrity of Pennsylvania, William L. Wilson, Josiah Quincy of Massachusetts, and Francis L. Stetson, among others, exchanged information during a working lunch. While Whitney probed, questioned, and doubted, each man reported on his state. They drafted membership of ranking convention committees, chose nominating speakers, the temporary and permanent chairmen, and checked detailed lists of delegates and platform suggestions. Cleveland, who knew of the meeting but remained at Buzzard's Bay, worried especially about the platform. He wanted no radicalism on either protection or the currency. George F. Parker briefed him on June 12, but Cleveland had already warned Whitney. "The platform on the money question *must* be right if I am to be in any way related to it." [84]

Whitney's dispatch illustrated the air of victory in Cleveland's camp, and showed how much organizational skill had developed since 1888. They needed delegates now, the trickiest part of all. But the whole task seemed relatively easy, especially since the Republicans would obviously fulfill predictions and renominate President Harrison.

The music of conflicting bands clashed as Republicans converged on Minneapolis. The loudest groups chanted:

> Blaine, Blaine, James G. Blaine,
> We had him once, we'll have him again.

The familiar white plumes, florid badges, and portraits preceded the vigorous Blaine men everywhere. Their talk and wares spilled through hotel lobbies, along rows of seats at the convention hall, and into press reports reaching Harrison. His supporters had a less familiar but equally determined slogan:

> Let every honest fellow from Maine to Oregon
> Let every honest fellow, unless he's a son-of-a-gun
> Let every honest fellow, unless he's a son-of-a-gun,
> Be sure and vote for Benjamin Harrison.

Blaine's silence encouraged phalanxes in the streets, and lent credence to whispers that bosses might yet stop Harrison with the hope that Blaine could win.[85]

Harrison's "Twelve Apostles" and allies worried less about Blaine than McKinley. The Governor's appearances produced applause, and Mark Hanna's impatient, forceful figure began to impress both delegates and party leaders. No one with McKinley's future prospects should welcome the nomination in an uncertain year, but the badges, posters, and Hanna were all there, with an informal headquarters. Vocal supporters urging another tariff campaign noted the logic of selecting the man identified with protection and prosperity, who now governed a major state. If the convention deadlocked, he was the obvious choice.[86] Hanna was especially active among western delegates, who seemed eager to follow McKinley after a complimentary first ballot vote for Harrison. The President's agents isolated McKinley on the platform as permanent chairman. He would "Garfield" the convention at his own risk.

Delegates and onlookers gathered in a new auditorium reeking of fresh paint, turpentine, and resin that dripped from the high ceiling, fouling hair and clothes. The heat was incredible, and sluggish currents of humid air frayed tempers. Men mopped brows with large handkerchiefs, and more than one statesman strolled around coatless. Some spectators swirled the smoky, sluggish air with palm-leaf fans. "It was a fan-fluttering convention," a young reporter wrote. He also noted the current of nervous expectation and tension in the hall. "I was amazed at the emotional heights to which the delegates worked up in that atmosphere."[87]

The proceedings opened on Tuesday, June 7, and every hint at Blaine's name provoked unruly demonstrations. Jacob Sloat Fassett's address as temporary chairman was almost extinguished in the maelstrom of cheering when he alluded to the Plumed Knight's record and personality. The next day brought McKinley's vigorous address as permanent chairman, stressing Harrison's record, protection, and reciprocity. His tumultuous reception, complete with rousing "peculiar applause," made Harrison's men apprehensive.[88] At the third day's evening session, Foraker reported a terse platform, and delegates spent another weary night before the nominating speeches.

On Wednesday, June 10, Colorado sent Senator Edward O. Wolcott to the platform, to name Blaine in a brilliant flash of spread-eagle oratory. When he finished, the faithful cheered their fading hero for nearly half an hour, in a demonstration that amazed even cynical reporters. "Like the chorus of an anthem, with measured solemnity, the galleries shouted 'Blaine! Blaine! James G. Blaine!' Myriads of stamping feet kept a barbaric rhythm, while plumes and banners waved, and women with flags and scarfs filled the atmosphere with motion and color of light," ex-Senator John J. Ingalls recalled. But it was a farewell, not a rallying call, and many observers cried as they waved white plumes, carried helmets atop state standards, and called out their hero's name until they were hoarse and exhausted. "That gigantic demonstration was at once a salutation and a requiem. The Republican party there took leave of their dying leader, and bade him an eternal farewell." [89]

Even Chauncey Depew's celebrated style was anticlimactic as he seconded Harrison's name, after a brief nominating speech from Richard W. Thompson. The President's well-ordered ranks held firm, determined to equal the Blaine demonstration in noise if not enthusiasm. When Depew finished, they played out all the rituals. A small group carried a huge portrait of Harrison down the center aisle, flanked by state standards. Confetti and buttons showered from the galleries. Ladies waved large handkerchiefs, while men tossed hats in the air. The cheering was infectious and a girl in gray aided the Harrison cause with an oft-repeated Indian war whoop, recalling the President's grandfather, "Old Tippecanoe!"

Seconding speeches and procedural confusion bored and irritated the delegates, until balloting began under considerable tension. McKinley entertained the roll call motion, then settled into a chair, idly waving a large palmetto fan. He grew visibly nervous when a complimentary vote came his way, and increased the pace of fanning. When Ohio cast ballots for him, he challenged the count, but Foraker silenced him on a point of order. The tally gave Harrison an easy first ballot victory with 535⅙ votes, to 182⅙ for Blaine, and 182 for McKinley. The convention released remaining tension in cheers, and applauded the procession of statesmen pledging loyalty and hard work in the coming campaign.[90]

That evening, the gathering surprised observers by replacing Vice-President Morton with Whitelaw Reid. The choice was a puzzle, for Reid added little to the ticket, and Harrison seemed unnecessarily callous toward Morton. The President was not close to Morton, and disliked his Senate rulings and lethargy during the Fifty-first Congress. Tom Platt, who distrusted Reid, mistakenly thinking him a reformer, probably wanted him defeated with Harrison. Reid hastily protested his unworthiness to Morton, and denied wanting the position. Morton did not actively seek renomination, as Jacob Sloat Fassett noted. "I think I may safely say, however, that there were two factors operative against you. First, the apathy of the Harrison people, and second the aggressiveness of the Reid people. Then too, some of your best friends did not know that it would be a kindness to put you on a ticket, the head of which had been made by such unconscionable use of federal patronage." [91]

The Administration won its candidate, platform, and the nucleus of a campaign organization, but the excitement and tension of 1888 that helped the GOP to victory was gone. Harrison credited his success to a "faithful and unstampedeable band of friends," especially Depew and Michener,[92] but the party's other leaders were indifferent or hostile. Only an extraordinary emergency or a deft harmonizer could keep them from dozing during the campaign. "Harrison's selection for a second term caused a chattering of the teeth among warm-blooded Republicans of the East," Tom Platt wrote. ". . . many of the New York delegation, including myself, wrapped ourselves in overcoats and earmuffs, hurried from the convention hall, and took the first train for New York." [93] Matt Quay was not enthusiastic. When a group of reporters sought his views, he glanced languidly out the window at shimmering heat waves: "It looks as though it might snow." Alger thought "it looks like sledding on bare ground, at present." As usual, Tom Reed was more candid. "Well, perhaps he is as good a man to get licked with as anybody," he wrote Lodge.[94]

For the moment, more people congratulated McKinley than praised Harrison. When he left the hall, the smiling and courtly Ohioan heard people say: "Well, you'll be nominated by acclamation in 1896 anyway." [95] Enthusiastic admirers waved at the carriage bearing him to a hotel. As it swayed to a stop, part of the crowd carried the mortified Governor into the lobby. Amused reporters noted McKinley's look of pained dismay, as he realized his genial captors had inadvertently raised his trouser cuffs to reveal gartered legs. Restored to his feet, the Major said a hasty farewell, and joined friends in consuming large quantities of iced water. Hanna mixed apprehension and relief: "My God, William, that was a damned close squeak!" [96]

Hanna's remark did not clarify McKinley's motives, but made the point; in 1896, non-machine party elements would come to him. Hanna had also displayed managerial skills. McKinley unquestionably had a large and growing popular following. Hanna was touchy about veiled hints at disloyalty to Harrison. "I do not consider that Governor McKinley was placed in any false position by what was done," he hotly wrote Sherman. "I do not consider that the administration have any right to criticize his actions because his friends—and I was at the head of it—took the responsibility of doing just what we did. Governor McKinley's position today as the result of all that transpired at Minneapolis is in the best possible shape for his future. His bearing and conduct and personal magnetism won the hearts and respect of everybody." [97] Sherman promised to mollify Harrison, noting: "I have conversed with several members of the convention, and believe you were nearer success with McKinley than you were aware of." [98] The whole affair whetted Hanna's desire for victory. It was "an impolitic thing to nominate him" in 1892, but Ohio would produce a president in four years. [99]

Despite the chill around Republican prospects, the traditional rituals unfolded. On June 20, McKinley led the party's most distinguished leaders to notify Harrison. The brief speeches stressed Republican achievements and promises for more success. The President revealed no grudges. When the speakers finished, a man jumped on an antique chair, and gave three cheers for Harrison, in which all joined. The company then lunched on sweetbreads, lobster, fish, salads, ice cream and sherbet molds, and a large array of tidbits. Summer's heat did not dull appetites. The following day, a similar group boarded a special train for White Plains, and Reid's mansion, "Ophir Farm." From the station, they drove in elegant carriages toward the tall flagpole marking the house, and heard band music before they sighted the elaborate, castellated pile. After an elegant luncheon, speeches, and a group photograph, the statesmen returned to plan victory. [100]

It was all colorful and impressive, even to hardened cynics, accustomed to the sights and sounds of power. They liked band music and White House receptions as well as patronage and appropriations. Most insiders thought the ticket would lose. The marginal agrarian and labor voters that produced victory in 1888 were restless and unpredictable. Still, a dignified campaign would save something for the future, and no one of consequence was likely to bolt. And predictions about the Democrats were always risky. Cleveland seemed a sure winner, but even as Republicans chose their candidates, the opposition gathered in Chicago amid warnings of a political Donnybrook.

Cleveland's supporters arrived in Chicago chanting a catchy ditty:

> Grover, Grover,
> Four more years of Grover;
> In we'll go,
> Out they'll go,
> Then we'll be in clover.

William C. Whitney appreciated the thought, but he was not a man to cut corners at the last moment. New York's vital delegation threatened a bitter-end fight against Cleveland. Reformers like Watterson wanted a firm declaration for a revenue tariff, which Cleveland thought would lose the East. Westerners wanted a free silver plank, but Cleveland favored a straddle. One or two minor candidates still had hopes, if Cleveland stalled. Whitney worked from a headquarters suite in the Palmer House, the essence of courtesy to reporters, purveying a refreshing candor and exuding confidence.

He met the Cleveland planning committee on Friday, June 17, four days before the convention opened. Men from some twenty states appeared, armed with lists of delegates, reports of disaffection or potential alliances, and gossip useful both for Cleveland's nomination and the campaign. Whitney was the meeting's moderator, firmly but courteously drawing out each man. Next evening, another ten states sent representatives. Whitney remained cool and demanding, watching each man through pince-nez, absently rubbing a pocket-watch, but not missing a discrepancy. On Sunday, they canvassed again, and faced a more tense chief that night. Each man listed his delegates, and offered final suggestions. Whitney shifted nervously in a chair, and occasionally paced the floor. Cleveland needed 607 votes to win, and agents counted about 600. It seemed safe enough. The elegant New Yorker leaned back and smiled. "Well, that will do. There is no longer any doubt of the result, and no further question in my mind." [101] The platform was still uncertain, and Watterson's radicals got the National Committee to choose a doubtful Kentuckian as temporary chairman, but the delegates mattered most for now. A cub reporter named Theodore Dreiser haunted hotel bars and lobbies, taking each "statesman" at his own word. A candid southerner said Cleveland had the nomination, but the convention would pay the usual homage to a few favorite sons. Whitney radiated self-assurance: "I can't keep the votes back. They tumble in at the windows as well as at the doors." [102]

Gorman's friends also conferred in an ormolu hotel suite. The Marylander was a Democratic Garfield. His Border background, congressional skill, and moderation on both silver and the tariff were recommendations to a deadlocked convention. Though discounting his chances, Gorman early analyzed the party's situation. Democrats would win, he told Atlanta's Evan P. Howell in April, by "indicting the Republicans for their 'McKinley Bill,' their bad financial legislation, the 'Force Bill,' and their extravagance, . . ." [103] Gorman was not a stalking-horse for Hill, though the New Yorker finally offered to support him to beat Cleveland. On June 19, a group of anti-Cleveland men vainly urged Gorman to challenge Whitney. That would divide the party and ruin his chances for 1896, a much more tempting prospect.

The public knew little of these machinations, and did not let bad weather or conflicting rumors dampen spirits. Delegates and spectators sat in a "wigwam" of rather simple lines, with five flagpoles around a gabled entrance. The building was a huge semicircle, the speakers' platform against one wall, and balconies resting on columns twined with bunting. Flags, banners, and portraits hung from every vantage point. Ladies dotted galleries with colorful clothes, and cheered like men. Tammany's braves arrived with a large mock tiger that roared and writhed on command. Its escort drank freely while the paper beast growled at Grover Cleveland. Inside the hall, band music struggled toward the high ceiling, making more noise than harmony. A German conductor who knew music better than history, led a vigorous rendition of "Marching Through Georgia" when that state's delegation appeared.[104]

Tuesday, June 21, passed in routine business. The second day brought the keynote speech from William L. Wilson, whose presence indicated Cleveland's strength. The evening session heard William F. Vilas report a compromise platform, while angry men like Watterson sat with folded hands. Vilas mentioned Cleveland, and provoked a twenty-minute demonstration. "Rank after rank of coatless men, of sometimes hatless men, rose by hundreds, thousands, aye, by tens of thousands, almost with a wild acclaim that grew from the noisy into the impressive, from the impressive into the awful, as it increased," a reporter wired his paper.[105] Don Dickinson led the parade, carrying Michigan's banner among milling delegates. A portrait of Hill caused scuffles and angry words. New York delegates sat expressionless, reading newspapers or talking to each other. Cleveland would not win without a fight.

When the demonstration subsided, the assembly reviewed the platform's substance. It condemned the McKinley Act "as the culminating atrocity of class legislation, . . ." attacked "sham reciprocity," and promised to repeal both. But it was not free trade, and tortuous qualifications promised to save American industry in new schedules. The silver plank was equally ambiguous, favoring both metals while denouncing the Sherman Act as "a cowardly makeshift," but urging "All currency at par with gold." A floor fight followed. Easterners defeated free silver amendments, but Watterson and other reformers bitterly attacked Cleveland's moderate tariff proposals, and won a firmer pledge to reduction with a vote of 564–342. Whitney might control the nomination, but he did not rule the party. Cleveland insisted on a "*plain* and *right* financial plank," but every state convention from Virginia to Texas had endorsed free silver. Its defeat embittered some western and southern Democrats, who threatened to bolt the ticket if another refuge appeared.[106]

Many exhausted delegates wished to avoid a night of alternating boredom and exertion, but the Cleveland leaders wanted to maintain their momentum, and proceeded to the nominations. New York would not present Cleveland, and the honor passed to his native New Jersey. An unenthusiastic Governor Leon Abbett emphasized tariff reform, and named "the nominee of the people, the plain, blunt, honest citizen, the idol of the Democratic masses, Grover Cleveland." While he talked, the former President's men passed noisemakers, banners, and bottles down restless rows of delegates and spectators. "A storm of tropical violence" broke outside, drumming an incredible rain on the temporary roof, but Cleveland's men paraded, howled, cheered, and contorted "like hired mourners at an oriental funeral." Dickinson carried his standard past the New York delegation, and ugly words filled the air.[107]

The usual seconding speakers tried to follow, but rain made the roof a bass drum, smothering every sound, until the chairman withdrew and delegates waited for the storm to subside. The roof of green lumber and tar paper admitted showers of water that ruined clothes, washed down posters and bunting, and sent people scampering for shelter. The evening wore on through confusion and disarray. William H. DeWitt of New York nominated Hill, though water-spouts sent him running across the stage several times, while reporters huddled under umbrellas and folded newspapers. The New Yorkers made Hill a champion of party regularity, the one man who could carry the Empire State. "We love him not merely for the enemies he has made, but for the enemies he has conquered." Iowa presented Horace Boies, with Watterson's second, and other favorite sons appeared in the columns. When nominations ended after midnight, disorder filled the hall as many delegates urged adjournment to dry off and rest.

Then "there came a shrill cry from the New York delegation, . . ." and a figure struggled toward the platform through milling and confused delegates. A chorus of speculation mingled with thunder and lightning to give Tammany's silver-tongued orator, W. Bourke Cockran, his greatest moment. As one of the era's finest set-piece orators, he produced a scene vivid in memories of old men decades later. The Cleveland delegates proposed to see it through, and let Cockran launch a last charge against him. Head back, speaking with a cadence that matched the weather's drama and rhythm, he summed up the case against Cleveland with remarkable candor. "He had something to say, and he said it with art and seeming conviction," Theodore Dreiser recalled. "He had presence too, a sort of Herculean, animal-like effrontery." [108]

Cockran argued that Cleveland represented personalism. The party could not trust him; his independent friends were a standing menace to unity. "If we be not accorded the nomination that we ask for from the state of New York [Hill], give us any citizen in this United States who is a Democrat. Give us some man who will not raise up against us any active hostile force within our own ranks." Hisses, boos, and heavier objects greeted the speech, while water ran down the walls and showered on stage. Lightning produced a lurid effect, and thunder rattled the building, but Cockran marched through the indictment. "I have said that I believe he [Cleveland] is a most popular man— let me say a man of extraordinary popularity—every day in the year except one, and that is election day." This hint at a Tammany bolt produced more groans, hisses, and catcalls.[109]

When Cockran finished, the chair controlled the tumult enough for balloting. The clerk droned through the states, while men marked score sheets on their knees and telegraphers rattled the results to distant night editors. Whitney stood near the operator sending the figures to Buzzard's Bay. As his men held firm, he gave a small victory whoop, and tossed his straw hat toward a telegrapher. "It is a funeral," a Hill man said gloomily. Cleveland received 617⅓ votes, 10 more than the necessary two thirds. Hill gathered 114, including New York's 72, 27 from the South, 5 in the Northeast, 3 of Colorado's, 6 from Ohio, and

1 from New Mexico. Cleveland won votes from every state except New York, Iowa, Colorado, Idaho, Montana, and Nevada. Horace Boies had 103 midwestern votes. At 4:40 A.M., the exhausted delegates adjourned, after sitting all night without sleep or food.

It was calmer at Buzzard's Bay, as dawn colored the eastern sky and lighted the water and forests near Cleveland's summer home. In the gun room at "Gray Gables," Cleveland and his wife read telegraph reports with a small group of friends. The candidate seemed unperturbed. At the tension's height, he suddenly went outside, set fishing lines to dry, and everyone noted nonchalantly that his nomination coincided with the dawn's first light.

In Chicago, the convention's last session chose Adlai E. Stevenson for Vice-President on Cleveland's instructions. Many delegates favored Indiana's Isaac Grey, largely because the Hoosier State was more doubtful than Illinois, but Stevenson liked free silver, and appealed to spoilsmen who remembered "Adlai and his Axe" in the Post Office Department. He might also mollify Hill, as a tacit promise not to ignore regulars. The departing delegates and appraising newsmen credited Whitney's efficient organization with the victory. ". . . the ferocious tiger of the New York jungles was only a poor old alley cat when W. C. Whitney started in to shoot," a reporter wrote later. The New Yorker knew it would not be an easy campaign. He wrung hasty promises from Hill's men not to bolt, and offered to soften Cleveland's attitude; but the rift was there. Whitney would work with the regulars, Cleveland against them.[110]

As in 1884 and 1888, Cleveland won because of a small band of devoted lieutenants, who stressed his merits as a symbol for a reform crusade to hide Democracy's conflicting interests. This role was only partly accurate, however. Cleveland embodied tariff reform, but refused to make it radical. He bitterly opposed the rising silver feeling. Most westerners and southerners wanted to win, and compromised silver in hopes of later rewards. Cleveland's opponents were weak and confused, scattering strength through a dozen states and as many candidates. Hill's opposition was almost a blessing, letting Cleveland remain publicly aloof from intra-party battles, while symbolizing "good government" as friends attacked Tammany and alleged bosses like Gorman. But the party had only superficial unity, its various interests rose from the common source of rhetoric and the need to win. The interests were dangerously independent; only a tactful harmonizer could hold them together, and that was not Cleveland's best role. The long-predicted third party movement now appeared, threatening Demo-

crats in the South and Republicans in the Midwest, with national
results even the wisest man did not prophesy that hot July.

Unsettling reports of party division came from the South and West
during the spring of 1892. The agrarian press adopted a bitter tone,
and gained wide if not deep circulation. Various signs in 1891 pointed
toward a third party embracing discontented farmers and marginal
reformist and labor groups. Protesters like Tom Watson of Georgia
hoped for Democratic collapse as the "people" turned to a new political organization: [111]

> Little drops of Grover,
> Little grains of Dave,
> Make their busted party
> Mighty hard to save.

It was mostly talk. No new party was likely to gain a majority of either
old party's voters, but southern Democrats that spring called the Alliance "a demon in their rear." [112] Politicians feared the effect of any
agrarian revolt at all levels. "The people seem to be running wild into
the third party. . . ." a North Carolina congressman wrote his wife. "I
have never known such a doubtful condition of politics." [113] Many
Democrats blanched at the prospect of another Cleveland campaign.
"I have never discovered any differences in the Cleveland administration of the finances of the country, and the Republican administration,"
a North Carolinian said. "I cannot and will not support Cleveland. . . .
Cleveland Democracy is no better than the enemy." [114] Silver clearly
appealed more than tariff reduction as a nostrum for falling crop prices
and appreciating debts. In the Midwest, agrarian successes of 1890
seemed a reasonable foundation for further work in 1892 and possible
triumph in 1896. After all, the Republican party won in 1860 after
losing only one presidential contest. The silverites continued newspaper propaganda, pamphlet mailings, congressional speeches, and
conventions.

Genuine Populist leaders like Leonidas Polk, pledged to a lasting
third party, opposed local fusion that would blur their separate identity
and future impact.[115] Polk died suddenly in the spring, but his heirs
expected fireworks and action from the delegates arriving in Omaha
in July to write a platform and choose a ticket for the People's Party,
U.S.A. The party's movers and shakers were an assorted group of intellectuals, agrarians with rough hands and ready tongues, professional
reformers and organizers from the old Grange and new Alliance. They
divided on tactics and demands, but shared the fiery enthusiasm common to reform movements not yet weary of fighting human caution

and institutional inertia. The convention, gathered for a "second Independence Day," seemed to fulfill earlier promises.

The platform combined old and new demands, cloaked in phrases that unsettled politicians who knew the appeal of words to American voters. It opened with Ignatius Donnelley's lurid preamble, dividing America into two classes, the very rich and very poor; foretelling a coming apocalypse unless Populism triumphed; and simplifying American history into two conspiracies, one for and one against the people. The platform mixed altruism with practical politics, a desire to build for tomorrow and an urge to win today. It demanded free coinage, an enlarged banking system, a graduated income tax, government ownership of communication and transportation, and regulation of land monopoly.

These planks sounded more radical than they actually were. The rest of the platform promised a free ballot without federal regulation; liberal veterans' pensions; restriction of immigration that competed with labor; the initiative and referendum; a single six-year term for president and vice-president; and direct election of senators. The document emphasized almost as an after-thought the alleged ties between labor and agriculture, and frankly sought to ally all dissatisfied groups in a single party.* The platform satisfied most Populists, though some wished more moderation, while southerners wanted all-out war. Its rhetoric promised radicalism, but specific suggestions offered the safety of familiarity. The "respectable" press was harsh. *Bradstreet's*, not surprisingly condemned the "Cassandra-like tone. . . ," and the *Baltimore American* labeled Donnelley's work "a farrago of nonsense." [116]

Polk's death left Walter Q. Gresham as the new party's most discussed presidential contender, but he hastily assured both Republican and Democratic friends that he was not encouraging such talk.[117] His judicial rulings against railroads made him popular with some farm and labor groups, but Gresham did not want a nomination from a party he could not altogether support. While the convention talked, he declined, and the honor passed to Iowa's James B. Weaver.

Weaver was born in Dayton, Ohio, in 1833, the fifth of thirteen

---

*Historians have been too generous in analyzing this famous document's subsequent impact on reform movements. It suggested almost nothing outside the mainstream of American reform. Its demands for agricultural subsidies were sweeping, but had appeared in American politics before. Its pitch to labor was artificial. The cause and effect relationship between these Populist demands and later enactments is hazy. Most of Progressivism and the New Deal would have come without the Populist precedents as such, though Populism was undoubtedly influential in *advertising* some new political demands. If the government ever acquires the railroads in the future, historians no doubt will ascribe the action to Populist precedent, ignoring other historic and immediate factors.

children in a typical frontier family. He lived in Michigan and Iowa, panned gold in California, kept a country store, carried mail, and studied law. He went from Democratic to Free Soil doctrine, and then to Republicanism, allegedly after reading *Uncle Tom's Cabin.* He fought with distinction at Fort Donelson, Corinth, and Shiloh. Brevetted a brigadier general, he returned to Iowa to espouse Methodism, Prohibition, railroad regulation, and easy currency. He ran for president on the Greenback ticket in 1880, and alternately represented that party, liberal Democrats, and Farmer-Laborites in the House between 1879–1881, and 1885–1889. He was less radical on the currency question than many contemporaries. Midwestern origins, political experience, and campaigning skill made him a logical compromise choice. Weaver was a curious combination of clay and iron, radiating a quiet kindness with individuals, but fiery with crowds. Opponents thought him dull behind his dignified whiskers, a reform-party hack, veteran of too many mixed crusades to attract new voters. They liked to list his affiliations, noting that as late as 1876, he was "a red-hot Republican." [118] "General" James G. Field of Virginia, actually a CSA major, balanced the ticket with the diffuse hope of ending sectionalism. It looked like a regular party slate.

The opposition treated Populism to elaborate disinterest or easy ridicule, greeting Weaver's nomination with "something closely approaching a sigh of relief." [119] He was a broader target for abuse and ridicule than Gresham. "The wicked politicians of the Republican and Democratic parties breathed easier and were with better appetites when the Gresham bogie disappeared, and they found their familiar old enemy, General Weaver, in the lead of the People's movement." [120] His candidacy might help southern Democrats by not offering a spectacular alternative to Cleveland. "He is not exactly the sort of a man who can frighten pharoah into fits, or bring convincing plagues upon the monopolistic oppressors of Israel," a middle-class journal noted.[121]

July became August, and campaign managers organized for fall's better weather. The Populists were active, but others kept repeating that noise was not everything. The third party did not seem especially threatening, but its tone worried observers. "No intelligent man could sit in that audience and listen to the wild and frenzied assaults upon the existing order of things without a feeling of great alarm at the extent and intensity of the social lunacy there displayed," a reporter wrote.[122]

Nothing seemed to stir men who were simply uninterested. "As yet, so far as I have observed, not so much as a shotgun has been fired in

honor of the President's nomination, from Maine to California," Foraker wrote Alger. "In other words, there is no enthusiasm whatever." 123 Neither candidate appeared to care. Harrison worried over
his wife's declining health. Cleveland fished in Buzzard's Bay, and
was irritable about the platform and pestering politicians. Publicly,
at least; privately, he corresponded with Whitney and friends, and
clearly did not want to lose. The masses dozed. "The two candidates
were singular persons," Henry Adams said, "of whom it was the common saying that one of them had no friends; the other, only enemies." 124 Even Tom Reed's blade seemed dull. His best suggestion
was a new slogan for Democrats: "The prophet and the ballot box—
both stuffed." 125

Michener and Harrison's other managers tried to arouse the party
with appeals to reason. "We must remember that we are not organizing a Sunday School convention or a prohibitionist meeting, but are
preparing for an assault upon the devil. In warfare of this kind, a good
long stick is more effective than a sprinkle of Eau-de-Cologne." 126
Local committees solicited funds from government workers, and tried
to raise money in business circles, but with indifferent success. The
President appreciated these efforts, but knew Platt was more important than a hundred lesser men. Things looked worst in New York, the
Midwest, and the Old Northwest. Republicans seemed strong in the
Far West. If New York's organization wheeled into line, more money
and energy might save doubtful states like Illinois, Indiana, and Wisconsin. Harrison warmed rather quickly. "I could readily see why
Republicans might think someone else might be a stronger candidate
or a better president . . . ," he assured Governor William R. Merriam
of Minnesota.127 Platt gave no sign of hearing such talk indirectly. "If
I should do in this campaign what I did in 1888, and be treated in the
same way, I would grill either Harrison or myself, most likely myself,"
he told Thomas H. Carter, chairman of the National Committee.128

Whitelaw Reid dealt surprisingly well with Platt, and two long conferences in early August at Ophir Farm calmed everyone's nerves.
Platt seemed willing to cooperate. "There were absolutely no promises,
direct or implied," Reid told John Hay, "and there is no dust on anybody's knees." 129 In mid-August, Harrison wrote Platt a remarkably
frank letter. He could not campaign because of Mrs. Harrison's health,
but was not avoiding Platt. While he would not make promises, the
President assured Platt of later cooperation if they won. He rebuked
tale-bearers who poisoned their relationship. "I have never intentionally done or omitted anything out of any personal disrespect, and any
such impression on your part is a mistake, the origin of which I will

not attempt to trace, but will venture to suggest that the fault may not have been wholly on one side." He held no grudges, but offered no regrets. "You will not expect me to apologize for getting the nomination, nor I to you for having tried to prevent it." [130] There must only be thought of party success. Democratic victory would mean less to New York than a second Harrison administration.

Platt visited the President and promised to work for the ticket. He admitted sulking, and thought more misunderstanding had passed between them than in any other political duo. He did not like being a party whipping boy between elections, and frankly wanted substantial rewards if he helped the GOP win again. He told reporters the New York organization was in the fight tooth and nail, and that Harrison was "broadminded and statesmanlike." [131] Late September produced a love feast at Cooper Union, with Platt, Warner Miller, Reid, and Depew on the platform. "Friends, there is harmony everywhere," Platt told the inquisitive after the meeting.[132] But promises, as Platt knew, were easier to make in 1892 than deliveries. Cleveland's following in New York was powerful despite internal divisions, and Harrison's attitude had angered many in the GOP organization.

Platt was not the only leader needing presidential attention. In Pennsylvania, Quay kept his machine in gear, but the party was safer there than in neighboring states. Reid was close to Harrison, but did not want to stump the country: "The speechmaker for this ticket is at the head of it." [133] That was all very well, but the President understandably would not leave his ailing wife, and Reid finally spoke in Ohio, Indiana, and Illinois, with bonus appearances in New York. The eternal "Blaine problem" remained. Genuine ill-health and family tragedy prevented Blaine from campaigning, but even a letter or speech might rouse Republicans more than a thousand lesser bugles. "Blaine needs tender treatment," William E. Chandler counseled Reid. "There was not enough tact used toward him. We need everybody to win, and even then the fight will be a desperate one." [134] Reid was once more the harmonizer, easier this time because of long friendship with the Plumed Knight. Early in September, Blaine wrote a lengthy public letter to Joseph H. Manley of Maine, reprinted as a newspaper article and pamphlet, supporting protection and defending reciprocity. But he would not campaign, breaking the rule only for a ceremonial appearance at Ophir Farm. He even explained in another public letter that he would not vote, having paired with a friend, thus saving a trip from Washington to his Maine polling place.

Harrison could neither placate Blaine nor stage a speaking tour. A long letter of acceptance was his chief contribution, defending tariff protection without over-praising the McKinley Act. Like Blaine, he bore down on reciprocity and all it implied, but the subject too easily became a string of uninspiring statistics. The *Nation* labeled the document a "combination of stump speech, a statistical report, a selection of clippings from a press-bureau, and a jumble of familiar editorials and 'scare' articles taken from loyal Republican papers." [135] That was harsh and wide of the mark, but Harrison's efforts were above the heads and immediate concerns of most undecided voters.

Mrs. Harrison's deepening illness damped the President's style. The family tried the remedy of cheer and quiet. "Mrs. Harrison is so much of an invalid as to require [much] of my time to assist her in the short walks and drives she takes daily," he wrote Platt, "and much more in efforts to cheer her up and lift her out of her nervous depression." [136] Her death on October 24 further removed Harrison from the already dull canvass. "The summer was one of great anxiety and pain," he later told a correspondent. "I was a leader in prison. Indeed, I was so removed from the campaign that I can scarcely realize that I was a candidate." [137] In any event, neither candidate would set the country aflame, or encourage underlings to personal attacks. After the fact, *Life* abandoned humor for wishful thinking: ". . . perhaps we are getting to be a more polite people, and the raw-head-and-bloody-bones style of electioneering has passed away from us for good." [138] Field agents of both parties thought otherwise, away from the gentle waters of Buzzard's Bay and the curious White House calm. After all, there were things like Populism and the Homestead strike to keep them tense.

The Homestead iron and steel works sat near the Monongahela River in Pittsburgh. Though Andrew Carnegie owned part of the property, management fell to Henry Clay Frick, a man who firmly believed in his own and industry's destiny. The plant expanded in the early 1890's, and attracted a variety of workers. The settlement around the plant contained grog shops, cheap storefronts, and poor housing. The management had contracts, due to expire on June 30, with skilled men in the Amalgamated Association of Iron and Steel Workers. But despite apparent prosperity, Frick lowered the wage rates of about a sixth of the labor force in a new contract. His refusal to negotiate or accept full unionization produced a strike and over-reaction on both sides early in July. The strikers left, talking of violence; management locked out old employees. Barbed wire, observation towers, and private guards—later including Pinkertons—protected strike-breakers: [139]

> There stands today with great pretense
> Enclosed within a white-washed fence
> A wondrous change of great import,
> The mills transformed into a fort.

Violence flared, including a serious battle between Pinkertons and strikers, while local and state authorities tried to confine the disorder. By mid-July, some union leaders approached Reid, a friend of Carnegie, to end the strike on any reasonable terms. They would come back merely for their old jobs. Carnegie remained in Scotland, giving Frick full authority to act.[140] On Saturday, July 23, an Anarchist named Alexander Berkman calmly shot and wounded Frick at his desk before a startled visitor realized there was any danger. They tried to disarm Berkman, who stabbed Frick several times during a rolling melee. After help arrived, a doctor bandaged Frick's wounds, but he refused to stop working and left that night at his usual time, recuperating at home for three weeks. "This incident will not change the attitude of the Carnegie Steel Company toward the Amalgamated Association," he said. "I do not think I shall die. But if I do or not, the company will pursue the same policy and it will win." He was right, as workers admitted. Despite their lack of connection with the assassin, labor leaders knew "the bullet from Berkman's pistol . . . went straight through the heart of the Homestead strike." [141]

As the initial public outcry against the assassin settled, prominent Republicans urged Frick to settle the strike. John E. Milholland, representing the GOP National Committee, called on Frick, who listened in bed, swathed in bandages. He bade Milholland goodbye with fresh determination. "I will never recognize the Union, never, never, never!" [142] Reid wrote Harrison of their frustration, but Frick refused to deal with the union even if Harrison requested it.[143] Though Frick later gave Elkins a $25,000 campaign contribution, he thought "it was a waste of money, but we wanted to do our duty and I hoped Mr. Harrison would be relected." [144] By early September, the plant was running at half-capacity with new workers, as the lockout succeeded. Chauncey Depew blamed Carnegie for the debacle, and thought Homestead embittered many eastern labor groups. The workers in Pittsburgh proposed to show the national Administration their power: [145]

> The mills of the gods grind slowly,
>   And they grind exceeding fine;
> And in the ides of November
>   You'll find us all in line.
> Our bullets made of paper,
>   We'll plunk them in so hot
> That the G.O.P. will wonder
>   If they ever were in the plot.
> For we are the people and
>   We'll occupy the land
> In spite of the Carnegies'
>   Or Pinkerton's brigands.

Railroad shutdowns in the East, as well as western mining strikes, also inevitably hurt the Administration in some labor circles.

Populists did not welcome industrial violence, but thought it was a hopeful sign for a farmer-worker party. The Populists were vocal in the Plains states and mountain boroughs, where normally Republican counties shifted into the third party's ranks. But the South naturally produced the campaign's greatest struggle. Cleveland had few ties there, despite past southern advisers, and snappish agrarian editors wearied quickly of his pious exhortations to downgrade the silver issue and raise the farmer's lot with tariff reduction. "Clevelandism seeks to get beyond the Republicans in the direction of compliance with the grasping demands of the moneyed and monopolistic interests of this [northeastern] section," a farm journal reported, tying sectionalism to economic complaints.[146] This attitude directly countered New England Democratic demands for a tariff war that avoided the currency question.[147]

Local correspondents warned Democratic campaign planners not to take the South for granted. The Populists' stand on currency, land, and transportation, plus some Negro votes, jeopardized the outcome for the first time since Reconstruction. All the once abstract political issues were now personal, and farmers faced irate creditors with new anger on both sides. "The people under the present financial pressure are restless, and ripe for change and experimentation," a friend wrote Alabama's Senator John T. Morgan. "The opposition to trusts and monopolies has been transferred to individual owners of property. The cry against corporations, gold-bugs, plug hats, etc. has so embittered the minds of the people, and so filled them with prejudice that they are ill-prepared to listen to the appeals of reason."[148]

Regulars counted on emotion to hold southern Democratic ranks. The national leadership emphasized the empty threat of a "force bill" if Harrison won. But hundreds, then thousands, of Alliance Democrats who could not accept Cleveland's stand on gold, moved to Populism. It was not an easy choice. The southerner who dropped Democratic allegiance even for a moment often became an outcast among neighbors, was denied credit at the country store, charged higher prices, and received lower prices for his crops. He symbolized threats to white rule in a society fearing the Negro more than depression or Republicanism. "It is like cutting off the right hand or putting out the right eye," a Virginian said of leaving the old party.[149]

Republican prospects in the three-cornered election enhanced Democratic violence. Nightriders, hired thugs who broke up meetings, newspaper wars, purchased votes, and even duels became common. If the Border states followed Harrison, the Republicans might make up for losses in the Midwest. Special bureaus sent speakers, literature, and money south, though many Republicans called the whole idea "moonshine." Southerners would never let Negroes vote, or count the ballots if they did; and southern Republicanism could not win without Negro votes. Of course, it worked both ways. Democrats used the Republican threat as another syllable in their appeal for unity and the "Old Cause." Hecklers punctuated General Weaver's speeches with cries of "A Vote for Weaver is a vote for Harrison!" A Nashville paper warned readers in no uncertain terms: "Any Democrat might just as well go straight into the Republican party as into the ranks of its active ally, the People's Party." [150]

Populist speakers dodged rocks to carry their message into the wilderness. "Read your bibles every Sunday and the Omaha platform every day in the week," General Field counseled audiences, as he gamely swung around the circle. It was a shoe-string operation, but the underdog role was not an unmixed evil. Populist speakers financed rides between stumps with collections that often gave country voters a rare sense of helping a national crusade. Many a farmer put his last quarter into Mrs. Lease's laundry basket after hearing a ringing indictment of the money power or bloated East.[151] Behind a vocal effort, the rural press carried Populist doctrine to an estimated 20 per cent of the voters. Determination compensated for poor organization and bitter foes. "Their [the farmers'] earnestness, bordering on religious fanaticism, has a touch of the kind of metal that made Cromwell's round-heads so terrible a force," the Dallas Morning News reported in June.[152]

Democrats pilloried Populists as rag-tag agitators, outsiders, and trouble-makers eager to gain power at the farmers' expense, but Democrats more than matched every Populist verbal indiscretion, duel, and knife-fight. Hecklers made Weaver's tour of Georgia a bitter gauntlet. In Waycross, only local supporters saved the party from physical attack. In Albany, "a howling mob" drowned his speech. Columbus staged a riot after hearing Democratic harangues on Weaver's supposed war atrocities against southerners. In Macon, the local populace jostled Weaver, his wife, and Mrs. Lease, and showered the group with rotten eggs, tomatoes, and rocks while a band played "Marching Through Georgia." Weaver spoke in Atlanta, but abandoned the tour because of a "spirit of organized rowdyism." [153] He blamed the troubles on city riff-raff. "The country people are uniformly respectful and anxious to hear," he insisted in the best agrarian tradition. Mrs. Lease noted tartly: "The fact was, Mrs. Weaver was made a regular walking omelet by the southern chivalry of Georgia." Tom Watson joined the chorus. "They [Democrats] call us the ragtag scum of creation. Thank God, we have never yet dreamed we could win our way to public favor by insulting women, and striking them in the face with eggs." The opposition endlessly discussed Populist incompetence: [154]

> Why should the farmer delve and ditch,
> Why should the farmer's wife darn and stitch?
> The government can make 'em rich,
>   And the People's Party knows it.
> So hurrah, hurrah for the great P.P.!
>   1 = 7, and 0 = 3,
>   A is B and X is Z
> And the People's Party knows it!

The bogey of Negro domination overshadowed all other arguments as the hot summer led to a violent Election Day. Left to his own devices, the Negro would probably vote Republican, but ancient servitude and fear of neighbors made him saleable. As one black voter told a prominent Virginian: "Major Page, don't you know that God made the Negro for sale to the highest bidder?" [155] Many Negroes also suspected Populism's shallow talk of racial equality, believing white agrarians would use them politically in a segregated social system. Most southern whites readily agreed with Virginia's Fitzhugh Lee. "It matters little whether a white voter is protectionist, free trader, tariff reformer, or prohibitionist; he sinks everything in his desire not to be controlled by the blacks." [156]

General Weaver sadly agreed in private. "There is but one issue in the South," he once told a friend. "That is competition to see who can most hate the Negro. The man that wins gets the nomination. The whole thing is a dead-drag on the country. . . . Slavery must be the greatest of crimes. Here we are, all these years after it has been abolished, and we are still paying the penalty for it." [157] The Democrats fused temporarily with some local Populists, bought off others, threatened Negroes, "colonized" many districts, and controlled the ballot count. The cities and towns were Democratic strong points, and most major newspapers bitterly assailed Populism. The Populists lacked the strength to adopt Democratic methods, and the numbers to win over fraud and intimidation.

Weaver and faithful aides toured the wheat states, silver camps and desert cities. California and Oregon gave him and other speakers a hearing, as both major parties often drained Populist strength with fusion arrangements based on post-victory promises. The Populists were making a showing with meager resources, threatening Republicans in the Midwest and Far West, but the Democrats would not lose the South, and by fall had surprising claims to a larger part of the country.

The Democratic party was always a looser coalition than the GOP, and every presidential campaign exposed its weakness. Cleveland's nomination heightened intra-party tensions in New York, the party's counterpart to the "Blaine problem" among Republicans. Cleveland was still heavy-handed in dealing with either friendly critics or outright foes, but he quickly called for unity, on his own terms. "I will, however, venture to say this: If we are defeated this year, I predict a Democratic wandering in the dark wilds of discouragement for twenty-five years," he wrote Watterson. [158]

Tammany Hall was a more pressing problem than southern Democrats. John Kelly died in 1886, passing leadership to Richard Croker. A shrewd man, intensely devoted to the organization, Croker spread authority among lieutenants and wished to integrate the Hall into the national party, with proper rewards. In Chicago, he told reporters Tammany was loyal. "We will return home and give the ticket our hearty support. It is a good ticket. We were for Hill, and we will give the nominee of this convention the same kind of support we gave the Senator here." He promised "sturdy support" of both Cleveland and the platform, naturally assuming that sensitive eastern ears picked up these bids for reciprocity. He liked and respected Whitney, because he had once helped Croker fight a false murder charge. [159]

Hill's reaction was another, and equally important matter. He showed no taste for unity taffy after Cleveland's nomination. "I am keeping quiet and saying nothing," he told friends.[160] He especially disliked the New York party's role as Cleveland imagined it. The former President seemed to excoriate it between elections, then demand subservience every four years in the name of harmony. "The treatment of the N.Y. delegation was most outrageous and makes our people bent on revenge as they now feel," he wrote a friend. "Gorman and everybody have been explaining it ever since they returned—but I think I know how it was." People would damn whatever he did. "If I should work ever so hard, and Mr. Cleveland should then fail, they will falsely accuse me of treachery. It is a difficult situation." He doubted the ticket would carry New York with tariff reform. At Buzzard's Bay, the candidate complained of too much attention from Watterson and too little from Hill. "Little Dave" declined to attend the formal notification ceremonies, and begged off serving on Whitney's special advisory committee. He seemed content to watch the state election, not at all sure that tariff reduction was either wise or possible.[161]

All this dissatisfaction called for at least a gesture from Cleveland. Whitney spent weeks organizing committees and raising funds, promising malcontents that Cleveland would reward their services, no matter what he said now. Cleveland preferred fighting party enemies to pacifying them. He badly wanted to win, but thought Tammany and Hill would cheat him. *"The thing is not right . . . ,"* he wrote Wilson Bissell. "I believe there is a lot of lying and cheating going on and unless the complexion changes we shall wake up, I think, the morning after election and find that we have been fooled by as base a set of cut-throats as ever scuttled a ship." Croker did not want Tammany to disappear in a personal party, and Cleveland would run a personal administration. Cleveland disliked passing campaign management to men "who have solemnly declared that I cannot carry New York," while his own friends took back seats.[162] It would not pay to publicize the party's need of New York's disparate groups, lest they later demand huge rewards.

Whitney continued his rounds, and even drafted a harmony letter for Cleveland to send Edward Murphy of Troy. That was too much. "I'll see the whole outfit to the devil before I'll do it," Cleveland said.[163] Whitney insisted, and was equally blunt. "The policy of getting everybody upon whom Hill relies and nullifying him is the true policy both for now and for the future," he told Cleveland. "It is no use to say not trust any of them. We have got to trust them; they have the organization and the power and by trusting them we can make them pull straight." [164] Like it or not, the talk affected the campaign. Cleveland was uncomfortable about it all by September. "The neglect of everything except tickling these men amounts to a craze at headquarters," he wrote Bissell again, "and in the meantime the campaign, it seems to me, limps and halts." [165]

A conference was the proper answer, however much Cleveland disliked the idea. On September 8, he arrived at New York's Victoria Hotel, jaw set and step firm, to meet Whitney and the Empire State leaders. He shook hands all around, and sat down to a luxurious dinner. The conversation lagged, but Whitney combined charm and common sense until after the meal, when "legs were crossed and business gotten down to." Everyone was frank without rudeness. Croker tried to be reasonable. William Sheean of Buffalo was a little more cross. Edward Murphy of Troy wanted straight answers. Cleveland listened, then dropped his hand on the table, quietly but firmly remarking: "No promises." The men looked at each other, then Croker said that no Administration could mortgage its future, but they at least wanted assurances, if not concrete promises. They had a right to expect reasonable payment for services rendered. Cleveland left them the distinct impression that he agreed. After all, Hill was notable for his absence at the conference; even if these men cooperated, the party was not safe in New York. Whitney smoothed over the rough places, and everyone soon seemed in line; obviously with crossed fingers, but in line nonetheless. Hill finally campaigned for the party, if not for Cleveland.[166]

Whitney still disliked the limelight, but ran the organization with verve and imagination. He managed Cleveland, and posted experienced men in key states to sift requests for money and observe local efforts. He even asked Cleveland to abandon his lofty epistles and get down to the hard business of educating the public. Though Cleveland refused to leave Buzzard's Bay, he wrote careful letters to party managers and selected reform organizations that indicated a keen desire to win. He would not repeat the foolish lethargy of 1888. Whitney followed Republican example in establishing special groups to add color to the impersonal contest. An Irish-Democratic Club, and the Democratic Wholesale Drygoods Club were only a few such. Whitney worried constantly about finances. "I am haunted now with the money fear," he wrote Cleveland early in August, well before large outlays began. "I shall do nothing else for the next month but try to organize a good finance committee." Whitney reputedly gave $250,000, and agents carefully solicited businessmen. The *New York World* raised funds, and state committees paid most of their bills for naturalizing aliens and spreading the good word of tariff reform and sound money. The national organization spent about $2,350,000, some $800,000 more than the Republicans.[167]

Cleveland worried more about the tariff problem than campaign mechanics. It could win or lose industrial states. "The tariff straddle in the original [Democratic] platform was just dull and cumbrous and wordy enough to have been written by Cleveland himself," John Hay told Reid, "and its upsetting by Watterson and Tammany was a delicious piece of monkey mischief."[168] Whitney also knew protection's appeal. "I would rather have seen Cleveland defeated than have had that fool free trade plank adopted."[169] Cleveland condemned Watterson and his reformers as obstructive, dangerous and personally offensive. "As for this fellow Watterson, the sooner he is given his place on the furthest back seat the safer we shall be. . . . I think I must just stand by the message of 1887 and if I make up my mind to that, I shall come pretty near saying so."[170] He did, in effect, by delaying the letter of acceptance until September 26, and talking tortuously of reducing rates without affecting American industry. As in the past, Democratic politicians ironically paid homage to protection while demanding its reform. He also opposed free coinage, leaving the clear impression that deflation on gold was better than silver legislation.

Cleveland hoped to carry the Midwest and Old Northwest on tariff reform tied to consumer prices. A special subcommittee under Dickinson coordinated efforts there, organizing propaganda for ethnic groups, and trying to play down local issues. Where possible, Democrats fused temporarily with Populist or dissident Republican groups, and by fall showed surprising progress. Cleveland appeared at Madison Square Garden for notification ceremonies in late July, but the burden of personal campaigning fell on Stevenson, and "Adlai and his Axe" showed to good effect in doubtful areas. His frank appeals to spoilsmanship were "the delight of the multitude . . . ," as the old campaigner "spoke right out in meeting, and did not mince his words."[171] He was particularly vocal in stressing the dangers of Republican rule while touring the Border and upper South, arguing in Richmond that beating a federal election law was "more important than a hundred tariff bills."[172] Countless speakers emphasized white man's rule, warning against federal inspectors and predatory marshals in state affairs if Harrison won. "No Force Bill! No Negro domination!" became the battle cry, though the New York Tribune rebuked such blatant bigotry. "Time and circumstances have diluted that sort of stuff to a thinness that makes dishwater a powerful compound by comparison."[173]

In the week before Election Day, Cleveland abandoned invisibility to appear at a mass meeting in a Jersey City ice-rink. But only the Populists seemed clamorous. Neither Harrison nor Cleveland raised men from their seats to frenzied cheering. As one observer noted, "each side would have been glad to defeat the other if it could do so without electing its own candidate." [174] "The contest has been singularly good natured," a magazine said in excusing the torpor. But the editor also noted significant reliance on party loyalty, organization, and new methods of propagandizing. Technology, faster communication, and a changing electorate emphasized literature, image-building, and advertising over personal campaigning. It was an important, if too little noticed step in nationalizing American politics, and placing party loyalty above individual whims.[175]

Harrison spent Election Day quietly in the White House. He read returns until after midnight, and stoically accepted defeat. The Clevelands and a few aides noted returns in their New York home. About midnight, "a swaying, clamorous crowd" arrived outside, and the President-elect spoke briefly about coming responsibilities. He, Parker, and Lamont stayed up until 4 A.M. As he rose to retire, Cleveland looked at his secretary. "Well, Parker, none of these men or all of them together know or realize as you and I do how this thing has been done." Parker noticed that Cleveland seemed more self-assured than ever.[176]

It was an impressive triumph. Cleveland won the South, and all mid-Atlantic states except Pennsylvania. He received 1 electoral vote in Ohio, 5 in Michigan, 1 in North Dakota, and 8 in California. He won Indiana, Illinois, and Wisconsin. Only New England, the upper Rocky Mountain states, Washington, Minnesota, and Iowa remained fully Harrison's. The President added 1 vote in California and 3 in Oregon. Cleveland ran nearly 400,000 popular votes ahead, with 5,555,426 to the President's 5,182,690, but congressional contests revealed soft spots in the sweep. Congress was safely Democratic, but the party lost House seats in Iowa, Massachusetts, Michigan, Nebraska, New York, Ohio, and Wisconsin, though reapportionment added some southern members. The Democrats would barely control the Senate; Populists lost 6 House seats. Mugwumps again ascribed victory to younger voters interested in issues rather than passions, but the *New York Tribune* credited the victory to Democratic organization, especially in New York. The country apparently favored tariff reduction, assuming the rates increased consumer prices. As in 1890, many people also briefly rebelled at Republican spending and federal power. ". . . the fraud pension deal was fully as strong a factor as tariff reform in inducing many Republicans to vote the Democratic ticket," a Minnesotan wrote Cleveland.[177]

The Populists drew much attention, and many sighs of relief from regular politicians. Weaver won 22 electoral votes, with just over a million popular ballots. He carried Kansas, Colorado, Idaho, and Nevada, with 1 vote each from Oregon and North Dakota, but the party failed to win substantial labor support, made no serious inroads east of the Mississippi, and won its largest margins in silver states. As former President Hayes noted: "The labor vote, holding the balance of power and better organized than ever before, joined the Democrats." [178]

Discontent resting on economic grievances, dislike of Republican personalities and some policies, and emotional apprehension gave the Democrats their chance. Senator Orville Platt privately offered an astute, if partisan analysis: [179]

> The Republican party has been defeated in this election because the Democrats have induced all the people in the country who think that they want something which they have not got, to vote the Democratic ticket in the expectation that that party in power will give them what they want. Socialists, anarchists, hoodlums, as well as farmers, laborers and people of small means, and the discontented everywhere, expect now that all their ideas, whether reasonable or wild, are to be carried out in practical legislation by the Democratic party.

His remarks contained much truth. The Democrats, not the Populists, won on the theme of discontent. "I made up my mind that if a change of administration would bring good times, I wanted a change," an upstate New York farmer said. "It may make things a good deal worse. But I am willing to try. If I find the Democrats have deceived me, I shall vote the Republican ticket again in 1896." [180]

The President was resigned. "For me there is no sting in it," he told Cornelius Bliss of New York. "Indeed, after the heavy blow the death of my wife dealt me, I do not think I could have stood the strain a reelection would have brought." [181] He gave no sign of realizing that his personality was a factor. He thought the Homestead strike, a wavering economy, and working-class resentment against corporate riches supposedly flowing from tariff protection beat the party. "The workingman declined to walk under the protective umbrella because it sheltered his employer also," he condoled with Reid. "He has smashed it for the fun of seeing the silk stockings take the rain. If he finds that the employer has a waterproof coat, while he is undefended, he may help us rig up the umbrella." [182] Most Republican leaders admitted an apparent public shift toward tariff reform. Harrison did not laud protection in his last annual message the following month. "The results of the recent election must be accepted as having introduced a new policy." He savored a dry observation: ". . . no emotion cools sooner than that of gratitude." [183]

The salad days seemed to be back for Democrats. If they fulfilled campaign pledges and speedily reduced the tariff, the era of balanced politics might be over. But it was a deceptive triumph. The temporarily discontented of all parties followed the Democratic standard; each must be rewarded. Southern Democrats admitted suppressing rather than pacifying Populist discontent. In the West, Democrats fused with agrarians for post-election rewards of patronage and power. This was especially dangerous, since Cleveland always refused to see the symbolic and party value of offices and rewards. Most Democratic voters favored tariff reform, but many also wanted the currency manipulation and agrarian relief that Cleveland opposed. Still, the victory was a great opportunity. Tact, careful rewards, and luck might revitalize the party.

A certain brooding quality briefly invaded the GOP; something more than bitterness at momentary defeat. The American people seemed fickle. Decades of organizing, nationalistic legislation, and campaigning seemed to produce pendulum politics for Ins and Outs. As if to mark this tiredness under the stress of long tension, two leading Republicans symbolizing much of their party's past died that snowy winter as the country awaited a second Cleveland Administration.

Rutherford B. Hayes seldom played a political role. He quietly pursued charity and educational work and appeared at solemn state events. The interior man loved ideas, and he enjoyed a long feast of reading and speculation, but committed his thoughts to a voluminous diary and discreet private correspondence. "For years I have had no time to read," he wrote an Ohio friend. "Now I am a reveller." [184] Mrs. Hayes' death in 1889 weakened his spirit, and he was content merely to "shove on to the end." He guided callers around the grounds, noting new trees, and watching birds flutter in the air. "Oh, Lucy wouldn't like that," he might say if a gardener did something wrong.[185] He died quietly on January 17, 1893, and snow softened the background of his funeral. Cleveland arrived, remarking that Hayes had promised to visit him, and he would now return the compliment a final time. Governor McKinley, so long Hayes' friend and protegé, led the state's delegation.

James G. Blaine could not attend the funeral. Poor health and emotional depression kept him secluded. The deaths of his son and daughter in 1890 had further sapped his strength. "We learn in these dispensations that there is something greater in this world than the indulgences of ambition," he sadly wrote Russell Alger.[186] He left office in a swirl of controversy; then silence. His other son, Emmons, died suddenly in Chicago on June 16, 1892. The Democratic national convention, in an unprecedented act, moved the party's condolences be sent.

He was out of office, but a Republican. The old charisma could still bring men to tears. James S. Clarkson spoke for millions while surveying the echoing Blaine headquarters in Minneapolis after Harrison's nomination. "It is the last time we shall ever see them," he said, picking up a white plume. "For five successive conventions, I have fought for Blaine. Do you realize what it means to me to see the end—without success?"[187] Blaine was still the Plumed Knight, and made a valedictory campaign address. Appearing at Ophir Farm to congratulate Reid, he spoke for the programs he and the party supported. He looked old and weak, white hair and beard stirring in a cool evening breeze. His eyeglasses reflected torchlight while he read from a slightly shaking paper. Two thoughtful watchers raised brands for more light, and caught him in a moment of wavering shadows.[188]

He accepted the party's defeat silently. Visitors still came to the Washington home, and his few walks attracted sightseers. He read, but talked little. In mid-winter he fell ill, and did not respond to treatment. His death on January 27 brought grief to his followers, and provoked fresh speculation about his historical reputation. But mourners cared less for posterity's judgments than for the vibrant human personality and his exciting ideas. Even opponents admitted he was always "a shadow afar off, and yet singularly near and vivid."[189] Blaine was a great party leader, superbly attuned to the men and measures of his time. He early formulated and popularized constructive nationalism, and set many important precedents in foreign policy. Despite intense personal appeal, he extolled the virtues of party loyalty, and was a prime mover in nationalizing politics and broadening the GOP's appeal. Many of that generation would always remember him.

XI

☆☆☆☆☆☆ ☆☆☆☆☆☆ ☆☆☆☆☆☆☆☆

The Democracy's Fall: 1893–1894

☆☆☆☆☆☆ ☆☆☆☆☆☆ ☆☆☆☆☆☆☆☆

Cleveland did not seek much advice in composing a second Administration. He doubted the wisdom of making ranking Democrats Cabinet officers or immediate subordinates. The public expected familiar and perhaps colorful statesmen, but successful politicians were not always good administrators in national departments.[1] They also had larger ambitions than Cabinet portfolios, and forceful men could threaten a president if they disagreed enough to resign. Cleveland formed a personal Administration, turning for suggestions to the small circle of men he knew and trusted. It was a characteristic but dangerous attitude. Unless he mollified opposing Democrats, used patronage to strengthen the whole party, and cultivated a larger public following, unexpected events could easily destroy his coalition.

The State Department naturally drew the greatest attention. Whitney declined the post because he was more interested in business than diplomacy. Cleveland turned next to Bayard, but the former Secretary dreaded the expense and partisan attacks. He preferred the first ambassadorship to Great Britain, which Cleveland duly awarded him. The choice fell ultimately to a surprising figure, Walter Q. Gresham, so recently a Republican, whose selection Cleveland somehow thought would please independent voters. Gresham had the surface talents for political success in America, but his career was a study in frustration. An Indianan, born in 1832, he worked up the usual frontier ladder of success, teaching school, and practicing law. He opposed slavery, preferring compensated extinction to abolition, but campaigned for Frémont in 1856. Entering the war as a private, he emerged a brevet major general. After opposing Reconstruction and the spoils system, he gained a strange reputation for independence based on anti-railroad bias and a brooding sympathy for a vaguely defined working class. He served President Arthur as Postmaster-General, and for one month as an interim Secretary of the Treasury. In 1884, he went on the Circuit Court bench in Chicago, and steadily expanded his newspaper reputation with decisions against corporations.

Gresham saw the world through deep-set, sad eyes, and his tone was an essay in resignation to fate, yet he shrewdly retained frontier mannerisms. He was no stranger to the spittoon, and often interviewed distinguished men in shirt-sleeves and open collar. His absentmindedness was legendary, and he once kept servants looking for his overshoes until they realized he was wearing them. Sympathizing with many reformist ideas, he lacked the will to act outside familiar patterns. He feared a coming war between Haves and Have-nots, but was full of apprehensive doubts rather than answers. "The labor question has come to stay; it cannot be ignored," he wrote a friend in 1892: [2]

> We are living under new conditions, conditions utterly unlike anything in the past. Labor-saving machinery has given capital an advantage that it never possessed before. What is an equitable division of the joint product of capital and labor, and who is to decide the question? I fear that settlement of the controversy will be attended with serious consequences. The laboring men of this country have intelligence and courage, and they firmly believe that they are oppressed. They are growing stronger daily, and unless capital yields, we will have collisions more serious than the one which occurred at Homestead. The right to acquire and hold property must be recognized.

He thus seemed an anomaly: a pessimistic frontiersman, a tired reformer, a man of action frozen in place.*

He feared the Republican party was growing old. If it did not grasp a new opportunity, national leadership would go by default to the hodgepodge Democrats, whose vision was even narrower. "Our boat will have to be rowed against the stream, while the Democratic boat will run with it," he told William E. Chandler in 1891.[3] If he could not be a Democrat, he might follow Cleveland, like many other independents. "I think, with you, that a Republican can vote for Mr. Cleveland without joining the Democratic party," he said in 1892.[4]

---

*This theme of impending strife recurs so often among politicians of the period that it may be worth noting their apprehensions did not come true. Despite the upheavals of 1894, the great majority of workers retained traditional political allegiances and shared in the industrial system's benefits after the political settlement of the 1890's. Except for brief moments during the depression of the 1930's, this fear of social warfare has not returned to many Americans. Of course, we may now be witnessing its revival around the race question, with undecipherable results.

Gresham was realistic while bidding the GOP goodbye. "I have no political ambition, but if I had, no one realizes better than I do that I have committed political suicide." [5] His apparent independent character and strange personality doubtless attracted Cleveland, who shared many of these qualities without the accompanying doubts.

Gresham did not enter the Administration easily. The offer took him by surprise, and he feared cutting all ties with his past. Despite pressure from Cleveland through friends like Carlisle, Fairchild, Dickinson, and Whitney, he wavered. Legend said he accepted only after Cleveland literally beckoned: "Come, Gresham, I need you." [6] The choice produced criticism. As Champ Clark said, it "slapped every Democrat betwixt the two seas squarely in the face." [7] Minnesota's Senator Cushman K. Davis later answered for Republicans, calling Gresham "that Old Welkin of diplomacy, that plantigrade pachyderm from the Wabash." [8] Though Cleveland admired Gresham, and learned to listen to his advice, he was a poor appointment. He had no party, had quarreled with ranking senators, disliked diplomacy's details, and was better at moralizing than acting.

Cleveland did little better politically with the important Treasury post. He turned almost instinctively to John G. Carlisle, now a senator from Kentucky. Carlisle was a familiar Democrat, tariff reformer, and as politicians went, a fiscal expert. His hardscrabble life as a farm youth gave way to a law practice in Covington, but he briefly linked rural and urban constituents in the national tariff debates of the 1880's. Cleveland apparently wanted to groom him for the presidential succession, and trusted his judgment while overrating his political skill. "He knows all I ought to know, and I can bear all we have to bear," the new President remarked.[9] That was part of the problem, for Carlisle would have to bear much in a war over the currency. He had favored silver as a congressman, hoping to submerge the issue quietly in tariff reform. Though an able orator, he was best at cool, dispassionate logic. He was detached, wearing "a sort of thoughtful, intent melancholy," most of the time, and tended to move with the majority in crises that threatened party unity.[10]

Geography dictated a New England appointment. Cleveland avoided taking prominent New Englanders from Congress or governorships since the party would need them in the tariff battle. When Senator George Gray of Delaware declined the Attorney-General's appointment, Cleveland turned to Richard Olney of Boston. He had met him only once, but Olney had well-advertised talents and political connections. He was a strange figure—publicly blunt, and privately exhibiting a puckish humor. A graduate of Brown University and Harvard Law School, he developed a lucrative corporate law practice that kept him out of personal argumentation in courtrooms. His dislike of people thwarted a career in local politics, but Olney knew the party's ranking managers, and obliquely advertised his talents. Late in January, he whimsically urged Whitney not to "forget how many people at the East —including numberless widows and orphans—are interested in railroads, and require and deserve a reasonable amount of consideration." [11]

Cleveland liked Olney, and respected his legal abilities. He preferred a southern Attorney-General, but thought Olney could fill either that post or the Navy Department. He desired the latter, for obvious reasons. ". . . I have thought that Mr. Olney's railroad clientage, while with such a man as he [is] no real objection, might in the estimation of the public make him a more desirable Secretary of the Navy than Attorney General." [12] But he left the choice to Olney, after sending him on a token errand to persuade John Q. Adams, a strange choice himself, to take the Navy office. When Adams refused, Cleveland demanded Olney's acceptance. "Nothing will now excuse you but the act of God or the public enemy." [13]

Olney's blunt, businesslike manner naturally attracted Cleveland. He was a small, busy man exuding "a forceful personality." The high-strung young Theodore Roosevelt crossed party lines to play tennis with "funny, gruff old Olney," but the Attorney-General seldom laughed. He armored internal doubts with efficient formality, liked rules, and expected obedience. When his daughter married a man he disliked, he simply barred her from the house. "He looks like a man rather tired of things in general," a caller reported.[14] Like Gresham, but for different reasons, Olney was a weak selection politically. He had no constituency, represented big business in the public mind, and confirmed suspicions that Cleveland was more interested in personal than party rule.

The Interior appointment went to Hoke Smith of Atlanta, who opposed Hill in Georgia, and advertised Cleveland's virtues in his paper, the *Atlanta Journal*. Smith had a modest reputation for wanting to smooth the harshest aspects of the industrial New South. He believed in tariff reform and "honest money" in an area sympathetic to silver. Ranking Bourbons like L. Q. C. Lamar and John B. Gordon praised his campaign work, and thought him safer than a rural southerner. His belief in administrative reform, and ties to the business community further recommended him to Cleveland. He was a reasonable choice from the confused South, but naturally drew press ridicule. Who had

ever heard of "Hoax Myth," the *New York Sun* asked. He well symbolized Cleveland's love of obscure people who would follow his lead.
"Now, suppose Mr. Cleveland had decided to give Fake Yarn a place
in his cabinet," Dana's sheet speculated.[15]

Daniel Lamont sought a higher place than private secretary. He
wanted to be more than "a colonel by courtesy," and asked Parker to
tell Cleveland he could not enter the Administration as a mere facto-
tum. The news surprised Cleveland, who characteristically thought
the private secretaryship more important than the War Department.[16]
But he satisfied "Dan's" wishes, and the appointment was sound
enough, barring a war. Cleveland needed Lamont, who understood
him, the party, and public opinion. "[Cleveland] had no equal in provoking men to wrath," Champ Clark recalled, "and Lamont no rival
in applying poultices and administering soothing syrup." [17] Whitney
saw him as a harmonizer within both the Administration and party.
". . . you will find Col. Lamont the sagest and wisest of advisers—
especially in all matters political," he counseled Gresham, now entering unfamiliar political terrain. "There is no man in the whole Democratic party who knows men as he does—the frauds and humbugs of
the party as well as those entitled to consideration." [18]

Cleveland added another close friend to his Cabinet in making
Wilson S. Bissell Postmaster-General. As a former law partner, adviser
on New York politics, and best man at Cleveland's wedding, Bissell
would not oppose presidential wishes in handling that department's
rich patronage. Cleveland put a southerner in the Navy Department,
Alabama's Hilary Herbert, who bore all the marks of southern political
success, including the usual war wounds. As a member of the national
House from 1877 to 1893, he gained notoriety in opposing the Federal
Elections Bill of 1890, editing a symposium titled *Why the Solid
South?* that proved the white man's right to rule. But his support for
a larger steel Navy pleased Democrats who favored an active foreign
policy. Cleveland filled the last seat at his Cabinet table with J. Sterling Morton of Nebraska in the Agriculture Department. Morton
boasted an active career in the Plains country's hurly-burly politics,
but did not really understand the area. He was fanatically devoted to
scientific farming, invented Arbor Day, and adopted as his seal a
bucolic tree with the motto: "Plant Trees." Morton mixed low tariff
and hard money views, and emphasized economy enough to suspend
the Department's distribution of free seeds.

Cleveland's immediate official family thus confirmed the opposition's
belief that an interregnum had not widened his view of politics. No

Cabinet member represented the country's changing mood. Gresham and Olney had no party but Cleveland. Herbert, Smith, and Carlisle did not speak for the restless South. Bissell and Lamont were Cleveland's personal friends. Morton did not voice agrarian needs or discontent. With his attitude toward politics, Cleveland could do little better. A leader with tact and patience might have formed an administration at least open to information from the discontented groups it must win to survive. Instead, he chose familiar men to enforce decrees, or obscure ones to accept his will.

Preparations for the inaugural proceeded into early March, but with a calmer tone than in 1885. The Harrison entourage radiated "a feeling of relief such as characterized the departure of but few administrations." [19] On a cold March 4, Cleveland delivered his inaugural address in "a blizzard-riddled wooden pen" at the Capitol.[20] The speech was brief, and its message simple. The new Administration would sustain the currency, revise the tariff without injuring the economy, and avoid "the unwholesome progeny of paternalism." That was the theme: "The lessons of paternalism ought to be unlearned and the better lesson taught that while the people should patriotically and cheerfully support their government, its functions do not include support of the people." [21]

Despite Cleveland's confidence, the country felt uneasy. The *Nation,* like other observers, expected action. "For the first time since Buchanan's day, there is no check to the rule of the Democracy." [22] Attention naturally focused on Cleveland, who must move quickly to stabilize the party's victory. All his old characteristics still dominated. He was "as hard-headed as ever," Senator J. N. Camden of West Virginia wrote a friend.[23] The President looked heavier, with thinner hair and a larger walrus mustache. He was abrupt even with distinguished callers. Cabinet meetings seemed a waste of time. If he grew bored, he merely ended the conversation, or turned away from guests to paperwork. His few public appearances were equally curt. He used the pronoun "I" freely, which irritated the press. One cartoonist drew a map of the United States resembling Cleveland's outlines, captioned: [24]

> My country 'tis of Me,
> Of Me I sing.

Office-seekers poured in on the new Administration and Cleveland condemned "the demoralizing madness for spoils" in the inaugural,

largely because it consumed time. A few surviving civil service reformers raised plaintive cries, but Vice-President Stevenson fed names
of deserving Democrats to the Post Office Department. As a former
First Assistant, he had "decapitated sixty-five Republican postmasters
in two minutes," which he always thought "the highest compliment
he had ever received."[25] Cabinet officers, congressmen, and state
leaders put petitions on the President's desk. His first response was a
consuming irritation. He complained to friends of time-wasting congressmen, and often worked between midnight and 4 A.M. "at the
business of the nation." He finally issued a public statement telling
people to stay away from Washington, and warning those who remained they would get nothing. He still condemned "this dreadful,
frightful, damnable office-seeking." But he also fell back on the tone
of wounded self-pity that covered a determination to thwart leaders
who might use patronage to their own advantage. "Sometimes the
pressure is almost overwhelming, and a president cannot always get
at the exact truth," he told a friend just before the inaugural, "but I
want you to know, and all my friends to know, that I am trying to do
what is right—I am trying to do what is right."[26] Office-seekers and
their official friends returned the hostility. Party leaders in the South
and West were especially apprehensive at Cleveland's slowness in
dividing the spoils. They must now fulfill the promises that made local
fusion possible in 1892. But the President delayed, as well he might.
The economy was clearly collapsing.

While the campaign developed in mid-summer, 1892, a few bankers
and businessmen warned of economic stagnation. Capital seemed
timid, uncertain of the future. Like most of life, economics lived on
the hope of future improvement and development. After the election,
Treasury income declined, exports of foodstuffs and raw materials
slumped, and long-term investment in railroads and plant expansion
stabilized. Boston, New York, and Philadelphia, the centers of trade
and finance, were jittery. Democrats feared the economy would break
with Cleveland's inauguration, saddling the party with an impossible
burden of public blame. Even a sharp but brief panic might trigger a
successful silverite attack on the currency.[27]

A dangerously overextended economy provoked these fears. In the
Mississippi Valley and beyond, "boomers" and developers overran
their markets, extending railroads into freightless territory, establishing towns without population, expanding farm acreage in the face of
declining prices—all for the future. Easy money and optimism let

every country town borrow for improvements it did not need. Declines in housing construction, slack export trade, financial stringency in Europe that affected American investments, and the change of political administrations weakened many economic sectors. A poor banking system, overextension in rails and steel, and nagging doubts about the dollar's stability sapped confidence. In April, the first shock waves radiated out from Boston and New York. Calls on fixed collateral dried up the money market, stock prices tumbled, and banks closed. "Men died like flies under the strain," Henry Adams recalled, "and Boston grew suddenly old, haggard, and thin." [28]

Most people saw the panic's symptoms, not its causes. Away from the centers of economic power, they naturally worried about lost jobs and low produce prices. An ugly mood replaced optimism as events tested men's basic assumptions and faith in the future. "Business is at a standstill," James J. Hill wrote Cleveland in June, "and the people are becoming thoroughly aroused. Their feeling is finding expression about as it did during the War of the Rebellion." [29] Many westerners thought Wall Street produced the panic with overspeculation. The businessman merited no special salvation; silverites would use the crisis to make their theories into law.

Men caught by the crisis felt an equal, if different, frustration and impotence. "People who are rich and *sound* when asked to pay up their percentage cannot do it, and we cannot sell their stocks," Henry L. Higginson of Boston wrote Olney in July.[30] Money was hiding. Most businessmen instinctively thought of confidence, the magic ingredient that kept the system expanding. If the government sustained gold, the panic would not become depression. "Do not forget how much imagination has to do with all business operations," Higginson reminded Olney, while asking for a statement on the gold standard.[31] On April 20, Carlisle announced that the Treasury would pay out gold "so long as it has gold lawfully available for the purpose." This ambiguous statement, which Cleveland approved, only increased apprehension and on April 23, the White House issued an unequivocal promise to sustain the gold standard.[32]

The Treasury's apparent resolve did not even brake the collapse. "And so the summer, big with approaching commercial disaster, came on," the *Forum* recalled.[33] Like most American phenomena, the crash was large. Between November, 1892, and August, 1893, some 33 stocks lost over $400,000,000 in value. Business liabilities increased almost tenfold in the same time. The collapse of "glamor stocks" and expansive concerns that symbolized technical progress eroded confidence. By

the end of 1893, 119 railroads with 28,000 miles of track were in receivership, including familiar and impressive names like the Union
Pacific, the Atcheson, Topeka and Santa Fe, and the Erie. In June,
1894, 156 railroads were in receivership, with 30,000 miles of track,
and assets and debts of nearly $2,500,000,000. At the end of 1893, 642
banks were closed.

After the first shock, the nation seemed to doze, like "a patient suffering from a low fever of the financial type." [34] Breadlines gradually
appeared. Westerners returning to eastern and southern homes intensified relief problems for local government and private charity. Like all
great depressions, this one spared nobody. The professional and common laborer both lost jobs. Stockholders' income vanished or shrank;
farmers, lawyers, small and large businessmen suffered. "Just say that
I'm done," a bankrupt businessman told young Theodore Dreiser.
"This panic has finished me. I could go on later, I suppose, but I'm
too old to begin all over again. I haven't any money now, and that's all
there is to it." [35] The country agreed heartily with the *Los Angeles
Times* at New Year's: "Thank the Lord! 1893 is in the hands of a re-
ceiver." [36]

Many public spokesmen and newspapers repeated by rote the sunny
optimism they hoped would arrest the economy's tailspin, but insiders
in both politics and business feared the worst was yet to come. Doubts
about the gold standard and the prospect of a long battle over tariff
reform curtailed investment. Timidity, political uncertainty, and business ruin took the usual toll in human lives. In cities like Chicago and
New York, 1894 brought the spectacle of unemployed men sleeping in
parks, along railroad tracks, on piers, and at railroad stations. Breadlines, soup kitchens, relief stations distributing coal and old clothes
took on a permanent appearance.

In the South and Plains states, farm prices fell below the cost of
production, and money was a curiosity outside cities and towns. A
rural work force felt the impact of industrial depression for the first
time in southern textile mills, coal mines, and new towns. Farther
west, farmers lost even their seed for future crops; cattle went to
market for a few dollars; unsalable repossessed machinery sat in
sheriff's lots. State government supplied some relief on slender resources, but exodus became a way of life. In January, 1894, an estimated 2,500,000 men looked for work; in July, 1894, the economy ran
at three-fourths of capacity. "As the months went by, a strange blight
fell upon the country," the *Washington Post* said, "it came as a fog
comes up out of the sea, foretold by a leaden line along the horizon

and enveloping everything in its cold and deadly touch . . . money withdrew itself from the channels of trade; mills closed, business became stagnant, uncertainty and fear spread like a pall over a hitherto prosperous land." [37]

But the country remained intrinsically rich, and a helter-skelter relief system provided a marginal existence for millions. The federal government had no program,* but states, cities, and private charities raised and spent substantial sums. Popular belief in self-help did not forbid simple acts of neighborly help in both city and country, or inhibit government expenditures altogether. The middle class, religious groups, elected officials, and individual citizens responded surprisingly well in spite of strained resources, indicating the depression's impact throughout society.†

A bewildered people inevitably sought scapegoats. The President and his party quickly filled the bill; soup kitchens became "Cleveland Cafes." The crisis sharpened the silverites' and Populists' conspiracy theory. "In obedience to the demands of the bondholders everywhere, Mr. Cleveland deliberately proceeded to create the panic of 1893 after his inauguration," Nevada's Senator Stewart insisted. In retrospect, Cleveland called the Nineties "these luckless years," and alternately hoped to revive the economy with minimal legislation, or simply to leave office a whole man.[38]

Eastern businessmen convinced the Administration that a crisis of confidence triggered the depression. Quick action to save the gold standard would restore confidence, even if silver purchases did not in fact threaten economic soundness. The Sherman Act symbolized the currency's weakness; the issue must be settled.[39] Cleveland was un-

---

*Cleveland's supporters clung doggedly to their views of free enterprise and self-help. A Pennsylvania manufacturer wrote the President: "While the people are tinctured with the virus of protectionism and paternalism, while they agree with ex-president Harrison that 'it is one of the highest aims of government to so regulate affairs as to provide them work', we can expect little else [but criticism]. Harrison spoke of the pathetic sight of men out of work, forgetting that a far more pathetic sight is to see the destruction of their manhood and independence under the system he would inaugurate." (See A. B. Farquhar to Cleveland, November 13, 1893, Cleveland LC.)

†Professor Norman Pollack overstates the opposite case: "Populists stood almost alone in the 1890's in befriending the men who had been chewed up by the economic system and spewed out over the dark landscape of unemployment and hunger—the men derisively labelled tramps and vagabonds by a society unwilling to concede that the concentration of wealth was accompanied by widespread social misery." The Populists did their share of relief work, but lacked funds, and were more prone to rhetoric and demands for legislative panaceas than to concentrated charity. (See Pollack, The Populist Mind, 329.)

certain. He dreaded a pitched battle with Congress that might wreck the party and kill tariff reform. Perhaps the economy would right itself, as in the past. "Call an extra session NOW!" the *Atlanta Constitution* implored in June.[40] The same pleas came in steady streams from businessmen. Late in June, New York's Democratic banker August Belmont offered advice: [41]

> I think now that the trouble has already gone quite beyond the expectation of both yourself and everyone. From a political point of view, delays will help the formation of plans by the enemies of sound money and the enemies of tariff reform for the defeat and embarrassment of your administration. It would appear that, if it is possible to repeal the silver bill, it should be done while the enemies are on the run.

Cleveland made a serious error in avoiding an immediate special session of Congress to revise the tariff before attacking the currency question. Tariff reform was his basic campaign pledge and the Democratic party was more united on this than on any currency program. Even a quick effort at reduction would calm some fears; success would give the Democrats something to stress while debating silver. It was worth a gamble. Cleveland missed the timing, and the currency debate's sharp personal conflicts and symbolic meanings magnified his worst political attitudes—and for the first time in his life, the President was seriously ill.

Cleveland was singularly unlucky in choosing running-mates, even admitting the necessities of politics. Thomas A. Hendricks, his first Vice-President, died eight months after taking office in 1885. Allen G. Thurman did not win in 1888, but at seventy-five had little vigor. Adlai E. Stevenson spoke for Democrats leaning toward silver inflation. If he succeeded Cleveland, the party and country would change fiscal policies. The prospect worried some friends. "I wish you had Congress in session *now*," Ohio's Michael Harter wrote the President in June, 1893. "*You* may not be alive in September. It would make a vast difference to the United States if you were not." [42] He was closer to the mark than any man knew, for as he wrote, Cleveland faced a possibly fatal operation.

On May 5, the President complained of a rough spot on the roof of his mouth, but did not seek medical aid until June 18. Doctor R. M. O'Reilley, the regular physician for ranking government officials, summoned specialists from Philadelphia and New York. They diagnosed cancer, possibly a result of cigar smoking, and urged an immediate operation. Lamont hastily arranged a secret operation to avoid news-

paper speculation about Cleveland's recovery that would further unsettle the economy. On June 30, the President summoned Congress
into special session for August 7, and left for New York. Subordinates
assumed he meant to rest at Buzzard's Bay, and no one outside his
immediate circle knew of the operation. That evening, he quietly
boarded his friend E. C. Benedict's yacht, the *Oneida,* and exclaimed: "Oh, Doctor Keen, those office-seekers! They haunt me in
my dreams!" [43]

The following day, while the boat steamed up the East River, sur-
geons removed a large part of his upper right jaw and palate, including two teeth. He survived the ordeal well, and recuperated at Buzzard's Bay through July, receiving a few callers, and under strict
family supervision. Cleveland was a docile patient, guilty of only
minor dietary lapses. He soon talked almost normally, with an artificial
jawpiece, and showed no external scars. Only a loss of weight and
slight pallor revealed his illness. Late in July, he discussed fiscal matters with the Treasury's Charles S. Hamlin, who assumed the cotton
padding in Cleveland's mouth protected a dental operation. That was
what the press reported, and officials honestly denied rumors of a more
serious illness. "The newspaper reports in regard to his health are
very much exaggerated," Carlisle wrote Ambassador Bayard, "as he
simply had one of his attacks of rheumatism and suffered somewhat
from a decayed tooth." [44] Cleveland stoically accepted the cloak-and-
dagger secrecy, but burst out to the visiting Attorney-General: "My
God, Olney, they nearly killed me." [45] He returned to Washington on
August 5, two days before Congress convened, apparently well, and
looking better for the weight loss. He needed all the energy he could
command. The Congress now assembling five months after the inauguration would determine the fate of his whole term.

The Sherman Act was a political compromise, workable in prosperous times when men did not doubt the purchasing power of dollars
or the symbolic meanings of money, but depression naturally called
into question the varying merits of all United States currency. Under
tension, faith in gold as the world's symbol of value confronted earnest
belief in silver inflation, and an American rather than world standard.
Senator Sherman had no illusions. "I voted for it, but the day it became a law, I was ready to repeal it, if repeal could be had without
substituting in its place absolute free coinage." [46] The Harrison Administration enjoyed relative prosperity after the law passed in 1890,
but Treasury officials always worried about the Act's requirement to

redeem silver certificates "in coin." In practice, that meant gold; and
each note commanded multiple redemptions, in what Cleveland called
"an endless chain" draining the gold reserve. On January 29, 1891,
Secretary of the Treasury William Windom, warned the New York
Board of Trade against inflation, ending with a pointed quotation:
"He that loveth silver shall not be satisfied with silver." With this, he
collapsed and died of a heart attack, as if to summarize the subject's
passions.

His successor, Charles Foster of Ohio, had equal difficulty in maintaining a safe gold reserve. President Harrison attempted to arrange
another international conference but no major power was interested,
evidence of silver's declining status. In December, Foster's annual
report warned that blanket gold redemption could not continue forever. In February, 1893, he maintained the $100,000,000 gold reserve
only through appeals to bankers, bookkeeping devices, and delayed
payments of government bills. In that month, the Treasury engraved
plates for a bond issue, and left Cleveland a slender margin in the
reserve.

Publicly, the new Administration eagerly awaited successful tariff
reform; privately, the President's counselors feared the silver issue
would swallow everything.[47] Sherman argued that only Democratic
opposition prevented immediate repeal or modification of the existing
law. "If the Democratic party will furnish a contingent of ten senators
in support of the repeal of the silver act of 1890, it will pass the Senate
within ten days," he wrote in January.[48] Senator Allison was nearer
the mark in denying "the slightest chance that the Sherman law will
be repealed during this session." [49] The Republicans would leave that
hot potato to Cleveland.

He originally hoped to spend his first months carefully planning a
tariff bill, while doling out offices. But the panic, ill-health, and party
discontent prevented a September session to reform the tariff. On
August 8, Congress heard his blunt message asking for repeal of the
Sherman Act's purchase clause, and tacit endorsement of the single
gold standard. He firmly believed repeal would restore business confidence and stabilize the economy. As usual, Cleveland did not mince
words, warning that speed was essential. Lengthy debate would only
increase uncertainty and reward speculators in silver. Asking for bipartisan support, and opposing fiat money, he concluded: "The maxim
'He gives twice who gives quickly' is directly applicable." The message produced widely different responses. Urban papers like Reid's
Tribune, regardless of party, generally favored repeal, but grim silver-

ites braced for a protracted struggle. Some argued that Cleveland deliberately created an emergency to enrich speculating friends with a stock panic, and to turn opinion against silver by tying it to depression.[50]

Cleveland never publicly discussed why he accepted the single gold standard. He probably hoped this vagueness would raise the issue above politics. A different leader, more attuned to the problem's political foundations, would have explained it. In failing to do so, the Administration enhanced the sinister aura of conspiracy around the currency question. Cleveland was also willing to destroy radical Democrats, and aid eastern elements he trusted. Thinking the crisis would unify Democrats, and that repeal would restore prosperity, he utterly misjudged the issue's impact. Westerners and southerners warned against this facile optimism that reflected the President's isolation from the country's real desperation.[51] Populists almost welcomed the contest, realizing silver's appeal in hard times, and its use as an opening wedge for a broader reform program. ". . . when Mr. Cleveland forces the issue, he will get the worst of it," Tom Watson predicted. "I think he will draw off into his party all those men up there in the North and East, while the liberal and truly Democratic elements in the South and West will gravitate together with the Populists." [52]

As the House opened debate, Administration spokesmen endlessly argued that repeal would restore confidence. ". . . much of our present trouble is the result of senseless fright," Gresham told friends, "and I think the passage of the repeal bill would do much good in getting rid of that fright." [53] Republican congressional leaders supported repeal, but doubted it would either end the depression or scotch the silverites. Many Republicans were in a curious position. "The very men who now denounced from Wall Street this compromise [of 1890], were shouting 'Hallelujah!' for their deliverance by it from free coinage," an irate congressman shouted.[54] The Republicans intended to make political capital; they would favor repeal, and not rule out future pro-silver legislation. Gresham's tinge of bitterness was understandable to those familiar with the ironies of politics. "The Republicans took great credit for the passage of the Sherman Law, and they now blame the party in power for its evil effects." [55]

The GOP also had intra-party problems. Westerners might follow silver out of the party if it meant more to them than party regularity. The depression hit the sparsely settled and economically weak Mountain and Plains states especially hard. Whole towns vanished under falling ore prices and the money panic that dried up eastern investment. Relief funds were scarce, and the banker, cattleman, miner, farmer, and businessman equally felt the shock of depression. A subsidy would obviously help the area, and government recognition would maintain silver's price and its circulation in a rising economy. The silverites now staged conventions and protest meetings, with full press coverage of the most lurid rhetoric since the war. In Chicago, the American Bimetallic League heard Colorado's Governor Davis Waite exclaim that the people would rule, if they must "wade through seas of blood, yea, blood to the horses' bridles." [56] Silver leaders feared the depression would provoke permanent legislation against the white metal, a double blow to western economies. The House might repeal, but the Senate would filibuster. "There is every prospect of a lengthy, angry and heated debate," Senator Stewart promised Collis P. Huntington.[57]

The bitter House debate let agrarian Democrats excoriate Cleveland, while he identified enemies and denied them patronage, congressional authority, and party management. In early August, the Democracy's decline was well underway as westerners and southerners threatened to bolt if the party adopted the gold standard or represented only the hated East. The struggle produced some possible new leaders for 1896, including Nebraska's William Jennings Bryan. His great speech of August 16 summarized the President's opposition, and warned of party breakdown. "Cleveland might be honest," Bryan noted, "but so were the Indian mothers who with misguided zeal threw their children in the Ganges." [58] Across the Capitol, Populists like Nebraska's Senator William V. Allen inflated their conspiracy thesis, attacking "that hoard of insolent, aggressive, and ravenous money-changers and gamblers of Lombard Street and Wall Street, who for private gain would . . . turn the world back into the gloom of the Dark Ages, with all its attendant evil and misery." [59] Opposition was fruitless. The President withheld patronage and promised future rewards for loyalty. Republicans supported repeal, and the House struck out the purchasing clause on August 28, with a sectional vote of 239–108.

The Senate was a greater obstacle because of rules favoring endless debate, silverite power, and Cleveland's poor relations with its members. He ruthlessly used the patronage lever that usually moved congressmen. Adherance to gold was now his test of loyalty to Democratic principles. Even before the inauguration he turned a grim face to talk of party harmony on any but his own terms. "One thing may as well be distinctly understood by professing Democrats in Congress, who are heedless of the burdens and responsibilities of the incoming administration, and of the duty our party owes to the people," he wrote

Carlisle. "They must not expect me to 'turn the other cheek' by rewarding their conduct with patronage." [60]

From his first days back in office, Cleveland subjected all appointments to the test of personal loyalty. Congressmen unwilling to pledge future votes left his presence empty-handed and venegeful. Stormy personal confrontations only made him reply in kind. "He was very indignant with silver men," Charles S. Hamlin reported, "especially senators; [and] said if they wanted a fight he would give them one." [61] He assumed an air of dry superiority with associates and callers. "It is, however, my judgement that we ought not to incur too much fatigue in our efforts to gratify at this time those who bitterly oppose our political attempts to help the country and save our party." [62] He did not realize that enemies he made now would scuttle tariff reform and other meaningful party programs.

This patronage policy and its attendant personalism were disastrous since Cleveland refused to honor his subordinates' earlier promises to factions that reluctantly accepted appeals for party unity during the campaign of 1892. In the West and South, the party's following disintegrated in the face of unfulfilled pledges and economic disaster that both seemed to prove the Democratic party was a refuge only for men of Cleveland's frame of mind. Much of politics was a matter of style and timing. A soft touch and calm answer might accomplish more than favors or threats, but Cleveland had no capacity for patient, human dealing. Isolated from the party's edges, he saw only the center of events. To worsen matters, he adopted an open air of contempt toward honest and desperate opponents, complaining of "the vexatious opposition in the Senate" as if it had no basis but personal spite. "I can take care of the Senate," he told a group of visiting politicians, "they are a lot of damned old patronage brokers." Cleveland expected an aroused eastern press to support firmness, and, as he told Gresham, drive senators to repeal. The Secretary of State thought he was more likely to drive them out of the party. [63]

Cleveland's attitude drew bitter fire from fellow Democrats. Senator John Tyler Morgan of Alabama condemned colleagues who behaved like birds in cuckoo clocks, responding automatically to White House chimes. The mail was less than flattering, if Cleveland bothered to read it. "What are you but a damned goldbug contractionist?" an anonymous correspondent asked. "What are you but a damned imposter, a hypocrite and an enemy to humanity?" A speaker in Arkansas drew cheers from a rustic audience by attacking "The 360-pound tool of plutocracy, . . ." an insult by 100 pounds, even to Cleveland. [64]

The President obviously could not lead a repeal fight in the Senate and reluctantly passed the task, with a virtually blank check for patronage, to Indiana's Senator Daniel W. Voorhees. "The Tall Sycamore of the Wabash" was an uncertain ally, having favored silver in the past, but he liked the Senate, and especially his Finance Committee chairmanship, and risked future defeat for present power. Voorhees tried not to alienate those who felt political pressure from the folks at home. He supported unconditional repeal, but wanted ample party caucuses and free discussion. "For my part, I do not regard a vote for the repeal of the Sherman Act as any test at all of a man's position on the question of the proper coinage and use of silver money," he wrote Cleveland, reflecting senatorial opinion.[65] Cleveland thus confronted the Senate with weak leadership, a divided party, and no reservoir of popular appeal.

Silverites of both parties entered the contest with loud cries. "In a test of physical endurance the men who have camped out on the plains and mountains of Colorado, Montana, Idaho, and the veteran campaigners of the South are certainly able to 'stay with' and wear out the votaries of 'sweetness and light' and 'culchaw' from the effete East," trumpeted the *Cheyenne Daily Leader* as a filibuster developed.[66] It was a romantic view. Years of terrapin, champagne, and quail had sapped the western senators' hardihood, and even legitimate stamina would not be likely to bridge the patronage gap and other chasms. Through September and October, the senators talked, while silver's friends stored sleeping cots, foodstuffs, and other necessities for a siege near the Senate chamber. Business languished, money markets weakened, and confidence evaporated as silverites consumed weeks in repeating old arguments to empty galleries and an irate eastern press. ". . . nobody cares to hear or read their dreary speeches again," the *Nation* snapped. Like many predecessors, Cleveland thought senatorial courtesy reached "the extreme." Commercial papers despaired of action in time to avoid a depressed winter. Even normally cynical humor magazines like *Judge* condemned "This Government of the silver senators, for the silver senators, by the silver senators." [67] As unconditional repeal seemed hopeless, leaders in both parties tried to fashion a workable compromise.

Gorman led moderate Democrats. Unlike Cleveland, he doubted the merit of driving silverites from the party. The Administration had better bend than break. He favored modifying silver purchases to help restore confidence, but feared that total repeal would be political suicide. In the deadlock of words, Republicans seemed willing to share the blame and divide the honors in a bipartisan plan. On October 21,

37 of the 44 Democratic senators signed a letter to Voorhees that reflected Gorman's views. They would end silver purchases on October 1, 1894; coin the seigniorage, the government's profit between the price it paid for bullion and the dollar it minted; retire all paper below $10 denomination except silver issues; and oppose an issue of gold bonds. Hope spawned enough false rumors to let some think Cleveland would not protract unsettling debate for repeal. Sherman doubted he would wreck the Democratic party. "I am impressed [that] he will yield to a fair compromise," he said on October 5. "If he does not, he will destroy his party, and his administration will be broken down." [68] It was a reasonable view for Sherman, but reflected more experience in Ohio politics than any understanding of Cleveland.

Once the President embraced a single gold standard, compromise seemed both morally wrong and tactically dangerous. It would invite further gold drains, continue the party's internal struggle, and further weaken business confidence. He also saw political gains for his wing of the party. A compromise would redound to Republican credit. "I cannot help but feel that there is great danger of our friends the enemy getting more credit with the country than we," he wrote Vilas in August.[69] In mid-October, he refused even to see a group of Democratic senators favoring moderation. On October 23, as the Cabinet discussed Gorman's plan, he staged an impressive tantrum, pounding the table until he almost hurt his hand. The silverites better understood his position. "Mr. Cleveland would sign no bill for any further use of silver as money," Senator Stewart wrote Collis Huntington. "He is utterly opposed to any further coinage of silver on any terms or conditions." [70] Oregon's Republican Senator John Mitchell was equally realistic. "What the President and those who are allied with him want is a single gold standard, pure and simple, with silver completely demonetized." [71] Carlisle lobbied among former colleagues, and no Administration spokesman offered to compromise, while Cleveland withheld patronage.

The silver bloc weakened steadily under the combined pressures of public opinion, party stress, and presidential adamance. One day, late in the debate, Senator Isham G. Harris of Tennessee walked over to Fred Dubois, his colleague from Idaho. "Dubois, I told you that we would stand by you until hell froze over. We have had another look at our hand and must lay down." [72] On October 24, Voorhees assured Cleveland "There is no wavering in our lines," and the Senate repealed the purchase clause six days later.[73] Republicans voted 26–12; Democrats divided 22–22; and 3 Populists opposed repeal. The total vote of

48–37 gave a comfortable margin to so controversial a measure. The Republicans won a strange but significant political victory. They repealed one of their own laws, but seemed bipartisan and still friendly to future silver legislation.

An extraordinary bitterness enveloped the Democratic party. Cleveland especially condemned Gorman as a literal heretic from honest principles. The President gained a little praise from some businessmen, fellow gold Democrats, and the genteel press. Even Senator Allison later thought it "God's mercy" that a man of Cleveland's strong will was in office during the crisis. Some Democrats were not so sure. The debate irrevocably split the party, and Cleveland ostracized opponents, deepening their bitterness. "Those of us who represented the sentiments of our people in the extra session of Congress on the silver question," Senator Richard Coke of Texas wrote home, "are as completely cut off from any participation in the counsels of the administration, or in the giving out of patronage, as if we belonged to the Republican party." [74] Men like Richard P. Bland had about "as much influence with the party now in control as the letter 'p' in pneumonia." [75]

Silverites reciprocated, warning Cleveland not to travel west or south if he valued life. The attitude was bipartisan. "The people of Idaho don't desire to secede or fight," one man noted, "but we would like to have John Sherman's head in an ore sack." [76] Repeal did not produce recovery or save the gold reserve. It ended silver purchase but did not retire existing silver notes. Uncertainty over future Democratic policies, and the lingering threat of tariff reform replaced the Sherman Act as the investors' bogey-man. Wise men and cynics had not expected much else. "All men of virtue and intelligence know that all the ills of life—scarcity of money, baldness, the common bacillus, Home Rule, . . . and the potato bug—are due to the Sherman Bill," John Hay wrote Henry Adams wryly. "If it is repealed, sin and death will vanish from the world . . . the skies will fall, and we shall all catch larks." [77]

The repeal fight not only disrupted the Democratic party; it also stymied any revision of the currency or banking system while Cleveland was president. His enemies awaited 1896, and from both conviction and hatred, rebuffed all compromise monetary legislation. They lacked strength to override opponents, and settled into a guerilla war that naturally benefitted Republicans. "I have done with all compromises . . . ," Richard Bland said. "Free coinage or nothing." [78] In March, 1894, Bland pushed through a bill to coin the Treasury's silver seigniorage, hoping to enlarge the currency and heal some party wounds. At prevailing rates, the Treasury would gain $55,000,000 if it coined silver dollars. The bill's large congressional majority indicated an almost desperate desire for a ceremonial gesture to the silverites. Most political observers thought Cleveland would sign it. Prominent Democrats appealed to him personally. Bland tried persuasion, but met presidential candor: "Well, Bland, you do give me more trouble than any good man in the country." [79] He vetoed the bill on March 29, with a stinging indictment of silver, and prevented its repassage. This was logical to him, but politically unwise and unnecessary. Silver dollars did not threaten the gold reserve. The amount involved would not provoke inflation, might soothe some silverites' feelings, and could even illustrate the quantity theory of money's doubtful merits by failing to affect the situation.

Repeal of silver purchase was probably wise. The depression illustrated bimetallism's instability when paper money commanded endless redemption, and psychological fears eroded public and foreign confidence in the dollar. A ceremonial act was in order. But Cleveland's manner unnecessarily divided the country. Simple ending of silver purchases would not strengthen confidence in the gold standard. The greenbacks and existing silver certificates still commanded full redemption. It was more sensible to seek legal cancellation of currency after its first redemption, then coin silver dollars which did not require gold backing. This might have helped the economy, and would have calmed political storms at least temporarily.

But Cleveland wanted to purge silver Democrats, almost as if to atone for past sins of favoring silver purchases. More importantly, his hopes for repeal's effects on prosperity could only hurt Democrats when they failed to materialize. Now at loggerheads with congressional and party leaders, the President could do nothing constructive for almost a full term. Four later bond sales saved the gold standard, but emphasized his lack of political skill. However logical or necessary, unexplained bond sales to bankers and syndicates only underscored his financial ties in the popular imagination, and reinforced agrarian desires to form a new party without his followers. [80] Cleveland also rejected Hawaiian annexation, partly because he distrusted it, but also to thwart a popular Republican policy. He thus alienated internationalist Democrats, and sympathetic moderate Republicans. The depression winter of 1893–1894 ground down on the country. Seven months after taking office, Cleveland was a man without any significant political following. Only the reality of his office made him a force in American politics. The Democratic party resembled the celebrated one-hoss shay, steadily going to pieces in public. And the explosive tariff issue haunted both parties.

Cleveland opposed radical tariff reduction, but his inaugural address emphasized the problem, and most interests expected serious changes. Carlisle's presence in the Treasury reassured some businessmen, who favored administrative reform and doubted that he wanted radical changes. They conveniently ignored his lack of power on Capitol Hill, where Congress made financial legislation. Depression and the bitter repeal fight effectively nullified Cleveland's congressional and party influence, and spread fear and hesitation through Democratic ranks. Tariff reform was dangerous. A long debate would reveal the party's internal weakness, vent destructive spite, and create animosity among both businessmen and workers. Inaction would infuriate the party's agrarians, however. A compromise would satisfy neither. Nearly everyone stalled, as the Atlanta *Constitution* complained: [81]

> It's funny 'bout this tariff—how they've lost it, or forgot;
> They were rushin' it to Congress once; their collars were so hot
> They could hardly wait to fix it 'till we harvested a crop:
> Was it such a burnin' question that they had to let it drop?
>   O, we'd like to know—
>   Seein' such was so—
>   Where's the tariff, tariff, tariff
>   Of a year or so ago?

Republicans who had predicted Democratic hard times silently smiled. Whatever the Democrats did would help the GOP's image.

Depression sharpened opposition to reform, especially in industrial centers and among farmers serving urban areas. Much of the press, as usual, condemned a "British policy," and even reformers like Edward Atkinson wanted to wait until prosperity returned. Democrats divided bitterly, protectionists looking to the Senate to thwart any radicalism. States with "colonial" economies producing for home consumption favored protection more than ever. Californians wanted high rates on citrus, fruits, ores, and beef products, but reductions on their imports. Rocky Mountain silverites wanted protection for wool, ore, and hides. Southerners still alternated between blatant sectionalism and nagging desire for reform.[82] Warnings of cracking party unity flooded into the White House and upon congressional leaders. As usual, tariff reform paid homage to protection in deciding what duties to raise and lower. From first to last through the long debates, Republicans steadily gained public support by favoring the McKinley Act, pointing to Democratic disunity, and blaming hard times on reform's unsettling economic effects.

Tariff reformers, especially southerners, could not logically complain about poor representation on the Ways and Means Committee, which leaned heavily toward agrarian interests, importers, and manufacturers seeking free raw materials. Tom Reed was its only forceful Republican, and he preferred to play out the rope his foes eagerly grasped. William L. Wilson of West Virginia chaired the group, and held hearings through most of September. Like most Democratic reformers, he dismissed testimony as "the customary rubbish," but went through the motions to pacify opponents and gain time for friends writing schedules.

The fifty-year-old Wilson was a logical choice to manage the House bill; he would not entertain radicalism, and hoped to balance the arguments over protection within the party. He came to support tariff reform through study. He fought in the Confederate army, practiced law in Charles Town, and taught classical languages in college. From 1883 to 1895, he spoke for tariff reform in the national House, catching Cleveland's eye, and earning a reputation among fellow solons for calm but incisive debate. "Reed wielded the battle-axe," Champ Clark recalled, "Wilson, the Damascus blade." [83] Cleveland wanted to pay Wilson from his own pocket as a special assistant, but hesitated to take him from House leadership. Wilson, later Postmaster-General from 1895 to 1897, admired Cleveland but had no illusions about his lack of political skill. "Many a young fellow who grew alienated from him personally and politically in the House, [and] other Democrats in the Senate, could have been kept personally friendly by a casual invitation to lunch, or a formal invitation to dinner, a stroll together or a carriage drive." [84]

Wilson believed protection raised consumer prices, penalized agriculture, and aided trusts, but like most Democrats, he generally opposed federal regulation and subsidy. He condemned "the renaissance of ultra-Federalism we are suffering under Harrison and the Republican party . . . ," and talked easily of self-reliance, small government, and localism.[85] "The Democratic party is not a party of high government or much lawmaking," he said truthfully in 1891. "It is founded on the doctrine that the progress of freedom means not an increase, but a diminution of governmental restraints and interference, and that our prosperity is to be sought and our highest destiny reached, more by individual efforts than by laws." [86] It was a good statement of party differences.

Wilson unveiled his bill late in November, 1893. It slightly lowered

most industrial rates, and juggled minor items. It did not threaten
steel or other heavy industry, but favored eastern manufacturers wanting cheap raw materials. The free list included wool, coal, lumber,
sugar, sacking, and iron and copper ores, and was loaded with political
dynamite. Free sugar denied revenue to the Treasury and repeal of
the McKinley Act's bounties angered important Louisianans and western beet growers. Free wool and lumber irritated the Midwest and
West. Free ores nettled southerners and westerners. Reductions on
items farmers purchased, and favors to selected northeastern manufacturers made the bill seem as sectional as any past effort. Depressed
industries now feared competing with cheaper foreign goods. Radicals
like Roger Q. Mills thought the measure only "a Sabbath day's journey
on the way to reform." Jerry Simpson spoke for many agrarians in
calling it "only a robber tariff in a little less degree than the McKinley
Bill." [87] As usual, the Republicans united on protection, and expected
support from powerful Senate Democrats like Gorman, Hill, and
Murphy.

In the annual message of December 4, Cleveland counseled speedy
action and appealed for party unity over local interests, but practical
leadership fell to warring congressmen. Wilson reported the measure
on December 19, and opened debate on January 8. His fellow Democrats had added a tax on personal and corporate incomes above $4,000
a year, and raised levies on tobacco and whiskey to increase revenue.
Cleveland and Carlisle favored a corporate income tax to avoid alienating eastern supporters, who correctly saw the income tax as a sectional measure. Populists claimed the idea's authorship, but western
and southern spokesmen had introduced over sixty similar bills since
the wartime tax lapsed in 1872. The levy was obviously aimed at the
Northeast and industrial interests, as Democrats admitted, and raised a
host of diverse enemies. "The Democrats are in favor of an income tax
for the reason that Democrats, as a rule, have no incomes to tax," the
Los Angeles Times said. Cranky individualists like the New York Sun's
writers and readers labeled it "an overt act of communism, . . ." invading individual privacy. Business interests naturally opposed it as a
drain on capital and a penalty on success. Mugwumps condemned it
as another exaltation of federal government. It was sectional, inquisi-
torial, would open the door to larger government expenditures, and
hamper competition by exposing business secrets.[88]

On February 1, Wilson made a last formal speech on the subject,
impressing visitors with both his earnestness and obvious physical
exhaustion. Fellow Democrats cheered the effort, and while he clutched

a basket of red roses, colleagues carried him out of the chamber on their shoulders. The vote of 204–140 was partisan; 122 Republicans, 17 Democrats, and 1 Populist opposed it, while 196 Democrats and 8 Populists favored the bill. Despite precarious health, Wilson tried to address the New York Board of Trade on February 3, but sat down amid a vicious turmoil as spectators hissed, booed, and cried "Cuckoo!" [89] The bill angered most of the business community, and made workingmen uneasy.

The income tax was an added burden for Democrats to explain. They should have followed Cleveland's inclination and restricted it to corporations, or made it a separate measure; and he should have pressed them to do so, instead of behaving as if it were not presidential business. Whatever the House bill's merits or liabilities, either as reform or moderate protection, its political results were disastrous to an already weak Democratic party. Any such measure inevitably cost political support amid depression. Republicans were united, and their dire predictions about "tariff tinkering" seemed to come true. The GOP now acquired among the electorate a compelling identification with prosperity that firmly set it on the road to long-term political success. In time-honored fashion, the Senate promised a long debate and serious modifications that might finally ruin Cleveland's party.

On January 31, Gorman publicly warned that the Senate would make its own bill, implying that reformers could take the upper house's wisdom or the existing McKinley Act. Senator Voorhees, nominally in charge of the measure as chairman of the Finance Committee, eliminated hearings to save time. "The country needs action, action," he told the press.[90] The bill went immediately to a special subcommittee: James K. Jones of Arkansas, Vest of Missouri, and Mills of Texas, the last a special adviser. The Democrats needed every vote, and Populist help, to pass any measure, but Hill would not accept an income tax. Senators Caffrey and Blanchard would protect Louisiana's sugar. Morgan and Pugh wanted higher rates on Alabama's iron. Faulkner of West Virginia would save coal from the free list. White of California fought for truck produce and fruits. Butler and Irby of South Carolina championed rice. Smith of New Jersey watched industrial schedules. Murphy of New York joined Hill both to raise rates and thwart Cleveland. The House bill could not possibly pass. The special subcommittee gave way to Senator Jones' effort simply to pacify everyone and save something from the wreckage.

The President did not help. In January and February he irritated

Hill and the Senate by nominating two New Yorkers to the Supreme Court without asking Hill's advice. The Senate rejected them, and Cleveland finally settled for Edward D. White of Louisiana. He had no desire to deal with Hill, calling him "David B. D———d!" Weary advisers, attuned to party needs and public opinion, gave up the struggle to educate Cleveland. "Oh, if Mr. Cleveland had only allowed us from the beginning to go to senators and mollify them, how much better it would have been!" Gresham exclaimed.[91] Cleveland's open contempt for senators seeking rate increases produced an apocryphal but likely story. His wife allegedly roused him in the night: "Wake up, Mr. Cleveland, wake up, there are robbers in the house." The President stirred and replied automatically: "I think you are mistaken. There are no robbers in the House, but there are lots in the Senate." [92] Before the Senate started formal debates, many saw that leadership would go by default to independent members who could force a compromise in the name of party harmony and tacitly repudiate the Administration.

The confused discussion dragged through March and April, until Jones began framing conciliatory amendments to catch votes. He thought Cleveland accepted the strategy. On April 9, Hill lambasted the income tax amendment, and favored increased protection on many articles. The New York legislature voted thanks, thus rebuking Cleveland and reform. Early in May, Jones turned in his omnibus package, belatedly discovering that Cleveland was unhappy with the whole procedure. Over 400 amendments adjusted rates on products important to local interests. The Senate bill proposed a duty on raw sugar, and provoked a confused investigation of the sugar lobby's efforts to influence senators. The new measure taxed coal and iron ore, and added significantly to House rates on many items, but retained the income tax. A procession of Democrats like Gorman, Brice, Hill, and Jones defended it as wise, expedient, and the best they could do.

Time dragged and confusion increased. Republicans sat tight. The public grew weary, then angry. Congressional talk seldom pleased the nation; certainly not during a depression. A year of Cleveland's administration had passed in violent debate around repeal, panic and depression, and unfinished tariff bills. "Congress is hard at work digging post-holes," *Judge* reported in February, "and burning the posts that were designed to go in them." [93] Local politicians, desperately trying to hold their followers, turned on Congress with fury. "Where in the microscopic field of fogies and fungi did we pick up this Congress anyway?" an outraged Californian wrote Secretary Morton. "Is there any folly that rattle-brains conjure that does not find advocates among the members, who endlessly mouth the shibboleth 'I am a Democrat,' while supporting ideas no more fitted to Democratic principles than a plow is to the uses of a piano." [94]

The average citizen soon agreed with an Omaha paper: "If any man says 'tariff' to you, shoot him on the spot." [95] Reformers were weary and discouraged; some preferred the McKinley Act to an un-Democratic measure that invited party dissension and Republican ridicule. Henry Cabot Lodge, now a senator, knew the Democrats would pass a protectionist bill. As summer arrived, he thought they would settle for almost anything. "The fact is, . . . They are merely trying to pass something which they can call a tariff." [96] It did seem that way, as weeks passed, with Democratic leaders divided and the President apparently helpless.

Meanwhile, as the Senate talked, the long-predicted industrial war between Haves and Have-nots seemed at hand. As Cleveland feared, 1894 was a genuine "time of troubles."

Spring only marked depression's first anniversary. Breadlines, unemployment, and vagabondage had increased during a hard winter. Local authorities and private charities coped with distress, but the national government's inaction, political bitterness, and confusion fed a growing fear of revolution. Populists used violent rhetoric. "Foreign" ideas like anarchism, syndicalism, and socialism suddenly developed spokesmen and followings. The press naturally inflated their importance, increasing the public's jitters. Wandering tramps alarmed and irritated a society committed to the ideals of work. Men saw in passing hobos the dreaded spectacle of what they might become. Strikes and industrial disorders increased fears of unassimilated immigrants in cities. Most newspapers, reflecting a middle-class bias, offered the simple cure of repression. "The best meal to give a regular tramp is a leaden one," a New York sheet suggested. A Chicago paper thought hand grenades would be "a valuable lesson" to strikers and hobos.[97]

Various "armies" of unemployed men advertised demands and panaceas, and invited nervous ridicule. When "Kelly's Army" left San Francisco to demonstrate in Washington, local papers sneered that the men expected "to find bread to the right of them, meat to the left of them, and pie in front of them, on the rest of the eastward charge." [98] The country's apprehension obscured the "army's" true composition. A rough poll of Kelly's group revealed that two-thirds were American citizens. Of the foreign-born, two-fifths were from British countries.

Miners were most numerous of the 83 trade unions represented. There were 240 Populists, 218 Republicans, 196 Democrats, 81 undecided, and 11 independents. Protestantism claimed 358; Catholicism 280; and atheism or religious uncertainty, 114. Though feverish imaginations raised up conquering hosts, probably not more than 10,000 men were ever on the road at one time.[99]

The phenomenon produced a major spokesman in "General" Jacob S. Coxey of Massillon, Ohio. Though well-to-do from quarry investments, Coxey sympathized with the unemployed. His years of jostling over rough country roads also produced a proposal that would create jobs, increase the currency, and improve transportation. He became a bi-cycling enthusiast, and leader in the "good roads movement." In 1892, congressional friends introduced his measure to issue $500,000,000 in legal tender notes to finance new roads. The scheme would employ all able-bodied applicants at $1.50 for an eight-hour day. Coxey elabo-rated the idea in a dream on New Year's, 1894. It combined localism and federal support, allowing any state, county, or municipality to issue non-interest bearing bonds up to half its assessed valuation, as collateral for United States legal-tender notes to finance public works. The idea found few followers in government or politics. It would in-volve an enormous sum, further confuse the currency, and provide unprecedented made-work.

Early in the spring of 1894, Coxey told Carl Browne he would "send a petition to Washington with boots on," and began organizing a march of the unemployed to ask Congress to enact his public works project. Browne was among the first of a band of mountebanks, show-men, cranks, and genuine reformers coalescing around Coxey. Known as "Old Greasy" because of an unwillingness to bathe, he wore a buck-skin suit, long beard, and curly locks befitting a medicine show. He was an itinerant cartoonist and sign painter, who often carried a large banner with a picture of Christ that strangely resembled himself, over the legend: "Peace on Earth, Good Will to Men. He Hath Risen, But Death to Interest on Bonds." Browne had a "Financial Panorama" that illustrated the gold conspiracy with appropriate pictures. He was a Theosophist, believing that everyone was a composite of all preceding humanity, each bearing a little of Christ's soul. He called Coxey the "Cerebrum of Christ," and himself the "Cerebellum of Christ." Others like Christopher Columbus Jones, Kelly, and parts of his army, planned to start to Washington on Easter Sunday, 1894.[100]

Populists and silverites struggling with the tariff and currency ques-tions in Congress begged Coxey not to upset public opinion already suspicious of radical change. Senator Stewart feared a bloodbath.

"Abandon the folly of marching an unarmed multitude of starving laborers against the modern appliances of war under the control of a soul-less money trust," he pleaded.[101] The pathetic group left Massillon in good order on Sunday, March 25, in as strange a procession as ever moved on the nation's capital. "General" Coxey rode with his wife and infant son, "Legal Tender" Coxey. "Humble Carl" Browne carried his signs. One "Cyclone" Kirtland, a Pittsburgh astrologist, followed; so did an Indian half-breed named Honore Jaxon, in a white Buffalo Bill outfit. Douglass McCallum of Chicago was the best dressed man, sporting a white plug hat and fur coat, distributing copies of his pamphlet *Dogs and Fleas, by One of the Dogs*. "Oklahoma Sam" Pfrimmer, and "Weary Bill" Iller brought up the rear with rank-and-file privates. Some of the men looked tough, but most were only unemployed and taking a chance. Lurid tales of thieving, rapine, and pillage preceded the "army," but its worst offences concerned chicken coops, bumming free train rides, and sitting in town squares until local authorities raised provisions to send the men elsewhere. The press naturally covered the event like a foreign invasion. ". . . for every two sloggers in Coxey's ranks there was at least one reporter," a cynical newsman recalled.[102]

The procession attracted ridicule, fear, sympathy, and hostility. Who knew what it represented? Would the unemployed form irregular armies to prey on the countryside or challenge government? Over-speculation produced over-reaction. "People along the line of march talk worse than members of the 'army', who speak in a very moderate manner," a correspondent wrote Cleveland's secretary.[103] The *New York Sun* affected a dry cynicism. "A city that has seen the Wilson Bill and the Income Tax Bill is not to be disturbed by an incursion of common cranks." [104] Secret Service detectives mingled with the army's privates, and reported their progress, however. The staff increased protection around the White House until reporters dubbed it "Fort Thurber," after the President's secretary. Excited commentators predicted the men would loot the Treasury vaults, turn Congress out of the Capitol, and fight in the streets. On May 1, Coxey, fellow leaders, and the 400 remaining marchers, tried to present a petition, but confronted Capitol police and curiosity seekers. After a scuffle, the leaders went to jail briefly and paid small fines for trespassing on the grass. Bitterness pervaded the army's ranks, as the men left Washington. "We are going to our homes, where we will continue to do all in our power to condemn the administration of Grover Cleveland . . . ," a marcher said, throwing a verbal clod at the White House.[105]

Attorney General Richard Olney thought the army "an eccentric and ephemeral demonstration," but feared it was the vanguard of more serious disturbances.[106] Coxey's Army was intrinsically pathetic, but it strengthened public desire for law and order. The "tramp movements" opposed Cleveland, but probably gave him momentary popularity. The various groups hurt Populism, since most people saw Coxey's Army as a microcosm of the third-party movement, filled with whimsical cranks, quacks, and conflicting ideas.

That spring's tensions broke further west in Chicago, an inevitable source of discontent since hungry men and restless labor elements filled the sprawling city whose factories and railroads served the entire nation. Pullman, Illinois, sat on the city's edge, the personal creation of George M. Pullman. The head of the Pullman Company was a success in the American tradition, rich as patent-holder and inventor of many railroad luxuries, especially the sleeper and diner cars that bore his name. He combined a desire for profit with paternalism in a model village for his workers, attempting to furnish life's luxuries and necessities at a profit. The town was a showcase for passing philanthropists, who saw in it the promise of a stable industrial order that regulated dangerous tensions in both business and labor without sacrificing the rights of either. But Pullman was not a philanthropist; his tenants furnished a profit from rent, utilities, and services. Above all, he wanted quiet gratitude, best expressed in unwillingness to strike or even grumble.

Magazine writers and hasty observers passing through on the train considered the village "a bright and radiant little island in the midst of the great tumultuous sea of Chicago's population; a restful oasis in the wearying brick-and-mortar waste of an enormous city." [107] Pullman's employees were not so enthusiastic; nor were some businessmen and politicians who saw the makings of another Homestead. Senator Sherman compared the Pullman Company to the odious Sugar Trust. The vigorous, shrewd Mark Hanna, no stranger to making a living in industry or maintaining good relations with labor, later dismissed empty enthusiasm about Pullman. "Oh, hell!" he would snort. "Model ———! Go and live in Pullman and find out how much Pullman gets sellin' city water and gas ten percent higher to those poor fools! A man who won't meet his men half-way is a God-damn fool!" [108] Many businessmen privately sympathized with the employees. "As a very prominent railroad man said to me yesterday at the Club: the town of Pullman is not American," a friend wrote Secretary Gresham. "The people do not like to be prescribed to certain walks on the street, to have their churches built for them, and their graveyards made ready for them. In fact, a man at Pullman can neither keep a chicken nor a dog nor any living thing. It is more rigid than the laws of Russia." [109] Early in May, 1894, employees struck against wage cuts and layoffs, and asked railroaders to join a sympathy strike.

The call did not arouse the labor world. Hard times inhibited strikes, since management easily recruited strikebreakers in a depressed labor market. The newly formed American Railway Union could offer the quickest help, but its president and pioneer labor organizer, Eugene Victor Debs, doubted the wisdom of a contest that might wreck the union. But his sympathies were clear when he reported to his men after personally investigating and condemning Pullman's arrangements. An emotional convention voted to strike, and Debs tried to keep the walkout peaceful. By late June, most rail traffic was stalled west of Chicago. Pullman moved his family to seclusion in fashionable El- beron, New Jersey, then disappeared into a cottage in the Thousand Islands. Strikers often guarded railroad property to avoid violence that would harm their cause. The union moved mail trains on schedule, to avoid confronting federal authorities. They were willing to negotiate for Pullman's workers, but met refusal from his subordinates: "We have nothing to arbitrate." As the strike worsened and Chicago ex- pected violence, railroad companies pooled resources in a General Managers' Association. It furnished information to local and state au- thorities, blacklisted strikers, guarded property, and influenced federal authorities.

In the national capital, Attorney General Olney was ready to act. He gathered information for himself, the Army, and President Cleve- land as the strike developed. At the mercy of telegraph dispatches and biased observers, Cleveland thought the strike "a very determined and ugly labor disturbance . . . ," but he was not Olney's dupe. Both men and their subordinates watched mail delivery and government com- munication, and retained contact with local federal authorities. In late June, the Treasury suspended gold shipments by train. Secret Service operatives reported from around the country. Military officers ended leaves, returning quietly to units that might control mob violence. Most significantly, federal officials were openly allied with railroad officers in Chicago, as special counsels and even as deputies protecting railroad property.

On July 2, a federal court enjoined strikers from interfering with mail transit or interstate commerce. The Chicago police maintained order reasonably well, and the state militia was on guard outside the city, where it suppressed minor violence. The sweeping injunction, "a

Gatling gun on paper," as Debs later called it, neither ended the strike nor calmed tempers. On July 3, local authorities and the government's special operatives telegraphed Olney for federal troops, describing mobs burning railroad property and endangering the whole city. Late that afternoon, the President ordered federal soldiers into the city from Fort Sheridan, without the consent of Illinois or Chicago authorities.

The strike, which the nation's press covered loudly if not well, now took on historic dimensions. It quickly became a microcosm of the contest within the Democratic party, between angry workers and established social groups and federal and local authority. It naturally polarized around two equally determined and important figures, Cleveland and Illinois' Democratic Governor John P. Altgeld. The Governor cut a strange figure in the Midwest's turbulent Democratic politics and business world. His close-cropped head and mustachioed face fairly invited the cartoonist's cruelty. A pre-war German immigrant, he had moved through odd-jobs, farm life, schoolteaching, and simple idling, but focused a desire for power on politics and business that made him famous and wealthy. "I commend you to the goddess of ambition," he once told a group of visitors. "She teaches the great virtues of labor, aggression and perseverance."

That ambition took him into Illinois' executive mansion after a shrewd campaign as the workingman's friend, complete with the obligatory carnival atmosphere. "I want power," he once said, "to get hold of the handle that controls things. When I do, I will give it a twist." He was an excellent campaigner, ratifying traditional political deals, and building a legend as the poor man who made good. But the inner man he so carefully controlled sometimes broke through the outer person who played the world's game by its rules. He had a fierce sense of justice that in 1893 made him pardon the anarchists imprisoned after the Haymarket Riot of 1886. They had received patently unfair trials, and Altgeld minced no words in condemning their persecutors. Respectable society and the press unloosed a corrosive scorn that inevitably made him the villain of 1894. As the pardoned men walked to freedom, much of the press echoed the *New York Sun's* sentiments: [110]

> O, wild Chicago, when the time
> Is ripe for ruin's deeds,
> When constitutions, courts and laws
> Go down midst crashing creeds,
> Lift up your weak and guilty hands
> From out the wreck of states,
> And as the crumbling towers fall down,
> Write ALTGELD on your gates!

Altgeld had presidential ambitions, but knew that foreign birth and controversy would deny him the prize. If he could not be King, he would be Warwick. He planned to control many midwestern delegates at the Democratic National Convention in 1896.

Altgeld now communicated with alerted militia units and Chicago authorities from an office fitted like a war room. In Washington, Olney and his staff considered both Altgeld and Mayor Carter Harrison friends of the strikers. They cared little for Altgeld's boast: "If it becomes necessary, I could and would put 100,000 men into the city of Chicago inside of five days. The whole state would answer to the call as one man." [111] The appearance of token federal soldiery, on obscure legal basis, provoked a brief, bitter telegraph debate between Altgeld and Cleveland. On July 5, the Governor denied the President's right to use federal troops without state consent, and insisted they were unnecessary. They would only break the strike, and intensify ill-feelings. Cleveland greeted this "remarkable dispatch" with a familiar authoritarian self-righteousness. Though he thought the telegram "irrelevant and, in some parts absolutely frivolous," the President tersely explained his legal and constitutional rights and the hour's necessities. He did not silence Altgeld. The following day, the Governor sharply attacked Cleveland's analysis and actions. The President swept aside all cavils with a sharp response bound to win public favor: "While I am still persuaded that I have neither transcended my authority nor duty in the emergency that confronts us, it seems to me that in this hour of danger and public distress, discussion may well give way to active efforts on the part of all in authority to restore obedience to law and to protect life and property." [112]

The dialogue disappeared in a violent outburst of press condemnation of Altgeld. The *Chicago Tribune* only typified the outrageous vindictiveness that swept over him. "This lying, hypocritical, demagogical, snivelling Governor of Illinois does not want the law enforced. He is a sympathizer with riot, with violence, with anarchy." [113] The flash of federal bayonets and glint of blue uniforms coincided with fresh disorder. Between July 5 and July 7, mobs destroyed hundreds of railroad cars, razed the central roundhouse, and part of the Columbian Exposition burned in a roaring fire. Itinerants, railroad agents, and lawless mobs caused much if not most of the damage, but the ARU got the blame. The handful of federal troops were unequipped for their task, and often wandered in strange streets until policemen directed them to disturbances. State troops and local police quelled the mobs, but federal soldiers and Cleveland won credit in the press and most of the public mind. Chicago's importance as a shipping point for food, livestock, mail, and industrial products increased the public's apprehension. As foodstuffs spoiled, prices rose, and reports of mob rule filled the nation's press, most Americans undoubtedly opposed the strikers.

Olney moved swiftly and heavily. He was a political and philosophical conservative, but not the anti-labor villain he seemed to foes. His information was poor and sporadic, reinforcing a tendency to rashness. Cleveland approved his actions, and was fully informed of the strike's progress. With the same information, most presidents probably would have acted like Cleveland. His use of federal troops was not so questionable as the open alliance between federal agents and the railroads, and his unwise refusal to consult state authorities. Leaders in other states, like Governor Hogg of Texas, condemned Cleveland's use of troops without consent of local authorities. Federal intervention, failing ARU resources, confusion, and public disapproval ended the strike. Debs stood trial for conspiracy to interrupt the mails and interstate commerce, and served a short jail sentence that helped make him a Socialist. Railroads blacklisted strikers, and the ARU died.

The strike's results eddied through the nation's politics for years. Most skilled, organized workers steadily employed during the depression emotionally supported "law and order," but marginal groups bitterly turned against Cleveland. The propertied middle class, professionals, and businessmen supported the President without later voting Democratic. The vindictive press ruined Altgeld's career, but many radicals hoped the strike dramatized the power of entrenched corporate wealth, with ties to a Democratic Administration that opposed agrarian and labor demands. But for the moment, a spasm of fear and hostility gripped most of the public. One of Gresham's correspondents again reported all-too-typical reaction. Most workingmen, he wrote, thought the courts and government sided with capital and against them. Economically sound citizens were outraged at the other extreme: Cleveland was too lenient, and state authority bankrupt: [114]

> Many of my intelligent friends say Mr. Debs should be hung without trial or jury, and that platoons of 'foreign devils' should be shot down, and that would settle them. The citizens seem mad, and the courts seem mad and crazy, and the congress, and senate are in the same state of frenzy. If this keeps on long, fire and sword will devastate the country. The poor are very largely in the majority, and in an internecine war would sweep the country with flame. The sword would be impotent without the masses to use it.

A special investigating commission later blamed all participants, but was not easy on the railroads and courts, or on federal authorities.

The political results were profound. Though momentarily silenced, Altgeld lost little power or popularity among fellow anti-Cleveland Democrats. With other men from the mountains and plains, he grimly determined to topple Cleveland. Early in 1895, he refused to attend a Jefferson's Birthday dinner at the Iroquois Club in Chicago, assuming speakers would praise the national Administration. "To laud Clevelandism on Jefferson's Birthday is to sing a *Te Deum* in honor of Judas Iscariot on a Christmas morning!" he exclaimed.[115] That sense of personal affront, philosophical division, and the need of party realignment now pervaded Cleveland's Democratic opposition.

Coxey's Army, depression, the Pullman strike, and a national case of the jitters inevitably hurt the Democrats. Amid the confusion and conflicting advice, Congress finished its tariff labors. The law bade fair to make the McKinley Act seem wonderful, and completed the Democracy's cycle of destruction.

Depression, strikes, apparent industrial warfare did not stop the Senate tariff debates. Bored newsmen and spectators in the galleries sat through endless discussions of duties on sugar, the income tax, free silver, and presidential prerogatives. The President seemed helpless to speed action or thwart protectionist Democrats, and Republicans steadily developed the theme of Democratic legislative incompetence. On July 3, while federal troops prepared to enter Chicago, Senator Harris of Tennessee told Cleveland he must accept the Senate bill or nothing. That day, the measure passed 39–34, with 12 abstentions, and went to a conference committee. It now sported 634 amendments; coal, sugar, and iron ore gained duties; wool, lumber, and copper remained free. Other alterations favored manufactured articles.

The Senate-House conferees mired in confusion and bitterness. Days passed without results, and Senator Hill laconically watched waiters carry food and refreshments into the committee room. "Men who are in agreement and making progress never send for sweet milk and corn bread," he noted drily, "when you see the trays carrying a decanter and a box of cigars, you can bet that an agreement has been reached."[116] On July 15, Senator Brice announced that the conferees were deadlocked, and three days later the group reported they could not agree on a bill. Only some extraordinary public pressure could produce a measure.

On July 19, a weary House gathered to hear Wilson explain the situation. Summer heat, social violence, and party confusion frayed tempers and many observers expected trouble. It came when Wilson, pale from exhaustion and excitement, read a letter from Cleveland, dated July 2, declaring war on his party enemies and in effect asking the public somehow to compel genuine tariff reform. Sentences fell heavily into a charged atmosphere. Cleveland hoped the House would rebuke the Senate, devise a genuine reform bill, and stand pat. He wanted free raw materials to expand foreign trade and lift the depression. He attacked the sugar lobby, and by implication, every Democratic senator who favored a sugar revenue duty. The income tax was unfortunate, but he would accept it as the party's apparent will. He dealt heavy blows to fellow Democrats: [117]

> Every true Democrat and every sincere tariff reformer knows that this bill in its present form and as it will be submitted to the conference falls far short of the consummation for which we have long labored, for which we have suffered defeat without discouragement, which, in its anticipation, gave us a rallying cry in our day of triumph, and which, in its promise of accomplishment, is so interwoven with Democratic pledges and Democratic success that our abandonment of the cause of the principles upon which it rests means party perfidy and party dishonor.

Party perfidy and party dishonor fairly leaped from the pages into congressional sensibilities. Outrage dominated the conversation in corridors and cloakrooms at both ends of the Capitol. Republican Lemuel Quigg, a Platt lieutenant, thought it "an unprecedented and amazing performance." He saw that the letter defeated tariff reform; no congressman would bow to such Executive attacks. "He says they [Democratic opponents] are dishonest in their position. To yield will be to admit it. He says they are traitors to the Democratic party. To yield will be to admit that." [118]

The next day, Senator Vilas, presumably after conferring with Cleveland, introduced a resolution to recommit the bill until the sugar duties came down. Gorman warned that this meant no bill, and further disruptive talk. Cleveland actually believed the letter would bring public opinion to the reformers' side, and greeted Vilas with a hopeful attitude. Vilas was not so cheerful, and suggested the President talk with Brice and Gorman. "If you choose you can tell them to come," Cleveland said. "I will not send for them." Brice later appeared, was noncommittal, and rose to go without discussing the tariff. When Cleveland asked about it, the Ohioan suggested he write Gorman for a conference. Cleveland balked. "I said to myself, I'll see him damned before he gets a note from me which he can show around, [saying] that I had sent for him." The ever-tactful Lamont urged the President to write Gorman that Brice wanted him to come to the White House. That bypassed Cleveland's touchy ego, and Gorman arrived on Monday, July 23. They had little to say. The Marylander doubted that congressional leaders could enlarge the free list. It was this bill or nothing.[119] He left, saying he would speak that afternoon on Cleveland's letter to Wilson, and on the bill's whole history.

In a lengthy discourse, with support from various Democratic colleagues, Gorman dissected the President's wavering stand on a compromise tariff, arguing that he had agreed, however reluctantly, to every step the moderates took. He thus rejected Cleveland's talk of party perfidy and dishonesty. At the same time, Gorman urged fellow Democrats to accept the conference committee's bill. It at least partially redeemed the party's platform, lowered some duties, and was better than the McKinley Act. Rejection would ruin the party. He promised to support separate revenue bills later to correct errors or salve disappointments if the measure now passed. The party must end the subject on some reasonable note, or die in a welter of talk and public disgust.[120]

Vilas withdrew his motion, and the House apologetically concurred by a partisan vote on August 13. Cleveland received divided counsels about signing the measure. A few diehards urged a veto. Let both the McKinley Act and Democratic principles stand. Other Democrats advised him to sign it; it was the best they could do, and was better than the existing law. "Much has been developed which has shocked and surprised you and me," he wrote Wilson, "and I have within the last hour found myself questioning whether or not our party is a tariff-reform party."[121] On August 27, the bill became law without his signature, another open sign of contempt for his party's handiwork. In private letters, Cleveland condemned "the communism of pelf," lobbyists, and trusts that allegedly defeated reform. He naturally refused to see that his own weak leadership contributed to the result. The debacle pleased Republicans. Tom Reed said he had heard of men eating crow, but never of their importing the crow. The business community and public wanted calm. In a muffled coup de grâce, the Supreme Court invalidated the income tax early in 1895.[122] The Democrats had nothing to show for their tariff labors.

The Democracy drifted. Men in the Administration were weary; those outside it were vengeful. The President and Congress did not speak. Cleveland devoted his energies to saving the gold standard with bond issues. The party had no more programs. "How confused the future of our politics looks to me now," Wilson wrote a year later. "The magnificent army which we rallied . . . to carry out the reform of the tariff, has been so long involved in internecine war that it seems a collection of hostile camps." [123] In April, Tom Reed had penned a dry but not premature epitaph: "We did have an interesting time with the Democracy," he wrote Foraker, "but then they are always interesting." [124]

Since they pinned so much hope on reform, the Wilson-Gorman Tariff was a complete fiasco for the Democrats. Repeal of the Sherman Act provoked an essentially intra-party war. The tariff debates openly arrayed Democrats both against each other and united Republicans, who shone to good advantage in the public mind. The debates and their result confirmed for many voters what Republicans had long said of the opposition's ineptitude. "We are on the eve of a very dark night, unless a return of commercial prosperity relieves popular discontent with what they [the people] believe Democratic incompetence to make laws," Francis L. Stetson admitted to his friend in the White House.[125]

The Democrats seemed divided and untrustworthy, supporting neither reform nor stability, and provoking costly delay. Republicans appeared unified, almost bipartisan in crisis, committed to industrial protection and the home market idea, especially compelling in a depression. The Democrats' changes in the tariff seemed to penalize consumers and the industrial sector without benefitting anyone. Free wool and lumber alienated major groups who seemed ready to vote Democratic after 1892, and looked like concessions to a few northeastern manufacturers to westerners who already disliked that section's political dominance. The Democrats' stubborn refusal to adopt even a modest reciprocity program in the new tariff gave Republicans a major opportunity to stand for protection with suitable modifications to expand overseas trade. The whole clamor set the stage for one of the bitterest and most significant off-year elections in American history.

Summer moved inexorably toward fall's congressional elections while industrial armies stirred, strikes paralyzed and dismayed large areas, and Congress talked. Local Democratic leaders expected a sweeping defeat. Voters seemed full of rage and despair, eager to turn out every office-holder connected with the last year's events and Cleveland's Administration. Bitterness and frustration cut several ways, as Democrats battled each other and the Populists. The contestants fought before an almost visible backdrop of frustrations. A year's depression produced major strikes in the New South's industrial areas, and deepened back-country poverty. Senseless crimes like lynching, night-riding, and Negro-baiting revealed pent-up hostility in much of the white community. All the disaffected elements that heeded calls for party unity in 1892 and voted for some kind of reform, now turned against the national Administration with a vengeance. Tom Watson, Populist candidate for a Georgia seat in the House, savored his predictions come true. "Two years ago we were fed upon the ambrosia of Democratic expectations," he told enthusiastic audiences. "Today we are gnawing the cobs of Democratic reality." [126]

National attention focused on the normally Republican Midwest, now repentant for its brief flirtation with the Democracy in 1892. GOP regulars were out in force. Every Republican who could raise his voice and point a finger was on the hustings. Major national figures foraged into the South, along the Border, and through the pro-silver West. Tom Reed sounded the party's keynote: "Prosperity does not perch upon uncertainty; it can never ripen fruit as long as these noisy boys are shaking and clubbing the tree." [127] Even former President Harrison thawed enough to speak, and introduced Governor McKinley to an Indianapolis audience with a comment that struck fire: "We were told in the old times that the rich were getting richer and the poor poorer; and to cure that imaginary ill, our political opponents have brought on a time when everybody is getting poorer." [128] Backing up the speakers, literature emphasized Republican identification with prosperity through the tariff, moderation on the currency, and party unity that produced nationalistic legislation.

Governor William McKinley was the campaign's hero. Capitalizing on widespread popularity, growing stature as a constructive moderate, and long identification with protection and prosperity, the Ohioan conducted a vivid tub-thumping campaign that carried him from New England to Colorado and into the South. He received over 2,500 invitations to speak in local contests, and filled 371 engagements in 16 states, speaking 23 times in one day while crossing Nebraska. He conferred with important local politicians, and tactfully reminded them of his popularity and the issues of 1896. A quiet staff compiled index cards, plotted routes, and noted favors due. There was no denying his genuine appeal to the masses, and the significance of issues he discussed so well.

Democrats had no illusions about the outcome, and almost agreed with Tom Reed. "The Democratic mortality will be so great next fall that their dead will be buried in trenches and marked 'Unknown.'" [129] He was right. In the Fifty-fourth Congress, 104 Democrats would face 245 Republicans in the House; and 44 Republicans would probably control the 39 Democrats and 6 Alliance senators. In 24 states, no

Democrats won national office; 6 others elected only 1 Democrat each. "Honey Fitz" Fitzgerald was the lone Democratic congressman in New England. Wisconsin, Illinois, and New York went back to Republicanism, along with most of the Plains states and Far West where Populism seemed strong in 1892. The results repudiated Cleveland and emptied Congress of Democratic leaders. Conservatives like William L. Wilson, William M. Springer of Illinois, and William D. Bynum of Indiana went down to defeat. The voters also turned out more liberal Democrats like Richard P. Bland and William Jennings Bryan.

The returns disappointed Populists who eagerly awaited the voters' disgust with both old parties. Southern Democrats openly counted out, defrauded and intimidated Populist opponents. "We *had* to do it!" one exclaimed. "Those d———d Populists would have ruined the country!" [130] The Populist congressional bloc remained static—something of an accomplishment—but southern radicals had to accept minor victories in state and local contests or risk open warfare over ballot-counting. The movement's midwestern wing did no better. Democrats fused with Populists where possible, absorbing radicals. The Republicans easily beat quarreling factions, where "middle-of-the-road" Populists retained separate identities and rebuffed fusion. The Populists did poorly in urban areas, had no appeal to workers, did not capture significant Negro allegiance in the South, and could not beat local interest in fusion. Much of the West frankly wanted tariff protection. It all puzzled reformers like Ignatius Donnelley, who banked too heavily on the American voter's willingness to change allegiances. "Why they should go back on us, with wheat at 45 cents a bushel, is something no man can understand," he said. The "crank image" of Populism also hurt, especially after 1894's climatic disorders. Donnelley admitted the People's Party "must satisfy the average mind that we are reasonable and right" to win in 1896. [131]

The elections left a rump Democratic party in powerless enclaves around the country, identified with a discredited Administration, leaderless in national politics. The party would simply drift toward 1896. Many Democrats stayed home, increasing the margin of Republican gains. Cleveland was the nation's and party's scapegoat. "Nine-tenths of [the Democrats] are angry with Cleveland, angry with Congress, . . . and angry because cotton is 5 cents a pound," a North Carolinian wrote. "The party is torn to pieces by dissensions." [132] The loose Democratic coalition that unified briefly around discontent in 1892, collapsed from depression and the party's failure to perform in office. The Administration now seemed identified with conservative wealth and nostalgia for a fictitious past; the captive of men "who put on dress suits and talk at banquets on great subjects." [133]

The elections were historic, not only for reviving the GOP, but for indicating long-term trends. A third party was unlikely. In the middle of a depression, voters returned to familiar programs Republicans had espoused for decades. Depression was the catalyst that ended the GOP's long search for a national majority. The party's doctrines and leaders seemed more attuned to change than Democrats, and clearly more able to function than Populists. They represented the urban-industrial constituency that rose in the 1880's and triumphed in the 1890's. There were twists of irony. The federal spending that hurt Republicans in relatively prosperous 1890, helped them in depression. Funds for pensions, internal improvements, and other subsidies made sense in 1894. Republicans won this first round of enduring national success by emphasizing past performance, nationalistic programs, new leadership, and issues like protection and sound currency, all symbolizing stable growth in a familiar pattern.

A temporary calm followed the election. The nation was tired. Politics were stymied in a lame-duck session. A hostile Congress would face Cleveland for two more years, while he independently saved the gold standard. The economy rose and fell slightly in a depressing alternation between hope and despair. Administration officials noted quietly that Republicans had yet to face the silver question. Most Republicans agreed with Tom Platt. "I still believe it is the true policy of the Republican party to make protection the leading issue in the next campaign, and any attempt to crowd the free silver issue to the front should be frowned down." [134] That was easier said than done; free silver might realign both parties. It threatened the Democrats most, since the Administration challenged the silverites, but the subject baffled contemporary observers who did not swallow the silver thesis unthinkingly. Maine's Republican Senator William P. Frye well summed up a common dilemma in the winter of 1894: [135]

> There is such a disagreement between men who ought to understand the financial questions that it makes one's brain buzz to read their opinions. Since I have been in Congress, I have seen nearly all of the predictions of financial men come to grief. I was here throughout the refunding process, and every attempt to reduce the rate of interest was declared to be dangerous; bonds would not be floated at par at such low rates, etc., etc.; and yet we succeeded every time in establishing a lower rate. When the Bland Bill was passed, everybody seemed to think the price of silver would increase, but it decreased. When the

Sherman Bill became law, we all knew that silver would appreciate rapidly, as that law provided for the purchase of the entire product; yet silver went down. Now, where is wisdom to be found in these financial questions? I am a bi-metallist, but I have very serious doubts about the propriety of the United States going into free coinage alone. Of course, an international agreement would settle this thing, and if the horrors of gold mono-metallism are such as you describe, can other countries stand it any great length of time? Will not their eyes be opened as yours have been?

His argument had many merits, and reflected the bewilderment of able and honest politicians who tried to solve the question for majority benefit, but he overlooked the appealing simplicity of free silver in any heated campaign that obscured deeper issues.

Other men did not share these doubts. Their allegiance to silver overrode party loyalty, and powerful Democrats and Republicans now advertised their cause for 1896. Men like Senator Stewart assumed both major parties would favor gold. If the depression continued, dissatisfied elements could form a new party around silver inflation that offered a cure-all for hard times. Through 1895, silver men staged conventions, wrote pamphlets, and subsidized speakers and newspapers, challenging both parties to adopt silver in 1896 or collapse. Many Democrats saw silver's virtues for the first time; it might cover all other weakness, like tariff reform in the past.

Critics revived old charges of bonanza kings subsidizing an effort to win a permanent subsidy for their product. It was partly true, but no conspiracy of mine owners alone produced thousands of eager listeners for people like Bryan.[136] Spasmodic economic recovery heightened silver's appeal, and politicians did not refrain from over-simplifying its merits. Men with fixed debts and falling incomes easily believed that more money would bring good times. By early 1896, the President's friends and traveling agents reported near-hysteria in depressed farming areas; silver was sweeping all before it, and an educational campaign might come too late.

The election of 1894 and rising silver sentiment only stiffened Cleveland's resolve to maintain the gold standard. His attitude and policies drove party leaders and voters from the party. "It is simply impossible for us to come together," Senator Vest of Missouri wrote of the Democratic party's two wings in 1895.[137] Cleveland hoped to save a remnant of virtue to rebuild the old party when the seizure of radicalism passed, but his few efforts to stem the tide revealed his isolation from reality. In October, 1895, he toured the Cotton States Exposition in Atlanta, talking the homilies of patience, hard work, and courage in the nation's most economically stricken area.

Cleveland still used the appointment power to his faction's advantage. After 1894, he named lame-ducks to federal offices over the protests of local politicians. He also removed critics. "In the interest of good government, such officeholders must not be surprised if they are summarily dealt with." [138] He had no practical relations with Congress. Senator Brice did not "propose to pull any more chestnuts out of the fire for Grover Cleveland." [139] When Governor Tillman rather meekly asked Cleveland to consult him about appointments in South Carolina, the President contemptuously gave the letter to the press. Tillman campaigned against Cleveland in 1894, and entered the Senate with a famous slogan: "When Judas betrayed Christ, his heart was not blacker than this scoundrel, Cleveland, in deceiving the Democracy. He is an old bag of beef, and I am going to Washington with a pitchfork and prod him in his old fat ribs." Alabama's Senator Morgan spoke for many in simpler terms: "I hate the ground that man walks on." [140]

Except for a brief flurry of support during the Venezuela crisis of 1895, Cleveland never regained significant popularity. His band of followers dwindled; summer soldiers avoiding guilt by association, none eager to stand beside a target. He turned to family matters, routine paper work, and personal investments for his retirement years. His mail shrank almost to that of an average citizen. He seldom spoke or traveled, increasing his isolation from change. Perhaps he never knew what the depression meant to people who daily attacked him. "I was a child of four during the panic of '93, and Cleveland has always been a sinister figure to me," Walter Lippman recalled. "His name was uttered with monstrous dread in the household." [141] The bitter criticism was often unjust, but he inevitably became a scapegoat for every man's ills.

Cleveland occasionally tried to "educate" the party back to his ideal of negative government, but no one was really listening. Eager crowds in the West and South heard new men like Bryan and old reliables like Bland extoll silver inflation's virtues. They wanted a party without the President's followers or ideas. A new Democratic party was rising. Whatever its weaknesses, it better represented the people ready to wear its label than did Cleveland's residual groups. It had a unifying and popular idea in free silver. Now it needed a leader.

XII

The Battle of the Standards

In 1896, Canton was a small, prosperous town in the rolling country-side of northeast Ohio; a center of commercial, legal, and political activity. A composite population lived off the iron fabrication, rail-roading, coal mining, oil refining, and farming that dominated that part of Ohio and neighboring Pennsylvania. It was also the focus of a congressional district and boasted a famous son, former Governor William McKinley, who represented the area in Congress from 1877 to 1891. "The Major" was prominent in national politics, and returned to his modest frame home on Market Street in January, 1896, after two terms in the Statehouse, but no one expected him to go to seed or resume law practice. "It is just plain Mr. McKinley of Canton now," the local paper reported, "but wait a little while." [1] Everyone knew that his calm affability was part of a determined drive for the Republican presidential nomination.

Now fifty-three years old, McKinley was an approachable figure, with ambitions that did not seem abrasive. He liked to drive a rig to the livery stable for talk and cigar-smoking with the boys. He fortified old friendships and made new ones in the countryside, sampling apple pies and testing new horses; he was an expert on both subjects, whose opinion the local populace respected. He was equally familiar in Chicago's elegant clubrooms and Washington's marble halls. He had friends in nearly every state, and a national legislative record. Defeat in the bitter contest of 1890 only helped elevate him to the governor-ship a year later. Depression merely added to his luster as the architect of protected prosperity in the much maligned Act of 1890 that bore his name. For a moment, he fell among the Panic's ruins, going publicly bankrupt for thoughtlessly endorsing a friend's business notes.

482

But amazed politicians saw him emerge from that debacle as the beneficiary of a private fund to pay the debts, with acclaim from voters unaccustomed to seeing an honest politician go broke in public.[2] He was a small-town man with considerable sophistication, and a political success who never let power or fame turn his head.

McKinley gained his informal title in the war with genuine bravery, entering the conflict as a boy who hated slavery and wished to save the Union, and emerging eager to succeed in law and politics. He married well in local society and established a successful law practice. He worked hard in local politics, and let friends like Rutherford B. Hayes advise on larger plans. Personal tragedy sharpened the appeals of public life as an outlet for his energy, and compensation for disappointment. Two children died in youth, and plunged his wife into a nervous illness that made her a semi-invalid. The energy and sympathy he lavished on her out of genuine affection helped balance a personality attuned to other people's needs and desires, and he developed a legendary charm and patience. Like his idol James G. Blaine, he approached everyone on their own terms, and treated both friends and opponents with respect and courtesy.

He retained a dignity and quiet self-assurance embodied in an erect stance and meticulous personal dress. His charm did not twist arms or slap backs, and he avoided familiarity that bred contempt. A detached fatalism colored his thinking, but did not inhibit honest ambition. Washington columnist Frank Carpenter noted his prominent nose and alleged Napoleonic features: "It is a watchful nose . . . that watches out for McKinley." [3] In most relationships, he subtly took slightly more than he gave, without creating animosity. Few men ever penetrated his self-sufficiency or understood his oblique political methodology. "In all my career, in business and in politics, I have never known a man so self-contained," Mark Hanna noted with a touch of bewilderment.[4]

Accident did not make him the leading Republican contender in 1896. He boasted a productive twenty-year career in a major state; identification with national legislation; a moderate, constructive view that made him familiar to most GOP leaders, and to larger audiences who heard him speak in many campaigns. He typified the popular self-made man wishing to keep the system open for others. His doubts about radical solutions for democracy's defects only reflected wisdom acquired in the political market-place, and he spent most of his life devising a system of politics and economics based on material security and social harmony. He disliked localism, and while playing the game of partisan rhetoric, could harmonize diverse interests even as a young congressman.

McKinley wanted to retain the system's mobility and diversity, to let men fulfill their talents. He championed tariff protection specifically and the Republican party generally because he rightly understood that both promoted national interests. Naturally and honestly echoing the rhetoric of responsible individualism, he did not seek to advance at society's expense. The belief that material security fostered social responsibility might be as idealistic as facile self-sacrifice based on man's alleged innate goodness and rationality, but it at least accepted limitations in democratic politics, and the understandable reluctance of men to abandon old ideals.

McKinley's interest in stable development, so typical of the era's attitude toward change, shaped his politics. Both his personality and career let him accept the slowness of representative party politics that operated for a nation of diverse interests. As an artful survivor of Ohio's cutthroat politics, he never rejected a fruitful compromise that did not obscure an ideal. Parties and nations could move no faster than constituents desired. The American system was not perfect, but it historically worked for the general good. Flexibility was its greatest virtue, since astute political leaders could shape the public "will." In the meantime, he did not reject conciliation. "We cannot always do what is best," he once realistically told a congressman, "but we can do what is practical at the time." [5] Politics, to him, functioned on two levels. Specifically, a leader must acquire support from key individuals who commanded larger followings. Generally, a leader persuaded constituents to follow policies he better understood from a broader view. It was not a unique attitude, but he raised it to an art form in a personal style that alienated few people while enfolding diverse elements into a constructive consensus.

Intuition and experience gave him two talents essential to any representative leader: patience to find ways around temporary obstacles without sacrificing a whole program, and tolerance of diverse views and people, whose advice he cheerfully heard without always following it. His rustic origins did not foster provinciality. When the bigoted American Protective Association attacked him for allegedly pro-Catholic sympathies, McKinley did not inflate the issue with a public rebuttal, but privately hoped the record would speak for itself: [6]

> The course of the [APA] is extraordinary in American politics, and I cannot but think that it will react upon its authors and others related to it. Think for a moment—the leaders of a secret order seeking

through its organization to dictate a presidential nomination. A committee sitting in secret judgement on a public man, and whose report and judgement are to be binding upon all its membership. It may hurt locally here and there, but in the broad sense it cannot hurt. But whether it does or not, we cannot afford for any stake to narrow our platform, or consent to countenance any abridgement of the constitutional guarantee of religious freedom.

He respected party government, and never put himself above the GOP as a whole. He understood that victory in 1896 could finally cement the Republican coalition so long a-building in his lifetime. McKinley meant "Republican party" in the best sense. Like most people, he knew the differences between the two parties. Democrats stood for localism and states' rights; Republicans fostered nationalism through economic funding, spending, and regulation. Like Mrs. Foraker, he could say tersely: "The Republican party had saved the Union. It was the Union." [7] This was not idle emotion. The idea of Union to men of his mind was more than victory in a past war. It was the watchword of constructive national action.

Some Republicans, and many Democrats, represented only business interests, but McKinley's background, personality, and constituency opened his mind to change and moderation. As a congressman, he favored civil service reform, federal protection of voting rights, and workable business regulation, reflecting the needs and aspirations of an expanding middle and working class. Like Mark Hanna, he had many friends in organized labor, and protection heightened his appeal in shops and factories. He visited the mines, warehouses, forges, and plants in his district, and got a warm welcome from most workers. His uncertain district, which Democratic legislatures regularly gerrymandered, was a blessing in disguise. He never had the luxury of safety. In American politics, a safe constituency was the kiss of death, since it isolated leaders from change and new demands. McKinley's whole congressional career sharpened his talents for compromise. In his own time, he was a liberal Republican, as many followers who later became reformers readily attested. "I always felt that McKinley represented the newer view," Robert La Follette recalled. "Of course, McKinley was a high protectionist, but on the great new questions as they arose he was generally on the side of the public and against private interests." [8] By 1896, the Ohioan well represented the elements that could give the GOP a long lease on life.

The need to persuade not command, to walk not stride, denied him the eloquence so common to reformist politicians, and he seemed more

passive than he was. He became "a marvellous manager of men," as
even the tart Henry Adams admitted, but could not advertise the
method without destroying its efficacy.[9] At the height of a fierce legislative or party battle, he would approach combatants with disarming
kindness. "Come now, let us put the personal element aside and consider the principle involved."[10] He had the good sense not to advertise
at other men's expense, and preferred an unexciting press to antagonism with party leaders. That was his watchword; no personal element
must disrupt the whole party. But he could be stubborn on principles.
"Back of his courteous and affable manner was a firmness that never
yielded conviction," La Follette noted again, "and while scarcely seeming to force issues, he usually achieved exactly what he sought."[11]
The detached and able Elihu Root later noted this quality with admiration: "He was a man of great power because he was absolutely
indifferent to credit, . . . *but McKinley always had his way.*"[12] He
respected other men's views, and understood their problems. If they
could not join him, he would wait and hope, but he never made personal loyalty a test of virtue. ". . . one of McKinley's strongest points
is his lack [of] and disapproval of sycophancy, either on his own part
toward others, or in his expectation of others," Wyoming's Francis
Warren wrote later.[13]

The congressional elections of 1894 took McKinley across the country on a speaking tour, and informally announced his candidacy. By
1895, the inevitable political stirrings produced a group of favorite
sons in both parties, but McKinley was the most logical Republican
contender in terms of talent, record, and origins. Few doubted his
standing with the public. "McKinley has a great diffused strength all
over the country," John Hay wrote, "and is, in his own mind, almost
certain of the nomination."[14] But "almost" was not good enough, and
friends knew the equal dangers of silence and inactivity. "A year is a
good while in American politics," Hay warned. Whitelaw Reid was
equally blunt. "A boom for '96 which starts in '93 is in danger of with-
ering before harvest time."[15] He knew, like Emerson, that every hero
in time becomes a bore.

Calmness, efficient organization, and quiet work among potential
delegates could prevent dangerous intra-party rivalry. That required
astute management, and McKinley had the best man in Marcus Alonzo
Hanna. He was six years older than his chief, and came to politics
from business. An attractive figure, he was candid and genial with
the rustic charm of a self-made man who never let success obscure the
world's realities. His hurrying figure, cane tapping the ground, a plume

of cigar smoke trailing behind, was familiar in Ohio political circles. He first met McKinley while the young Major defended some striking workers, and both men stood well with organized labor. His bluff paternalism never condescended. If he denied workers' requests, he explained in terms the men understood. Big Business meant Big Labor, and he did not object to mutual demands that did not threaten the prosperity of both.

Hanna's genius for organization suited McKinley's plans. They were really one political individual. Hanna's drive and energy complemented McKinley's charm, patience, and shrewd appraisal of men and public issues. Hanna brought valuable experience in state politics to McKinley's boom. He helped carry Ohio for Garfield in 1880, worked for Blaine in 1884, and managed Sherman's pre-convention effort in 1888. By 1892, he moved to McKinley's cause, realizing he had better prospects for success, but he also acted out of loyalty and affection. Despite his worldliness, Hanna rhapsodized over McKinley. "You are not mistaken in your opinion and standard of McKinley," he wrote an acquaintance in 1892. "He is all you believe him to be and as true as steel." [16] After success in 1896, he remarked simply: "I acted out of love for my friend and devotion to my country." [17]

The press and political opponents gave their relationship a tarnish which time never fully erased. Contemporary cartoons depicted Hanna as a cruel monster, "Dollar Mark," covered with the wealth of oppressive plutocracy. McKinley walked the pages of the opposition press as a monkey on his string. Many, and not only Democrats, imagined that Hanna was master when he was the servant, but those who looked closely understood his subordinate role. William Allen White said Hanna was "just a shade obsequious in McKinley's presence." Charles G. Dawes knew the Major gave the orders. Herman H. Kohlsaat, a perceptive Chicago publisher, thought his attitude toward McKinley was "always that of a big, bashful boy toward the girl he loves," a simile Hanna liked and repeated.[18] He was seldom informal, and never familiar, with McKinley, and often told friends that McKinley's morality made him a better man. Without the Major's steadying and broadening influence, Hanna might have been merely another boss, like eastern counterparts. He realized the limits of his political expertise, and left strategy to the candidate while he organized the army and planned the logistics. McKinley well knew their public caricature, but never answered slander. He admired Hanna, respected his talents, and appreciated his work, but emotion did not weaken his detachment.

Hanna's philosophy matched McKinley's. They were both Hamiltonians in believing broadly that men who owned should rule, but they wanted more men to own, and to rule in favor of all sectors of life, not merely business. Hanna did not trust businessmen in politics. They easily panicked, lacked insight into the total system, and tended to a dangerous snobbery. He and McKinley slowly gathered a group of aides committed to the ideals of silence and patient organization. All were intensely loyal, and able to blend into a system. None swore allegiance to a simple profit ethic.[19]

By 1895, Hanna virtually retired from business to build the boom, pledging $100,000 to avoid political liens. With customary directness and a certain naiveté, he approached eastern party leaders in time-honored fashion. Home from this first skirmish in the political war, he entertained McKinley and Myron Herrick in Cleveland, eager to display apparent success. The gentlemen sat down after an elegant dinner to smoke and talk of things to come. "I don't suppose you saw anything about that meeting yesterday in the papers, did you?" Hanna asked. He lit a cigar and faced McKinley. "Now, Major, it's all over but the shouting. Quay wants the patronage of Pennsylvania; Aldrich, of New England; Manley, of Maine. Platt wants New York, but he wants it in writing; you remember he was fooled on Harrison." He paused, and said innocently: "I think they are willing to leave this region to me."

McKinley watched cigar smoke curl toward the ceiling, then grew serious. "Mark, some things come too high. If I were to accept the nomination on those terms, the place would be worth nothing to me and less to the people. If those are the terms, I am out of it." Hanna raised his hands quickly. "Oh, no, not so fast: I mean that on those terms the nomination would be settled immediately, but that does not mean that their terms have got to be accepted. There is a strong senti-ment for you all over the country, and while it would be hard to lick those fellows if they oppose against you, damned hard, I believe we can do it." McKinley thought a while. "How would this do for a slogan: 'The Bosses Against the People'? How would that sound?" Altered shrewdly to "The People Against the Bosses," it became the movement's official call.[20] McKinley's political finesse was more sound than Hanna's hope for an easy success. It was better to cultivate public opinion than run with the bosses. McKinley knew that if he won the nomination without their support, he could secure fruitful party loyalty and larger public appeal.

Hanna's agents were working late in 1895, sounding opinion, furnish-ing propaganda, talking to key men. McKinley badges, buttons, post-ers, reprints of speeches, pamphlets, poured into likely places until one opponent exclaimed with the voice of experience: "McKinley has plastered the land with his literary bureau." [21] While other candidates waited on fate, McKinley perfected an organization that could also conduct the election campaign. "If Mr. Hanna has covered every district in the United States in the same manner that he did those in Alabama, McKinley will be nominated . . . ," William E. Chandler noted.[22]

McKinley limited his own public role to precise speechmaking and guarded interviews. Newsmen liked him, but he seldom said anything exciting. "He can be both communicative and guarded and not mix the two efforts," one said.[23] In 1894, he spoke widely in congressional contests, and in 1895 entered some state elections for politicians eager to repay the favor later. Like all professionals, he declined to meddle in local affairs. "I do not 'swing delegations,'" he told an inquirer. "That is out of my line." His calm advice was well suited to the touchy situation. "Look over the ground carefully; make a quiet but strong canvass of the delegates; be sure you have the strength, and if you have, then instruct." [24]

Like all successful men, McKinley was lucky as well as astute and careful. The depression raised his stature as the country's chief protectionist. To millions of voters, the tariff seemed the key to good times and orderly growth. McKinley's campaign title "The Advance Agent of Prosperity" was both logical and alluring. His organization boomed protection as a unifying theme, avoiding the currency question, until an opponent exclaimed bitterly: "McKinley is making his whole capital on the theory that he is the only protectionist." [25] A correspondent wrote the edgy Quay that "McKinley's whole point seemed to be to keep the tariff question to the front and to ignore the financial question." [26] The tactic reaped widespread support from business, labor, and middle-class Republicans. McKinley now claimed labor support. Labor delegations called on him in Canton, and Hanna's emissaries emphasized the Major's standing with the distressed working class.[27]

But silver would not down, despite the appeals of a tariff campaign. The long-winded Senator Stewart demanded a public statement of McKinley's attitude, and got silence for his trouble. Tom Reed publicly mused over the circus, "where there was always at least one first class acrobat who could ride two horses at once." Other antagonists labeled McKinley "a political trimmer," and "a prince of straddlers" on the silver issue. McKinley flatly rejected free silver, and would not publicly discuss his stand,[28] but backstage, Senator Sherman and others explained the Major's bimetallism. The staff compiled a pamphlet on

McKinley's record, and friends said he would run on the gold standard if the party unified around it. It was the safest and wisest course. An early declaration would effect not only his chances, but also the party's unity.

By late 1895, the boom had developed impressive momentum. Mc-Kinley made peace with Foraker in Ohio, promising to support him for a Senate seat in 1896 if "Fire Alarm" Joe would nominate him at the national convention. In March, the Ohio state convention endorsed McKinley, who avoided Sherman's traditional fate of heading a doubtful home delegation. The South provided delegates for a candidate who was both popular and effective. McKinley was no stranger there. Since the mid-1880's, he had carried the message of protection into that industrializing area. His speeches in 1892 and 1894 were popular. As Governor of Ohio, he toured many southern expositions, and supported Negro rights without alienating white Republicans. Hanna bought a pleasant cottage at Thomasville, Georgia, which the McKinleys visited in March, 1895. The politicos came and went amid southern warmth and the Major's legendary blandishments. He protested against newspaper accounts of nefarious dealings, remarking that the trip was only "a little rest and outing." The elegant pantomime fooled no one; southerners knew he was there "to discuss the condition of Little Miss Boomlet." [29] Conversations in Washington rounded out the tour, and Hanna even outranked McKinley as an honorary "Colonel."

It was all effective. Louisiana liked his stand on the sugar question. Florida appreciated the tariff on citrus. Alabama and Georgia wanted industrial protection. Texas, West Virginia, and Kentucky applauded him. He needed at least 435½ votes in the convention, and nearly half that number came from the South. The commotion also helped elsewhere. "McKinley seems to be trying the alternating current," Reed said sarcastically, "rushing south to fill northern newspapers with his southern gains, and north to fill southern newspapers with his gains in New England." [30] It cost money, but Hanna and a few friends paid the bills. McKinley did not like subscriptions, and most businessmen were not ready to support one protectionist over another.

By early 1896, the plan's outlines were clear. Fellow politicos suddenly awoke to an apparent *fait accompli*. Despite the happy prospect of beating depression-ridden Democrats, no Republican but McKinley was well underway. There was no dearth of contestants, however. Former President Harrison seemed a possible choice, despite his difficulties with party leaders. Silence lent consent to talk of at least a complimentary nomination. Platt hoped otherwise, but Hanna said bluntly: "I consider Harrison as much of a candidate as anyone, and I know the 'little game' his managers are trying to play." [31] Harrison assured everyone he took only "a citizen's interest in politics," but his name counted in some circles, and industrious friends were ready for a deadlocked convention.[32] His chilly air was still evident to callers and correspondents. He might take a draft, but little else. "I do not like to appear to be in the attitude of the little boy that followed the apple-cart up the hill, hoping the tail-board might fall out," he wrote Elkins.[33] In February, Harrison disclaimed interest in the nomination, and McKinley secured many of his followers in the crucial Midwest.

Eastern leaders now saw the danger of a popular candidate they could not control. Platt, Quay, and others hastily revived the "favorite sons game" that usually produced bargains. They made a tacit "combine" against McKinley, using state figures to hold large delegations. The most logical choice if McKinley failed was the taciturn Senator Allison of Iowa. His moderation, midwestern origins, and a large circle of well-disposed friends made him a potent dark horse if pre-convention maneuvers failed to create a majority. Any such combine made Hanna's organizational task harder, but also helped McKinley by proving the apparent truth of his slogan, "The People Against the Bosses." "The McKinley boom shows a curious and increasing vitality . . . ," John Hay said. Senator Mason of Illinois noted that ". . . nobody seemed to be for McKinley except the people." [34]

Allison's friends toured the Midwest in a private railroad car dubbed "the Davy Crockett," and the public heard of other familiar figures. Platt backed Levi P. Morton, now governor of the Empire State. A round of lavish banquets, newspaper reports, and long letters from the "Easy Boss" let Morton think he had a chance. Platt's lieutenants went south, but were laughed at by people already firmly in McKinley's camp. Elsewhere, they confronted other favorite sons. Morton was only a sheep in wolf's clothing, too obviously a front for Platt's bargaining to gain any popularity. In Pennsylvania, Quay held the big block of Keystone delegates for himself; he visited the Major in Canton, but reached no agreement.

Tom Reed was the biggest, if not the most logical candidate, and had lost none of his zest for the cutting edge. A friend said he was the party's logical choice, and Reed mixed a sour realism with wit: "The convention could do worse, and probably will." He claimed support from men like Joseph Manley, Nelson Aldrich, Henry Cabot Lodge, and other New Englanders. He staunchly supported protection, and seemed more firmly wedded to the gold standard than McKinley, but as spring came on, Reed wobbled a little. "He is trying to make a reputation as a conservative economist," Theodore Roosevelt said, "and has merely succeeded in giving the idea that he has turned timid." [35]

McKinley was equally strong and well known in New England. He spoke regularly in Boston, Hartford, Providence, and other cities congenial to protection. McKinley Clubs and protectionist organizations now sprang up with help from Canton, to erode the Speaker's strength. In New Hampshire, Hanna's men successfully challenged Senator Chandler. Redfield Proctor led neighboring Vermont into McKinley's camp, and the walls of Reed's Jericho began to tumble. Reed was simply not popular. A man of his acerbity could not raise a wide following. A safe constituency isolated him from changing public wishes and the skills of honest compromise. McKinley's gains in New England reflected popularity and organizational skills as well as Reed's weaknesses. "Now we can make no mistake about this," a bitter manager exclaimed, "McKinley has out-generalled us all to pieces." [36] And he *was* popular. New Hampshire's Senator Jacob Gallinger did not dread the prospect of Ohio's triumph. "I know McKinley reasonably well, and am bound to say that I think you do him unintentional injustice in your well meant criticisms," he wrote a critical editor. "I know him to be a scrupulously honest man, and if he makes mistakes it will be those of judgement rather than intention." [37] Reed remained bitter; the rare man the Major could not charm or reason into firm alliance.

As warm weather heralded the convention season, state after state committed delegates to McKinley. In Illinois, a skillful organization under Charles Dawes calmly, but totally, destroyed Senator Cullom's pretensions. In the Upper Midwest, and Far West they had good success, considering free silver's appeal. Newspaper coverage and praise from local leaders only emphasized McKinley's popularity. He was clearly the people's choice. "These McKinley fellows have almost taken our breath away by the enthusiasm they manifest for their candidate," an Indianan admitted.[38] The growing parade impressed Wyoming's realistic Francis Warren. "I tell you, West," he wrote a friend on the *Washington Post*, "McKinley is in it with the masses in nearly every state in the Union, from New Hampshire to Wyoming, and from Minnesota to the Gulf. The politicians are making a hard fight against him, but if the masses could speak, McKinley is the choice of at least 75% of the entire Republican voters in the Union, and I am not considered much of a McKinley man, either." [39]

McKinley inherited the political tendencies of a whole generation. The ideals of party unity and loyalty, outlined when Rutherford B.

Hayes sat in the White House, found a logical spokesman in the man who championed every aspect of Republican nationalism, and mastered the arts of political leadership in a confused and fragmented era. He was fatalistic about success; an air of predestination hung about his apparent victory. But he and Hanna insured that destiny with years of hard work, cultivation of mass opinion, and close attention to a new, widened industrial constituency. Success would have been difficult without Hanna's brilliant organizational skill, but McKinley's role in national politics, his record as a constructive moderate, his geographical position, and widespread personal appeal made him the logical Republican nominee in 1896. His organization capitalized on that popularity, but did not create it.

A few prescient men realized what McKinley's success symbolized. His nationalism and allegiance to party ideals and programs could let him redefine Republicanism. The days when regional bosses dictated presidential nominations without regard to party wishes or popular ideals were over. Nearly every first-time presidential candidate between Jackson and McKinley was a compromise to prevent party disruption. They were chosen on the inside; McKinley made his own choice inevitable from the outside. His victory would illustrate the force of public opinion in unifying and democratizing parties into workable national units, more concerned with legislating for the country than being battlegrounds for warring chieftains.

And so by June, most Republicans settled down for a safe campaign. The discordant and bankrupt Democracy had no leaders. The GOP seemed unified for an easy victory. But McKinley was never one to relax his grip. Who could say what a seizure of the free silver disease could do to the proverbial best-laid plans?

Four years of agitation, depression, and party fragmentation produced no national Democratic spokesman. The President was defunct as a party leader and events reinforced normal tendencies to favorite-son candidacies. State leaders dominated almost all independent Democratic parties in the South and Midwest, where Populism further complicated the situation. The Democratic party was ripe for an appealing dark horse, unconnected to conservative easterners, moderate enough to ally South and West and appeal to ambitious Populists. A striking personality and the unifying issue of free silver would cover disunity.

Exhaustion and ennui pervaded Cleveland's element. His subordinates spent their energy saving the gold standard and trying vainly to control state groups. They had little time for national politics. Cleveland alternated between feeling he should stay in ready reserve if the party regained its senses, and a quiet understanding of his isolation. Realism triumphed. "Any man with even the smallest knowledge of the conditions which surrounded my second administration knows that I could not have commanded the support of half a dozen delegates in the whole country." [40] He was less realistic in thinking subordinates could control the party, even if they lost the election. He unsuccessfully groomed Carlisle, Olney, and Whitney for the succession. Snide opponents suggested Whitney might "pour Standard Oil upon the troubled waters." In New England, a small but devoted group, with the President's blessings, promoted former Governor William E. Russell of Massachusetts. On convention-eve, Whitney actually thought he could nominate Russell with 1892's methods. [41]

Outside Cleveland's small circle, few conservative Democrats hoped to shape the party's immediate future. No likely candidate could beat McKinley, or escape identification with the unpopular Administration. Men like Don Dickinson wearily counseled passive resistance. They could only hope to fight another day, perhaps in 1900. The gold Democrats reassured each other with private attacks on "socialists, anarchists and demagogues" in the silver movement, [42] but silverites cared little for eastern opinion. They thought it odd that Cleveland's group did not notice how they quickly controlled the party's machinery. [43] There was no real intra-party battle. "The solemn, tearful, easterners have about as much influence . . . as an over-patient hen might have on a porcelain egg," a reporter wrote as nomination-time approached. [44]

For all their activity and loud pronouncements about impending victory, the "new" Democrats had no single leader. They talked most about past crusaders too familiar for a fresh beginning. Missouri promoted Richard P. "Silver Dick" Bland, but his boom had an ignominious beginning. He raised a kite in 1894 and fell under the Republican landslide; but he had battled for inflation and agrarian interests since the 1870's, a major silver act bore his name, and until defeat he led agrarian elements in the House. His wife was Catholic, and Missouri was not a key state. Followers ignored these minor liabilities and mailed his speeches, opened small offices, and touted him as an elder statesman deserving recognition from a new Democracy. In the meantime, he tilled his farm in Lebanon, Missouri, occasionally removing his coat to pose for photographers atop a hayrick or behind a plow. [45]

In Iowa, former governor Horace Boies awaited the call. A handsome, smooth man with the virtues of a muted rusticity, he had a

"Mona Lisa smile" on a face so dignified that he earned the title "Affidavit Boies." His state was important, but leaned to Republicanism. Boies was the farmers' and workers' friend in the statehouse, but he angered powers like Altgeld for supporting Cleveland during the Pullman Strike. He was not overly enthusiastic about silver, but his following in the national convention of 1892 had not yet evaporated.[46] The strongest Democrat seemed least available. Illinois' John Peter Altgeld could not overcome German birth, but worked hard to reshape a party he could influence, if not command. He leaned to Bland, but would play the game to the end. Whatever the result, he figured large for the moment in the party's realignment.

Understanding silver's unifying appeal, some practical men suggested a convenient solution to the party's disarray. Why not nominate a well-known silver Republican? And who better qualified than Colorado's Senator Henry M. Teller? He could command almost all Democrats, some Populists and enough dissatisfied silver Republicans to win. Opposition to the Federal Elections Bill in 1890 endeared him to many southerners. He was a moderate protectionist, which pacified westerners who feared that issue might disappear in a silver crusade. Teller might attract independents, if there were any, and need not say anything unfortunate in a campaign. Or so it appeared to some.

But Teller appealed to only a handful of silver leaders. Alabama's Senator Morgan promised to follow if Teller won the nomination, but pointed out an obvious problem. How would they answer conservative Democrats who jeered: "You are invited to leave your party and its honest money creed, and vote for a Republican in order to get an opportunity of paying your debts with inflated, unsound, and dishonest dollars, worth, in fact, only fifty cents"? Altgeld would not commit himself to an independent Republican, fearing "another Greely fiasco."[47] Teller's friends persisted until the convention, but without much heart. Missouri's Senator Francis Cockrell spoke the simple truth: ". . . the next Democratic president will be a Democrat and fill the offices with Democrats."[48] After leaving the Republican party in June, Teller announced he would accept but not seek the Democratic nomination. Friends hoped for a deadlocked convention, or simple luck.

It was an unusual situation. No one seemed to fit the party's needs, yet there was no dearth of confidence, talk, and propaganda as the convention approached in July. Most delegates were not sure what to do, but a few shrewd professionals saw that Nebraska's William Jennings Bryan was the most appealing dark horse. He had escaped national notice; youth and inexperience seemed his only ironic assets. Bryan was barely thirty-six, a product of Salem, Illinois, and a comfortable rural upbringing that included a degree from Illinois College in 1881. He practiced law in Jacksonville, Illinois, then moved to frontier Nebraska in 1887. In Lincoln, he was a shrewd small-town lawyer, mingling easily, seldom holding a grudge, fitting snugly into semirural life. His wife, a good organizer and ambitious lawyer, fortified his desires for public office, and he won a House seat in 1890 and 1892. In Congress, he gained a modest reputation for low tariff speeches. He never hid his light, and wangled a seat on the powerful Ways and Means Committee, which usually went to older hands. Defeated in the landslide of 1894, he went into journalism after vainly attempting to win a Senate seat, and systematically organized a quiet boom for the 1896 nomination.

Robert La Follette remembered Bryan as "a tall, slender, handsome fellow who looked like a young divine." A streak of the moralist preacher raised his political chances among a people attuned to the biblical phrase and Shakespearan stance.[49] He was a fine actor, with a justly famous voice, but was not a charlatan. Bryan believed in the out-dated Jeffersonian virtues he preached in the Hamiltonian world of 1896, and though he wore the air of a gifted amateur in politics, he was a better judge of public opinion than many more experienced Democrats. Between 1894 and 1896, he and a few friends systematically contacted most potential delegates, key editors, and local figures. He never pushed when he could gently pull, and was always on call for the good cause, facing hundreds of audiences and sharpening a style suitable to a larger theater. Divisions among Bland, Boies, Altgeld, and lesser leaders enhanced his chances as a suitable compromise choice. He was young, had a respectable but not burdensome record, came from the West, and understood the arts of conciliation. Though men thought otherwise at the time, neither fate nor accident created his position in the party. He faithfully represented the elements striving to master the Democracy.

The shock of depression, and belief in the values of monetary inflation turned Bryan from a promising career in tariff reform to champion silver. He also saw its political virtues. "I don't know anything about free silver," he said in 1892. "The people of Nebraska are for free silver, and I am for free silver. I will look up the arguments later." While he was a hereditary Democrat, Bryan did not snub the Populists. "I was born a Democrat and have strong Alliance tendencies," he assured would-be supporters in 1892.[50] Seeing the misery in depression's wake as he toured the West and South after 1893, and believing Cleveland's policies misguided, Bryan left the President's principles without abandoning the party. "[If] the Democratic party, after you go home, endorses your action [favoring Cleveland] and makes your position its permanent policy," he told the Nebraska state convention in 1894, "I promise you that I will go out and serve my country and my God under some other name, even if I must go alone." [51] That was unlikely, since he spoke for an increasing number of dissatisfied Democrats who might provide a formidable column to follow his lead.

Bryan read the depths of political feelings with charm and courtesy, but old hands smiled and thought him over-eager, the kind of pushy young man who ruins his chances. "You are young yet," Altgeld counseled. "Let Bland have the nomination this time. Your time will come." [52] Bryan was not discouraged. He mailed postcards, spoke, visited friends, and acquired political debts marked for payment in 1896. He thought Boies impossible; Bland would stall before reaching the great prize. That made him the compromise choice.

He kept reminding people of his position, but it was understandably hard to take him seriously. "Here was a young man barely thirty-six, living in a comparatively unimportant Republican state west of the Mississippi River, audaciously announcing his probable candidacy for the presidential nomination," one man recalled. "The very seriousness of the suggestion emphasized its absurdity." [53] At most, leaders thought of him for a congressional race, or in Bland's Cabinet. He went about his business, which included reporting the GOP convention late in June. Charles A. Towne of Minnesota met him on the street, saying: "We are going to Chicago to nominate Senator Teller; you had better come and help us." Bryan smiled. "I can't do it. I am going to be nominated at Chicago myself." [54]

Maybe. But even if this dream materialized, final victory was uncertain. The gold Democrats would not quit without a fight that could ruin a new Democracy. The Populists might pick up the pieces after all, as they had long predicted. McKinley would not be easy to beat, even with full unity and a major effort. The Republicans were giving the country another look at their strength at a national convention in St. Louis.

Canton wore an air of tense calm in mid-June, as townsfolk awaited their favorite son's triumph. The plain house on Market Street hosted newspaper reporters, and the staff still handled an enormous correspondence. McKinley checked details, saw visitors, and spoke by telephone to delegates in St. Louis. He seemed unruffled, teasing neighborhood children across the fence, chatting with the gardener who worried about the lawn. He sometimes took Mrs. McKinley for a quick drive. Canton was decked in bunting, and nearly every store displayed McKinley's portrait. Tourists could buy his bust in bronze, terra cotta, tin, marble, or parian. An endless array of souvenir canes, flags, handkerchiefs, dishes, and buttons was available.

The scene was much the same in St. Louis, which entertained the party's assembled wisdom in a hall 260 feet long and 180 feet wide, seating some 14,000 people. It had electric lighting and special facilities for reporters. The casual stranger might have thought it was McKinleyville, for the Major's followers dominated the city. Bartenders concocted a gold-colored McKinley drink of bourbon, lemon juice, and sugar. Arriving delegates passed under McKinley arches at their hotels, and waved to each other with McKinley bandanas. His subordinates had not relaxed. The trusted Perry Heath arrived early in June, attending to delegates. Hanna controlled the Credentials Committee, ready to endorse McKinley men in disputed delegations.[55]

The hullabaloo only confirmed the fact of McKinley's success, and party leaders were less interested in disputed delegations than the currency plank. Many Republicans misjudged silver's impact. "I do not think we will have any trouble with the money plank, although there will probably be some dissent," Foraker wrote a month before the convention. "The sentiment for free coinage will be so slight comparatively that it will not amount to anything." [56] Other voices in business and doubtful areas told a different story. "The people [in the South and West] are simply crazy upon the money question," a Democrat wrote Cleveland in 1895, "they cannot discuss it rationally." [57] Alger was equally blunt in the first week of June. "This money question is absorbing all others, and the commercial world is almost in a state of paralysis." [58]

Party leaders remained uncertain. A declaration for gold would alienate westerners; a straddle for old-fashioned bimetallism would anger the East; any plank would cost support. Henry Cabot Lodge got a drawling "The hell you say!" from Hanna after threatening a floor fight against a straddle.[59] Midwesterners around Allison wanted to declare for international bimetallism. It all irritated Hanna, who spent a good deal of time scratching hives that resulted from Missouri's heat and mosquitos. He knew Reed's men wanted to embarrass McKinley more than stand for gold. And everyone wanted credit for whatever emerged.

The Major's silence on the issue was profitable, but must now end. Opponents made much of his past pro-silver congressional record, but except when he supported free coinage during the Bland-Allison debates, McKinley was a firm international bimetallist, along with most politicians of both parties. He was a "trimmer" or "straddler" only to rabid "gold bugs" and free coinage men. A realist, he understood that phraseology meant a good deal. The party must stand by gold without ruling out possible future action for silver after the present crisis. That spring, McKinley authorized the gregarious and well-connected Whitelaw Reid to circulate his ideas on the platform among businessmen and eastern party leaders. In general, they favored a firm stand for gold. As the convention gathered in St. Louis, McKinley agreed, telling Indiana's Charles W. Fairbanks: "Tell our friends at St. Louis they can't make the platform too strong for me." [60]

Hanna carried a draft plank in McKinley's handwriting. It demanded gold and silver at par, arguing that the party would "welcome bi-metallism based upon an international ratio, but until that can be secured it is the plain duty of the United States to maintain our present standard, and we are therefore opposed under existing conditions to the free and unlimited coinage of silver at sixteen to one." [61] McKinley was ready for the gold standard, with proper guarantees for flexibility. Hanna must now fit it to the party's needs with the minimum of fuss and antagonism. Like McKinley, he let everyone talk, and gain credit for writing the plank. The wider the responsibility, the greater the enthusiasm and loyalty.

In after years, a whole folklore enshrouded the subject, like quarrels over the authorship of Shakespeare's plays. Reporters, politicians, and businessmen claimed credit for this or that particular clause. In 1901, Senator Chandler paid Lodge $100 for allegedly insisting on the words "which we pledge ourselves to promote" after the sentences dealing with an international agreement. Lodge took the money and the credit, but the whole performance reflected both McKinley's subtle touch and shrewd ideas. The final plank was unequivocal, but a masterpiece of harmonizing:

> The Republican Party is unreservedly for sound money. It caused the enactment of a law providing for the resumption of specie payments in 1879. Since then every dollar has been as good as gold. We are unalterably opposed to every measure calculated to debase our currency or impair the credit of our country. We are therefore opposed to the free coinage of silver, except by international agreement with the leading commercial nations of the earth, which agreement we pledge ourselves to promote; and until such agreement can be obtained, the existing gold standard must be maintained. All of our silver and paper

currency must be maintained at parity with gold, and we favor all measures designed to maintain inviolably the obligations of the United States, and all our money, whether coin or paper, at the present standard, the standard of the most enlightened nations of the earth.

Though Hanna skillfully "surrendered" to gain support from various factions, he denied that eastern business elements dictated the plank. As he insisted, "the plank defining the party's position was advocated by western men, drawn up by western men, and approved by me before any man from the East reached St. Louis." [62] The GOP's final adherance to gold had a surprising effect. It gave many people a unifying sense of urgency and tension. They welcomed relief from hesitation. The bimetallic clause, and the Republicans' past performance on compromise silver legislation, reassured those who could not accept Cleveland's simplistic gold standard. The party's stand was timely and right. The country must choose the international standard and industrialism, or an uncertain silver standard and agrarian rule.°

The gold plank precipitated an intra-party crisis, however. At the convention's third session, Senator Teller offered a free coinage substitute, and provoked a poignant and memorable scene. He was an original Republican, but could not abandon silver, even if it meant political ostracism. After a brief, tearful speech, he saw the convention defeat the substitute, 818½ to 105½. The Canton GAR band struck up "Silver Threads Among the Gold," as delegates awaited the finale. The Chair let Senator Frank Cannon of Utah read the silverites' valedictory. At the podium, Cannon threw back his curly locks and struck a proper pose. Hanna stirred irritably: "Perty, ain't he? Looks like a cigar drummer." [63] Hisses and boos disturbed Cannon's reading, and when he finished, a moment of silence presaged a storm. Hanna's harsh voice rang out over the delegates' heads: "Go! Go!" A tumult of shouting accompanied the little band of silverites who brushed past friends and marched out the exit. Teller paused to shake Foraker's hand, and many bade tearful farewells. The bolt's effects were hard to predict. But the

---

°The gold standard was not the "best" or "wisest" answer to mankind's fiscal problems, but it was a deeply significant fact of life in the 1890's. The United States could not reasonably have sustained the dollar's purchasing power at home, or its stature abroad on a silver standard. The nation's need for foreign investment, and participation in world trade underscored this fact. Historians still too-commonly note that the United States left the gold standard in a depression in 1933 without serious economic results, implying that the same held true for 1896. This overlooks, among other things, two basic facts: (1) the United States abandoned gold in conjunction with the world's leading powers, especially Great Britain, in 1933; and (2) the United States still settles international dollar balances in gold on demand.

importance of the scene was clear to one thoughtful man in the reporters' section who stood up and walked across several desk-tops to get a better view. His name was William Jennings Bryan.[64]

That afternoon brought nominating speeches, and the McKinley men braced for a vivid demonstration. Chauncey Depew named Morton; Lodge spoke for Reed; an Allison supporter put the Iowan to the test. In Canton, the Major's guests listened nervously to the telegraph, while reporters paced the porch and sprawled in wicker chairs. The relaxed candidate entertained his aged mother, wife, and neighbors with banter. "Are you ladies getting anxious about this affair?" he asked lightly on one trip between the sitting room and study.[65]

Foraker finally came to the podium for a spellbinding nominating speech. He attacked the Cleveland Administration as "one stupendous disaster . . . ," then outlined what the people wanted in a new president. His mention of McKinley halfway through the speech set off pandemonium, as delegates poured into the aisles blowing horns, waving banners, and cheering while hats, canes, and umbrellas flew to the ceiling. Hanna waved a McKinley handkerchief to the music of conflicting bands. In McKinley's library, the telephone operator described the scene, and the Major heard an eerie crackling, the sound of delegates demonstrating 600 miles away. The rest was anticlimax, as Foraker finished and the convention prepared to ballot.

The states behind McKinley stood firm while the clerk moved through the roll. In Canton, McKinley smoked and watched the figures. When Ohio's turn came, he was within 20 votes of victory, and the 46 Buckeye delegates gave him the nod. Rising quickly, he crossed to the sitting room and embraced his wife. "Ida," he said, "Ohio's vote has given me the nomination." In St. Louis, Hanna burst out compulsively: "I love McKinley! He is the best man I ever knew." He savored a victory that gave McKinley 661½ votes on a first ballot, to Reed's 84½, Morton's 58, and Quay's 61½. It was not so rich a moment for other men. Myron Herrick saw a familiar figure watching the setting sun, Thomas C. Platt. McKinley later discussed the triumph with his usual detachment: "It will occur to the close student of political events that, all things considered, it was desirable to take a man from the Middle West, and that a man who had twice carried Ohio during troublesome times previous to 1896 was entirely available as a candidate. I cannot subscribe to the idea that accident or luck had very much to do with making me President."[66]

Canton erupted, as factory whistles blared above people rushing down Market Street. As the faithful converged on the Major's lawn, a visitor fled through the back door with a timely admonition: "You have my sympathy." In minutes, 2,000 people arrived by train from nearby Alliance; 19 carloads of pilgrims flooded in from Massilon. Trains disgorged eager well-wishers from Akron, Niles, and other towns, and visitors kept McKinley on his porch until after midnight. Dawn revealed a litter of paper and some rifled wallets, attesting both to enthusiasm and the dexterity of Canton's pickpockets. Between 5 P.M. and midnight, McKinley spoke to 50,000 people, setting an early pattern for the campaign.[67]

The convention named New Jersey's Garret A. Hobart for Vice-President, McKinley's choice after Reed refused second place. Hobart was a shrewd fund-raiser, understood political habits in the mid-Atlantic states, and his tact and courtesy matched McKinley's. Hanna became National Chairman, placed efficient lieutenants in subordinate positions, and promised an effective campaign. Not everyone in the party liked the convention's work, but no one disputed McKinley's popularity with the masses, or his skill as a campaigner and spokesman on major political issues. Unless the Democrats defied most rational predictions, the GOP would win handily.

Early in June, William C. Whitney prepared for a European tour. He was tired, disheartened over politics, and wanted to see his son row in the Henley Regatta. For months he had doubted that any conservative Democrat could win the nomination, but pressure from Cleveland revived his hope that skillful organization and a rapid attack could save the party from radicalism. In mid-June, he saw his son off to Europe, then canceled his own trip. He would go to Chicago. As the delegates moved toward the Windy City, where the convention opened on July 7, Whitney's special train bore distinguished men to a showdown. He wanted a reasonable compromise on all important intra-party matters. He would settle for international bimetallism, expanded banking facilities, and William E. Russell's nomination.

The easterners alighting from their elegant train, filled with Whitney's wines and gourmet food, were strangers in a different land, however. They had no common ties to those who now controlled the party. No amount of entertaining or appeals to party harmony and reason swayed the angry western and southern delegates who were in the saddle and proposed to ride. Most of the "new Democrats" agreed with the acid Ben Tillman: "The silver men are running this affair, and they propose to run it in their own fashion. If the gold men don't like it, let them bolt. I hope they will." [68] Tension ran through every gathering, large or small, until one of Whitney's friends remarked half-fearfully: "For the first time I can understand the scenes of the French revolution!" [69] The impending crisis over silver momentarily fused discordant eastern elements. Hill and Whitney both lobbied in the name of reason. But it was not 1892; careful planning would not triumph over emotion and demands for party reorientation.

Attention naturally centered on the Resolutions Committee drafting a platform, where Hill argued for a moderate stand on gold and silver. But the westerners were in charge, and as Altgeld said, would write a document suitable to their section. Hill could only make a minority report, and speak to the convention. "Senator Hill, why don't you ever smile and look pleasant?" a man asked. "I never smile and look pleasant at a funeral," the New Yorker answered. [70]

As the party's fervor for silver intensified, William Jennings Bryan's confidence grew. After securing a position in Nebraska's delegation, he arranged with Senator Jones, the Resolutions Committee Chairman, to be last in a series of speakers debating the merits of silver and gold. The night before the convention faced the issue, Bryan and a group of friends watched the human procession from a restaurant. A Bland parade noisily passed, and the Nebraskan smiled. "These people don't know it, but they will be cheering for me just this way by this time tomorrow night. I will make the greatest speech of my life tomorrow in reply to Senator Hill." He reassured his wife: "I am the only man who can be nominated. I am what they call 'the logic of the situation.'" The idea of his victory still seemed fantastic. "Who will be nominated?" a reporter asked him the next day. "Strictly confidentially, not to be quoted for publication, I will be," Bryan said while nonchalantly eating a sandwich. [71]

The third day's session, July 9, promised to relieve the delegates' tension. If the gold men bolted, so be it; hopefully, the nominee would make up the difference with Populists and Republicans. Senator Jones reported the platform planks, and debate on the currency question opened. Tillman began with a violent, rambling attack on the national Administration, and the East. His language provoked shocked hisses even from sympathizers, but he was in no mood to compromise. "There are only three things in the world that can hiss," he snapped at the unruly crowd, "a goose, a serpent, and a man." Hill followed with an able argument. Stand for international bimetallism, he said; abandon lurid assaults on business that seemed to condemn all property. "Have you not undertaken enough, my good friends, now without seeking to put in this platform these unnecessary, foolish and ridiculous things?"

he asked. He warned of the obvious: No Democrat could win without carrying some of the East. Declarations for an income tax, assaults on Cleveland, and a campaign weighted toward agricultural interests opposing tariff protection would alienate much support.[72]

Bryan listened intently. Clark Howell of the *Atlanta Constitution* urged him to make "a big, broad, patriotic speech that will leave no taste of sectionalism in the mouth, and which will give a sentiment that will touch a responsive chord in the heart of the whole country." Bryan proposed to do just that, already marshalling phrases in his mind. "You will not be disappointed, . . ." he assured Howell.[73] Vilas and Russell followed Hill; then Bryan left his seat like an eager athlete. When the conflicting applause died, he began a justly famous speech, the measured phrases reaching every part of the hall. His impressive appearance, clear voice, and persuasive tone captivated a crowd that did not know him well.

Bryan had an empathy with audiences that let him drop words like bricks or feathers as the occasion required. He had mastered the Biblical allusion, dramatic pause, and artful gesture that so easily captivated Americans. He followed Howell's advice, and spoke for unity among the people he hoped to bring into a new party. His insistence that all producers were businessmen was an effort to dull the edge of many Democrats' attacks on wealth. Artful allusions to the mutual interests of workers and farmers covered their obvious differences with an appealing rhetoric pitched toward the underdog. His tone rose above conflicting facts into compelling oratory that defined the vague aspirations of millions.

In its structure and words, the speech was masterful politics, working toward harmony and conciliation while sounding progressive. Nothing better illustrated his own style, or the varied desires of the restless following he hoped to lead than the dramatic conclusion: "You shall not press down upon the brow of labor this crown of thorns, you shall not crucify mankind upon a cross of gold." Sunlight filtered onto him during the speech, and when he finished, Bryan raised his arms in a crucifixion stance, then lowered them slowly as the last syllable fell on the hushed and expectant crowd.[74]

Silver had its leader. Eager friends bore Bryan around the platform and offstage in triumph, while supporters carried state standards toward the front of the hall. Followers in the galleries demanded an immediate nomination; a triumphant new factor had entered the calculations. The cheering and tumult did not please Altgeld, who still favored Bland and a cautious campaign. He distrusted emotion that might not last until November. "It takes more than speeches to win real victories," he told Clarence Darrow. "Applause lasts but a little while. The road to justice is not a path of glory; it is stony and long and lonely, filled with pain and martydom. I have been thinking over Bryan's speech. What did he say, anyhow?" [75] Cynics downgraded Bryan's speech as quickly as enthusiasts mistakenly said it made him an overnight candidate, but Bryan could not have won without the address, and he voiced sentiments that united all elements of a potential new party. No easterner would have uttered them; no southerner had the grace for such a speech. From the mouth of an older man, these phrases would be weak and cynical, but Bryan's youth, origins, and obvious sincerity made them compelling.

The party adopted the radical platform. Bryan did not push his advantage, knowing it was the better part of valor to let the delegates choose him, and then appeal for party unity. Nomination speeches consumed the next day, and leaders like Altgeld fought a bitter rearguard action for favorite sons. Bryan won on the fifth ballot, though gold Democrats sullenly refused to vote. The happy tidings reached him in a barber's chair, and he alighted with a fresh shave and beaming smile, ready to face eager well-wishers. They followed him to the hotel, and even reverently tiptoed past the bed while he napped. The results pleased silverites. "Now we are even with old Cleveland," Senator Vest whispered when the clerk announced Bryan's nomination.[76] The new candidate revealed at least a touch of realism under his bland good nature. "I seem to have plenty of friends now, but I remember when they were very few." [77]

The convention chose Arthur Sewall of Maine, an elderly shipping magnate, for Vice-President. He was an eastern silverite, who would presumably add geographical weight and campaign funds to the ticket. Only tactful parliamentary rulings avoided a pitched brawl between triumphant silverites and angry gold men, who threatened to bolt. Would they stay home, follow McKinley, or make a separate ticket? No one knew as the delegates dispersed, bearing lively tales to the folks at home, and eager to upset careful Republican plans. The People's Party would further complicate matters. Its hopes of inheriting dissidents from both major parties now vanished, but it probably commanded enough support to elect Bryan in a close contest.

The Populists convened in St. Louis on July 22, alternating between a frank desire to win by endorsing Bryan, and fears of losing their separate identity. The delegates were poor, testifying vividly to the depression's impact on the West and South. Some had no shoes; others wore them only to meetings. Most ate at cheap lunch stands, and walked blocks or miles to save cab fare. The usual gathering of peripheral cranks embarrassed Populist leaders, and delighted newsmen interested in the bizarre, or seeking to smear the reform movement. So many sported beards that one suggested "some mysterious connection between Populism and hair." An eminent physician reported that most delegates displayed obvious signs of insanity, which well illustrated the state of medical diagnosis.[78]

Outside the convention hall, in hotel lobbies, and at state standards near the speakers' platform, earnest men debated the virtues of fusing with the Bryan ticket. "Middle-of-the-roaders" wished to remain independent and drive toward reform. Men with political experience preferred endorsing Bryan, given suitable promises of post-election rewards. "Democracy is that bourne from which no reform party returns, as yet," a radical insisted. But the hope of success with Bryan and the overriding issue of free silver attracted most Populists. "It was in the air that there must be union," Lloyd noted. This reflected an obvious dilemma. "If we fuse, we [the separate People's Party] are sunk; if we don't fuse, all the silver men will leave us for the more powerful Democrats." [79]

Older Populists and reformers frankly wanted a unified crusade, even if free silver momentarily engulfed more basic reforms. After victory, they argued, like other pragmatic politicians, a successful coalition could enact wider programs. For now, they must take advantage of popular response to a silver crusade and Bryan's personalism. General Weaver clung to realism after 1894. "I am a middle-of-the-road man, but I don't propose to lie down across it so no one can get over me. Nothing grows in the middle of the road." In 1895, he assured Bryan that Populist moderates "have had quite enough middle-of-the-road nonsense." [80]

Bryan carefully cultivated good relations with moderate Populists. He had won the Democratic nomination, and assumed that reason would produce fusion. Other silver leaders hoped so. Senator Teller urged a general reform crusade behind Bryan. Senator Stewart agreed. "The [Democratic] platform is radical enough for you or me," he wrote North Carolina's Senator Marion Butler, a moderate Populist. "Bryan is more of a Populist than a Democrat. . . . There was nothing left of the Democratic party at Chicago but the name." [81] While many Populists would swallow Bryan, most objected to Sewall. He was rich, only a nominal reformer, and represented the hated East. Moderates worked to endorse Bryan and secure a separate Populist vice-presidential candidate.

The convention was unruly. Cranky Texans often displayed firearms, and delegates harangued each other during the proceedings. Every man was his own philosopher. The sergeant at arms at one point could not quell disturbances because someone cut his suspenders. Though radicals charged fraud, no one forced the Populists to endorse free silver. Realists could not resist it. Although Bryan insisted he would not accept a Populist running-mate, leaders acted on the opposite assumption. They hoped to persuade the Democrats to drop Sewall after the fact; their failure to do so lent credence to charges that they abandoned Populist doctrine for momentary victory. The confused convention endorsed Bryan for President and named Georgia's Tom Watson for Vice-President. He was an unhappy, if necessary choice to appease radicals. A quick tongue and flaring temper underlined his inability to work for party unity.

Delegates left St. Louis in varying states of expectation or foreboding. Moderates embraced free silver and fusion from both expediency and enthusiasm. They knew the electorate would better respond to Bryan and one paramount issue than to a general reform program. Radical Populists were unhappy, threatening to fuse with Republicans for GOP support in local contests. Professional reformers like Lloyd and Donnelly disliked seeing Populists behave like other political mortals, eager to win elections.

It was a strange crusade, feeding more on enthusiasm than genuine resources. The endorsement was a mixed asset for Bryan. A separate Populist ticket probably would not have cost him much since most of the party's moderates seemed ready to vote for him. A full Populist slate would have won only radicals, whose loss would have made Bryan's campaign "respectable" to more important voters. The Democratic crusade now seemed a hybrid creature, holding only to free silver and personalism around an unknown man. Bryan probably could not gather farmers, workers, and small businessmen into a victorious coalition during one campaign. His mixed following would quarrel, underline its weaknesses, and help unite Republicans. In the summer doldrums, Republicans began fashioning a campaign that displayed their own appeals.

Tension did not govern Republican planning until July. McKinley's nomination seemed tantamount to election, and party leaders placidly enjoyed summer vacations and attended to private matters. In Canton, the candidate went about his business, including Sundays in church, where he heard at least one sermon from an applicable text: "Wherefore the rather, brethren, give diligence to make your calling and election sure: for if ye do these things, ye shall never fall." [82] Hanna was ready to organize when cooler fall campaign weather came. He visited Canton to map strategy, and talked genially to reporters. Success gave him no pretensions, and nearly everyone responded to his humanity, even when carrying out bluff orders and hard assignments. In Cleveland at a jolly victory parade, he waved a plume and sang songs. Spying a friend on the sidewalk, he winked broadly, pointed to his chest, and said humorously: "Big Injun! Me Big Injun!" [83] McKinley seemed unperturbed. In July, he told friends: "I am a tariff man, standing on a tariff platform. This money matter is unduly prominent. In thirty days you won't hear anything about it." William R. Day, an old and honored friend usually at hand with lucid advice, answered drily: "In my opinion, in thirty days you won't hear of anything else." [84]

Democratic fusion with Populists, rising silver sentiment, and Bryan's announcement that he would tour in an underdog campaign, roused Hanna. "The Chicago convention has changed everything," he warned McKinley. The national chairman rallied subordinates with refreshing candor: "Quit blowing, and saw wood." [85] He established a headquarters in New York, largely to gather funds and oversee eastern operations. From a special office in Chicago, able lieutenants like Dawes directed a campaign to save the Midwest. Hanna oversaw everything. "I will be in the saddle, so to speak, and be found at both places at different times," he told reporters. Businessman Cornelius Bliss handled the treasurer's duties; Henry Clay Payne directed the Chicago organization; state leaders like Platt, Quay, and Manley sat on the executive committee.

Hanna's vigor and common sense quickly impressed everyone. "He was candid, genial, and straightforward. No pretense, no intrigue, to gain his ends. He was openly for you or against you." [86] His subordinates fortified the impression of business efficiency. Dawes let printing contracts on bid, hired only competent staff members, screened special state organizations, and established a speakers' bureau to find talent. The whole intricate organization had no time-servers.

By early August, the strategy was clear. They would appeal to labor and established farmers everywhere. McKinley wanted a blanket campaign against silver until the last moment, when heavy emphasis on protection would change the pace and emphasize Republican identification with prosperity. The rising sense of urgency helped Hanna make truces with party leaders. He conferred with Reed's men, and calmly told them to raise $400,000. He recognized Platt's organization in New York. Hanna repeated the performance in Pennsylvania, and Quay did his usual yeoman service. In spite of all this, McKinley did not surrender to eastern bosses; he could manage them after victory. Hanna relied on the midwesterners who engineered the pre-convention boom and understood the crucial area. Neither Platt nor Quay dominated the organization.

Campaign funds became scarce. "I am afraid that we are mistaken in assuming that we are going to have more funds than in 1892," the worried Dawes wrote McKinley on August 1, after surveying bills for printing and transportation. "While the interest of the businessmen is greater in our contest, it is more difficult for them to spare the money for subscriptions." [87] A few wealthy men like John Hay sent personal donations, but appeals to the business community were often vain. Hard-pressed state organizations and local clubs could not pay their own bills.

Early in August, Hanna made the rounds in New York, but many good Republicans did not know him. His business and political reputation commanded more respect in the Midwest than East. A stroke of luck brought him to James J. Hill, who personally escorted him through the proper offices. In five days, the two collected enough money for immediate expenses, with pledges for more. A special committee oversaw funds. Banks and insurance companies were asked for a percentage of their income. Independent clubs and organizations raised smaller amounts in special campaigns. Few refused to pay when they saw Hanna and his efficient methods. By September, the money scare was over and Hanna was returning some contributions. Ultimately, some $3,500,000 flowed from the two headquarters, of which about $3,000,000 came from New York.[88]

The corn belt, wheat states like Nebraska and the Dakotas, and the Old Northwest received close attention. The managers wrote off the Rocky Mountain states, though Oregon and California seemed at least likely to go Republican. Boxcars laden with pamphlets for the hungry masses left Chicago hourly, and an intricate system of mailing kept post offices busy. Ghost writers produced pamphlets and wrote speeches for famous men. Hanna loved the excitement, vigor, and sense of accomplishment. By Election Day, the organization had sent out 250,000,000 documents. Some 5,000,000 families got McKinley material weekly. Over 275 different pamphlets went out in 5,000 freight packages and 1,500,000 mail packages from the Chicago office. The New

York office dispatched 20,000,000 pamphlets east and north of the Ohio
River. The technical improvements evident in the campaign of 1892
now came into their own. Heavy local newspaper coverage, with plates
and copy from GOP headquarters, was also a great help. By late
September, most field agents were confident of victory.

This activity drew unparalleled abuse on Hanna. Unable to attack
McKinley's probity, the Democrats lambasted his manager. Homer
Davenport's vicious and unjust cartoons of Hanna as a bloated monster went into millions of homes. Farm wives allegedly hid their children at the mention of his name. One morning, Nathan B. Scott saw
Hanna grow tense while reading a newspaper. The familiar bloated
figure stared up from the page. "That hurts," Hanna said suddenly.
"When I have tried all my life to put myself in the other fellow's place,
when I have tried to help those in need and to lighten the burdens of
the less fortunate than myself, to be pictured as I am here, to be held
up to the gaze of the world as a murderer of women and children, I
tell you it hurts." [89] Despite lurid charges, the Republicans did not
bribe their way to victory. McKinley bluntly warned leaders that he
would not countenance corruption. There was no need for it; skillful
propaganda would win voters. So morally squeamish a man as William
Allen White dismissed these charges. Hanna lavishly subsidized newspapers, advertisers, and speakers, but he hotly denied bribery or coercion. ". . . he must produce his proof of the charge he makes against
me," he said of one reporter, "or stand a self-convicted liar before the
people. He is a liar if he said that." [90]

While Hanna forged the organization and flooded the country with
literature and speakers, McKinley greeted delegations in Canton. He
soothed party chieftains in person and via the mails, including the icy
Harrison who refused to tour. "I cannot go about the country making
speeches," he snapped. "I have not the time, and I do not think it
would be appropriate." The Major's charm won out. Harrison spoke
in New York, coining an oft-repeated answer to silver inflation: "The
first dirty errand that a dirty dollar does is to cheat the workingman." [91]
McKinley also moved Reed. The Speaker disliked the Ohioan, but
hated free silver and Bryan more. He mercilessly hammered the Democrats, and subtly criticized everyone but himself. "He stirs the blood,
he stimulates the fancy, he actually flatters men by making them believe they have weak minds," a reporter noted.[92]

McKinley heard all advice, saw all callers. "I was more struck than
ever with his mask," John Hay wrote after an interview. "It was a
genuine ecclesiastical face of the fifteenth century. And there are idiots

who think Mark Hanna will run him!" [93] The Major rejected appeals for local recognition that might weaken party unity. "It has been my endeavor to keep free from all factional trouble," he gently admonished a maverick New Yorker. "Upon consideration, you will, I am sure, agree with me that I cannot refuse the aid of anybody." [94]

Conservative Democrats who could not follow Bryan and free silver were in a dilemma. They bemoaned the "mournful outcome of the Chicago convention . . ." but were reluctant to form a third party.[95] Cleveland preferred quiet, but Carlisle argued "that we cannot be silent during this fierce campaign." [96] The Administration's supporters were bitter, calling silverites "repudiators," "thieves," and "liars," among other things. They clung doggedly to the hope of saving something for 1900 or later. Most agreed with Hill: "I am a Democrat still, very still." [97] Conservatives did not underestimate Bryan's appeal, or the allure of "party regularity" among men understandably reluctant to vote Republican.

The Gold Democrats solved the problem with a third party, which ranking midwesterners outlined at a Chicago conference late in July. Bragg and Vilas of Wisconsin, John M. Palmer of Illinois, and William D. Bynum of Indiana, with the Administration's support, called for a convention in Indianapolis on September 2 and 3. They had financing from banks and corporations the Republicans could not tap, and hoped to draft Carlisle, Wilson, or even the President. For a supposedly defunct and fossilized group, the Gold Democrats displayed a remarkable vitality—even distemper. Few Populists could beat their oratorical style, or improve on their adjectives. Speakers belied elegant clothes and cultivated manners with ferocious assaults on Bryan, "an untried man, a demagogue, a word-juggler." They promised a hard-fought rear-guard action, with a platform that endorsed the gold standard, Cleveland's Administration, tariff reform, and law and order.[98]

Cleveland bluntly refused any kind of draft. "My judgement and personal inclinations are so unalterably opposed to your suggestion that I cannot for a moment entertain it," he wired an enthusiastic supporter.[99] The convention then named John M. Palmer for President, and Kentucky's former CSA General Simon Bolivar Buckner for Vice-President. Cleveland thought the result "a delicious infusion of fresh air." [100] Palmer's nomination pleased Republicans who subsidized Gold Democrats in Kentucky, West Virginia, Delaware, and other areas where a third party might tip the scales to McKinley. Independents and aging Mugwumps like Carl Schurz also spoke for sound money.

Cleveland remained publicly aloof, but helped the Gold Democrats behind the scenes, and he continued to purge doubtful followers. When Hoke Smith thought it better to have Bryan and white rule than a Republican victory, Cleveland accepted his resignation from the Cabinet with a cutting comment: "I suppose much was said about the 'local situation' in 1860." [101] Palmer and Buckner behaved like genuine candidates, touring the South and West in style, making colorful speeches and evincing good humor. Opponents styled the National Democracy "Yellow Bellies," "The McKinley Aid Society," "that little Indianapolis ticket," and "Hannarchists." [102] They got a mixed reception. Secretary Carlisle's former constituents in Covington, Kentucky, rotten-egged him. Colleagues feared anew for Cleveland's life. Palmer and Buckner often met jeering crowds at their train stops, and Palmer elaborately packed and smoked a corncob pipe while awaiting silence. Opponents beat on tin pans, blew whistles, shouted epithets, and thrust up huge pictures of Bryan, while the cheerful candidates waved to imaginary friends. The elderly statesmen spoke in Richmond, Mobile, Baltimore, Chicago, and to a cheering throng in Madison Square Garden. It was a brave effort, but did not match the style which Bryan and "new Democrats" displayed.

Bryan's campaign organized diffuse but powerful public yearnings in the midst of continuing depression. His youth, underdog role, the argument that inflation meant good times, and efforts to revive the Democracy endeared him to many who would not have noticed him in other campaign years. To millions, both pro and con, his nomination seemed "like the swinging of a firebrand in a powder mill." [103] Nearly every appearance produced a huge throng that intently followed his argument, gleaning catchwords and glittering phrases from arguments about mint ratios and silver values. The country was angry, nervous, eager for a release from tension. Bryan appealed the only way he could; not to intellect but to emotion. He was always the good evangelist, probably more interested in creating opinion than in power. He trusted the common man as deeply as he distrusted expertise and wealth. "There are plenty of good heads in this country," he insisted. "Education has multiplied intelligence; but I am looking for the man whose heart is sound and true." [104]

In a very real sense, Bryan was always an amateur, while McKinley was the professional politician. The desire for actual power is the professional's distinguishing mark, while the amateur prefers attention. Bryan never overcame the handicap of seeming transitory. To more liberal critics, he "could only run, stir up a fuss and fall back. His value was that of ambassador of the rural crowd." [105] The sense that America must choose between the agrarian past and industrial future made Bryan an ideal spokesman of transitional confusion. The astute young Willa Cather of Nebraska put it well: "So I think William Jennings Bryan synthesizes the entire middle west; all its newness and vigor; its magnitude and monotony; its richness and lack of variety; its inflammability and volubility; its strength and its crudeness; its high seriousness and self-confidence; its egotism and its nobility." [106]

Whatever the final judgment, Bryan brought more unity and success to his party than any other Democrat could have done, as he proved in a campaign tour that capitalized on his freshness in American politics. Returning home from Chicago, he thought of a tour to compensate for lack of funds and to cover the party's divisions. By September, his career seemed an unending progress through cheering crowds. Critics sneered at "this Baby Demosthenes," but huge audiences rewarded his efforts. He bore up well under a grueling routine, without a staff to manage scheduling, speech-writing, and briefings on local conditions. He slept almost anywhere, though speaking as often as thirty-six times a day. He sometimes ate six daily meals, and enjoyed a gin rubdown that served the double purpose of driving people from the car and relaxing his muscles. Like all good politicians, he enjoyed crowds, whose eagerness kept his speeches at a compelling level, though their substance naturally declined with time. He attended the inevitable picnics, barbecues, and fairs, and shook innumerable hands. Women held up babies to see him pass, and children crowded forward to touch him.

Bryan and his subordinates crisscrossed the South and West, and journeyed east to "the enemy's country" in early August. He would offset a rural reputation by accepting the nomination with a major speech in Madison Square Garden. The train stopped in Canton, where he and Bland shook hands with a startled McKinley. The Major was courteous, but could not resist a professional remark. "Bland, you should have been nominated; you were the logical candidate and the strongest man your party had." The Missourian could only shrug. "I am satisfied if my party is." [107]

The New York appearance was a fiasco. Bryan and Sewall were both tired, blazing heat engulfed the city, and Bryan disappointed eastern followers by reading a set-piece riddled with statistics and clichés. The scrape of departing feet drowned his justly famous voice, and he earned the derisive nickname, "Boy Reader of the Platte." [108] He did as poorly elsewhere in the East. Yale hecklers made him lose his temper and call them parasites and idle rich, but the colorful and tense incidents covered a deeper truth. Bryan had little if any appeal to labor and conservative immigrant groups. His eastern tour only fortified his image as a rural spokesman. None but the already converted seemed willing to follow a new man, free silver, and tariff reform.

The ever-pressing problem of party unity nagged managers and candidates behind the campaign tours and prepared speeches. The silver Republicans were in an awkward position; many could not accept Bryan's low tariff views, and all risked ostracism no matter who won. They were men without parties, disappointed now at their small influence in Bryan's crusade, fearful of becoming "the subject of the combined attack of the Democrats and Populists and McKinley Republicans," as Senator Teller early wrote Bryan.[109] But Democratic managers would not give them a voice in strategy, and party ties were so strong that few of the western Republicans admitted changing allegiance. "I am not a Democrat because I vote for Bryan," Teller said.[110]

All this was simple compared to cooperating with Populists. Moderates like Marion Butler worked out fusion tickets in most states, but no one was sure how victorious electors would actually vote in November. Westerners generally supported union, and quarreled sharply with southern opponents, adding to the confusion and costing energy spent on campaigning. Tom Watson and the vice-presidency were naturally the center of heated debate. Sewall would not leave the ticket no matter what Watson and the Populists said; Senator Jones, directing the ramshackle campaign, was more blunt. As an Arkansas Democrat, he disliked the Populists, and was tired of pacifying Watson. "They [the Populists] will go with the Negroes, where they belong. . . . Mr. Sewall will, of course, remain on the ticket, and Mr. Watson can do what he likes." [111]

Watson attacked Sewall as a gold bug in disguise, oppressor of his workers, and phony reformer. "He is a wart on the party. He is a knot on the log, he is a dead weight to the ticket." [112] Watson argued that Democratic treatment of Populists during the campaign only presaged what would follow victory. "They say we must fuse, but their idea of fusion is that we play minnow while they play trout; we play June-bug while they play duck; we play Jonah while they play the whale." [113] He disliked the inflation panacea, and feared defeat would doom the Populist program. He often started speeches explaining that he would not "make a little two-by-four silver speech." While many shrill voices agreed with him, the radicals never overcame their party's general desire to win with Bryan.

As if the Populists and Silver Republicans were not embarrassing and time-consuming enough, many of the "new Democrats" alienated voters with lurid charges and threats. Ben Tillman toured with his imaginary pitchfork, telling audiences that if the Democrats won, no judge who ruled against farmers and workingmen would be safe. Amid the disorder, a graphic poem made its way in roughly Shakespearean form: [114]

> Double, double, toil and trouble,
> Fire burn and cauldron bubble,
> Extract from a speech of Hoke,
> His consistency's no joke,
> Fork of Tillman, sock of Jerry,
> Peffer's whiskers, Sewall's ferry-
> Boat's that plow the sad salt waters,
> Blood from Waite's bootlegs and halters,
> Carl Browne's cartoons, Coxey's boomers,
> Mrs. Lease's blood-red bloomers,
> Crown of thorns and cross of gold,
> A tale of platform now is told.
> Double, double, toil and trouble,
> Chicago's platform's but a bubble!

Confusion and cross-purposes cost Bryan both sympathy and votes. Many potential supporters thought him better than his helpers. He was a man of good intentions, but parties ruled in America, and he must inevitably reward followers. Would Tillman sit in the Cabinet? Could Watson preside over the Senate? Would Populists direct Congress? Perhaps Altgeld would represent America at the Court of St. James's? Confusion and undirected energies in Bryan's coalition convinced many Americans that whatever his designs or intentions, he could not govern.

Lack of funds also handicapped the sketchy Democratic organization. Silver-mine owners paid much of Bryan's expenses, but could not equal Hanna's resources. Audiences donated nickels and dimes, but at one point tons of literature lay stacked in warehouses because the national committee could not pay freight charges. Democrats complained loudly that a flood of ill-gotten money smoothed McKinley's path, a charge sure to stick in case of defeat. The Republicans were undeniably affluent, but Bryan's managers used their estimated $500,000 campaign fund to good effect. The public had every chance to see and hear Bryan. His train traveled 18,000 miles, and he spoke nearly 600 times to an estimated 5,000,000 people in 27 states. Newspaper coverage, local organizations, and other Democratic leaders added impetus in every part of the country. There was no blackout against him.

Few observers denied Bryan's effectiveness as he crossed the country, shrewdly repeating the easily remembered phrases that brought him fame. He wove a concerted campaign against industrial America around the slogans of free silver, increased personal action, and the money power's alleged injustices. While he vainly tried to win voters outside the agrarian constituency, William McKinley was indulging in some highly effective personalism.

Bryan's tour and silver's obvious appeals worried Mark Hanna. He knew McKinley preferred a sober campaign stressing Republican responsibility, but in those first nervous days of June and July, when anything seemed possible, he suggested that McKinley take to the campaign trail. "We have got to get McKinley out on the road to meet this thing, and I wish you would go out to him . . . and map out a campaign for him," he told Herrick. Other advisers urged McKinley not to keep silent, but the Major was adamant, and shrewd. "Don't you remember that I announced that I would not under any circumstances go on a speechmaking tour?" he asked rather testily. "If I should go now it would be an acknowledgement of weakness. Moreover, I might just as well put up a trapeze on my front lawn and compete with some professional athlete as go out speaking against Bryan. I have to *think* when I speak." [115] He could not beat Bryan in the role of underdog. "If I took a whole train, Bryan would take a sleeper; if I took a chair car, he would ride a freight train." [116] It would be wiser to let Bryan bore the public. McKinley would stay in Canton, unruffled and dignified, the essence of experienced and responsible politics, while party organizers spread the GOP message with literature and other speakers. He left Canton for only three days during the campaign, to fill pre-convention speaking agreements.

The answer was a front-porch campaign, patterned after Harrison's successful effort in 1888. Though McKinley was wary of its dangers, he soon accepted the idea of visiting delegations. Each could return home with stories of the exciting pilgrimage, and redouble local campaign efforts. Any group could visit Canton simply by writing to make arrangements. The staff digested the organization's history, listed its visiting members, and arranged transportation. McKinley surprised visitors by knowing their names and family background. A felicitous inquiry about a wife's health, a chance remark about a delegation leader's son in school, an inquiry about affairs in some rural district all endeared him to the faithful who milled about the steps.

Delegation leaders often talked with McKinley in private before bringing their group, or sent the substance of their plans. He asked what they proposed to say. "Oh, anything that comes to mind," they usually replied. Ever mindful of 1884's three R's, the Major tactfully suggested that he approve their speech in advance. This also let him write a short response, tailored to each delegation and its locale. He dictated dozens of these talks, striding up and down the study, smoking constantly, seeking just the right words. No one ghost-wrote anything for him, and the whole process made his brief, pithy, front-porch speeches highly effective. They combined personal appeal and national issues, and were good reading as pamphlets and newspaper reports.

When a delegation appeared after marching up a crowded and colorful Market Street, it waited in awkward respect at the legendary porch. Cheers rent the air when McKinley stepped through the door and waved. The delegation spokesman talked while McKinley listened raptly, "like a child looking at Santa Claus." The assembled faithful watched the famous man and his house, while some took pictures with cumbersome black boxes. When the speaker finished, McKinley mounted a chair or decorated box, and replied vigorously. He then shook hands as guests filed across the porch, through the house, and went out the back door toward a waiting train.

Canton's public facilities expanded to meet the emergency. Restaurants and hot-dog stands multiplied; souvenir shops did a booming business. A whole staff of professional greeters and timetable artists provided bands and trains. Railroads offered special fares and extra runs. The city had to repave the streets and the Major's home almost vanished. The front yard looked as if "a herd of buffalo had passed that way," and pilgrims pried off so much wood that the house almost collapsed. The picket fence was long since gone, and grass went into scrapbooks like pressed flowers. On rainy days, a special "tabernacle" hosted visitors. McKinley had only to glance out the window to see yet another delegation of teachers, iron puddlers, school children, businessmen, or dock workers coming down the street, trumpets blaring. Between June 19 and November 2, he spoke over 300 times to 750,000 people from 30 states. In a single day, 16 delegations came from 12 states.

He repeated three basic themes to the audiences: Free silver would be inflationary, and threaten everyone's income and savings; prosperity rested on a Republican tariff policy for the home market, with an expanding export trade; the Democrats spoke for narrow class interests at a time when nationalism and political unity were vital. "We have but one political party which is united, and that is ours," he insisted, emphasizing Democratic dissension.[117] He persuasively argued that inflation threatened workers without corresponding benefits. They had no large debts to pay, and would pay increased prices for foodstuffs and fibers. "This money question presents itself to me in this homely fashion," he told one group: [118]

> If free coinage of silver means a fifty-three cent dollar, then it is not an honest dollar. If free coinage means a one hundred cent dollar equal to a gold dollar, as some of its advocates assert, we will not, then, have cheap dollars, but dollars just like those we now have, and which will be as hard to get. In which case free coinage will not help the debtor or make it easier for him to pay his debts.

He emphasized the basic fear of inflation that troubled many. "We do not propose to vote in favor of money, the value of which you have got to ascertain every morning by consulting the market columns in the newspaper." [119] Nor did he overlook the moral aspect, of equal concern to most Americans. Every debt should be honestly paid. The problem was how to start up the economic system; final political settlement of which party was to rule would restore confidence. He appealed for unity, and did not sound insincere, in view of his own origins and the GOP's past programs: [120]

> My countrymen, the most un-American of all appeals observable in this campaign is the one which seeks to array labor against capital, employer against employed. It is most unpatriotic and is fraught with the greatest peril to all concerned. We are all political equals here— equal in privilege and opportunity, dependent upon each other, and the prosperity of the one is the prosperity of the other.

This was effective among a people unwilling to believe in social classes, and stressing the virtues of individual competition.

Elsewhere, lesser campaigns developed the themes he enunciated in Canton. The Negro vote received special attention in Border states. A group of colorful superannuated Union veterans toured in a private car. Even the ladies came in special delegations, and one feminine visitor paid a high compliment: "I think Major McKinley is just lovely!" [121] McKinley carefully watched all campaign details, and Hanna's organization made no major decision without his knowledge and consent.

In August, he released the obligatory Letter of Acceptance that quickly became a popular pamphlet. It was a concise, forceful document, especially applicable to workers and wavering farmers. He stood firmly on the gold plank, and pledged himself to seek international bimetallism. In the meantime, he argued, the country could not go it alone. Bryan's election would produce a severe panic of indefinite duration, and weaken the dollar's power. He aimed most shots at inflation's effects on Americans:

> No one suffers so much from cheap money as the farmers and laborers. They are the first to feel its bad effects and the last to recover from them. . . . It [inflation] would fall with alarming severity upon investments already made, upon insurance companies and their policy holders, and upon savings banks and their depositors, upon building and loan associations and their members, upon the savings of thrift, upon pensioners and their families, and upon wage earners and the purchasing power of their wages.

He promised to settle the tariff question, and seek overseas markets through the reciprocity his name symbolized.[122] His firmness impressed gold advocates and bimetallists, and sowed doubt among some of silver's friends.

By September, the Republican campaign was stalling the silver drive. McKinley was right. Full organization, party harmony, a campaign of education with the printed and spoken word would more than counteract Bryan's thin emotional appeals. Notes of defeat already entered the private musings of some silverites. "I think [Bryan] is doing well," Senator Teller said, "and we are at least reaching the people and creating in their minds a spirit of inquiry that in the end will be valuable, even if this campaign results disastrously."[123]

In October, McKinley began to emphasize protection, and urged workers not to disrupt the industrial system with continued tariff agitation. A month before the election, polls in New York City showed that unskilled workers followed Bryan, but clerks, railway and shipping employees, and skilled workers were more Republican.[124] Bryan dismissed the tariff in his letter of acceptance, arguing that the currency overrode all other issues, but the home market idea appealed strongly to established farmers and producers of raw materials like wool, hides, ores, and specialty crops, even in the pro-silver West. McKinley reinforced that idea to almost every delegation that trampled his lawn. At his orders, speakers in agricultural areas touted protection, and the "Advance Agent of Prosperity." Every audience must "talk tariff, think tariff, dream tariff."[125] Upturns in exports and investment helped Republicans talk about returning prosperity that Bryan's victory would wreck.

This appeal was more effective than most observers realized. Mc-

Kinley knew protection could hold many who leaned toward silver: ". . . thousands of men who are somewhat tinctured with free silver ideas will keep within the Republican party, and will support the Republican nominee because of the fact that they are protectionists." [126] Prosperous farmers feared inflation's effects, and protection may have determined their allegiance. An astute visiting English observer noted this while touring the Old Northwest, where farmers producing poultry, dairy and meat products, and fresh vegetables were moving back to the GOP. "They are just depressed enough to want a change in the tariff, and just prosperous enough to shrink from upsetting the whole financial system of the country. McKinley offers change, but not too big a change, and so McKinley it is." Rising wheat exports, and other stirrings in agricultural markets convinced many farmers that prosperity was returning.[127]

Exhausted Republican managers saw victory in sight. Maine's big margin in her fall election raised hopes, and pollsters and newsmen detected a rising McKinley tide. McKinley continued his full speaking schedule until Election Day. Whatever the result, no one could say that either party had evaded the issues. The American people would know, as seldom before, just what they voted for or against.

November brought both renewed tension and universal relief that the campaign was ending. General Palmer told Gold Democrats he would not "consider it any very great fault if you decide next Tuesday to cast your ballot for William McKinley, . . ." [128] Bryan returned to Lincoln. On Election Day, the Major rose early and walked with his brother Abner some four blocks to the polling place, where they stood in line behind a group of workers to cast their ballots. McKinley met Hanna at the train station later in the day. As they set off for lunch and congratulations, the national chairman seemed "rosy, breezy, like a commercial traveller" to newsmen.[129] Special wires brought early returns to the Major, who smoked away the evening in his library. He occasionally took glad tidings to his anxious wife, and chatted with a small group of friends while aides tabulated figures. The early trends released pent-up tensions. Hanna predicted over 300 electoral votes.

McKinley sat at his desk all night, digesting returns and making notes for future reference. Cigar after cigar went into the ash tray. The sounds of hurrying feet reminded him of the months of tension and careful organization that produced this evening's results. Neighbors passed the house to serenade, cheer, or wave. Midnight came, and his lead solidified into victory. He pencilled on light green stationery the digits "241," the number of apparently safe electoral votes. An impressive victory was developing. The states from North Dakota to Maine were apparently his, including Delaware, Maryland, West Virginia, and most of Kentucky's divided electoral votes. In the West, he would carry Oregon and 8 of California's 9 votes. It was a safe majority in both popular and electoral counts.

A different story unfolded in Lincoln, Nebraska. A last night of campaigning preceded Bryan's return, and he was clearly exhausted. His children ran in and out of the room while he relaxed in a velvet smoking jacket with a pink carnation in the buttonhole. Loyal neighbors intermittently passed the house, singing jolly songs to cover apparent defeat. He had fought the good fight in what he termed "The First Battle." He almost feared victory. "If they elect McKinley, I will feel a great burden lifted off my shoulders." He was also realistic, later remarking: "I regard it in some respects as fortunate that I was not elected, considering the fact that for four years I would have been confronted by a gold Congress. No free silver bill would have been passed. My hands would have been tied." [130] He did not relish defeat, but planned to control the party and work for free silver and a reform program. In after-years, he recalled with pride that he polled 6,000,000 votes in his first campaign at the age of thirty-six.

An excited nation watched returns all night, for by common consent this was the most critical election since 1860. Western and southern farmers stamped in anger against the Money Power. Distinguished gentlemen in Wall Street sighed with relief. In Times Square, boisterous crowds magnified an attitude and performance common to nearly every city and town, blowing horns and ringing bells, reeling toward solace or celebration on rubber legs. A certain humor accompanied partisanship. In one small town, a triumphant Republican chided opposition ignorance by shouting that the Argentine Republic had gone for McKinley. "It's a d———d lie," a local Democrat answered, "for we just got word that it went for Bryan." [131]

After a brief but refreshing sleep, McKinley rose the next day to face Canton's pride and cheers. The posters, bunting, rutted street, and barren lawn seemed suddenly dated as he took his mother a bouquet of roses. Later in the day, he sorted through congratulatory telegrams, including an effusion from Buffalo Bill. On November 5, Bryan conceded defeat, though his managers charged that fraudulent returns and corruption elected McKinley. "We have submitted the issues to the American people, and their word is law," Bryan wired. At his home, he told reporters: "The fight has just commenced." [132]

Canton was not interested, as it indulged in fireworks, victory speeches, and a final rush on McKinley's home.

The President-elect was frankly tired. Critics charged that he stayed comfortably at home, receiving rigged delegations, while agents herded voters into his column with questionable means. This was false. His own calmness, and the organization's smooth efficiency only made the campaign seem easy. His hands ached, his throat was sore, his mind was tired from months of exertion. Now, an almost unnatural sense of relief and quiet filled the country. The "Battle of the Standards," so squarely joined and bitterly fought, was over.

A post-mortem inevitably followed. McKinley's 271 electoral votes to Bryan's 176, and his 7,100,000 popular votes to the Democrat's 6,500,000 provided a firm margin. Each candidate received more popular votes than any predecessor in his party. The total increase over 1892 indicated voter interest and party organization on all levels. McKinley was the first candidate since Grant to receive a clear national majority, but it was not a landslide. Republicans retained the national House, with 203 members to the Democrats' 121, and 21 Populists, with a few scattering. However, the new Senate would have 44 Republicans, 34 Democrats, 5 Populists, 6 Silverites and 1 Independent. Only McKinley's extraordinary skill as a political manager could control his first Congress.

Bryan calculated that 4,500,000 Democrats, 1,500,000 Populists, and 500,000 silverite Republicans voted his ticket, but like Jones, Altgeld, and many other Democrats, he believed the Republicans carried critical states by force and fraud. The "ifs" naturally fascinated him. A change of 962 votes in California, 1,059 in Oregon, 142 in Kentucky, 9,002 in Indiana, 2,826 in North Dakota, and 5,445 in West Virginia would have given him victory with 224 electoral votes. He thought the election results did not repudiate free silver. Republicans could play the numbers game with equal skill: McKinley lost North Carolina, Tennessee, and Virginia by about 19,000 votes each. Full Negro voting would undoubtedly have given him all three. Nebraska went to Bryan by a mere 12,000 votes and Kansas by only 14,000. McKinley lost South Dakota by about 200 votes, and Wyoming by about 300, indicating the effectiveness of his appeal and organization even in Bryan country.

McKinley's other margins were impressive. New England gave him two-thirds of her vote. He compiled large majorities in the mid-Atlantic states, and easily carried all five states of the Old Northwest. Within the context of state victories, he led in urban-industrial areas and among prosperous farmers. In states which Bryan carried, like Nebraska and Missouri, McKinley scored heavily in cities. Though Bryan did better than expected in northeastern cities, he captured only 40.61 per cent of the national urban vote, and 48.34 per cent of the rural vote. Prosperous farmers did not follow his lead; nor did conservative immigrant groups. McKinley's pledge to seek an international silver agreement kept many people in the GOP.[133] The belt of states around the Great Lakes, now partners in the established industrial system, voted for gold, protection, and Republican nationalism.

Democrats filled the papers with charges that Republicans intimidated voters. Factory owners told workers not to report if Bryan won; some mortgage companies either extended credit or threatened to curtail it. The business community's more shrill spokesmen saw anarchy, bloodshed, and total economic collapse in the wake of a Bryan victory. Employers undoubtedly tried to influence voters, but threats did not bring labor to McKinley. Few workers believed that businessmen would actually close their plants if Bryan won, but they could readily believe his victory would bring a crash, with unpredictable results. Labor frankly suspected agrarian rule, feared inflation, favored protection, and, like everyone else, wanted to settle the long-boiling political problem. Labor simply had little in common with Bryan's agrarian interests. Free silver appealed only to distressed farmers; there seemed no chance that Bryan could enact the rest of his program. The country had had enough of stalemate politics—and intimidation worked both ways. White Democrats and Populists obviously kept Negroes from the polls. Bribery, threats, and force were not strangers to Democratic city machines. As in past elections, these shady practices did not determine national victory.

Many observers praised the Gold Democrats for siphoning off Democrats in borderline states that went for McKinley, but this was an exaggeration. Palmer and Buckner provided a conscientious refuge for Democrats who otherwise would have voted for McKinley or stayed home. Their presence in the field testified more to the era's intense party loyalty than to actual influence.

Bryan naturally made mistakes, and drew some undeserved criticism. Many disliked the company he kept. He was sincere, and silver might be a good thing, but could he really govern? One midwesterner spoke for many people: "I like Bryan, but being honest, he will pay his debts to Altgeld, Tillman, Stone, Peffer, Cyclone Davis, and that crowd, and that will bankrupt him and the country, [and] therefore I will not vote for him." [134] Bryan also over-stressed free silver, as Hanna shrewdly saw: "He's talking silver all the time, and that's where we've got him . . . ." [135] While this obscured other issues and let Republicans attack him as a shallow one-idea man, Bryan could do little else to unify his coalition. The facts of political life imprisoned him, however willingly.

McKinley's brilliant generalship, the GOP's depth of organization, and skillful propagandizing, confirmed the party's cohesion and power to govern. Hanna had a simple formula for success: "I have kept them moving, kept them moving all the while. I have not given them a moment's rest." [136] McKinley conducted a remarkably effective campaign, whose echoes reached every corner of the country from his busy porch. He symbolized prosperity, boasted a long career as a constructive moderate from a major state, and was a shrewd analyst of political strength and weakness. He was a formidable and popular contender, who did not miss a step throughout the intense campaign.

The results confirmed the long-term trends clearly forecast in 1894. The Republicans did not win by bribing voters, threatening workers, or unfairly crushing opposition. They elected McKinley and laid the basis for a generation of national rule because the party deserved victory. The GOP triumphed on its past record, present proposals, and obvious ability to represent an industrial constituency of business, diversified agriculture, labor, and the professional middle class. After an intensive campaign devoted as much to reading, reason, and discussion as to emotion, a majority of the people endorsed Republican policies. Following a generation of bitter struggle, Republican nationalism triumphed at the polls. The GOP had come to stay.

☆☆☆☆☆☆ ☆☆☆☆☆☆ ☆☆☆☆☆☆☆☆☆☆

Conclusion

☆☆☆☆☆☆ ☆☆☆☆☆☆ ☆☆☆☆☆☆☆☆☆☆

Like his predecessors, William McKinley spent a winter forming an administration, but Americans were interested more in the working nationalism he symbolized than in his advisers. Concern about patronage did not decline among politicians, but the public was less intrigued than in 1860 or 1880. "The Advance Agent of Prosperity" fulfilled his party's promise in the years that followed, as the GOP became synonymous with expansive well-being. Prosperity, overseas expansion, a growing feeling of national pride and destiny illuminated McKinley's administration, and solidified Republican control of national politics. McKinley enlarged the new GOP coalition with extraordinary political skill, creating public support for new policies, and symbolizing harmonious times when almost every American could logically aspire to his particular dream of success.

The "New Democracy" around William Jennings Bryan seemed no better than the old elements that followed Grover Cleveland. It drifted, clinging passionately to ideas the people rejected. The free silver crusade blended into an opaque anti-imperialism, with equal results. Democrats still seemed concerned with issues and programs fitting a minority of the public's desires. Younger Democrats seemed frustrated, older ones bewildered. "The Democratic party as we knew it, is dead," Abram S. Hewitt wrote in 1900.[1]

The Democratic party only seemed to change its leadership and ideology with Bryan's accession. It remained heavily grounded in the South, devoted to agrarian interests, with marginal support from a few immigrant groups and laissez-faire businessmen who distrusted the national government. The dominant tone was still negativism, a belief in small government. The dogmas of localism, retrenchment, and antifederalism reigned as the Democracy dozed through the warm prosperity and growing nationalism of the McKinley-Roosevelt years. Despite the brief Wilson interregnum, Republicanism remained triumphant until it failed to solve a great depression. The Crash of 1929 re-shaped the Democratic party, which shone by comparison with a disordered GOP and because of Franklin D. Roosevelt's charisma and programs.

Fierce political struggles in the years between Hayes and McKinley produced this national party system, which paralleled similar national consolidation in economics, technology, and diplomacy. The total process changed each party and both parties within a national system. Republicans faced and mastered problems in their own house, best illustrated in the submergence of powerful local bosses like Roscoe Conkling into a national party structure and loyalty. Republicans learned to unify, organize, and harmonize diverse followers with issues like tariff protection, federal economic regulation, and the currency.

Elections after 1896 confirmed the trends that produced McKinley's first victory. The Congress chosen in 1898 remained Republican, and the party's margins grew with the twentieth century as people embraced expansion in all sectors of life and Theodore Roosevelt used the presidency's publicity to his party's advantage. Except Kentucky, every state McKinley carried in 1896 remained Republican until 1912. After decades of struggling to survive, the GOP seemed a permanent majority party. During those halcyon days, a youth could mature outside the South without knowing there was another party, and the GOP seemed as natural as the heavens to Ohio's young Brand Whitlock. "It was merely a synonym for patriotism, another name for the nation. . . . It was inconceivable that any self-respecting person should be a Democrat." [2]

Few people foretold that result in 1865 or 1877; a generation of hard work and commitment made it so. The appeal of local rule was very strong, and distrust of Republican federalism dominated the sidewalks of New York and back-country Alabama with equal force. But Republicans captured the new industrial constituency in cities and towns, consisting of businessmen, professionals, prosperous farmers, and skilled workers. The party leadership devised a system of organization that made every active voter feel important within a grand design.

The campaigns, laws, and events that marked this progress toward a functioning party system were hectic and colorful. Politics seemed deadlocked only to those who failed to understand the tension of creating a new constituency and ideology. Republicans triumphed in some measure because Democrats looked backward and rejected industrial America. Republican spokesmen were attuned to the era's changes. Drawn from the professions, education, business, and journalism, these men represented the larger masses of people eager to rise in an expanding system.

Republicans were remarkably effective within the publicly accepted ethic of the day. The party believed in federal spending for projects of regional and national importance. Republicans championed Negro rights while there seemed a chance to succeed, and rewarded Negroes with patronage and official recognition while Democrats trapped the freedmen in segregation. A few businessmen talked of nonexistent laissez-faire concepts, but Republican politicians were busy funding the national economy's major sectors. These policies developed western territories, expanded markets and transportation systems, opened vast areas to settlement, and outlined a national system for future growth.[3] As many people sensed in 1896, the settlement of who was to govern —agrarian or industrial interests—helped stabilize the industrial system that emerged in the 1880's, and triumphed in the 1890's.

Practicing politicians, like lesser mortals, do not live with theories and speculation, but men like William McKinley felt that a major phase of American political history matured in their lifetime. Responsible national party government was at last functioning after a century of bitter partisan struggle. That system would create and support both the legislative machinery and emotional attitudes for increased governmental action. From that generation nationalized politics was a crucial legacy which would touch every aspect of American life.

FALSTAFF MARSHALS HIS RAGGED REGIMENT.

"Falstaff" Cleveland rallies a motley army for the campaign of 1892. (*Judge*, June 18, 1892.)

Secretary of State Walter Q. Gresham. (Library of Congress.)

Secretary of State Richard Olney at his desk. (Library of Congress.)

Vice-President Adlai E. Stevenson, Chicago, 1893, (Library of Congress.)

HARPER'S WEEKLY

A JOURNAL OF CIVILIZATION

Vol. XXXVIII.—No. 1939.
Copr. 1894 by Harper & Brothers
All Rights Reserved

NEW YORK, SATURDAY, FEBRUARY 17, 1894.

CENTS A COPY
DOLLARS A YE

William L. Wilson, father of the Wilson Tariff Bill of 1894, at his House desk.
(*Harper's Weekly,* Feb. 17, 1894.)

Richard P. "Silver Dick" Bland of Missouri at his desk in the House. (*Harper's Weekly*, March 24, 1894.)

Senator Arthur Pue Gorman, moderate from Maryland, co-author of the Wilson-Gorman Act. (Library of Congress.)

David B. Hill, Governor of New York, 1885–91. (New York State Library.)

A cartoonist depicts the mountain of Cleveland bringing forth the mouse of a compromise tariff bill in 1894. (*Judge*, June 16, 1894.)

James B. Weaver, Populist presidential candidate, 1892. (Library of Congress.)

"We Demand Nothing but Justice." Typical members of "Kelly's Army" as they marched t Washington in the spring of 1894. (*Harper's Weekly*, May 5, 1894.)

Uncle Sam steps on "General" Coxey with the boot of Law and Order. (*Judge*, May 12, 1894.)

Scene of destruction in the Railroad Yards in Chicago during the Pullman Strike of 1894. (*Harper's Weekly,* July 21, 1894.)

"Too big a job for the little tugs." The Cleveland Administration's promised good times are stuck on the mudbank of insolvency. (*Judge*, May 4, 1895.)

Ignatius Donnelly, pugnacious Populist. (Minnesota Historical Society.)

Mary E. Lease, "The Kansas Pythoness." (Kansas State Historical Society.)

THOMAS E. WATSON, OF GEORGIA,
Populist Candidate for Vice-President.

Tom Watson, Georgia Populist. A popular campaign picture. (Library of Congress.)

"The Eagle Forgotten." John Peter Altgeld, Governor of Illinois, 1892–96. (Illinois Historical Library.)

William Jennings Bryan campaigning, c. 1896. (Library of Congress.)

The "Popogriff," symbol of the new Populist-Democratic alliance. (*Judge*, Oct. 24, 1896.)

"Boy Bryan on the Burning Deck." (*Judge*, Aug. 8, 1896.)

John Palmer, Gold Standard Democrat presidential candidate, 1896. (Illinois Historical Library.)

Marcus A. Hanna, influential Ohio politician and presidential adviser. (Ohio State Historical Library and Library of Congress.)

"HOW CAN HE LOSE ME?"

A typical anti-McKinley cartoon from the *New York Journal*, Oct. 18, 1896. (Library of Congress.)

Candidate McKinley addresses a crowd from the famous
front porch, 1896. (Ohio Historical Society Library.)

The Faithful parade down Market Street in Canton, 1896. (Ohio Historical Society Library.)

Ladies' Day at Canton in 1896, with Major and Mrs. McKinley in center. (Ohio Historical Society Library.)

Mother McKinley (center), Ida McKinley, and William McKinley entertain a visiting delegation in 1896. (Ohio Historical Society Library.)

William Jennings Bryan (left), and Mrs. Bryan (right), greet supporters from the platform of the campaign train, 1896. (Library of Congress.)

Key to Abbreviations

CR	*Congressional Record*
DPL	Detroit Public Library
DUL	Duke University Library
HML	Rutherford B. Hayes Memorial Library, Fremont, Ohio
HPSO	Historical and Philosophical Society of Ohio, Cincinnati
HSP	Historical Society of Pennsylvania, Philadelphia
IHS	Indiana Historical Society, Indianapolis
ISHL	Illinois State Historical Library, Springfield
ISDHA	Iowa State Department of History and Archives, Des Moines
LC	Library of Congress, Manuscripts Division
MHC	Michigan History Collection, Ann Arbor
MHS	Massachusetts Historical Society, Boston
NA	National Archives
NHHS	New Hampshire Historical Society, Concord
NHS	Nevada Historical Society, Reno
NUL	Northwestern University Library
NYHS	New York Historical Society
NYPL	New York Public Library
OHS	Ohio Historical Society, Columbus
SCHS	Stark County Historical Society, Canton, Ohio
SHSC	State Historical Society of Colorado, Denver
SHSW	State Historical Society of Wisconsin, Madison
SUL	Syracuse University Library
THC	Texas History Collection, Austin
UNCL	University of North Carolina Library
UPL	University of Pennsylvania Library

WLCL   William L. Clements Library, Ann Arbor
WRHS   Western Reserve Historical Society, Cleveland
WVUL   West Virginia University Library

Note: Manuscript collections are designated by the subject's name, followed by the abbreviation for the papers' location; e.g., Hayes HML means Rutherford B. Hayes papers, Hayes Memorial Library.

Bibliographical Note

The footnotes reveal my sources and suggest further reading on specific points, but a few brief remarks on recent parallel works may help the reader.

Primary Sources

Any adequate study of the Gilded Age must rest on primary materials, especially in political history. Manuscripts are voluminous but often frustrating. Major figures like William McKinley, James G. Blaine, and Thomas B. Reed left few or fragmentary papers. Southerners and westerners did not usually retain much correspondence. Some powerful men like William B. Allison left large collections of uneven value. The ease of transportation and communication was already letting politicians avoid written records and the private understanding appealed to a generation of men always uncertain of their political fates. Collections like those of Rutherford B. Hayes, Grover Cleveland, Benjamin Harrison, John Sherman, and Thomas F. Bayard are the foundation for any study of party politics, public policy, and foreign affairs. Any student who works through these materials is struck by the wide range of problems that came before national leaders, and the generally well-informed way in which they met them. The notion that these politicians were indifferent or irresponsible is untrue. Debates in the *Congressional Record* for the years 1877–1896 will bear comparison with those of any other generation. On important questions like civil service reform, fiscal policy, and foreign affairs, they reveal a responsible group of leaders, whatever their differences of view.

No student of the period can overlook newspapers. The press profited from new technical improvements, better newsgathering, editing, and analysis. Coverage of world and national events was outstanding in major city dailies like the *Washington Post, Chicago Tribune,* and all New York papers. Wire services furnished news to papers in secondary cities around the country,

531

and people of that generation were probably better read than our own. The era also produced a group of influential editors and reporters, whose political information was usually correct.

General Works

It has become popular to synthesize the Gilded Age, but we still know so little about its major problems that most such efforts are unsatisfactory. The largest general study remains that of Ellis P. Oberholtzer, *A History of the United States Since the Civil War*, 5 vols. (New York: Macmillan Co., 1917–1937). Despite its length, the work is uneven and one-dimensional, useful largely as a quarry of facts. James Ford Rhodes, an important contemporary, covered the period in Volumes VII and VIII of his *History of the United States*, but that too is dated.

The most famous political study is Matthew Josephson, *The Politicos, 1865–1896* (New York: Harcourt-Brace, 1938). Though Josephson's work has influenced most textbook writers and popularizers, it is of doubtful merit. He dismissed politics as sound and fury, and his erroneous idea that nothing divided parties except spoils remains a favorite view with popularizers who dislike research. Harold Underwood Faulkner presented a more balanced but still incomplete discussion in *Politics, Reform and Expansion, 1890–1900* (New York: Harper and Brothers, 1959). Samuel P. Hays, *The Response to Industrialism, 1885–1914* (Chicago: University of Chicago Press, 1957), is an interpretive overview that has influenced a revival of interest in the Gilded Age during the last decade. Hays' argument that people and institutions responded to industrialism in the context of older ideals is sound, but the book is thin and only briefly touches politics.

Ray Ginger offered a slightly different emphasis in *Age of Excess: The United States From 1877 to 1914* (New York: Macmillan Co., 1965). About half the book interprets the late nineteenth century, focusing on culture, social behavior and discontented groups. Ginger argues that American leaders avoided domestic problems because they had no answers, and wished to find overseas outlets for the industrial system's growing surplus production. While many important people believed the nation was approaching overproduction, it is well to remember that the crisis never occurred. By 1900, such talk subsided as prosperity returned; however important the idea was to a few leaders, it did not affect many people. A strong tone of disenchantment with majority rule and popular taste flavors Ginger's work. He is best in dealing with culture, where he can sympathize with ideals and artists while condemning audiences. He is weakest in dealing with politics and diplomacy. The pungent bibliographical essay is often more acute than the text.

People in the era were deeply concerned with salvaging tested standards amid great change in all aspects of life, and Robert H. Wiebe used that theme in *The Search for Order, 1877–1920* (New York: Hill and Wang, 1967). The book presents nothing new on politics, and a purely analytical style makes it difficult to read without background. Though he offers a few useful insights, as in seeing that the country consisted of "island communities," Wiebe does not develop his major points systematically. The book is weakest on diplomacy and politics, and most interesting in discussing social thought.

Though uneven in coverage, the symposium *The Gilded Age: A Reappraisal* (Syracuse: Syracuse University Press, 1963), edited by H. Wayne Morgan, contains much information on many aspects of the period.

Biography

The biographical literature easily confounds the legend that the Gilded Age was an era of dull men and issues, and remains a major source for political historians. In alphabetical order by subject, the following books are valuable: Harry Barnard, *Eagle Forgotten: The Life of John Peter Altgeld* (Indianapolis: Bobbs-Merrill Co., 1938), is perceptive about Altgeld's personality and covers the major events of his career. Leland L. Sage, *William Boyd Allison: A Study in Practical Politics* (Iowa City: State Historical Society of Iowa, 1956), is valuable for information on national finance, presidential campaigns, and Republican politics. It does not, however, show very well just how influential Allison was in legislative or party affairs. George F. Howe, *Chester A. Arthur* (New York: Dodd, Mead and Co., 1934), is necessarily thin because of fragmentary Arthur papers.

The era's most fascinating figure, and a great party leader, James G. Blaine, awaits a genuinely exhaustive biography. Lack of papers hampers the project, and any potential biographer must understand psychology to deal well with Blaine. Gail Hamilton, *Biography of James G. Blaine* (Norwich, Conn.: Henry Bill Pub. Co., 1895), was authored under a pseudonym by a cousin, Mary Abigail Dodge. The book reproduces valuable letters and apparently reflects Blaine's views on many points. Edward Stanwood, also a kinsman, wrote a brief life, *James Gillespie Blaine* (Boston: Houghton Mifflin Co., 1905). The standard biography is David Saville Muzzey, *James G. Blaine: A Political Idol of Other Days* (New York: Dodd, Mead and Co., 1934), which suffers not so much from lack of information as from an ambivalent attitude toward Blaine.

Paolo Coletta has filled a major gap with the first volume of his biography, *William Jennings Bryan. I. Political Evangelist, 1860–1908* (Lincoln: University of Nebraska Press, 1964). Richard S. West, Jr., *Lincoln's Scapegoat General: A Life of Benjamin F. Butler, 1818–1893* (Boston: Houghton Mifflin Co., 1965), is weak on Butler's political career, a subject worth a separate monograph. James A. Barnes, *John G. Carlisle: Financial Statesman* (New York: Dodd, Mead and Co., 1931), is a major work useful for the tariff controversies of the 1880's, Democratic politics, and Cleveland's financial programs. Leon Burr Richardson, *William E. Chandler, Republican* (New York: Dodd, Mead and Co., 1940), is full of information on the Republican party.

The period's only Democratic president has received much attention. Allan Nevins, *Grover Cleveland: A Study in Courage* (New York: Dodd, Mead and Co., 1932), is a monumental work, though its too-favorable view of Cleveland has rightly been attacked. Nevins did not analyze Cleveland's failure to control the Democratic party, and accepted the doubtful proposition that he was a great president. A useful alternate view is developed in Horace Samuel Merrill, *Bourbon Leader: Grover Cleveland and the Democratic Party* (Boston: Houghton Mifflin Co., 1957).

Donald Barr Chidsey wrote an impressionistic life of Roscoe Conkling in *The Gentleman From New York* (New Haven: Yale University Press, 1935). Conkling deserves a new study, but left no significant papers, forcing students to rely on newspapers. A secondary but important senatorial figure is covered in James W. Nielson, *Shelby M. Cullom: Prairie State Republican* (Urbana: University of Illinois Press, 1962). Protestors and radicals always attract historians, and Martin Ridge has covered one of the era's most colorful and enigmatic in *Ignatius Donnelley: The Portrait of a Politician* (Chicago: University of Chicago Press, 1962). Oscar D. Lambert, *Stephen Benton Elkins* (Pittsburgh: University of Pittsburgh, 1955), is thin and unsatisfactory, the more so since Elkins left voluminous papers pertaining to both his political and business affairs.

President Garfield's career prompted a good deal of attention, and he left substantial papers useful for both Ohio and national politics. The Michigan State University Press is publishing his diary, but the basic printed source remains Theodore Clarke Smith, *The Life and Letters of James Abram Garfield*, 2 vols. (New Haven: Yale University Press, 1925), which is full of extracts from manuscripts. The standard life, Robert G. Caldwell, *James A. Garfield: Party Chieftain* (New York: Dodd, Mead and Co., 1931), is thinner, though more interpretive. Maryland's leading Democratic senator is covered in John R. Lambert, *Arthur Pue Gorman* (Baton Rouge: Louisiana State University Press, 1953). The study is sound, but necessarily hampered by poor Gorman papers. Unfortunately, there is no adequate study of U. S. Grant's political career after 1877, though the current publication of his papers by Southern Illinois University Press should help remedy this in time. William B. Hesseltine, *Ulysses S. Grant, Politician* (New York: Dodd, Mead and Co., 1935), has some useful information on the presidential boom of 1880. Cleveland's second secretary of state merits a good biography, but students rely now on a pietistic account, Matilda Gresham, *Life of Walter Quintin Gresham*, 2 vols. (Chicago: Rand McNally and Co., 1919).

Herbert Croly wrote a good authorized biography in *Marcus Alonzo Hanna: His Life and Work* (New York: Macmillan Co., 1912). In the absence of major Hanna papers, it remains a primary source. The book should be supplemented with Thomas Beer, *Hanna* (New York: Alfred A. Knopf, 1929), a bright, cynical work of considerable value because Beer's father was a friend of Hanna.

Benjamin Harrison is the subject of a multi-volume study by Harry J. Sievers, whose *Benjamin Harrison. II. Hoosier Statesman, 1865–1888* (New York: University Publishers, 1959), details Harrison's senatorial career, and the presidential boom and campaign of 1888. Volume III, *Benjamin Harrison: Hoosier President* (Indianapolis: Bobbs-Merrill Co., 1968), covers the presidency and Harrison's retirement years. Both volumes are unbalanced, with too much attention to family life and personal details, and too little to politics and diplomacy. Harrison's eventful administration is probably worth a monograph, which his rich personal papers make possible. President Hayes is the subject of several works, and Hamilton J. Eckenrode, *Rutherford B. Hayes: Statesman of Reunion* (New York: Dodd, Mead and Co., 1930), was the standard life for many years. It has been superseded by Harry Barnard, *Rutherford B. Hayes and His America* (Indianapolis: Bobbs-Merrill Co., 1954). The book is gracefully written and rests on prodigous research, but focuses heavily on Hayes' personality, while slighting the presidential years.

Herbert J. Bass has studied an important state figure in *'I Am A Democrat': The Political Career of David Bennett Hill* (Syracuse: Syracuse University Press, 1961). The book is a welcome addition to a slowly growing body of literature that discusses state politics in a national context. John A. Garraty's *Henry Cabot Lodge* (New York: Alfred A. Knopf, 1953), is valuable largely for post-1900 events, but has some information on the Federal Elections Bill, the campaign of 1896, and Republican politics. A study of Lodge's role as a national and state leader before 1900 would offer many constructive insights into how the GOP won and retained its constituency in the Gilded Age.

Two works on the 25th President are important. Margaret Leech, *In the Days of McKinley* (New York: Harper and Bros., 1959), emphasizes family and social life, though it contains valuable information on his administration. The book is well written, but crowded with petty detail and only summarizes the pre-1896 story. H. Wayne Morgan, *William McKinley and His America* (Syracuse: Syracuse University Press, 1963), is a full-scale life, with two chapters on the presidential boom and campaign of 1896.

The story of easily the most acid man in the period is told in William A. Robinson's *Thomas B. Reed, Parliamentarian* (New York: Dodd, Mead and Co., 1930). The "Czar" unhappily left no papers, but his scattered letters are a delight to researchers in far-flung archives. The influential publisher of the *New York Tribune* is covered in an old fashioned authorized biography, Royal Cortissoz, *The Life of Whitelaw Reid*, 2 vols. (New York: Charles Scribner's Sons, 1921), useful chiefly for the correspondence it reprints. Since Reid left voluminous papers, he deserves a better study. The same is true of Claude M. Fuess, *Carl Schurz, Reformer* (New York: Dodd, Mead and Co., 1932).

Unfortunately, there is no good study of John Sherman, the most important congressional figure in the period. Until Professor Jeannette Nichols completes her biography, readers must use Winfield Scott Kerr's superficial *John Sherman*, 2 vols. (Boston: Sherman, French and Co., 1908). Another important senatorial figure is dealt with in Dorothy Ganfield Fowler, *John Coit Spooner: Defender of Presidents* (New York: University Pubs., 1961). Spooner's papers are voluminous and valuable for the 1890's. Elmer Ellis, *Henry Moore Teller: Defender of the West* (Caldwell, Idaho: Caxton Printers, 1941), is one-dimensional, reflecting the lack of significant Teller papers, but useful for western and national politics.

The dominant Democrat of the 1870's is studied in Alexander C. Flick, *Samuel Jones Tilden: A Study in Political Sagacity* (New York: Dodd, Mead and Co., 1939). Another such exhaustive study is probably unnecessary, but a short, pungent account of Tilden as a political leader is in order. Mark Twain was not a politician, but an outstanding new biography is important to everyone working in the period. Justin Kaplan's *Mr. Clemens and Mark Twain* (New York: Simon and Schuster, 1966), is based on full research and reflects hard thinking and a conscious effort to retain the context of Twain's era. There is much useful information in Horace Samuel Merrill, *William Freeman Vilas: Doctrinaire Democrat* (Madison: State Historical Society of Wisconsin, 1954). The book is good for the first Cleveland administration, and the Gold Democrat movement of 1896. An opposite figure is studied in C. Vann Woodward, *Tom Watson: Agrarian Rebel* (New York: Macmillan Co., 1938). Mark D. Hirsch wrote an invaluable book in *William C. Whitney: Modern Warwick* (New York: Dodd, Mead and Co., 1948). It is a mine of information on the Democratic party from Tilden through Cleveland's second term, especially important for all three Cleveland booms and campaigns, the New Navy, and the Gold Democrat movement of 1896. The tortuous subject of tariff reform may be approached through Festus P. Summers, *William L. Wilson and Tariff Reform* (New Brunswick, N.J.: Rutgers University Press, 1953).

Many of these subjects now need revision, and many more have never been adequately studied. Lack of sources, for instance, makes it difficult to study Matthew S. Quay or Thomas C. Platt, though patient newspaper research would reveal much about the men and their respective states. Among Mugwumps, neither E. L. Godkin nor George William Curtis is the subject of a modern biography. Prominent congressional leaders like Justin S. Morrill, Nelson W. Aldrich, and Thomas F. Bayard deserve fresh treatment as political leaders. Such diverse contemporaries as Richard Olney and Richard P. Bland lack adequate biographies. In short, much remains to be done, and with modern attitudes and techniques, each biography should help fill out the larger picture of national party politics.

Political Studies

Fragmentary sources and complex issues have hindered research on party politics. There is background information in Eugene Holloway Roseboom, *A History of Presidential Elections* (New York: Macmillan Co., 1957). There is no reliable history of the Democratic party, but George H. Mayer covers some of the GOP story in *The Republican Party, 1854–1964* (New York: Oxford University Press, 1964). The book tends to narrate surface events, but is a useful guide. The same is true of Malcolm Moos, *The Republicans* (New York: Random House, 1956), though it is a sprightly and often penetrating work. Wilfred E. Binkley, *American Political Parties: Their Natural History* (New York: Alfred A. Knopf, rev. ed., 1945), has many calm and constructive suggestions about American politics in general, and the late nineteenth century in particular. While it does not deal with politics as such, Leonard D. White, *The Republican Era, 1865–1900: An Administrative History* (New York: Macmillan Co., 1958), is a guide to the responsibilities and achievements of the federal bureaucracy.

Works by several younger scholars have helped reorient discussions of party politics and the role of government. Ari A. Hoogenboom, *Outlawing the Spoils: A History of the Civil Service Reform Movement* (Urbana: University of Illinois Press, 1961), modifies the older view that Mugwump virtue fought political fraud. Hoogenboom criticizes reformers' motives, and shows political purpose behind Hayes' attacks on Conkling, but fails to set this fully in the larger perspective of nationalizing party politics. David J. Rothman, *Politics and Power: The United States Senate, 1869–1901* (Cambridge: Harvard University Press, 1966), details the growth of party discipline and responsible government in the upper house. Rothman's profiles of senatorial origins and interests are useful, though he often overstates the case in a book that is much too long. There is some acute criticism of the Cleveland Democracy in J. Rogers Hollingsworth, *The Whirligig of Politics: The Democracy of Cleveland and Bryan* (Chicago: University of Chicago Press, 1963).

Several studies of local politics are important to the national story. Seymour J. Mandelbaum, *Boss Tweed's New York* (New York: John Wiley and Sons, 1965), is difficult to read but offers fresh information about human communication in urban politics that has ramifications for the national story. His discussion of the limitations of "boss power" is illuminating. The traditional narrative story is recounted in Alexander B. Callow, Jr., *The Tweed Ring* (New York: Oxford University Press, 1966). Careful biographies of two leading Tammany sachems, John Kelly and Richard Croker, would be a relatively painless way to enter the tangle of urban-ethnic politics within the national Democratic party, but would require enormous newspaper research.

Among state studies, Harold F. Gosnell, *Boss Platt and His New York Machine* (Chicago: University of Chicago Press, 1924), has many insights into how an apparently all-powerful leader must accommodate followers and win converts. Geoffrey Blodgett's brilliant book, *The Gentle Reformers: Massachusetts Democrats in the Cleveland Era* (Cambridge: Harvard University Press, 1966), is a model synthesis of facts and analysis. A lucid, finely written discussion of the Mugwump mentality, it also delves into clashing ideologies, ethnic problems, and social tensions in an old society confronting change. Two books by Howard F. Lamar detail political developments in frontier areas, *Dakota Territory, 1861–1889* (New Haven: Yale University Press, 1956); and *The Far Southwest, 1846–1912* (New Haven: Yale University Press, 1966). Lewis L. Gould, *Wyoming: A Political History, 1869–1896* (New Haven: Yale University Press, 1968), is an excellent analysis of how a party is built with patronage and recognition. A forthcoming study of California in roughly the same period by R. Hal Williams will add to our knowledge of party structure and appeal.

The South is the subject of much research. C. Vann Woodward, *Origins of the New South, 1877–1912* (Baton Rouge: Louisiana State University Press, 1951), remains an outstanding summary. Two books on the Republican party are important: Vincent P. DeSantis, *Republicans Face the Southern Question: The New Departure Years, 1877–1897* (Baltimore: Johns Hopkins Press, 1959), details GOP efforts to build a southern party. Stanley P. Hirshson, *Farewell to the Bloody Shirt: Northern Republicans and the Southern Negro, 1877–1893* (Bloomington: Indiana University Press, 1962), deals largely with northern attitudes toward the race question. Hirshson overstates the role of economic factors in terminating northern efforts to guarantee Negro rights, and neither he nor DeSantis adequately emphasizes that southerners used the bloody shirt tactic longer than northerners, and to greater effect. Both authors probably overemphasize its importance in the

1880's, when most Americans were simply no longer interested in the Negro, and were voting self-interest as they defined it on issues like protection.

Full-scale studies of individual elections have been slow to appear. Herbert J. Clancy, *The Presidential Election of 1880* (Chicago: Loyola University Press, 1958), is a pedestrian work that does not place this important election in the context of reorienting the GOP around new issues and fresh leadership attuned to public desires and party management. No scholar has fully studied the colorful election of 1884, one of the most confused in American history. The details of Cleveland's sex life, and of Blaine's alleged personal corruption have obscured for historians, as they did for contemporaries, the battle's true significance to both parties. Relevant biographies contain some information on the election of 1888, but two dissertations are worth consulting. Edward Arthur White, "The Republican Party in National Politics, 1888–1891" (Wisconsin: 1941), details pre-convention maneuvering. C. J. Bernardo, "The Presidential Election of 1888" (Georgetown: 1949), is a useful narrative. George Harmon Knoles, *The Presidential Campaign and Election of 1892* (Palo Alto: Stanford University Press, 1942), is the standard work.

The "Battle of the Standards" has attracted considerable attention. Stanley L. Jones, *The Presidential Election of 1896* (Madison: University of Wisconsin Press, 1964), is the definitive account, reflecting prodigious research and careful analysis. Jones' footnotes and bibliography are a convenient guide, and his admiration for William McKinley's political style is a good contrast to outdated views. Paul W. Glad combines intellectual and political history in *McKinley, Bryan and the People* (Philadelphia: J. B. Lippincott Co., 1964). The book focuses on the intellectual origins and symbolism of major candidates. Though a useful introduction, it is too pro-Bryan, and is ambivalent toward the American political system. Glad's conclusion that many people doubted the ability of politics to change society probably reflects more of his own time than of 1896, when people expected much less of politics. The election's historiography is discussed in Gilbert C. Fite, "William Jennings Bryan and the Campaign of 1896: Some Views and Problems," *Nebraska History*, 47 (September, 1966), 247–64.

Many farmers lived on the edge of the industrial system during the Gilded Age, but agrarians have prospered in historical literature. Two books provide basic information for understanding the technical growth of agriculture. Fred A. Shannon, *The Farmer's Last Frontier: Agriculture, 1860–1897* (New York: Holt, Rinehart and Winston, 1945), is an encyclopedic account touching almost all aspects of the farmers' lot, though its judgments on politics, railroads, and marketing are debatable. A brief, well-written account by Gilbert C. Fite, *The Farmer's Frontier, 1865–1900* (New York: Holt, Rinehart and Winston, 1966), is especially useful for discussions of risk farming, mechanization, and daily life.

The Populist movement has attracted sustained attention, attesting to historians' interest in protest groups. The standard factual account, not likely to be superseded, is John D. Hicks, *The Populist Revolt* (Minneapolis: University of Minnesota Press, 1931). John S. Spratt, *The Road to Spindletop: Economic Change in Texas, 1875–1901* (Dallas: Southern Methodist University Press, 1955), is a valuable study in depth of an agrarian economy's response to new economic forces. Spratt's observations on the shallow ideal of self-sufficiency, and on transportation and marketing problems are shrewd. The failure of Populism to appeal in areas producing diversified crops is demonstrated in Roy V. Scott, *The Agrarian Revolt in Illinois, 1880–1896* (Urbana: University of Illinois Press, 1962). Populist political activity is studied in Robert F. Durden, *The Climax of Populism: The Election of 1896* (Lexington: University of Kentucky Press, 1965). Though Durden favors too much of Populist rhetoric, he shows that moderates in the movement did not wish to abandon traditional modes of appeal and operation, and were fairly successful in 1896.

Richard Hofstadter was the first systematic critic of Populist mythology, arguing in *The Age of Reform: From Bryan to F.D.R.* (New York: Alfred Knopf, 1955), that agrarians were often authoritarian, anti-Semitic, and backward-looking. This sparked a lively debate, and Norman Pollack, *The Populist Response to Industrial America: Midwestern Populist Thought* (Cambridge: Harvard University Press, 1962), is the most forthright rejoinder, but rests on thin evidence. Pollack's argument that Populist leaders were proto-Marxians seeking a cooperative society is unconvincing, and involves fine definitions of Populism. The charge of anti-semitism is answered in Walter T. K. Nugent, *The Tolerant Populists: Kansas, Populism, and Nativism* (Chicago: University of Chicago Press, 1963), who argues in effect that Populists were no more bigoted than Democratic and Republican neighbors. But the book has wider application in discussing forces that made some farmers leave old party allegiance in an era when people clung fiercely to political labels. Nugent's essay, "Some Parameters of Populism," *Agricultural History*, 40 (October, 1966), 255–70, summarizes most of his important findings. The same periodical for April, 1965, contains essays by Professors Norman Pollack, Irwin Unger, Oscar Handlin, and J. Rogers Hollingsworth that highlight current interpretations. An article by Theodore Saloutous, "The Professors and the Populists," *Ibid.*, 40 (October, 1966), serves a similar purpose.

The current debate over Populism's origins, nature, and achievements has produced valuable information and analysis, but overemphasizes its contemporary importance. We still know little about farmers who remained Republicans and Democrats. Despite a plethora of books on cowboys and Indians, there are few sound studies of cattle and sheep raising in the national economic context. Gene M. Gressley, *Bankers and Cattlemen* (New York: Alfred A. Knopf, 1966), takes a good step in the right direction, discussing origins and patterns of investment, and western attitudes toward various economic policies. We also ought to know more about specialty crops like sugar, rice, citrus, and urban-oriented dairy and poultry farming in both an economic and political context.

Economic Policy

The present study only touches lightly upon economic questions, but obviously uses important work on national development. All students of the period will profit greatly from Edward C. Kirkland's masterful summary,

Industry Comes of Age: Business, Labor, and Public Policy, 1860–1897 (New York: Holt, Rinehart and Winston, 1961). The book rests on prodigious research in manuscripts, state and federal documents, the press, and theoretical writings. Written with grace and a dry wit, it offers a welcome antidote to the shallow "Robber Baron" thesis, and successfully depicts the era as it saw itself, and also in the light of historical judgment. Kirkland rightly emphasizes the basic economic good the era produced, and the extended bibliographical essay is invaluable. Two other slender books by the same author deal with the ideology, motivations, and social views of the businessmen: *Business in the Gilded Age: The Conservatives' Balance Sheet* (Madison: University of Wisconsin Press, 1952); and *Dream and Thought in the Business Community, 1860–1900* (Ithaca: Cornell University Press, 1956). Kirkland's recent biography of a leading railroad executive, *Charles Francis Adams, Jr., 1835–1915: The Patrician at Bay* (Cambridge: Harvard University Press, 1965), contains information on the movement for regulation. A new study by Louis M. Hacker, *The World of Andrew Carnegie, 1865–1901* (Philadelphia: J. B. Lippincott, 1967), emphasizes economic development, with a refreshing Hamiltonian viewpoint. The work is uneven, and Hacker's analysis of politics is often debatable. But the book has much valuable information and interpretation on fiscal policy, tariff protection, Populism, railroad development and regulation, banking, and corporate growth.

Railroad regulation has elicited more interest among historians than any other business activity because it involved public policy, popular attitudes, and politics. Unfortunately, no one has tackled the baffling problem of actual railroad influence in politics on either the state or national level in any systematic way, but Thomas C. Cochran edited and analyzed a vital collection of primary materials in *Railroad Leaders, 1845–1890: The Business Mind in Action* (Cambridge: Harvard University Press, 1953). Lee Benson, *Merchants, Farmers and Railroads: Railroad Regulation and New York Politics, 1850–1887* (Cambridge: Harvard University Press, 1955), argues that eastern shippers and merchants were more influential in securing federal regulation than western agrarians. This is a sound enough view, though much of the argument is in older works by Solon Justus Buck, and Chester McA. Destler. The idea that many businessmen sought federal regulation to avoid harsher local control, and to increase profits in a unified system is repeated in Gabriel Kolko, *Railroads and Regulation, 1877–1916* (Princeton: Princeton University Press, 1965). The entire debate will no doubt continue because of what the railroad symbolized, and interested students should not overlook Edward A. Purcell, Jr., "Ideas and Interests: Businessmen and the Interstate Commerce Act," *Journal of American History*, 54 (December, 1967), 561–78.

Two major works are necessary to understanding of the movement against trustification: Hans B. Thorelli, *The Federal Anti-Trust Policy: Origination of an American Tradition* (Baltimore: Johns Hopkins Press, 1955); and William Letwin, *Law and Economic Policy in America: The Evolution of the Sherman Anti-Trust Act* (New York: Random House, 1965). The latter takes the Sherman Act seriously, showing the limitations of legal precedent that surrounded its drafting, and the lack of trained staff and public support that hindered its enforcement.

The currency question produced more sound and fury than any other political issue in the Gilded Age, but its complexity retarded historical investigation until recently. The first major work to challenge the older view that the rich business community wanted a gold standard, while poor agrarians wanted a paper-silver system, was Robert P. Sharkey, *Money, Class and Party: An Economic Study of Civil War and Reconstruction* (Baltimore: Johns Hopkins Press, 1959). The book is difficult reading, but has invaluable information on government fiscal policy, business and the tariff, and popular attitudes for and against managed currency. The most comprehensive and provocative account for the 1870's is Irwin Unger, *The Greenback Era: A Social and Political History of American Finance, 1865–1879* (Princeton: Princeton University Press, 1964). Resting on primary sources, the study shows how apparently divergent groups often united on similar views for both moralistic and practical reasons. It also demonstrates that politicians were usually independent of business control, and moved by a wide range of motives. Walter T. K. Nugent, *Money and American Society, 1865–1880* (New York: The Free Press, 1968), discusses group interests and moralistic rhetorical attitudes toward the money question. The book is especially valuable for giving the American problem a world setting, in discussing various efforts at international agreement. Its chief weakness is unrealistic criticism of the era's dominant ethics and attitudes. It is a trifle unhistorical to argue that men should have abandoned time-honored allegiance to redeemable money in favor of irredeemable paper, especially during a period of vast change when monetary stability had important emotional overtones. Critical scholars have not demonstrated that any alternative policy was actually possible, given the American people's clear acceptance of common ideas about progress, growth, and morality.

Despite great public interest in monetary questions, tariff protection was probably more important in politics. The tariff issue was vital in arranging constituencies within each major party. Contrary to most historical judgment, protection appealed to many interest groups in labor and agriculture, as well as business. To study its actual economic effects, however, is almost impossible, because of poor statistics and the difficulty of contriving a comparative model. Most contemporary critics contrasted British and American tariff policy, but Germany is probably a better example because of similar home markets, industries, and political pressures. Most studies of the subject are polemical. The fullest coverage in a non-economic vein is still Edward Stanwood, *American Tariff Controversies in the 19th Century*, 2 vols. (Boston: Houghton Mifflin Co., 1903). Despite its protectionist viewpoint, the work contains many sidelights on the tariff's role in economics and party politics that historians have overlooked. Protection probably generated more jobs, higher wages, and fewer price increases than we have been led to believe. Its most important effect, however, was to create re-investment capital, speeding up the whole process of industrialization. In any event, the home market idea was politically appealing throughout most of American history. The basic attack on protection is Ida Tarbell. *The Tariff in Our Times* (New York: Macmillan Co., 1911). a shallow tract from the Muckraker Era. The standard scholarly account is Frank W. Taussig, *The Tariff History of the United States*, 5th ed. (New York: G. P. Putnam's Sons, 1910), though its generalizations are open to some question.

Foreign Policy

The most glamorous events in American foreign policy occurred after 1896, but developed throughout the Gilded Age. Interest in America's current role as a world power has sparked re-examination of the whole problem. Foster Rhea Dulles, *Prelude to World Power: American Diplomatic History, 1860–1900* (New York: Macmillan Co., 1965), is a bland general introduction. The New Navy's role in politics and diplomacy is traced in Walter R. Herrick, Jr., *The American Naval Revolution* (Baton Rouge: Louisiana State University Press, 1966), which deals best with administrative policy during the Harrison years. Alice Felt Tyler's *The Foreign Policy of James G. Blaine* (Minneapolis: University of Minnesota Press, 1927), is still the basic account, but a full scale re-examination of Blaine's foreign policy is much overdue. Charles Callan Tansill, *The Foreign Policy of Thomas F. Bayard, 1885–1897* (New York: Fordham University Press, 1940), exhausts the subject, but a shorter, more critical account of Bayard's whole career would be very useful. David M. Pletcher, *The Awkward Years: Foreign Policy Under Garfield and Arthur* (Columbia, Mo.: University of Missouri Press, 1962), is a major work with wider application than its time span indicates. Pletcher examines tariff reciprocity, Pan-Americanism, the influence of domestic politics, and growth of departmental staff within the context of innovation and change.

The tortuous Hawaiian imbroglio is developed in relevant biographies and general studies, and in two detailed works by William Adam Russ, Jr.: *The Hawaiian Revolution, 1893–1894* (1959); and *The Hawaiian Republic, 1894–1898* (1961), both published by the Susquehanna University Press, Selinsgrove, Pennsylvania. The view from Honolulu is described in Merze Tate, *The United States and the Hawaiian Kingdom* (New Haven: Yale University Press, 1965). And Julius W. Pratt, *Expansionists of 1898: The Acquisition of Hawaii and the Spanish Islands* (Baltimore: Johns Hopkins Press, 1936), is still valuable.

The most publicized re-examinations of expansionism have come from younger scholars influenced by William Appleman Williams. His own *The Tragedy of American Diplomacy*, rev. ed. (New York: Delta Books, 1961), states in general terms the basic economic interpretation now finding vogue. Williams argues that "informal imperialism," spurred by a search for overseas markets, lay behind American expansionism. In this view, expansion robbed America of the chance to build a cooperative domestic society, and unnecessarily involved the nation in international power rivalries. This argument has the merit of seeing a developing policy, where earlier scholars erroneously saw chance and blunder. But it over-states the influence of businessmen in policy formation, partly because scholars who accept this thesis are seldom familiar with domestic political methods and power arrangements. Furthermore, it is doubtful that most Americans really wanted the cooperative society Williams wishes had arisen with industrialism. The economic thesis is developed in depth in Walter LaFeber, *The New Empire: An Interpretation of American Expansion, 1860–1898* (Ithaca: Cornell University Press, 1963). The book is hard reading, but valuable for three long introductory chapters analyzing the intellectual, strategic, and economic motives behind expansionism. But it too over-emphasizes the search for markets. The theme is carried to the Orient in Thomas McCormick, *China Market* (Chicago: Quadrangle Books, 1967), which focuses on the Philippine question and the Open Door policy. Market-seeking is a more obvious and important factor in America's China policy than as a cause of the Spanish-American War. And while important men and groups may have economic motives, they seldom stir nations as a whole, and certainly did not persuade the American people of expansionism's virtues in 1898. A businessman or business journal, furthermore, may develop a brilliant critique for economic expansion that never reaches a president or diplomat who adopts a similar policy for different reasons.

Placing American foreign policy in a global context is a formidable challenge, most recently attempted by Ernest R. May in *Imperial Democracy* (New York: Harcourt, Brace and World, 1961). Though valuable for its multi-archival information, and for exploding several myths, the book is ambivalent, and May accepts the idea that America accidentally drifted into world power.

The most salutary recent study of these foreign affairs is John A. S. Grenville and George Berkeley Young, *Politics, Strategy and American Diplomacy: Studies in Foreign Policy, 1873–1917* (New Haven: Yale University Press, 1966), a series of provocative essays resting on the theme that domestic politics and military strategy rather than economic motives shaped American foreign policy. The authors properly downgrade the influence of A. T. Mahan, and upgrade that of his predecessor, Admiral Stephen B. Luce. They show that Henry Cabot Lodge was not a Jingo, and prove beyond reasonable doubt that strategy and informed policy, not Theodore Roosevelt's whimsy, took Commodore Dewey to Manila Bay. The authors are corrosive in judging Cleveland, and have a high regard for McKinley.

The origins and results of the Spanish-American War are a separate empire of scholarship, but a few titles may be helpful. Most of the works mentioned above deal with the subject, and H. Wayne Morgan, *America's Road to Empire: The War with Spain and Overseas Expansion* (New York: John Wiley and Sons, 1965), is a convenient guide with a moderate position. Lester D. Langley, *The Cuban Policy of the United States: A brief History* (New York: John Wiley and Sons, 1968), is a clear analysis of this complex problem, with good treatment of the Ten Years' War, and the decision to intervene in 1898. Robert L. Beisner, *Twelve Against Empire: The Anti-Imperialists, 1898–1900* (New York: McGraw-Hill, 1968), is a collection of analytical profiles of leading anti-expansionists, centered on the treaty fight of 1898–99, and the election of 1900. The book is intellectual rather than diplomatic history. Beisner is fundamentally anti-expansionist, but does not disguise the lack of practical alternatives these people offered in 1898. Nor does he ignore the darker side of their opposition to empire, including a rather blatant racism. The most recent effort to analyze the forces that made expansion appeal so widely in American life is Ernest R. May, *American Imperialism: A Speculative Essay* (New York: Atheneum, 1968). A welter of information often obscures the book's theme, that crucial American opinion-making groups drew on European precedents and attitudes for their decisions.

In one way or another, most recent students have questioned the wisdom and motives of American expansionism. The most systematic critique has come from those who feel it thwarted the good life at home. They argue that "informal imperialism" may begin without force, but leads to armaments and confrontations with other powers in the struggle to hold markets. This is especially detrimental to long-term relations with developing countries. Some of this criticism is valid, but only offers untestable alternatives that never developed, and it leaves unanswered the general question of why the nation as a whole favored expansion, suggesting no other course but impractical isolationism or impossible altruism. Nor does it assess at their true worth the humanistic motives that statesmen and lesser folk mixed with desires for fame, power and even markets. That many of these hopes and assumptions were naive should not detract from their contemporary importance in men's thinking.

Cultural Studies

A few recent works on culture help in studying any of the era's problems. Jay Martin, *Harvests of Change: American Literature, 1865–1914* (New York: Prentice-Hall, 1967), is an outstanding example of scholarly condensation without loss of clear analysis. The book offers many insights for non-literary historians, and is especially important in discussing regional culture. Werner Berthoff, *The Ferment of Realism: American Literature, 1884–1919* (New York: The Free Press, 1966), though sometimes difficult reading, is a good exposition of main currents in literary Realism and Naturalism. H. Wayne Morgan, *American Writers in Rebellion: From Mark Twain to Dreiser* (New York: Hill and Wang, 1965), has relevant introductory chapters on Twain, Howells, Garland, and Norris. Louis J. Budd has written an incisive and often delightful book in *Mark Twain: Social Philosopher* (Bloomington: Indiana University Press, 1962). In *The Victorian Mode in American Fiction, 1865–1885* (East Lansing: Michigan State University Press, 1965), Robert Falk offers a clear, formal presentation of the major themes in American writing during the period. Larzer Ziff discusses some intriguing possibilities for literary development, and analyzes new literature in *The American 1890's: Life and Times of a Lost Generation* (New York: Viking Press, 1966).

Notes to Chapters

Prologue

1. See John J. Ingalls, *A Collection of the Writings of John James Ingalls* (Kansas City, Missouri: Hudson-Kimberly Publishing Co., 1902), 384–85; *New York Tribune*, March 2, 1877.

2. *New York Tribune*, March 5, 1877; Harry Barnard, *Rutherford B. Hayes and His America* (New York: Bobbs-Merrill Co., 1954), 403.

3. Judson Kilpatrick to W. T. Sherman, December 16, 1876, W. T. Sherman LC.

4. *Washington Capitol*, February 18, 1877, in Charles C. Tansill, *The Congressional Career of Thomas Francis Bayard, 1869–1885* (Washington: Georgetown University Press, 1946), 198.

5. Charles Richard Williams, *The Life of Rutherford Birchard Hayes . . . ,* 2 vols. (Columbus: Ohio Historical Society, 1928), II, 1; Alphonso Taft to Hayes, December 6, 1876, Hayes HML.

6. *New York Tribune*, March 2, 3, 1877.

7. William H. Crook, *Through Five Administrations* (New York: Harper and Brothers, 1910), 218–20.

8. Rutherford B. Hayes Diary, March 14, 1877, HML. Hayes' diary exists in several forms, both printed and in manuscript. To avoid confusion, I will cite it by date, from the original copy in HML.

9. Edna Colman, *White House Gossip From Andrew Johnson to Calvin Coolidge* (New York: Doubleday, Page and Co., 1927), 105ff.

I

Hayes: Harmony and Discord

1. Frank G. Carpenter, *Carp's Washington* (New York: McGraw-Hill, 1960), 3.
2. *Ibid.*, 111.

3. James Bryce, *The American Commonwealth*, 3rd ed., 2 vols. (New York: Macmillan Co., 1893), I, 76.

4. William H. Crook, *Memories of the White House* (Boston: Little, Brown and Co., 1911), 109; Hayes Scrapbooks, Vol. 115, p. 197, HML.

5. Hayes Diary, October 4, 1892, HML.

6. Thomas C. Donaldson Memoirs, June 27, 1879, HML.

7. Hayes to W. H. Smith, August 24, 1864, Hayes HML.

8. Quoted in Frank Krebs, "Hayes and the South," (Unpublished Ph.D. Dissertation, Ohio State University, 1951), 144.

9. Hayes Diary, October 12, 1875, HML.

10. *Ibid.*, January 5, 1892.

11. *Ibid.*, September 24, 1876.

12. *Washington Post*, January 7, 1878. Cf., Donaldson Memoirs, May 6–9, 1879, HML; Chauncey M. Depew, *My Memories of Eighty Years* (New York: Charles Scribner's Sons, 1924), 102; Hayes to W. H. Smith, March 29, 1881, HML.

13. Hayes Diary, October 23, 1881, HML.

14. Hayes to Editor, *New York Morning Advertiser*, September 30, 1892, in *Bulletin*, American Iron and Steel Association, 27 (March 1, 1893), 66.

15. Schurz to W. M. Grosvenor, March 29, 1877, in Carl Schurz, *Speeches, Correspondence and Political Papers*, 6 vols. (New York: G. P. Putnam's Sons, 1913), III, 410.

16. Hayes Diary, April 3, 1879, HML.

17. Barnard, *Rutherford B. Hayes*, 487.

18. Williams, *Rutherford B. Hayes*, II, 303–304, nl.

19. *New York Tribune*, March 10, 1877; *Washington Post*, December 13, 1877.

20. Chester L. Barrows, *William M. Evarts* (Chapel Hill: University of North Carolina Press, 1941), 339; *Letters of Mrs. Henry Adams* (Boston: Houghton Mifflin Co., 1936), 303; Donaldson Memoirs, November 8, 1877 and April 28, 1877, HML.

21. David S. Barry, *Forty Years in Washington* (Boston: Little, Brown and Co., 1924), 38–39.

22. Donaldson Memoirs, April 28, 1877, HML.

23. Daniel Ryan, *Masters of Men* (Columbus: McClelland Co., 1915), 56; Claude M. Fuess, *Carl Schurz* (New York: Dodd-Mead, 1932), 237; Irwin Unger, *The Greenback Era* (Princeton: Princeton University Press, 1964), 282; O. O. Stealey, *Twenty Years in the Press Gallery* (New York: Publishers Printing Company, 1906), 393.

24. Williams, *Rutherford Birchard Hayes*, II, 413–14, nl.

25. *Ibid.*, 302–305.

26. Crook, *Memories*, 118–19; Williams, *Rutherford Birchard Hayes*, II, 299–303; Lewis Mumford, *The Brown Decades* (New York: Dover Publishing Company, 1955), 214; Leonard Alexander Swann, *John Roach, Maritime Entrepreneur* (Annapolis: United States Naval Institute, 1965), 100–101.

27. Julia Stoddard Parsons, *Scattered Memories* (New York: B. Humphries and Co., 1938), 50; *Letters of Mrs. Henry Adams*, 260.

28. Williams, *Rutherford Birchard Hayes*, II, 306–308; Colman, *White House Gossip*, 123; Crook, *Memories*, 116; Canton (Ohio) *Repository*, February 15, 1878.

29. Schurz, *Speeches*, IV, 181.

30. Hayes Diary, February 29, 1879, HML; Donald Barr Chidsey, *The Gentleman From New York, A Life of Roscoe Conkling* (New Haven: Yale University Press, 1935), 235; Colman, *White House Gossip,* 114, 124.

31. Barnard, *Rutherford B. Hayes,* 479ff.

32. Hayes Diary, January 16, 1881, HML.

33. *Washington Post,* January 10, 1887.

34. Julia B. Foraker, *I Would Live It Again* (New York: Harper and Brothers, 1932), 74.

35. Hayes to Thomas C. Donaldson, March 10, 1891, in Williams, *Rutherford Birchard Hayes,* II, 314–15, nl.

36. Crook, *Memories,* 175; Parsons, *Scattered Memories,* 44.

37. *New York Tribune,* March 5, 1877.

38. T. Harry Williams, *Hayes of the Twenty-Third* (New York: Alfred Knopf, 1965), 5–7.

39. Hayes Diary, February 25, 1887, HML.

40. Hayes to Mrs. Hayes, July 2, 1864, Hayes HML.

41. *Galveston News,* May 27, 1877.

42. C. Vann Woodward, *Reunion and Reaction* (Boston: Little, Brown and Co., 1951), 25.

43. Vincent P. DeSantis, *Republicans Face the Southern Question* (Baltimore: The Johns Hopkins Press, 1959), 123ff.

44. August Meier, *Negro Thought in America, 1880–1915* (Ann Arbor: University of Michigan Press, 1964), 21.

45. James M. McPherson, "Coercion or Conciliation? Abolitionists Debate President Hayes's Southern Policy," *New England Quarterly,* 39 (December, 1966), 486.

46. *Cincinnati Commercial,* March 13, 1877.

47. Randall to Bayard, March 9, 1877, Bayard LC.

48. Hayes Diary, March 14, 1877, HML.

49. *Ibid.,* March 16, 1877.

50. *Ibid.,* March 20, 1877.

51. *New York Herald,* March 16, 1877.

52. Hampton to Hayes, April 27, 1877, Hayes HML.

53. Hayes Diary, April 22, 1877, HML.

54. Kellar to Hayes, April 20, 1877, Comly to Hayes, April 30, May 11, 1877, all in Hayes HML.

55. See DeSantis, *Republicans Face the Southern Question,* 61–62; *New York Tribune,* March 7, 1877; James A. Garfield Diary, March 11, 1877, Garfield LC.

56. Blaine to Reid, April 12, 1877, Reid LC.

57. Albert Bigelow Paine, *Th: Nast, His Period and His Pictures* (New York: Macmillan Co., 1904), 355.

58. *Harper's Weekly,* 21 (May 19, 1877), 382.

59. Hayes Diary, April 1, 1880, HML.

60. Hayes to W. D. Bickham, May 3, 1877, Hayes HML.

61. See Stanley P. Hirshson, *Farewell to the Bloody Shirt* (Bloomington: Indiana University Press, 1962), 38–39.

62. Krebs, "Hayes and the South," 178–88.

63. Hayes Diary, November 3, 1877, HML.

64. Sherman to Robert O. Herbert, June 19, 1879, Sherman LC.

65. Woodward, *Origins of the New South*, 46; Hayes to Guy Bryan, March 28, 1880, Hayes HML; DeSantis, *Republicans Face the Southern Question*, 91; Albert V. House, Jr., "President Hayes' Selection of David M. Key for Postmaster General," *Journal of Southern History*, 4 (February, 1938), 87–93.

66. *New York Times*, April 15, 1877; Donaldson Memoirs, July 23, 1879, HML; Olive Hall Shadgett, *The Republican Party in Georgia from Reconstruction Through 1900* (Athens, Georgia: University of Georgia Press, 1964), 141–42.

67. James A. Garfield Diary, April 6, 1877, Garfield LC; Woodward, *Origins of the New South*, 47; Schurz, *Speeches*, III, 384–87.

68. *New York Times*, March 4, 1879.

69. *New York Tribune*, December 19, 1877.

70. Theodore Clarke Smith, *Life and Letters of James Abram Garfield*, 2 vols., (New Haven: Yale University Press, 1925), II, 665.

71. James A. Garfield Diary, March 4, 1878, Garfield LC.

72. Smith, *James Abram Garfield*, II, 659; James A. Garfield Diary, October 26, 1877, Garfield LC.

73. *Nation*, April 12, 1877, p. 172.

74. Hirshson, *Farewell to the Bloody Shirt*, 46–49; Sherman to S. J. Kirkwood, November 7, 1878, Sherman LC; James A. Garfield Diary, November 6, 1878, Garfield LC.

75. *Cincinnati Commercial*, March 29, 1877.

76. *New York Tribune*, January 4, 1879.

77. *New York Times*, January 27, 1879.

78. Chandler held that Hayes deliberately sought to "break down the party utterly" with lenience to the South and civil service reform; Chandler to Reid, March 4, 1878, Reid LC. Conkling thought Hayes wanted "to create a party of his own in the South"; *New York World*, April 17, 1878. Neither man discussed the President's purpose in all this, or what profit a rump party would bring him.

79. Samuel Rezneck, "Distress, Relief and Discontent in the United States During the Depression of 1873–1878," *Journal of Political Economy*, 58 (December, 1950), 494–512.

80. John Sherman, *Recollections . . .*, 2 vols. (Chicago: Werner Co., 1895), I, 582.

81. *The Nation*, July 26, 1877, p. 49.

82. "Fair Wages," *North American Review*, 125 (September, 1877), 322–24.

83. Hayes Diary, August 5, 1877, Hayes HML.

84. Hayes to Schurz, September 15, 1876, Hayes HML.

85. *New York Times*, March 29, 1877.

86. Ari Hoogenboom, *Outlawing the Spoils*, (Urbana, Illinois: University of Illinois Press, 1961), 21ff.

87. Gerald W. McFarland, "The New York Mugwumps of 1884," *Political Science Quarterly*, 78 (March, 1963), 40–58; Gordon S. Wood, "The Massachusetts Mugwumps," *New England Quarterly*, 33 (December, 1960), 435–51; Geoffrey Blodgett, *The Gentle Reformers: Massachusetts Democrats in the Cleveland Era* (Cambridge: Harvard University Press, 1966), 7.

88. William M. Armstrong, *E. L. Godkin and American Foreign Policy, 1865–1900* (New York: Bookman Associates, 1957), 35, 207, n101.

89. Paul P. Van Riper, *History of the United States Civil Service* (Evanston, Illinois: Row, Peterson and Co., 1958), 85.

90. Blodgett, *The Gentle Reformers,* 42.

91. Bristow to Schurz, March 8, 1877, in Schurz, *Speeches,* III, 409.

92. William L. Riordan, *Plunkitt of Tammany Hall* (New York: E. P. Dutton and Company, 1963), 12–14.

93. Blodgett, *The Gentle Reformers,* 66.

94. A. R. Anderson to Allison, November 29, 1876, Allison ISDHA.

95. Thomas Collier Platt, *Autobiography* (New York: B. W. Dodge Co., 1910), 89.

96. W. M. Dickson to W. K. Rogers, March 25, 1878, Hayes HML.

97. William Elsley Connelley, *The Life of Preston B. Plumb* (Chicago: Browne and Howell Co., 1913), 257ff; George S. Boutwell, "The Political Situation," *North American Review,* 136 (February, 1883), 160; *St. Louis Globe Democrat,* February 20, 1880.

98. *New York Sun,* March 16, 1877. Cf., Dorothy Ganfield Fowler, *The Cabinet Politician* (New York: Columbia University Press, 1943), 167–68; M. K. Turner to Hayes, March 9, 1877, Hayes HML.

99. James D. Richardson, *A Compilation of the Messages and Papers of the Presidents, 1789–1897,* 10 vols. (Washington: G.P.O., 1897), VII, 450–51.

100. *New York Tribune,* April 18, 1888.

101. *Cincinnati Commercial,* October 30, 1877.

102. Alfred R. Conkling, *The Life and Letters of Roscoe Conkling* (New York: Charles L. Webster and Co., 1889), 583. See his note to Whitelaw Reid, August 21, 1879, thanking him for denying lies about his private life, reprinted in Royal Cortissoz, *The Life of Whitelaw Reid,* 2 vols. (New York: Charles Scribner's Sons, 1921), I, 372. He wrote for the same purpose to a Democratic opponent, Samuel J. Randall, on February 21, 1883, Randall UPL.

103. Chidsey, *The Gentleman From New York,* 272. Mrs. Conkling was a sister of Horatio Seymour, New York's Democratic wartime governor.

104. Conkling, *Life and Letters of Roscoe Conkling,* 414.

105. *Ibid.,* 636.

106. Barnard, *Rutherford B. Hayes,* 289; Chidsey, *The Gentleman From New York,* 208–209; George Frisbie Hoar, *Autobiography of Seventy Years* (New York: Charles Scribner's Sons, 1903), I, 243.

107. Chidsey, *The Gentleman From New York,* 222–23; Sherman to Hayes, December 12, 1876, March 8, 1881, Hayes HML; *New York Tribune,* March 6, 1877; Hayes Diary, April 19, 1888, HML; Platt, *Autobiography,* 83–84; *Chicago Tribune,* December 23, 1877.

108. James Ford Rhodes, *History of the United States . . . ,* 8 vols. (New York: Macmillan and Co., 1919), VIII, 138; DeAlva Stanwood Alexander, *A Political History of The State of New York,* 3 vols. (New York: Henry Holt and Co., 1909), III, 402–403.

109. Donaldson Memoirs, January 5, 1880, HML; Hayes Diary, April 19, 1888, HML.

110. Halstead to Hayes, February 22, 1877, Hayes HML.

111. *New York Tribune,* September 7, 1877; R. C. McCormick to Sherman, September 7, 1877, Sherman LC; George Frederick Howe, *Chester A. Arthur* (New York: Dodd, Mead and Company, 1935), 47ff.

112. William Hartman, "The New York Custom House: Seat of Spoils Politics," *New York History,* 34 (April, 1953), 149–63; Leonard D. White, *The Repub-*

lican Era, 1869–1901 (New York: Macmillan Co., 1958), 118–19; *Commercial and Financial Chronicle,* 24 (June 2, 1877), 505; John W. Andrews to W. K. Rogers, June 11, 1877, Hayes HML.

113. Sherman to Justin S. Morrill, December 14, 1878, Morrill LC; and to S. J. Kirkwood, November 7, 1878, Sherman LC; George F. Howe, "The New York Custom House Controversy, 1877–1879," *Mississippi Valley Historical Review,* 18 (December, 1931), 350–63.

114. Norton to Hayes, July 22, 1877, Hayes HML; *New York Tribune,* September 7, October 17, 1877.

115. Smith to L. Pickering, August 1, 1878, Smith OHS; Hoogenboom, *Outlawing the Spoils,* 156–57.

116. *New York Tribune,* September 15, 18, 1877.

117. Conkling, *Life and Letters of Roscoe Conkling,* 530–31, 551–52.

118. *New York World,* September 25, 1877; Conkling, *Life and Letters of Roscoe Conkling,* 550.

119. *New York World,* September 27, 1877; Conkling, *Life and Letters of Roscoe Conkling,* 658, 538–50.

120. Depew, *My Memories,* 80; Edward Cary, *George William Curtis* (New York: Houghton Mifflin Co., 1894), 258.

121. *New York Tribune,* September 27, 1877; *New York World,* September 28, 1877; *New York Herald,* November 9, 1877.

122. Hoogenboom, *Outlawing the Spoils,* 162–63; Sherman, *Recollections,* II, 682ff; *Washington Post,* December 13, 1877. The Senate vote was 31–25, with only 6 Republicans sustaining the nominations.

123. Quoted in Hoogenboom, *Outlawing the Spoils,* 168–69.

124. Hayes to William Henry Smith, December 8, 1877, Hayes HML.

125. Sherman, *Recollections,* II, 684; *Washington Post,* February 4, 1879.

126. Howe, *Chester A. Arthur,* 92.

127. *Nation,* February 20, 1879, p. 128.

128. Hayes Diary, February 4, 1879, Hayes HML.

129. *Ibid.,* July 13, 14, 1880.

130. Chidsey, *The Gentleman From New York,* 270.

131. Ryan, *Masters of Men,* 19.

132. C. E. Henry to Garfield, February 28, 1880, Garfield LC.

133. Sherman to Richard Smith, June 14, 1880, Sherman LC.

134. *Nation,* April 14, 1892, p. 275.

135. *Puck,* 7 (May 26, 1880), 205.

136. See Jeannette P. Nichols, "John Sherman: A Study in Inflation," *Mississippi Valley Historical Review,* 21 (September, 1934), 181–94.

137. Sherman to W. Sprague, January 15, 1884, Sherman LC.

138. Ryan, *Masters of Men,* 21. Cf., Allan Nevins, *Abram S. Hewitt* (New York: Harper and Brothers, 1935), 402; Unger, *The Greenback Era,* 322–23.

139. For the quotations in order, see Arthur Krock (Ed.), *The Editorials of Henry Watterson* (New York: Doubleday, Doran and Co., 1923), 50; Sherman, *Recollections,* I, iv; *Nation,* November 22, 1877, p. 312; William V. Shannon, *The American Irish* (New York: Macmillan Co., 1963), 77.

140. *Cincinnati Commercial,* December 6, 1877; the anatomy is confused.

141. *Rocky Mountain News,* December 6, 1877; February 24, 1878; *Cincinnati Commercial,* January 4, February 1, 1878; *Chicago Tribune,* December 24, 1877.

142. George Waite to Hayes, November 16, 1877, Hayes HML. Cf., Chester McArthur Destler, *American Radicalism, 1865–1901* (Chicago: Quadrangle Books, 1966), 7; *Nation,* November 8, 1877, p. 280, and December 4, 1884, p. 477.

143. See Sharkey, *Money, Class and Party,* 267ff; Unger, *The Greenback Era,* 155; *Chicago Tribune,* December 24, 1877.

144. John T. Morgan, "The Political Alliance of the South with the West," *North American Review,* 126 (March–April, 1878), 309–22.

145. Smith to Hayes, July 9, 1879, Smith OHS.

146. Wilson Vance to Schurz, March 24, 1878, Schurz LC. Cf., Bonsall to Benjamin F. Butler, April 25, 1877, Butler LC; *New York Tribune,* November 7, 1877.

147. *Chicago Tribune,* January 7, 1878.

148. John Walsh to Hayes, November 16, 1877, Hayes HML.

149. See Paul M. O'Leary, "The Scene of the Crime of 1873 Revisited: A Note," *Journal of Political Economy,* 68 (August, 1960), 388–92; Allen Weinstein, "Was There a 'Crime of 1873'?: The Case of the Demonetized Dollar," *Journal of American History,* 54 (September, 1967), 307–20; Walter T. K. Nugent, *The Money Question During Reconstruction* (New York: W. W. Norton, 1967), *passim,* esp. Chapter 5; and the same author's *Money and American Society: 1865–1880* (New York: The Free Press, 1968), 140–71.

150. *Cincinnati Commercial,* October 1, 1877; Sharkey, *Money, Class and Party,* 156–57; Unger, *The Greenback Era,* 59–60, 118, 332–33; Edward C. Kirkland, *Industry Comes of Age: Business, Labor and Public Policy, 1860–1897* (New York: Holt, Rinehart and Winston, 1961), 36ff.

151. Charles Nordhoff to Edward Atkinson, February 19, 1878, Atkinson MHS; John V. Farwell to William Henry Smith, January 25, 1878, Smith IHS; Warner Bateman to Sherman, October 11, 1877, Sherman LC; *Nation,* February 7, 1878, p. 85.

152. Sharkey, *Money, Class and Party,* 288ff.

153. Unger, *The Greenback Era,* 148–53; Hayes Diary, February 6, 1878, HML.

154. *Commercial and Financial Chronicle,* 28 (January 4, 1879) 1; Sherman, *Recollections,* II, 604–605, 620–24.

155. Unger, *The Greenback Era,* 120–26, 144–46; Hayes Diary, November 5, 1877, HML.

156. Garfield Diary, October 31, 1877, Garfield LC.

157. *Washington Post,* December 11, 1877.

158. Harold A. Haswell, Jr., "The Public Life of Congressman Richard Parks Bland," (Unpublished Ph.D. Dissertation, University of Missouri, 1951), 77–97.

159. *Beatrice Webb's American Diary,* 16.

160. Allison to Edward Atkinson, March 8, 1867, Atkinson MHS.

161. Sherman, *Recollections,* II, 620–21.

162. Haswell, "Richard Parks Bland," 87–88; Unger, *The Greenback Era,* 362; *Rocky Mountain News,* February 17, 1878; Leland L. Sage, *William Boyd Allison* (Iowa City: State Historical Society of Iowa, 1956), 143–57.

163. *Washington Post,* December 8, 1877, and February 23, 26, 1878; *Chicago Tribune,* January 29, 1878; *Cincinnati Commercial,* February 18, 25, 1878; *Rocky Mountain News,* February 28, 1878; Unger, *The Greenback Era,* 356; Hayes Diary, February 3, 17, 26, HML.

164. *Washington Post,* March 1, 1878; Crook, *Through Five Administrations,*

237; Hayes Diary, March 1, 1878, HML. The international conference convened in Paris, talked, and true to historic form, dispersed in the summer of 1878.

165. Hayes Diary, May 15, 1891, HML; John Sherman, "Resumption of Specie Payments," *North American Review*, 125 (November, 1877), 420–26.

166. Garfield to Edward Atkinson, April 16, 1878, Atkinson MHS; Sherman, *Recollections*, II, 660.

167. Robert McElroy, *Levi Parsons Morton* (New York: G. P. Putnam's Sons, 1930), 80–81; Stoddard, *As I Knew Them*, 87.

168. Sherman to Warner Bateman, January 20, 1879, Sherman LC.

169. Hayes Diary, November 12, 1878, HML.

170. *The Education of Henry Adams* (New York: Modern Library, 1931), 261.

171. *Carp's Washington*, 12–15; *New York Times*, February 12, 1880.

172. Bryan to Hayes, June 25, 1879, Hayes HML.

173. Smith, *Life and Letters of James Abram Garfield*, II, 679–80.

174. See David Saville Muzzey, *James G. Blaine* (New York: Dodd, Mead & Co., 1934), 140–42; James G. Blaine, *Political Discussions, Legislative, Diplomatic and Popular* (Norwich, Connecticut: The Henry Bill Publishing Company, 1887), 246–59.

175. Garfield to Burke A. Hinsdale, May 20, 1879, in Mary L. Hinsdale (Ed.), *Garfield-Hinsdale Letters* (Ann Arbor: University of Michigan Press, 1949), 426.

176. Quoted in Smith to A. B. Howard, April 4, 1879, Smith OHS.

177. Hayes Diary, March 31, 1879, HML.

178. Garfield Diary, March 28, 1879, Garfield LC; Hayes Diary, March 30, 1879, HML.

179. Curtis W. Garrison, "Conversations with Hayes: A Biographer's Notes," *Mississippi Valley Historical Review*, 25 (December, 1938), 369–80.

180. *New York Tribune*, July 5, 1879.

181. *New York Herald*, July 3, 1879.

182. Hayes Diary, July 3, 1879, HML.

183. Hayes Diary, December 29, 1881, and Hayes to Guy Bryan, March 26, 1880, HML.

184. Hayes Diary, March 12, 1878, HML.

185. Barnard, *Rutherford B. Hayes*, 496.

II

Presidential Sweepstakes: 1880-Style

1. Robert Underwood Johnson, *Remembered Yesterdays* (Boston: Houghton Mifflin Co., 1923), 215.

2. *New York Tribune*, February 23, 1866, in William B. Hesseltine, *Ulysses S. Grant, Politician* (New York: Dodd, Mead & Co., 1935), 63.

3. Adam Badeau, *Grant in Peace* (Hartford, Connecticut: S. S. Scranton Co., 1887), 73–74; Justin Kaplan, *Mr. Clemens and Mark Twain: A Biography* (New York: Simon and Schuster, 1966), 121.

4. Matilda Gresham, *Life of Walter Quintin Gresham*, 2 vols. (Chicago: Rand McNally Co., 1919), II, 494.

5. Claflin to W. E. Chandler, August 22, 1870, Chandler LC.

6. *New York Tribune,* March 5, 1873.

7. Paine, *Th: Nast,* 351.

8. *New York World,* June 8, 1865.

9. Harry Thurston Peck, *Twenty Years of the Republic, 1885–1905* (New York: Dodd, Mead & Co., 1906), 108–109.

10. Grant to E. F. Beale, July 7, 1878, copy in Grant LC.

11. Badeau, *Grant in Peace,* 316.

12. *St. Louis Post-Dispatch,* August 19, 1879.

13. *St. Louis Globe-Democrat,* February 28, 1880.

14. *Nation,* August 22, 1878, pp. 108–109.

15. *New York Herald,* December 9, 1878.

16. See Hesseltine, *Ulysses S. Grant,* 431.

17. Williams, *Rutherford Birchard Hayes,* II, 235–36.

18. Badeau, *Grant in Peace,* 524–25; Kaplan, *Mr. Clemens and Mark Twain,* 224–26.

19. Chidsey, *The Gentleman From New York,* 276.

20. Grant to Badeau, August 30, 1879, in Badeau, *Grant in Peace,* 318.

21. Grant to E. F. Beale, October 24, 1879, copy in Grant LC.

22. See *New York Times,* January 23, 1880; *Nation,* April 17, 1879, p. 255.

23. Hirshson, *Farewell to the Bloody Shirt,* 59–60; Hesseltine, *Ulysses S. Grant,* 91; Raymond B. Nixon, *Henry W. Grady* (New York: Alfred A. Knopf, 1943), 165; *Nation,* November 20, 1879, p. 335; *St. Louis Globe-Democrat,* June 11, 1880.

24. Chidsey, *The Gentleman From New York,* 168–69.

25. James G. Blaine, *Twenty Years of Congress,* 2 vols. (Norwich, Connecticut: The Henry Bill Publishing Co., 1884–1886), II, 599.

26. Cortissoz, *Whitelaw Reid,* II, 18–19.

27. *Nation,* February 12, 1880, p. 105; *Harper's Weekly,* May 29, 1880, p. 338; E. Dunbar Lockwood to Schurz, April 14, 1880, Schurz LC.

28. Conkling, *Life and Letters of Roscoe Conkling,* 586–87; Chidsey, *The Gentleman From New York,* 280–81; *Nation,* March 4, 1880, p. 165; *New York Sun,* February 26, 1880; *Washington Post,* May 3, 1880; *Frank Leslie's Illustrated Weekly,* June 5, 1880, p. 218.

29. Parsons, *Scattered Memories,* 66.

30. Blaine to Murat Halstead, April 8, 1880, Halstead HPSO.

31. W. H. Smith to Murat Halstead, November 8, 1879, Smith OHS; Badeau, *Grant in Peace,* 319–20; Sherman, *Recollections,* II, 766; *Harper's Weekly,* January 10, 1880, p. 18; *Cincinnati Commercial,* January 1, 1880; Elihu B. Washburne to John A. Logan, April 30, 1880, Logan LC.

32. Donaldson Memoirs, December 20, 1879, HML.

33. *New York Times,* May 8, 1880.

34. Connelley, *Preston B. Plumb,* 245–47.

35. Wharton Barker to Garfield, April 6, 1880, Barker LC.

36. Thomas H. Sherman, *Twenty Years With James G. Blaine* (New York: The Grafton Press, 1928), 39. Sherman was Blaine's private secretary.

37. Ingalls, *Writings,* 417–18.

38. *CR,* 45th Congress, 3rd Session, 239.

39. Garfield Diary, April 19, 1880, Garfield LC.

40. See the astute appraisal of an editorial foe, *New York Sun,* June 13, 1884.

41. Sherman, *Twenty Years With James G. Blaine,* 159; Harriet S. Blaine

Beale (Ed.), *Letters of Mrs. James G. Blaine,* 2 vols. (New York: Duffield and Co., 1908), I, 185.

42. Foraker, *I Would Live It Again,* 132; Sherman, *Twenty Years With James G. Blaine,* 126; Crook, *Through Five Administrations,* 260–61; Charles Edward Russell, *Blaine of Maine: His Life and Times* (New York: Cosmopolitan Book Co., 1931), 2; Brand Whitlock, *Forty Years of It* (New York: D. Appleton and Co., 1914), 50–51.

43. Ingalls, *Writings,* 438.

44. Matthew Josephson, *The Politicos* (New York: Harcourt, Brace, 1938), 336.

45. Muzzey, *James G. Blaine,* 97.

46. Blaine to Garfield, February 13, 1881, in Gail Hamilton, *Biography of James G. Blaine* (Norwich, Connecticut: Henry Bill Publishing Co., 1895), 501; Blaine to S. B. Elkins, February 10, 1881, Elkins WVUL.

47. A. K. McClure, *Old Time Notes of Pennsylvania,* 2 vols. (Philadelphia: John C. Winston Co., 1905), II, 566–67; Blaine to J. W. Foster, December 24, 1891, Foster LC; Sherman, *Twenty Years With James G. Blaine,* 13; Whitlock, *Forty Years of It,* 50; Russell, *Blaine of Maine,* 378; Paine, *Th: Nast,* 420–21; Charles R. Flint, *Memories of an Active Life* (New York: G. P. Putnam's Sons, 1923), 159.

48. *Nation,* February 19, 1880, p. 127; *New York Times,* February 20, 1880.

49. See Hamilton, *James G. Blaine,* 152; Chidsey, *The Gentleman From New York,* 90–92.

50. Cortissoz, *Whitelaw Reid,* II, 15–17.

51. *Ibid.,* 21; Typescript Memo, October 15, 1879, copy in Smith OHS; Garfield Diary, May 23, 1880, Garfield LC; Chandler to Mrs. Blaine, January 17, 1880, Blaine LC; *Frank Leslie's Illustrated Weekly,* April 10, 1880, p. 83; McClure, *Old Time Notes,* II, 506; *Letters of Mrs. James G. Blaine,* I, 170.

52. *New York Times,* February 15, 1880.

53. Blaine to Halstead, April 23, May 3, 1880, Halstead HPSO; Hamilton, *James G. Blaine,* 503; Sherman, *Recollections,* II, 773.

54. Garrison, "Conversations With Hayes," *passim.*

55. Garfield Diary, July 1, 1879, Garfield LC; Sherman to Richard Smith, June 14, 1880, Sherman LC; Sherman, *Recollections,* II, 729–31.

56. *Ibid.,* II, 730.

57. *Harper's Weekly,* April 24, 1880, p. 258.

58. Sherman, *Recollections,* II, 769; White, *The Republican Era,* 110.

59. Shadgett, *The Republican Party in Georgia,* 79.

60. Ellis Paxson Oberholtzer, *A History of the United States Since the Civil War,* 5 vols. (New York: Macmillan Co., 1918–1937), IV, 77, n2.

61. Sherman to Warner Bateman, June 1, 1880, Sherman LC.

62. *Nation,* February 26, 1880, p. 145.

63. *Harper's Weekly,* May 22, 1880, p. 322; Grant to Fred Grant, June 8, 1880, Conkling LC; Selig Adler, "The Senatorial Career of George Franklin Edmunds," (Unpublished Ph.D. Dissertation, University of Illinois, 1934), 165.

64. John A. Garraty, *Henry Cabot Lodge* (New York: Alfred A. Knopf, 1953), 65; Hayes Diary, April 1, 1878, HML; Hoar, *Autobiography,* I, 385–88.

65. Stealey, *Twenty Years in the Press Gallery,* 268; *New York Tribune,* July 26, 1880; Hayes Diary, August 6, 1885, HML; Edward Chase Kirkland, *Charles Francis Adams, Jr.* (Cambridge: Harvard University Press, 1965), 109.

66. Robert Kelly, "The Thought and Character of Samuel J. Tilden: The Democrat as Inheritor," *The Historian,* 26 (February, 1964), 176–205.

67. Alexander Clarence Flick, *Samuel Jones Tilden* (New York: Dodd, Mead and Company, 1938), 299.

68. Herbert J. Bass, *"I Am A Democrat": The Political Career of David Bennett Hill* (Syracuse: Syracuse University Press, 1961), 7.

69. F. P. Mitchell, *Memoirs of An Editor* (New York: Charles Scribner's Sons, 1924), 294.

70. Flick, *Samuel Jones Tilden,* 530.

71. Blaine, *Twenty Years,* II, 572ff. Cf., John Bigelow, *Letters and Literary Memorials of Samuel Jones Tilden,* 2 vols. (New York: Harper and Brothers, 1908), I, 273; Alexander B. Callow, Jr., *The Tweed Ring* (New York: Oxford University Press, 1966), 238, 254, 296; Schurz, *Speeches,* III, 259.

72. Eaton to Sherman, July 29, 1876, copy in Sherman LC.

73. Mitchell, *Memories of An Editor,* 262, 300.

74. *Washington Post,* January 12, 1878; *St. Louis Globe-Democrat,* March 23, 1880; Ward to Bayard, June 3, 1879, Bayard LC.

75. Nevins, *Abram S. Hewitt,* 435.

76. John Bigelow, *The Life of Samuel J. Tilden,* 2 vols. (New York: Harper and Brothers, 1895), II, 265.

77. *St. Louis Globe-Democrat,* March 18, 1880.

78. *Ibid.,* June 13, 1880.

79. Flick, *Samuel Jones Tilden,* 445.

80. Allan Nevins, *Grover Cleveland* (New York: Dodd, Mead and Co., 1932), 112–13.

81. M. R. Werner, *Tammany Hall* (New York: Doubleday, Doran, 1928), 276–77.

82. *New York Sun,* April 21, 1880; *New York Times,* April 21, 1880; *New York Tribune,* April 24, 1880; Herbert J. Clancy, *The Presidential Election of 1880* (Chicago: Loyola University Press, 1958), 72–73.

83. *St. Louis Globe-Democrat,* March 22, 1880.

84. *New York Times,* June 20, 1880.

85. *New York World,* June 22, 1880; Carl Brent Swisher, *Stephen J. Field* (Washington: Brookings Institution, 1930), 286ff; *New York Herald,* June 22, 1880; Dallas Sanders to Samuel J. Randall, June 7, 9, 1880, Randall UPL.

86. Stealey, *Twenty Years in the Press Gallery,* 34, 201.

87. Bayard Diary, July 3, 1895, Bayard LC.

88. W. H. Pratt to Bayard, April 22, 1888, *ibid.*

89. Bayard to Pendleton King, November 29, 1883, *ibid.*

90. Garland to Bayard, September 29, 1879, *ibid.*

91. *St. Louis Globe-Democrat,* March 8, 1880.

92. Tansill, *Congressional Career of Thomas Francis Bayard,* 243ff.

93. Bayard to David A. Wells, December 3, 1879, Wells LC.

94. Bayard to Samuel Barlow, November 15, 1878; to August Belmont, March 7, 1879; John Hunter to Bayard, February 16, 1880; and Perry Belmont to Bayard, March 1, 1880; all in Bayard LC.

95. James A. Barnes, *John G. Carlisle, Financial Statesman* (New York: Dodd, Mead and Co., 1931), 47.

96. *Philadelphia Press,* August 18, 1886; see also the description of a speech in the *New York Tribune,* February 9, 1884.

97. *New York Times,* January 31, 1884; J. C. Morgan to Randall, November 23, 1882, Randall UPL; *New York Tribune,* November 14, 1882; *Nation,* April 17, 1890, p. 305; Ida Tarbell, *The Tariff in Our Times* (New York: Macmillan Co., 1911), 83–84.

98. *New York Times,* December 2, 1883.

99. Tansill, *The Congressional Career of Thomas Francis Bayard,* 247ff; *St. Louis Globe-Democrat,* February 21, 1880; George Cotton to Randall, June 4, 1889, Randall UPL; John B. Haskin to Randall, April 17, 1880, *ibid.*

100. Clancy, *The Presidential Election of 1880,* 68–69; Mary R. Dearing, *Veterans in Politics: The Story of the G.A.R.* (Baton Rouge: Louisiana State University Press, 1952), 152–53, 156, 201, 222; Hancock to Sherman, June 23, 1880, W. T. Sherman LC.

101. *St. Louis Globe-Democrat,* March 22, 1880.

102. Robert G. Caldwell, *James A. Garfield* (New York: Dodd, Mead and Co., 1931), 17.

103. *Ibid.,* 62.

104. Alexander K. McClure, *Recollections of Half a Century* (Salem: The Salem Press, Inc. 1902), 106; Chidsey, *The Gentleman From New York,* 296; Crook, *Through Five Administrations,* 256–57.

105. Ingalls, *Writings,* 398.

106. Smith, *Life and Letters of James Abram Garfield,* II, 790ff.

107. Caldwell, *James A. Garfield,* 340.

108. Smith, *Life and Letters of James Abram Garfield,* II, 656.

109. Garfield Diary, April 26, 1876, Garfield LC.

110. Russell, *Blaine of Maine,* 372.

111. Garfield Diary, May 13, 1878, Garfield LC.

112. Sherman, *Recollections,* II, 807.

113. Smith, *Life and Letters of James Abram Garfield,* II, 888.

114. Garfield to Burke A. Hinsdale, March 28, 1879, Garfield LC.

115. Smith, *Life and Letters of James Abram Garfield,* II, 944.

116. Clancy, *The Presidential Election of 1880,* 34–36.

117. Garfield Diary, May 31, 1880, Garfield LC.

118. Colman, *White House Gossip,* 133.

119. Garfield to Harmon Austin, April 16, 1880, Garfield LC.

120. *Cleveland Herald,* June 2, 1880.

121. Garfield to Harmon Austin, April 16, 1880, Garfield LC.

122. Garfield to Harmon Austin, February 14, 1880, *ibid.*

123. Garfield to Mrs. Garfield, June 2, 1880, and Garfield Diary, May 28, 1880, both Garfield LC.

124. I have used the *New York Times,* May 24–June 10, 1880 for describing the convention and its aftermath; see also *Proceedings of the Republican National Convention, . . . 1880* (Chicago: Jno. B. Jeffery Printing and Publishing House, 1880), hereafter cited as *GOP Proc. 1880;* Rhodes, *History,* VIII, 116.

125. *Ibid.,* 115–17; William C. Hudson, *Random Recollections of an Old Political Reporter* (New York: Cupples and Leon, 1911), 95.

126. Clancy, *The Presidential Election of 1880,* 85–86, 115–16; Blaine to Chandler, June 1, 1880, Chandler LC.

127. William Dennison to Sherman, June 2, 1880, Sherman LC.

128. Shelby M. Cullom, *Fifty Years of Public Service* (Chicago: A. C. McClurg and Co., 1911), 123ff.

129. *New York Times,* June 3, 1880; Alexander, *Political History,* III, 438–39.

130. *GOP Proc. 1880,* p. 81.

131. Platt, *Autobiography,* 102; *GOP Proc. 1880,* p. 34ff; Clancy, *The Presidential Election of 1880,* pp. 90–92; Conkling to Garfield, June [?] 1880, Garfield LC.

132. Rhodes, *History,* VIII, 119.

133. *GOP Proc. 1880,* pp. 160ff.

134. *Ibid.,* 175ff; Depew, *My Memories,* 121; Hamilton, *James G. Blaine,* 484.

135. *Chicago Inter-Ocean,* June 7, 1880.

136. *GOP Proc. 1880,* pp. 179ff.

137. *Cleveland Herald,* June 6, 1880.

138. *GOP Proc. 1880,* pp. 184ff; Stoddard, *As I Knew Them,* 108–109; Chidsey, *The Gentleman From New York,* 289–90; Depew, *My Memories,* 121; *St. Louis Globe-Democrat,* June 7, 1880; Clancy, *The Presidential Election of 1880,* p. 104; Halstead to Sherman, June 6, 1880, Sherman LC.

139. Connelley, *Preston B. Plumb,* 245–47.

140. Hayes Diary, June 15, 1880, HML.

141. *GOP Proc. 1880,* pp. 195–201.

142. See *Los Angeles Times,* February 11, 1894; Charles Emory Smith, "How Conkling Missed Nominating Blaine," *Saturday Evening Post,* 172 (June 9, 1901), 2–3; Platt, *Autobiography,* 113; *New York Herald,* June 4, 1888; Clancy, *The Presidential Election of 1880,* pp. 117ff.

143. Smith, *Life and Letters of James Abram Garfield,* II, 983–84; Blaine, *Twenty Years,* 666; Cortissoz, *Whitelaw Reid,* II, 25–26; Depew, *My Memories,* 122; McClure, *Recollections,* 109–10.

144. Clancy, *The Presidential Election of 1880,* 119; Chidsey, *The Gentleman From New York,* 293–94; McElroy, *Levi Parsons Morton,* 105–106; Stoddard, *As I Knew Them,* 110–12; Alexander, *Political History,* III, 443.

145. Hudson, *Random Recollections,* 97–98; McElroy, *Levi Parsons Morton,* 105–106; *New York Herald,* June 4, 1888.

146. *St. Louis Post-Dispatch,* June 9, 1880.

147. Sherman to Warner Bateman, June 9, 1880, Sherman LC; Sherman, *Recollections,* II, 886.

148. Blaine, *Twenty Years,* 666–67.

149. Fuess, *Carl Schurz,* 272–73.

150. *Nation,* June 17, 1880, 445–49.

151. Sherman to J. Kilpatrick, June 12, 1880; to C. A. Trimble, June 12, 1880; to Rush Sloan, January 31, 1883, all in Sherman LC.

152. Conkling, *Life and Letters of Roscoe Conkling,* 608–609.

153. *New York Sun,* June 9, 1880; McClure, *Recollections,* 110; Orville Babcock to Adam Badeau, June 27, 1880, Badeau LC; Conkling, *Life and Letters of Roscoe Conkling,* opposite 609.

154. Hayes to George W. Jones, June 11, 1880, Hayes HML.

155. Williams, *Rutherford Birchard Hayes,* II, 240, nl.

156. *Frank Leslie's Illustrated Weekly,* June 26, 1880, p. 278.

157. George Bates to Bayard, June 21, 1880, Bayard LC; *New York Times,* June 22, 1880.

158. See *Official Proceedings of the National Democratic Convention . . . 1880* (Dayton: Daily Journal Book and Job Room, 1880), viii-ix, cited hereafter as *Dem.*

Proc. 1880; New York Herald, June 24, 1880; William R. Barlow, "Cincinnati Hosts the Democrats in 1880," Cincinnati Historical Society *Bulletin,* 22 (1964), 145–61.

159. *Dem. Proc. 1880,* 43.

160. *New York Herald,* June 17, 1880; *St. Louis Globe-Democrat,* February 25, 1880.

161. Flick, *Samuel Jones Tilden,* 457ff; Bigelow, *Samuel J. Tilden,* II, 272; *New York Times,* June 21, 1880.

162. *New York Tribune,* June 21, 22, 1880.

163. *Harper's Weekly,* 24 (July 10, 1880), 433.

164. Hudson, *Random Recollections,* 109–10.

165. David A. Wells to Manton Marble, October 30, 1880, Marble LC.

166. *Dem. Proc. 1880,* p. 5.

167. *Ibid.,* 69ff; *New York Times,* June 24, 1880.

168. *Dem. Proc. 1880,* pp. 71ff.

169. *Ibid.,* 85–89.

170. Bigelow, *Samuel J. Tilden,* II, 272; *Dem. Proc. 1880,* 107–14.

171. H. L. Bryan to Bayard, June 26, 1880, Bayard LC.

172. Ward to Bayard, June 28, 1880, *ibid.*

173. *Dem. Proc. 1880,* pp. ix, 121–22.

174. *Ibid.,* 127–29.

175. *Nation,* July 1, 1880, p. 1.

176. Weed to Tilden, June 25, 1880, in Bigelow, *Letters and Literary Memorials of Samuel J. Tilden,* II, 599–600.

177. Tilden to S. C. Johnson, July 2, 1880, Tilden NYPL; *New York Herald,* June 26, 1880.

178. Hampton to Bayard, June 26, 1880, Bayard LC.

179. George H. Armstrong to Randall, June 25, 1880, Randall UPL.

180. *New York Times,* June 25, 1880.

181. *Harper's Weekly,* July 10, 1880, p. 434.

182. *Nation,* July 1, 1880, pp. 4–5.

183. *New York Times,* June 25, 1880.

III

Campaigns and Feuds: 1880–1881

1. Parsons, *Scattered Memories,* 68; Caldwell, *James A. Garfield,* 292.

2. M. P. Curran, *Life of Patrick Collins* (Norwood: Norwood Press, 1906), 82; Garfield to Schurz, July 6, 1880, Schurz LC; McClure, *Old Time Notes,* II, 512.

3. *New York Times,* June 12, 1880; Howe, *Chester A. Arthur,* 111ff.

4. Garfield to Whitelaw Reid, June 29, 1880, in Smith, *Life and Letters of James Abram Garfield,* II, 996–98.

5. Garfield to Blaine, June 29, 1880, Garfield LC.

6. Hoogenboom, *Outlawing the Spoils,* 138–39.

7. Smith, *Life and Letters of James Abram Garfield,* II, 999–1000; Chandler to Garfield, June 14, 1880, Chandler LC; Chandler to Garfield, February 17, 1881, Chandler NHHS.

8. Garfield to Blaine, June 29, 1880, Garfield LC.

9. *Harper's Weekly*, July 31, 1880, p. 482.

10. *Nation*, July 15, 1880, 235.

11. Reid to Garfield, June 12, 1880, in Cortissoz, *Whitelaw Reid*, II, 35.

12. Quoted in James M. Tyner to Louis T. Michener, September 21, 1888, Michener LC.

13. Smith, *Life and Letters of James Abram Garfield*, II, 1046.

14. Blaine to Garfield, July 4, 1880, in Hamilton, *James G. Blaine*, 486–87.

15. Rhodes, *History*, VIII, 200.

16. Conkling to Morton, August 1, 1880, Morton NYPL.

17. *New York Times*, July 19, 1880; *GOP Proc. 1880*, pp. 302–304.

18. Cortissoz, *Whitelaw Reid*, II, 37.

19. Chandler to Garfield, July 24, 1880, Garfield LC.

20. Dorsey to Garfield, July 26, 1880, *ibid.*

21. Garfield to Chandler, July 26, 28, 1880, *ibid.;* Garfield to Blaine, July 30, 1880, in Hamilton, *James G. Blaine*, 487–88.

22. Garfield Diary, August 5–12, 1880, Garfield LC.

23. See Platt, *Autobiography*, 125–27; *New York Herald*, May 11, 1881; Chidsey, *The Gentleman From New York*, 306; Cortissoz, *Whitelaw Reid*, II, 37–38; George C. Gorham in *New York Herald*, June 4, 1888; Conkling, *Life and Letters of Roscoe Conkling*, 611.

24. Platt, *Autobiography*, 128ff; Garfield Diary, August 5–6, 1880, Garfield LC; Conkling, *Life and Letters of Roscoe Conkling*, 612–13; Paine, *Th: Nast*, 487; *New York Herald*, May 11, 1881; McElroy, *Levi Parsons Morton*, 110.

25. Murat Halstead, "The Tragedy of Garfield's Administration," *McClure's Magazine*, 6 (February, 1896), 275.

26. Garfield Diary, August 9, 1880, Garfield LC.

27. *Frank Leslie's Illustrated Weekly*, August 28, 1880, p. 426; Curtis to Hayes, August 15, 1880, Hayes HML; Reid to Garfield, August 15, 1880, Garfield LC.

28. Reid to Garfield, August 31, 1880, Reid LC; Chauncey Filley to D. G. Swain [?], Garfield LC; R. C. McCormick to Chandler, August 13, 1880; Chandler LC; Conkling to Morton, August 29, 1880, Morton NYPL; *New York Herald*, May 11, 1881; Conkling, *Life and Letters of Roscoe Conkling*, 614–15.

29. *Ibid.*, 614; *Frank Leslie's Illustrated Weekly*, April 29, 1888, p. 163; Platt, *Autobiography*, 132–33.

30. *Nation*, October 21, 1880, p. 453; *New York Sun*, October 20, 1880.

31. Grant to Logan, August 12, 1880, Logan LC.

32. Garfield to Harmon Austin, September 23, October 6, 1880, Garfield LC; Foraker, *Notes*, I, 143–44.

33. Garfield's Diary entry for September 28, 1880, merely recounts the party's visit. Platt, *Autobiography*, 134–35, is the chief source for the dramatic front-yard embrace. Conkling, *Life and Letters of Roscoe Conkling*, 622ff, disavows the idea of a "Treaty of Mentor," saying Conkling avoided being alone with Garfield. Williams, *Life and Letters of James Abram Garfield*, II, 1033–34, quotes Garfield's secretary as saying the two men were never alone and the front-yard confrontation "was a deliberate lie." George C. Gorham, in an obituary article on Conkling in the *New York Herald*, June 4, 1888, agrees there was no treaty.

34. Platt, *Autobiography*, 134–35.

35. Johnson Brigham, *Blaine, Conkling and Garfield: A Reminiscence and a*

Character Study (Des Moines: The Prairie Club, 1915), 21; T. B. Connery, "Secret History of the Garfield-Conkling Tragedy," *Cosmopolitan* 23 (June, 1897), 150–51.

36. Cortissoz, *Whitelaw Reid*, II, 38; William Roscoe Thayer (Ed.), *Life and Letters of John Hay*, 2 vols. (Boston: Houghton Mifflin Co., 1915), II, 441.

37. Grant to E. F. Beale, October 22, 1880, copy in Grant LC.

38. *Dem. Proc. 1880*, pp. 515ff; Almira Russell Hancock, *Reminiscences of Winfield Scott Hancock* (New York: Charles L. Webster Co., 1887), 171.

39. Randall to Hancock, June 26, 1880, Randall UPL.

40. J. J. McElhone to Randall, June 26, 1880, *ibid.*

41. John Hunter to Bayard, July 17, 1880, Bayard LC.

42. *Dem. Proc. 1880*, pp. 161–68.

43. *New York Times*, July 31, 1880.

44. Hancock to Bayard, August 31, 1880, Bayard LC; and to English, September 1, 1880, English IHS.

45. Dudley to Garfield, September 9, 1880, Garfield LC; Stilson Hutchins to Chandler, November 30, 1880, Chandler NHHS; Rhodes, *History*, VIII, 135; Garfield to Morton, September 3, 1880, and September 28, 1880, in McElroy, *Levi Parsons Morton*, 113–16.

46. Hayes Diary, June 15, 1880, HML.

47. Barry, *Forty Years in Washington*, 80.

48. *New York Sun*, June 9, 1880.

49. Donaldson Memoirs, June 16, 1880, HML.

50. Garfield to Reid, September 2, 1880, Garfield LC.

51. Garfield Diary, September 13–15, 1880, *ibid.*; Garfield to Morton, September 17, 1880, in McElroy, *Levi Parsons Morton*, 114–15.

52. Hudson, *Random Recollections*, 112.

53. Jewell to Garfield, September 14, 1880, Garfield LC.

54. Clancy, *The Presidential Election of 1880*, pp. 219–20. Democratic apprehension was especially strong in Pennsylvania, New Jersey, Indiana, and Connecticut.

55. Stanwood, *American Tariff Controversies*, II, 200ff.

56. Edwin Cowles to Garfield, October [?], 1880, Garfield LC.

57. Clarence Lee Miller, *The States of the Old Northwest and the Tariff* (Emporia, Kansas: Emporia Gazette, 1949), 135–36; Flint, *Memories*, 258–59.

58. Smith, *Life and Letters of James Abram Garfield*, II, 1039–41; Nevins, *Abram S. Hewitt*, 435–36; Filley to D. G. Swain, October 24, 25, 1880, Garfield LC; *New York Sun*, October 30, 1880.

59. Garfield Diary, Ocotber 30–November 3, 1880, Garfield LC.

60. Hancock, *Reminiscences*, 172–73.

61. *Ibid.*, 174–75; David Lindsey, *"Sunset" Cox, Irrepressible Democrat* (Detroit: Wayne State University Press, 1959), 194.

62. Howe, *Chester A. Arthur*, 129–30; Chandler to Garfield, February 17, 1880, Chandler NHHS.

63. Blaine, *Twenty Years*, 669–70; Garfield to Morton, November 8, 1880, Morton NYPL; Garfield to Charles Foster, November 8, 1880, Garfield LC.

64. Blaine, *Twenty Years*, 679.

65. *Puck*, November 10, 1880, p. 152.

66. *Frank Leslie's Illustrated Weekly*, November 20, 1880, p. 182.

67. Garfield Diary, November 8, 1880, Garfield LC.

68. Schurz to Garfield, December 10, 1880, in Hamilton, *James G. Blaine*, 490–91.

69. Blaine to Garfield, December 10, 1880, *ibid.*, 490–91.

70. Garfield to Blaine, December 19, 1880, *ibid.*, 493.

71. Williams, *Life and Letters of James Abram Garfield*, II, 1053, 1058–59; Garfield Diary, November 27, 1880, Garfield LC.

72. Blaine to Garfield, December 10, 1880, in Hamilton, *James G. Blaine*, 490–91.

73. Sherman to Garfield, January 21, 1881, Garfield LC.

74. Blaine to Garfield, December 24, 1880, in Hamilton, *James G. Blaine*, 495–96. Cf., McElroy, *Levi Parsons Morton*, 121; Sage, *William Boyd Allison*, 165ff; Garfield Diary, November 16, 1880, Garfield LC.

75. *Ibid.*, December 13, 1880.

76. Dorsey to Garfield, December 16, 1880, *ibid.*

77. Muzzey, *James G. Blaine*, 182; Cortissoz, *Whitelaw Reid*, II, 53; Hamilton, *James G. Blaine*, 497–98; Sherman to Garfield, January 23, 1881, Garfield LC.

78. *New York Herald*, May 11, 1881; Connery, "Secret History of the Garfield-Conkling Tragedy," 151; Garfield Diary, February 16, 1881, Garfield LC.

79. McElroy, *Levi Parsons Morton*, 122–29; Connery, "Secret History of the Garfield-Conkling Tragedy," 152–53.

80. Garfield Diary, November 4, 1880, Garfield LC.

81. *New York Herald*, March 5, 1881.

82. Garfield Diary, March 24, 1881, Garfield LC.

83. *Ibid.*, March 3–4, 1881.

84. Reid to Elizabeth Mills, March 3, March 5, 1881, in Cortissoz, *Whitelaw Reid*, II, 56–57; Caldwell, *James A. Garfield*, 329; Smith, *Life and Letters of James Abram Garfield*, II, 1083.

85. Garfield Diary, January 17, 27, February 10, March 1, 4, 1881, Garfield LC.

86. Barnard, *Rutherford B. Hayes*, 500.

87. Crook, *Through Five Administrations*, 256.

88. Sherman to Garfield, February 16, 1881, Garfield LC; Hayes Diary, January 16, 1881, HML.

89. *New York Herald*, June 4, 1888.

90. Garfield Diary, March 8, 1881, Garfield LC.

91. Clarence H. Cramer, *Royal Bob: The Life of Robert G. Ingersoll* (Indianapolis: Bobbs, Merrill Co., 1952), 199; Hamilton, *James G. Blaine*, 514.

92. Badeau, *Grant in Peace*, 330.

93. Smith, *Life and Letters of James Abram Garfield*, II, 1093–95, 1108ff.

94. Rhodes, *History*, VIII, 144, n4; Cortissoz, *Whitelaw Reid*, II, 55, 58–59.

95. Sherman, *Twenty Years With James G. Blaine*, 28; Chidsey, *The Gentleman From New York*, 329–30.

96. Alexander, *Political History*, II, 466; Cortissoz, *Whitelaw Reid*, II, 44–47; *New York Tribune*, January 3, 1881; Sherman to Garfield, January 23, 1881, Garfield LC.

97. Cortissoz, *Whitelaw Reid*, II, 49–51; Alexander, *Political History*, III, 468, n5; George C. Gorham in *New York Herald*, June 4, 1888.

98. *Letters of Mrs. Henry Adams*, 256.

99. Cortissoz, *Whitelaw Reid*, II, 54.

100. Platt, *Autobiography*, 149–50; *New York Herald*, May 11, 1881; Garfield Diary, March 20–22, 1881, Garfield LC.

101. Matthew P. Breen, *Thirty Years of New York Politics* (New York: n.p., 1899), 656; *New York Herald*, June 4, 1888.

102. Garfield Diary, March 22, 23, 1881, Garfield LC.

103. Chidsey, *The Gentleman From New York*, 330–32; *New York Tribune*, May 17, 1881; George S. Boutwell, *Reminiscences of Sixty Years in Public Affairs*, 2 vols. (New York: McClure, Phillips and Co., 1902), II, 274; *Letters of Mrs. James G. Blaine*, I, 286–87.

104. Garfield to Reid, March 30, 1881, in Cortissoz, *Whitelaw Reid*, II, 61–62; see also William Henry Smith to Hayes, April 7, 1881, Hayes HML; Garfield to Burke A. Hinsdale, April 4, 1881, in *Garfield-Hinsdale Letters*, 488ff.

105. Blaine to Reid, March 31, 1881, Reid LC.

106. Alexander, *Political History*, III, 472ff.

107. Smith, *Life and Letters of James Abram Garfield*, II, 1132–34. Garfield noted: "He seems to have forgotten that he is only one citizen, and hence is unconsciously insolent."

108. Dawes to Mrs. Dawes, April 30, 1881, Dawes LC; Henry L. Dawes, "Conkling and Garfield," *Century Magazine*, 47 (January, 1894), 343–44.

109. T. B. Connery, "The Secret History of the Garfield-Conkling Tragedy," 145–62.

110. *New York Herald*, June 4, 1888; Garfield Diary, April–May, 1881, *passim*, Garfield LC; Chidsey, *The Gentleman From New York*, 339.

111. Connery, "Secret History of the Garfield-Conkling Tragedy," 159.

112. Howe, *Chester A. Arthur*, 146; Dawes to Mrs. Dawes, May 16, 1881, Dawes LC.

113. Garfield Diary, May 16, 1881, Garfield LC.

114. *Ibid.*, May 20, 1881.

115. *Ibid.*, May 25–31, 1881.

116. Garfield to Jacob D. Cox, May 22, 1881, in Smith, *Life and Letters of James Abram Garfield*, II, 1136.

117. *Nation*, June 2, 1881, p. 379.

118. Garfield Diary, June 9, 1881, Garfield LC.

119. *Albany Argus*, July 2, 1881; *New York World*, July 2, 1881; *Washington Post*, July 1, 2, 1881.

120. Garfield to Sherman, November 15, 1880, in Sherman, *Recollections*, II, 789.

121. *Washington Post*, July 3, 1881; *New York Herald*, July 4, 1881.

122. Hamilton, *James G. Blaine*, 538–39; Crook, *Through Five Administrations*, 271.

123. Smith, *Life and Letters of James Abram Garfield*, II, 1184–85; Chidsey, *The Gentleman From New York*, 352ff; *Washington Post*, July 3, 1881; Howe, *Chester A. Arthur*, 150–52; Harry J. Sievers, *Benjamin Harrison: Hoosier Statesman* (New York: University Publishing Co., 1959), 200; Caldwell, *James A. Garfield*, 349ff.

124. Platt, *Autobiography*, 162–65; Colman, *White House Gossip*, 147; *Washington Post*, July 3, 1881; J. W. Thompson to Sherman, July 4, 1881, Sherman LC; Hayes Diary, July 3, 1881, HML; Hayes to Sherman, July 7, 1881, Hayes HML; *Nation*, July 7, 1881, p. 1; Oberholtzer, *History*, IV, 128–29; Bayard to Henry Gassaway Davis, July 3, 1881, in Charles M. Pepper, *The Life and Times of Henry Gassaway Davis* (New York: Century Co., 1920), 266.

125. Crook, *Memories*, 155; Smith, *Life and Letters of James Abram Garfield*, II, 1195–96.

126. *Ibid.*, 1193–94.

127. *Ibid.*, 1191; Chandler to Mrs. Blaine, July 18, 1881, Blaine LC.

128. Arthur to MacVeagh, July 26, 1881, MacVeagh HSP.

129. Howe, *Chester A. Arthur,* 1–3, 154.

130. *Washington Post,* September 21–25, 1881.

131. George C. Gorham in *New York Herald,* June 4, 1888; Stoddard, *As I Knew Them,* 114.

132. Ingalls, *Writings,* 343.

133. Conkling, *Life and Letters of Roscoe Conkling,* 659, 676–77.

134. William A. Croffutt, *An American Procession, 1855–1914* (Boston: Little, Brown and Co., 1931), 257–58. The Declaration uses the phrase "a decent respect to the opinions of mankind."

135. Chandler to Mrs. Blaine, July 18, 1881, Blaine LC.

IV

Arthur

1. Sherman to Hayes, January 3, 1882, Hayes HML.

2. *New York Post,* April 2, 1900.

3. Howe, *Chester A. Arthur,* 7.

4. *Ibid.,* 15ff; Francis Butler Simkins, *The Tillman Movement in South Carolina* (Durham: Duke University Press, 1926), 28.

5. *New York Times,* November 19, 1886.

6. Howe, *Chester A. Arthur,* 21.

7. *Letters of Mrs. James G. Blaine,* I, 294.

8. Ingalls, *Writings,* 435.

9. Stealey, *Twenty Years in the Press Gallery,* 27.

10. Platt, *Autobiography,* 182.

11. Crook, *Through Five Administrations,* 276–78.

12. *Letters of Mrs. Henry Adams,* 300.

13. Richardson, *William E. Chandler,* 356; Howe, *Chester A. Arthur,* 173.

14. *New York World,* April 20, May 19, 1884; *Letters of Mrs. James G. Blaine,* I, 294.

15. Hugh Bradley, *Such Was Saratoga* (New York: Doubleday, Doran and Co., 1940), 200; Colman, *White House Gossip,* 160; Howe, *Chester A. Arthur,* 174.

16. *New York Tribune,* April 16, 1882.

17. Eckenrode, *Rutherford B. Hayes,* 335.

18. *Letters of Mrs. James G. Blaine,* II, 8; *Letters of Mrs. Henry Adams,* 356.

19. Andrew D. White, *Autobiography . . .,* 2 vols. (New York: Century Co., 1905), I, 193.

20. *New York Times,* September 23, 1881.

21. *Nation,* October 20, 1881, p. 301.

22. Chidsey, *The Gentleman From New York,* 360–61; *Washington Post,* October 8, 1881.

23. Howe, *Chester A. Arthur,* 244.

24. *New York Times,* October 1, 1881.

25. Badeau, *Grant in Peace,* 336, 338–39; Robert M. Ogden (Ed.), *Diaries of Andrew D. White* (Ithaca: Cornell University Library, 1959), 241; Platt, *Autobiography,* 180–81.

26. Depew, *My Memories*, 116.

27. Hudson, *Random Recollections*, 127.

28. *New York Times*, September 25, 1881.

29. Hayes to William Henry Smith, December 14, 1881, Hayes HML.

30. David M. Pletcher, *The Awkward Years: American Foreign Relations Under Garfield and Arthur* (Columbia: University of Missouri Press, 1962), 19; *Carp's Washington*, 83.

31. Quoted in Armstrong, *E. L. Godkin and America Foreign Policy*, 166–67.

32. Limitations of space forbid discussing anything but the results of this tortured problem. For background information see Muzzey, *James G. Blaine*, 184–224; and Alice Felt Tyler, *The Foreign Policy of James G. Blaine* (Minneapolis: University of Minnesota Press, 1927), 107–64. Pletcher, *The Awkward Years*, 40–101, offers new insights. Frederick S. Pike, *Chile and the United States, 1880–1962* (Notre Dame: University of Notre Dame Press, 1963), is hostile to the United States. See Russell H. Bastert, "A New Approach to the Origins of Blaine's Pan-American Policy," *Hispanic American Historical Review*, 39 (August, 1959), 375–412. I depart slightly from Bastert's interpretation in placing more emphasis on Blaine's interest in trade, and less emphasis on the State Department's origination of the problem. Blaine spelled out his own views, emphasizing stability and economics, in an article for the *Chicago Weekly Magazine*, September 16, 1881, printed in Muzzey, *James G. Blaine*, 206–207.

33. *Letters of Mrs. James G. Blaine*, I, 258, 269, 270.

34. John Watson Foster, *Diplomatic Memoirs*, 2 vols. (New York: Houghton Mifflin Co., 1909), II, 263–64.

35. *New York Sun*, January 17, 1882.

36. Quoted in Muzzey, *James G. Blaine*, 222.

37. Foster, *Diplomatic Memoirs*, II, 264; *Nation*, December 15, 1881, p. 461, and December 29, 1881, p. 506.

38. *Letters of Mrs. James G. Blaine*, I, 293–95.

39. Blaine, *Political Discussions*, 407–10.

40. *Letters of Mrs. Henry Adams*, 342.

41. See Russell H. Bastert, "Diplomatic Reversal: Frelinghuysen's Opposition to Blaine's Pan-American Policy in 1882," *Mississippi Valley Historical Review*, 42 (March, 1956), 653–71; Pletcher, *The Awkward Years*, 83–86; LaFeber, *The New Empire*, 48.

42. *Letters of Mrs. James G. Blaine*, II, 31.

43. Blaine to Garfield, February 13, 1881, Garfield LC.

44. Chandler to Garfield, February 17, 1881, *ibid.*

45. Caldwell, *James A. Garfield*, 335ff.

46. MacVeagh to James, August 27, 1881, MacVeagh HSP.

47. Arthur to MacVeagh, November 7, 1881, Arthur LC; Howe, *Chester A. Arthur*, 192.

48. J. Martin Klotsche, "The Star Route Cases," *Mississippi Valley Historical Review*, 22 (December, 1935), 407–18; *Nation*, June 21, 1883, p. 356.

49. *Ibid.*, April 19, 1888, p. 311.

50. *Cincinnati Inquirer*, August 3, 1882.

51. *Nation*, August 10, 1882, p. 101.

52. Hoar, *Autobiography*, I, 405ff; *New York Tribune*, November 14, 1882.

53. *Washington Post*, June 16, 1882.

54. Folger to James B. Butler, September 11, 1882, Folger NYPL.

55. *New York Tribune,* October 3, 1882.

56. *Washington Post,* September 8, 1882.

57. Folger to J. B. Butler, October 13, 1882, Folger NYPL.

58. *Washington Post,* November 8, 1882.

59. *New York Tribune,* November 8, 1882.

60. *Washington Post,* November 8, 1882.

61. *New York Tribune,* November 9, 1882.

62. *Washington Post,* September 8, 15, 1882.

63. Badeau, *Grant in Peace,* 546–47; *Letters of Mrs. Henry Adams,* 414.

64. Garfield Diary, March 26, 1881, Garfield LC.

65. William Dudley Foulke, *Fighting the Spoilsmen* (New York: G. P. Putnam's Sons, 1919), 91.

66. *Nation,* December 7, 1882, p. 480.

67. Schurz, *Speeches,* IV, 87.

68. *New York Sun,* July 24, 1884; see also *CR,* 47th Congress, 2nd Session, 277–80; *Harper's Weekly,* January 20, 1883, p. 34.

69. *CR,* 47th Congress, 2nd Session, 245, 275.

70. *Ibid.,* 661, December 27, 1882.

71. Van Riper, *History of the United States Civil Service,* 107–108.

72. *Ibid.,* 111–12.

73. Stanwood, *American Tariff Controversies,* II, 256; Kirkland, *Industry Comes of Age,* 294.

74. *New York Tribune,* April 30, 1883.

75. Stoddard, *As I Knew Them,* 214.

76. Hayes to B. A. Hayes, January 23, 1873, Hayes HML.

77. *Speeches and Addresses of William McKinley . . .* (New York: D. Appleton and Co., 1893), 17; cited hereafter as McKinley, *Speeches* (1893). See also H. Wayne Morgan, *William McKinley and His America* (Syracuse: Syracuse University Press, 1963), 59–64.

78. See H. Wayne Morgan, "William McKinley and the Tariff," *Ohio History,* 74 (Autumn, 1965), 215–31.

79. McKinley, *Speeches* (1893), 96.

80. This is an important point; see Miller, *The States of the Old Northwest and the Tariff,* 137–39; Richard H. Barton, "The Agrarian Revolt in Michigan, 1865–1900," (Unpublished Ph.D. Dissertation, Michigan State University, 1958), 109; Kenneth E. Hendrickson, "The Public Career of Richard F. Pettigrew of South Dakota, 1848–1926," (Unpublished Ph.D. Dissertation, University of Oklahoma, 1962), 131–32; Norbert Robert Mahnken, "The Congressmen of the Grain Belt States and Tariff Legislation, 1865–1900," (Unpublished Ph.D. Dissertation, University of Nebraska, 1942), 142.

81. Morrison to David A. Wells, September 7, 1884, Wells LC.

82. Quoted in Sidney Fine, *Laissez-Faire and the General Welfare State* (Ann Arbor: University of Michigan Press, 1956), 67.

83. *Nation,* January 5, 1882, p. 3.

84. Tarbell, *The Tariff in Our Times,* 98.

85. *Nation,* December 7, 1882, p. 475.

86. *Boston Daily Advertiser,* January 6, 1883.

87. Samuel W. Bell to Randall, February 16, 1883, Randall UPL.

88. *CR,* 47th Congress, 2nd Session, 3737.

89. Hewitt to Edward Atkinson, February 26, 1883, Atkinson MHS; Morrison

to Edward Atkinson, September 15, 1883, *ibid.;* Nevins, *Abram S. Hewitt,* 425; Pletcher, *The Awkward Years,* 155.

90. Crook, *Through Five Administrations,* 278–79; *Nation,* April 4, 1884, p. 353; Badeau, *Grant in Peace,* 339.

91. Schurz, *Speeches,* IV, 297–304.

92. *Carp's Washington,* 30.

93. Howe, *Chester A. Arthur,* 260.

94. Hirshson, *Farewell to the Bloody Shirt,* 107; Vincent P. DeSantis, "Negro Dis-satisfaction With Republican Policy in the South, 1882–1884," *Journal of Negro History,* 36 (April, 1951), 148–59; Going, *Bourbon Democracy,* 53.

95. Chandler to Blaine, October 2, 1882, cited in DeSantis, *Republicans Face the Southern Question,* 155–60.

96. Woodward, *Origins of the New South,* 102ff; Shadgett, *The Republican Party in Georgia,* 87–89, 145; DeSantis, *Republicans Face the Southern Question,* 159–70; Paul Casdorph, *A History of the Republican Party in Texas* (Austin: Pemberton Press, 1965), 47.

97. *Nation,* February 28, 1884, p. 177.

98. Harrison C. Thomas, *The Return of the Democratic Party to Power in 1884* (New York: Columbia University Press, 1919), 146–47; *New York Tribune,* May 21, 1884; Blake McKelvey, *Rochester: The Flower City, 1855–1890* (Cambridge: Harvard University Press, 1949), 296; *New York Times,* May 21, 1884; Badeau, *Grant in Peace,* 339; Schurz, *Speeches,* IV, 202; Swank to Morrill, May 6, 1884, Morrill LC.

99. W. T. Sherman to John Sherman, May 7, 1884, Sherman LC.

100. Blaine to Sherman, May 25, 1884, W. T. Sherman LC.

101. Sherman to Blaine, May 28, 1884, *ibid.*

102. Sherman to Blaine, June 7, 1884, in Hamilton, *James G. Blaine,* 626–27.

103. Boutwell, *Reminiscences,* II, 263.

104. Sherman to William T. Sherman, January 29, 1884, in Rhodes, *History,* VIII, 210.

105. Sherman to Joseph B. Foraker, May 8, 16, 25, 1884, Foraker HPSO; Stephen B. Elkins to John A. Logan, May 24, 1884, Logan LC; Sherman to Richard Smith, May 13, 1884, Sherman LC; Cortissoz, *Whitelaw Reid,* II, 94–95; Ryan, *Masters of Men,* 19.

106. Reid to Blaine, October 28, 1881, in Cortissoz, *Whitelaw Reid,* II, 77.

107. *Ibid.,* 91.

108. *Letters of Mrs. James G. Blaine,* II, 90.

109. *New York Times,* February 12, 1884.

110. *Nation,* March 20, 1884, p. 244; *New York Sun,* January 3, 1884.

111. *New York World,* April 2, 1884.

112. Ingalls, *Writings,* 437; Boutwell, *Reminiscences,* II, 263; *New York Sun,* May 5, 1884; John Sherman to Murat Halstead, March 13, 1884, copy in Halstead HPSO.

113. Blaine to Elkins, August 26, 1883, in Oscar Doane Lambert, *Stephen Benton Elkins* (Pittsburgh: University of Pittsburgh Press, 1955), 93.

114. *New York World,* March 22, 29, 1884.

115. *New York Times,* February 5, 1884; William Penn Nixon to Shelby Cullom, February 3, 1884, Cullom ISHL.

116. *New York World,* May 23, 1884; Justin S. Morrill to Redfield Proctor,

April 26, 1884, Morrill LC; Elkins to Blaine, April 23, 1884, Blaine LC; *New York Tribune,* April 1884, *passim;* William McKinley to A. L. Conger, April 11, 1884, McKinley HML.

117. Platt, *Autobiography,* 181. The title "Senator," if Conkling used it, was a courtesy; Platt was not elected again until 1896. Cf., W. W. Phelps to Blaine, June 9, 1884, in Hamilton, *James G. Blaine,* 627.

118. *New York Tribune,* April 12, 1884; McClure, *Old Time Notes,* II, 549; *New York World,* April 9, May 21, 1884; Blaine to Reid, April 21, 1884, Reid LC; *Washington Post,* April 29, 1884.

119. *Carp's Washington,* 30.

120. *New York World,* April 7, 1884.

121. Sherman, *Twenty Years With James G. Blaine,* 91–92.

122. James C. Olson, *J. Sterling Morton* (Lincoln: University of Nebraska Press, 1942), 283.

123. Barnes, *John G. Carlisle,* 63.

124. Lindsey, *'Sunset' Cox,* 229; *New York World,* November 30, 1883.

125. *New York Sun,* January 5, 1884; G. Wooley to Randall, February 14, 1884, Randall UPL; *New York Times,* January 4, 1884.

126. Henry Watterson, *'Marse Henry',* 2 vols. (New York: Doubleday, Doran and Company, 1919), II, 122.

127. *Chicago Tribune,* March 24, 1883; David Earl Robbins, "The Congressional Career of William Rawls Morrison," (Unpublished Ph.D. Dissertation, University of Illinois, 1963), 253; *New York Sun,* March 21, 1883; *New York Tribune,* March 20, 1884; Lewis Wesley Rathgeber, "The Democratic Party in Pennsylvania, 1880–1896," (Unpublished Ph.D. Dissertation, University of Pittsburgh, 1955), 117.

128. William D. Kelley, "The Treasury Surplus," *The Forum,* 4 (October, 1887), 143.

129. *Harper's Weekly,* January 26, 1884, p. 54; *New York Tribune,* February 5, 1884. Both sources are discussing the bill Morrison later introduced.

130. J. G. Priest to Randall, February 11, 1884, clipping attached, Randall UPL.

131. Franklin Ruffin to Randall, March 7, 1884, *ibid.*

132. Barnes, *John G. Carlisle,* 83–84.

133. *Washington Post,* May 7, 1884.

134. Lyman to Atkinson, May 10, 1884, Atkinson MHS.

135. *New York Tribune,* April 9, 1884.

V

The Democracy Revives—Barely

1. *New York Times,* January 18, 1884.

2. *Ibid.,* March 15, 1884.

3. Bigelow, *Letters and Literary Memorials of Samuel J. Tilden,* II, 635ff.

4. *New York Sun,* March 12, 1884, quoting the *Atlanta Constitution;* W. S. Groesbeck to Tilden, April 29, 1884, Tilden NYPL.

5. *Harper's Weekly,* March 22, 1884, p. 182.

6. Nevins, *Grover Cleveland*, 146–47.

7. Bayard to Henry G. Davis, April 9, 1884, in Pepper, *Henry Gassaway Davis*, 267–78.

8. *New York Tribune*, April 2, 1884, quoting and describing the *Sun* interview and its circumstances.

9. *Ibid.*, May 18, 1884.

10. *Washington Post*, April 17, 19, 1884.

11. *New York Times*, April 5, 1884.

12. McClure, *Old Time Notes*, II, 23; Robinson, *Thomas B. Reed*, 108–109, 113.

13. John R. Read to Randall, February 22, 1884, Randall UPL.

14. John R. Read to Randall, March 2, May 4, June 2, 1884, *ibid.*

15. *Carp's Washington*, 32.

16. Pepper, *Henry Gassaway Davis*, 137; *Nation*, July 10, 1884, p. 26; C. Walrath to Bayard, June 11, 1884, Bayard LC.

17. *New York Times*, July 12, 1884.

18. *New York Tribune*, July 12, 1884.

19. *New York Sun*, May 14, 1884.

20. Hirsch, *William C. Whitney*, 227.

21. In order: J. N. Matthews to Cleveland, May 19, 1884, Cleveland LC; *Nation*, June 19, 1884, p. 515; *New York Tribune*, May 26, 1884.

22. Nixon, *Henry W. Grady*, 217; Edith Dobie, *The Political Career of Stephen Mallory White* (Palo Alto: Stanford University Press, 1927), 52; *New York World*, March 29, 1884.

23. See Brown, *Irish-American Nationalism*, 54; Richard S. West Jr., *Lincoln's Scapegoat General: A Life of Benjamin F. Butler, 1818–1893* (Boston: Houghton Mifflin Co., 1965), 42–43, 102, 372–73, 409.

24. McElroy, *Grover Cleveland*, I, 20.

25. George F. Parker (Ed.), *Writings and Speeches of Grover Cleveland* (New York: Cassell Publishing Co., 1892), 537; cited hereafter as Cleveland, *Writings* (1892).

26. McElroy, *Grover Cleveland*, I, 17; George F. Parker, *Recollections of Grover Cleveland* (New York: Century Co., 1909), 23.

27. Depew, *My Memories*, 124.

28. Gamaliel Bradford, "Grover Cleveland: His Characteristics," *Atlantic*, 126 (November, 1920), 654–55.

29. Nevins, *Grover Cleveland*, 66, 129; Charles H. Armitage, *Grover Cleveland as Buffalo Knew Him* (Buffalo: Buffalo Evening News, 1926), 67.

30. Robert Kelly, "Presbyterianism, Jacksonianism and Grover Cleveland," *American Quarterly*, 18 (Winter, 1966), 615–36.

31. Nevins, *Grover Cleveland*, 765.

32. Willard L. King, *Melville Weston Fuller* (New York: Macmillan Co., 1950), 112.

33. William Allen White, *Masks In A Pageant* (New York: Macmillan Co., 1928), 116.

34. Daniels, *An Editor in Politics*, 10.

35. Hirsch, *William C. Whitney*, 185.

36. *New York Tribune*, September 23, 1882; Armitage, *Grover Cleveland as Buffalo Knew Him*, 152ff.

37. McElroy, *Grover Cleveland*, I, 49; *Albany Evening Journal*, April 10,

1883, cited in Nevins, *Grover Cleveland*, 118; Parker, *Recollections of Grover Cleveland*, 67.

38. *Ibid.*, 340–43; Flick, *Samuel Jones Tilden*, 487.

39. James McGurrin, *Bourke Cockran* (New York: Charles Scribner's Sons, 1948), 54.

40. Armitage, *Grover Cleveland as Buffalo Knew Him*, 179.

41. *New York Sun*, January 5, 1883.

42. *New York Times*, January 31, 1884.

43. Hudson, *Random Recollections*, 242.

44. *Ibid.*, 151; Nevins, *Grover Cleveland*, 96ff; Cleveland to Whitney, March 9, 1884, Whitney LC.

45. Pletcher, *The Awkward Years*, 261; *New York World*, January 4, 1883; *Washington Post*, July 17, 1884.

46. Manton Marble to Tilden, June 15, 1884, Marble LC; Merrill, *Bourbon Leader*, 65.

47. *New York World*, May 24, 1884; see also William Dorsheimer to Cleveland, May 13, 1884, Cleveland LC.

48. M. P. Curran, *The Life of Patrick A. Collins* (Norwood, Mass.: Norwood Press, 1906), 84.

49. *New York Times*, July 8, 1884.

50. John Bigelow to Randall, June 6, June 10, 1884, Randall UPL.

51. Bigelow, *Letters and Literary Memorials of Samuel J. Tilden*, II, 647ff; Tilden to Smith M. Weed, February 13, 1885, Tilden NYPL; *New York Times*, February 12–14, 1884.

52. DeAlva S. Alexander, *Four Famous New Yorkers* (New York: Henry Holt, 1923), 31.

53. *Harper's Weekly*, March 29, 1884, p. 199.

54. *New York Times*, April 14, 1884; Edmunds to Morrill, August 26, 1884, Morrill LC.

55. *Washington Post*, April 29, 1884.

56. *New York World*, May 2, 1884, italics added.

57. *New York Sun*, June 2, 1884.

58. Rhodes, *History*, VIII, 208; Lambert, *Stephen B. Elkins*, 95.

59. *New York Tribune*, May 31, 1884; Edward Nelson Dingley, *The Life and Times of Nelson Dingley, Jr.*, (Kalamazoo: Ihling Bros. and Everard, 1902), 242ff; *New York Sun*, June 4, 1884.

60. *Proceedings of the Eighth Republican National Convention . . . of 1884* (Chicago: Rand McNally Co., 1884), 3–10, 37ff; cited hereafter as *GOP Proc. 1884*.

61. *Ibid.*, 97ff; Muzzey, *James G. Blaine*, 282; Henry Cabot Lodge (Ed.), *Selections from the Correspondence of Theodore Roosevelt and Henry Cabot Lodge, 1884–1919*, 2 vols. (New York: Charles Scribner's Sons, 1925), I, 69, 72; Ryan, *Masters of Men*, 38; *Nation*, June 12, 1884, p. 494.

62. Foraker, *I Would Live It Again*, 79–80.

63. Foster, *Diplomatic Memoirs*, II, 267.

64. *Harper's Weekly*, June 14, 1884, p. 374.

65. Champ Clark, *My Quarter Century of American Politics*, 2 vols. (New York: Harper and Brothers, 1921), I, 286. Cf., Sherman to Foraker, June 9, 1884, Sherman LC; *Nation*, June 12, 1884, p. 495; Theodore Roosevelt, *Autobiography* (New York: Charles Scribner's Sons, 1926), 105; Elting Morison, *et al.* (Eds.), *The*

Letters of Theodore Roosevelt, 8 vols. (Cambridge: Harvard University Press, 1951–1954), I, 71.

66. H. C. Burleigh to Arthur, June 9, 1884, Arthur LC.

67. *New York Times,* June 10, 1884.

68. McElroy, *Grover Cleveland,* I, 76ff; *Nation,* July 10, 1884, p. 24; West, *Lincoln's Scapegoat General,* 386ff; *New York Tribune,* July 8, 1884; *New York Sun,* July 6, 1884; Hirsch, *William C. Whitney,* 233.

69. *New York Times,* July 9, 1884; Bulletin Number 2, July 8, 1884, Bayard LC; McGurrin, *Bourke Cockran,* 55; *Official Proceedings of the National Democratic Convention . . . 1884* (New York: Douglas and Taylor's Democratic Printing House, n.d.), 5–7; cited hereafter as *Dem. Proc. 1884.*

70. *Ibid.,* 97ff.

71. *Ibid.,* 150ff; *New York Times,* July 11, 1884; *New York Tribune,* July 11, 1884.

72. Watterson, '*Marse Henry*', II, 122; Olson, *J. Sterling Morton,* 295; Charles Edward Russell, *Bare Hands and Stone Walls* (New York: Charles Scribner's Sons, 1933), 39.

73. *Dem. Proc. 1884,* pp. 195ff; West, *Lincoln's Scapegoat General,* 387–88.

74. *Dem. Proc. 1884,* pp. 226ff; Denis Tilden Lynch, *Grover Cleveland: A Man Four-Square* (New York: Horace Liveright, 1932), 201; *New York Times,* July 12, 1884.

75. Hudson, *Random Recollections,* 172–73; Lynch, *Grover Cleveland,* 203.

76. *Dem. Proc. 1884,* pp. 228ff; McClure, *Recollections,* 126.

77. *New York World,* July 12, 1884; *Nation,* July 17, 1884, p. 44; Nevins, *Grover Cleveland,* 154.

78. *New York Sun,* July 12, 1884.

79. Henry L. Bryan to Bayard, July 15, 1884, Bayard LC.

80. Olsen, *J. Sterling Morton,* 301.

81. *New York Tribune,* July 12, 1884.

82. *New York Sun,* July 14, 1884; T. F. Gallagher to Bayard, July 12, 1884, Bayard LC.

83. Blodgett, *The Gentle Reformers,* 1.

84. Tansill, *The Congressional Career of Thomas Francis Bayard,* 318ff; Blodgett, *The Gentle Reformers,* 10; Cary, *George William Curtis,* 289–90.

85. Muzzey, *James G. Blaine,* 270ff; Blaine, *Political Discussions,* 109.

86. Schurz, *Speeches,* IV, 212–15.

87. Bayard to Davis, July 18, 1884, in Pepper, *Henry Gassaway Davis,* 270; *Nation,* June 12, 1884, p. 496, listed some of the important bolting papers to that date, including: *Brooklyn Union, Boston Advertiser, Boston Transcript, Boston Herald, Springfield Republican, Syracuse Herald, Rochester Post-Gazette, Flushing Times,* in addition to the ones Bayard named and others.

88. Thomas, *The Return of the Democratic Party to Power in 1884,* p. 240.

89. Theodore Lothrop Stoddard, *Master of Manhattan: A Life of Richard Croker* (New York: Longmans, Green, 1931), 77–78.

90. *Nation,* November 6, 1884, p. 387; *Harper's Weekly,* July 5, 1884, p. 426.

91. See Curtis to Cleveland, October 20, 1884, Cleveland LC. The quotation is from Cleveland to the New York Civil Service Reform Association, October 24, 1884, in *Writings* (1892), 42.

92. *New York Times,* October 26, 1884.

93. Hamilton, *James G. Blaine,* 584.

94. Kirkland, *Charles Francis Adams, Jr.,* 103.

95. *Minneapolis Tribune,* October 11, 1884.

96. *New York Tribune,* July 11, 1884. The 'Boston Tizer' is, of course, a rival newspaper, the *Boston Advertiser.*

97. *Ibid.,* July 28–30, 1884.

98. Cortissoz, *Whitelaw Reid,* I, 330.

99. Pepper, *Henry Gassaway Davis,* 271.

100. *New York Sun,* July 17, 1884; *Dem. Proc. 1884,* pp. 281ff; *New York Times,* July 26, 1884; *New York Tribune,* July 13, 14, 1884.

101. Peck, *Twenty Years of the Republic,* 76.

102. Cleveland to Lamont, August 11, 1884, in Cleveland, *Letters,* 40.

103. See *New York Sun,* September 7, 1884; *New York World,* September 13, 1884; McGurrin, *Bourke Cockran,* 69ff; Thomas, *The Return of the Democratic Party to Power in 1884,* p. 220; Robert H. Mucigrosso, "Tammany Hall and the New York Irish in the 1884 Presidential Election," (Unpublished M.A. Thesis, Columbia University, 1961), 100ff.

104. John R. Lambert, *Arthur Pue Gorman* (Baton Rouge: Louisiana State University Press, 1953), 79; Charles Willis Thompson, *Party Leaders of the Time* (New York: G. W. Dillingham Co., 1906), 111; Alfred Henry Lewis, *Richard Croker* (New York: Life Publishing Co., 1906), 297ff.

105. *New York World,* July 8, 1884.

106. The basic story is in Nevins, *Grover Cleveland,* 162ff.

107. Beecher to Carl Schurz, July 29, 1884, in Schurz, *Speeches,* IV, 222; Nevins, *Grover Cleveland,* 171; *New York Sun,* September 1, 1884.

108. James Freeman Clarke to Cleveland, September 1, 1884, Cleveland LC; Cleveland to Wilson S. Bissell, September 11, 1884, in Cleveland, *Letters,* 42.

109. J. F. French to Mr. Williams, August 24, 1884, copy in Cleveland LC.

110. Mark A. DeWolf Howe, *Portrait of An Independent: Moorfield Storey* (Boston: Houghton Mifflin Co., 1932), 150.

111. Cortissoz, *Whitelaw Reid,* II, 111. Cf., Schurz, *Speeches,* IV, 274; *Nation,* August 7, 1884, pp. 106–107; Hayes Diary, November 11, 14, 1884, Hayes HML.

112. Lambert, *Arthur Pue Gorman,* 105.

113. Cleveland to Lamont, August 14, 1884, in Cleveland, *Letters,* 41.

114. Hudson, *Random Recollections,* 185ff.

115. *Puck,* August 24, 1884, p. 54.

116. To sample the attacks on Blaine, see Muzzey, *James G. Blaine,* 311; *New York World,* September 24, October 1, 17, 1884; George Juergens, *Joseph Pulitzer and the New York World* (Princeton: Princeton University Press, 1966), 248–49, 313, n60.

117. Dearing, *Veterans in Politics,* 305–307; McElroy, *Grover Cleveland,* I, 93–94. The quotation is from the *New York Sun,* August 7, 1884, and see issues of September 12, 15, 1884. *Judge,* November 8, 1884, p. 2, has an incredible attack on Cleveland's morals. Cf., Lynch, *Grover Cleveland,* 232.

118. Armitage, *Grover Cleveland as Buffalo Knew Him,* 194.

119. *New York Sun,* September 7, 1884.

120. Parker, *Recollections of Grover Cleveland,* 338–39.

121. *New York Sun,* October 20–23, 1884.

122. Peck, *Twenty Years of the Republic,* 255.

123. *New York Times,* July 24, 1884.

124. Bayard to Henry G. Davis, August 27, 1884, in Pepper, *Henry Gassaway Davis*, 271.

125. West, *Lincoln's Scapegoat General*, 389; Chandler to Mrs. Blaine, June 8, 1884, Chandler NHHS; Blaine to Elkins, July 27, 1884, in Edward Stanwood, *James G. Blaine* (Boston: Houghton Mifflin Co., 1905), 285.

126. Hans L. Trefousse, "Ben Butler and the New York Election of 1884," *New York History*, 37 (April, 1956), 185–96.

127. Hamilton, *James G. Blaine*, 578; Curran, *Patrick Collins*, 93.

128. *Nation*, November 6, 1884, p. 387.

129. *New York Times*, September 20, 1884.

130. *New York Sun*, July 15, 1884.

131. *GOP Proc. 1884*, pp. 32–33, 35–36, 41; Nevins, *Grover Cleveland*, 174–75; Connelley, *Preston B. Plumb*, 276–77.

132. Quoted in William Frank Zornow, *Kansas: A History of the Jay-Hawk State* (Norman: University of Oklahoma Press, 1957), 191–94.

133. Chandler to Reid, September 25, 1884, Reid LC; see also Thomas W. Pittman to Cleveland, November 2, 1884, Cleveland LC.

134. Muzzey, *James G. Blaine*, 307.

135. Foraker, *I Would Live It Again*, 82; Dearing, *Veterans in Politics*, 296ff; *Nation*, July 24, 1884, p. 61; *New York Times*, July 23, 1884.

136. Ewing to Blaine, August 23, 1884, in Muzzey, *James G. Blaine*, 309; Pletcher, *The Awkward Years*, 240.

137. *New York Herald*, July 8, 1884.

138. John Boyle O'Reilley to Manning, November 25, 1884, Cleveland LC; Robert D. Parmet, "Cleveland, Blaine and New York's Irish in the Election of 1884," (Unpublished M.A. Thesis, Columbia University, 1961), 50, 61.

139. *Washington Post*, June 9, September 19, 1884; Muzzey, *James G. Blaine*, 307.

140. Blaine to Elkins, July 27, 1884, in Stanwood, *James G. Blaine*, 284–85.

141. The remark varies; I have used it as stated in Chidsey, *The Gentleman From New York*, 374.

142. *Ibid.*, 376; *New York Sun*, September 2, 1884; *New York World*, October 13, 1884; *Washington Post*, November 3, 1884.

143. *New York Times*, July 19, 1884.

144. *Harper's Weekly*, July 26, 1884, p. 474.

145. *Nation*, July 24, 1884, p. 61.

146. Blaine to Reid, July 27, 1884, Reid LC.

147. Muzzey, *James G. Blaine*, 311.

148. T. B. Boyd, *The Blaine and Logan Campaign of 1884* (Chicago: J. L. Regan Co., 1884), 52; *New York Times*, September 21, 1884.

149. M. Woodhull to Chandler, September 29, 1884, Chandler LC.

150. Hamilton, *James G. Blaine*, 612.

151. Boyd, *The Blaine and Logan Campaign of 1884*, pp. 79–80, 117, 163ff; J. Leonard Bates (Ed.), *Tom Walsh in Dakota Territory* (Urbana: University of Illinois Press, 1966), 9–11; Bradford, "James G. Blaine," *passim*.

152. *Puck*, October 1, 1884, p. 66.

153. Reid to Blaine, October 8, 1884, Reid LC; Muzzey, *James G. Blaine*, 314–15; Elkins to Chandler, October 26, 1884, Chandler LC; B. F. Jones to Elkins, August 31, 1884, Elkins WVUL; McElroy, *Grover Cleveland*, I, 98.

154. Stoddard, *As I Knew Them*, 132–34. Cf., *New York World*, October 30, 1884; Boyd, *The Blaine and Logan Campaign of 1884*, pp. 190ff; *New York Times*, October 30, 1884.

155. Frank W. Mack, "'Rum, Romanism, and Rebellion': How James G. Blaine was Defeated by a Phrase," *Harper's Weekly*, 48 (July 23, 1904), 1140–42.

156. See Hudson, *Random Recollections*, 207–209, from which this account is drawn. Hudson's remarks may be slightly inflated, but seem basically accurate. See also Oscar S. Straus, *Under Four Administrations* (Boston: Houghton Mifflin Co., 1922), 38–39; Lambert, *Arthur Pue Gorman*, 107–12.

157. *New York Sun*, November 7, 1884.

158. Blaine, *Political Discussions*, 461–62.

159. Depew, *My Memories*, 144–45.

160. *Ibid.;* Hudson, *Random Recollections*, 212; Cullom, *Fifty Years of Public Service*, 119. This second view matches the present author's suspicions, and was first documented in David G. Farrelly, "'Rum, Romanism and Rebellion' Resurrected," *Western Political Quarterly*, 8 (June, 1955), 262–70.

161. *Nation*, June 21, 1888, p. 497. *New York World*, November 14, 1884, gives some contemporary adverse reactions.

162. *New York Tribune*, October 30, 1884; *New York Sun*, October 30, 1884, is surprisingly fair covering this and the Burchard incident. Cf., Boyd, *The Blaine and Logan Campaign of 1884*, pp. 184–89; Blaine, *Political Discussions*, 457.

163. Juergens, *Joseph Pulitzer and the New York World*, 103, n34, notes that the cartoon contains people who did not actually attend the banquet, indicating it was made up beforehand.

164. Swann, *John Roach*, 196–97; *New York Tribune*, July 22, 1884; Lynch, *Grover Cleveland*, 263ff.

165. Nevins, *Grover Cleveland*, 180; *Nation*, November 6, 1884, p. 338; Lynch, *Grover Cleveland*, 263ff.

166. *New York Tribune*, November 4, 1884.

167. Sherman, *Twenty Years with James G. Blaine*, 94–96.

168. *Letters of Mrs. James G. Blaine*, II, 120–21.

169. William Gorham Rice, "Cleveland's First Election," *Century Magazine*, 84 (June, 1912), 299–304; Armitage, *Grover Cleveland as Buffalo Knew Him*, 207; Hirsch, *William C. Whitney*, 243–44; Lambert, *Arthur Pue Gorman*, 111–12; Lewis, *Richard Croker*, 303; *New York Herald*, November 6–9, *passim*, 1884.

170. Nevins, *Grover Cleveland*, 186.

171. McElroy, *Grover Cleveland*, I, 97–98; *Washington Post*, November 8, 1884.

172. Lynch, *Grover Cleveland*, 279; Oberholtzer, *History*, IV, 209.

173. Arthur Hood to Cleveland, November 19, 1884, Cleveland LC; Abram S. Hewitt to Cleveland, November 19, 1884, *ibid.; Washington Post*, November 21, 1884; Ray Ginger, *Age of Excess* (New York: Macmillan Co., 1965), 107; Woodward, *Tom Watson*, 115.

174. Hamilton, *James G. Blaine*, 589; Blaine to Elkins, November 7, 1884, in Lambert, *Stephen B. Elkins*, 101–102.

175. Chandler Diary, November 16, 1884, Chandler NHHS; Muzzey, *James G. Blaine*, 324.

176. *Letters of Mrs. James G. Blaine*, II, 120.

177. Lambert, *Stephen B. Elkins*, 102.

178. Stanwood, *James G. Blaine*, 292–93; Sherman, *Twenty Years With James G. Blaine*, 95.

179. Blaine to Francis Fessenden, November 17, 1884, quoted in F. B. Loomis to James S. Clarkson, November 17, 1884, Clarkson LC.

180. Quoted in William Penn Nixon to William Henry Smith, November 12, 1884, Smith OHS.

181. *New York World*, November 17, 1884, has a long and astute interview with Blaine. Schurz's comments are in a letter to Cleveland, January [?], 1885, Schurz LC. The Irish vote has never been analyzed, but Brown, *Irish-American Nationalism*, 140–42, makes tentative suggestions. Mucigrosso, "Tammany Hall and the New York Irish," 96–97, has some information.

182. See Seth M. Scheiner, *Negro Mecca* (New York: New York University Press, 1966), 180–83; August Meier, "The Negro and the Democratic Party, 1875–1915," *Phylon*, 17 (Second Quarter, 1956), 173–91; Elsie M. Lewis, "The Political Mind of the Negro, 1865–1900," *Journal of Southern History*, 21 (May, 1955), 189–202.

183. *Washington Post*, November 18, 1884; Thomas, *The Return of the Democratic Party to Power*, 219; Hamilton, *James G. Blaine*, 632; Muzzey, *James G. Blaine*, 306; Connelley, *Preston B. Plumb*, 277; William G. Carleton, "Why Was the Democratic Party in Indiana a Radical Party, 1865–1890?" *Indiana Magazine of History*, 42 (September, 1946), 207–28.

184. Pepper, *Under Three Flags*, 359–60, says Blaine later blamed Stalwarts for defeat. Cf., Mucigrosso, "Tammany Hall and the New York Irish," 94. *Washington Post*, November 26, 1884, has the Conkling response on the recount. *New York World*, November 10, 1884, credits Conkling with the defeat. The *New York Sun*, quotation is from the November 8, 1884, issue. The *Washington Post* quotation is from the November 25, 1884, issue. John Richardson to John Sherman, November 8, 1884, Sherman LC, is a sample letter blaming Stalwarts but arguing it is their last moment of power. See also Lee Benson, "Research Problems in American Political Historiography," in Mirra Komarovsky (Ed.), *Common Frontiers in the Social Sciences* (Glencoe, Illinois: The Free Press, 1957), esp. 123–45.

185. *New York Tribune*, November 17, 1884.

186. Paine, *Th: Nast*, 507.

187. W. R. Morrison to David A. Wells, December 14, 1884, Wells LC.

188. Hayes to Mrs. Hayes, November 12, 1884, Hayes HML.

189. E. F. Webb to Blaine, November 11, 1884, in Muzzey, *James G. Blaine*, 324, n3.

190. Cleveland to Wilson S. Bissell, November 13, 1884, in Cleveland, *Letters*, 47–48.

191. S. M. Phelps [?] to Bayard, November 10, 1884, Bayard LC.

VI

Spoilsmen and Reformers: 1885–1887

1. Nevins, *Grover Cleveland*, 198.

2. Stealey, *Twenty Years in the Press Gallery*, 34.

3. W. T. Thompson to Whitney, December 8, 1884, Whitney LC; Tilden to

George Hoadly, December 5, 1884, Tilden NYPL; Bigelow, *Samuel J. Tilden*, II, 306, 314.

4. Randall to Tilden, December 17, 1884, Tilden NYPL.

5. Tilden to Smith M. Weed, February 13, 1884, and to Manning, February 14, 1885, both *ibid*.

6. Flint, *Memories*, 256–57; Bigelow, *Letters and Literary Memorials of Samuel J. Tilden*, II, 666–67.

7. *Nation*, February 26, 1885, p. 167.

8. Lucius Beebe, *The Big Spenders* (New York: Doubleday, 1966), xiii; *New York Herald*, February 3, 1904.

9. McElroy, *Grover Cleveland*, I, 104; L Q. C. Lamar to Cleveland, February 6, 1885, and Alfred Colquitt to Cleveland, November 28, 1884, both Cleveland LC.

10. Thurman to Bayard, March 5, 1885, Bayard LC.

11. Horace Samuel Merrill, *William Freeman Vilas* (Madison: State Historical Society of Wisconsin, 1954), 65–66.

12. Cleveland to Wilson S. Bissell, September 24, 1885, Cleveland LC.

13. McElroy, *Grover Cleveland*, I, 106.

14. Nevins, *Grover Cleveland*, 198; Blaine to Reid, March 6, 1885, Reid LC.

15. Merrill, *Bourbon Leader*, 24.

16. *Carp's Washington*, 37–38.

17. McClure, *Recollections*, 115.

18. Barnes, *John G. Carlisle*, 91; Colman, *White House Gossip*, 170–71; *Washington Post*, March 2–6, 1885.

19. C. W. Moulton to W. T. Sherman, May 9, 1884, W. T. Sherman LC.

20. Alfred Mason, Jr., to W. T. Sherman, May 15, 1884, *ibid*.

21. Grant Note, July [?], 1885, copy in Grant LC.

22. Grant Note, Item 2351, Volume 14, Series I, C., undated, *ibid*.

23. Grant Note, July 8, 1885, *ibid*.

24. S. S. Cox, *Three Decades of Federal Legislation* (Providence: J. A. and R. A. Reid, 1885), 673.

25. Crook, *Memories*, 173–74.

26. Parsons, *Scattered Memories*, 78.

27. *Carp's Washington*, 39–40.

28. Bradford, "Grover Cleveland," *passim*.

29. McClure, *Recollections*, 127; McElroy, *Grover Cleveland*, I, 112; Cleveland to Bissell, December 14, 1885, *Letters*, 95–96.

30. Lewis, *Richard Croker*, 266–67.

31. Hilary Herbert, "Grover Cleveland and His Cabinet at Work," *The Century Magazine*, 85 (March, 1913), 740–44; Stealey, *Twenty Years in the Press Gallery*, 28–31.

32. Parker, *Recollections of Grover Cleveland*, 117–20, 262; Stealey, *Twenty Years in the Press Gallery*, 29; Nevins, *Grover Cleveland*, 127; *Carp's Washington*, 41; Lamont to Don M. Dickinson, January [?], 1887, Dickinson LC.

33. Clark, *My Quarter Century*, I, 252ff.

34. Parker, *Recollections of Grover Cleveland*, 357.

35. *New York Herald*, June 9, 1886. He added: "I used those words and thought they would please the western taxpayers, who are fond of such things."

36. *Washington Post*, June 11, 1887; Merrill, *William Freeman Vilas*, 126ff.

37. Watterson, '*Marse Henry*,' II, 118.

38. Peck, *Twenty Years of the Republic*, 72; McElroy, *Grover Cleveland*, I, 100.

39. Martin Ridge, *Ignatius Donnelley* (Chicago: University of Chicago Press, 1962), 223–24.

40. Clark, *My Quarter Century*, I, 243ff.

41. Stoddard, *As I Knew Them*, 150.

42. Charles Francis Adams, Jr., "What Mr. Cleveland Stands For," *The Forum*, 13 (July, 1892), 663.

43. *Nation*, May 21, 1885, p. 411.

44. Curtis to Lamont, March 16, 1885, Cleveland LC.

45. Cleveland to Schurz, March 23, 1885, in Schurz, *Speeches*, IV, 363–64.

46. *Ibid.*, 402–403; Richard Watson Gilder, *Grover Cleveland: A Record of Friendship* (New York: The Century Co., 1910), 163.

47. Parker, *Recollections of Grover Cleveland*, 259.

48. Cleveland to Eaton, September 11, 1885, in *Letters*, 74–76; see also Bayard to Schurz, May 8, 1886, in Schurz, *Speeches*, IV, 439–42.

49. Grover Cleveland, *Presidential Problems* (New York: The Century Co., 1904), 39ff.

50. McElroy, *Grover Cleveland*, I, 162–63.

51. Cleveland to Wilson S. Bissell, June 25, 1885, in *Letters*, 64–65.

52. George M. Ray to Cleveland, November 24, 1884, Cleveland LC.

53. *Carp's Washington*, 120.

54. Tilden to Manning, June 19, 1885, Tilden NYPL.

55. James Smith to Cleveland, February 23, 1885, Cleveland LC.

56. Cleveland, *Presidential Problems*, 42.

57. Stoddard, *Master of Manhattan*, 77–80; Lynch, *Grover Cleveland*, 408; Wood, "The Massachusetts Mugwumps," *passim*.

58. Morton to A. J. Sawyer, March 27, 1887, in Olsen, *J. Sterling Morton*, 328–29.

59. Peck, *Twenty Years of the Republic*, 78.

60. Schurz to Bayard, May 20, 1886, in Schurz, *Speeches*, IV, 444.

61. Cleveland to Wilson Bissell, November 25, 1885, in Cleveland, *Letters*, 94.

62. McElroy, *Grover Cleveland*, I, 178; Cleveland, *Presidential Problems*, 47ff.

63. The message quoted is dated March 1, 1886, in Richardson, *Messages and Papers*, VII, 4967.

64. Sievers, *Benjamin Harrison: Hoosier Statesman*, 286ff.

65. Peck, *Twenty Years of the Republic*, 148.

66. Dearing, *Veterans in Politics*, 114, 190–96.

67. Cullom, *Fifty Years of Public Service*, 221.

68. The vetoes, in order quoted, are dated June 21, 22, 23, 1886, in Richardson, *Messages and Papers*, VIII, 5020ff.

69. Thomas, *The Return of the Democratic Party to Power in 1884*, 235; *Nation*, July 1, 1886, p. 1; *ibid.*, July 15, 1886, p. 48, P. L. Robertson, "Cleveland's Constructive Use of the Pension Vetoes," *Mid-America*, 44 (January, 1962), 33–45; Lewis, *Richard Croker*, 265–66; *Washington Evening Star*, May 8, 1886; *New York Mail and Express*, June 26, 1886; *Chicago Inter-Ocean*, June 26, 1886.

70. Sam Ross, *The Empty Sleeve: A Biography of Lucius Fairchild* (Madison: The State Historical Society of Wisconsin, 1964), 203–208; Dearing, *Veterans in Politics*, 344ff.

71. Everett Walters, *Joseph Benson Foraker* Columbus: Ohio Historical Society, 1948), 53; McElroy, *Grover Cleveland*, I, 206–207; Dearing, *Veterans in Politics*, 347–51.

72. Barnes, *John G. Carlisle*, 118; Cleveland, *Letters*, 143–46; Cleveland, *Writings* (1892), 398–401, 406–407.

73. McElroy, *Grover Cleveland*, I, 217.

74. *Carp's Washington*, 45.

75. Cleveland to Mary Cleveland Hoyt, April 19, 1886, in Cleveland, *Letters*, 106–107; *Washington Post*, November 17, 1884.

76. *Nation*, August 19, 1886, p. 148.

77. See Nevins, *Grover Cleveland*, 309–10.

78. Cleveland, *Writings* (1892), 345–46.

79. Bradford, "Grover Cleveland," *passim*.

80. McElroy, *Grover Cleveland*, I, 285–86; Crook, *Memories*, 192.

81. Cleveland to Mrs. Whitney, December 12, 1888, Cleveland LC.

82. Thomas C. Cochran, *Railroad Leaders, 1845–1890* (Cambridge: Harvard University Press, 1953), 188, 189, 195, 298–99, 445, 493; David J. Rothman, *Politics and Power: The United States Senate, 1869–1901* (Cambridge: Harvard University Press, 1966), 200ff.

83. Cochran, *Railroad Leaders*, 182, 355; Gabriel Kolko, *Railroads and Regulation, 1877–1916* (Princeton: Princeton University Press, 1965), 39.

84. Gilman M. Ostrander, *Nevada: The Great Rotten Borough, 1859–1964* (New York: Alfred Knopf, 1966), 86–87.

85. *Commercial and Financial Chronicle*, 17 (June 6, 1885), 666–67. Kirkland, *Industry Comes of Age*, notes the East-West, and urban-rural conflict. Lee Benson, *Merchants, Farmers and Railroads: Railroad Regulation and New York Politics, 1850–1887* (Cambridge: Harvard University Press, 1955) is influential in arguing that eastern mercantile shippers rather than western and southern farmers promoted federal regulation. This idea, however, can be found in two older pro-farmer studies: Solon Justus Buck, *The Granger Movement* (Cambridge: Harvard University Press, 1913), 122, 230; and Chester McArthur Destler, *American Radicalism, 1865–1901* (New London: Connecticut College Monographs, 1946), 4. See also Gerald D. Nash, "Origins of the Interstate Commerce Act of 1887," *Pennsylvania History*, 24 (July, 1957), 181–90; Edward A. Purcell, Jr., "Ideas and Interests: Businessmen and the Interstate Commerce Act," *Journal of American History*, 54 (December, 1967), 561–78.

86. James W. Neilson, *Shelby M. Cullom: Prairie State Republican* (Urbana: University of Illinois Press, 1962), 90; Kirkland, *Industry Comes of Age*, 117–18; Benson, *Merchants, Farmers and Railroads*, 208, 215; Gerald D. Nash, "The Reformer Reformed: John H. Reagan and Railroad Regulation," *Business History Review*, 29 (June, 1955), 189–96. Theodore Lyman to Edward Atkinson, December 19, 1884, Atkinson MHS, has an amusing description of Reagan as "a cross between a Sioux Indian and a fighting Irishman. He has about as much idea of the laws of commerce, and especially their *power*, as a grizzly bear." See also *Chicago Inter-Ocean*, May 14, 1886, urging Reagan to drop simple prohibition; and Ben H. Proctor, *Not Without Honor: The Life of John H. Reagan* (Austin: University of Texas Press, 1962), 218–60.

87. Cullom, *Fifty Years of Public Service*, 227; *New York Herald*, January 30, 1887; Neilson, *Shelby M. Cullom*, 95ff.

88. Kirkland, *Industry Comes of Age,* 125.

89. Kolko, *Railroads and Regulation,* 43–44.

90. James E. Anderson, "The Emergence of the Modern Regulatory State: A Study of American Ideas on the Regulation of Economic Enterprise, 1885–1917," (Unpublished Ph.D. Dissertation, University of Texas, 1960), 243–45.

91. Robbins, "William Rawls Morrison," 287; Kirkland, *Charles Francis Adams, Jr.,* 63.

92. Thomas M. Cooley Diary, March 7, 1888, Cooley MHC.

93. *Washington Post,* January 17, 1887.

94. Tilden to Conrad Jordan, May 15, 1885, in Bigelow, *Samuel J. Tilden,* II, 294.

95. McElroy, *Grover Cleveland,* I, 162–63.

96. Nevins, *Grover Cleveland,* 302.

97. Tilden to Cleveland, February 28, 1885, in McElroy, *Grover Cleveland,* I, 110.

98. For details of this story, see John A. S. Grenville and George Berkeley Young, *Politics, Strategy and Diplomacy: Studies in Foreign Policy, 1873–1917* (New Haven: Yale University Press, 1966), 44–51.

99. Morrison to Marble, December 24, 1885, February 3, 1886, Marble LC.

100. Manning to Marble, February 15, 1886, *ibid.*

101. Manning to Marble, March 20, 1886, *ibid.*

102. Robinson, *Thomas B. Reed,* 155–57.

103. C. T. Russell, Jr. (Ed.), *Speeches and Addresses of William E. Russell* (Boston: Little, Brown and Co., 1894), 226, 233.

104. *Kansas City Times,* April 16, 1888.

105. *Beatrice Webb's American Diary,* 54–55.

106. Bayard to Don M. Dickinson, July 11, 1891, Dickinson LC. I wish to thank Mr. Hal Williams of Yale University for drawing this quotation to my attention.

107. Allen J. Going, "The South and the Blair Bill," *Mississippi Valley Historical Review,* 44 (September, 1957), 267–90.

108. Quoted in William Ivy Hair, "The Agrarian Protest in Louisiana, 1877–1900," (Unpublished Ph.D. Dissertation, Louisiana State University, 1962), 180.

109. Russell, *Speeches,* 294–95.

110. J. L. M. Curry to Robert C. Winthrop, September 1, 1886, in Woodward, *Origins of the New South,* 64.

111. Rathgeber, "The Democratic Party in Pennsylvania," 74–75, 364ff.

112. The veto is dated February 16, 1887, in Richardson, *Messages and Papers,* VII, 5142.

113. Cleveland, *Presidential Problems,* 11; Nevins, *Grover Cleveland,* 270.

114. Schurz to Cleveland, December 15, 1886, in Schurz, *Speeches,* IV, 463–64; almost the exact language is used in *Nation,* September 10, 1885, p. 210.

115. Curran, *Patrick A. Collins,* 97ff.

116. *New York Herald,* June 17, 1886; *New York Tribune,* June 17, 1886; *Philadelphia Press,* June 28, 1886.

117. *New York Herald,* January 3, 1887; *Louisville Courier-Journal,* November 4, 1886; *Washington Post,* December 16, 1886; Nevins, *Abram S. Hewitt,* 459–60.

118. Vilas to Wells, June 24, 1886, Wells LC. Cf., Morrison to Wells, May

28, 1884, *ibid.;* M. W. Packard to Morrison, February 6, 1885, Morrison ISHL; Edward Atkinson to W. C. P. Breckinridge, July 20, 1886, Breckinridge Family LC; Sherman to Morrill, September 25, 1885, Morrill LC.

119. Joseph Medill to Shelby Cullom, January 18, 1888, Cullom ISHL; Mahnken, "The Congressmen of the Grain Belt States and Tariff Legislation," 277–78; Homer Clevenger, "Agrarian Politics in Missouri, 1880–1896," (Unpublished Ph.D. Dissertation, University of Missouri, 1940), 161–73; R. R. Bowker to Morrison, October 26, 1885, Cleveland LC; Nevins, *Grover Cleveland,* 288ff; Blodgett, *The Gentle Reformers,* 74–79.

120. Howard R. Smith, "The Farmer and the Tariff: A Reappraisal," *Southern Economics Journal,* 21 (October, 1954), 152–61; Kirkland, *Industry Comes of Age,* 187; Hoadly to Cleveland, November 22, 1887, in Cleveland, *Letters,* 165–66; Robert D. Leiter, "Organized Labor and the Tariff," *Southern Economics Journal,* 28 (July, 1961), 55–56.

121. Morrison to D. A. Wells, February 10, 1887, Wells LC; Barnes, *John G. Carlisle,* 95.

122. James Charn to W. C. P. Breckinridge, December 12, 1886, Breckinridge Family LC.

123. Swank to Justin S. Morrill, December 1, 1886, Morrill LC.

124. McElroy, *Grover Cleveland,* I, 268; Watterson, *'Marse Henry,'* II, 122; Tarbell, *The Tariff in Our Times,* 140–41.

125. Cleveland to Wilson S. Bissell, September 2, 1887, in Cleveland, *Letters,* 149–51; *New York World,* September 7, 1887; *Washington Post,* October 1877, *passim;* Whitney to Cleveland, November 9, 1887, and F. G. Flower to Cleveland, October 26, 1887, both in Cleveland LC.

126. Richardson, *Messages and Papers,* VII, 5165–76.

127. *Washington Post,* December 8, 1887.

128. Clark, *My Quarter Century,* I, 280–81.

129. *Nation,* November 8, 1888, 368.

130. *Washington Post,* December 7, 1887.

131. J. F. Hanson to Randall, December 10, 1887, Randall UPL.

132. *Ohio State Journal,* March 2, 1888.

133. *Philadelphia Press,* December 8, 1887.

134. Stoddard, *As I Knew Them,* 153.

135. Whitney to Cleveland, December 11, 1887, Whitney LC.

VII

The Tariff Wars: 1888

1. *New York Tribune,* December 8, 1887.

2. Hay to Blaine, December 8, 1887, in Muzzey, *James G. Blaine,* 367.

3. *New York Times,* December 8–12, 1887; *New York Herald,* December 9–10, 1887; James Parton, "Defeated Presidential Candidates," *The Forum* 6 (January, 1889), 509.

4. *New York Herald,* December 7, 1887.

5. Grady to Randall, December 21, 1887, and Randall to Grady, January 6, 1888, both in Randall UPL.

6. *Nation*, January 26, 1888, p. 61.

7. Tarbell, *The Tariff in Our Times*, 156–57; Summers, *William L. Wilson and Tariff Reform*, 78.

8. *Ibid.*, 79–82.

9. *Nashville American*, January 15, 1888.

10. *Washington Post*, April 17, 1888.

11. *Louisville Courier-Journal*, June 15, 1888.

12. Barnes, *John G. Carlisle*, 135.

13. Septimus Hall to Johnson N. Camden, February 12, 1888, in Festus P. Summers, *Johnson Newlon Camden* (New York: G. P. Putnam's Sons, 1937), 417–18; Rathgeber, "The Democratic Party in Pennsylvania," 183.

14. *Chicago Inter-Ocean*, July 22, 1888.

15. The presidential election of 1888 is intrinsically fascinating, and I refer the reader to two dissertations. Edward Arthur White, "The Republican Party in National Politics, 1888–1889," (Unpublished Ph.D. Dissertation, University of Wisconsin, 1941) is valuable on pre-convention maneuvering. Carmelo J. Bernardo, "The Presidential Election of 1888," (Unpublished Ph.D. Dissertation, Georgetown University, 1950), is especially good on organization and analysis of the campaign's progress.

16. Charles B. Farwell to Walter Q. Gresham, February 9, 1888, Gresham LC; Oberholtzer, *History*, V, 16, 25.

17. *Nation*, March 4, 1886, p. 181; Hamilton, *James G. Blaine*, 595; *Brooklyn Eagle*, June 18, 1886; *Washington Post*, April 9, 10, 1887; Stanwood, *James G. Blaine*, 309; *Life*, 11 (February 23, 1888), 104.

18. Hayes to Fanny Hayes, December 18, 1887, Hayes HML.

19. Harrison to Wharton Barker, November 25, 1886, Barker LC.

20. Plumb to Harrison, October 1, 4, 1887, Harrison LC.

21. B. F. Jones to Elkins, April 25, 1888, Elkins WVUL.

22. Blaine to Reid, October 11, 1887, in Cortissoz, *Whitelaw Reid*, II, 113. Cf., Clarkson to Elkins, May 18, 1888, Elkins WVUL.

23. M. A. Dodge to Elkins, January 24, 1888, copy *ibid.*

24. M. A. Dodge to Elkins, April 15, 1888, *ibid.;* Erastus Brainerd to Gresham, April 2, 1888, Gresham LC.

25. Muzzey, *James G. Blaine*, 366ff.

26. Eugene Hale to Blaine, February 27, 1888, Blaine LC; *New York World*, February 26, 1888; *Cincinnati Commercial-Gazette*, May 14, 1888; Hamilton, *James G. Blaine*, 605.

27. *New York Times*, May 30, 1888.

28. *Atlanta Constitution*, May 14, 1888.

29. Gresham, *Walter Quintin Gresham*, II, 571.

30. *Nation*, May 3, 1888, p. 358.

31. Blaine to Morton, April 28, 1888, in McElroy, *Levi Parsons Morton*, 170–71.

32. Blaine to Harrison, July 19, 1888, Harrison LC, says as much *after* Harrison's nomination. Elkins to Michener, March 26, 1888, copy *ibid.*, typifies the ambivalent Elkins attitude. Michener to Barker, May 10, 1888, Barker LC, assures him that Harrison's men will have Blaine's support; and Barker to Sherman, June 14, 1888, Sherman LC, warns the Ohioan of this. Harrison's own views are sum-

marized in an autobiographical memorandum printed in Volwiler, *Correspondence*, 296–97.

33. Sherman to Barker, January 20, 1888, Barker LC.

34. Jones to Elkins, April 30, 1888, Elkins WVUL.

35. Barry, *Forty Years in Washington*, 41–42; *Washington Post*, March 6, 1888.

36. Elkins to L. T. Michener, March 26, 1888, Michener LC. Cf., B. F. Jones to Elkins, May 21, 23, 28, 1888, all in Elkins WVUL.

37. *Reminiscences of Senator William M. Stewart* (New York: Neale Publishing Co., 1908), 292; A. M. Jones to Sherman, June 4, 11, 1888, Sherman LC.

38. Elkins to Harrison, February 14, 1888, Harrison LC.

39. Alger to Reid, May 25, 1888, Reid LC; Alger to Foraker, April 23, 1888, Foraker HPSO.

40. Michener to Elkins, June 9, 1888, Elkins WVUL; Alger to W. T. Sherman, February 6, 1889, John Sherman LC, item 47592, Vol. 537, misfiled; Hanna to Sherman, June 15, 1888, *ibid.*

41. Blaine to Elkins, March 1, 1888, Elkins WVUL.

42. Michener to Elkins, April 5, 1888, *ibid.*; Joseph Medill to Gresham, April 19, 1888, and John W. Foster to Gresham, April 29, 1888, both Gresham LC; *Harper's Weekly*, June 16, 1888, p. 426.

43. E. W. Halford, "Making a President," *Frank Leslie's Illustrated Weekly*, 128 (March 8, 1919), 332, 351; *Louisville Commercial*, April 7, 1888; *Chicago Herald*, April 21, 1888.

44. *Minneapolis Tribune*, April 8, 1888; Hoar, *Autobiography*, I, 411–13; Allison to Morton, July 4, 1888, Morton NYPL; Sage, *William Boyd Allison*, 204–29; Charles Edward Russell, *These Shifting Scenes* (New York: Hodder and Stoughton, 1914), 119.

45. Harry Barnard, *Eagle Forgotten: The Life of John Peter Altgeld* (Indianapolis: Bobbs, Merrill, 1938), 330.

46. L. T. Michener, "The National Convention of 1888," typescript in Michener LC.

47. McClure, *Old Time Notes*, II, 574.

48. White, *Masks in a Pageant*, 72.

49. Cullom to Chandler, September 28, 1900, Chandler LC.

50. Barry, *Forty Years in Washington*, 90–91; *New York Sun*, May 12, 1884.

51. Stoddard, *As I Knew Them*, 165.

52. Hayes to Manning Force, December 20, 1891, Hayes HML.

53. Foraker, *Notes*, I, 425; George Hoadly to Cleveland, July 3, 1888, Cleveland LC.

54. Harrison to James Johnson, January 8, 1892, Harrison LC; Harrison to Elkins, January 23, 1890, Elkins WVUL.

55. Sievers, *Benjamin Harrison: Hoosier Statesman*, 302.

56. Harrison to W. P. Fishback, April 29, 1882, Harrison LC; E. J. Halford, "General Harrison's Attitude Toward the Presidency," *Century Magazine*, 84 (June, 1912), 307.

57. Michener to Barker, March 3, 15, 1888, Barker LC; Halford, "Making a President," 332, 351; Michener to Hay, February 24, 1888, E. G. Hay LC.

58. Charles Hedges (Ed.), *The Speeches of Benjamin Harrison* (New York: Lovell, Coryell, and Co., 1892), 9–24; cited hereafter as Harrison, *Speeches* (1892).

59. Blaine to Elkins, March 1, 1888, in Lambert, *Stephen B. Elkins*, 120.

60. Harrison to Elkins, February 18, 1888, and Michener to Elkins, February 27, 1888, both in Elkins WVUL.

61. Elkins to Harrison, February 27, 1888, Harrison LC.

62. Elkins to Michener, March 21, 1888, *ibid.*

63. Elkins to Michener, April 7, 1888, Michener LC.

64. Michener to Elkins, April 10, 1888, Elkins WVUL.

65. A. T. Volwiler, "Tariff Strategy and Propaganda in the United States, 1887–1888," *American Historical Review,* 36 (October, 1930), 76–96; Platt, *Autobiography,* 205; Michener to Hay, May 21, 30, 1888, E. G. Hay LC.

66. Lynch, *Grover Cleveland,* 357–59.

67. Smith to Hayes, June 9, 1888, Smith OHS.

68. *Philadelphia Press,* April 11, 1888.

69. *Philadelphia Times,* February 5, 1888; *Life,* 11 (February 23, 1888), 104.

70. *Official Proceedings of the National Democratic Convention . . . 1888* (St. Louis: Woodward and Tiernan Printing Co., 1888), 76ff; cited hereafter as *Dem. Proc. 1888.*

71. Clark, *My Quarter Century,* II, 216–17; Lambert, *Arthur Pue Gorman,* 140–41; Charles S. Hamlin Diary, December 28, 1896, Hamlin LC.

72. *Dem. Proc. 1888,* pp. 93ff.

73. See John S. Hare, "Allen G. Thurman: A Political Study," (Unpublished Ph.D. Dissertation, Ohio State University, 1933), 304; *Frank Leslie's Illustrated Weekly,* 66 (June 16, 1888), 274; Breen, *Thirty Years of New York Politics,* 714; Oberholtzer, *History,* V, 5; *Judge,* June 23, 1888, p. 166; Hoadly to Cleveland, July 3, 1888, Cleveland LC.

74. *Puck,* June 20, 1888, p. 284.

75. Rush Sloan to Sherman, June 30, 1888, Sherman LC.

76. Edward A. White, "A Woman Promotes the Presidential Candidacy of Senator Allison, 1888," *Iowa Journal of History* (July, 1950), 221–46.

77. *Washington Post,* June 17, 1888.

78. Sherman to Hanna, June 19, 1888, Sherman LC.

79. Stoddard, *As I Knew Them,* 156–57; *Chicago Tribune,* June 20, 1888; Russell, *These Shifting Scenes,* 116.

80. *Proceedings of the Ninth Republican National Convention . . . 1888* (Chicago: Blakely Printing Co., 1888), 11ff; cited hereafter as *GOP Proc. 1888.*

81. *Public Opinion,* June 30, 1888.

82. *Nation,* June 28, 1888, p. 520.

83. *Harper's Weekly,* July 7, 1888, p. 486.

84. *GOP Proc. 1888,* pp. 112ff; Morgan, *William McKinley,* 113.

85. Depew, *My Memories,* 131–32.

86. Bates, *Tom Walsh in Dakota Territory,* 182–83; Stoddard, *As I Knew Them,* 232–33; *New York Herald,* June 24, 1888. Benjamin Butterworth to Sherman, June 22, 1888, Sherman LC, outlines McKinley's dilemma, and the growing move for him in and out of the Ohio delegation.

87. Walters, *Joseph Benson Foraker,* 72–74; Hanna to Sherman, Item 29429, Sherman LC; Morgan, *William McKinley,* 118.

88. Muzzey, *James G. Blaine,* 378.

89. Rhodes, *History,* VIII, 317.

90. Sievers, *Benjamin Harrison: Hoosier Statesman,* 351.

91. Michener to Harrison, June 17, 1888, copy in Michener LC; Halford, "General Harrison's Attitude Toward the Presidency," 305–306.

92. C. B. Farwell to Gresham, June 5, 1888, Gresham LC.

93. Gresham, *Walter Q. Gresham*, 599–600; Stephenson, *Nelson W. Aldrich*, 71–72; Morgan, *William McKinley*, 118–22.

94. Michener, "The National Convention of 1888," typescript, Michener LC; *New York World*, June 7, 26, 1888; Adlai E. Stevenson, *Something of the Men I Have Known* (Chicago: A. C. McClurg Co., 1909), 48.

95. See, *New York Sun*, June 26, 1888; Foraker, *Notes*, I, 390, quoting the *Brooklyn Eagle;* Blaine to Reid, July 6, 1888, in Cortissoz, *Whitelaw Reid*, II, 117–18; Mrs. Blaine to Walker Blaine, July 10, 1888, in *Letters of Mrs. James G. Blaine*, II, 211; Blaine to Elkins, July 8, 1888, Elkins WVUL.

96. Sherman to Platt, August 13, 1890, Sherman LC; Sherman, *Recollections*, II, 1029–30; Dunn, *From Harrison to Harding*, I, 69.

97. Harrison to Foraker, July 11, 1888, Foraker HPSO; Harrison to Reid, July 10, 1888, copy in Harrison LC.

98. Hamilton Wilcox to Lamont, June 26, 1888, Cleveland LC.

99. *Dem. Proc. 1888*, pp. 140ff.

100. *New York World*, June 7, 1890.

101. Parker to Lamont, August 18, 1888, Cleveland LC.

102. Cleveland, *Letters*, 399–400.

103. Whitney to Mrs. Whitney, August 11, 1888, Whitney LC; Robert Bolt, "Donald M. Dickinson and the Second Election of Grover Cleveland," *Michigan History*, 49 (March, 1965), 35.

104. George F. Parker to Lamont, August 18, September 6, 1888, Walter Thayer to Lamont, October 15, 1888, all in Cleveland LC.

105. *Atlanta Constitution*, June 23, 1888.

106. Brice to Lamont, August 4, September 11, 1888, H. A. Hurlburt to Don Dickinson, March 8, 1888, John H. Reagan to Cleveland, July 8, 1888, all in Cleveland LC; *Chicago Tribune*, September 15, 1888.

107. Wilson S. Bissell to Lamont, October 3, 1888, Cleveland LC.

108. Cleveland, *Writings* (1892), 19ff.

109. William Ivins to Lamont, August 10, 1888, Cleveland LC.

110. Stoddard, *As I Knew Them*, 158–59.

111. *Washington Post*, June 27, 1888.

112. Quay to Barker, July 17, 1888, Barker LC; Harrison to Clarkson, October 27, 1888, Harrison LC; Preston B. Plumb to Harrison, July 3, 1888, *ibid.*, Harrison to Barker, October 17, 1888, Barker LC.

113. White, *Masks In A Pageant*, 32–33; Harold F. Gosnell, *Boss Platt and His New York Machine* (Chicago: University of Chicago Press, 1924), 319.

114. *Ibid.*, 348; Josephson, *The Politicos*, 244; Lemuel Eli Quigg, "Thomas Platt," *North American Review*, 191 (May, 1910), 668–77; Bryce, *American Commonwealth*, II, 111; Thompson, *Party Leaders*, 96.

115. Roosevelt, *Autobiography*, 313–20.

116. McClure, *Old Time Notes*, 456ff, 479.

117. Platt, *Autobiography*, 213; McDougall, "Pictures in the Papers," 67–73; Pepper, *Under Three Flags*, 257–58.

118. Platt, *Autobiography*, 211; Stackpole, *Behind the Scenes*, 104–105; Mitchell, *Memoirs of An Editor*, 429–30; Sherman to Harrison, July 13, 1888, Harrison LC; Michener to Elkins, July 30, 1888, Elkins WVUL.

119. McClure, *Old Time Notes*, II, 571; *Boston Globe*, October 23, 1888; *New York World*, March 2, 1889; Herbert Adams Gibbons, *John Wanamaker*, 2

vols. (New York: Harper Brothers, 1926), I, 259; Clarkson to William Loeb, Jr., August 19, 1906, Roosevelt LC.

120. Harrison to Reid, October 9, 1888, Reid LC.

121. Harrison to Sherman, July 9, 1888, in Sherman, *Recollections*, II, 1030.

122. Harrison, *Speeches* (1892), 31.

123. Stoddard, *As I Knew Them*, 169; Michener, "Harrison's Speeches of 1888," typescript in Michener LC.

124. Harrison to Alger, September 14, 1888, Alger WLCL.

125. Harrison, *Speeches* (1892), 37–38, 106–107, 177–78.

126. *Ibid.*, 73–74, 156, 181, 187; James Tyner to Michener, September 21, 1888, Michener LC.

127. Harrison to Morton, October 29, 1888, Morton NYPL.

128. Harrison, *Speeches* (1892), 135.

129. Sherman to Harpster, July 25, 1888, Sherman LC.

130. Cullom, *Fifty Years of Public Service*, 244; Sherman to Harrison, September 12, 1888, Sherman LC.

131. Harrison, *Speeches* (1892), 132.

132. C. S. Casey to Cleveland, August 3, 1888, Cleveland LC; Edward T. James, "American Labor and Political Action, 1865–1896," (Unpublished Ph.D. Dissertation, Harvard University, 1954), 419–23.

133. McKinley to Morton, July 19, 1888, Morton NYPL. Cf., Miller, *The States of the Old Northwest and the Tariff*, 178–79; Mahnken, "Congressmen of the Grain Belt States and the Tariff," 174; B. F. Jones to Elkins, April 25, 1888, Elkins WVUL.

134. Swank to Allison, September 26, 1888, Allison ISDHA; *Bulletin,* National Association of Wool Manufacturers, XVIII, p. 264; Volwiler, "Tariff Strategy and Propaganda . . . 1887–1888," *passim;* Tarbell, *The Tariff in Our Times,* 178; *Nation,* September 13, 1888, p. 202.

135. James McCutcheon to Lamont, July 9, 1888, Cleveland LC.

136. W. F. Sheean to Lamont, October 3, 1888, Cleveland LC. Cf., Richard Gibbons to Bayard, June 27, 1888, and Turner Oliver to Bayard, June 14, 1888, both in Bayard LC.

137. *GOP Proc. 1888*, pp. 255–62.

138. Fowler, *The Cabinet Politician,* 205–206; Van Riper, *History of the United States Civil Service,* 132; Cary, *George William Curtis,* 309–11; *Washington Star,* June 26, 1888; *Nation,* June 28, 1888, p. 521; *Atlanta Constitution,* June 9, 1888.

139. Quay to Harrison, September 6, 1888, Harrison LC; Foulke, *Fighting the Spoilsmen,* 46–47; Harrison, *Speeches* (1892), 113–14; *Indianapolis Journal,* August 30, 1882.

140. Brown, *Irish-American Nationalism,* 139; James, "American Labor and Political Action," 459; Bass, '*I Am A Democrat,*' 114ff. Nevins, *Grover Cleveland,* 437–38, argues that Quay "colonized" New York with voters from Pennsylvania, and bought Negro voters within the City. He says nothing of similar Democratic activities and does not substantiate the charges.

141. Josephson, *The Politicos,* 425; English to Cleveland, July 8, 1888, and Parker to W. U. Hensel, June 26, 1888, both in Cleveland LC.

142. Sievers, *Benjamin Harrison: Hoosier Statesmen,* 417–21.

143. [?] Graham to E. G. Hay, November 9, 1888, E. G. Hay LC.

144. *New York Tribune,* June 26, 1888.

145. Harrison, *Speeches* (1892), 77.

146. *New York Herald*, September 12, 1888. Cf., Michener to Elkins, July 30, 1888, Elkins WVUL.

147. Harrison, *Speeches* (1892), 170–72; *Chicago Tribune*, August 18, 1888.

148. Muzzey, *James G. Blaine*, 148.

149. Adee to Bayard, February 22, 1888, Bayard LC.

150. Patrick Collins to Cleveland, August 2, 1888, Cleveland LC.

151. Whitney to Mrs. Whitney, August 11, 1888, Whitney LC.

152. Dorothy Ganfield Fowler, *John Coit Spooner: Defender of Presidents* (New York: University Publishers, 1961), 112–13.

153. *New York World*, August 29, 1888; Ernest R. May, *Imperial Democracy* (New York: Harcourt-Brace and World, 1961), 11, quoting the London *Times; Toronto Globe*, August 24, 1888.

154. The letters' texts are printed in *New York Tribune*, October 21–25, 1888, with profuse comment. The standard work on the subject is Theodore C. Hinckley, "George Osgoodby and the Murchison Letter," *Pacific Historical Review*, 27 (November, 1958), 359–70. Otis to Sherman, February 19, 1889, Sherman LC, and Otis to Harrison, January 1, 1889, Harrison LC, hold that Osgoodby acted without knowledge or consent of local Republicans. Hinckley does not emphasize that Osgoodby planned to use any damaging reply. A similar letter from other sources went to the Mexican Minister, Matias Romero, who promptly informed Bayard; see Tansill, *The Foreign Policy of Thomas F. Bayard*, 355, n104.

155. Bayard to Edward J. Phelps, March 7, 1886, Phelps to Bayard, December 28, 1888, both Bayard LC; Stephen Gwynn (Ed.), *The Letters and Friendships of Sir Cecil Spring-Rice*, 2 vols. (New York: Houghton Mifflin Company, 1929), I, 57.

156. *New York Herald*, October 24, 1888.

157. *New York Tribune*, October 24, 1888.

158. Memo of Cabinet meeting, October 25, 1888; Sackville-West to Bayard, two letters, October 25, 1888, all in Bayard LC.

159. Memo, October 26, 1888, *ibid.;* Bayard to Cleveland, October 25, 1888, Cleveland LC; *New York Herald*, October 26, 1888.

160. John Boyle O'Reilley to Cleveland, October 25, 1888, and Leverett Saltonstall to W. C. Endicott, October 27, 1888, both in Cleveland LC; *Philadelphia Press*, October 31, 1888; Samuel Farling to Bayard, October 26, 1888, Bayard LC. The quotation is from Nugent, *The Tolerant Populists*, 116.

161. Oberholtzer, *History*, V, 68; James F. Muirhead, *America: The Land of Contrasts* (London: John Lane, 1898), 140–41.

162. Cleveland to Bayard, October 26, 1888, Cleveland LC; *New York World*, October 29, 1888.

163. Bayard to Phelps, October 26, 1888, Bayard LC, explains again the need for speed. Phelps to Bayard, October 28, 1888, *ibid.*, explains the delay. *New York World*, October 31, 1888, covers the cabinet meeting that decided to dismiss the Minister. Charles S. Cambell, Jr., "The Dismissal of Lord Sackville," *Mississippi Valley Historical Review*, 44 (March, 1958), 635–48, argues the United States was too precipitate in dismissing Sackville under international law and custom, but ignores the politics involved. The quote is in *New York Herald*, November 1, 1888.

164. James, "American Labor and Political Action," 461.

165. Hayes Diary, November 9, 1888, Hayes HML.

166. Bass, *'I Am A Democrat,'* 121–26.

167. Parker, *Recollections of Grover Cleveland*, 342–43.

168. *Washington Star*, November 7, 1888. Cf., *Atlanta Constitution*, November 11, 1888; *Judge*, 15 (Noember 24, 1888), 101; Hirshson, *Farewell to the Bloody Shirt*, 166–70.

169. Olson, *J. Sterling Morton*, 329.

170. *New York World*, January 12, 1888.

171. *New York Sun*, November 13, 1888.

172. *New York Herald*, November 15, 1888; McElroy, *Grover Cleveland*, I, 300–301; Hoogenboom, *Outlawing The Spoils*, 261–62; *Birmingham Herald*, November 7, 1888.

173. *Nation*, November 22, 1888, p. 406.

174. *New York World*, November 25, 1888; Bates, *Tom Walsh in Dakota Territory*, 204–205.

175. McClure, *Old Time Notes*, II, 572–73.

VIII

The Billion-Dollar Congress: 1889–1891

1. Hawley to Harrison, December 27, 1888, Harrison LC.

2. Sherman, *Recollections*, II, 1031–32.

3. Weed to Whitney, November 19, 1888, Whitney LC.

4. Elijah W. Halford, "How Harrison Chose His Cabinet," *Frank Leslie's Illustrated Weekly*, 128 (April 19, 1919), 574, 594.

5. Volwiler, *Correspondence*, 2, 299–300; Halford, "How Harrison Chose His Cabinet," 574, 594; Michener to Hay, March 23, 1901, E. G. Hay LC.

6. Blaine to Reid, July 6, 1888, in Cortissoz, *Whitelaw Reid*, II, 118.

7. Blaine to Elkins, November 8, December 6, 1888; Walker Blaine to Elkins, December 18, 1888, all in Elkins WVUL.

8. John L. Stevens to Harrison, December 28, 1888, in Volwiler, *Correspondence*, 12. Cf., Foster, *Diplomatic Memoirs*, II, 250–51; Walter Wellman to Gresham, January 12, 1889, Gresham LC.

9. McElroy, *Levi Parsons Morton*, 177.

10. Blaine to Alger, January 1, 1889, Alger WLCL.

11. Oberholtzer, *History*, V, 85.

12. Stoddard, *As I Knew Them*, 174.

13. *Nation*, January 31, 1889, p. 81.

14. *Chicago Tribune*, January 30, 1889.

15. Volwiler, *Correspondence*, 297–99.

16. Platt to Alger, December 25, 1888, Alger WLCL.

17. Harrison to Elkins, February 2, 1889, Elkins WVUL.

18. Harrison to Elkins, February 4, 1889, *ibid.;* Halford, "How Harrison Chose His Cabinet," 574, 594.

19. Platt, *Autobiography*, 206.

20. Harrison to Elkins, February 23, 1889, Elkins WVUL.

21. Volwiler, *Correspondence*, 300; *New York World*, March 6, 1889.

22. Gibbons, *John Wanamaker*, I, 260–89, 304–29; White, *The Republican Era*, 261–63.

23. Harrison to Blaine, February 1, 1889, Harrison LC; Halford, "How Harrison Chose His Cabinet," 574, 594.

24. Harrison to Barker, February 5, 1889, Barker LC.

25. Harrison, *Speeches* (1892), 190ff; Foraker, *I Would Live It Again*, 134–35.

26. *New York Tribune*, March 4–6, 1889; Younger, *John A. Kasson*, 348; Colman, *White House Gossip*, 198–99; Peck, *Twenty Years of the Republic*, 166.

27. Crook, *Memories*, 177, 198.

28. Irwin H. Hoover, *Forty-Two Years in the White House* (New York: Houghton Mifflin Co., 1934), 5–7; Elijah W. Halford, "Family Life in the White House," *Frank Leslie's Illustrated Weekly*, 129 (September 20, 1919), 452, 466.

29. Volwiler, *Correspondence*, 3; George F. Hoar to Barker, June 6, 1891, Barker LC. For an example of Harrison's insistence on detail, see Lewis L. Gould, "Francis E. Warren and the Johnson County War," *Arizona and the West*, 9 (Summer, 1967), 131–42.

30. Foster, *Diplomatic Memoirs*, II, 253.

31. Stoddard, *As I Knew Them*, 166.

32. Colman, *White House Gossip*, 212; Crook, *Memories*, 206ff.

33. *Carp's Washington*, 305.

34. Halford, "Family Life in the White House," 452, 466; Gibbons, *John Wanamaker*, I, 328.

35. Colman, *White House Gossip*, 200; Crook, *Memories*, 233–34; *Washington Post*, July 8, 1890.

36. Foraker, *I Would Live It Again*, 132–33.

37. Hoar, *Autobiography*, I, 413–14.

38. Walter Wellman to Gresham, March 20, 1889, Gresham LC; Platt, *Autobiography*, 252; Quigg to Reid, May 24, 1892, Reid LC.

39. Blaine to Elkins, April 15, 1889, Elkins WVUL.

40. *Nation*, March 14, 1889, p. 216; Festus P. Summers (Ed.), *The Cabinet Diary of William L. Wilson, 1896–1897* (Chapel Hill: University of North Carolina Press, 1957), 235.

41. Cullom, *Fifty Years of Public Service*, 250–51.

42. Sherman, *Recollections*, II, 1032; Hoar, *Autobiography*, II, 46.

43. Harrison to Elkins, January 23, 1889, Harrison LC.

44. Clark, *My Quarter Century*, I, 290.

45. *New York World*, June 21, 1889.

46. Cullom, *Fifty Years of Public Service*, 249.

47. James S. Clarkson, "The Politician and the Pharisee," *North American Review*, 152 (May, 1891), 619.

48. Clarkson to Michener, May 29, 1890, Michener LC.

49. Dearing, *Veterans in Politics*, 393; Tanner to Sherman, January 5, 1889, W. T. Sherman LC.

50. Harrison to Blaine, February 11, 1889, contains the quotation, and Blaine to Harrison, February 13, 1889, repeats the arguments for a special session, both in Harrison LC.

51. *Nation*, January 9, 1890, p. 24.

52. L. White Busbey, *Uncle Joe Cannon* (New York: Henry Holt Co., 1927), 166–67. Cf., Morgan, *William McKinley*, 123–28.

53. Clark, *My Quarter Century*, I, 278.

54. Kaplan, *Mr. Clemens and Mark Twain*, 360; Platt, *Autobiography*, 213; Robinson, *Thomas B. Reed*, 77; Dunn, *From Harrison to Harding*, I, 300.

55. Robinson, *Thomas B. Reed*, 19.

56. *Ibid.*, 271.

57. Dunn, *From Harrison to Harding*, I, 302.

58. Robinson, *Thomas B. Reed*, 271.

59. *Ibid.*, v.

60. Stealey, *Twenty Years in the Press Gallery*, 410.

61. Robinson, *Thomas B. Reed*, 147.

62. *Ibid.*, 174.

63. *Ibid.*, 171.

64. Reed to Barker, February 20, 1894, Barker LC.

65. *Beatrice Webb's American Diary*, 31.

66. Leon A. Harris, *The Fine Art of Political Wit* (New York: E. P. Dutton Co., 1964), 223.

67. Joseph G. Cannon, "Dramatic Scenes From My Career in Congress. II. When Reed Counted a Quorum," *Harper's Monthly*, 140 (March, 1920), 433–41; Robert M. La Follette, *Autobiography* (Madison: La Follette Publishing Company, 1911), 96–97; Robinson, *Thomas B. Reed*, 196–216; McKinley, *Speeches* (1893), 387; Rhodes, *History*, VIII, 343.

68. Dunn, *From Harrison to Harding*, I, 71.

69. *CR*, 51st Congress, 1st Session, 1208–36.

70. La Follette, *Autobiography*, 110; McKinley, *Speeches* (1893), 445–46; *Washington Post*, December 28, 1889.

71. Cleveland to Carlisle, April 7, 1890, in Cleveland, *Letters*, 221–22.

72. *CR*, 51st Congress, 1st Session, 835.

73. Louis A. Coolidge, *An Old Fashioned Senator: Orville H. Platt* (New York: G. P. Putnam's Sons, 1910), 230.

74. *Letters of Mrs. James G. Blaine*, II, 252–54.

75. Garraty, *Henry Cabot Lodge*, 147.

76. Cullom, *Fifty Years of Public Service*, 252–53; Parsons, *Scattered Memories*, 84.

77. Hamilton, *James G. Blaine*, 683.

78. *Ibid.*, 700; Foster, *Diplomatic Memoirs*, II, 4.

79. Harrison, *Speeches* (1892), 87, 112.

80. Harrison to Reid, September 27, 1888, Harrison LC.

81. Robinson, *Thomas B. Reed*, 236; *Baltimore Sun*, June 17, 1890.

82. Russell, *Speeches*, 227–28, speaking in Boston, 1886.

83. James Atkins to Sherman, March 8, 1887, Sherman LC.

84. Richard Welch Jr., "The Federal Elections Bill of 1890: Postscript and Prelude," *Journal of American History*, 52 (December, 1965), 511–26.

85. Stealey, *Twenty Years in the Press Gallery*, 349.

86. Woodward, *Origins of the New South*, 254–55.

87. See Meier, *Negro Thought*, 38, 77; Leslie H. Fishel, "The Negro in Northern Politics, 1870–1900," *Mississippi Valley Historical Review*, 42 (December, 1955), 466–89; *New York World*, June 1, July 1, 1890; John H. Purnell to Sherman, July 19, 1890, Sherman LC; Woodward, *Origins of the New South*, 219.

88. Seymour Mandelbaum, *Boss Tweed's New York* (New York: John Wiley and Sons, 1965), 48; DeSantis, *Republicans Face the Southern Question*, 199–202; Ellis, *Henry Moore Teller*, 201; T.V. Powderly, "The Federal Election Bill," *North American Review*, 151 (September, 1890), 257–73; Spooner to J. M. Smith, July 20, 1890, Spooner LC. The quote is in Hoar to Sherman, August 26, 1890, Sherman LC.

89. Richardson, *William E. Chandler,* 412.

90. Michener to Halford, October 1, 5, 1889, Harrison LC.

91. Sherman to L. J. Gartrell, July 26, 1890, Sherman LC.

92. Fowler, *John Coit Spooner,* 138.

93. Coolidge, *An Old Fashioned Senator,* 232–34.

94. Effie Mona Mack, "The Life and Letters of William M. Stewart," (Unpublished Ph.D. Dissertation, University of California, 1930), 63–64, 72, 76–77, 227ff; Stewart, *Reminiscences,* 297ff.

95. Spooner to Jeremiah Rusk, January 27, 1891, Spooner LC. See also Garraty, *Henry Cabot Lodge,* 120, for Lodge's view. Warner Bateman to Sherman, January 26, 1891, Sherman LC, typifies the outcry against "western rotten boroughs." Shadgett, *The Republican Party in Georgia,* 150, quotes Harrison. Vincent P. DeSantis, "Benjamin Harrison and the Republican Party in the South, 1889–1893," *Indiana Magazine of History,* 51 (December, 1955), 279–302, summarizes the President's policy.

96. L. T. Hunt to Sherman, January 6, 1891, Sherman LC.

97. Michener to Halford, November 5, 26, 1889, Harrison LC.

98. Barry, *Forty Years In Washington,* 92. Idaho and Wyoming were not represented in the Senate until December, 1890, after passage of the Sherman Act.

99. Stewart to H. B. Kelly, March 11, 1890, Stewart NHS.

100. Philip F. Buckner, "Silver Mining Interests in Silver Politics, 1876–1896," (Unpublished M.A. Thesis, Columbia University, 1954), 9ff; Stewart to [?] Lord, March 29, 1888, to Harrison, April 20, 1889, and to W. D. Marvel, February 3, 1890, all in Stewart NHS; Newlands to Harrison, June 5, 1890, Harrison LC; Barnes, *John G. Carlisle,* 221, n1.

101. Stewart, *Reminiscences,* 293; Mack, "William M. Stewart," 210–11, 213–14; *Salt Lake City Tribune,* May 15, 1890; Elmer Ellis, *Henry Moore Teller* (Caldwell, Idaho: Caxton Printers, 1941), 189; Arthur B. Darling (Ed.), *The Public Papers of Francis G. Newlands,* 2 vols. (Boston: Houghton Mifflin Co., 1932), I, 18.

102. *New York World,* June 6, 1890; *Wall Street Journal,* April 16, 1890, typifies this ambivalent business attitude. Cf., Kirkland, *Industry Comes of Age,* 39. Blaine to Harrison, August 22, 1890, Harrison LC, reports conversations with businessmen favoring more silver for the fall money market; see also Lodge to E. B. Haskell, April 30, 1890, Lodge MHS. Platt is quoted in *Nation,* May 8, 1890, p. 365.

103. Hanna to Sherman, June 16, 1890, Sherman LC.

104. *Rocky Mountain News,* April 24, 1890; Mack, "William M. Stewart," 222.

105. See Stewart's remarks in *CR,* 51st Congress, 1st Session, 7022; *Nation,* July 17, 1890, p. 41; R. P. Bland, "A Janus-Faced Statute," *North American Review,* 151 (September, 1890), 344–53; *New York Sun,* July 14, 1890.

106. Typescript of conversation with Hayes, dated December 14, 1887, Smith HML.

107. Arthur P. Dudden, "Antimonopolism, 1865–1890: The Historical Background and Intellectual Origins of the Anti-Trust Movement in the United States," (Unpublished Ph.D. Dissertation, University of Michigan, 1950), 124–25; Kirkland, *Industry Comes of Age,* 196–97; Alfred D. Chandler, "The Beginnings of 'Big Business' in American Industry," *Business History Review* 33 (Spring, 1959), 1–31; Jack Blicksilver, "A Study of Some Defenders and Certain Aspects of the Defense

of Big Business in the United States, 1880–1900," (Unpublished Ph.D. Dissertation, Northwestern University, 1955), 117; Dudden, "Anti-Monopolism," 49, 127–28.

108. This is well stated in Blicksilver, "A Study of Some Defenders . . . of Big Business," 398–99.

109. Sanford D. Gordon, "Public Opinion as a Factor in the Emergence of a National Anti-Trust Program, 1873–1890," (Unpublished Ph.D. Dissertation, New York University, 1953), 110–17; Dudden, "Anti-Monopolism," 96ff; Blicksilver, "A Study of Some Defenders . . . of Big Business," 1–55; William Letwin, *Law and Economic Policy in America: The Evolution of the Sherman Anti-Trust Act* (New York: Random House, 1965), 69–70. The Reed quote is in *Beatrice Webb's American Diary*, 22.

110. Gordon, "Public Opinion as a Factor in the Emergence of a National Anti-Trust Program," 173–74, 282–84; Blicksilver, "A Study of Some Defenders . . . of Big Business," 370; Dudden, "Anti-Monopolism," 285–87.

111. James B. Weaver, *A Call to Action* (Des Moines: Iowa Printing Co., 1892), 24.

112. Letwin, *Law and Economic Policy*, 76ff; Spooner to A. A. Arnold, December 22, 1889, Spooner LC; Arthur P. Dudden, "Men Against Monopoly: The Prelude to Trust-Busting," *Journal of the History of Ideas*, 18 (October, 1957), 587–93.

113. *New York Sun*, February 23, 1890.

114. Sherman, *Recollections*, II, 1071ff. His principal set-speech of March 21, 1890, is in *CR*, 51st Congress, 1st Session, 2457ff. Cf., Dudden, "Anti-Monopolism," 534–35.

115. *CR*, 51st Congress, 1st Session, 3146–47; Letwin, *Law and Economic Policy*, 98.

116. *Wall Street Journal*, April 2, 1890.

117. Spooner to E. Coe, April 14, 1890, Spooner LC.

118. Thompson, *Party Leaders*, 32; Stealey, *Twenty Years in the Press Gallery*, 175.

119. Stephenson, *Nelson W. Aldrich*, 9, 24, 29, 31, 32, 41.

120. Dunn, *From Harrison to Harding*, I, 44; Muzzey, *James G. Blaine*, 445.

121. Blaine to Harrison, July 24, 1890, Harrison LC.

122. Morrill to James M. Swank, November 24, 1884, and September 15, 1889, Swank HSP; Coolidge, *An Old Fashioned Senator*, 235–37, n1.

123. Flint, *Memories*, 117; Reed to McKinley, January 30, 1892, McKinley LC.

124. Stanwood, *American Tariff Controversies*, II, 278–79; James Laurence Laughlin and H. Parker Willis, *Reciprocity* (New York: Baker and Taylor, 1903), 185–87.

125. Muzzey, *James G. Blaine*, 450.

126. *New York Tribune*, August 30, 1890.

127. LaFeber, *The New Empire*, 117.

128. Warner M. Bateman to Sherman, August 5, 1890, Sherman LC.

129. LaFeber, *The New Empire*, 117.

130. H. V. Boynton to Halstead, July 30, 1890, Halstead HPSO.

131. Sherman, *Recollections*, II, 1084–85; Fred Wellborn, "The Influence of the Silver Republican Senators, 1889–1891," *Mississippi Valley Historical Review*, 14 (March, 1928), 462–80.

132. Barnes, *John G. Carlisle*, 186; H. Wayne Morgan, "Western Silver and the Tariff of 1890," *New Mexico Historical Review*, 35 (April, 1960), 118–28.

133. Samuel Lee to Sherman, August 4, 1890, Sherman LC.

134. John A. McCurdy to Sherman, January 19, 1890, *ibid.*

135. Sherman to Smith, September 26, 1890, Smith OHS.

136. Foster to Sherman, July 22, 1890, Sherman LC.

137. Clarkson to Allison, September 11, 1890, Allison ISDHA.

138. A. Dewey to Sherman, June 8, 1890, Sherman LC.

139. Hicks, *The Populist Revolt,* 159, 166–67; Scott, *The Agrarian Movement in Illinois,* 61; Ingalls, *Writings,* 21.

140. Howard F. Lamar, *Dakota Territory, 1861–1889* (New Haven: Yale University Press, 1956), 274.

141. Callow, *The Tweed Ring,* 211.

142. Robinson, *Thomas B. Reed,* 249.

143. *Ibid.,* 241.

144. For criticism of spending, see Elkins to Reid, November 14, 1890, Reid LC; *Baltimore Sun,* November 12, 1890; *New York Sun,* December 1, 1890; *Cleveland Plain Dealer,* November 5, 1890. The Lodge quote is from Garraty, *Henry Cabot Lodge,* 122.

145. Dunn, *From Harrison to Harding,* I, 72; Clark, *My Quarter Century,* I, 223.

146. Scott, *The Agrarian Movement in Illinois,* 18; Woodward, *Origins of the New South,* 203–204; Russell, *Speeches,* 349; Haynes, *Third Party Movements,* 239.

147. John B. Elam to Halford, January 8, 1891, Harrison LC.

148. New York *Herald,* December 9, 1890.

149. Bayard to Schurz, March 9, 1889, in Schurz, *Speeches,* V, 18.

150. Grenville and Young, *Politics, Strategy and Diplomacy,* 10.

151. LaFeber, *The New Empire,* 58.

152. Anonymous to Chandler, 1883, Chandler LC.

153. Pletcher, *The Awkward Years,* 116–36; Haswell, "Richard Parks Bland," 139; Foster Rhea Dulles, *Prelude to World Power* (New York: Macmillan Co., 1965), 124.

154. William Dana Orcutt, *Burrows of Michigan,* 2 vols. (New York: Longmans, Green, 1917), II, 9.

155. Hirsch, *William C. Whitney,* 267–68, 272–73, 292, 324ff gives the most favorable interpretation of Whitney. Swann, *John Roach, passim,* esp. 134, 149, 209–37, argues convincingly that the Cleveland Administration used Roach as a scapegoat to punish Chandler and gain political publicity.

156. Harrison to Elkins, January 13, 1889, Elkins WVUL.

157. Walter R. Herrick, Jr., *The American Naval Revolution* (Baton Rouge: Louisiana State University Press, 1966), 39ff; LaFeber, *The New Empire,* 122; Grenville and Young, *Politics, Strategy and Diplomacy,* 11; *New York World,* November 26, 1891.

158. Blaine to Harrison, August 10, 1891, Harrison LC; Harrison to Reid, October 21, 1891, Reid LC; O. H. Platt to Barker, January 28, 1885, Barker LC.

159. For details, see Tyler, *The Foreign Policy of James G. Blaine,* 174–75; Volwiler, *Correspondence,* 302; Pike, *Chile and the United States,* 62ff; LaFeber, *The New Empire,* 112–21; Dulles, *Prelude to World Power,* 40–43.

160. See Tyler, *The Foreign Policy of James G. Blaine,* 128–65; Pike, *Chile and the United States,* 73ff.

161. *Ibid.,* 74.

162. Harrison to Blaine, October 31, 1891, Harrison LC.

163. Andrew Carnegie, *Autobiography* (New York: Houghton Mifflin Co., 1920), 350–53; Albert T. Volwiler, "Harrison, Blaine and Foreign Policy, 1889–1893," American Philosophical Society *Proceedings*, 79 (1938), 637–48.

164. Blaine to Harrison, January 29, 1892, Harrison LC.

165. Pike, *Chile and the United States*, 73ff.

166. *Chicago Herald*, January 30, 1892. Cf., *New York Sun*, January 28, 1892.

167. Rhodes, *History*, VIII, 378–79. Cf., Grenville and Young, *Politi.., 'trategy and American Diplomacy*, 96.

168. Harrison, *Speeches* (1892), 289ff; "Tour of the President to the Pacific Coast . . . 1891," typescript from Mrs. Harrison's handwriting, copy in Harrison IHS.

169. See Robert C. Cotner, *James Stephen Hogg* (Austin: University of Texas Press, 1959), 358–59.

170. Swann, *John Roach*, 114; Harrison to J. B. Houston, August 6, 1891, Harrison LC; Kirkland, *Industry Comes of Age*, 296ff; Sherman, *Twenty Years With James G. Blaine*, 164.

IX

The Restless Farmers

1. Clarkson to Harrison, May 5, 1891, Harrison LC.

2. See William D. Sheldon, *Populism in the Old Dominion* (Princeton: Princeton University Press, 1935), 36ff; Scott, *The Agrarian Movement in Illinois*, 78–79.

3. Buck, *The Granger Movement*, 288–89; John S. Spratt, *The Road to Spindletop: Economic Change in Texas, 1875–1901* (Dallas: Southern Methodist University Press, 1955), 44, 70–73.

4. Ralph Adam Smith, "A. J. Rose: Agrarian Crusader of Texas," (Unpublished Ph.D. Dissertation, University of Texas, 1938), 273ff.

5. Woodward, *Origins of the New South*, 50.

6. Richard Harvey Barton, "The Agrarian Revolt in Michigan, 1865–1900," (Unpublished Ph.D. Dissertation, Michigan State University, 1958), 51ff.

7. Woodward, *Origins of the New South*, 246–55.

8. See the remarks quoted in Norman Pollack, *The Populist Response to Industrial America* (Cambridge: Harvard University Press, 1962), 87–88.

9. Nugent, *The Tolerant Populists*, 96–97.

10. John Chamberlain, *Farewell to Reform* (New York: John Day Co., 1932), 4.

11. Stuart Noblin, *Leonidas LaFayette Polk: Agrarian Crusader* (Chapel Hill: University of North Carolina Press, 1949), 79, 96, 138.

12. Sheldon, *Populism in the Old Dominion*, 22.

13. Barton, "The Agrarian Revolt in Michigan," 29, 205.

14. Theodore Saloutous, *Farmer Movements in the South, 1865–1933* (Berkeley: University of California Press, 1960), 85.

15. Kirkland, *Industry Comes of Age*, 389.

16. Smith, "A. J. Rose," 126–224; Buck, *The Granger Movement*, 274ff; C. W. Macune, "The Farmers' Alliance," Typescript, Texas History Collection,

University of Texas, 30; Ridge, *Ignatius Donnelley*, 264; Destler, *American Radicalism*, 20.

17. See Hicks, *The Populist Revolt*, 186–204.

18. Noblin, *Leonidas LaFayette Polk*, 209.

19. *Ibid.*

20. Hicks, *The Populist Revolt*, 206.

21. Olson, *A History of Nebraska*, 235.

22. Hicks, *The Populist Revolt*, 27.

23. Olson, *A History of Nebraska*, 211ff.

24. Hendrickson, "The Public Career of Richard F. Pettigrew of South Dakota," 105–106.

25. Nugent, *The Tolerant Populists*, 55.

26. H. J. Fletcher, "Western Real Estate Booms, and After," *Atlantic Monthly*, 81 (May 1898), 689–704.

27. Gressley, *Bankers and Cattlemen*, 65, 143–45.

28. Elizabeth N. Barr, "The Populist Uprising," in William E. Connelley (Ed.), *A Standard History of Kansas and Kansans*, 2 vols. (Chicago: Lewis Publishing Co., 1918), II, 1138.

29. Gilbert C. Fite, *The Farmers' Frontier, 1865–1900* (New York: Holt, Rinehart and Winston, 1966), 200.

30. Spratt, *The Road to Spindletop*, 131; Clevenger, "Agrarian Politics in Missouri," 33–38.

31. Allen G. Bogue, *Money at Interest: The Farm Mortgage on the Middle Border* (Ithaca: Cornell University Press, 1955), 144, 274ff.

32. *Ibid.*, 146–50, 183, 272–74.

33. Barr, "The Populist Uprising," 1150.

34. Hicks, *The Populist Revolt*, 55–56.

35. Russell, *Bare Hands and Stone Walls*, 27–28.

36. See the perceptive contemporary article by Rodney Welch, "The Farmer's Changed Condition," *The Forum*, 10 (February, 1891), 689–700.

37. C. Wood Davis, "Why the Farmer is Not Prosperous," *The Forum*, 9 (April, 1890), 231–41.

38. Eric Goldman, *Rendezvous With Destiny* (New York: Alfred A. Knopf, 1952), 37–38.

39. Alex M. Arnett, *The Populist Movement in Georgia* (New York: Columbia University Press, 1922), 72–73.

40. *Ibid.*, 61.

41. Ginger, *Age of Excess*, 68.

42. There is an excellent analysis in Walter T. K. Nugent, "Some Parameters of Populism," *Agricultural History*, 40 (October, 1966), 255–70; and in Nugent, *The Tolerant Populists*, 94–95.

43. Roscoe C. Martin, *The People's Party in Texas* (Austin: University of Texas Press, 1934), 61ff.

44. Raleigh, *Progressive Farmer*, April 28, 1887, cited in Hicks, *The Populist Revolt*, 54.

45. Noblin, *Leonidas LaFayette Polk*, 192–93.

46. Carl Henry Chrislock, "The Politics of Protest in Minnesota, 1890–1901; From Populism to Progressivism," (Unpublished Ph.D. Dissertation, University of Minnesota, 1955), 24–25, 30–59.

47. J. R. Dodge, "The Discontent of the Farmer," *Century Magazine*, 43 (January, 1892), 447–56, is a surprisingly shrewd article, and contains many of the "revisionist" ideas in recent historiographical treatment of Populism; see also the perceptive editorial in the *Washington Post*, April 16, 1890.

48. The letter of Dr. E. L. Sturtevant to Randall, February 5, 1884, Randall UPL, from the Agricultural Experiment Station at Geneva, New York, is very interesting on this matter.

49. Scott, *The Agrarian Movement in Illinois*, 3.

50. Octave Thanet, "The Farmers in the North," *Scribners Magazine*, 15 (March, 1894), 323–39.

51. Spratt, *The Road to Spindletop*, 13–14.

52. Robert S. Dykstra, "Town-Country Conflict: A Hidden Dimension in American Social History," *Agricultural History*, 38 (October, 1964), 195–204; Saloutous, *Farmer Movements in the South*, 75–76; Woodward, *Origins of the New South*, 177.

53. Blodgett, *The Gentle Reformers*, 176.

54. William Vincent Allen, "Western Feeling Towards the East," *North American Review*, 162 (May, 1896), 588–93; Henry Littlefield West, "Two Republics or One?", *ibid.*, 162 (April, 1896), 509–11.

55. Francis Butler Simkins, *Pitchfork Ben Tillman, South Carolinian* (Baton Rouge: Louisiana State University Press, 1944), 326.

56. Stanley L. Jones, *The Presidential Election of 1896* (Madison: University of Wisconsin Press, 1964), 38.

57. Barton, "Agrarian Revolt in Michigan," 30; see also Buck, *The Granger Movement*, 3; Stanley Parsons, "Who Were the Nebraska Populists?" *Nebraska History* (June, 1963), 83–99; David F. Trask, "A Note on the Politics of Populism," *ibid.*, 46 (June, 1965), 157–161.

58. Fred H. Haynes, *James Baird Weaver* (Iowa City: State Historical Society of Iowa, 1919), 255.

59. *Los Angeles Times*, January 3, 1894; and Unger, *The Greenback Era*, 202.

60. Buck, *The Granger Movement*, 16–18; Chrislock, "The Politics of Protest in Minnesota," 27–29.

61. Simkins, *Pitchfork Ben Tillman*, 2–3, 105, 151–54; Francis Butler Simkins, *The Tillman Movement in South Carolina* (Durham: Duke University Press, 1926), 52–53.

62. Woodward, *Origins of the New South*, 191, 194.

63. Hicks, *The Populist Revolt*, 132.

64. Russell B. Nye, *Midwestern Progressive Politics* (East Lansing: Michigan State University Press, 1951), 73.

65. Connelley, *A History of Kansas*, II, 1148–49.

66. Hair, "Agrarian Protest in Louisiana," 362–64.

67. Hicks, *The Populist Revolt*, 286; C. Vann Woodward, *Tom Watson: Agrarian Rebel* (New York: Macmillan Co., 1938), 178.

68. Edward Keating, *The Gentleman From Colorado* (Denver: Sage Books, 1964), 53–54.

69. William Allen White, *Autobiography* (New York: Macmillan Co., 1946), 218–19.

70. *Judge*, February 10, 1894, p. 82.

71. Chamberlain, *Farewell to Reform*, 24.

72. Ridge, *Ignatius Donnelley*, 26.

73. Zornow, *Kansas*, 207–208; Karel Denis Bicha, "Jerry Simpson: Populist Without Principles," *Journal of American History*, 54 (September, 1967), 327–38.

74. Martin, *The People's Party in Texas*, 99, 113–40, 141–61, 179–81, 220, 226–27, 231–35; Woodward, *Origins of the New South*, 235–90; Robert F. Durden, *The Climax of Populism: The Election of 1896* (Louisville: University of Kentucky Press, 1965), 1–22; Albert D. Kirwan, *Revolt of the Rednecks* (Louisville: University of Kentucky Press, 1951), 85–102.

75. Martin, *The People's Party in Texas*, 88.

76. Parker, *Recollections of Grover Cleveland*, 208.

77. Cotner, *James Stephen Hogg*, 431–32.

78. *New York Sun*, July 27, 1890.

79. Norman Pollack (Ed.), *The Populist Mind* (New York: Bobbs, Merrill Co., 1967), 5.

80. Chrislock, "The Politics of Protest in Minnesota," 63–64.

81. Connelley, *A History of Kansas*, II, 1138.

82. Pollack, *The Populist Mind*, 34.

83. Connelley, *A History of Kansas*, II, 1117.

84. L. L. Polk, "The Farmers' Discontent," *North American Review*, 153 (July, 1891), 5–12.

85. Hicks, *The Populist Revolt*, 81–83.

86. Weaver, *A Call to Action*, 5. It seems unnecessary to reproduce a chain of documentation for this conspiracy thesis, since anyone reading Populist literature finds it in abundance.

87. *Ibid.*, 441.

88. See Theodore Saloutous, "The Professors and the Populists," *Agricultural History*, 40 (October, 1966), 235–54.

89. Benjamin Orange Flower, *Progressive Men, Women and Movements of the Past Twenty-Five Years* (Boston: New Arena, 1914), 61–62.

90. Weaver, *A Call to Action*, 6.

91. Roger V. Clements, "The Farmers' Attitude Toward British Investment in American Industry," *Journal of Economic History*, 15 (1955), 151–59.

92. Hair, "Agrarian Protest in Louisiana," 229–34, details a raid of Louisiana farmers on Jewish stores in one community. Unger, *The Greenback Era*, 211, has important remarks on the general subject. Nugent, *The Tolerant Populists*, 109–15, 193–94, is rational. Paul S. Holbo, "Wheat or What? Populism and American Fascism," *Western Political Quarterly*, 14 (September, 1961), 726–36, is a balanced statement. *Agricultural History* for April, 1965 is devoted to Populism, and is a good cross-section of current controversies in historiography. See also John Higham, "Anti-Semitism in the Gilded Age," *Mississippi Valley Historical Review*, 43 (March, 1957), 559–78.

93. Noblin, *Leonidas LaFayette Polk*, 19.

94. Atkinson to David A. Wells, July 6, 1882, Wells LC.

95. Ridge, *Ignatius Donnelley*, 321.

96. Haswell, "Richard Parks Bland," 161–62; Daniels, *Tar Heel Editor*, 500.

97. William Jennings Bryan, *The First Battle* (Chicago: W. B. Conkey Co., 1896), 81.

98. Hicks, *The Populist Revolt*, 316.

99. Quoted in Kirkland, *Industry Comes of Age*, 38.

100. Hicks, *The Populist Revolt*, 204.

101. Jones, *The Presidential Election of 1896*, p. 33; John B. Clark, *Populism in Alabama, 1874–1896* (Auburn, Alabama: Auburn Printing Co., 1927), 164, n1.

102. Francis Thurber to William A. Croffut, December 5, 1885, Croffut LC.

103. Smith to Hayes, June 20, 1885, Smith OHS.

104. O. H. Platt to Barker, May 24, 1885, Barker LC.

105. Barker to Charles Stone, May 11, 1892, *ibid.*

106. Hayes Diary, March 18, 1886, HML.

107. McKinley, *Speeches* (1893), 218.

108. Cullom to Barker, June 3, 1891, Barker LC.

X

"Grover, Grover, Four More Years"

1. E. W. Halford, "In and Out of the White House," *Leslie's Magazine*, 128 (May 31, 1919), 854, 870.

2. Hamilton, *James G. Blaine*, 702.

3. Volwiler, *Correspondence*, 301.

4. Harrison to Allison, May 23, 1891, Harrison LC.

5. Proctor to Harrison, June 1, 1891, Harrison LC.

6. Muzzey, *James G. Blaine*, 465.

7. White, *Masks in a Pageant*, 97–98.

8. *Nation*, January 28, 1892, p. 61.

9. Michener to Halford, August 10, 1891, Harrison LC.

10. Tanner to Cullom, December 30, 1891, Cullom ISHL.

11. Smith to W. W. Phelps, January 15, 1892, Smith OHS.

12. Michener to "My Dear Dad," [*sic*] July 30, 1891, Harrison LC.

13. Dingley, *Nelson Dingley, Jr.*, 343ff.

14. C. B. Farwell to Cullom, January 11, 1892, Reid LC.

15. Blaine to Reid, January 13, 1892, Reid LC.

16. Blaine to Clarkson, February 6, 1892, in Russell, *Blaine of Maine*, 424; *New York Times*, February 8, 1892.

17. Sherman to F. F. D. Albery, May 19, 1892, Sherman LC.

18. Sherman to E. Rosewater, May 25, 1892, *ibid.*

19. Sherman to Hanna, May 5, 1892, *ibid.*

20. E. G. Rathbone to Halford, March 7, 1892, Harrison LC.

21. Hanna to Sherman, April 7, 1892, Sherman LC.

22. Alger to Foraker, March 1, 1892, Foraker HPSO.

23. Thomas Richard Ross, *Jonathan Prentiss Dolliver* (Iowa City: State Historical Society of Iowa, 1960), 101.

24. Hanna to Sherman, June 9, 1892, Sherman LC.

25. Charles Boynton to Harrison, June 9, 1892, Harrison LC.

26. Reed to Foraker, May 8, 1892, Foraker HPSO; Cortissoz, *Whitelaw Reid*, II, 176; Alexander, *Four Famous New Yorkers*, 183.

27. Alger to Foraker, March 1, 1892, and May 23, 1892, Foraker HPSO.

28. Platt to Barker, November 20, 1891, Barker LC.

29. Reed to Foraker, May 10, 1892, Foraker HPSO; Platt to Barker, May 20, 1892, Barker LC.

30. *New York Tribune,* June 2, 1892; *New York Herald,* June 1, 1892.

31. O. H. Platt to Barker, June 14, 1892, Barker LC.

32. E. W. Halford, "Harrison in the White House," *Leslie's Magazine,* 128 (May 3, 1919), 671, 685.

33. Russell, *These Shifting Scenes,* 214–16; Depew, *My Memories,* 134–35.

34. Halford, "General Harrison's Attitude Toward the Presidency," 310.

35. Halford, "Harrison in the White House," 671, 685.

36. Stanwood, *James G. Blaine,* 339–40.

37. Peck, *Twenty Years of the Republic,* 287.

38. E. W. Halford, "In and Out of the White House," 854, 870; George Harmon Knoles, *The Presidential Campaign and Election of 1892* (Stanford: Stanford University Press, 1942), 50; Michener to B. F. Tracy, May 30, 1892, Tracy LC.

39. Donald Marquand Dozer, "Benjamin Harrison and the Presidential Campaign of 1892," *American Historical Review,* 54 (October, 1948), 49–77; *New York Tribune,* June 2, 1892.

40. *New York Sun,* May 31, 1892.

41. Dunn, *From Harrison to Harding,* I, 91; Richard F. Pettigrew, *Imperial Washington* (Chicago: Charles H. Kerr Co., 1922), 217; Russell, *These Shifting Scenes,* 219.

42. Peck, *Twenty Years of the Republic,* 252.

43. Parker, *Recollections of Grover Cleveland,* 24; Cleveland, *Letters,* 203–205.

44. *Washington Post,* March 16, April 21, 1890.

45. *Nation,* December 19, 1889, p. 484; Parker, *Recollections of Grover Cleveland,* 128.

46. Gilder, *Grover Cleveland,* 29.

47. Parker, *Recollections of Grover Cleveland,* 151ff; McElroy, *Grover Cleveland,* I, 310; Cleveland, *Writings* (1892), 374.

48. Cleveland to Russell, July 23, 1891, and Lamont to Cleveland, July 27, 1891, both Cleveland LC; Merrill, *William Freeman Vilas,* 175.

49. Cleveland to D. Cady Herrick, July 26, 1891, in Cleveland, *Letters,* 263–64.

50. Cleveland to John G. Prather, April 3, 1891, Cleveland NYHS.

51. Cleveland to Lamont, October 13, 1891, Cleveland LC.

52. *New York Tribune,* October 12, 1891.

53. *New York Sun,* September 9, 1891.

54. Cleveland, *Writings* (1892), 101–102.

55. *Ibid.,* 104.

56. Cleveland to Whitney, March 19, 1892, Whitney LC.

57. Cleveland to Herbert, March 27, 1892, Herbert UNC.

58. *New York Sun,* April 10, 1892.

59. James K. McGuire, (Ed.) *The Democratic Party of the State of New York,* 3 vols. (New York: United States History Co. 1905), II, 79.

60. Cox, *Journey Through My Years,* 31; Clark, *My Quarter Century,* I, 346.

61. Bass, *'I Am A Democrat,'* 247.

62. Lewis, *Richard Croker,* 290–92.

63. McGuire, *The Democratic Party,* II, 84; Platt, *Autobiography,* 193; Herbert J. Bass, "The Politics of Ballot Reform in New York, 1880–1890," *New York History,* 42 (July, 1961), 253–71; Dunn, *From Harrison to Harding,* I, 137–38.

64. *Nation,* February 4, 1892, p. 79; *ibid.,* February 11, 1892, p. 100; Armstrong, *E. L. Godkin,* 12; Steevens, *Land of the Dollar,* 65.

65. Cleveland to Lamont, September 13, 1890, in Cleveland, *Letters,* 231–33.

66. Cleveland to Wilson S. Bissell, November 8, 1890, *ibid.,* 234–36.

67. Dickinson to Fairchild, January 31, 1892, Fairchild NYHS.

68. Hill to Marble, January 22, 1892, Marble LC.

69. *New York World,* February 3, 1892; *Philadelphia Press,* February 2, 1892.

70. Dickinson to Cleveland, September 24, 1903, Cleveland LC.

71. *New York Sun,* February 22, 1892.

72. *Chicago Herald,* March 12, 1892.

73. Nevins, *Grover Cleveland,* 482; *Nation,* March 24, 1892, p. 222; Dewey W. Grantham, Jr., *Hoke Smith and the Politics of the New South* (Baton Rouge: Louisiana State University Press, 1958), 45.

74. Knoles, *The Presidential Campaign and Election of 1892,* p. 24.

75. *Louisville Courier-Journal,* February 23, 1892.

76. Watterson, *Editorials,* 69–72.

77. Cleveland to E. C. Benedict, March 29, 1903, in Cleveland, *Letters,* 567–68.

78. Cleveland to Bragg, March 9, 1892, in Cleveland, *Writings* (1892), 549–50.

79. *New York Herald,* March 15, 1892.

80. Charles S. Hamlin Diary, April 30, 1892, Hamlin LC. Cf., Summers, *William L. Wilson,* 130.

81. Parker, *Recollections of Grover Cleveland,* 136–53.

82. Whitney to Cleveland, June 12, 1889, Cleveland LC.

83. Fairchild to Wilson, March 26, 1892, Fairchild NYHS.

84. Cleveland to Vilas, May 12, 1892, in Cleveland, *Letters,* 284, illustrates the plan's development. The meeting is reported in Parker, *Recollections of Grover Cleveland,* 156ff, and Hirsch, *William C. Whitney,* 391ff.

85. Russell, *Blaine of Maine,* 409; *New York Herald,* June 7, 1892.

86. W. J. Arkell to Halford, June 6, 1892, Harrison LC.

87. *Art Young, His Life and Times* (New York: Sheridan House, 1939), 146–47.

88. *New York Herald,* June 9, 1892; *Proceedings of the Tenth Republican National Convention . . .1892* (Minneapolis: Harrison and Smith, Publishers, 1892), 27ff; cited hereafter as *GOP Proc. 1892.*

89. Ingalls, *Writings,* 441–42.

90. H. H. Kohlsaat, *From McKinley to Harding* (New York: Charles Scribner's Sons, 1923), 7.

91. Halford, "In and Out of the White House," 854, 870; Allison to Morton, June 25, 1892, Redfield Proctor to Morton, June 18, 1892, Fassett to Morton, July 12, 1892, all in Morton NYPL; McElroy, *Levi Parsons Morton,* 199–202.

92. Dozer, "Benjamin Harrison and the Presidential Campaign of 1892," 68.

93. Platt, *Autobiography,* 246–47.

94. Pettigrew, *Imperial Washington,* 217; Alger to Foraker, June 22, 1892, Foraker HPSO; Reed to Lodge, July 2, 1892, Lodge MHS.

95. Oberholtzer, *History,* V, 186–87.

96. Kohlsaat, *From McKinley to Harding,* 8–9.

97. Hanna to Sherman, June 14, 1892, Sherman LC.

98. Sherman to Hanna, June 17, 1892, *ibid.*

99. Joe Mitchell Chappele (Ed.), *Mark Hanna: His Book* (Boston: Chapple Publishing Co. 1904), 51.

100. *GOP Proc. 1892,* pp. 155–62.

101. Parker, *Recollections of Grover Cleveland,* 159–62.

102. Theodore Dreiser, *Newspaper Days* (New York: Horace Liveright, 1931), 56, 58; Peck, *Twenty Years of the Republic,* 291; John Payne to Whitney, June 20, 1892, Whitney LC; Pepper, *The Life and Times of Henry Gassaway Davis,* 146.

103. The quotation is from Gorman to Howell, April 9, 1892, Gorman SUL. Cf., Lambert, *Arthur Pue Gorman,* 168–79; Dunn, *From Harrison to Harding,* I, 94–95.

104. Dreiser, *Newspaper Days,* 48–53; Young, *Life and Times,* 148–49.

105. *New York Herald,* June 23, 1892.

106. *Official Proceedings of the National Democratic Convention . . . 1892* (Chicago: Cameron, Amberg and Co. 1892), 25ff, cited hereafter as *Dem. Proc. 1892;* Stanwood, *American Tariff Controversies,* II, 313–14; Hirsch, *William C. Whitney,* 393–94.

107. *Dem. Proc. 1892,* pp. 102ff; *Review of Reviews,* 6 (August, 1892), 3–8; Robert Bolt, "Donald M. Dickinson and the Second Election of Grover Cleveland," 28–39.

108. Parker, *Recollections of Grover Cleveland,* 164–65; Dreiser, *Newspaper Days,* 61.

109. *Dem. Proc. 1892,* pp. 145–55.

110. Russell, *Bare Hands and Stone Walls,* 40; *New York Tribune,* January 12, 1893; Dunn, *From Harrison to Harding,* I, 97; Hirsch, *William C. Whitney,* 394.

111. Hicks, *The Populist Revolt,* 241.

112. *Nation,* March 17, 1892, p. 201.

113. Noblin, *Leonidas LaFayette Polk,* 278.

114. *Ibid.,* 283.

115. *Ibid.,* 279.

116. *Bradstreet's* 20 (July 9, 1892), 433; Nye, *Midwestern Progressive Politics,* 78.

117. Gresham to Barker, July 6, 1892, Barker LC.

118. Russell, *Bare Hands and Stone Walls,* 71; Ridge, *Ignatius Donnelley,* 347; Haynes, *James Baird Weaver,* 91.

119. Noblin, *Leonidas LaFayette Polk,* 293.

120. Haynes, *Third Party Movements,* 263ff.

121. *Review of Reviews,* 6 (August, 1892), 9.

122. Arnett, *The Populist Movement in Georgia,* 142–43.

123. Foraker to Alger, June 20, 1892, Alger WLCL.

124. Adams, *Education,* 320.

125. Robinson, *Thomas B. Reed,* 390.

126. Michener to Halford, July 1, 1892, Harrison LC.

127. Harrison to Merriam, June 13, 1892, *ibid.*

128. Halford, "In and Out of the White House," 854, 870.

129. Reid to Harrison, August 5, 6, 1892, Harrison LC; Cortissoz, *Whitelaw Reid,* II, 182.

130. Harrison to Platt, August 17, 1892, in Platt, *Autobiography,* 247–51.

131. *New York Tribune,* September 5, 1892.

132. *New York Herald,* September 29, 1892.

133. Cortissoz, *Whitelaw Reid,* II, 179.

134. Chandler to Reid, June 13, 1892, Chandler LC.

135. *Nation,* September 15, 1892, p. 193.

136. Harrison to Platt, August 17, 1892, in Platt, *Autobiography,* 248.

137. Harrison to W. O. Bradley, November 16, 1892, Harrison LC.

138. *Life,* 20 (November 10, 1892), 262.

139. Leon Wolff, *Lockout* (New York: Harper and Row, 1965), 85; Burton J. Hendrick, *Life of Andrew Carnegie,* 2 vols. (New York: Doubleday, Doran and Co., 1932), I, 405.

140. *Ibid.,* 406ff.

141. *Ibid.,* I, 397ff; Wolff, *Lockout,* 188.

142. George Harvey, *Henry Clay Frick* (New York: Charles Scribner's Sons, 1928), 150ff.

143. Reid to Harrison, August 4, 1892, with memorandum filed under date August 1, 1892, Harrison LC.

144. Harvey, *Henry Clay Frick,* 157.

145. Wolff, *Lockout,* 196–97.

146. Woodward, *Origins of the New South,* 243.

147. Summers, *William L. Wilson,* 117; Edward Atkinson to W. C. P. Breckinridge, January 12, 1891, Atkinson MHS.

148. John P. Ralls to Morgan, September 9, 1892, Cleveland LC.

149. Saloutous, *Farmer Movements in the South,* 125; Woodward, *Origins of the New South,* 244; Woodward, *Tom Watson,* 289.

150. Arnett, *The Populist Movement in Georgia,* 150; *Nashville Daily American,* August 28, 1892, in DeSantis, *Republicans Face the Southern Question,* 233.

151. Sheldon, *Populism in the Old Dominion,* 76; Haynes, *James B. Weaver,* 319.

152. Martin, *The People's Party in Texas,* 194–200; *Dallas Morning News,* June 25, 1892.

153. Knoles, *The Presidential Campaign and Election of 1892,* 187ff.

154. Haynes, *Third Party Movements,* 265; Connelley, *A History of Kansas,* II, 1170; Woodward, *Tom Watson,* 235; Hicks, *The Populist Revolt,* 248.

155. Sheldon, *Populism in the Old Dominion,* 102, n51.

156. Lee made the statement in a New York City interview, on March 19, 1888; Sheldon, *Populism in the Old Dominion,* 48.

157. The date of Weaver's remark is unspecified; see Russell, *Bare Hands and Stone Walls,* 74.

158. Cleveland to Watterson, July 15, 1892, in Watterson, *'Marse Henry',* II, 140–41.

159. *New York Herald,* June 25, 1892; *New York Tribune,* July 7, 1892; Hirsch, *William C. Whitney,* 82–83.

160. Hill to Manton Marble, June 24, 1892, Marble LC.

161. Bass, *'I Am A Democrat,'* 236–38; Summers, *William L. Wilson,* 147; Charles S. Hamlin Diary, August 1, 1892, Hamlin LC; Knoles, *The Presidential Campaign and Election of 1892,* 157–59.

162. Cleveland to Bissell, July 24, 1892, in Cleveland, *Letters,* 295–96.

163. Cleveland to Bissell, August 10, 1892, *ibid.,* 302.

164. Whitney to Cleveland, August 22, 1892, *ibid.,* 303.

165. Cleveland to Bissell, September 4, 1892, *ibid.*, 305–306.

166. Hirsch, *William C. Whitney*, 402ff; Nevins, *Grover Cleveland*, 496–97; *New York Tribune*, September 9, 1892.

167. Hirsch, *William C. Whitney*, 407–10; Whitney to Cleveland, August 11, 1892, Cleveland LC; Merrill, *William Freeman Vilas*, 192–94; Charles S. Hamlin Diary, June 12, 1892, Hamlin LC; Knoles, *The Presidential Campaign and Election of 1892*, p. 137.

168. Cortissoz, *Whitelaw Reid*, II, 181.

169. Hirsch, *William C. Whitney*, 398.

170. Cleveland to Whitney, July 9, 1892, Whitney LC.

171. Clark, *My Quarter Century*, I, 260–61.

172. Sheldon, *Populism in the Old Dominion*, 87–88.

173. Grantham, *Hoke Smith*, 52; *New York Sun*, June 24, 1892; *New York Tribune*, September 6, 1892.

174. Muzzey, *James G. Blaine*, 481, n1.

175. *Review of Reviews*, 6 (November, 1892), 387–89.

176. *New York Herald*, November 9, 1892; Parker, *Recollections of Grover Cleveland*, 171–73.

177. *Nation*, November 10, 1892, p. 346; *New York Tribune*, November 9, 1892; H. C. Howard to Cleveland, January 14, 1893, Cleveland DPL.

178. Hayes Diary, November 9, 1892, HML.

179. Platt to Barker, November 15, 1892, Barker LC.

180. *New York Tribune*, November 21, 1892.

181. Harrison to Bliss, November 14, 1892, Harrison LC.

182. Dunn, *From Harrison to Harding*, I, 97–98; Harrison to Reid, December 5, 1892, in Cortissoz, *Whitelaw Reid*, II, 188.

183. *New York Tribune*, November 10, December 7, 1892.

184. Hayes to J. M. Comly, November 19, 1882, Hayes HML.

185. Foraker, *I Would Live It Again*, 75.

186. Blaine to Alger, April 6, 1891, Alger WLCL.

187. Dunn, *From Harrison to Harding*, I, 93–94.

188. *New York Tribune*, October 14, 1892; Foraker, *I Would Live It Again*, 81.

189. Bradford, *Journal*, 191; Mitchell, *Memoirs of An Editor*, 321.

XI

The Democracy's Fall: 1893–1894

1. Parker, *Recollections of Grover Cleveland*, 184.

2. Gresham to Morris Ross, August 1, 1892, Gresham LC.

3. Gresham to Chandler, May 21, 1891, Chandler LC.

4. Gresham to Bluford Wilson, October 24, 1892, in Gresham, *Walter Quintin Gresham*, II, 672–73.

5. Gresham to Joseph Medill, November 7, 1892, *ibid.*, II, 676.

6. *Ibid.*, II, 680–81; Barnes, *John G. Carlisle*, 209.

7. Clark, *My Quarter Century*, I, 233.

8. Davis to Lodge, March 18, 1895, Lodge MHS.

9. Parker, *Recollections of Grover Cleveland*, 175; McElroy, *Grover Cleveland*, II, 6.

10. Marcosson, *Adventures*, 21; Barnes, *John G. Carlisle*, 161; La Follette, *Autobiography*, 51; Stealey, *Twenty Years in the Press Gallery*, 235.

11. Olney to Whitney, January 27, 1893, Olney LC.

12. Cleveland to Lamont, February 19, 1893, Lamont LC.

13. Henry James, *Richard Olney* (New York: Houghton Mifflin Co., 1923), 4ff.

14. Grantham, *Hoke Smith*, 59; *Los Angeles Times*, January 7, 1894; Roosevelt, *Letters*, I, 393; Barnes, *John G. Carlisle*, 210; *New York World*, February 24, 1893.

15. Gordon to Fairchild, May 24, 1892, Fairchild NYHS; Parker, *Recollections of Grover Cleveland*, 177; Grantham, *Hoke Smith*, 51; *New York Sun*, March 3, 1893.

16. American Iron and Steel Association, *Bulletin*, 17 (February 22, 1893), 57; Parker, *Recollections of Grover Cleveland*, 177.

17. Clark, *My Quarter Century*, I, 239.

18. Whitney to Gresham, March 6, 1893, Gresham LC.

19. Hoover, *Forty-Two Years*, 11.

20. Peck, *Twenty Years of the Republic*, 306–308.

21. *Washington Post*, March 5, 1893.

22. *Nation*, March 9, 1893, p. 172.

23. Camden to James G. Fair, April 18, 1893, in Summers, *Johnson N. Camden*, 465.

24. Clark, *My Quarter Century*, I, 254; Peck, *Twenty Years of the Republic*, 325–28.

25. Horace White to Cleveland, March 29, 1893, Cleveland LC; Schurz, *Speeches*, V, 138–39; Roosevelt, *Letters*, I, 241, n3.

26. Rhodes, *History*, V, 410–11; Armitage, *Grover Cleveland as Buffalo Knew Him*, 239; McElroy, *Grover Cleveland*, II, 8.

27. Lamont to Cleveland, February 19, 1893, Cleveland LC.

28. White, *Autobiography*, 170; Charles Hoffman, "The Depression of the Nineties," *Journal of Economic History*, 16 (June, 1956), 137–64; Douglas W. Steeples, "Five Troubled Years: A History of the Depression of 1893–1897," (Unpublished Ph. D. Dissertation, University of North Carolina, 1961), 24; Adams, *Education*, 338.

29. Hill to Cleveland, June 15, 1893, Cleveland LC.

30. Higginson to Olney, July 11, 1893, Olney LC.

31. Barnes, *John G. Carlisle*, 245, n1; Higginson to Olney, April 17, 1893, Olney LC.

32. Cleveland, *Letters*, 322, n2, 324; Garraty, *Henry Cabot Lodge*, 135, n7.

33. *The Forum*, 17 (April, 1894), 132.

34. *Nation*, June 22, 1893, p. 448.

35. Dreiser, *Newspaper Days*, 315.

36. *Los Angeles Times*, January 7, 1894.

37. Hoffman, "The Depression of the Nineties," 102–16; *Washington Post*, August 19, 1894.

38. Samuel Rezneck, "Unemployment, Unrest and Relief in the United States During the Depression of 1893–1897," *Journal of Political Economy*, 61 (August, 1953), 324–25; *Los Angeles Times*, January 17, 1894; Stewart, *Reminiscences*, 313; Cleveland, *Presidential Problems*, 80.

39. See James J. Hill to Cleveland, June 23, 1893, Cleveland LC.

40. *Atlanta Constitution*, June 29, 1893.

41. Belmont to Cleveland, June 26, 1893, Cleveland LC.

42. Harter to Cleveland, June 21, 1893, *ibid.*

43. The basic primary source for this episode is W. W. Keen, "The Surgical Operations on President Cleveland in 1893," *Saturday Evening Post*, 190 (September 22, 1917), 24–25, 53–55; see also Nevins, *Grover Cleveland*, 528ff.

44. Carlisle to Bayard, July 28, 1893, Bayard LC.

45. McElroy, *Grover Cleveland*, II, 29–31.

46. Sherman, *Recollections*, II, 1070.

47. Carlisle to Edward Atkinson, December 26, 1892, Atkinson MHS.

48. Sherman to John M. Carson, January 13, 1893, Sherman LC.

49. Allison to R. P. Clarkson, January 27, 1893, in Sage, *William Boyd Allison*, 255; he referred to the session ending on March 4, 1893.

50. *New York Tribune*, August 9, 1893; Stewart, *Reminiscences*, 314.

51. Daniels, *Editor in Politics*, 49.

52. Woodward, *Tom Watson*, 248–49.

53. Gresham to F. P. Schmidt, August 16, 1893, Gresham LC.

54. *CR*, 53rd Congress, 1st Session, 1052.

55. Lodge to Edward Atkinson, August 17, 1893, Atkinson MHS, and Lodge to A. Amis, June 14, 1894, Lodge MHS, both outline this strategy. Reed to Joseph G. Cannon, July 1, 1893, Cannon ISHL, and Reed to J. C. Burrows, July 1, 1893, in Orcutt, *Burrows of Michigan*, II, 22–23, contain good inside attitudes. See *Review of Reviews*, 8 (October, 1893), 371–72, for congressional opinion. Jeannette P. Nichols, "The Politics and Personalities of Silver Repeal in the United States Senate," *American Historical Review*, 41 (October, 1935), 26–53, is the best summary of the debates. The quotation is from Gresham to D. W. Voyles, August 4, 1893, Gresham LC.

56. Buckner, "Silver Mining Interests," 44–46; *New York Tribune*, August 3, 1893; Ridge, *Ignatius Donnelley*, 322–23.

57. See Mack, "William M. Stewart," 236.

58. Coletta, *William Jennings Bryan*, I, 83–87; Bryan to Jesse D. Carr, May 22, 1903, in McElroy, *Grover Cleveland*, II, 34; Goldman, *Rendezvous With Destiny*, 33.

59. *CR*, 53rd Congress, 1st Session, 788–89.

60. Cleveland to Carlisle, January 22, 1893, in Cleveland, *Letters*, 314–15.

61. Charles S. Hamlin Diary, August 18, 1893, Hamlin LC.

62. Cleveland to Henry Thurber, August 20, 1893, Cleveland LC.

63. Cleveland, *Presidential Problems*, 135–36; Dunn, *From Harrison to Harding*, I, 118; Gresham, *Walter Quintin Gresham*, II, 708.

64. *Ibid.*, II, 706; "Washingtonian" to Cleveland, May 20, 1893, Cleveland DPL. This collection contains much obscene mail to Cleveland apparently saved by Don M. Dickinson. The last quote is in Clevenger, "Agrarian Politics in Missouri," 243–45, 256.

65. Voorhees to Cleveland, August 14, 1893, Cleveland LC.

66. *Cheyenne Daily Leader*, September 22, 1893.

67. *Nation*, September 7, 1893, p. 163; Cleveland to Richard Watson Gilder, July 27, 1902, in Cleveland, *Letters*, 558; *Commercial and Financial Chronicle*, 57 (October 7, 1893), 572; *Judge*, November 11, 1893, p. 290.

68. Gorman to Whitney, January 3, 1893, Whitney LC; Lambert, *Arthur Pue Gorman*, 194–97; Nichols, "The Politics and Personalities of Silver Repeal . . .," 41.

69. Cleveland to Vilas, August 13, 1893, in Cleveland, *Letters*, 330.

70. Stewart to Huntington, September 3, 1893, in Mack, "William M. Stewart," 237.

71. Mitchell to Wharton Barker, September 7, 1893, Barker LC.

72. Dunn, *From Harrison to Harding*, I, 121.

73. Voorhees to Cleveland, October 24, 1893, Cleveland LC.

74. Coke to James S. Hogg, December 7, 1893, Hogg THC.

75. Clevenger, "Agrarian Politics in Missouri," 256.

76. Barnes, *John G. Carlisle*, 435.

77. Hay to Adams, October 2, 1893, in Thayer, *Life and Letters of John Hay*, II, 101–102.

78. *St. Louis Globe-Democrat*, November 1, 1893.

79. John B. Gordon to Cleveland, March 15, 1894, Cleveland LC, well illustrates southern desire for the bill. Coletta, *William Jennings Bryan*, I, 91–92, summarizes congressional efforts at harmony. Byars, *An American Commoner*, 295, has the quote.

80. The famous bond sales are an important subject, but limitations of space forbid treatment here; fortunately, they are covered well in Barnes, *John G. Carlisle*, 287–424.

81. Quoted in American Iron and Steel Association, *Bulletin*, 27 (November 22, 1893), 339. See H. M. Putney to Chandler, February 5, 1894, Chandler LC, for a graphic description of opinion among New England workers and businessmen. The *Los Angeles Times*, January 6, 1894, bitterly condemns the Wilson Bill in hard times. Summers, *William L. Wilson*, 163–64, has some comments from cautious reformers.

82. *Birmingham Age Herald*, November 8, 1893. Cf., American Iron and Steel Association, *Bulletin*, 27 (May 3, 1893), 129; A. Engelhardt and Sons, Inc., to W. C. P. Breckinridge, January 27, 1894, Breckinridge LC; Alfred Stofer to Henry Thurber, July 25, 1894, Cleveland LC; *Philadelphia Ledger*, November 10, 1893; M. C. Butler to Watterson, October 14, 1903, Watterson LC.

83. Clark, *My Quarter Century*, I, 353.

84. Parker, *Recollections of Grover Cleveland*, 181–84; Summers, *William L. Wilson*, 205–206.

85. Wilson to W. C. P. Breckinridge, April 22, 1889, Breckinridge LC.

86. *New York World*, February 8, 1891.

87. *New York Sun*, November 28, 29, 1893; *Baltimore Sun*, November 28, 1893; *New York World*, November 30, 1893; Simpson to W. S. Harwood, December 30, 1893, Cleveland DPL.

88. See in order, *Atlanta Constitution*, May 5, 1893; *Los Angeles Times*, January 22, 1894; *New York Sun*, May 2, July 2, 1894; *Bradstreet's*, 22 (January 27, 1894), 53; American Iron and Steel Association, *Bulletin*, 27 (May 31, 1894), 163; *Nation*, January 11, 1894, p. 25; *Harper's Weekly*, January 13, 1894, pp. 26–27.

89. Daniels, *Editor in Politics*, 74; Paul Bourget, *Outre-Mer: Impressions of America* (London: T. Fisher, Irwin, 1895), 372; *Washington Post*, February 6, 1894.

90. *New York Times*, February 7, 1893.

91. Merrill, *Bourbon Leader*, 187ff; *Los Angeles Times*, March 18, 1894; Nevins, *Grover Cleveland*, 571–72.

92. McElroy, *Grover Cleveland*, II, 110–11.

93. *Judge*, February 17, 1894, p. 98.

94. John P. Irish to J. Sterling Morton, April 27, 1894, Cleveland LC.

95. *Omaha World-Herald,* July 4, 1894.

96. Lodge to F. Richards, Jr., July 2, 1894, Lodge MHS.

97. Woodward, *Tom Watson,* 261.

98. Donald L. McMurry, *Coxey's Army* (Boston: Little, Brown & Co., 1929), 150.

99. *Ibid.,* 187–88, 242.

100. *Ibid.,* 30ff; A. Cleveland Hall, "An Observer in Coxey's Camp," *Independent,* 46 (May 17, 1894), 615.

101. Stewart to Coxey, March 24, 1894, in Mack, "William M. Stewart," 259ff. Cf., Ridge, *Ignatius Donnelley,* 329–30.

102. McMurry, *Coxey's Army,* 41ff; Chamberlain, *Farewell to Reform,* 32–33; Dunn, *From Harrison to Harding,* I, 139.

103. *Washington Post,* April 18, 1894; James, *Richard Olney,* 36–37; W. P. Hazen to Henry T. Thurber, May 24, 1894, Cleveland LC.

104. *New York Sun,* March 17, 1894.

105. H. Jones to Cleveland, April 30, 1894, Cleveland LC; Daniels, *Editor in Politics,* 57; *Nation,* May 24, 1894, p. 377. The quotation is in *Washington Post,* August 8, 1894.

106. *Philadelphia Evening-Telegram,* June 20, 1894.

107. Barnard, *Eagle Forgotten,* 280–81.

108. Almont Lindsey, *The Pullman Strike* (Chicago: University of Chicago Press, 1942), 26; Beer, *Hanna,* 132–33.

109. E. W. Phelps to Gresham, July 16, 1984, Gresham LC.

110. See Barnard, *Eagle Forgotten,* 18, 27, 61, 125, 152, 159, 245; Whitlock, *Forty Years of It,* 65–66; *Beatrice Webb's American Diary,* 100–102.

111. James, *Richard Olney,* 204; Caroline Lloyd, *Henry Demarest Lloyd,* 2 vols. (New York: G. P. Putnam's Sons, 1912), I, 147ff.

112. The correspondence is printed in Cleveland, *Letters,* 357–62. Cleveland's quotations, reactions, and plans are in *Presidential Problems,* 109ff. For a mildly dissenting view of the strike, see Stanley Buder, *Pullman: An Experiment in Industrial Order and Community Planning, 1880–1930* (New York: Oxford University Press, 1967), esp. pp. 147–204.

113. *Chicago Tribune,* July 7, 1894.

114. R. M. Johnson to Gresham, July 24, 1894, Gresham LC. Lloyd, *Henry Demarest Lloyd,* I, 146, has some comments from radicals. H. P. Robinson, "The Humiliating Report of the Strike Commission," *The Forum,* 18 (January, 1895), 523–31, contains useful information and an accurate apocalyptic tone.

115. Barnard, *Eagle Forgotten,* 350.

116. Nevins, *Grover Cleveland,* 579; *New York World,* July 12, 1894.

117. Cleveland, *Letters,* 354–57.

118. Quigg to Oscar Hofstadt, July 19, 1894, Quigg NYPL.

119. The conversation is recorded under the date February 7, 1897, in Summers, *The Cabinet Diary of William L. Wilson,* 224–25.

120. Lambert, *Arthur Pue Gorman,* 230ff; Gorman to Charles F. Crisp, August 9, 1894, Gorman SUL.

121. See Nevins, *Grover Cleveland,* 585–86; McElroy, *Grover Cleveland,* II, 114–15; Daniels, *Editor in Politics,* 75; Cleveland, *Letters,* 362. The quotation is from *ibid.,* 363.

122. See Cleveland to Thomas C. Catchings, August 27, 1894, *ibid.,* 364–66; *Washington Post,* August 14, 1894; *New York Evening Post,* September 28, 1894;

Paul, *Conservative Crisis and the Rule of Law,* 159–84; Gerald G. Eggert, "Richard Olney and the Income Tax Cases," *Mississippi Valley Historical Review,* 48 (June, 1961), 24–41.

123. Blodgett, *The Gentle Reformers,* 194ff.

124. Reed to Foraker, April 25, 1894, Foraker HPSO.

125. Stetson to Cleveland, October 7, 1894, in Cleveland, *Letters,* 369.

126. Ward and Rogers, *Labor Revolt in Alabama,* 123; Arnett, *The Populist Movement in Georgia,* 178.

127. William L. Wilson and Thomas B. Reed, "The Issues of the Coming Elections," *North American Review,* 159 (October, 1894), 385–94.

128. Benjamin Harrison, *Views of An Ex-President* (Indianapolis: Bowen-Merrill Co., 1901), 384.

129. Daniels, *Editor in Politics,* 57.

130. Arnett, *The Populist Movement in Georgia,* 184.

131. Destler, *American Radicalism,* 207–209; Buckner, "Silver Mining Interests," 56; Paolo E. Coletta, "Bryan, Cleveland and the Disrupted Democracy," *Nebraska History,* 41 (March, 1960), 1–27; Ridge, *Ignatius Donnelley,* 340.

132. Clevenger, "Agrarian Politics in Missouri," 266–67, estimates the stay-at-home Democratic vote at 15 per cent. Cf., Jones, *The Presidential Election of 1896,* p. 49.

133. *Ibid.,* 52. Cf., Adolph S. Ochs to Henry T. Thurber, November 10, 1894, Cleveland LC; Roper, *Fifty Years of Public Life,* 81; Summers, *Johnson N. Camden,* 491.

134. Platt to Barker, June 7, 1895, Barker LC.

135. Frye to Barker, December 4, 1894, *ibid.*

136. Ben Tillman to Barker, January 21, 1896, and A. J. Warner to Barker, November 17, 1894, *ibid.;* Stewart to R. C. Chambers, February 4, 1896, in Mack, "William M. Stewart," 264–65; J. Rogers Hollingsworth, *The Whirligig of Politics: The Democracy of Cleveland and Bryan* (Chicago: University of Chicago Press, 1963), 35–37, lists many of these silverite activities. Jones, *The Presidential Election of 1896,* 63, has information. Coletta, *William Jennings Bryan,* I, 100–108, details Bryan's tours.

137. Vest to Barker, February 1, 1895, Barker LC.

138. Cleveland to John M. Stone, April 26, 1896, Cleveland LC.

139. Merrill, *Bourbon Leader,* 198.

140. Woodward, *Origins of the New South,* 279.

141. Walter Lippman, *Drift and Mastery* (New York: Prentice-Hall, 1961), 135.

XII

The Battle of the Standards

1. Canton *Repository,* January 15, 1896. Much of my analysis of McKinley, and some of the information in this chapter, derive from my book, *William McKinley and His America,* 183–248, and my article, "William McKinley as a Political Leader," *Review of Politics,* 28 (October, 1966), 417–32. I concentrate here on his pre-presidential career, and the analysis should be supplemented with the remarks

in, among others, Grenville and Young, *Politics, Strategy and American Diplomacy,* 239–47; LaFeber, *The New Empire,* 327–33; Paul S. Holbo, "Presidential Leadership in Foreign Policy: William McKinley and the Foraker-Turpie Amendment," *American Historical Review,* 72 (July, 1967), 1321–35.

2. See H. Wayne Morgan, "Governor McKinley's Misfortune: The Walker-McKinley Fund of 1893," *Ohio Historical Quarterly,* 69 (April, 1960), 103–20.

3. *Carp's Washington,* 178.

4. *Mark Hanna: His Book,* 58.

5. Grenville and Young, *Politics, Strategy and American Diplomacy,* 240.

6. McKinley to William M. Osborne, April 17, 1896, in Jones, *The Presidential Election of 1896,* p. 143.

7. Foraker, *I Would Live It Again,* 140.

8. La Follette, *Autobiography,* 127.

9. *The Education of Henry Adams,* 373–74.

10. La Follette, *Autobiography,* 92–93.

11. *Ibid.,* 133.

12. Charles S. Olcott, *Life of William McKinley,* 2 vols. (Boston: Houghton Mifflin Co., 1916), II, 346.

13. Warren to Melvin Nichols, February 22, 1898, courtesy of Mr. Lewis L. Gould.

14. Hay to Reid, May 2, 1895, Reid LC.

15. Cortissoz, *Whitelaw Reid,* II, 199.

16. Hanna to John Hopley, June 29, 1892, Hopley, OHS.

17. Olcott, *William McKinley,* I, 303.

18. White, *Autobiography,* 295; Charles G. Dawes, *A Journal of the McKinley Years* (Chicago: R. R. Donnelley and Sons, 1950), 368; Kohlsaat, *From McKinley to Harding,* 96.

19. The standard life of Hanna is Herbert Croly, *Marcus Alonzo Hanna* (New York: Macmillan Co., 1912). It should be supplemented with Thomas E. Felt, "The Rise of Mark Hanna," (Unpublished Ph.D. Dissertation, Michigan State University, 1960). Thomas Beer, *Hanna* (New York: Alfred Knopf, 1929), has a good deal of first-hand anecdotage, since Beer's father was a friend of Hanna.

20. T. Bentley Mott, *Myron T. Herrick: Friend of France* (New York: Doubleday, Doran and Co., 1929), 59–61; Kohlsaat, *From McKinley to Harding,* 30–31.

21. Reid to Hanna, May 4, 1896, Reid LC; Smith to A. B. White, February 15, 1896, White WVUL; Smith to Dawes, April 9, 1896, Dawes, NUL; Clarkson to Allison, March 20, 1896, Allison ISDHA.

22. Chandler to R. A. Moseley, June 3, 1896, Chandler LC.

23. Canton *Repository,* May 4, 1896.

24. McKinley to J. M. Cullers, April 1, 1896, and to John Grant, April 2, 1896, to Robert Alexander, December 18, 1895, to John Mason, April 25, 1896, all in McKinley LC.

25. Clarkson to Allison, April 4, 1896, Allison ISDHA.

26. Hamilton Disston to Quay, April 1, 1896, Quay LC.

27. McKinley to E. R. Holman, April 16, 1896, McKinley LC.

28. Hanna to Foraker, April 2, 1896, Foraker HPSO; *Ohio State Journal,* March 28, 1896; McKinley to Kohlsaat, May 23, 1896, McKinley LC.

29. *Atlanta Constitution,* March 21, 1895.

30. Reed to Lodge, April 9, 1895, Lodge MHS. Cf., Shadgett, *The Republican Party in Georgia,* 122ff, 131.

31. Albert Boardman to Tracy, June 20, 1895, Tracy LC; E. G. Hay to Mrs. Hay, December 10, 1895, E. G. Hay LC; Hanna to John Hay, October 7, 1895, Hay LC.

32. Harrison to John Wanamaker, November 7, 1895, Harrison LC.

33. Harrison to Elkins, February 3, 1896, Elkins WVUL.

34. Hay to Reid, February 15, 1896, Reid LC; Olcott, *William McKinley*, I, 307.

35. Morgan, *William McKinley*, 198–200; Roosevelt to Anna Roosevelt Cowles, March 9, 1896, in Roosevelt, *Letters*, I, 520.

36. George Lyman to Lodge, April 30, 1896, Lodge MHS.

37. Gallinger to Charles Marseilles, May 30, 1896, Gallinger NHHS.

38. Jones, *The Presidential Election of 1896*, p. 118.

39. Warren to H. L. West, April 4, 1896, courtesy of Mr. Lewis L. Gould.

40. Parker, *Recollections of Grover Cleveland*, 315–16.

41. Hirsch, *William C. Whitney*, 476–79; Blodgett, *The Gentle Reformers*, 207ff.

42. Dickinson to Cleveland, March 31, 1896, Cleveland LC; Summers, *Cabinet Diary of William L. Wilson*, 108–109.

43. Blodgett, *The Gentle Reformers*, 205–206.

44. *San Francisco Chronicle*, July 10, 1896, in Coletta, *William Jennings Bryan*, I, 143.

45. Jones, *The Presidential Election of 1896*, pp. 180–81; Haswell, "Richard Parks Bland," 242–50; *Review of Reviews*, 14 (August, 1896), 138–39.

46. Merrill, *Bourbon Leader*, 150; Haynes, *Third Party Movements*, 360, 363.

47. See Ellis, *Henry Moore Teller*, 269, 274; Francis Newlands to Teller, July 8, 1896, Teller SHSC; Jones, *The Presidential Election of 1896*, pp. 89–90; Morgan to Teller, July 4, 1896, Teller SHSC; Altgeld to William Carroll, June 16, 1896, Barker LC.

48. Dunn, *From Harrison to Harding*, I, 183.

49. La Follette, *Autobiography*, 345.

50. Coletta, *William Jennings Bryan*, I, 73, 75.

51. Jones, *The Presidential Election of 1896*, p. 41. Cf., Bryan to W. B. McHugh and others, February 15, 1894, Cleveland LC.

52. Barnard, *Eagle Forgotten*, 367ff.

53. Charles M. Rosser, *The Crusading Commoner* (Dallas: Mathis, Van Nort and Co., 1937), 21; Coletta, *William Jennings Bryan*, I, 114.

54. Dunn, *From Harrison to Harding*, I, 184.

55. *New York Tribune*, June 6, 1896; Joseph Shafer, "The Presidential Election of 1896," (Unpublished Ph.D. Dissertation, University of Wisconsin, 1941), 106.

56. Foraker to James H. Wilson, May 12, 1896, Foraker HPSO.

57. A. B. Farquhar to Henry Thurber, May 2, 1895, Cleveland LC; Kenesaw M. Landis to Lamont, May 23, 1896, Lamont LC; Beer, *Hanna*, 157n.

58. Alger to McKinley, June 4, 1896, McKinley LC.

59. Reed to Lodge, June 12, 1896, Lodge MHS; Dunn, *From Harrison to Harding*, I, 178.

60. Olcott, *William McKinley*, I, 312; Coolidge, *An Old Fashioned Senator*, 196–97.

61. Olcott, *William McKinley*, I, 312–13; *Mark Hanna: His Book*, 62–63.

62. Even Coletta, *William Jennings Bryan*, I, 119, credits McKinley with the "master stroke" of including the pledge to promote bimetallism. Cf., Peck, *Twenty Years of the Republic*, 486–87; Morgan, *William McKinley*, 554, n181; Jones, *The Presidential Election of 1896*, pp. 166ff.

63. White, *Autobiography*, 276–78. Cf., *Official Proceedings of the Eleventh Republican National Convention . . . 1896* (n.p., 1896), 75–100; cited hereafter as *GOP Proc. 1896*; Ellis, *Henry Moore Teller*, 245–46, 259; Jones, *The Presidential Election of 1896*, pp. 172–73.

64. Dunn, *From Harrison to Harding*, I, 181; Coletta, *William Jennings Bryan*, I, 118–19.

65. Margaret Leech, *In the Days of McKinley* (New York: Harper and Brothers, 1959), 81.

66. *New York Tribune*, June 21, 1896; *GOP Proc. 1896*, pp. 129–31; Mott, *Myron T. Herrick*, 61–62; Dunn, *From Harrison to Harding*, I, 228.

67. *Canton Repository*, June 19, 1896.

68. Flower, *Progressive Men and Women*, 103–105; *Beatrice Webb's American Diary*, 61; Simkins, *Pitchfork Ben Tillman*, 332–33.

69. Nevins, *Grover Cleveland*, 700.

70. Barnard, *Eagle Forgotten*, 359–60; Bryan, *The First Battle*, 197; Coletta, *William Jennings Bryan*, I, 122–23.

71. Rosser, *Crusading Commoner*, 37–41.

72. *Official Proceedings of the Democratic National Convention . . . 1896* (Logansport, Indiana: Wilson, Humphries and Co., 1896), 190ff; cited hereafter as *Dem. Proc. 1896*. The most fanatical silverites perversely agreed, wishing silver to be the *only* issue in the campaign. Senator Stewart thought the platform was "unfortunately loaded . . . down with an attack on the judiciary and other outside matters which embarrassed the canvass."; Stewart, *Reminiscences*, 323–24.

73. *Atlanta Constitution*, July 11, 1896.

74. Rosser, *Crusading Commoner*, 45ff; C. S. Thomas to Teller, July 14, 1896, Teller SHSC; Coletta, *William Jennings Bryan*, I, 141; Clarence Darrow, *The Story of My Life* (New York: Charles Scribner's Sons, 1932), 91.

75. *Ibid.*, 92.

76. McElroy, *Grover Cleveland*, II, 224.

77. Rosser, *Crusading Commoner*, 56–57.

78. Henry D. Lloyd, "The Populists at St. Louis," *Review of Reviews*, 14 (September, 1896), 298–303; Jones, *The Presidential Election of 1896*, pp. 249ff; Woodward, *Tom Watson*, 294. The Populist convention and campaign of 1896 are best covered in Durden, *The Climax of Populism, passim*.

79. Lloyd, "The Populists at St. Louis," 298–303; Lloyd, *Henry Demarest Lloyd*, I, 259.

80. Haynes, *Third Party Movements*, 349; Haynes, *James Baird Weaver*, 366ff; Weaver to Bryan, January 31, 1895, Bryan LC.

81. Stewart to Butler, July 14, 1896, Stewart NHS.

82. II Peter 1:10; *Canton Repository*, June 22, 1896.

83. Croly, *Marcus Alonzo Hanna*, 207.

84. Olcott, *William McKinley*, I, 321.

85. Rhodes, *History*, IX, 18–19; Coletta, *William Jennings Bryan*, I, 183.

86. Stoddard, *As I Knew Them*, 262; White, *Autobiography*, 291–92; Beer, *Hanna*, 156; Marcossen, *Adventures*, 18–19.

87. Dawes to McKinley, August 1, 1896, McKinley LC.

88. Croly, *Marcus Alonzo Hanna*, 220–21; Dawes, *Journal*, 106; Jones, *The Presidential Election of 1896*, p. 282.

89. Morgan, *William McKinley*, 229; Foraker, *I Would Live It Again*, 91–92.

90. Canton *Repository*, October 27, 1896.

91. Harrison to E. G. Hay, September 8, 1896, E. G. Hay LC; Harrison to Powell Clayton, August 10, 1896, Harrison LC; McKinley to Harrison, October 7, 1896, and Hanna to Harrison, October 10, 1896, both *ibid.; New York Times*, August 28, 1896.

92. McKinley to Herrick, August 10, 1896, Herrick WRHS; *Washington Post*, October 27, 1896.

93. Thayer, *The Life and Letters of John Hay*, II, 152–53.

94. McKinley to E. L. Osborne, August 26, 1896, McKinley LC.

95. T. P. Hall to Dickinson, July 20, 1896, Lamont LC; Charles S. Hamlin Diary, July 9, 1896, Hamlin LC; Hirsch, *William C. Whitney*, 505.

96. Cleveland to Hoke Smith, July 15, 1896, in Cleveland, *Letters*, 447; Barnes, *John G. Carlisle*, 465.

97. Steevens, *Land of the Dollar*, 33, 61; Bass, *'I Am A Democrat'*, 245.

98. *Proceedings of the Convention of the National Democratic Party . . . 1896* (Indianapolis: Sentinel Printing Co., 1896), 10ff, 26–30, 45, 64ff, 86–87.

99. Elbridge Gerry Dunnell, "The Rise of the 'National Democracy'," *Review of Reviews*, 14 (October, 1896), 434–45, 650.

100. Cleveland, *Letters*, 456–57.

101. *Ibid.*, 451–53.

102. Woodward, *Origins of the New South*, 287; Daniels, *Editor in Politics*, 179; Arndt M. Stickles, *Simon Bolivar Buckner: Borderland Knight* (Chapel Hill: University of North Carolina Press, 1935), 409–10; Steevens, *Land of the Dollar*, 105; Sheldon, *Populism in the Old Dominion*, 132.

103. White, *Autobiography*, 279.

104. Roper, *Fifty Years of Public Life*, 86; Darrow, *The Story of My Life*, 94; Paul W. Glad, *The Trumpet Soundeth: William Jennings Bryan and His Democracy, 1896–1912* (Lincoln: University of Nebraska Press, 1960), 29.

105. Chamberlain, *Farewell to Reform*, 234.

106. Jones, *The Presidential Election of 1896*, p. 361, n9.

107. Byars, *An American Commoner*, 298.

108. *Dem. Proc. 1896*, pp. 400ff; Coletta, *William Jennings Bryan*, I, 164; Oberholtzer, *History*, V, 414–16; *New York World*, August 13, 1896; Summers, *The Cabinet Diary of William L. Wilson*, 134.

109. Teller to Bryan, July 30, July 22, Teller SHSC.

110. Teller to William Van Nostrand, September 3, 1896, *ibid.*; Elmer Ellis, "The Silver Republicans in the Election of 1896," *Mississippi Valley Historical Review*, 18 (March, 1932), 519–35.

111. *New York World*, September 19, August 3, 1896.

112. *Ibid.*, September 8, 16, 1896.

113. Woodward, *Tom Watson*, 311.

114. Sheldon, *Populism in the Old Dominion*, 129–30.

115. Mott, *Myron T. Herrick*, 64.

116. Timmons, *Portrait of An American*, 56.

117. Glad, *McKinley, Bryan and the People*, 187.

118. Canton, *Repository*, September 18, 1896.

119. *Ibid.*, September 30, 1896.

120. *Ibid.*, August 18, 1896.

121. Beer, *Hanna*, 161–62; *Cleveland Plain Dealer*, October 2, 18, 1896.

122. *GOP Proc. 1896*, pp. 146ff; *New York Tribune*, August 27, 28, 1896.

123. Teller to Brooks Adams, September 3, 1896, Teller SHSC.

124. See *New York World*, September 24–28, 1896.

125. *Dem. Proc. 1896*, p. 436. Senator Stewart early feared protection's impact on the campaign; see Stewart to S. C. Jack, February 10, 1896, Stewart NHS; Canton *Repository*, August 14, 1896. The quote is in Stoddard, *As I Knew Them*, 241–42.

126. McKinley to H. H. Kohlsaat, August 5, 1896, McKinley LC.

127. Steevens, *Land of the Dollar*, 159–61. The point is noted in Mahnken, "The Congressmen of the Grain Belt States and Tariff Legislation," 210, and in Gilbert Fite, "Republican Strategy and the Farm Vote in the Presidential Campaign of 1896," *American Historical Review*, 65 (July, 1960), 787–806.

128. *Nation*, November 5, 1896, p. 337.

129. *New York World*, November 4, 1896.

130. Coletta, *William Jennings Bryan*, I, 189–90.

131. Atherton, *Main Street on the Middle-Border*, 213–14.

132. Canton *Repository*, November 5, 8, 1896.

133. Hollingsworth, *The Whirligig of Politics*, 99; Howard Roberts Lamar, *The Far Southwest, 1846–1912* (New Haven: Yale University Press, 1966), 197; Durden, *The Climax of Populism*, 129ff; Hendrickson, "Richard F. Pettigrew," 206–207. I have summarized the election's statistical significance; for more information, and sometimes different views, see: Jones, *The Presidential Election of 1896*, pp. 332–50; Glad, *McKinley, Bryan and the People*, 195–208; Shafer, "The Presidential Campaign of 1896," 436ff; James A. Barnes, "Myths of the Bryan Campaign," *Mississippi Valley Historical Review*, 34 (December, 1947), 367–404; William Diamond, "Urban and Rural Voting in 1896," *American Historical Review*, 46 (January, 1941), 281–305; Gilbert C. Fite, "William Jennings Bryan and the Campaign of 1896: Some Views and Problems," *Nebraska History*, 47 (September, 1966), 247–64.

134. James A. Barnes, "Illinois and the Gold-Silver Controversy, 1890–1896," Illinois State Historical Society, *Transactions* (1931), 55.

135. Beer, *Hanna*, 153.

136. Glad, McKinley, *Bryan and the People*, 195.

Conclusion

1. Hirsch, *William C. Whitney*, 509.

2. Whitlock, *Forty Years of It*, 27.

3. Carl N. Degler, "The Great Reversal: The Republican Party's First Century," *South Atlantic Quarterly*, 65 (Winter, 1966), 1–11.

Index

Aldrich, Nelson W., 349

Alger, Russell, 285, 400

Allison, William B., 49; and Garfield's Cabinet, 125ff; and boom in 1888, 286, 323, 349, 452

Altgeld, John Peter, 470ff, 495, 497

Arthur, Chester Alan, as Collector of New York, 32, 35–36; and vice-presidency in 1880, 94ff; and campaign of 1880, 107ff; aides Conkling and Platt, 136; and Garfield tragedy, 138–41; background and character, 143–46; and social life, 146ff; and national politics, 150–51; and tariff commission idea, 171; and presidential boom of 1884, 173ff; and South, 174–75

Barker, Wharton, 65, 117, 303

Barnum, William H., 98, 294, 300

Bayard, Thomas Francis, 20, 39; background and character, 79–80; and campaign of 1880, 114, 189; on Mugwumps in 1884, 210–12, 240; and Democratic philosophy, 269, 315ff, 356, 361

Blaine, James Gillespie, 22, 52; on Grant, 58; background and character, 63–69; as party leader, 67–68; and boom of 1880, 70ff; and Conkling, 70–71; on Tilden, 75; and tariff issue, 116–17, 121–22, 137–38; talents as Secretary of State, 151ff; and

Chile in 1881, 152–53; and Pan-Americanism in 1881, 154–55; and GOP losses in 1882, 161; seeks nomination in 1884, 177ff; and Grant in 1884, 179; in campaign, 201ff; and personal scandals, 215ff; on Butler, 219–20; and Conkling in 1884, 223; and tariff issue in 1884, 224; and Delmonico dinner, 229–30; and "Three R's," 228–30; and campaign funds, 230n; and significance of 1884 election, 234–35; travels, 277ff; and GOP nomination in 1888, 281ff; on Harrison, 284; on Harrison's nomination, 299; in campaign of 1888, 312–13; and Cabinet post, 321ff; and tariff reciprocity, 349–53; and Chile in 1891, 360ff; and GOP nomination in 1892, 395ff; resignation, 401–402, 413–14, 426–27; death, 439

Blaine, Harriet Stanwood (Mrs. James G.), 66; on Arthur, 144, 148; and election of 1884, 232–33, 337, 402

Blair Education Bill, 269ff

Bland-Allison Act, 47–49, 343

Bland, Richard Parks, 48–49, 388, 458–59, 494, 497, 513

Boies, Horace, 410–11, 420, 494–95

Bragg, Edward S., 205–206, 405, 411

Brice, Calvin, 300–301, 473

Bryan, William Jennings, on free silver, 387–88, 454, 480, 495–97; nominated in 1896, 503ff; and Populists

613